William Dorsey's Philadelphia
and Ours

William Dorsey's Philadelphia and Ours

ON THE PAST AND FUTURE OF THE BLACK CITY IN AMERICA

Roger Lane

NEW YORK   OXFORD
OXFORD UNIVERSITY PRESS
1991

Oxford University Press

Oxford New York Toronto
Delhi Bombay Calcutta Madras Karachi
Petaling Jaya Singapore Hong Kong Tokyo
Nairobi Dar es Salaam Cape Town
Melbourne Auckland

and associated companies in
Berlin Ibadan

Published by Oxford University Press, Inc.,
200 Madison Avenue, New York, New York 10016

Library of Congress Cataloging-in-Publication Data
Lane, Roger.
William Dorsey's Philadelphia and ours : on the past and future
of the Black city in America / Roger Lane.
p. cm.   Includes bibliographical references and index.
ISBN 0-19-506566-2
1. Afro-Americans—Pennsylvania—Philadelphia—History.
2. Afro-Americans—Pennsylvania—Philadelphia—History—Sources.
3. Philadelphia (Pa.)—History. 4. Philadelphia (Pa.)—History—
Sources. 5. Dorsey, William Henry—Archives. I. Title.
F158.9.N4L36   1991
974.8'1100496073—dc20   90-41311

9 8 7 6 5 4 3 2 1

Printed in the United States of America
on acid-free paper

To William Henry Dorsey

Acknowledgments

A book as long as this, dealing with the modern as well as the current history of Philadelphia and other cities, requires a great deal of help. The list of people to whom I owe a debt begins with three fellow historians. Harry Silcox, principal of Abraham Lincoln High School, first brought the William Henry Dorsey Collection to my attention, and again shared his knowledge of Philadelphia's 19th-century black history, his collections, and his own published and unpublished work. Charles R. Blockson, curator of the Blockson Collection of Afro-Americana at Temple University, has been a matchless source of information about the men and women of Dorsey's generation and their descendants. Charles A. Hardy III, too, who has interviewed dozens of surviving veterans of "The Great Migration" of the 1910s and 1920s, has helped to locate individual people as well as to put the earlier period in context.

The staff of the Historical Society of Pennsylvania, which has inherited the remaining records of Dorsey's American Negro Historical Society, has been, as always, professional and helpful; so have the several Philadelphia county and city agencies which contain the records of the past, notably the Municipal Archives under the direction of Ward Childs. Victoria Parker, Secretary of St. Thomas Church, combed the church's archives for relevant records. David Assolino, of the Van Pelt Library of the University of Pennsylvania, is courteous curator of the census and other raw records collected by the Philadelphia Social History Project, which under the direction of Theodore Hershberg in the 1970s did so much to influence the direction of urban history generally.

Academic Vice President Vernon Clark and librarian Karen Humbert, of Cheyney University, helped make the whole of the Dorsey Collection accessible; Dorothy Wesley-Porter and Sulayman Clark helped to unravel its history.

William Dorsey's surviving descendants and their friends took a strong interest in the project, notably his granddaughter Virginia Ramsey Chew, her friend Dorothy Warrick-Taylor, her niece Felicia Blue, and above all the family historian Dr. Preston Johnson, who contributed not only his knowledge and memories but a number of family papers and photographs.

Many of these people also contributed their views about the current state of the black city. My own impressions, as gathered over many years of living in and near Philadelphia, and attending political rallies, weddings, funerals, ball-games, concerts, and other events, were also supplemented by those of many others, some of them prominent citizens, some wholly anonymous, whom I met, primarily in the late 1980s, through joint participation in radio talk shows, television panels, workshops, conferences, and lectures on the subject. Among those who submitted to formal scheduled interviews, sometimes more than once, were: Elijah Anderson, associate director, Center for Urban Ethnography, University of Pennsylvania; Harry A. Bailey, Jr., chair, Philadelphia Civil Service Commission; Paul Bennett, executive editor, Philadelphia Tribune; Joseph Boulware, grand secretary, Grand and United Order of Odd Fellows; Councilman George Burrell; Councilwoman Augusta Clark; Father Robert DuBose, pastor of St. Thomas P.E. Church; Theodore Hershberg, director, Center for Greater Philadelphia; Curtis Jones, director, Minority Business Enterprise Council; Eric King, research director, Urban League of Philadelphia; David W. Lacey, president, Philadelphia Private Industry Council; Claude Lewis, columnist, Philadelphia Bulletin; Jerrilyn McGregory, Philadelphia Folklore Project; Rev. William P. Moore, Jr., president, Black Clergy of Philadelphia and Vicinity; Father Paul M. Washington, former pastor, Church of the Advocate.

Research assistance was provided by David Babbit, John Connor, Clinton Johnston, Sandra Kaiser, Eric Pollack, Abigail Porter, and Mary Beth Salerno.

The manuscript was read and criticized by Herbert Hill, Preston Johnson, Eric Monkkonon, and Nell Irvin Painter; but while many of their suggestions were incorporated, the opinions expressed remain wholly my own.

The typing was done cheerfully by Marguerite Wagner; Howard Hoffman and Kurt Kaydk helped solve nagging technical problems on computer. Friend, neighbor, and photographer Joan Kanes contributed her expertise. Sheldon Meyer of Oxford University Press was encouraging, while Stephanie Sakson-Ford served as a vigilant and helpful copyeditor.

My wife, finally, Marjorie Merklin, helped me more on this project than on any other, serving as primary copyeditor, resource person, and, with some assistance from our daughter Joanna, spiritual advisor.

Haverford   R.L.
September 1990

Contents

    to William Henry Dorsey   309

    PART IV   WILLIAM DORSEY'S CITY AND OURS

12. Survivals and Evolution: The Black City Today   337

13. Transition: From There to Here   354

14. A Common Destiny: Prospects for the Black City   374

    APPENDIX I. The William Henry Dorsey Collection
        at Cheyney State University   411

    APPENDIX II. Sources for William Dorsey and His Family   413

    APPENDIX III. Philadelphians Most Noted
        in the Dorsey Collection   416

    APPENDIX IV. "Elite" Philadelphians, 1860s and 1890s   420

    Notes   423

    Index   459

    Illustrations follow page 190

Introduction

This book is an attempt to illumine much of the history and some of the condition of modern black Americans through the story of those who settled in one place, the City of Philadelphia.

The significance of this Philadelphia story begins with the simple fact that the great majority of African-Americans today live in cities, products of the long journey that over the past century and a quarter has transformed an overwhelmingly rural people, locked in slavery, into an overwhelming urban people, still searching to better a troubled state of freedom. Slavery, the starting point, is of course the secular equivalent of original sin in this country, ultimate source of much of the tragic side to our history and society. But the problems that sin begat have inevitably changed with time. The world made by slave and slaveowner has been richly and even vividly illumined for millions of Americans over the past generation, but it is no fault of either scholar or artist that the portrait is increasingly one of a remote and faded society. And while it was Civil War which most dramatically changed that society, what really killed it was less that one event than the long slow process of urbanization itself, one which passed an important milestone when, within the lifetimes of most of today's adults, the census of 1960 showed that we had reached the current situation in which proportionately more black than white Americans live in cities.

The place to look, then, for the origins of the contemporary African-American condition is no longer the plantation but the city. And for an historian, the time to look is the time of the new beginning ushered in by Civil War. The thirty-five or forty years between the Emancipation Proclamation and roughly the turn of the century were by any measure the most hopeful in the history of black Americans. And while for the great rural majority the joy which greeted the death of slavery was tempered by political and social reverses later in the period, there were no such obvious setbacks among those who moved to northern cities. It was then that urban blacks, although still a small minority both of their own race and of city-dwellers generally, began to build their own civilization out of the familiar old materials, European, southern, and African, together with a number of new ones peculiar to their new legal, social, and economic condition. Citizens at last, equal in law but not yet in practice, they had to find what it meant to be "Afro-American," the term that they used then and that I will use throughout the historical sections of this book. The issues for black Philadelphians a century ago—many of them simply irrelevant to an earlier time, or a less cosmopolitan setting—involved integration and separation, opportunity and discrimination, education and power, identity and culture, class and community, in ways that their descendants still live with and have not yet resolved.

One reason for choosing Philadelphia as the place in which to explore these issues is that while every city has its distinctions, this one may be said to represent the rest better than any other.

Historic Philadelphia, to begin with, during the crucial long generation between the Civil War and our own century, was not so much "typical," as compared with Chicago, New York, and other northern cities, as archetypical, in many ways the metropolitan headquarters of Afro-American urbanity. The late 19th century, more than any other time, was one in which the black experience in the city was truly cosmopolitan, the result not simply of railroad and telegraph but of the central political and military history of the era. While the great majority—close to 90 percent of all Afro-Americans—remained rural and southern, the pioneers who populated the city remained in touch with those left behind as well as with each other. Particularly in places not far from the Mason-Dixon line (southern border of the Commonwealth of Pennsylvania and only minutes by rail from Philadelphia), working men and women migrated back and forth with opportunity and the seasons. The majority of those who lived in the North had come themselves from the South, or had relatives there. A host of institutions, churches, lodges, and newspapers knit the leadership together, creating a network that spread across the country. During the 1860s and 1870s especially, the turbulent and promising time of Civil War and Reconstruction, first the Union Army and then the Republican party created opportunities for ambitious northerners to travel, visit, and help make history among their fellows to the South.

What made Philadelphia archtypical was partly that it had the largest Afro-American population of any northern city—Chicago and New York would not match it, either absolutely or relatively, until sometime in the 20th century— but also that it was central to the cosmopolitan web that tied so much of black America together. Its geographic location contributed to this central position. During the height of the urban-industrial era too, the Quaker City attracted immigrants from all over to work in its industries, the most varied in the nation;

if blacks were not generally welcomed into its factories they hoped still to share in its prosperity as they flocked north throughout the period.

Philadelphia was also home to the two biggest black-run organizations of the period, both of which continually established new outposts across the country. National headquarters of the Grand and United Order of Odd Fellows had been moved to the city shortly after its American establishment in the 1840s. The significance of the first black church and indeed denomination was even greater. Close by the original "Mother Bethel" in the Fifth Ward was the African Methodist Episcopal Book Concern, the only Afro-American publishing house in the country, while the weekly *Christian Recorder,* and then the *A.M.E. Review,* attracted many of the leading writers of the era. The fact that the AME was an Episcopal church, too, its bishops and pastors regularly rotated across the country, was especially important. Especially during the 1860s and 1870s, war and postwar reconstruction opened opportunities to bring the message of deliverance, secular as well as sacred, to millions who had previously been denied the right to join a black church. Meanwhile the continual stream of emissaries to and from Mother Bethel, soldiers of Christ and sometimes of the new Republican party, further insured that the city was the center of black institutional and intellectual life.

The intellectual dimension was nurtured further by several distinguished local educators and schools. While the Institute for Colored Youth, founded shortly before the Civil War, was theoretically managed by a board of white Quakers, it was operated by black principals and teachers. No other school in the country sent as many teachers south, in the heady days just following the Civil War, or abroad, as diplomats, in the decades which followed; its students or staff included the first Afro-American woman to win a degree from any four-year college in the country, the first man to graduate from Harvard, and the first Ph.D., this one from Yale. The city's several medical schools meanwhile not only served ambitious local men and notably women but drew students from, and later sent pioneering doctors to, places all across the nation and even Africa.

Philadelphia had a reputation for leadership in business as well as the professions, which also helped attract the ambitious. In the period between 1865 and 1900 the city's leading black doctor, and first lawyer, were both men who had spent their earliest years among the colony of Canadian refugees from fugitive slave laws. From the other direction Caribbean migrants had long been established among the local elite, further adding to the city's position as the one with the best perspective from which to view the whole of the contemporary black experience in America.

What makes it uniquely possible to recapture at least some of that experience, finally, is that many of those Philadelphians who lived through it also worked to understand and preserve it, notably William Henry Dorsey, to whom this book is dedicated. The city has never lacked for able Afro-American historians, but he was in many ways the first, and his newly discovered collection has often served as the base upon which others, consciously and unconsciously, have built their works. Much of this book, too, follows in this tradition by drawing heavily, although not exclusively, on Dorsey's hundreds of scrapbooks and biographical files for its basic portrait of the late-19th- and early-20th-century city. Thus Part I introduces the Dorsey Collection itself, and the ways in which contemporary newspapers treated the major national events, cultural phenomena, and stereotypes which shaped the lives of Dorsey's contemporaries. Part II looks more closely at the economic and civic life of Philadelphia's Afro-Americans, the occupations and activities of wage-earners, criminals, entrepreneurs, educators, intellectuals, and politicians. Part III is devoted to the ways in which all of these people defined themselves in terms of class and community, in church and at play, in relation to others and among themselves.

The concluding section departs from this formula in using the City of Philadelphia to look not at the Afro-American past but the African-American present and even future. Any reader of Dorsey's or other historical records must of course see them from the perspective of the present. That simple fact is implicit in most histories; I will make it explicit in Part IV of this one, based not on the experiences of William Dorsey and his contemporaries but on my own, and ours.

Generations of history and of urban migration have of course dramatically changed the context and nature of black city life. But together with wholly unprecedented conditions and issues there is despite all this change a great deal of continuity, as both small notes and larger themes from the late 19th century are still echoed in the late 20th. And if today's Philadelphia no longer enjoys the kind of distinction it had a century ago, having long since lost its claim as metropolitan headquarters of the black experience, that may be for this purpose not a weakness but a strength. As mass communications and centralized authority have flattened the differences among cities, the fact that their black populations, especially, share so many of the same characteristics means that no place and yet everyplace is typical. And all of them, like Philadelphia, are descended from their predecessors in ways that force a historian to refect on then and now.

William Dorsey's Philadelphia and Ours

Part I

THE MEDIUM AND THE MESSAGE: THE DORSEY COLLECTION AND THE BLACK PORTRAIT IN THE POPULAR PRESS

Much of black urban history is still murky simply because of the scarcity of records needed to reconstruct it. During the 19th century certainly, blacks as historical actors were scarcely visible to the dominant white population, clearly not in charge of the major political and economic decisions that shaped their lives. Most, too, did not leave the kind of formally written sources, letters, diaries, and reminiscences, of which traditional history is built. But while there are some of the same gaps in the Philadelphia story as in those of other cities, it can be told better than most because of several unique advantages. W. E. B. Du Bois, who published his great study of *The Philadelphia Negro* in 1899, is only the best known of a series of observers who have traced the black experience from colonial times to the present. But for the raw material of history nothing is more important than the unique collections left by the members of the American Negro Historical Society, above all its custodian William Henry Dorsey.[1]

Dorsey was named the Society's "custodian" perhaps because his own contributions were central to it, certainly bigger than those of any other member. Some aspects of his life, and his family's, remain as obscure as those of other and less eminent urban blacks. As much as can be known will be woven, with his neighbors', throughout this book, as part of the occupational, political, religious, and cultural history his legacy has enabled. But its outlines are appropriate here, in the introduction to Part I, as part of the background to the 388 scrapbooks and 914 biographical files at the heart of the Dorsey Collection.[2]

William Henry Dorsey was born in 1837, the oldest child and only son of one of the most prominent members of Philadelphia's mid-19th-century black elite. His father, Thomas J., had escaped from slavery in Maryland before marrying Louise Tobias, a free woman from Pennsylvania, and establishing one of the leading catering firms in the city. The son, with his sisters Sarah and Mary Louise, grew up in a household increasingly used to the relative wealth and status conferred by this success story. He in turn married and had six surviving children of his own. But like many others in his position he chose not to pursue the family business; instead William Henry Dorsey listed himself as "artist" in Philadelphia's city directories almost until his death in 1923, and especially from the early 1870s on to about 1903 he appointed himself a kind of recorder for posterity, busily gathering evidence about the activities of Afro-Americans in the city and across the nation. His granddaughter and others recall him much as he appears in the last surviving photograph, apparently taken when he was in his sixties, as a big man, with the high cheekbones and reddish color of an Indian, a somber "loner" whose personality was well-suited to the essentially solitary activities of painting and collecting.[3]

The collecting habit usually shows itself early, and while the scrapbooks are dated mainly from the late 19th century Dorsey may have exercised it in other ways as a boy and then young man. He collected as well as created paintings, especially portraits of notable blacks, together with coins, autographs, catalogues, books, letters, and artifacts. The scrapbooks themselves reflect an enormously wide-ranging curiosity about the ancients, archaeology, natural history, crime and scandal, literature and the stage. More than half, however, and far more than half of the total number of pages involved, are devoted to peoples of color—Native Americans and Pacific Islanders as well as Africans—to add to the core of about 140 devoted wholly to Afro-Americana.

What makes this core of books especially valuable is the same devouring curiosity which marks the rest of the collection. Dorsey was in fact a natural "social" historian generations before the historical profession caught up. He lived at a time when history was narrowly defined in terms both of subject and approach; it was mostly, as the cliché has it, about "great white men," and beyond that the leading journal declared simply that "History is Past Politics, and Politics, Present History." His fellows in the American

Negro Historical Society, while of course rejecting the "white" criterion, were still committed to a narrowly didactic program, dedicated to showing the Progress of the Race mostly through the achievements of its most notable members. But Dorsey had a wider vision: while his books are full of the activities of outstanding Philadelphians, as well as such national figures as Frederick Douglass and Booker T. Washington, they also contain long membership lists for the Hodcarriers Association, recipes for possum and terrapin, a great deal of crime news, observations about barbering and chimney sweeping, the game of craps, minstrelsy, and cakewalk.[4]

The books include official reports, posters, menus, tickets, and ballots as direct souvenirs of his own life and times. But Dorsey was especially addicted to the daily and weekly papers, which he clipped and sometimes marked with his own marginal comments. These contemporary papers and periodicals, the staple of scrapbooks and files, are the subjects of Part I.

Chapter 1

Of Politics, Religion, and Popular Culture

While not precisely a Golden Age of Journalism, the period covered by William Dorsey's scrapbooks was one of fully free expression, and surely in technical terms the most innovative span in the history of the newspaper business. Full of cocksure conclusions, often scurrilous and fiercely partisan, the journals of the day were almost wholly unfettered by modern fears of libel law, or by modern restrictions in the name of sensitivity or taste. In other respects, however, the years between roughly 1873, when Dorsey began to clip out items in number, and 1903, when he largely stopped, represent the development of the newspaper (although not the publishing) business into a recognizably modern form.

The history of the Philadelphia *Inquirer*, locally the only surviving daily from the period, is fairly representative. Founded in 1869, it was published through the early 1870s under a rigid format, eight pages long, six days a week—no news on the Sabbath—with no single headline wider than any of its invariable six columns. It added a Sunday edition in 1889, graphics in 1885, wide headlines in 1893, photographs in 1899. By the mid-1890s the journal's layout, its editorial and sports pages, its special Sunday supplement full of special features and graphic department store advertising, had made it into something closely resembling its contemporary incarnation. The difference between then and now is less visual than economic: while the *Inquirer* today is the only daily in town—with the quasi-exception of the tabloid *Daily News*, published cooperatively by the same corporation—a century ago it had to share the market not with broadcast media but with six, eight, or ten other daily newspapers at any given time.

During the same period, although the Afro-American population of the city was according to somewhat suspect census figures no more than about 21,000 in 1870 and perhaps 70,000 in 1904, the black community managed to produce several journals and many journalists of its own. *The Christian Recorder,* official organ of the AME church, was published continuously beginning in 1843. It was joined at various times by a single short-lived secular daily and at least 21 weeklies of varying longevity, one of which, the Philadelphia *Tribune,* founded in 1883, is the oldest black paper still in business.[1]

Most of these local journals are represented in the Dorsey scrapbooks, together with dozens of others, daily, weekly, and monthly, black and white, ranging from Boston to San Francisco. The ones most commonly used, outside of Philadelphia, are from the cities of New York and Washington, and various smaller places across the state of New Jersey. The eclectic, geographically widespread nature of the collection is reinforced by the contemporary editorial habit, especially before the advent of the wire services in the 1880s, of reprinting excerpts and sometimes whole articles from other journals across town or around the country.

The whole collection may be arbitrarily split into two categories, one dealing with events or hard news, the other with what may loosely be classified as features, each of which was treated differently. With the important exception of issues bearing directly on race, miscegenation, and lynching, subject of the next chapter, the amount and nature of hard news not surprisingly varied with the perceived importance of the black population. Given political and demographic changes, what that meant is that, discounting the general explosion in the amount of newsprint, there was over time proportionately less coverage of black subjects coming out of Washington and points south, and more out of northern cities and of course Philadelphia itself. With some exceptions, blacks in the "hard" news category were treated in the newspapers (if not by the newsmakers) with reasonable respect.

This is less true of the other category, which—again excepting race and lynching—involved a mélange of items including sentimental fiction, features on music and art, "darkey" jokes and dialect poetry, the observation of habits and mores. Some of this might be classified, broadly, as the stuff of culture, or folklore; more of it must be classified as the stuff of stereotype. There were two observable trends in this kind of coverage over time. One was simply the product of changes in the journals themselves, which made stereotyping not worse but more vivid and less escapable. The other was the gradual encroachment of urban themes and materials onto a portrait, or caricature, that had been mostly rural and southern in origin.

Afro-American news of national importance in this period was mostly made in Washington, or the rural South. If the big city represented the future of the race, its immediate present was still overwhelmingly identified with the millions of slaves newly freed by the Civil War. Blacks in 1870 were numbered at nearly 13 percent of the nation's population; 90 percent of those lived in the South, while the 22,000 officially counted in Philadelphia, a little over 3 percent of the city's residents, were both absolutely and relatively the largest group in the urban North. And while black Philadelphians were only marginally able to affect events to their south, those events were crucially important to them, the giant backdrop against which their own activities were played out. They kept abreast, then, in part through their own rich network of personal contacts, in part, like their neighbors, through reading the papers.[2]

The national news in general was bitterly discouraging. Historians disagree about the reasons for the failure of what is conventionally called "Reconstruction," but they do agree that it failed to create a socially healthy situation either for the blacks or indeed most whites. The Civil War had clearly changed the relationship between the races in general and master and slave in particular, but it had not in itself transformed them, and the actual shape of a society without slavery was not defined for some years. That shape was determined, state by state, only after a series of complex battles among a number of divided and fractious forces including not only the ex-slaves and the former leaders of the old South but the federal government and army, northern opportunists and idealists of both races, and the poor white majority. Despite high hopes, in the early years, that the freedmen would be able to help both to create a genuinely New South and not incidentally to consolidate a Republican national majority, the violent intransigence of the older southern leadership, in combination with various allies, wore down the national government and put down the blacks. The white leadership could not re-create the antebellum era exactly, and in an era of railroad and industrial growth in many ways did not want to. But in terms of race relations the society that they did succeed in reconstructing, over the whole period of forty years, was as much like the old one as possible: conservative, sharply stratified, racially divided, with blacks granted only a kind of limited and politically impotent citizenship, and little access to economic opportunity.

Increasing numbers of historians are coming to believe that this outcome represents the greatest single missed opportunity in our national history, one with tragic long-term consequences. Black Philadelphians at the time were equally aware of the stakes involved, but less aware of the decisive nature of each successive downward turning point, and with some dramatic exceptions continued through most of the period to imagine that the situation might be reversed. The southern black as voter, a major player in the national arena and constantly, vividly in the news in the first decade after the war, did not fully fade until the 1890s into something like an "invisible man." The process of turning potential into impotence was a long and slow one, partially hidden by gains of various kinds to the north, and confusing countertendencies in the South itself.

In retrospect it is clear that the black cause was lost sometime between 1866 and 1877, the year in which the last federal troops were symbolically withdrawn from the last southern states, and as the price for electing President

Rutherford B. Hayes the Republican party essentially surrendered the South to their old Democratic opponents. The Dorsey scrapbooks from this period are heavily political in emphasis, as he and his contemporaries in the Afro-American community closely monitored legislation and elections. But they do not include much from the earliest years, the immediate postwar period in which the situation was most fluid and hopes ran highest. While some items date from before young "Bill" was born, suggesting that the collecting mania may well be hereditary, there are relatively few from the first four decades of his life. He established his courage in 1859, at the age of 22, with a personally dangerous journey to the slave state of Georgia to marry Virginia Cashin, but the family responsibilities which set in with the arrival of a son later that year were compounded by five more children during the 1860s. All this not only kept him out of the Civil War but combined with the apparent lack of any regular job to keep him from spending the effort and expense involved in collecting newspapers in number. The major events of his early manhood, including the passage of the Civil Rights Acts of 1875 and the disputed Tilden-Hayes Election of 1876–77 are all covered, but only barely. The collection thickens notably only just afterward, in the late 1870s, as the four surviving children grew up, Dorsey entered his forties, and his father died and left him a legacy to help support his habit.

Much of the old political fire still smolders in the late-19th-century items which make up the bulk of the collection. But in general most of the newspapers Dorsey clipped had muted the more extreme partisanship of the 1860s and early 1870s, with Republican journals conceding that Reconstruction had been mishandled, while even in the South a few Democratic or independent editors could agree that the black citizen was in some limited sense "a man and a brother." A compact example of the prevailing tone after Reconstruction may be provided by coverage of a single incident, which beginning in the spring of 1880 was declared one of the three major news stories of the season, rivaling the elections for President in this country and prime minister in Great Britain. It involved the ordeal of a single young man, Johnson C. Whittaker, one of the first black cadets admitted to the U.S. Military Academy at West Point.[3]

The case of Cadet Whittaker officially opened early in the morning of the 6th of April 1880, when the officer of the day discovered him tied to his bed hand and foot, some of his hair cut, his nightgown bloodied, one ear slit and mutilated. In addition to an Indian club, also bloodied, a search of the room revealed a curious warning note: "look out; keep awake; you will be fixed—a Friend." Whittaker himself, dazed at first, was able only to remember that he had been seized by three unidentified men who beat and trussed him, and then proceeded to act on the suggestion of one of them: "Let's mark him the way we do hogs down South!"[4]

The New York *Times* headlined its story "Outrage at West Point"; the

New York *Herald,* the same day, cited inconsistencies in Whittaker's account, some doubt as to the tightness of the rope, and the obvious skepticism of the Point's commanding officer, General J. M. Schofield, who was especially at pains to deny that any of the other cadets could have been involved. Schofield volunteered that Whittaker was in academic trouble, and suffering from acute loneliness since the graduation of Henry Flipper, the academy's first Afro-American graduate and a better student. And although at first insisting that he had no opinion, and must properly reserve opinion until a proper court of inquiry had made a proper report, he predicted that the outcome of any such inquiry would be Whittaker's "dismissal in disgrace, of course."[5]

Dorsey's favorite white newspaper throughout the 1870s and early 1880s was the Philadelphia *Press,* which championed Whittaker from the first, and the early weeks of the inquiry swung most of the other local papers to his side as well. The case was covered closely, with generous swatches of verbatim testimony, as the inquiry ranged about to include, among other subjects, the relationship between cadets and surrounding civilians of both races in the nearby town of Newburgh and villages such as Wappinger's Falls. One dispute centered about whether a group of Whittaker's classmates had gathered after taps in a Highland Falls saloon and threatened to "fix" him; there was enough smoke to prompt the U.S. attorney to arrest the bartender on a charge of perjury, simply for denying that he served young men in uniform.[6]

But the real focus for sympathetic papers in the early days was the conduct of the military academy itself, beginning with its court of inquiry. The officers, it became clear, had opened Whittaker's mail in order to find, for example, that his mother back in Charleston could not make the rent. Above all, no one either in authority or among his peers had protested the fact that the young black man, alone at the Point, was totally ostracized by the corps. "No one has ever spoken to me other than officially," he testified, prompting the Troy *Times* to wonder whether those commissioned graduates beseiged in Colorado by "murderous Utes," back in '77, had found it in themselves to greet the black company which had marched 90 miles to their rescue in not much more than 24 hours.[7]

Late in April Whittaker's defense was buoyed further by the testimony of his mentor, Professor Richard Greener, an Afro-American educated at Philadelphia's Institute for Colored Youth, who had earlier taught him at the University of South Carolina. Greener was especially struck by the contrast between his own warm experiences as a pioneer at Harvard, where he had had white friends, roommates, and much respect, and the boorish frigidity at the military academy.[8]

But during the final weeks of the inquiry the pendulum of opinion in the press swung back as a result of expert testimony about the knots which had bound Whittaker when found, the superficial nature of his wounds, and above all the handwriting on the note itself, which was apparently written on half a sheet which matched another in Whittaker's drawer. On May 29 the court of inquiry officially declared his story a hoax, designed to cover fear of academic failure—Whittaker had already been set back a year. Some black leaders, such as Albion Tourgee, regretfully accepted this verdict, although narrowly, placing ultimate blame for the incident on the racism of the academy itself. Others, including Greener and Mississippi senator Blanche K. Bruce, refused to let the matter drop. In the fall of 1880 General Schofield's conduct won him dismissal from the Point, and at the very end of December it was announced that the whole matter would be reopened through a formal court-martial.[9]

The court-martial, stretching like the original inquiry over a period of two months, reviewed essentially the same evidence and reached the same conclusion in March of 1881, finding Whittaker guilty of perjury, recommending a dishonorable discharge, a $1 fine, and a year of imprisonment at hard labor. President Chester A. Arthur, however, overturned the verdict on the grounds that the handwriting testimony had been improperly introduced. Whittaker was then restored to endure another round of cadet status, under conditions all too easy to imagine, until the Secretary of War, in March of 1882, announced his discharge from the military academy for "academic deficiencies."[10]

Dorsey's scrapbook on the case contains 165 pages of clippings from 3 New York, 4 Pittsburgh, and 9 Philadelphia papers; the *Afro-American People's Advocate* of D.C.; the Elmyra, N.Y., *Daily Bulletin;* in addition to reprints from *Harper's Weekly* and other journals. Several of the papers were at least capable of changing their minds, in either direction. Beyond that a survey of press opinion conducted by the Philadelphia *Evening Bulletin* on May 17, 1880, just after circumstantial evidence apparently wounded Whittaker's personal case severely, is worth citing. The *Bulletin* itself reserved judgment. The New York *Tribune*, like the Philadelphia *Press*, believed that while things were not going well the young man might still vindicate himself. The New York *Times* thought him probably guilty of shamming, but that the atmosphere at the Point made his wild story by no means improbable, and that he had invented it only because he was "isolated and friendless, and driven into an abnormal state of mind." The Philadelphia *Inquirer* and the *North American* agreed that the incident should not interfere with the movement to place more black cadets in the academy. (It was widely recognized that these young men needed mutual support, and that their numbers would not be likely to grow under the existing system of congressional appointment. Iowa's Senator Allison had already proposed, on April 26, an early version of affirmative action, under which the President would be authorized to select some twelve cadets at large, at least two of them Afro-American.)[11]

The New York *Herald* and *World*, in contrast to the *Times*, both believed that Whittaker's apparent humiliation vindicated their own consistent skepticism, and the Philadelphia *Times* thought an apology was owed Schofield and the white cadets. None of these papers commented on the wider issue of the treatment of blacks—which they had not defended directly—or on the separate but related issue of black admissions. The Philadelphia *Record*, however, was not so reticent on the second point: under the headline "No Place for Colored Boys" it went on to say that it was "gross cruelty to place them there in competition with the selected youth of a superior race," and that the behavior of these future officers and gentlemen, while the result of "an unhappy prejudice of color," was not likely to change "at least in the present generation." (The last qualification represents some softening of the same paper's position with respect to Lt. Flipper, three years earlier, when it had declared social prejudice "a law of nature.")[12]

This range of opinions is reasonably representative of mainstream northern coverage of formal legal or political news involving Afro-Americans during the late 1870s and early 1880s. Five of the papers surveyed, generally Republican in politics, were at least prepared to sympathize with young Whittaker as an individual, and clearly sympathized with him as one of the symbolic pioneers at the Point. The four others, generally Democratic or Independent, were willing if not to endorse at least to condone blatantly racist behavior, and in the case of the *Record* to express its own racist opinions.

Color was important to all, not simply black and white but each shade in between. More toward the beginning of the period than the end, perhaps because of the novelty of having to deal with Afro-American actors at all, it was conventional to note that "Mr. Frederick Douglass," for example, "is not a negro but a mulatto." The very first and sympathetic New York *Times* piece on Whittaker typically thought it essential to describe his "not very kinky" hair and freckles, and to conclude that he had "a complexion so light that he could not be identified as a colored man while parading with the cadets."[13]

Beyond physical description there was however no attempt in this instance to stereotype behavior, to ascribe the actions or position of any individual to the nature of the race as a whole. In terms of most news and comment—again holding the purely racial and lynching issues for later—this too held for most journals through most of the period. It is hard, however, in view of what was happening in the country at large, and indeed elsewhere in the same newspapers, not to smell the kind of hypocrisy noted by the Pittsburgh *Daily Post* in the Whittaker case. After pointing out that the great majority of West Point's cadets had come from northern homes, most of those—in view of appointment procedures—Republican, it went on further to note that "the devilish spirit of caste is daily condemned in vigorous editorials and daily enforced and strengthened by the publishers of the aforesaid editorials."[14]

In any case, over the next generation political and hard news coverage did not grow more racist but in the North rather less. Frederick Douglass was treated with at least as much dignity as most other public figures. Otherwise the declining number of nationally known black southern politicians allowed increasingly meager opportunities for caricature. It was no coincidence that

Booker T. Washington, who succeeded Douglass on the latter's death, in 1895, as the leading spokesman for his race, deliberately courted a modest public image. In strong contrast to the bold costume and social behavior earlier displayed by Mississippi senator Hiram K. Revels, for example, or Louisiana's poker-playing Governor P. B. S. Pinchbeck, a white southern planter in all but racial law and custom, Washington in this era would provide no grist for gossip.

The problem with political news then was not that it grew more racist but that it got both objectively worse and thinner. During the Civil War and Reconstruction, sectional issues, and with them the place of Afro-Americans within the larger society, had been recognized as politically central. By the 1880s and after, as Reconstruction faded, so did national consciousness of black issues. After the Whittaker case, stretching from 1880–82, Dorsey devoted an entire scrapbook to only one more national episode not directly involving lynching or similar "outrage." Late in January 1890—the last year, it would turn out, for generations to come, in which federal legislation on behalf of black voting rights or education was seriously debated in Congress—Senator John J. Ingalls of Kansas delivered a dramatic oration denouncing the conduct of race relations to the South. Dorsey opened a new book with a full page of excited, front-page coverage by the Afro-American *Richmond Planet;* the items which follow, mostly short clippings from the sympathetic Philadelphia *Press,* weary *Bulletin,* and skeptical *Record,* fill only ten pages of what is the shortest scrapbook in the collection.[15]

In general each successive stage in the long erosion of nationally guaranteed civil or political rights is less clearly marked in Dorsey's books. When the federal Civil Rights Act of 1875, forbidding racial discrimination in places of public accommodation, was struck down by the Supreme Court in 1883, on the grounds that private discrimination was not a fit subject for state interference, this was still major news. Thirteen years later the court climaxed a number of intervening findings with *Plessy v. Ferguson,* which permitted the states to establish "separate but equal" facilities of their own. But *Plessy,* while familiar now to schoolchildren as the target of the landmark 1954 decision outlawing segregation in public education, went almost unnoted at the time, and most of Dorsey's coverage is taken not from the mainstream but the black press.[16]

It is then no coincidence that black papers, growing in number, provided Dorsey with more and more of his national news and comment. And it is the black press, too, which provides much of the color and invective missing from increasingly perfunctory coverage elsewhere. This is especially true after the early 1880s, when the relatively restrained *People's Advocate* was replaced, as Dorsey's favorite black source from out of town, with the New York papers *Globe, Freeman,* and *Age.* These three were all successively edited by T. Thomas Fortune, whose shifting positions and alliances combined with an angry talent for mockery to lead him at one time or another to denounce a long series of rival "Race Men," in terms that neither they nor his readers could easily forget.[17]

In dealing with hard news and features from the Afro-American community of Philadelphia itself, the journalistic conventions followed by the local white papers in the late 19th century generally mirrored those used in covering events elsewhere, but with two important exceptions. In the first place the news from Philadelphia did not fade but grew continually in importance, matching the growth of the community itself in terms not only of numbers but of distinction. However depressed, and affected, later in the period, by events to the south, black Philadelphians generally continued to make important gains in many areas, including education, desegregation, and entrance into the professions. And in the second place, for related reasons, much of the reportage was either written or at least gathered by black journalists and other sources in the community itself.

The professional leaders of that community—licensed doctors, lawyers, ministers of mainstream congregations—were universally treated, in the news and editorial columns of white papers, with respect and in the case of some notables a good deal more than that. Others, in context, were targets of fun— this was not an age in which politicians, in particular, were objects of reverence. Only one local figure of importance—always identified as "Majah" James Teagle, at various times barber, politician, sportsman, impresario, and restaurateur—was consistently victim of a light mockery based in part on his "colored" dialect, much as the same papers treated "Squire" James McMullin, in some respects his counterpart in the Irish community.[18]

The first such reference to "the Majah" ("I, J. H. Teagle, are not no ways connected with the restaurant at 242 South 12th Street") occurs in the March 9, 1879, edition of the "Walks About Town" column regularly published by the *Sunday Leader*. Its author, Daniel P. Adger, writing as "Palmetto," was one of several part-time black journalists who contributed regularly to white papers. The practice was in fact pioneered in Philadelphia when Col. John W. Forney, editor of the *Press*, hired T. Morris Chester as the first Afro-American correspondent for a daily paper. Beginning in the 1870s the sort of column that Adger contributed to the *Leader* might be found as well in the Sunday editions of not only the *Press* but the *Mirror* and *Item*, written by Alexander Davis, H. P. and Samuel O. Williams, and others. Much like equivalent "Philadelphia Letter" columns in the out-of-town black papers, these gossipy "penny-a-line" efforts tended to be brisk recitations of social events and the doings of the local elite. But these and other kinds of news were subjects of longer pieces also, and a number of Afro-American men and women, notably John Stephen Durham, Florence Lewis, and Gertrude Mossell, worked as regular reporters or correspondents for mainstream papers.[19]

Even without Philadelphia's own black press, then, coverage of routine events in the Afro-American community—political meetings, sermons and ordinations, lodge conventions, balls, plays, and concerts, major funerals always, by the 1890s a few weddings—was considerably fuller than it is now, in *Daily News* or *Inquirer,* at a time when the black population averaged far less than one-fifteenth its present size. And of the thousands of these and more significant news items collected by William Dorsey—whose whole collection includes much that is unflattering and even ugly—only two were written in a way clearly objectionable to contemporary black sensibilities.

The surprise is that the straight news columns only twice printed the kinds of tags and sentiments found often enough in ordinary discourse, and indeed elsewhere in the papers. Perhaps it was mere carelessness, failure to clean up a reporter's in-house notes, that led an editor at the *Times,* in 1892, to pass an otherwise routine story out of the Seventh Ward under the heading "Coon Voters Revolt." A bit of investigative reportage by the reforming *North American,* in 1899, was more clearly deliberate. On interviewing a black juror who had been given a patronage job after voting to acquit U.S. senator Matthew Quay of a bribery charge, the reporter listed his apparent qualifications as expertise in shooting craps, wielding razors, eating watermelons, and swinging a banjo "through a full three-quarters of a circle without missing a note."[20]

While there were two other objectionable pieces included in the Dorsey Collection, both were the work of black reporters working on white papers, people whose sometimes difficult position will be described in a later chapter dealing more fully with black journalists. Otherwise the generally respectful way in which Afro-Americans were treated by the news and editorial columns of northern white newspapers represents a kind of a formal triumph over more ordinary language and attitudes. But 19th-century readers of course found the same people in other sections of the same papers, in features, short news items, and pictures which came closer to spanning the full range of their own feelings.[21]

Some of those feelings were shaped by an Afro-American stereotype which long preceded and would long survive the period. The stereotype itself is thoroughly familiar, and it may in fact be argued that some of its elements are universal, that Russian landlords and southern planters regarded serfs and slaves respectively with much the same mixture of affectionate contempt and exasperation. It is clear at least that bigotry in the United States has had a limited imaginative range: Irish immigrants in the middle of the 19th century, according to one historian, were thought: "apelike . . . childish and emotionally unstable; ignorant, indolent, primitive, politically naive, greedy, musical, amusing, likeable at a distance, impulsive and never able to calculate ahead; and excessively lustful."[22]

But while useful to a point, the perspective suggested by the common or banal nature of much stereotyping does not allow for either the power or the full range of images surrounding Afro-Americans, a people with a truly unique place in our culture and history. The stereotype, or stereotypes, are too complex to be drawn from any single standard model simply by making a few specific substitutions, banjos for fiddles, watermelon and fried chicken for boiled cabbage and ham. At the same time, while most popular materials to which white readers were exposed were in some way shaped by stereotype, this was by no means true of all. Blacks were targets of caricature but also simply objects of curiosity, sometimes sources of sentiment and even delight—again saving fear and attendant emotions for the following chapter.

William Dorsey was of course alert for evidence of distinction, for the kinds of items which would show that Afro-American athletes, artists, scholars, soldiers, or musicians could excel in the dominant white arena itself. And he found much of it.

For the athletes, the term "arena" was not simply metaphor, in that boxing was more important than any other sport in pitting black against white in contests whose overtones were too obvious to be thought merely symbolic. There is no evidence that Dorsey himself was a sportsman. His name appears nowhere on the roster of four teams fielded by the Pythian Baseball Club in the 1860s, his peers among the city's black elite, organized by his friend and near-exact contemporary "Jake" White, Jr. No Dorsey is listed as either participant or spectator in any sporting item in his collection. But if not an athlete he was proudly black, and so in some respects a boxing fan almost by definition.[23]

The first of his three scrapbooks largely devoted to the Manly Art begins with an excerpt from Pierce Egan's classic *Boxiana; Or, Sketches of Ancient and Modern Pugilism*, first published in London during the early 19th century. It deals with the career of the ex-slave Tom Molineaux, who, "unknown, unnoticed, unprotected, and uninformed," had arrived in London to seek his fortune in 1808. Winning several bouts over the next two years, and a reputation as a "Tremendous Man of Color," he earned the right to challenge the Englishman George Cribb, coming very close in the first of their two matches to winning what would have been the first World's Championship of any sort awarded to a black man. Egan's volume being too valuable to cut and paste, the entire section, in a tribute unmatched in any other scrapbook, is copied patiently in thirteen pages of longhand.[24]

The item which follows is one of dozens in this and other books devoted to the Australian heavyweight Peter Jackson, first of his race since Molineaux to reach the same heights in his chosen sport. Jackson first visited the United States in 1888 to box the "colored" champion George Godfrey, but it was impossible to keep him confined within racial bounds. After a visit to London, during which he "paralyzed" Jem Smith, the "so-called Champion of the World"—the actual title as unclear a century ago as it has often been of late—he was judged ready to take on the great John L. Sullivan for the "World's Championship." Back on this side during 1890, challenging Sullivan and destroying a series of lesser white opponents, Jackson pulled in huge crowds of blacks who—a generation before Jack Johnson and two before Joe Louis— "regarded him as a modern Samson of their race and a vindication of their claim as equal in muscular prowess to the whites."[25]

A sensitive giant, who wrote poetry and aspired to play Othello, the charismatic boxer stopped short of Shakespeare but did put on theatrical performances which alternated scenes from "Uncle Tom" and rounds of "scientific exhibitions" with local challengers, the latter a way of evading the facts that prize-fighting itself was illegal in most states. A great favorite with the sporting public, Jackson was a genuine international celebrity, fluent in both French and Danish, who soon outgrew his native country and spent much of his prime shuttling the Atlantic by steamship. Although "The Great John L." managed to duck his challenge throughout 1890, the *Illustrated News* exploited public curiosity with a series of sketches in which it simulated a battle between the two. Jackson did finally earn a bout with Sullivan's successor, Jim Corbett, in May of the following year. But that much-touted match in San Francisco went 61 rounds to a universally disappointing draw, and despite a number of feints and near-things over the next few years it was as close as the big Australian ever got to a championship.[26]

In the meantime, with much less advance ballyhoo, Boston's George Dixon, "Little Chocolate," fighting at the bantamweight of 115 pounds, had already broken the barrier in June of 1890 by taking a world's title from Nune Wallace at London's Pelican Club. And unlike Jackson, the smaller man proceeded to stay at the top of his profession for a number of years, at various weights, and clearly pioneered in establishing Afro-Americans as the dominant force in the sport.[27]

The sociological significance of all this was immediately clear to contemporary sports reporters. Professional prize-fighting has always drawn its champions and victims from among the poorest and most desperate of ethnic groups, and in the 19th century, excepting the occasional Jackson or Corbett, it was not far removed from brawling. American cities, during the middle decades of the century, had often been wracked by interracial fighting which pitted the Irish, newly arrived and still insecure, against the even newer, much outnumbered, and yet more insecure Afro-Americans. By the 1890s, just as they were finally replacing the Irish in the worst and heaviest of urban laboring jobs, the blacks were replacing them in the prize ring also, their older battles in the streets displaced by newer contests conducted under the Marquis of Queensbury's rules. To complete the transformation, it was remarked that the mentors, managers, and trainers of the rising black challengers, including Jackson's Sam Fitzpatrick and Dixon's Tom O'Rourke, were themselves often retired Irish pugs.[28]

John L. Sullivan, bareknuckled hero of the laborers just off the boat, had been openly racist, refusing in his prime to even consider fighting "pigs, niggers, hogs and dogs." "Gentleman Jim" Corbett, symbol of a new and less crude generation of Irish Americans, had met Peter Jackson for the right price and called him "gentleman" in turn.[29]

And the working press in general applauded. In many ways the sports pages of the 1890s resemble those a century later more than any other section of the newspapers, partly in their insistence that, whatever the (sometimes noted) prejudices of their readers, their only concern was that "the better man win every time, whether he be red, white, or blue." The inescapable concern with color was of course reflected in nicknames: every city had its own Black "Spider," "Pearl," or "Cyclone," its equivalent of "Muldoon's Pickaninny," in the era when Afro-Americans were beginning to take over the game. And the *Item,* in 1894, was concerned that one reason why "weight for weight, it seems impossible to beat a colored man" was that their red ribs, black eyes, and bruises remained invisible to judges awarding points. But even a mostly white audience at Philadelphia's Ariel Club rooted for Dixon in a match against a local boy, Jack Lynch; the little "darkey fighter" had beat a Britisher for the title, after all.[30]

Next to boxing, and close to the opposite social pole, the other major arena of athletic competition that was opening for blacks was intercollegiate. As professionalized spectator sports began to take hold in the later 19th century, many colleges smelled the potential in dollars and prestige that might come to those which fielded successful teams. And prior to athletic competition there was competition for athletes, including Afro-Americans, who in Philadelphia were sometimes awarded scholarships to run track or play football by the end of the century. Perhaps these young men could dream of the good fortune earned by William Lewis, in 1903 first of his race to be appointed an Assistant U.S. Attorney, in Boston, supposedly because President Theodore Roosevelt, a fellow Harvard man, was impressed with his play at "centre-push."[31]

Neither they nor any other black athletes, however, could hope for success in professional sports apart from fighting. There are few more striking illustrations of the irrationalities of racial prejudice than its application to athletics. Historically it was always weakest in boxing, a sport in which two men alternately beat and embrace each other, literally mixing blood, sweat, tears, and spittle, and it was beginning to weaken in some intercollegiate athletics, theoretically the pastime of gentlemen students who belonged to the same club. At the same time it was tightening in a number of other areas which involved much less physical or social intimacy.

One of the few which stayed open was marathon walking, in which contestants traveled as far as they could go in three or six days, for purses of several thousand dollars. This was another sport in which blacks were beginning to succeed Irish Americans: the U.S. record in 1879 was set in a New York City match won by Frank Hart, known as "O'Leary's Smoked Irishman" after his trainer, the ex-champ. (Dorsey somewhat redundantly noted in the margin that Hart was "col'd.") But marathon walking, for perhaps obvious reasons, was never a major professional sport, and seems to have died of its own weight until revived, in recent years, on a decidedly amateur basis.[32]

The loss of thoroughbred racing was more serious. Through the 1880s and early 1890s the sport had been open to and even dominated by Afro-American jockeys like Isaac Murphy and George Simms, southerners often, who had spent their lives in and around the stables. But these men were resented and pushed out by other jockeys in a campaign which accelerated sharply around 1895, and by the turn of the century it was rare to find black men competing on the major tracks.[33]

The fact that bicycle racing was only born, with the bicycle craze itself, in the 1890s, a decade of exclusion generally, meant that in contrast to horse racing Afro-Americans never enjoyed a time when they were generally accepted. Although "Major" Marshall Taylor won some honors in the period, white "wheelmen" from the first sought to bar black competitors from professional associations and tournaments, and Taylor remained nearly unique.[34]

Far more important, symbolically and actually, was the longer, slower, process of pushing Afro-Americans out of professional baseball. Baseball, from the time of the formal organization of the National League in 1876, has been not only "the national pastime" but from the beginning the biggest and most successful of professional spectator sports. Black Philadelphians felt the sting of exclusion early, when their own Pythians challenged the local Athletics, who had won an intercity title from other white clubs, for what would in effect have been the Championship of the World as of 1867. Despite generally good relations the match was never held, and indeed the black club was barred from the statewide federation formed just two years later.[35]

There was still some hope, however, as late as 1886, when William Dorsey began to compile a book devoted to the "Giants," a club formed only a few years before across the river in Trenton, New Jersey. Several of these Giants, notably Shepard Trusty, "unquestionably the finest colored pitcher in the country," were native Philadelphians, or had played with the Active, Orion, or other Philadelphia teams. Trusty and his mates may have moved out of the bigger city because the Sabbath laws, prohibiting play on the one day when working people could ordinarily watch, were notoriously stricter on the Pennsylvania side of the Delaware. In any case the Jersey club played several successful exhibitions against National League teams during '86, but were unable to join any permanent league of their own. And although after leaving Trenton they were often allowed, for some decades to come, to continue these exhibitions while thinly disguised as the famous "Cuban" Giants, the rules were tightened as the years passed. Some white teams for a time were able to use an occasional black player at home, or in northern cities, holding him out against Baltimore or St. Louis. All that was ended in the 1890s when "gentlemen's agreements" against hiring Afro-Americans were succeeded by formal prohibitions written into league constitutions. Dorsey had long since lost his interest in the game.[36]

It was of course naïve of Peter Jackson's early fans, or of Dorsey's friend the historical columnist Carl Bolivar, ruminating years after in the *Tribune*, to imagine that proof of athletic ability would lead to full acceptance of black Americans generally. But it is true at least that the sportswriters of the era were willing to accept that ability on its own terms, however racist they may have been in other areas of their lives. Certainly there is nothing in the Dorsey scrapbooks to suggest approval of the segregation of sports; those accounts which go beyond simple description are almost universally disapproving. Within the sporting fraternity, quite apart from win and lose, not to play the game at all was clearly against the rules. In contrast the issues suggested by newspaper coverage of "serious" black music and musicians, secular and especially sacred, were far more complex than the relatively straightforward issues of exclusion versus opportunity in sports. Attitudes toward musical performance depended not only on the nature of the music but on its real or imagined origins, and the context in which it was heard.[37]

There was never any doubt about Afro-American ability to sing and play serious European music—musicality, and imitativeness, were parts of the stereotype. Truly distinguished performers had been recognized long before the Civil War, including the Philadelphia bandleader Frank Johnson, whose command performance at Windsor Castle remained a legend in his hometown for generations after, and the Mississippi-born Elizabeth Greenfield, trained in the Quaker city, who won international fame as "The Black Swan." But Johnson died young, in the 1840s, and Greenfield, nearly 70 by the time William Dorsey began seriously to collect reviews, had long since lost her extraordinary three-and-a-half octave range and retired to teach music and occasionally sing in the low-key atmosphere of the Home for Aged and Infirm Colored Persons.[38]

Philadelphia in the late 19th century was rich in classically trained black musicians, and Johnson's baton was not dropped but passed on to a series of able local successors. Other black performers and indeed composers in the European tradition visited the city often enough. Most famous between 1870 and the early 20th century were the extraordinary Thomas Greene Wiggins, "Blind Tom," and the singers Madame Selika, Bessie Lee, Flora Batson, and "Black Patti," Sisseretta Jones. But much like the great Shakespearean Ira Aldrich, for whom Dorsey named a son, these people were all honored less in their own country than abroad.[39]

In the United States, at least in cities with big black populations, concert appearances by black artists posed social problems hard for contemporaries to overcome. Dorsey's collection includes dozens of concert bills and advertisements for such performances, the most important held in the magnificent auditorium at the Academy of Music. But the Academy was opened to Afro-Americans only in 1877, too late for the city's own "Black Swan." And visitors such as Madame Selika, heralded by handbills full of praise, always shared the stage with local black performers as parts of mixed bills usually held for the benefit of one or another Afro-American church. Whites did come to these shows, and were indeed important sources of revenue, but clearly many potential concertgoers were wary of the enthusiastic black crowds who packed the hall, and while the occasions were noted they never ran more than one night. The visitors with top billing got fees of perhaps $25, they were not seriously reviewed, and they had to share the next morning's news account with the behavior of the audience itself, and the local amateurs.[40]

These serious artists then were not scorned but essentially ignored, or treated perfunctorily, by white audiences and newspapers. The few items about Blind Tom in the white journals stressed less the genius than the prodigy, the illiterate born handicapped and slave, while Dorsey's items about Selika, Batson, Jones, and their peers are taken almost wholly from the black press. The standard classical repertory was available from many sources; what white audiences wanted from black folks in concert was not Shubert but spirituals, and no other performers rivaled the popularity of the Fisk Jubilee Singers.[41]

White Americans had been hearing tunes taken, at some distance, from Afro-American music at least since the 1830s, as part of the standard minstrel repertoire. But the chorus from Fisk College, from their impromptu opening tour in 1871, for the first time exposed northern audiences to something else entirely, and as close to the originals as a secular setting would allow. Their success was immediate, and they were almost as immediately followed by imitators. The group had been sent north in the first place as part of an effort to raise money for the school, but Fisk was not the only struggling new institution in the South, and it had neither a monopoly on strong young voices nor a copyright on the even stronger musical tradition which inspired them. The Jubilee Singers included ten young men and eight women; some of the other places could at first mount no more than a quartette to perform at small gatherings of potential givers. But all of them first fed and then drew upon a real appreciation of the songs and perhaps the singers themselves.[42]

Songs and singers were as hard to separate as genuine concern and the notorious sentimentality of the era. The story of Fisk itself, and of the wider southern struggle for education and opportunity, was almost as much a part of Jubilee Singers' mystique as the quality of their voices. A reporter for the New York *Herald,* noting that President Chester A. Arthur was observed weeping quietly during a special White House performance in February of 1882, was not sure whether the President was simply responding to the strains of "Steal Away to Jesus" or to the story, which he had been pointedly told, of the way in which the singers had been refused rooms in every hotel in the nation's capital.[43]

The religious element in the appeal of this kind of Afro-American music is in any case undeniable. This was still a time in which Monday morning's newspapers—often following a day off for the Sabbath—were dominated by accounts of services held in each and every major church the previous day; black spirituals reached the North during a decade in which the mix of song and sermon served up by the revivalists Moody and Sankey played to an estimated one million Philadelphians in the course of just eight weeks. Virtually every white man and woman who had worked to abolish slavery in the decades before the Civil War had been inspired directly by religious belief, and in some ways that belief was even more important in the postwar decades. "Science," as understood in the late-19th-century heyday of Social Darwinism, was then used not to attack but to buttress the idea of white Anglo-Saxon superiority, and it took either uncommon sense or a strong belief in Christian brotherhood to resist it.[44]

A final and in some ways related basis for the appeal of the spirituals was their well-publicized origin as traditional and yet spontaneous creations of entire religious communities or congregations. Throughout the 19th century romantic intellectuals in general and composers in particular were fascinated by "folk" expression, tales or tunes that sprang direct from the people themselves. Afro-American spirituals seemed to be "our" equivalent to these materials, certainly to listeners on the other side of the ocean, where they were at least as well received as over here. Anton Dvořák's use of black materials in his symphony *From the New World* was no passing fancy. During 1894, the year in which the symphony premiered, the Czech composer was director of the National Conservatory in Washington, and had sought out the genuine roots of minstrelsy, among other things, in the course of his research on Afro-American music. Insatiably curious, unsatisfied with what he was able to observe, he wanted on the one hand to see more blacks singing and dancing in the old "authentic" manner, "as their forefathers did," and on the other more stretching their capabilities through performing in grand opera. Mrs. Jeannette Thurber, the Conservatory's president, believed that "we may all look forward to the negro race taking the lead in American music"; for Dvořák, clearly, the day had come already.[45]

Only his expertise and intensity set the trained musician apart from the amateur anthropologists whose accounts of black folkways were a staple of the northern press throughout the period. The form was often "A Letter from the South," in which the visitor recorded local manners and mores in three basic keys: amused, appalled, and straightforward. "Voodoo," as example, fell under the category of superstition or even crime, but about the Christian religion, and song, authors were almost universally enthusiastic. A typical account, "Scenes Witnessed at a Colored Revival in Savannah," noted that "the negro is strong on revivals, and on funerals he is simply immense." Writing in 1886, the author was faithful to the romantic convention that the death of slavery had led to a significant loss of religious vitality and other aspects of the picturesque. But the music, still, was "rapturous," the words "startlingly vivid":

> "Jesus my all to heaven is gone—
> Is anybody here gittin' ready?
> He whom I fix my hopes upon—
> Is anybody here gettin' ready?[46]

In fact similar observances were continually held north as well as south of the Mason-Dixon line. The counties surrounding Philadelphia, even the wooded areas of the city itself, were often home to Sunday and sometimes week-long camp meetings of a kind familiar throughout rural America. These events were reported, too, but in ways that contrasted sharply with the treatment given their analogues to the south or to ordinary religious services generally. Editors were confident that camp meetings in Glenolden, Red Bank, or Media would make colorful copy, much of the color provided by reporters who shared the dominant attitude that these occasions were a kind of circus. In fact white spectators and listeners often made up a majority of those in attendance, loosely circulating with equally casual blacks around the ring of faithful ones who surrounded the principal exhorter. In the midst of hawkers selling candies and watermelon, ginger pop and cigarettes, perhaps bringing more potent refreshments of their own, these people showed little appreciation of the "folk" and not much more respect for their religion. Or as Brother Hinton put it to visitors at Morford's Woods, New Jersey, as rendered by an amused representative of the *Sun*, "I see before me, a-laughin' and a-whisperin', young women whut hez hed thousans' spent on their eddications, and yet dey cum here to 'spose dier ignunce."[47]

And when the show moved out of the outskirts and into the heart of the city itself, the attitude toward it slid down another notch from mere amusement to distaste. Under the heading "Ear-Splitting Worship," a local paper in July of 1890 described the year-round mission run by the Reverend Isaiah Brown out of a dilapidated little building located in a narrow corridor between Lombard and Minster streets ironically named Pleasant Valley. The building itself was decorated, by this account, with "pasted lithographs of such Scriptural episodes as are most imposing to people of modest intellect." Services were held "every night after it has become too dark to sell bananas, and all day Sunday." In the hot months, as the congregation spilled out into the alley and sang straight up into the air, the neighbors could not escape the words:

> Oh Lord bress my soul,
> Lord and the prophets;
> Oh, Lord bress my soul,
> Bless my soul oh Lord.[48]

The next step followed naturally from the direction increasingly taken by the newspaper business in the 1890s, as the kind of amused contempt with which the papers treated the Pleasant Valley Mission was joined by outright sensationalism. The same double standard was at work, as what was seen as folkish in the South was seen as freakish in the North. The ancient Christian ceremony of foot-washing, as example, was colorful copy when practiced by a black Baptist congregation in Philadelphia, but reported reverentially when introduced into American Catholic ritual by the Bishop of Washington in 1894—a difference which the *Tribune* was quick to note. And when a pastor in upstate Dunbar, Pennsylvania, reportedly engaged in the ritual slaughter of a lamb during the Passover / Easter season of 1896, the New York *World* gave it a full two-page story, "A Living Sacrifice at a Modern Altar," with a huge illustration of a white-bearded black man doing a bloodstained imitation of the Prophet Moses.[49]

But while it is possible to identify tendencies, it remains impossible to find any unbroken rules in newspaper coverage of Afro-American religion. A series of baptisms performed by the newly arrived Church of God and the Saints between January and April of 1903 virtually called out for sensational treatment: the little flock was still not much bigger than the Reverend Isaiah Brown's, and its rituals demanded total immersion in the wintry Delaware River. Hundreds of shivering onlookers watched the first of these, as the Reverend Abel Dixon cut through eight inches of ice to accommodate Jane Short, whose age was variously estimated as between 88 and 100 years; when interviewed by the *North American,* Mrs. Short noted simply that if she had known beforehand that it would feel so good she would have done it all decades before. A columnist for the *Bulletin,* in April, was genuinely moved by the immersion of two men, one white and one black:

> The performance of the rite at such a time and such a place was an instance of touching, if not also impressive, devotion to the faith that was in them, and of the literal adherence to the rude and simple forms of one of the earliest ceremonies which the apostles ascribe to their master.[50]

One reason why reportage was so various in tone was then simply that Afro-American themes tapped into so many emotional wellsprings inside the white majority, many of them in conflict. A second and even simpler was that much of the space devoted to blacks consisted of miscellaneous brief items that were themselves quite various.

Some stories kept recurring. One type involved a legally black woman or her children's sudden inheritance from an old slavemaster, lover or father. The testator's white family was always doubly annoyed, both embarrassed and out of pocket; the papers usually suggested that the right thing had been done at last.

A full scrapbook was devoted to 177 clippings reporting the deaths of alleged centenarians. Afro-American longevity was evidently an article of faith, starting point of a simple formula: Aunt or Uncle ———, believed the oldest inhabitant in the city, state, or nation, was dead at the age of 133 years. In accounts written before about 1880 s/he had once seen/served/nursed George Washington. After a series of premature announcements that the old person in question was in fact the very last of what had evidently been an army of the first President's slaves, the papers took the man-bites-dog approach of reporting, for example, that "she never claimed to have nursed George Washington," until the *Times* surrendered altogether by announcing that a gala reunion of surviving servitors would be held at the Columbian Exposition of 1893.[51]

Far more important, and scattered throughout the collection, were reports of distinction of every sort. The Afro-American papers seem especially interested in honors won abroad, a regimental surgeon made Companion of the Bath, the Chief Justice of St. Nevis knighted, a Danish doctor appointed president of the medical department of the University of Copenhagen. In the United States itself there was always good news of some kind, whether from across the continent, where the only black at the University of Idaho won the Watkins Medal for Oratory in 1898, to the City of Philadelphia itself, where the Lippincott Prize of the Academy of Fine Arts was one of many honors showered on the artist Henry Ossawa Tanner.[52]

It was news of another sort when an Italian consular official "astonished" white Washington by surrendering his seat to an elderly black woman on the streetcar, and news too when a Virginia man was pulled off a trolley in Philadelphia and arrested for calling an elderly black woman "nigger." It was news when five Princeton men quit the school after a group of Afro-Americans at the Theological Seminary were allowed into a lecture by the college's President Joshua M'Cosh, and news too when M'Cosh declared that the logical skills of the students at Lincoln University matched those he had seen anywhere, at home or abroad.[53]

But while Afro-Americans were featured in most types of those unclassifiable short items which crowded the bottom pages of newspapers everywhere, as heroic soldiers, two-headed infants, mathematical prodigies, and the like, the type in which they figured most often, however, was not news but feature: the late 19th century was the heyday of printed "darkey" jokes, sayings, and dialect poems. These were in fact so common that, with its literally thousands of examples, the Dorsey Collection may be seen as a kind of giant anthology of the three forms.

Racial and ethnic jokes are virtually all intended to show the ignorance of their targets. But within this broad similarity there were specific forms associated with each group. The Irish Bull, common in the 19th century, stressed linguistic near-misses, paradoxes that often combined what was thought a characteristic tendency to exaggerate with a wholly unconscious or revealing wisdom. Thus the classic defense of a Philadelphia politician: "Half the lies told about him are not true."[54]

The typical "darkey" joke, like the Irish Bull, involved the misuse of language, and often again the tendency to exaggerate. But the stress was not on paradox but malapropism, the result of overreaching, or failure of an "uppity" attempt at educated diction. While dialect is optional in the Bull—the example above requires none—it is essential to the polysyllabic confusion of the darkey joke. Many in the newspapers were passed off as real exchanges experienced by the teller, in this case the lawyer in a divorce case:

> Q: "Did you love her?"
> A: "*Love* her, sah? Ah jest *analyzed* her!"[55]

Not all darkey jokes followed this form, however, and some suggest a kind of subversive cleverness in dealing with white folks. Thus a slave's logical defense when accused of stealing the master's rice:

> "Well, masser, does I belong to you or does I not?"
> —"Yes, you belong to me."
> "An don't dat rice belong to you?"
> —"Certainly."
> "Well, den, if I take dat rice and eat it, it belong to you still?"[56]

While only a minority of jokes involved this kind of reversal, or any other features of interest, the dialect poems and aphorisms were more varied. A piece in *Lippincott's Magazine* perceptively noted that unlike genuine "Black English," for example, what passed as dialect in the papers was only an attempt at phonetic rendering of ordinary speech, and could make anyone sound silly. But genuine or not, it was inescapable. Black entertainers, whether professionals or such amateurs as Caroline LeCount, principal of Philadelphia's Catto School, routinely told Irish as well as Afro-American stories in dialect; the journalist Gertrude Mossell attempted a little mock-Confucian "tickee-shirtee" Chinese in the *Freeman*. And the *Press*, in 1881, managed to squeeze three different accents into a single story on the reception given the city's first black cops:

> "Jes's luk at him!"
> "Niver did I expect to see the loikes o' thot. A nagar polaceman!"
> "By Jove, Chawley, old boy, this is the—ah—African officer, you know."[57]

Dialect forms, then, if never quite neutral, were too universal to be considered mere instruments of ridicule. Black dialect as used in "Aphorisms from the Quarters," for example, was simply a way of expressing folk wisdom, as invented by (usually white) literates. These one-liners could of course be directed at the uppity: "Hi l'arnt nigger ain't much service at the logrolling." But most had no specifically Afro-American content at all, and might as easily be used to represent the sentiments of any rural people: "Cussin' de weather is mighty po' farmin'," or "Tall tree made de sq'uell sassy."[58]

Dialect poetry, finally—whether by Paul Dunbar or other authors of either race—was a truly flexible form. Sometimes sentimental, sometimes didactic, it too could be used simply to reinforce stereotypes about laziness or other vices. But most examples were not simply stereotypical. And the more interesting were used the way that the contemporary Irish humorist Peter Finley Dunne used "Mr. Dooley's" rich brogue, to establish, with great sophistication, the native wit of the unsophisticated.

The best examples involved social or political commentary, and the Spanish-American War of 1898 inspired several of them, as it did Mr. Dooley. The aphorism could be used to make a point: "Dey ain't no Christianity in war, but dar's more prayin' done when war gwine on den in time er peace." The black press was especially alert to the racism involved less in the war itself than in the imperialist ambitions it inspired in much of the dominant population. One weapon was satire, displayed at its best in a powerful parody of Rudyard Kipling's famous "The White Man's Burden," evidently submitted to the Philadelphia *Tribune* by its correspondent in Cape May, a person known only as Ferguson. The title was "Drap Dat Bundle, White Man," and the cadence followed the original:

> Drap dat bundle, white man
> Yer burden is too great
> I'se speakin' but in kindness,
> Wid not one smitch o' hate.
> You started down de ages,
> To 'dopt another class.
> Two hundred years dey served you,
> No thanks! But let dat pass. . . .[59]

Afro-American dialect in print, then, could be used in several ways, often double-edged. But printed dialect had less social impact than the versions presented on the minstrel stage, origin of many of the darkey jokes which circulated in bar-rooms as well as the songs sung 'round the parlor piano. Minstrel humor had an important role in playing to and even creating stereotypes. But the nature of the stereotypes did change over the late 19th century, and so did the place of black materials in American popular culture generally. Both changes can be seen through the history of popular songs, one of the areas in which William Dorsey was considered an authority by his peers.

Much of American popular song from its beginnings was taken from black sources, at enough distance and with enough dilution so that it is hard to tell the work of Stephen Foster, who did "Old Folks at Home" in the 1850s, from the "Carry Me Back to Old Virginny" and "(Oh Dem) Golden Slippers" written by the Afro-American James Bland nearly a generation later. Both men were minstrels, performers of their own music, and deeply part of the enormously popular minstrel tradition which from the 1840s into the 1880s alternated a plaintively sentimental view of the plantation black, represented usually by soft guitar music, and the happy-go-lucky "darkey" featured on the banjo.[60]

In some sense the Foster-to-Bland succession is symbolic of one important strain in the history of minstrelsy. Before the Civil War it was hard to present actual blacks on stage, impossible to mix them with white performers; by the 1870s it was possible and the 1880s routine to do either or both, and job opportunities for Afro-American singers, dancers, and comics widened as a result. But by that time the minstrel form was set so firmly that performers of whatever complexion must, by tradition, smear their faces with burnt cork; the early cultural historian Alain Locke noted that the process was one in which whites had begun by imitating blacks, and was then picked up by blacks imitating whites imitating blacks.[61]

An interview with Charles Callendar, the most successful minstrel-show manager of the early 1880s, gives some insight into this evolution. Having dealt with players of both races, Callendar noted that the blacks sang better, were easier to deal with—slavery had made them used to obeying orders—and of course took more naturally to dialect. They were also more popular, and earned more money than whites—the comedian Billy "Cudjo" Kersands and the Philadelphia native L. L. Brown could command up to $150 a week. But it was hard to teach them to clog dance, and they had to be restrained from breaking out of the hallowed forms, and forced to stick to "what people would expect to come naturally from colored people."[62]

One reason for the growing success of Afro-American minstrels was that reviewers, as part of the wider romantic interest in the folk, ironically thought them more authentic than the whites who had pioneered in their places; the adjective "genuine" was always a feature of playbills and advertisements. The Philadelphia dailies in 1879 were universally enthusiastic about the appearance of Jack Haverly's troupe, whose spring engagement lasted two weeks, at a time when live entertainment in the big city was richly various, and most concert or dramatic performances lasted only a single night and few as long as seven. Part of the appeal, in this latter age of "megatharian" minstrel shows, was the sheer size of Haverly's production, with its one hundred voices in chorus. But the fact that real blacks were doing the old comic and slapstick routines had the added advantage of persuading reporters that they were not only enjoying the frivolity but somehow gaining insight into the "genuine negro character" by witnessing these folk in their native plantation habitat.[63]

The minstrel show had always provided a clownishly sentimental version of the Old South, and so of slavery, perhaps never more strongly than in an era when Civil War passions were mostly dead, in the North, and Reconstruction moribund. The *Press*—fiercest Republican champion of the black in politics—

was delighted with Haverly's tambourines, jawbones, and "side-splitting slave sketches." The next day the reviewer went on to reflect that "the ordinary actual colored man of the South was, and is still, in a large measure, nothing more or less than a grown-up child." All of the other eight city dailies chimed in with similar praise; only the *Sunday Transcript* held its applause, noting the ironic black takeover of a genre through which "the Southern plantation-negro . . . has been mercilessly caricatured and burlesqued by his white brother in burnt cork."[64]

The contemporary black attitude was ambivalent. One reader wrote to the *People's Advocate* to denounce those who went to "nigger minstrel shows" for in effect laughing at their own degradation. But this was an age much less sensitive to stereotyping than our own, and the issue was never really important in the black press, which continued to print its own darkey jokes and dialect. People like James Bland, too, minstrel composers and artists, were objects of some pride as a result of their success. Instead of objecting to the whole minstrel tradition, the evidence suggests that most drew a rather finer line.[65]

The entertainment programs put on by Philadelphia's own Afro-Americans featured much dialect material, self-mockery, and such basic staples of stereotype as watermelon-eating contests. But some elements of minstrelsy were conspicuously left out. And it is these which distinguish an evening at the Rittenhouse Assembly rooms with the General Dabney E. Maury Chapter of the local Daughters of the Confederacy, for example, and anything sponsored by, say, Bethel AME Church: the Confederate ladies best liked those songs and skits "that carried one back to real plantation days," a time and place to which Mother Bethel's parishioners had absolutely no intention of returning.[66]

The best example of Afro-American objection to any romantic rendering of the slave experience occurred when in 1887 a number of community leaders and politicians refused, apparently as one, to participate in a parade to celebrate the centennial of the Constitution of the United States. The event evoked especial pride in the Quaker City, where the original convention had taken place, and the Republican organizers could normally count on at least some of these men to jump at their bidding. But the plan was to illustrate one hundred years of progress by contrasting a refined drawing-room tableau, used to represent contemporary black conditions, with a slave cabin from 1787, complete with ragged but happy folks singing "plantation songs." Neither end of this scenario, it was wisely judged, would play well before the Afro-Americans of the Seventh Ward, where the proposed procession might have to wend its way through a brick shower.[67]

A less dramatic but culturally more important way of rejecting the slave past was musical, the abandonment of banjo and fiddle in favor of urban instruments such as the accordion and especially the piano. A piece in the Chicago *Herald* in 1892 struck the still dominant note of regret at this loss of tradition. But by that time others had discovered that urban blacks were folk too, and had characteristic traditions of their own. Learned pieces occasionally looked beyond the rural South to describe and analyze the game of craps, for example, which was, like playing the daily numbers lottery, or "policy," a pastime of the town or better the city, and unlike policy was clearly post–Civil War in origin.[68]

Those who looked could find work songs, too, well north of the cotton fields. In Washington, following an official ban on the blowing of horns within the city limits, people like newsboys and ash collectors took to advertising their presence or wares in characteristic singsong cadences. A piece written in 1893 supplied musical notation to the chant used by the slopmen at the back door. "Come erlong, Come erlong, Come erlong now!" A Philadelphia story, some years earlier, illustrates some of the perils of amateur collecting. The chanty used by old John Davis's chimney sweeps sounded a little too pat:

> Glory! Glory! Up we go!
> Sweep him Chimney clean!
> Who's for de Udder Shore, 'lula!
> Gib him pork and bean.

It turned that it was composed from scratch by Davis's son—a minstrel.[69]

In fact, of course, the characteristic songs of the city, like the younger Davis's little ditty, were only indirectly folk products. Unlike the Davis piece, toward century's end they began to break with earlier traditions in sounding new and characteristically urban notes.

A four-volume collection of pieces by Afro-American songwriters, published in 1897, inspired a reflective article by the black journalist John Edward Bruce, "Bruce Grit," which helps to illustrate the key transition to a distinctively black city music. The piece begins by citing the authority of William Henry Dorsey on the origins of "Listen to the Mocking Bird." The little tune, "as familiar to Americans as 'Hail Columbia,'" Bruce commented, "will hold its own with 'Annie Laurie,' or 'The Last Rose of Summer,' and will live as long as either of them." Although published in 1855 by a white man, Septimus Winner, "Mocking Bird" was actually composed by "Whistling Dick" Millburn, whom Dorsey had often heard near his own home in the Eighth Ward.[70]

Most of the compositions Bruce admired were much like "Mocking Bird"—with its telling comparison to the two Celtic airs—in their resemblance to contemporary white productions. Blind Ned wrote schottisches, others marches and quadrilles, and most Afro-American musicians the kind of sentimental songs most popular in the period. The prolific Gussie S. Davis, who had already sold 375 pieces to sheet-music publishers by 1895 (he got no royalties), carried the romantic fascination with death virtually to the point of necrophilia in "The Fatal Wedding," and especially "In the Baggage Coach Ahead."[71]

Bruce's list illustrates the pervasive influence of Afro-American music in

several ways. As the other side of the fact that white composers often wrote in
an Afro-American vein, many of the Afro-Americans, not only Bland and
Davis but younger men like Ernest Hogan, were perfectly capable of turning
out the sort of "Pretty Little Kate McCoy" waltzes that were associated with
Irish Americans in the 1890s, so that much of their work was and remains
hidden from view. More important, it is possible nearly a century later to apply
the test-of-time standard that Bruce himself suggested. And if his own three
choices for immortality seem ironically a little off, "Oh, You Can't Get to
Heaven" is still sung around summer camp fires; "A Hot Time in the Old
Town" is played at football rallies; and "The Cat Came Back," continually
evolving, remains a favorite at folk festivals. Most important, despite his own
evidently conservative tastes, Bruce included several examples of a significant
new type, neither rural nor southern in origin, known generically as the "coon
song." And while the musical content and significance of these songs belong in
a later chapter, their appearance in the 1890s illustrates something about the
new urban image and the process of stereotyping.[72]

William Randolph Hearst's New York *Evening Journal*, in the summer of
1899, printed an exchange with a reader who objected to the use of the word
"coon." The reader suggested that the *Journal*, having recently sworn off
"Sheenie" in reference to Jews, should then take the next step and stop calling
Afro-Americans after four-footed beasts. The editor's reply began with the
claim that "the colored people themselves" had probably invented the offending term, and certainly used it. He went on to claim—falsely—that the *Journal*
never used it anyway except as part of song titles or verbatim testimony in
court, and concluded with a peroration based on the biblical text "Ye shall not
see My face, unless your brother be with you."[73]

In fact the Hearst papers and their sensationalist competitors in the 1890s
were deeply involved in stereotyping. A new emphasis on graphics meant that
straight or even sympathetic news stories involving Afro-Americans were
increasingly illustrated with little cartoon figures, while a little later the ability
to reproduce photographs opened new opportunities to give caricature a veneer
of realism. The Philadelphia *Times* illustrated a "Coon Heaven" feature in
1899 with a half-page photo of a grinning youngster with a face-full of
watermelon; the text suggested that a constant supply of melons would cure all
racial problems, as "the darkey would be completely disarmed, and incapable
of giving vent to his inherent baseness."[74]

But while the *Times* piece, in context, referred to southern blacks, more
and more pieces in New York, Philadelphia, and elsewhere dealt with those
who lived in the city itself, people who called out different sentiments and
required a different stereotype. No northern paper would casually use the
word "nigger," but while the old shuffling southern "darkey" was never fully
retired, for the local news and features he was increasingly replaced by another

figure, the urban "coon." Visually the darkey was ragged and humble, the coon elegant and haughty, dressed in bowler hat and spats, with cards popping out of his pockets and a razor up his sleeve, often in company with a proud woman in tight dress, high heels, and plumed hat. If not always a change for the better, it was a real change, and its impact was measured by the immense popularity of the "coon songs" among both black and white audiences in the late 1890s. [75]

Given the sheer weight of this rising flood of racist material, contemporary blacks had no way of stemming it effectively. Their own standards were entirely personal and themselves beginning to change; use of the word "coon," like others, was supremely a matter of context. Ernest Hogan, author of "All Coons Look Alike to Me" was himself proudly Afro-American, and there was no apparent question about singing and dancing to his song and others like it at black affairs in Philadelphia. In contrast, a group of young white men who chanted the title at churchgoers on a Sunday were courting serious injury and won some. But for the still small and relatively powerless urban minority, there were few such opportunities to deal with racism in such a physically satisfying way. Deliberate insult was common enough on the streets, but in its own way easier to deal with than the confusion, shifting standards, insensitivity, and ambiguity which marked most white treatment of black subjects in the popular press. [76]

The ways in which Afro-American life were sketched in the newspapers and popular journals of the later half of the 19th century were then various and often self-contradictory. They were also curiously segregated, with very different attitudes coexisting in different sections of the same papers. The hard news, in the dominant northern press, was generally given straight, whether its content was mostly discouraging, from the South and Washington, or more hopeful, from Philadelphia and other northern cities. The more personal, colorful, or even malicious notes were more often sounded by black reporters or papers.

The restraint involved in treating black news with any measure of dignity is shown in the much broader range of attitudes suggested by the treatment of other and miscellaneous items, those dealing with various aspects of black culture in the South and increasingly the urban North. These features and short news pieces typically involved some mixture of two black figures or images which, while certainly different, were essentially ranged along the same spectrum, and could be blended in many ways. At one end was an object of essentially favorable attention, even imitation, often inspiring or inspired by religious or romantic sentiment. At the other was the familiar caricature, generally viewed with condescending amusement.

But there was a third image as well, not so easily blended as the other two. Only a few items on the entertainment, short news, and feature pages, notably those dealing with the new sexual element in the "coon songs," even suggested its existence. But the "inherent baseness" which inspired so much contemporary white fear and violence was central to the full journalistic portrait of the Afro-American in the late 19th century, and the subject of the following chapter.

Chapter 2

Of Race, Sex, and Lynching

It may be argued that from the beginning there was a chicken-egg relationship between prejudice and American racial oppression, or even that racial attitudes grew up, after the fact, to justify a domination that preceded them. It is true at least that some specific stereotypes were conveniently tailored to specific social situations, as Thomas Jefferson's insistence that blacks are better suited to work under a hot sun than whites, require less sleep, and feel loss and other emotions less keenly. But the evidence is overwhelming that racial prejudice is even wider than racial oppression. And the fact that hostility to blackness, in particular, is built into the whole Indo-European family of languages has given hostility to Afro-Americans a character wholly different, in kind and degree, from the prejudice which dominant white Protestants have historically directed at other ethnic and even racial groups.[1]

Two conditions helped to make the effects of prejudice especially painful in the years covered by William Dorsey's collection of clippings. First, in an age when science was enjoying more prestige than ever before, what passed for scientific knowledge of race was not helpful but hurtful, and gave apparent sanction to deep white fears of miscegenation or "amalgamation." Second, once legal domination through slavery and "black codes" was ended, and the Reconstruction effort had failed, race relations in the southern states were redefined largely through illegal violence. As peaceful coexistence seemed hopeless, forecasters turned to increasingly grim predictions about the future. By the late 1880s and 1890s the lynching phenomenon, drawing on racial and sexual fears, was seriously affecting the image and condition of blacks not only in the southern states but all across the country.

Popular journalism reflected the ambivalent and even contradictory feelings of white Americans toward black, as shown in the previous chapter. Confusion was one of the hallmarks, too, of the racial information and misinformation published throughout the period, with many items contradicting each other as well as the editorial positions of the papers which printed them. But in dealing with the sensitive issues of sex and violence, the press went beyond merely reflecting popular attitudes to the point of shaping or inciting them, even in areas like Philadelphia, which did not experience lynching directly.

Especially frustrating for the leadership of the city's black community was the fact that with slavery ended and the Fourteenth and Fifteenth amendments to the Constitution opening the promise of equal citizenship, only racial discrimination prevented their full inclusion in the wider society. And despite substantial gains, dramatic exceptions, and the usual contradictions, that discrimination worsened with the lynching phenomenon, and threw them continually on the defensive.

It would be hard to exaggerate the amount of racial nonsense published in the mainstream press between the 1870s and the early 20th century. Scholars may now distinguish among a variety of contemporary scientific or quasi-scientific positions on the issue. There were intellectual differences between the more optimistic neo-Lamarckians, who believed in relatively rapid racial evolution, and the hereditarian neo-Darwinists, who thought change proceeded at a glacial pace; between the polygenists, who believed that the races were distinct species, and the monogenists, who did not; between the contributions of serious ethnologists such as Lewis Henry Morgan and popularizers such as the Social Darwinist John Fiske. But readers were less often exposed to coherent syntheses than to random snippets from evidently respectable authorities:

- Professor Blumfield, of Johns Hopkins University, proclaimed in 1890 that the dark color of Afro-Americans resulted from oxygen's tendency to dissolve in the warm air of their original homeland, thus leaving unoxidized carbon deposits in the skin.
- Doctors at a convention of the International Surgical Association in 1897 discussed the significance of the fact that black people do not sneeze.
- While American physicians were skeptical of a Viennese colleague's claim, in 1899, that he could "bleach" any African with electric shock treatments, they refused to reject it outright since "it is well known . . . that negroes are much more susceptible to the action of electricity than white men."
- French scientists, in the same year, debated the implications of the fact that blacks are born white—a matter thought significant by both theologians and evolutionists searching for the "original man"—before concluding that they are not, in fact, born white.[2]

For many people similar questions were not merely academic. The Philadelphia *Times* reported in 1899 that when Emma Addison was bitten, in the course of a domestic dispute, she was terrified that her husband might be a "blue-gum nigger," whose bite was poisonous. Policemen, in both New York and Philadelphia, were also scared about this extra risk; doctors at Hahneman Hospital, after treating a case resulted from an especially violent arrest, told reporters that "anatomical research has shown that certain classes of the Ethiopean race have small poison sacs or cells under the gums which in certain circumstances eject poison."[3]

But acutely personal anxiety more often struck those bitten not literally but metaphorically: whites who loved or were at any rate married, or thinking of marriage, to someone who might have a racial "taint." At a time when the name and work of Gregor Mendel were still wholly unknown, ignorance of genetics was almost as complete as ignorance of racial characteristics themselves. The void was filled among other things with the lore surrounding blacks who turned white, or vice-versa, one of the staple short items in the papers. One such boy was put on exhibition in Philadelphia in the winter of 1881; an older man, "Uncle Tom," discovered by a Dr. Lindsey the following year, was still touring in 1894, when he was shown at the city's Jefferson Medical College. Why did these mysterious biological changes occur? Perhaps for the same reason as all those black babies born to apparently white parents, or mixed twins to black ones—that is, a result of the "blood" passed on, undetected, by some remote ancestor of the other race. This sort of "reversion" was the subject, in fact, of serious scholarly correspondence, in 1869, between two of the country's leading scientists, Louis Agassiz and Thomas Cope.[4]

When an anonymous reader asked the *Inquirer*'s advice column, in the spring of 1894, for a sure way to tell white from black—"certain reasons make me most anxious to find out"—s/he was told to examine hair samples under a microscope. The suggestion was one of the rare pieces of relatively sound information, on this delicate question, in the whole of the Dorsey Collection. First of the more usual tests was supplied by old Judge Mackey, father of a maverick South Carolina congressman, when the younger man's death in 1884 revealed that he had secretly married Vickey Sumter, an "octaroon" from Philadelphia. The Judge dismissed the charge. Miss Sumter had merely been raised, as an orphan, by kindly colored people; the crescents at the base of her fingernails were white, rather than purple, irrefutable proof of the purity of her own ancestry. The advantage of this test was its simplicity; in an age of public prudery, with women especially covered from ankle to shoulder and virginity at marriage not uncommon, the other commonly cited telltale mark—a dark stripe running down the spine of those afflicted with black blood—was, presumably, sometimes discovered too late.[5]

After the possibility of "reversion," a second reason for anxiety about miscegenation—the word itself alien and vaguely threatening—was that mixed children were thought sickly. The purely physical vitality of blacks was part of the national folklore, as witnessed by the army of record-breaking centenarians whose deaths were regularly reported in the papers. But while the infusion of

white blood was supposed to make them more intelligent—one reason for the
insistence on recording precise skin color was to explain ability in terms of
observably Caucasian ancestry—there was a price for this in terms of lung
diseases, infertility, and other symptoms of constitutional delicacy.[6]

In the summer of 1872, when there was still some hope for a meaningful
Reconstruction in the South and for full civil rights everywhere, delegates to
the Republican party convention in Philadelphia demanded among other things
the repeal of state laws forbidding miscegenation, on the ground that American
citizens should have the right to marry whomever they chose. But all the
southern states, and many to the north, continued to carry these on their
books; it is surprising only that Pennsylvania, which had deprived black
citizens of the vote in 1838, and only reallowed it under pressure of the
Fifteenth Amendment in 1870, had never passed such a prohibition. In fact
cases of legal miscegenation remained fascinating enough to be reported as
news throughout the period. Usually—although there were no fast rules in
anything governing race relations—the stories suggested that the reporters
shared the distaste that made the event newsworthy to begin with.[7]

"A Revolting Case of Miscegenation" was the *Bulletin*'s headline over a
brief story about the 1879 marriage, in upstate McKeesport, of a black farmer
and a "pretty" local girl. Col. Forney's *Press* thought it "A Strange Infatua-
tion" which brought two Bostonians together in 1884. In 1894 a public display
of affection, in St. Louis's Union Station, between a black male and a veiled and
possibly white female was enough to bring in the police, who fortunately
discovered that the woman, indeed wife, was acceptably dark. In such a social
atmosphere, with vigilantes tarring and feathering a white girl in Ohio for
consorting with a black, "White Caps" threatening the same in rural Pennsylvania, and loose talk of lynching a married couple in southern New Jersey, even
the law was not enough. Stories from all over the North reported that court
clerks refused to issue licenses except under pressure, that magistrates refused
to perform mixed marriages even in places, such as Detroit, with reputations
for enlightened race relations. A couple in Illinois required a writ of mandamus, in 1898, to get the proper authorities to allow their wedding. And when
one partner in an existing marriage learned the awful truth about the other only
after the fact—an event, in the stories, sometimes precipitated by the birth of a
"coal-black" child—the revelation could lead to insanity in Ohio, suicide in
Texas, murder-suicide in Oklahoma.[8]

Truly hostile reaction was not universal. White Philadelphians in general
kept their heads; mixed marriages were not uncommon locally, and the
occasional coverage given them was at worst satirical rather than hysterical.
When, on two separate occasions, the distraught fathers of white teenagers
sought to have Afro-American suitors arrested on various charges, the *Item*
noted that, however wrongheaded, the young women in question seemed
genuinely infatuated. The heaviest local coverage was given a story which

nearly developed into a small international incident. When Martin Hamilton was sent from Philadelphia to Glasgow, in the summer of 1897, as part of a street-paving crew, he fell in love with Maggie Woods, the landlady's daughter. When he sent for her the following September, however, immigration officials detained her on Ellis Island when they learned what she intended; it took several days and the personal intervention of several prominent Afro-Americans to get Woods released and a Presbyterian ceremony properly performed. All six Philadelphia stories in the Dorsey collection treated the incident as they would any other case of Young Love Triumphant; the *Item*, while remarking, grudgingly, that Hamilton was "moderately good-looking, so far as his race goes," concluded with a line from Bobby Burns: "A man's a man for a' that."[9]

A fundamental distaste for miscegenation was then sometimes leavened with amusement or balanced with conventional sentimentality. But neither of these was a real defense against a racism bolstered by the authority of contemporary science. The only effective counters were religious conviction and common sense, both of them stronger in the Afro-American community than among their dominant neighbors. That there was really only a single human race was simply an article of faith, a necessary corollary to belief in "the fatherhood of God and the brotherhood of man." And among a people who had experienced it over many generations, miscegenation was an everyday fact of life, and if often manifest in ugly ways neither fearful nor mysterious.

The precise proportion of Caucasian genes in the Afro-American population remains a matter of speculation. Two modern historians who attempted an estimate for the slave population of 1860 counted only those noted as "mulatto" in the census, a figure which depends on the trustworthiness of answers that sensitive owners, at the height of the Victorian era, gave to plantation visitors who asked for the number of resident slaves and next, in effect, for the proportion of those born of illicit unions between women without legal rights and powerful white persons unknown. Afro-Americans had their own guesses as to how many had white ancestors; the editor of the Washington *People's Advocate*, in 1879, put it at three-quarters. Whatever the figure, nothing infuriated articulate blacks more than the hypocrisy proclaimed when "a descendent of some African prince of the blood royal looks into a mirror and blushes at the features which tell him that in his veins flows along with that of the despised race the finest blood of the South." While whites, drawing again on the authority of science, proclaimed that "social antipathy" between the races was a "law of nature," the obvious answer was to turn the argument inside out, and to note that the law of sexual attraction overrode all others.[10]

Blacks themselves were by no means united on the subject of intermarriage. Frederick Douglass, who lost his first wife in 1882, was insistent the next year on the importance of marriage as a means of integration, and in fact took a white second wife early in the following year. (His response to public criticism was that the first time he had married someone of his mother's race, the second of his father's.) Bishop Henry McNeal Turner, on the other hand, was only the fiercest of several who took the negative side in a formal debate among several leading intellectuals held in Washington's Bethel Church in the winter of 1896. At less-exalted levels, while cities such as Philadelphia were too big to have any kind of unified reaction, smaller communities, as in southern New Jersey, took more distinctive positions. A majority of the inhabitants of Gouldtown were supposed to be of mixed descent, and many continued to marry across racial lines; interracial couples, after an initial stir, were reportedly tolerated in New Brunswick; but "White Caps" drove a married pair out of Mount Holly in 1890, and it was the resident black community whose hostility to a couple from Massachusetts forced them to leave West Asbury Park in the same year.[11]

But however mixed their feelings otherwise, leading blacks were nearly united in their insistence that the laws against miscegenation were bad social policy in practice as well as insulting in principle. The social-policy argument was that legal barriers simply encouraged the production of bastards. As a minor note, the fact that slave marriages were always held invalid in court continued to cause trouble long after abolition, creating problems of inheritance for the children and sensitizing literate blacks in general to the need for firm legal unions. Far more important, the experience of centuries had shown that interracial sex was inevitable, and would triumph over all; the only choices were to let it remain exploitative and furtive, or to bring it into the realm of choice.[12]

Both the importance of symbolism for blacks and the corresponding sensitivities of whites were illustrated by a marriage ceremony held in the offices of the *Christian Recorder,* in May of 1882, and its coverage in the Philadelphia *Press.* The principals were James Shaw, a British-born widower of 48, and Emma Jones, 22, both residents of Delaware, which denied them the right to marry. Although Shaw was clearly not a member of any AME congregation, and Jones was a stranger to the city, the occasion was thought important enough to warrant not only the offices of the Reverend Theodore Gould, pastor of Mother Bethel, but the added presence of the Reverend Levi Coppin and indeed the Right Reverend Daniel A. Payne, senior bishop of the denomination. The *Press,* although editorially the most integrationist of local white papers, chose to violate all of the usual rules governing coverage of mainstream religion and leadership in the local Afro-American community. Its account cruelly mocked the event, the accents of the "polychromatic loafers" who turned out for it, and the appearance of the "parti-colored" couple themselves, stopping just short of insulting the three clergymen directly.[13]

Miscegenation, and the issues surrounding it in the late 19th century, went well beyond the issue of individual choice. It was central, too, to the more fundamental and notably dismal debate about the racial future of the United

States. The debate was ultimately about politics, but it was governed by the assumptions of Social Darwinism, set off by statistics from the southern states and several cities, and colored by notions of black sexuality that contradicted much of the rest.

In the years just following the Civil War, it was the fear of Afro-American fertility which underlay one of the scenarios of Democratic politicians: that the freedmen, if not restrained, would not only dominate southern elections but flood the northern labor market as well. But what the 1870 census seemed to show was just the opposite: the southern black population officially grew at the modest rate of less than 8 percent, far less than under slavery, and less than the white gain, in the same states, of about 12 percent. What these figures then suggested was the fulfillment of the basic premise of Social Darwinism: that the inferior race, once released from the "protection" of slavery and thrown on its own into the great "struggle for life," was dying out. Indeed the difference between black population gains in the first decade of freedom and the last of slavery—when, in the South, the total increase had been over 25 percent—pointed to two satisfying conclusions. First it justified, ex post facto, the essential benevolence of a slave regime which had kept its people fat and healthy; second, if projected, the percentages would soon point down rather than up, signaling that the black race was on the way to extinction.[14]

These assumptions were apparently shattered by the returns from 1880, which officially recorded a truly remarkable black gain in the South of 35 percent over 1870. Isaiah Wears, the leading black orator in Philadelphia, delighted his audience with the observation that "the race had not died out, as had been prophesied. They were rather kind of 'dyed in.'" Others suggested commonsensically that the census itself was flawed. During 1870, especially, violent conditions in the South had prevented any kind of accurate count. If that one were ignored, the difference between 1860 and 1880 would show, roughly, the same kind of generally healthy gains that had marked the whole period since the formal abolition of importation from Africa, when natural increase alone accounted for growth in the Afro-American population.[15]

But common sense was never the strength of the Social Darwinist perspective, and its proponents were resilient. Some still pinned their hopes on the next, or 1890, census, which should show a marked decline among "shiftless" rural blacks. Others, who feared that the black increase would instead outpace the white, were reassured in 1889 by "Greybeard," the staunchly Republican southern correspondent of the *Press*, who argued that while Afro-American fecundity was higher than white, it was matched or exceeded by the death rate. The returns finally showed a 14 percent increase in both South and nation, settling nothing.[16]

But if the gross figures did not support the Social Darwinist argument, there was another and more helpful set. As early as the 1870s it was clear that Afro-Americans were increasingly leaving the farm for the city. And if the city was the future, it did not work. There was much statistical evidence to show that the urban black environment was lethal, that death rates in the city were two and even three times higher than those for whites. In fact, black urban populations, like those in medieval cities, were unable to reproduce themselves: the death rate so exceeded the official birth rate that growth was dependent wholly on in-migrants from the countryside. The accelerating movement toward Richmond, Washington, and Philadelphia, then, was in effect migration into a death trap, and might yet accomplish the extinction of the race.[17]

A modern social historian might quarrel with some of the statistics in question, not much more reliable than those from the census. But it remains true that black urban birth rates were relatively low and death rates appallingly high; the weakness of the extinction argument lay not in the raw figures but in the explanation for them. As the *People's Advocate* pointed out as early as 1878, the problem was not heredity but environment, not that Afro-Americans were constitutionally weak but simply that they were poor: it was the lack of good food and doctors, of heat in the winter and air in the summer that was killing them in cities. Professor Kelly Miller of Howard University expanded on the same theme a generation later; on closer examination the two-to-one racial difference in urban death rates was in large part due to differences in infant mortality, with the familiar deprivations of poverty compounded by parental ignorance and the lack of municipal sanitation in slum areas.[18]

These and similarly sensible observations did not put the issue to rest. And one favorite explanation tied the Social Darwinian and the miscegenation arguments neatly together. While the Afro-Americans stubbornly refused to fade away, and indeed many were making undeniable progress against all odds, the progress was entirely the work of the mixed bloods among them, and due to their Caucasian inheritance. Racial mixture, however, was only buying a little time; although mulattoes were evidently not quite as sterile as mules, "Gray-beard" explained in 1886 that four generations would be enough to extinguish their fertility. While pure-blooded blacks had a certain primitive vitality, just as whites had more advanced constitutions, the elimination of people in the middle would leave Afro-Americans to sink to their proper level, as hewers of wood and drawers of water, no longer engaged in the kind of direct competition with superior whites which was then causing racial friction.[19]

This was an old scenario. One black response, back in the 1860s, had been to suggest that if indeed mulattoes were doomed to extinction, the whites could speed up the whole process if they would only act on its inherent logic: "Let them reverse their policy and encourage, for a time, the amalgamation they have hitherto opposed, and, with patience, they can have a white man's government." Satire was no more effective than sense, however, and a genera-tion later, in the 1890s, grim predictions about the Afro-American future were more widespread, and authoritative, than ever.[20]

In the December 1891 issue of the *North American Review*, Professor

James Bryce published some "Thoughts on the Negro Problem," which William Dorsey dutifully pasted into his scrapbook collection. Lord Bryce had visited the United States eight years earlier, and the resulting two volumes on *The American Commonwealth* won him a reputation as the most perceptive foreign observer since Alexis de Tocqueville half a century earlier. Much like Tocqueville he could foresee no happy ending to the racial problems of the United States; unlike Tocqueville, as an established member of a great imperialist power in the age of Social Darwinism, he firmly believed that Afro-Americans were naturally "inferior in intellect, in tenacity, in courage, in the power of organization and cohesion." Clearly the racial situation in the southern states was deeply troubling, but after his most recent visit he could see no merit in any of the solutions then under discussion: "amalgamation" would set back the white race, which detested the very subject; mass deportation to Africa was wholly impractical; federal protection against lynching and electoral violations would only arouse white southerners. An immediate political problem had been created by the great mistake of granting blacks the vote. While it might be solved—Bryce was no democrat—by an educational qualification that would eliminate 90 percent of the black electorate and much of the white, the Americans were not likely to adopt any such restriction. There was some hope that more prosperity would ease tensions, and blacks could make some moral and educational gains. But basically the main thing for the majority was to patiently await yet more census returns, confident that a "terribly high" death rate and declining birthrate were already making the Afro-American population "relatively far weaker" than before.[21]

Lord Bryce's vision was distinguished from a number of others in part by his own humanitarian and essentially optimistic nature. The *Literary Digest*, on examining "The Future of the Afro-American" in August of 1898, could see no hope for a dying race except as foot soldiers, commanded by white officers, in the new tropical possessions which the United States was about to acquire. Some predictions involved a kind of racial Armageddon, a war of genocide. And one such piece in the *North American Review* was enough to set the usually mild-tempered Gertrude Mossell, personally as well accepted as any black in Philadelphia, to suggest that white hypocrisy was driving young people right out of the Christian faith, and to urge, herself, that the race take up arms to defend itself.[22]

The great rise in the incidence of lynching, toward the end of the century, was both cause and reflection of the growing concern about racial coexistence in the 1890s. While interracial violence was as old as American history, lynching was in significant ways different both from the more familiar race riots and from the confrontations which had marked the course of Reconstruction to the South, not least in the way it was treated in the established press.

"Race riots"—usually in fact the armed invasion of black neighborhoods or settlements—had long been common in the North as well as the South; Philadelphia in particular, through the middle of the century, had been notable for these murderous affrays. But the last major riot in the Quaker City occurred in 1871, when the novel sight of Afro-Americans at the polls enraged Irish Democrats downtown. In general, in the North, most issues involving political or civil rights were settled peaceably over the following thirty years, a period not coincidentally marked by the more cooperative behavior and predictable economic conditions brought on by a maturing industrial revolution. Race riots, then, always condemned by the established press, tended to fade in number and intensity.[23]

Reconstruction had meanwhile brought new forms of violence to the South, the assassination of Afro-American editors and politicians, urban riots of the northern kind, sometimes shootouts between gangs of armed men. These "outrages," as they were generally called by Republican papers, were universally recognized as part of a wider political struggle for power. But with the end of Reconstruction, another form of white aggression seemed to call for another kind of explanation.

The first lynching "scorecard" included in the Dorsey Collection was published by the Afro-American *Richmond Planet* in November of 1889. The number of incidents in which whites killed blacks reached a peak in the following decade at well over a thousand, and the accompanying news accounts came to dominate the scrapbooks themselves. It is impossible to tabulate the number exactly, in part because the verb "to lynch" was often debased in the popular press, and in part because the phenomenon took many forms. In the rural South, the lines between legal posse, search party, simple gathering, and lynch mob were nearly nonexistent, and it is hard to classify cases in which a group of men went looking for a suspected wrongdoer and then shot him. If lynching is defined strictly as extra-legal execution, carried out by a group and intended to punish crime or other offense, then there were still great variations in terms of the size and social composition of the groups, the weapons used, and the degree of forethought or barbarity involved in the act itself. Perhaps above all there was variation in the nature of the precipitating incidents, and in the motives, both conscious and unconscious, of the executioners. One of the few possible generalizations is that lynching grew up with the process of driving Afro-Americans from political power in the South, at a time when they were increasingly helpless. Another is that, despite the range of behavior for which victims were actually executed, with only a minority involving allegations of rape, the newspapers contributed to an overwhelming popular association between lynching and the defense of white women.[24]

Part of the reason for this is that the upsurge in lynching occurred just in the period, beginning in the late 1880s and peaking in the 1890s, when the "new" or "yellow" journalism associated with Joseph Pulitzer and William Randolph Hearst was inspiring imitators all over the country. It is no coincidence that

William Dorsey turned increasingly to Pulitzer's New York *World* and after 1895 to Hearst's *Journal*. While the two could seize on any passing incident, and their role in heating up the Spanish War fever of 1898 is the stuff of historical legend, it was lynching that most reliably provided the daily bread and butter of sensationalist coverage for newspapers everywhere. The word "daily" is no exaggeration. In a decade that averaged over one hundred each year, a lynching was often good for three or more separate stories, first when a crime occurred and retaliation was anticipated, next when the event actually took place, finally when in the aftermath it was dissected, denounced, or otherwise debated.

Lynchers and newspapers each in effect played the other's game. Southern mob lynchings, in particular, were often barbaric enough to require little sensationalist embellishment. In keeping with the general practice of "segregation," in which different images of or policies toward Afro-Americans were reserved for different parts of the same papers, northern editorialists in general denounced lynching, and certainly torture, but the actual news stories were forwarded by southern correspondents confident that the right thing had been done to the right parties. Headline writers shared the same confidence, so that in one of scores of such examples the reforming *North American* carried the story of how a mob in Texas slowly roasted one man alive under the banner "How a Fiend Died." While the Philadelphia *Times* condemned the whole practice, its own story on the Mississippi killing of a black who had actively denounced a lynching the day before concluded that "relations between the whites and blacks had been strained, but the summary treatment of Durett has quieted things."[25]

Racial prejudice and excitement about violence were emotions clearly shared by all mobs and many readers. And in an age of sexual repression, when fears about black sexuality and miscegenation were equally widespread, allegations of interracial "outrage" gave license to exploit them, even in newspapers reluctant to use the word "rape" directly. Just as a mob near Texarkana ceremonially handed the first match to the farmer's wife who had accused the young black man strapped to a pole above a woodpile, the New York *Journal* delighted in fanning flames on its own. In October of 1897 it printed the lavishly illustrated first-person narrative of young Katie Clum: "I saw a small dirty room with a cot in one corner. I felt sickened and would have fallen but the negro caught me. Then I fainted. God was merciful . . . ," a formula which allowed both Clum to repress any memory of the assault and her readers to supply their own imagined details. The headline over all this—actually a quote from an accompanying article by the pro-lynching activist Miss Hallie Erminie Rives, author of *Smoking Flax*—was "Lynch This Man!"[26]

Philadelphia's Afro-American community felt the heat in many ways. Despite the great educational advances and occupational strides of its own elite, a long series of victories in the local battle for desegregation and dignity, and a secure if minor place in the city's politics, it was never immune from problems that afflicted the race anywhere in the country.

The local community, to begin with, had thick roots and many ties below the Mason-Dixon line. William Dorsey's father Thomas, as noted, was an escaped slave. William himself, born in the city, was one of a minority of the Philadelphia elite who had not migrated in from rural areas, usually in the South. And he was further unlike many of his peers in that he apparently never went south on some long-term adventure of his own. His contemporary Theophilus J. Minton, for example, also the oldest son and heir of one of the city's three leading caterers, took his wife to Columbia, South Carolina, in the late 1860s, where he studied law and worked with Congressman Robert Elliot. So many Philadelphians left town during the same period that the somewhat shaky official census may have recorded a net loss in the black population, from 22,630 in 1860 to, perhaps, 20,550 in 1870. It is impossible to fix the number exactly, but perhaps 2000 may have served in the army or navy, while others went south to find their fortunes as educators, editors, clergymen, lawyers, or politicians amongst the newly freed millions who could use their sophistication and expertise.[27]

The tide ran the other way in the late 1870s and 1880s, with the 1876 election and its aftermath as pivotal in private lives as in national politics. Several Philadelphians were entangled in South Carolina congressional politics alone. Joseph Hayne Rainey, born in Georgetown, lived for many years and was married in the Quaker City before returning to his native state, where after a series of wartime adventures he won a seat in the First Congressional District as the first Afro-American to serve in the House of Representatives. Meanwhile young Stephen Gipson, born in Philadelphia's Fifth Ward, graduated in 1869 from Lincoln University, and immediately went south to teach school. Within a short time he had won a position as school commissioner in Rainey's Georgetown County, where he made a friend and political ally of another young northerner, George W. Offley. Offley, originally from Hartford and a few years older than Gipson, had also run off to the South at 14, joining General Daniel Sickles's invading army before his father brought him briefly back. Slipping away again, this time into the Union navy, he signed on a New Bedford whaler after the war and following that as a privateer, fighting in one of Cuba's recurrent civil wars. Captured by the same U.S. navy which had first launched his nautical career, he was put ashore in South Carolina in the same year as Gipson. He too moved a long way in a short time and wound up as a Macon County auditor. When Gipson, in the Byzantine course of Reconstruction politics, was shot by Congressman Rainey's brother, he fled north to teach in Maryland; Offley experienced a religious conversion, and went on to several ministries for the AME Zion church, combined with teaching jobs in North Carolina and then rural Pennsylvania. The two old friends—Gipson a fiery city councilman, Offley a noted revivalist—were reunited with each other, and with Joseph Rainey's widow Susan, in Philadelphia during the late 1880s. There they were shortly joined by T. J. Minton, who had left Columbia at about the same time as the supporting federal troops, served for a time as private secretary to the governor of Indiana, then as a lawyer with the United States Treasury Department, returning home only in the 1890s to take his place as the leading Afro-American of the Quaker City bar.[28]

Other Philadelphians, while typically returning for visits, remained in the South to pursue their careers: Lincoln graduate William W. Still, son of the city's most famous black abolitionist, as a South Carolina lawyer; Jonathan Gibbs as, at one time, Florida's secretary of state; John R. Lynch as an active Mississippi politician. The Institute for Colored Youth had been proud to claim more southern teachers during Reconstruction than any other institution in the country, and continued for many years after to send the majority of its graduates below the line. These young people, mostly children of the local elite, Bantons, Wests, Ramseys, and Lewises, found more opportunities than were available locally, but often returned to spend their summers in the city. But perhaps above all it was the continuing travels of officials of the African Methodist Episcopal Church which kept Philadelphians continually in touch with events to the south.[29]

The Reverend G. W. Offley's Carolina conversion was hardly an isolated event. When as part of their new freedom southern blacks were given the power to choose their own churches, they deserted white ones en masse and joined black. None was more important than the AME, which had effectively been barred from the Old South under slavery. But when the Confederacy was invaded the church sent its own soldiers of Christ to move in with the federal armies. The denomination then "exploded" in terms of both numbers and territory covered, growing twentyfold from a membership of perhaps 20,000 northerners in 1860 to 400,000 Afro-Americans all over the nation by 1880.[30]

The experience of Henry McNeal Turner was archetypal. As a free young South Carolinian he had first joined the regular Methodist Episcopal denomination, but switched to the AME some years before his appointment as Union army chaplain in 1863. As a politician in Reconstruction Georgia, Turner earned a reputation as "the most antiwhite—and most disliked—Negro member" of the State Assembly before moving to Philadelphia, in the pivotal year 1876, as manager of the AME Book Concern. On becoming bishop in 1880, a job that demanded continual shuttling between Philadelphia and points north, west, and especially south, he joined his Episcopal colleagues as an important spokesman on all racial issues. AME officials all moved in several worlds, one of them defined by political geography: generally treated in the North with the outward respect, at least, that their positions required, they were still classified as "colored" in the South, and their visibility kept them continually in the news as they experienced, first-hand, the tightening of segregation. It was the Reverend W. H. Heard—like Turner a native southerner, who had split his early years between Georgia and South Carolina before moving to Pine Street, to take charge at Mother Bethel—who brought the most important racial case ever heard by the Interstate Commerce Commission. When thrown out of a railroad car in 1887, four years after the Supreme Court had thrown out the Civil Rights Act of 1875, Heard appealed to the new commission, which he and others hoped would prove more protective than the Supreme Court; the ICC finally ruled only that railroads must provide separate or Jim Crow cars for those barred from first-class travel.[31]

At any given time, then, Philadelphia was home to many people who knew southern racism and violence directly. The number was continually swelled by migrants at every social level; since the city's Afro-American population, like those in other urban areas, did not grow naturally, the officially recorded rise to 63,000 by century's end resulted entirely from migration, mostly from the South. And at the same time the lynching epidemic migrated with them, to New Jersey, Pennsylvania, and Delaware, surrounding all of the city's black inhabitants, and preventing them from ever feeling genuinely secure.

The line between gathering and lynch mob was not in fact much thicker in rural South Jersey than in Alabama. The area was dotted with black settlers, many of them, Stills and Dorseys, related to cousins in the city, but the land was owned mostly by small white farmers. In the winter of 1886, following the arrest, near Eatonville, of a 65-year-old ex-jockey and longtime petty thief for the improbable rape of a white girl, the suspect was hanged from the jailhouse door. While the lynchers were named in the original accounts, and boasted of the crime, what the *Press* called "Efforts of the Authorities Not to Find Out Who Killed Mingo Jack" defeated investigation, as county officials refused to pay the expenses of detectives assigned to the case. Perhaps there was some embarrassment two years later when Richard Kearney, a white condemned killer with a record of sexual assaults, confessed to the original rape. In any case, no one boasted openly when in 1890 a black South Jersey jailbreaker, trailed by bloodhounds, was shot dead by pursuers. And in the following year, proceedings involving Frank Lingo, accused of rape and murder, were allowed to go peacefully into what were perhaps the most celebrated trials, and certainly the most racially explosive, in that era of New Jersey's history, and occupy three full scrapbooks in the Dorsey Collection.[32]

The trials began, in a sense, in September of 1889, when the body of Annie LeConey was found in her farmhouse near Merchantville. Suspicion naturally fell on a black farmhand, Francis Lingo, with a long criminal record. Born a slave in Maryland (he was not sure whether in 1857 or 1860), Lingo escaped indenture to his former master and fled to Delaware. In his new state he once got a year in jail for assault on a white woman, a sentence sandwiched between two others for theft. The first of these earned him two years, and under the Delaware code an additional one hundred lashes and an hour in the pillory; the second time he broke jail and fled back to Maryland, where he earned five more years for burglarizing a store, and thence to New Jersey, where he picked up yet another two for robbing a farmhouse. After being arrested for the LeConey murder, Lingo was then freed, despite the loud suspicions of the local white community, and indeed became the state's star witness against young Annie's Uncle Chalkey. The prosecution argued that LeConey had killed his niece for her property; the jury, in March of 1890, in effect repudiated Lingo by returning a verdict of not guilty.

That murder was then still unsolved when on the following September 25, just a year after Annie LeConey was killed, another local farmer, John Miller, reported that his wife had not returned from a train trip. A search party found her the next day in a bushlot, fully clothed, her hand bitten and throat cut; the body later yielded "evidence of outrage." The Millers' chief hand, who apparently knew about Mrs. Miller's scheduled trip and route, was Frank Lingo. After several people identified him as having been around the bushlot close to the estimated time of the murder, it was found further that his hand was cut or scratched, and small bloodstains were located both on his clothes and on a razor found at his home. Jailed in the cell that Chalkey LeConey had occupied the previous year, Lingo too was tried the following March, with LeConey a most conspicuous spectator; his two court-appointed lawyers called in a third, ex-Judge John W. Wescott, the man who had earlier sentenced him for theft.

Wescott's defense was based on two main points. He tried, first, to show that the prosecution's schedule was flawed, that various people had seen Lingo shooting craps or otherwise occupied too close to the estimated time of the murder to have allowed him to do it. The fact, too, that almost no blood had been found in the bushlot, although Mrs. Miller's body was virtually drained from the broad arterial wound, suggested that she had been killed elsewhere and only later dumped on the spot where she was found. The jurors came in with a guilty verdict on March 20; Wescott did not give up.

The old judge first came to the state supreme court in February with a private detective, J. P. Campbell, to bolster a theory which in some ways paralleled the state's case in the earlier LeConey murder. Campbell claimed that in order to win her confidence he had literally seduced Mary Collins, the murdered woman's sister, who then confessed to him that John Miller had killed Annie back at the house, and that Mary had then helped him dispose of the body. The justices were not moved, and the country indicted Campbell for perjury. Wescott continued campaigning, however, until the supreme court agreed to a new trial, which opened in November of 1892.

Given this second chance, and flanked by five other volunteers from the Camden County Bar, Wescott was still unable, in the opinion of the press corps, to shake John Miller. The testimony was much as before, absent the prosecution's two forensic experts, who had died between trials; the state of their art had not allowed them in any case to establish anything more than that the blood on Lingo's clothes and razor had come from a mammal rather than, say, a chicken, and that Annie Miller, a married woman, had had sexual intercourse before her death. There was then little reason to expect a different verdict, and indeed the jury, when polled later, agreed that they were ready to convict. But this time Justice Garrison halted the trial after the prosecution had finished, before ever hearing Wescott's defense. The county's own witnesses, he ruled, had in effect supported Lingo's alibi, so placing him in various places and at various times that he could not have been alone with Mrs. Miller for the period required. He then directed an acquittal.

The fact that Judge Garrison was a Democrat made this even more unexpected, and further helps to illustrate the rule that it is no more possible to make easy generalizations about justice than about any other aspects of race relations in the period. The aftermath, however, will come as no surprise to anyone familiar with the sensibilities of an era in which prurience about violence, if not sex, was given even freer reign than in our own. During the 1890s the walls of Manhattan's Tenderloin Club were graced with a composite photograph entitled "A.M.-P.M.," the first half featuring three smiling young black men; the second, the same trio hanged from a tree in rural Virginia. Following an incident in Franklin Park, New Jersey, in which a white farmer shot two black intruders who, he said, had killed his wife and child, a New York showman paid the man $500 to exhibit his bedroom furniture; two others bid $1000 each for the heads of the dead killers. And within days of his acquittal Francis Lingo was on display with his wife, child, and a lecturer on the case at Forepaugh's Dime Museum in Philadelphia. While he had to share the bill with Dockstader's Original Colored Minstrels and Prof. Welten's Cat Circus, the *Item* agreed that he was the main attraction, and whenever introduced as " 'a victim of circumstances' there was a yell which could be heard blocks away." Among the visitors was William Henry Dorsey; a friend in South Camden had marked two newspaper drawings as the best available likenesses, but the artist came to make the comparison in the flesh, noting in the margin that "he looks very much like the picture in the front of this book—slim—brown in color— rather pleasanter than the portrait mentioned. . . ."[33]

Pennsylvania's first lynching, two years later, occurred under different circumstances from most of the racial violence which continued to trouble South Jersey. Afro-Americans in many areas upstate were not longtime agricultural laborers but recent imports, brought in all-male gangs to work the mines or on the roads, often in conflict with local citizens or other Hungarian or Italian labor gangs. In February of 1894 Richard Prior, foreman of such a railway crew, was arrested for killing a local merchant and his family near Stroudsburg. Two weeks later an armed mob "warned out" the rest of the crew, and in mid-March, with his cell door left suspiciously unlocked, Prior escaped with a crowd not far behind. Spotted finally by Benjamin Burns, a local black man who had to plunge through a frigid mill race to make the catch, the fugitive was hanged to an oak tree with a block and tackle from a nearby slaughterhouse. Everyone seemed to know his part, perhaps as a result of having read the stories from down South; a collection was taken for Burns, who was also given the rope, following tradition, to sell off in 25-cent sections while other souvenir hunters chopped up the oak. Although the earliest news accounts mentioned several names, notably Burns's, a coroner's inquest concluded that Prior had been murdered by "a person or persons unknown."[34]

This event, routine in all but its geographical setting, was much less disturbing to Philadelphia's black community than another, subject again of a full Dorsey scrapbook, which began with events on June 16, 1903, in Old Christiana Hundred, a few miles outside of Wilmington, Delaware. When 17-year-old Helen Bishop died of a throat wound shortly after being found, raped and beaten, on her route home from Wilmington High School, the police arrested George White, a local farmhand whose nine prior years in prison included five for the murder of a white man. Talk of lynching was immediate as White was moved from jail in Wilmington to the New Castle County workhouse. After several demonstrations, one of them led by a black man, a crowd estimated at 4000 men, again including a number of blacks, stormed the place at 1:30 the morning of the 23rd. Despite resistance from special police and guards, who wounded several and killed one boy, the leaders reached White, took him to a prearranged spot, and burned him at the stake.[35]

As the newspapers analyzed the event in the aftermath, they generally agreed that beyond the murder itself two developments had brought on the lynching. First, on June 18, the state supreme court had refused to order any trial until the regular September term, judged much too long a delay by angry local citizens. Next, although Miss Bishop's father, a Christian minister and school principal, had urged patience and the need for legal judgment, a fellow minister, pastor of Olivet Presbyterian Church in Wilmington, took an entirely different line. The Reverend Robert P. Elwood, a young newcomer, later described as intensely ambitious to make his mark in the city, denounced the high court's delay at a mass meeting held the night of the 21st. Waving a handful of leaves stained with the girl's blood, quoting the U.S. Constitution on the need for a speedy trial, Elwood asked rhetorically whether White should be lynched. His answer was of course an impassioned "yes!"—if the law's delay or technicalities or indeed anything else should stand in the way of legal execution, quibbles his audience was in no mood to hear.

On the morning of White's murder Wilmington's Protestant ministers called for a united meeting at the YMCA; there, while the representative of Olivet Presbyterian remained conspicuously absent, they unanimously denounced the "revolting and fiendish crime" of the night before. Philadelphia's daily papers were equally united in condemnation. But in fact most had at one time or another expressed sentiments very like those of young Elwood, who had come to Wilmington not from the South but from New Jersey, where he had grown up in an atmosphere in which the emotions which underlay lynching, and the word itself, were continually and carelessly exploited in the popular press.

Lynching was common enough; rumored lynchings, or talk of lynchings, were far more common. Nineteenth-century Americans, even in big cities, were by no means as dependent as we are now on organized police forces, and it was common for citizens to chase and catch criminals on their own, often attracting helpful crowds in events routinely called "near-lynchings." Any violent crime could be made to produce lynch talk, from offended friends or relatives of the victim, passersby, newspaper readers, or indeed newspapers. "Deserved Lynching" was the headline over a local story describing a white cop's rape of a black teenager, an opinion voiced also by a judge in the District of Columbia and a magistrate in New York City in referring to accused black killers brought before them.[36]

In the case of Stroudsburg's Richard Prior, in 1894, the *Item* attributed the mob's actions precisely to the alleged flaws in the legal process that the Reverend Robert Elwood cited nine years later: corruption, favoritism, and delay. Although it was hard to argue that any of these were likely to operate in favor of black rapists or killers, in a decade when the modal murder trial came up within weeks of the event and occupied a single morning, the paper insisted that "murderers instead of being regarded as dangerous to the masses become the pets of the law," and "mob law is a protest of the public against [the] system." The New York *World* agreed that "legal delays and quibbles" were the real problem. While the *Times* stopped short—they all did—of urging mob action directly, it did note that "the penalties of law have little influence in deterring the ignorant and brutal class of negroes, while . . . mob law does in some measure terrify and restrain them."[37]

What happened during the 1890s was that, in the North, the earlier political model of racial tension was replaced by a newer version, born in the South, that obviously appealed to deep white emotions on both sides of the Mason-Dixon line. Southern papers themselves were indignant, even taunting, when, for example, a mob in Ripley, Indiana, broke into a jail to hang five black men accused of attempted burglary. The Indianans' real offense, one suspects, was that they had debased the act of lynching itself, which ought properly to be reserved for *the* crime. Certainly the discussion was increasingly carried on in these terms, and—whatever the real issue behind any given act—the defense rested on the need to protect white women from black lust.[38]

The Wilmington Lynching in 1903 combined most of the classic elements, magnified only in size. On the afternoon of June 24 an inept coroner's inquest was held as somewhere between 3000 and 5000 demonstrated around it; it resulted in the release of Arthur Corwell, the only man ever arrested in the affair, and the usual verdict blaming "persons unknown." Police Chief Black estimated that 8 of 10 residents of Wilmington supported the mob; those around the courthouse went into a frenzy when Corwell appeared, and after beating several black bystanders moved toward an actual attack on the black district before drifting away. Governor John Hunn did not, on the morning of the 25th, believe it necessary to call the militia; that night a crowd of about 400 black men beat some whites and exchanged shots with the police, resulting in the third death and several serious injuries. As small fights continually broke out and more armed confrontations threatened over the next several days, Governor Jelks of Alabama wrote the *North American* to suggest that nothing like the Wilmington situation could occur in "the more populous parts" of his own more enlightened state.[39]

The Philadelphia press was genuinely frightened by the size and fury of a mob so few miles away, and published huge graphic specters of "Anarchy" to vie with pictures of a frenzied Reverend Robert Elwood. But while the fears were doubtless real, and the editorials strong for law and order, nothing new was learned. The *Inquirer* suggested "that the law is as a rule all too lax in dealing with murderers." Elwood's pile of private congratulations more than balanced his editorial condemnations, both from all over the country; while formally censured, later, by his Presbytery, he was strongly supported by his congregation. The local papers were filled with letters from "A Mother of Daughters" and other bloodthirsty representatives of what the *Bulletin* called "the very large number of Philadelphians who justify the lynching, although far from being law-breakers themselves." When it was alleged—the state of local records made it impossible to confirm—that George White had once served a term for assaulting a white woman, the *Record* endorsed a suggestion in the *Press* that all convicted rapists should be castrated before release from prison. Later in the year a northern cleric, the Right Reverend William M. Brown, newly installed as Episcopal bishop of Arkansas, expressed much prevailing sentiment: "While I do not justify lynching, I can find no other remedies adequate to repress the crime for which it has been made a punishment by the people of the South."[40]

Meanwhile black reaction to events in Wilmington, like white, essentially summed up attitudes that had been developing over the previous fifteen years.

There were Afro-Americans, and some others, who attempted sophisticated explanations for the whole lynching phenomenon. While neither Marx nor Freud were yet familiar, black and white observers both understood some of the elements of any modern analysis. Christopher Perry of the *Tribune* ironically quoted the racist Irish-American agitator Dennis Kearney as explanation for violent behavior in anyone: "Feed me and I am a good citizen. Starve me and I am a fiend." Certainly Afro-Americans were fully aware of the tensions, guilts, and hypocrisies involved in everything related to interracial sex. Poverty, racism, and a weak state were cited as underlying reasons for lynching, as they are now; but none of these was new, and cannot fully explain the upsurge that dates specifically from the late 1880s.[41]

An unanswered question is whether in fact individual black attacks on whites were increasing during the late 1880s and 1890s. Southern whites said yes, and one modern historian has echoed the argument that a new generation, never subject to the close surveillance and intimidation of slavery, was in fact more aggressive than its parents. In the 1890s this was usually an argument for repression, but the anti-lynching crusader Ida Wells Barnett in effect inverted it. In her 1894 pamphlet, "The Reason Why," Barnett pointed out that since southerners had routinely left doors unlocked and women alone on plantations before and during the Civil War, the notion of an inherent black lust for white women was clearly a recent myth. As part of an attack on the whole system of caste and class in the southern states she argued the allegation was a specific product of the postwar years, an excuse for practicing the politics of racial intimidation.[42]

Rape, even alleged rape, was in fact at issue in only a minority of interracial lynchings. Beyond that it is at this date impossible to guess at the actual incidence of sexual assault, or even whether it was rising or falling. The modern women's movement has taught us how unreliably low are the official figures, for reasons partly involving fear and shame of a kind that were even more powerful in the Victorian era. To balance this, in the atmosphere of the 1890s, there were suggestibility and hysteria, on the part of sexually inexperienced women, and among those involved in interracial affairs the need for cover-up, even the possibility of blackmail.

As part of the complexity surrounding interracial issues of all kinds, it must be remembered that in most places notions of justice, and common sense, were never fully overcome. Rape was not an uncommon crime in Philadelphia, but very few incidents involving black males and white females were in fact prosecuted, all of them quietly. A number, perhaps the majority, of the most potentially inflammatory accusations were formally dismissed. Thus Robert Gills, in September of 1891, was accused by a white 15-year-old and freed by a magistrate; allegations against Alfred Watkins by an 11-year-old girl in 1897 were contested in court by her own father; Agent Watson, of the Society for the Protection of Children from Cruelty, warned a judge not to credit the word of a 12-year-old in 1899, while doctors, later in the same year, testified against the claims of a 14-year-old. Early in 1903, the same year as the Wilmington Lynching, a jury in upstate Taylortown took ten minutes to find a black man not guilty of the rape of the three-year-old daughter of two old-family local physicians.[43]

Perhaps the clearest example of the use of sexual emotions for political ends occurred not in Wilmington, Delaware, but a few years earlier in the North Carolina town of the same name. Wilmington's Afro-Americans had joined white Republicans and Populists in an 1897 election that replaced a Democratic government with an interracial coalition. In November of 1899, in answer to disparaging remarks about black morals made by the wife of Senator Felton, editor A. H. Manley of the weekly Wilmington *Record* printed an editorial judged so offensive that local whites not only destroyed his office and sent him fleeing for his life but went on a violent rampage that drove hundreds of blacks out of the town, not incidentally returning political power to the old Democratic regime.[44]

In Philadelphia, where Manley eventually settled and became a leading champion of civil rights, local ministers and the Afro-American League sponsored fully five indignation meetings in the fall of 1899, the largest at a "mobbed" Academy of Music on December 1. While the Dorsey scrapbook on the Wilmington affair is 153 pages long, much of it devoted to debate over the offending editorial in the *Record,* the dominant press, north and south, was apparently reluctant to quote from it directly, and it was thought a coup for one anonymous and possibly black paper to reproduce it. Manley—himself almost white, obvious product of several generations of miscegenation—had simply written that poor whites practiced much the same sexual behavior as blacks, and that further there were "fiends" of both races. The truly inflammatory passage, however, was the one in which he suggested that many black "rapists" were in fact sexually attractive to white women, and that sometimes the allegation of assault turned reality upside down.[45]

Black journals and speakers sometimes took the Ida B. Wells position on lynching, as when the Tribune argued that it was "rising above one's station" that really incited southern violence. But Manley's editorial, however it may have echoed private sentiments, stood virtually alone. Several Afro-American papers, notably the *Star of Zion,* in fact agreed with local whites in blaming the *Record* for setting off the Wilmington explosion, and although Dorsey, in the margins, denounced this as "infamous," few were willing to follow Manley across the line he had violated. When not only rape but miscegenation of any sort was illegal, it was simply not possible to discuss interracial sex in rational fashion, or to conduct a debate in terms of the often treacherous nature of criminal accusations and statistics.[46]

For Philadelphia's Afro-American community the whole situation was doubly frustrating. Its leaders were essentially helpless, physically far from the action, emotionally close, directly affected. If the stereotyping represented by minstrel songs and coon shows bothered few of them, it was because they were continually faced with a far deeper kind of racism, one they shared with no other group. The continual battle to open jobs and public places had little to do with banjos and watermelons. When Philadelphia's police fought integration it was explicitly because they could not face physical closeness, the sharing of table space and bunks; when the order went down to "Clear them niggers out" of the line at the Walnut Street Theater it was because they were supposed to smell bad; when a lawyer objected, in court, to a detective's giving a glass of

water to a black man who had fainted on the stand, or when restaurants forced
to open service dramatically broke dishes used by black patrons, the message
was clear. Most Afro-Americans, certainly the city's doctors, teachers, and
lawyers, could easily confound the comic stereotypes in person. But there was
no way of clarifying the mysteries the dominant race thought hidden in the
"blood," or in the loins.[47]

However helpless the Philadelphians, they never stopped doing what they
could, showing their solidarity, expressing their anger and even fury. The five
meetings held to protest the events in North Carolina's Wilmington were
among scores held during the decade. While white churchmen passed supportive resolutions, and a few Republican politicians might join elderly white
abolitionists on the dais, these congregations were almost entirely black: to fill
repeatedly the Academy of Music, at great expense, was to mobilize close to 10
percent of the city's adult Afro-Americans in a single place.[48]

Anger was an emotional necessity. During the height of Ida Wells's
campaign in the summer of 1894 a group of clergymen convened in Indianapolis called for ministers all over the country to use their pulpits to urge
Afro-Americans to arm themselves to fight back. T. Thomas Fortune, in
Philadelphia to help organize the protests over North Carolina's Wilmington,
made a reportedly "rabid" speech to a meeting of pastors, again vowing to
fight. Four years later, in the heat of the Sunday after the lynching in Delaware,
the Reverend Montrose V. Thornton of Wilmington preached a sermon which
expressed a not uncommon thought in uncommonly strong language. Noting
that some of the leading citizens of his city had supported White's murder,
Thornton announced that although once "charitable to whites" he was no
longer: "The white man in face of his boasted civilization stands before my eyes
tonight the demon of the world's races, a monster incarnate. . . . "[49]

After anger, hope was an emotional necessity too. Faith gave hope in the
long term, but even faith was often strained. The mild-mannered Christopher
Perry, editor of the *Tribune*, Republican politician, and officeholder, wrote in
1893 that he believed in "the Providence of God," but that if "justice to black
and white alike is to be an unknown virtue in this professedly christian country,
then . . . in place of the meek-faced christian . . . will be heard the inces-
sant tramp of the Nihilist . . . insisting on an entire revolution." The dream
of federal intervention was dying by that date, with no hope under the
Democratic administration of Grover Cleveland. It was entirely dead six years
later, with no improvement under the Republican William McKinley, whose
inertia inspired Perry to call him "the poorest excuse for a statesman that Ohio
has ever produced." For dramatic, immediate relief the Reverend William
Phillips, of Zion Baptist, suggested in 1899 an appeal to foreign powers,
perhaps to Germany, on the model of United States intervention in Cuba the
summer before. And Wilmington's Reverend Montrose Thornton in 1903,
only partly, it seems, as a device to rebuke the evident hypocrisy of the

American stand on the barbarities of czarist Russia, actually sent a petition to the Russian embassy asking for help.[50]

But intervention was clearly fantasy. And in late-19th-century America so it seemed was armed resistance in the South, a suggestion often brought up and on second thought abandoned. Given the imperative need to do something, the position that responsible leaders fell back on, perhaps again inevitably in the atmosphere of the 1890s, was conciliation. In terms of lynching, what this meant in practice was abandonment of the kind of response suggested by some of the arguments of Wells and Manley, and meeting instead with white racists on their own ground, conceding the terms of the debate at the outset.

After Wilmington in 1903 this meant of course that Philadelphia's AME ministers matched their denunciation of George White's burning death with another of "the utterances of Reverend M. V. Thornton, inciting the people to organize for bloodshed." The Reverend Matthew Anderson, writing an open letter of denunciation to his fellow Presbyterian Robert Elwood, only voiced the sentiments of any Christian pastor by including the statement that "no one deplores the crime of which White was accused more than myself." The tactical statement most characteristic of the era was rather the one made by the Reverend George Alexander McGuire of St. Thomas P.E., whose previously scheduled talk to a crowd of 2000 Afro-Americans at the graduation ceremonies of Wilmington's Howard School included a plea for the graduates to "ostracize such brutes in their own race."[51]

Again and again, black spokesmen like McGuire endorsed the southern defense of lynching, in effect, by blaming black "brutes" and "fiends" and urging their respectable brethren to restrain them by whatever means. In the year 1899 alone, the 71st Annual Conference of AME Zion unanimously condemned "those worthless negroes whose shiftlessness leads them into the commission of heinous crimes"; Howard Professor Kelly Miller, speaking at the Bethel Literary and Historical Society, stressed that the key to end lynching was to stop raping; and the Philadelphia *Tribune*, echoing the same sentiment, urged that "for conscience's sake, let us begin to do something to stop the downward grade of our people."[52]

It is easy a century later to see the futile and even self-defeating nature of this approach. But it was far too widespread to blame it on a few weak-willed accommodationists. The Reverend H. C. C. Astwood, as the AME church's superintendent of missions a bitter critic of American racism and imperialism in Cuba, was one of those who, in discussing the lynching epidemic in 1899, denounced "the criminal classes of our race . . . emboldened at the sympathy they get from time to time." And there was in the whole era no fiercer critic of white America than the redoubtable Bishop Henry McNeal Turner, whose language sometimes rivaled the Reverend M. V. Thornton's, who insisted that powerful historical change is usually the work of "fanatics," presumably like himself, and who in 1894 called for blacks to organize secret vigilante associations to rid themselves of the criminals who were destroying the reputation of the race as a whole.[53]

White Americans in the late 19th century had little perspective on either racial or cultural differences, and did not themselves fully understand the reasons for the fearful racism which inspired many of them. Blacks had some better understanding of the motives behind the violence too often directed at them, but no one had any real grasp of the future of race relations.

What appeared to be scientific theory, sometimes bolstered by official statistics, suggested to many educated whites that problems would be solved by the extinction of the inferior race. Thoughtful blacks, faced with the rise of both racist science in the books and racist violence on the ground, had no coherent alternative to offer. Most believed, it seems, in some combination of faith in divine Providence, party politics, or the eventual triumph of common sense, but the often maddening developments of the late 1880s and 1890s shook confidence in every one of these. Certainly there was nothing in the national news, from Washington or the South, to provide any grounds for hope for the future of the race as a whole. What perhaps saved them from despair was the fact that, certainly in places like Philadelphia, real life was more complicated than what appeared on the printed page, and that the daily business of living and making a living was more pressing than speculation about the future.

Part II

OCCUPATIONS AND
MAKING A LIVING

The intention of the next several chapters is to tell much of the story of late-19th-century black Philadelphia through the history of its several occupational groups. An occupation in this sense, and especially an occupational history, is about a source of income but also about the conduct of a life, as "artist," "laborer," "lawyer," "laundress," "politician," or "teacher," and in many cases about the way in which each occupation shared and shaped the wider history of the community.

In purely economic terms the three most important things about that community are that it was poor, that it offered limited opportunities, and that both of these problems were directly related to racial discrimination. The poverty was shared with other groups, but the racial discrimination and the limited opportunities made the black experience unique from bottom to top. What united these extremes was that top and bottom both were shut out of the dominant development of the era, the urban-industrial revolution which was transforming the economy of Philadelphia and the nation.

The late 19th century was a golden age of city building everywhere, a time when the urban skyline was transformed by high-rise buildings born of structural steel, the work inside revolutionized by typewriters and telephones. In Philadelphia as elsewhere this was when businessmen and governments built the features, some of them now in decay, that for most of a century Americans associated with urbanity itself: electric streetcars and zoos, ballparks and department stores, universities and museums.

The economic vitality that enabled all of this was driven by an industrial and transport system symbolized by the famous Pennsylvania triad of steel, oil, and railroads. Philadelphia meanwhile consolidated its position as the nation's leading industrial center, its official population nearly doubling in the thirty years between 1870 and 1900, from about 674,000 to 1,294,000. The city was then first in the most important textile business, and first too in the number and variety of skilled enterprises of all kinds, as thousands of local companies built steamships and locomotives, watches, wallets, and baby carriages. As the new blue-collar army of mill and factory workers grew in size it was joined by an even newer one of white-collar clerks and typists, telephone operators and salespeople.[1]

The Afro-American population meanwhile grew even faster than the whole, roughly tripling officially from something more than 20,000 in 1870 to over 63,000 by the turn of the century. But economically it did not keep pace at all. As of 1900, one study of the census figures has shown, there was an enormous gap between the occupational distributions of Philadelphia's blacks and whites. Fully 76 percent of African-Americans, for example, worked in either unskilled laboring or domestic and personal service jobs, compared with just 28 percent of white immigrants, and 12 percent of native whites of native parentage. The combined figures for white-collar jobs—professionals, clerks and salespeople, owners and executives—were for blacks 4, immigrants 15, and natives 35 percent; for manufacturing of all kinds, blacks 8, immigrants 47, and natives 40 percent.[2]

There is no single "Philadelphia Story" leading to these results in the chapters which follow. Occupational groups, indeed individuals, followed many different paths in the late 19th century, some moving up and others down. But the fact that the number of occupations open to blacks was relatively so small helps to make it easier than for their white contemporaries to generalize about their experience. The limited choices created by discrimination combined with poverty to make the lines between rich and poor much closer together than among whites, a condition which allowed many men and women to move out of one income category into others. Whatever their jobs at any given moment, virtually all had to share many of the same attitudes and insecurities, the same neighborhoods, the same need for resilience in the face of trouble. Most, too, had to face and deal with an underground or criminal economy that was also a part of the black experience. And mutual interdependence of many sorts assured that the condition of the great majority at the bottom of the income scale affected all.

To move beyond these generalizations into more telling detail is often treacherous. The occupational figures given above, although a reasonably good representation of the legitimate occupational hierarchy in Philadelphia and other cities at the turn of the century, are in fact misleading. In the absence of other and more personal information it has often been necessary to do Afro-American social and economic history "by the numbers," the numbers themselves provided by the United States census. No historian can do without this tool entirely. But it must be recognized that it is crudely unreliable, and to dress up the results with apparently authoritative columns of figures, decimal points within percentages, suggests an entirely false precision.

The census was among other things a kind of barometer of Afro-American trust in white authority, and not surprisingly it was generally low. The census of 1860, to begin with, was an especially suspect enterprise from the black perspective. The previous decade had begun with passage of a radically biased Fugitive Slave Act, which inspired many migrants to come to the big city and hide, not always successfully. As conflict over the place of Afro-Americans helped to push the nation toward Civil War, the Pennsylvania State Legislature twice during the 1850s passed resolutions aimed at solving the problem by shipping them back to Africa, a position endorsed also by Philadelphia's leading newspaper. And then in the summer of 1860 a group of strange white men fanned out through the city's black district to ask, "How many people live here? What color are they? What are their names?"[3]

No later census was taken under quite that big a cloud, but there were always reasons, on both sides, to shadow the exercise every time. No blacks did any of the counting before 1890, and while there were a number of places where a respectably dressed white man might be welcomed as a customer, or mark, this was not usual in the daytime, and for most households, then as now, such a visitor was more likely an agent of the law, or the landlord, than the bearer of good news. On the other hand these same visitors, low-level and temporary patronage employees of the government, could not have looked forward to searching through "Razor Avenue," "Bloody Row," "Bull's Run," "Soapfat Alley," and the other twisted courts and corridors that made up much of the Fifth and Seventh wards.

Given the intense overcrowding in Afro-American neighborhoods, with far more people and even families living in places than observers from other areas would expect, it is hard to imagine that the census takers would probe beyond the monosyllables they were likely to get from whomever they might find at home.

Even among the more respectable, the results may be illustrated by the ways in which the surviving descendants of Thomas and Louise Dorsey were counted and classified in 1880. William Henry, his wife Virginia, and their five children were properly located at 1231 Locust Street. His light color was noted as "B" for "black," hers "M" for "mulatto," both designations switched in other enumerations. Her Alabama birthplace was given as Georgia, in other censuses as Pennsylvania. Their son Ira was classified as daughter "Ida"; he had been "Eva" in 1870. Down the street at 1033 meanwhile William's "mulatto" younger sister Mary Louise, given as "Minnie," was listed as a married woman, although using the Dorsey name. She was living with a black "moulder" and a 12-year-old daughter Nellie, also given as "B," although newspaper descriptions and official records describe her as adopted, white, blue-eyed, and blond. None of the rest of Mary's family appears anywhere, although her husband Robert Harlan, Jr., and two natural daughters, Louise and Carrie, were almost certainly living in the city at the time, and two nephews, John C. and Dorsey Seville, whom she kept as legal guardian on the death of her sister Sarah, were even more surely in residence.[4]

One reason for hiding from or misleading The Man might be an illegal or shameful occupation; while some enumerators did sometimes list a few "prostitutes," for example, among the people they did count, it is generally impossible to find the pimps and madams, gamblers and numbers runners, bootleggers and thieves who made up much of the urban economy. But the wider dimensions of the problem may be suggested by trouble at the other end, the undercount of the city's Afro-American leadership.

Appendix III lists some 36 men and women whose prominence got them most often in the news. Of 24 such people mentioned at least 12 times each in the Dorsey Collection and in a period that suggests that they were residents of the city in 1880, only 20 can be found in the census of that year, while of the 20 resident in 1870, 6 are missing from a computerized printout of black names and occupations. There may have been professional reasons for the young tough destined to be the black city's most famous dance-hall and saloon proprietor to duck the count, but the other absentees include such eminent respectables as a future bishop of the AME church, together with the leading poet, outstanding public school educator, and most noted abolitionist in the community.[5]

A final problem, less stubborn than the one posed by the census but still troubling to most modern readers, is the fact that dollar figures from the late 19th century cannot be translated easily into equivalents in the late 20th. In general the period between 1870 and 1900 witnessed a significant deflation, as the economic system as a whole was still competitive, and improvements in transportation and productivity combined to drive prices down. The resulting increase in real wages was important even to those members of the working class, such as blacks, who were otherwise denied the benefits of the industrial revolution. But the wage and price changes between 1870 and 1900 were far smaller than those which divide that time from our own, and which have proceeded too unevenly to smooth out with precision. What does it mean, in modern terms, that ordinary whiskey in the late 1880s was worth 5 cents a shot, and the best cost 20 cents? That live-in domestic servants earned $2 to $4 a week, stevedores 20 cents an hour, government clerks $1000 a year? That a chicken—feet, feathers, and all—cost 12 cents a pound, and a four-room house rented for $10 a month? Over the past century in general wages for unskilled labor have moved up relatively more than for skilled, housing costs more than food, and there are a host of budget items, from auto insurance through withholding taxes, that simply cannot be compared.

For the period as a whole, one recent historian has suggested that a "working-class" income was one which fell below about $900, "middle-class" between $900 and $3500, and "upper-class" above $3500. But while a good guide to the levels of household incomes in general, these figures cannot be applied directly to urban Afro-Americans, with their far lower earnings. Among black Philadelphians, while status was granted on many grounds not strictly economic, the term "elite" may be applied to anyone with a white-collar job, and to a number of manual workers as well, although most members of this "elite" would qualify only as "working-class" by the definition above.

Perhaps for the black population, then, the best baseline is a kind of poverty line, or carefully constructed "minimum adequate standard of living budget" for a Philadelphia family of five in the year 1880. That yearly budget comes to a little less than $650; its approximate as of 1990, although by no means an exact equivalent, is the official poverty line for the same family, or something over $1200. The 1880 figure is probably high, and the 1990 low, for purposes of comparison, but as a rule of thumb for interpreting incomes in the following chapters, it will work simply to multiply late-19th-century dollar figures by a number between 20 and 25 to yield their rough equivalents in 1990 dollars.[6]

Chapter 3

The "Unskilled" Majority

No complex analysis is needed to explain the economic situation facing the majority of Afro-Americans in Philadelphia. The problem was poverty, caused mostly by limited job opportunities, and resulting from simple racism openly applied. In a period of unprecedented expansion, black workers were simply shut out of the contemporary urban-industrial revolution. While it was sometimes slow work, in Philadelphia and across the country, to push them out of the older manual trades, it was much easier to keep them out of the newer ones from the very beginning, so that while a few carpenters or painters hung on, there were in 1900 no Afro-American boilermakers, locomotive engineers, streetcar conductors, or sheetmetal workers.

Most important, factory jobs were considered too good for blacks, in painful contrast to the European immigrants who competed with them. No single difference between Afro-Americans and the foreign-born is greater, according to the census figures shown earlier in the introduction to Part II, than the percentages of the two groups involved in manufacture of any kind. Nearly half of the immigrants worked in this vital new sector of the economy, more than five times the proportion of blacks, who were in practice hired only in the oldest, non-factory areas, such as brick making. Of the 90 percent of the Afro-American population who worked with their hands, as of 1900, below the white-collar line, the great majority of those counted in the straight economy at all were then stuck in just two categories, "unskilled labor" and "domestic and personal service." And while not absolutely worse off than they had been in 1865 or 1870, the result of exclusion was that their relative position was continually eroding, as new opportunities lifted successive waves of immigrants up and past them. At the opening of the 20th century most blacks in Philadelphia were still doing the kind of jobs that had been done by the bottom layer of urban society in the Middle Ages.

But while this basic story is a simple one, the actual economic situations of the community's black men and women were as varied as life itself. "Domestic and personal service" and "unskilled labor" are both broad categories which do little to describe the very different skills and conditions of the often highly able people lumped into them. Each of these situations, in practice, changed with time. And the simple labels do not do justice to the ingenuity with which different groups tried to cope with the insecurity and discrimination which afflicted them all.

Contemporary observers were fully aware of the importance of black exclusion from industrial work. In 1893, in the midst of a growing concern about black crime, Christopher Perry's *Tribune* published an article which summed the opinions of "most Philadelphia newspapers." Crime was rising, the papers agreed, because "the relative industrial position of the negro in the community is sinking. . . ." Victims of what the *Press* called "a relentless prejudice," Afro-Americans were "shut out of machine shops and most, if not all, factories." The movement from south to north, moreover, was no escape; in terms of skilled jobs the situation was worse on Philadelphia's side of the Mason-Dixon line, and "in New York, Brooklyn, Boston and Chicago the same tendencies are evident." And to add to the frustration, the kind of organization that offered a solution to some white workers appeared to many blacks a part of the problem.[1]

The question of who was responsible for job discrimination, and why, did not much trouble white journalists. "A relentless prejudice" required no explanation; even the majority who officially opposed it thought of racial prejudice as given, a fact of nature. As to whose prejudice it was that barred blacks from factory and other skilled jobs, the Philadelphia press was confidently united. The problem, they argued continually, lay with white "mechanics," especially but not exclusively those organized in unions. Employers in contrast were not directly at fault, but simply gave in to workingmen who often acted on their constant threat to walk off any job that hired black labor next to them.

There are obvious problems with accepting this analysis, beginning with the anti-union sentiment shared by most newspapers. The same year, 1877, which saw a formal end to federal attempts at Reconstruction in the South, witnessed the nation's greatest labor strike to date, a clash which began, in effect, with resistance to wage cuts on railroads and evolved into a series of bloody confrontations among police, state militias, and crowds sympathetic to the workingmen's cause in several eastern and midwestern cities. The two developments together symbolically marked a real shift in the concerns of the middle and upper classes, from issues of race and section, black versus white, to issues of class, workingmen versus employers.[2]

One result was that Afro-Americans were seen, in some limited ways, as potential weapons in the battle against immigrant workingmen. This was a period in which strikes were often seen as "A Chance for the Negro." Republican papers like the *Evening Telegraph* contrasted faithful colored workingmen with "the haughty Huns, sensitive Russians, noble nihilists, distinguished dynamiters and other foreigners" who usually got the jobs. The Democratic *Record*, on the other hand, had its own political agenda in mind when it suggested that constantly urging blacks to learn skills was hypocritical: "Will their benevolent advisers inform the black men how they are to break through the trades-unions?" The point on which virtually all agreed was that "there is much less prejudice against the employment of colored mechanics in the South than there is in the North."[3]

In fact the late 19th century was a period in which modern unions were only beginning to organize, and still weak. Employers were not then notable for giving in to their demands, and only the most skilled of traditional tradesmen, in contrast to factory hands, were commonly able to dictate their conditions of work. The managers of mills and mines often cynically manipulated ethnic and racial divisions in the work force, using blacks to break strikes and then abandoning them afterward.

Despite these caveats, however, the black historian Carter Woodson has pointed out that in virtually every case where black men or women won entry into new jobs they did it first as strikebreakers. And although the little working-class dramas of shop and mill did not often attract the press, the more publicized breakthroughs in the period all involved employers willing to defy white workers. When Mayor Samuel King of Philadelphia, in 1881, hired three black policemen, several officers quit the force, a sequence repeated nine years later when the Board of Charities hired a black nurse for the almshouse in the face of a petition signed by 48 white ones, several of whom then resigned. Among private employers, Midvale Steel, during the 1890s, was unique in hiring Afro-Americans to work directly in the steelmaking process; tradition called for all labor gangs to be employed under a foreman from their own ethnic group, and the break was led by the efficiency expert Frederick R. Taylor, one of the principal villains of the contemporary labor movement. Conversely baseball's St. Louis Browns defied their owner in refusing to play a scheduled exhibition against the "Cuban" Giants in 1887, just as white workers successfully struck against the hiring of two black motormen by the Philadelphia and Western Streetcar Company in 1898.[4]

Prejudice on the job has historically taken different forms, under different conditions, with different economic results. In late-19th-century America blacks did not usually complain about "wage discrimination," that is, less pay for the same work, but absolute "job discrimination," that is, systematic reservation of whole categories for whites only. In some cases, as in South Africa, where blacks were and are in the majority, "wage discrimination" may profit an employer or industry. Economic historians are less agreed as to whether employers benefited from "job discrimination" as practiced in the American South, where whites were a clear but not overwhelming majority. On the one hand they may have more or less consciously used a black "reserve army" to divide the working class along racial lines. On the other they were denying themselves potentially useful black skills, and giving up the possibility of direct competition for the same jobs. But whatever the case to the south, there seems to be no good reason, on purely economic grounds, for employers to discriminate in a northern city whose work force was over 90 percent white.[5]

Certainly job discrimination cost employers in terms of lost black skills; the major irony about the pool of black "unskilled labor" was in fact how rich it was in ability. One of the most important results of screwing down the lid on opportunity was that the black occupational pyramid was artificially crushed flat, its top layers pushed close to the bottom, the bottom filled with people "overqualified" for the jobs they held and unable to move up. Black Philadelphia was full of men and women with skills they simply were not allowed to use. And the occupational histories of the more successful entrepreneurs described in the following chapter show that most of them had worked, at some point in their lives, as janitors, waiters, bootblacks, and agricultural or other laborers, all jobs the census classified as unskilled.[6]

Philadelphia's Afro-Americans were also clearly more literate than foreign immigrants, and in English. School attendance was not compulsory during most of the period, but there had always been other ways for eager Americans to learn, and while in 1880 perhaps 60 or 70 percent of black children went to school, the census suggests that 80 to 90 percent of adults could read and write. It was entirely possible for William Still to write a book, William Scott to become a university trustee, and Gilbert A. Ball to quote Shakespeare without benefit of a single day served in class. While both school attendance and literacy were improving with time, it is unusual even among the older generations represented in the Lebanon Cemetary records, for example, to find men or women who could manage no more than an "X" in signing legal documents. At the very bottom of the economic ladder, meanwhile, the hundreds of ordinary laborers who registered for manual training classes around 1890 could all spell their names, addresses, and occupations, with a few telling variations such as "hard-carrier."[7]

The very ability of these black men and women was reason for white workers to avoid competing with them directly, just as it was reason for businessmen to hire them. But economic reason did not dominate the pattern of discrimination in Philadelphia or anywhere.

The ideology and rationale of labor unions in the period was still unformed, and their role unclear. One traditional American ideal, that membership in a republican "commonwealth" transcended the idea of different and competing "classes," was easily joined to older Christian ideas of universal brotherhood.

The alternative was in practice not often represented by those who saw the economic world in terms of class conflict, but rather by those who saw it much as medieval guildsmen had. Such men—women were not then involved—were quite willing to fight and strike. But like the true guildsman they assumed that members of the same trade ought to be joined in a kind of confraternity in which shared work was only part of shared social and perhaps even religious lives. While this was obviously an ideal unsuited to the 19th-century United States, some notion of union as fraternity, with overtones of ethnic and social homogeneity, had a continuing appeal to the working class.

Different organizations had different visions of what a union should be. But more important than the split between rival organizations, in general, was the split between all national organizations or conventions and the local unions which sometimes gathered under their umbrellas. The urge to combine was as old as wage labor itself, but the attempt to represent the whole of the working class was new in the post–Civil War period. Central organizations, often prompted by sympathetic members of the middle class, wanted political power and influence through numbers, an aim that fit well with the rhetoric of union across all lines. Local groups wanted to keep their trades to themselves, to work, and after work perhaps to drink, among familiar faces. And while even the more conservative national organizations worked to broaden this parochial vision, their efforts were still far from successful, and in the late 19th century it was the local organizations which held what power labor had, including the power to set membership rules.

None of the "national" organizations which attempted to speak for the whole of the working class ever won more than a fraction of it in any case, and the great majority of wage-earning Americans belonged to no unions at all. Given the wide prejudice against blacks, and in Philadelphia against unions generally, it was especially hard to bring black Philadelphians into broad-based organizations of any kind.

The first attempt was made by the National Labor Union, in the late 1860s. The NLU officially stood for black equality, but it was less an organization than an annual convention of reformers, and had no wish to offend the actual union members in attendance by insisting that they apply the principle in practice. In March of 1869 its black ambassador, Isaac Myers of Maryland, spoke to five hundred members of the Colored Hodcarriers Association at Philadelphia's Liberty Hall. But while the men cheered his views on Reconstruction to the south they did not apparently share his enthusiasm for the NLU, already then in decline. And when Myers himself, later that same year, organized a separate National Labor Convention of Colored Men, the only Philadelphians on the 34-member committee which issued the call were Isaiah Wears, then a barber, and the Reverend B. T. Tanner, neither of them workingmen. The next two annual sessions, which dealt less with specifically workers' issues than with general protests against southern injustice, had no prominent representatives at all from the largest black community in the northern states.[8]

The Knights of Labor, immediate successor to the NLU, was born in Philadelphia as a secret society. But it began to appeal to blacks only when it went public in 1879, under the leadership of Terence Powderly, mayor of Scranton, who urged that all workingmen were brothers regardless of color. That policy was most dramatically evident seven years later at the Richmond Convention of 1886, when a district delegation from New York conspicuously supported a black fellow member, refusing to stay in segregated quarters and otherwise defying local custom in public and private. But few of Philadelphia's Afro-Americans were ever involved in the Knights, and while publicity from Richmond helped organizational efforts among southern blacks, the Knights had already reached their peak, and were unable afterward to halt a progressive national decline.[9]

The American Federation of Labor, meanwhile, finally broke with the Knights in 1886, and while there were a number of reasons for the split it seems no coincidence that it was made only a short time after the dramatic events in Richmond that year. Composed largely of elite craft unions, especially in the building trades, the AFL was the first to ignore larger reform efforts, confine itself to the issues of wages, hours, and working conditions—"More. Here. Now."—and abandon the idea of universal brotherhood in favor of a hard if limited struggle against employers as a class. Growing late in the century, just as the Knights declined, it was by the 1890s the leading labor organization in the country, its membership of roughly a million in 1900 representing a small but well-placed fraction of the work force. The national leadership always insisted that it welcomed all persons regardless of color. But the AFL was a loosely decentralized federation, and retreated in practice when challenged from below; at the opening of the new century it officially embraced a policy of recognizing, at best, separate "Jim Crow" locals in areas where its constituent unions insisted on excluding Afro-Americans.[10]

In this bleak atmosphere W. E. B. Du Bois reported late in the 1890s that the Cigarmakers, ironically the home union of AFL president Samuel Gompers, was the only one in Philadelphia with a substantial black membership. That situation was clearly abnormal, perhaps the result of migration, during the 1880s, of unionized workers from Tampa and even Cuba. Some other unions, like the Typographers, admitted a few Afro-American members. And there were bloody, sometimes deadly, but always unsuccessful battles to establish the integrated International Longshoremen's Association along the city's waterfront. Otherwise the city's blacks were on their own.[11]

Leading Afro-Americans, certainly through the 1880s, did not oppose the effort to organize workers into unions. Most to the contrary still hoped that blacks might be allowed to join, and objected only to the color bar that kept them out. As late as 1894 the *Christian Recorder* petitioned British labor leader John Burns for his help in removing the "whites only" clauses in AFL constitutions. But the strain by then was obvious, and that same year the *Sunday World* published a report (incorrect as it turned out) that the Knights of Labor was supporting a proposal to deport black Americans back to Africa.[12]

Mutual suspicion was encouraged by the simple fact that most leading Afro-Americans, politicians, editors, and ministers were also members of the Republican party. And although the Grand Old Party had won their allegiance through Civil War, and kept it afterward more through default than through economic policy, it was also increasingly the party of the nation's factory owners, and so increasingly hostile to unions. As unions in turn grew increasingly hostile to blacks, party identification made it easy to adopt a conservative view of the role of black workers.

Perry's *Tribune* is a good example of this trend and the reasons for it. During the troubled depression summer of 1894, when blacks were brought into upstate mines in place of foreign workmen fighting against cuts in pay, Perry noted that a fellow black editor, opposed to the strikes, had had his home in Punxatawney blown up by dynamite. Later in the same year, in commenting on the use of southern black strikebreakers in the coke fields, the *Tribune* reprinted an article taken mostly from the Pittsburgh *Dispatch*. While the *Dispatch* had reported that many of these imported southerners were of course "of the lazy and worthless kind," it agreed with a survey of employers which found that "what education he has gotten in the school and mechanical trades has not spoiled the negro as a worker." It would be good business, not charity, in short, to bring in more Afro-Americans to do the unskilled work of the North, at the same time thinning the overconcentration in the South which was creating racial tensions. In contrast to the striking miners, "the dregs of the population in Poland and Bohemia," these were people who "understood American institutions," made no trouble, and through hard times had shown their traditional "patience, adaptability, and perserverance."[13]

In practice, too, with the possible exception of those involved in the brief but fierce riverfront battles of the 1890s—newspaper accounts do not clarify the issues, or identify the sides involved—Philadelphia's own black workers made no organized trouble for their employers. The Hodcarriers, notably, the biggest of black associations, were "not . . . very active," according to W. E. B. Du Bois, writing in the late 1890s. While these men were in effect forced to quit work whenever the bricklayers walked out, this was sometimes a source of resentment. And on the rare occasions when they made the news they did so not because of any economic activity but because they were either gathered, for example, to hear Professor Richard Greener talk about southern lynchings or to plan a social event.[14]

In effect then the union, officially "Association," was not a union in the modern sense, or in the sense represented by those joined in the AFL. It seems rather much like the other occupational associations formed by black Philadelphians after the Civil War, beginning with the Coachmen's, dating from 1868, continuing through the Caterers', the Private Waiters', the Barbers', and finally in 1884 the waiters and others joined in the Hotel Brotherhood. In terms of activities it is hard to tell those which involved employers, such as the Caterers', from those which mixed employers and wage-earners, such as the Barbers', or those such as the Hotel Brotherhood which in theory included employees in the hotel trade only.[15]

Du Bois claimed that the Hotel Brotherhood "is conducted on the lines of regular trade unions," basically by making territorial arrangements with potential white competitors. But there is no other evidence for this. The real nature of the organization is suggested by the fact that George Sharper, at his death, was cited as an especially active member from the beginning. Hotel work of any kind is one of the few jobs missing from Sharper's long résumé as given in the next chapter; at the time when he served as chairman and manager of the Brotherhood's Eighth Anniversary Ball, in 1892, he had for some years been running a private dectective agency, as well as a Seventh Ward political club.[16]

Sharper's management of the affair at the Academy of Music was in fact an important contribution to the organization. In practice the annual ball (or in the case of the Caterers', the reception) was the most newsworthy activity of any of these associations. In the Dorsey Collection, or the black press, they appear almost exclusively as social clubs, their semiprivate banquets and especially public balls of interest far beyond the circles of their own membership. For the members themselves, in return for dues, these clubs paid benefits to the sick, funeral expenses for the dead, and otherwise provided support and encouragement. What they did not do, and were in no position to do, was collectively to challenge their employers, to bargain or demand. Above all during the late 19th century there is no record in the Dorsey Collection or anywhere else of these or other black groups in the city joining together to strike.[17]

When Philadelphia's black workingmen did join together, then, they did so in a spirit closer to guild or fraternity than to union. This was ironically the same spirit, with its emphasis on social functions and homogeneity, which helped create the color bar that kept them out of broader or more militant white organizations. But there was no choice. Never really able to trust their employers, rejected by other workingmen, the city's blacks had to face the working world with either the limited support they could find among their fellows or else entirely alone.

Despite the hostility and the obstacles, a handful of Philadelphia's Afro-Americans, following the rule that few rules were absolute, were qualified to work at skilled industrial jobs. While most who identified themselves as craftsmen—carpenters, for example—were either unable to work or worked episodically and alone, as independent entrepreneurs, the situation in manufac-

turing was more complex. In fact, the 1870 census lists well over 250 occupations for black men and women. But many simply describe the same job under
different titles; more than 100 of them had only single entries, and 70 more
included less than five people. Most of these were people in skilled manufacturing work, listed as "varnisher" or "wheelwright," "saddlemaker," "carpet-
cutter," "furrier," or "dyer." Each entry represents an individual story,
usually involving a white craftsman, teacher, or employer willing to defy
prevailing custom. But each was an exception also. No matter how the census is
analyzed the number of jobs open to black Philadelphians, given the enormous
variety of small mills and factories in the city, was far smaller than for whites,
and especially the number of jobs worked by significant numbers of people.
Above all the trend was dramatically down; when Du Bois counted the number
of occupations in the Seventh Ward, not exactly but roughly comparable with
the list from the 1870 census, a generation earlier, the total was about 130, or
less than half of what it had been a generation earlier.[18]

By the middle of the 1890s then the result of being shut out of the growing
industrial center of the city's economy was that the great majority of Afro-
American men had to work in the older sectors, along the margins, or in the
interstices. Nearly four out of every five over the age of 21 worked as either
laborers or servants of one kind or another, jobs that analysts of the census
classified as "unskilled," although in many cases they would have objected to
that demeaning description.[19]

Of the 3,850 men Du Bois counted, the largest single group was "laborers"
at 1,454 a total which included the stevedores, teamsters, hodcarriers, and
hostlers of what he called its "select class," which was a somewhat smaller
group at 602 than what he called the "common class" at 852. The difference
reflects the fact that Du Bois visited the city just at a time when the nature of
heavy laboring work open to black men was changing.[20]

Through the 1870s Afro-Americans did not as yet generally do the kind of
heavy construction now associated with city contracts. An article in 1873 noted
that they were "mostly debarred by the Irish," traditional and often violently
hostile competitors through the mid-century decades, from the rough work of
digging sewers, laying pipes, building bridges, and working on municipal
projects such as Philadelphia's monumental City Hall, begun two years earlier
and destined to provide another twenty years of labor. Three years after, in
1876, a local politician was cited as a "friend of the race" simply for supplying a
couple of dozen men with jobs grading streets. Most laborers meanwhile could
not count on the kind of steady work that would be there for weeks or even
days on end, but had to scrabble for odd jobs, rarely steady or long-lasting.[21]

Although there was a tiny black farm settlement known as "Guinea Hill,"
near Holmesburg in the twenty-third Ward, most local farmhands then as now
worked in truck gardens, many of them across the river in South Jersey. The
demand by definition varied sharply with the rhythms of the agricultural year.

Stevedores made good wages, at 20 cents an hour, but the money was paid only for time actually spent loading or unloading. Meanwhile they had to endure long stretches of waiting for their ships to come in, and hoping that they would actually be chosen at the daily waterfront lineups. The uncertainties of the public porters were even more extreme; they stood by, with straps and sometimes dollies, dressed in distinctive top hats and aprons, weaving rope mats to kill the time between carrying jobs that sometimes lasted no more than a few minutes.[22]

The curse of all such work, next to the physical strain, was this kind of insecurity. Employment was at best seasonal; although the railroads had eased the ice-bound paralysis of transport in wintertime they had not yet ended it, and most laboring work of all kinds was dependent on good weather. The one advantage that blacks held over the Irish-born was that some at least were able to go back home, retreating to southern farm country in the coldest months. But while pay might reach well above $10 in good weeks, the long periods of dead time meant that laborers in the city, including the generally better-paid white majority, earned no more than an estimated $336 a year in 1880, little more than half a family's minimum maintenance budget.[23]

Many other black workingmen shared the uncertainties that plagued the laborers. Among them were the hucksters and peddlers, an important group earlier but down to 37 men in the Seventh Ward by Du Bois's day; the 134 teamsters; and the declining number who worked as newsboys, bootblacks, and paper boys. Carl Bolivar, the community's historical columnist, remembered that earlier in the period, before electric trolleys and elevated tracks, when Philadelphia was still a "walking city," full of open markets, the streets had been crowded with people living off their wits. The line between those who sold goods and those who sold their labor was often artificial in a way that no count can capture, as with the public porters who offered woven mats to those passersby who had no need to rent their backs, the carters who sold market items, the farmhands who sold truck. Stevedores were not the only ones who needed strong arms and a willingness to do battle; success in shining shoes or selling penny papers was supremely dependent on location, and winning control of the right corner often meant fighting off white competitors.[24]

Food vending and street music were especially identified with Afro-Americans. West Indians, dressed all in white, carried trays of pastries downtown. Natives sold, among other things, herbs out of buckets, jelly donuts, coconut cakes, "Baltimo' Crrraabs!" in summertime, Christmas wreaths and especially soup in winter, "Peppery Pot, Smokin' Hot!" One man tried to beat the competition by selling peanuts in the park with the help of two animals: the dog did tricks on the donkey's back while their master played the guitar and yodeled. Others, with fiddles or banjos, would play anything on request—although a white man who asked for the Confederate anthem "Dixie" was also asking for a fight.[25]

Sometimes there was an air of desperation in all of this hustling for change: one man had to be enjoined by the court from grabbing baggage, unasked, out of the hands of passengers at the 30th Street Station, hoping to earn tips, and sometimes a passerby was assaulted for refusing a beggar. All those who worked the streets, whether hucksters, entertainers, or laborers, were struggling at lonely jobs whose very nature underlined their insecurity. The expert calculation is that in 1880 an adequate diet for a family of five would cost $336.44 a year, precisely 44 cents more for food alone than the average laborer brought in. Given further that the "average" included whites as well as blacks, and that by definition something close to half of all laborers earned even less, it is clear that a large number of Afro-Americans could not cope entirely on their own. [26]

In this they were hardly alone; perhaps half of all Philadelphians might be classed as "very poor" in 1880. But the black situation was extreme: by the calculations Du Bois made in the mid-1890s fully 90 percent of the families of the Seventh Ward fell below the line set by the "minimum adequacy budget." The need for charity soup kitchens in the three coldest months, and free medical care for the bottom fifth of the population, was built into the expectations of the industrializing city. These most desperate needs were generally met by a combination of private and city sources regardless of race. But Afro-Americans, by contemporary accounts, were notable for avoiding the two most extreme endpoints: the county almshouse and the pauper's grave. [27]

Among the reasons were a low rate of serious alcoholism combined with a sense of shame, even fear, about taking some kinds of charity. One paper noted in 1890 that "a completely intoxicated colored man is rarely seen, even in the lowest haunts." The observation, obviously intended as contrast to the Irish, is in fact borne out by the relatively low proportion of Afro-American arrests for drunkenness, and deaths from alcohol-related diseases. At the same time whites as well as blacks reportedly gave the rare door-to-door beggars a careful hearing since so few resorted to this except when in real need. Real need was often defined by the death of a near relative; charity wards and the poorhouse inspired "a superstitious horror of a pauper's burial or running the risk of the dissecting table." [28]

Besides skirting the trap of dependence on the then-prevailing drug, the surest way to avoid either fate was through some kind of insurance. With the usual forms of protection denied by discriminatory premiums, Afro-Americans had to rely either on small white-run firms, often fraudulent or shaky, or better again on mutual help. Perhaps nothing distinguished the city's blacks from other equally poor people than the number who belonged to mutual benefit societies. While the larger subject belongs in a later chapter, the societies in question might be fraternal, Odd Fellows and Masons, church-connected like the Sons of St. Thomas, or organized on occupational lines like the several associations such as the Private Waiters'. Beyond these there were literally hundreds of benefit societies in the city, many operated by small circles of friends without formal titles or wider affiliations at all. It took no great organizational hierarchy to administer the simple rules involved. While the amounts varied, all functioned in much the same way: in exchange for dues, perhaps 50 or 75 cents a week, the better ones provided $5 in weekly benefits to the sick, and up to $75 in funeral expenses. The problems that inspired them were common to all, and the tradition was to combat the isolated nature of much black employment by dealing with them cooperatively in groups.[29]

One index of the economic misery that afflicted black Philadelphia is that coachmen, waiters, and other personal servants, at 1,079 the second largest group of male workers in Du Bois's count, were widely thought an elite. Much as in 18th-century England, the attractions of service were the simple assumption of security combined with such elementary matters as access to food and shelter. Given the racial stigma which they had to bear in any case, the drawback of social stigma did not discourage Afro-Americans as much as others. And most of the other drawbacks did not apply to men as strongly as to women.[30]

A hundred years later, in the memories of elderly black men and women still active in the late 20th century, the noun that best fit the social attitude of the servants of William Dorsey's generation is not shame but pride, even snobbery. The southern migrants who flocked to this and other northern cities during the "Great Migration" of the World War I years and after were often in conflict with the so-called "O.P.s," or Old Philadelphians, already on the ground. Many migrants felt rejected by O.P. society, which they thought dominated by "house servants" or their descendants, conscious of their light color, heavily concentrated among the Episcopal and other white churches, and in general all too snobbish toward fellow blacks.[31]

Most of all this is simply an elaborate social myth. The phrase "house servant" as an insult goes back to the alleged hostility between the slaves in the "Big House" and the majority in the fields, and so does the rest of the "O.P." caricature. In fact the social structure of black Philadelphia in the late 19th and early 20th century was not dominated by "servants." While many of its leaders had spent some time as valets, pullman porters, or waiters, of the prominent citizens most often cited in the Dorsey Collection, and listed in Appendix III, only one, the headwaiter Hans Shadd, in last place, was primarily identified with such a job. While it is true that in the wider sense most successful entrepreneurs, for example, had literally or figuratively to cater to white customers, as shown in Chapter 4, to say that many of the community's leaders were descended from servants is not much more meaningful than to note that virtually all were descended from slaves.[32]

The one clearly accurate element in the "O.P." caricature is that many of the men listed under "personal service" jobs were at least proud and in some cases truly snobbish about what they did for a living. The hotel waiters, for example, thought of themselves as skilled workers. Serving the elaborate, sometimes twelve-course meals of the day, recalling the separate orders of twelve patrons at a table, remembering the faces and preferences of repeat visitors—all were accomplishments they thought deserved recognition. In the mid-century decades Afro-American men dominated the waiting business not only at Philadelphia's better places, black-owned restaurants such as Augustin's as well as the Continental Hotel, but also at fashionable resort spas such as Saratoga and Long Branch. If the work literally required bowing to white whims, it was not thought too demeaning by most. The Hotel Brotherhood's Annual Ball, in 1892, was attended by many of the community's social leaders, including William Dorsey, and so was the ceremony to honor Philadelphia's most popular headwaiters, in a contest sponsored by the Afro-American *Sentinel* in 1890. Although none of the four contest winners could be classified among the most prominent, all were variously active in church, lodge, or political affairs. Both the origin and the nature of their private social tastes are betrayed by the prizes won: James Ashe took home a complete silver service, John Barranger a gold watch, George Anderson a silver fish set, and L. C. Nicholson a silver soup service.[33]

Private coachmen were an equally elite group, even more likely than hotel waiters to be chosen for their bearing in uniform. In the 1890s, Isabel Eaton's survey of domestics put the Seventh Ward's 76 coachmen, who often doubled as butlers, at the top of the wage hierarchy, with salaries ranging between $5 and $14 a week and averaging $8.58, or well over $400 a year, not including perks. Physical size was one of the bases for premium pay, partly no doubt because the ability to order big men in uniform was especially gratifying to fashionable employers, partly as a heritage of the day, not then far distant, when coach and footmen were required to protect the master or mistress on excursions through rowdy streets.[34]

It is impossible in Eaton's survey to distinguish the "private waiters" within the whole group of 387 classed as "waiters" with no other adjectives. The group was less well paid than coachmen, with a range of $2 to $9 weekly, an average of $6.14, and so not much more than $300 a year, roughly in the laborer's class. But with board and perhaps room in addition, most, although a bare majority, of these men were able to marry.[35]

The rest of the male servants included 109 butlers, 47 cooks, 23 bell and errand boys, 4 valets, and 31 men who did "general work." Cooks in Eaton's survey earned about what private waiters did, although at the very top $15 a week beat even the coachmen, and would average about $750 a year. Those who did general work ranked at the bottom of the hierarchy, with a wide range between $1 and $10 a week, depending presumably on age, expertise, and the generosity of employers. The average was $5.38, or less than $300 annually.

Most would include janitors with servants; those in big apartment houses lived in. Despite their classification as unskilled, they often had considerable expertise in maintaining and repairing furnaces, and so earned relatively good wages. The ones who worked in public buildings, such as schools, had to win their jobs through politics; others had several private buildings in charge, and traveled from one to the other twice daily.[36]

All servants had to put up with restrictions which many found intolerable. While in general far fewer men than women actually lived in the households they served, the majority still did. They were then continually "on call," and none in Eaton's survey ever got so much as a full day off, the usual rule being a half-day holiday during the week and another on Sunday, or alternate Sundays.[37]

But hundreds of men still found the job attractive, more so than women. One of the most basic reasons was that, after all, they could quit service entirely. The alternatives, however limited, at least existed, in any of the variants of common labor, or perhaps in some other low-level work such as the brickyards, whose 159 black workers represented the most employed in manufacture as of the census of 1870. Another reason for job satisfaction was that men were used only in rich households with a greater division of servile labor, and so easier to work in. And they were richer too in food, warmth, the possibilities of travel to the shore or mountains in summer, gifts of castoff clothing, perhaps a small bequest at some later point in life.[38]

All of these benefits, none of them easily weighed at a distance but most very tangible to the beneficiaries, helped to divide male servants from their laboring fellows. And so above all did security. While the lost freedoms and other indignities that made up the price of servitude are hard to measure, it is roughly possible to measure length of service. And in contrast to the hours, sometimes minutes, at best seasons which measured most laboring jobs, the average male servant in the Eaton survey had worked fully four and a half years at his job, another reason to counter the usual stigma with pride.[39]

For women in service, however, conditions were different. While married white women in the late Victorian age usually worked only in the home rather than out in the money economy, blacks could not afford even this modest and sometimes ironic "freedom." Given the low earnings of the men, most women worked because they had to, whatever their marital status. And their choice of jobs was far more limited than even the narrow range available to men. Du Bois's careful calculation for the Seventh Ward, as of 1890, suggests that only 17 percent of women over 21 enjoyed a "housewife" status, without other paid work. Of the remaining number, nearly 90 percent worked at personal service jobs, with hard competition and lack of alternatives holding wages very low.[40]

The lack of alternatives is shown most strikingly by the fact that of the 2,857 employed women Du Bois counted, just one was listed as "factory employee," in an unskilled job. Either formal education or capital was required of most of the 140, or less than 5 percent, who worked at entrepreneurial, learned, or clerical jobs, all of which will be dealt with later. Of the 221, or about 7.5 percent, in the "skilled trades," aside from the 6 hairdressers, 4 "shrouders of the dead," 3 milliners, and the 1 each listed as apprentice, barber, manicurist, and typesetter, fully 204 were listed as "dressmakers," but it is not clear how skilled or enviable this job really was.[41]

The problem of raising healthy children in decent conditions affected all black Philadelphians. Low wages obviously prevented the great majority from enjoying the ideal Victorian family, with a father working out and a mother staying home. The mother, and often the children, had to add their own earnings to the father's in order to live at all; even with these additions, no more than about 1 in 10 of the families in the Seventh Ward reached the modest standards set by the "minimum adequacy budget" of $643. And women's work, while essential, created nearly as many problems for poor families as it solved.[42]

Live-in servitude, the single biggest occupation, posed serious obstacles to any kind of family life, and so, for mothers of small children, did the varieties of day work that were nearly as common. One way to deal with this was to work in the household itself, like many of the 48 "seamstresses" in the Seventh Ward. While Du Bois unaccountably did not list laundresses separately, probably several dozen women specialized in washing clothes, many of these, too, at home. But the biggest homework category was comprised of those 204 "dressmakers."[43]

William Henry Dorsey's wife Virginia, living in the adjacent Eighth Ward, was not counted among the 204, but she was a dressmaker too, an occupation which may have been based less on skilled training than sheer necessity, or a choice made in terms of family priorities. The Dorsey family enjoyed the elite status won by William's father Thomas, who also left them their houses on Dean and later Locust streets, the latter especially a prestigious address. But the younger Dorseys, however privileged in comparison to most of their peers, never had the kind of wealth enjoyed by their parents.

William Henry Dorsey traveled all the way to Savannah, Georgia, to marry Alabama-born Virginia Cashin on February 21, 1859, when she was just twenty-one, and shortly brought her back to the city. Thomas Rembrandt Dorsey was born five months later, and died the following March; Van Dyke followed in 1861, Toussaint L'Overture in 1862, dying two years later, Virginia in 1865, Ira in 1867, Sadie in 1869. William, meanwhile, apparently had no regular salaried job until his appointment as a messenger in 1879. The young couple, unlike the elder Dorseys, never had a servant, and unlike many Afro-American families did not take in boarders to help meet the rent. Bachelor boarders, Du Bois noted, were often a bad influence on youngsters, corrupting boys and seducing girls, a piece of wisdom that, himself a naïve and prudish newlywed at the time of writing, he may well have picked up from the more experienced Dorsey, one of the few family men among his local advisers. In any case Virginia began advertising herself as a dressmaker in the city directory of 1872, when she had four children under 10, and kept working through the birth of Thomas, the next year, and John in 1881.[44]

It is not clear how successful she or other black dressmakers were without either formal training or any continuous source of orders, but there are some clues in the events of the summer and fall of 1890. Industrial clothes making then employed far more white women than any other occupation in Philadelphia, increasingly Jewish refugees from Eastern Europe, among the poorest of immigrants. When even these people, put off by the notorious conditions in the industry, were driven to strike in August of 1890, it occurred to the wife of the Reverend B. F. Christian, newly installed at Shiloh Baptist, that blacks might be able to replace them. While she took several women into her own Erie Avenue home for training, he took the idea to several older hands who in turn took it to the Blum brothers, spokesmen for the manufacturers. And when after two quiet weeks Gabriel Blum announced that the industry would now open to Afro-American women, the response was enormous, on two different levels.[45]

Christopher Perry, who had made the rounds with the Reverend B. F. Christian; the old Abolitionist Robert Purvis; and several other community leaders were ebullient. The lawyer T. J. Minton announced that "this, to my mind, is a turning point in the history of the colored people of this town." The opening was in fact an opening wedge: "Now the women have got a chance and I think the day of the colored tradesman is approaching." Following an announcement from Afro-American pulpits on August 25, the *Times* reported that on the corner of 12th and Locust, less than a block from the Dorseys, who then had two daughters in their twenties, some 500 women were lined up for work at six o'clock next morning. Their clothes and manner suggested that they had all come from "the better class," the paper believed, and community support was shown by little American flags hung from neighborhood houses.[46]

But nothing came of it. The Blum brothers were gracious, but they did not expect the newcomers actually to take places in the factory, and instead sent some of them home with piecework assignments. The Reverend Mr. Christian and his wife actually rented space for them to sew in, or in some cases take lessons, and many women continued for some time to combine homework and hope. But if there had ever been a chance it was lost with the strike, which petered out unconditionally over the next several weeks. As the Jews returned, the blacks were left, by October, with nothing but the empty promises of the previous summer. While strikebreaking did lead to permanent employment in some other times and places, it never worked for either sex in Philadelphia; the only women who ever got a foothold in manufacture, in this era, were the sixty who slaved in the late 1880s at making artificial flowers, a job located squarely at the bottom of the industrial scale.[47]

There was nothing for most then but domestic and personal service. And because there was nothing else, conditions for women were far less attractive than those for men. Wages, to begin with, were lower. The whole group may be divided in two, as Du Bois did. The word he used for one, usually applied only to men doing back work, was "laborers," some 1,234 in the Seventh Ward, overwhelmingly "day workers," with a few waitresses, public cooks, and "office maids," distinguished from the other group, the 1,262 "domestic servants" who lived in. But Isabel Eaton found little difference between those who got room and board and those who did not; the irrationality of the market in fact gave a slight edge, in terms of money earned, to the live-in servants over those who went home each night.[48]

Black women often did heavy work, even janitorial work; Du Bois counted 22 in the Seventh Ward, and one was still working, in 1903, at the age of 72. These janitors earned more than any other female domestics, averaging $4.06 a week according to Isabel Eaton's survey, but this meant only about $200 a year. Among live-in servants all the other sub-specialties—lady's maids and chambermaids, laundresses, child's nurses, and cooks—made less than that. "Errand girls," in the lowest category, averaged only $100 a year, and some were paid nothing at all except "living and tips."[49]

By far the largest category did "general work," for a little more than $150 a year. These women, in contrast to the men, usually worked in homes with no other servants, responsible for everything: not only the cooking, cleaning, and mending, minding the children and waiting on table, but sometimes the jobs usually given to men—tending the furnace, scrubbing the stoop, and sweeping the walk. Their work was truly never done.[50]

Du Bois's puritanism, Eaton's sex, and the conventions of academic publishing prevented either of them from mentioning the sexual harassment that was also, too often, a part of the job. But contemporary papers did list "lack of protection from insult" as one of the drawbacks. Philadelphia in the late 19th century was not slave country, and white employers could be prosecuted for beating black maids, and were. But mistreatment was far more common than formal complaint. And if the master sometimes made special demands, it seems that the mistress, too, according to an account of the interview process, was more likely to be truly imperious with a woman than a man:

"Do you wear glasses all the time? I don't allow my girls to wear glasses."

"Have you got on a ring? You'll have to take that off."

"I don't allow my girls to wear wigs or bangs. Stand up and let me see how big you are. . . ."[51]

Not all jobs were so difficult. A generous employer made much difference, and the papers were full of stories of elderly Afro-Americans who had saved, and perhaps with wise advice invested, considerable sums of money over a lifetime of service. The New York *Sun*, in August of 1888, granted the elusive title of "richest colored woman in the country" to Elizabeth Gloucester, who had begun an investment career as a maid in Philadelphia before moving to New York to specialize in real estate. That was of course a nearly unique success, but Miss Holly Henry's obituary in the *Tribune* next month told a less uncommon story. Henry, nearly 90, having retired many years before from service to a family in the elite Eighth Ward, left a life's savings of $5000: some to her own church, St. Thomas P.E., some to historic Mother Bethel, most to the Home for Aged and Infirm Colored People, although she herself had spent her last years in her own house on South Tenth Street.[52]

But servitude was a kind of lottery, and there were long odds against landing the kind of position that Henry had won. Most women did not enjoy the same security as men, the average job lasting a full year less, or three and a half years total. Uncertainty in other things, the range of pay and working conditions, was also greater than for men. And the need for most to live in, continually on call, with behavior monitored and visitors screened, to have the whole situation in short so largely dependent on the character and personality of the master or mistress—all of this must have reminded many of the slavery which they or their ancestors had fled.[53]

While the situation of black male servants was better than for women, it took a turn for the worse during the last two decades of the 19th century. What had once been a near monopoly of the best uniformed jobs, both in Philadelphia and in the resort communities, began to disintegrate sometime in the late 1870s or 1880s. At the same time contemporaries believed that wages for ordinary servants and waiters were dropping under the pressure of competition and black population growth, a situation only partly relieved by new opportunities for laborers.[54]

The first problem, progressive loss of the most prestigious and visible jobs, resulted from the increasing importation of British or Swedish coachmen, nannies, butlers, and footmen. Neither the Private Waiters' Association nor the Hotel Brotherhood, both of which joined the older Coachmen's Association just when this was beginning to happen, were able to stop the loss. And more analytical observers were unable at the same time to explain it.[55]

Du Bois and Isabel Eaton followed the *Tribune* in agreeing that fashion was one important key; especially in an age of nouveau-riche admiration for Old World manners, the prestige that went with hiring men and women in uniform was multiplied when they were white. But there was some disagreement as to whether or not the imports actually did better work than the Afro-Americans whose jobs they took. J. S. Stemmons, a community leader who had himself worked as a waiter, voiced the usual view, in 1903, that head to head and on average black waiters and other servants were better than whites, who could move up if they had real ability. Du Bois argued from the same condition that Afro-Americans felt trapped, and so were chronically restless, full of self-pitying resentments and complaint. Some clue may be offered by relative pay scales; Eaton's survey found little difference between the wages of imported white women and native blacks, but a marked difference among men. Women, it may be inferred, were hired to work, and both groups worked equally well; men were hired in large part to look impressive, and the twin assumptions of racism and snobbery gave the edge to white over black.[56]

And at the same time that Afro-American Philadelphians were suffering this loss to immigrants brought in over them, they were losing, too, to southerners brought in under them. Many domestics had traditionally migrated to resort country in the summertime, some on their own, others perhaps on furlough from households that needed less staff to live more "simply" in Northeast Harbor or Long Branch. But in towns along the Jersey shore, the *Times* in 1890 reported that Philadelphians were being replaced by waiters from Maryland and Virginia; the reason was simply that these southern competitors would take both lower wages and, with less complaint, more racial indignities than the men from the northern city. Stemmons in 1903 reported a decline in wages over the previous fifteen years, as black waiters then averaged less than $250 a year as the result of southern in-migration.[57]

The Afro-American population growth that concerned Stemmons and others in the post–Civil War decades was in fact the beginning of a long trend, in Philadelphia and other cities, that has lasted into the present. Up to then the official statistics had grown very unevenly. The percentage of blacks in Philadelphia County had peaked early, around 1810, when their official total of 10,552 reached nearly 9.5 percent of the whole. Over the next thirty years immigration from Europe outmatched natural black growth. And in the mid-century decades, between 1840 and 1870, when the hungry Irish poured in and fought for the jobs on the bottom of the ladder, the total number of Afro-Americans had almost stalled altogether, moving only from an official 19,833 to 22,147, and falling from 7.4 to 3.3 percent of the whole population of the city. It was only at that point, with the Civil War ended and Irish immigration slowed in turn, that blacks began to migrate heavily into the city again.[58]

Black gains began consistently to outrun white only after 1870. While the city itself, as noted, grew impressively from an official 674,000 to 1,294,000 between that date and 1900, an increase of 91 percent in just thirty years, its Afro-American population in the same period leapt up from 22,000 to 63,000, a percentage growth more than twice that for the city as a whole. Since urban blacks then had such small families, the increase was wholly due to in-migration. The newcomers, mostly from the nearest southeastern states, Virginia, Maryland, and the Carolinas, were both pushed by worsening racial tensions and pulled by the promise of higher wages. Many of the skilled men among them found on arrival that they had to abandon their trades in the North. But they did earn higher wages, by southern standards, for the unskilled work they got, and by the 1890s they found laboring jobs of a kind that black Philadelphians had not done before.[59]

As of 1890, while the political leaders of the local black community welcomed the increased voting power that came with the influx—the saloonkeeper and ward lieutenant Gil Ball estimated that the number of voters in his Seventh Ward had grown to 2600, from just 900 in the election of 1882—others worried about the economic impact. While all agreed that in addition to the right to vote the newcomers found better schools and treatment in general, the employment situation was not so promising. As Common Councilman Constantin Hubert pointed out, given the continued blockage in skilled work, all of them had to scrabble for common labor, competing with the dockers, hodcarriers, and waiters already on the scene. But even at that time the situation was beginning to shift, and over the next decade wholly new fields were opened to black men.[60]

What happened was that two separate developments converged in the late 1890s and the early 1900s. One was that the process of city building by then required even more massive amounts of back work for a series of new projects, to cover cobblestone streets with asphalt, lay electric trolley tracks, dig subways, and above all overhaul the City of Philadelphia's water system through a series of reservoirs and filtration plants. At the same time the traditional relationship between blacks and white immigrants was changing dramatically, as the Irish laborers who used to do this kind of long-term work no longer challenged for it.

At the leadership level during the 1870s and 1880s there were signs of genuine rapprochement between Irish and blacks. The Fenian hero and poet John Boyle O'Reilly, editor of the Boston *Pilot,* then the leading Irish Catholic paper in the country, believed that the church should be working among blacks to the south. He was involved, too, in a series of warm exchanges with his Afro-American counterpart T. T. Fortune, in the *Freeman.* Fortune for his part had long believed that the two groups, "subjects of a similar oppression" and "*in fact* the laboring men of the country," had much to gain from union. Professor Richard Greener, in the same spirit, served during 1886–87 as secretary to the Irish Parliamentary Fund, which raised a reported $150,000 to help Charles Stewart Parnell in his fight for home rule. Eight years later the orator Isaiah Wears was officially invited to speak at a testimonial in honor of Philadelphia's Archbishop Ryan, and although too ill to manage that, did write out a letter, its gracious tone perhaps outweighing the somewhat backhanded suggestion that the Catholic church was related to the Protestant much as the Old World to the New.[61]

Historically the enmity between the two groups had been brutally deadly.

The Election Riot of 1871, in which an Irish mob had fatally shot two black men and hacked another to death with an axe or axes, was the climax of more than three decades of vicious persecution. But while fighting continued after 1871, it was much toned down. By the 1890s, just as the tradition was being sublimated in the prize-ring, the invitation "Hey, nigs, why don't you fight us?" or a giant's boast that "I can lick all the niggers in Pulaski-town" involved no deadly weapons. By the 1920s these contests had become, by earlier standards, little more than symbolic ritual; an old man, years later, remembering that the Irish youngsters of Grey's Ferry were far tougher, but in a fight fairer, than southern white men, recalled their astonishment when a cornered black youth actually pulled out a knife.[62]

The easing of racial friction with the Irish had a number of causes. Perhaps the determined efforts of church leaders, editors, and politicians had an effect; certainly the growing size of the black community made it impossible to invade in safety. And most surely economic tensions were eased as the Irish moved past the blacks and up the ladder. In every census after 1850 the proportion of unskilled laborers among them dropped steadily; already by 1870, with famine a memory and immigration much slowed, fewer than 25 percent of the Irish-born and 8 percent of the second generation were listed as laborers in the census. The direct result was that by the 1890s there was no longer a felt need to monopolize the pick-and-shovel work on the city's new construction projects, and the blacks were given a chance.[63]

Southern blacks had long been used to this kind of labor, done by gangs of men under supervision. In Philadelphia, as late as 1894, it was novel to see 18 or 20 men working and singing on the busy corner of 8th and Walnut, cooking hoe cakes and bacon in the street at lunchtime. Within the decade the novelty had worn off, and in addition to smaller gangs there were fully 600 men living in six giant barracks near the Torresdale filter beds alone, with similar encampments near the Queen Lane Reservoir and other sites in and near the city.[64]

But while no one was able to deny them their jobs outright, there was never any real peace for Afro-Americans, and they still had to fight, this time with the Italians. Since the blacks were already well established by the time these latest competitors began to arrive in the late 1880s, they were never outnumbered as they had once been by the Irish. But since neither group was able to establish a monopoly of unskilled labor, they worked nearby, in separate gangs, and lived nearby, in separate quarters, and found themselves continually in conflict.[65]

The Dorsey Collection is full of stories, mostly from the 1890s, about black-Italian battles all over the East, South, and Midwest. Since especially in the early years Italian immigrants, unlike black, left their own women behind, they fought in part over black women, and sometimes white. In Philadelphia, Frank Monroe, in January of 1898, was with typical irony allowed to attend a dance given by a union, the Cloakmakers', that he was not allowed to join; on the way home he was assaulted by a group of Italians who had followed him out. When in the following battle he killed one of them the jury ruled that it was self-defense. Scott Irwin was also acquitted in the killing of Frank Paladino the following April. That case was unusual only because the relationship between the two men broke two customary rules, as both had worked in an ethnically mixed group, and the black as foreman to the white; Paladino and two others had attacked Irwin after being fired.[66]

But the most important fights were those which pitted groups not against single men but against other groups or gangs. Many of the cases in the newspapers were labeled "riots," and erupted at work, sometimes as a result of quarrels on the job, sometimes quarrels over the job. Blacks fought Italians, among others, in the course of the murky waterfront battle sparked when more blacks than whites won jobs in June of 1898, during a slowdown blamed on the war with Spain. They fought head to head at the Queen's Lane Reservoir, and again while digging the subway in the center of the city. Perhaps the most significant local battle occurred across the Delaware in Camden, when in April of 1899 black gangs earning $1.25 a day laying trolley tracks were laid off in favor of Italians at $1.10. The result was neatly summarized in a sentence: "Italy met Africa in a labor riot in Camden yesterday, and Africa won in a hot fifteen minutes." The city's mayor sided with the blacks—there were few local Italian voters—and they kept the jobs. More than that, as a result of this wholly spontaneous action, the next day they demanded $1.50, by a few hundred yards the closest thing to a black strike in Philadelphia recorded in the entire Dorsey Collection, although the result remains unknown.[67]

But if the blacks were able physically to face down the Italians in this and other confrontations, they were not usually able to win better conditions. On the truly giant projects there was above all a double standard in housing. While Afro-American workers at Torresdale were crowded into barracks, the Italians were allowed to build their own little shacks because "their nature will not allow them to congregate a hundred or so in a house." The result of barracks living was among other things disease. In 1892, a pair of two-story brick buildings, each of which housed sixty black men near the Falls of the Schuyl-kill, were condemned as filthy and hazardous by the board of health. The men were deprived of their stoves, in late December, and quarantined for some time as the result of diphtheria, the city paying for their food but not for lost wages. Eleven years later the threat was smallpox, still a major killer. An infection was first found in January 1903 among 400 blacks working near Oak Lane; two weeks later 1000 men at Torresdale were vaccinated and quarantined, report-edly hungry in their barracks and doubtless cold as well.[68]

Afro-Americans working in gangs of course fought more than the Italians, and were visited by more than disease. Recruits from specific southern locations joined with those they came up with and, as young men will, often battled with other gangs from other places; the Philadelphia police noted that the city men, from Baltimore and especially Washington, were more dangerous than those from deeper in the rural South. And the addresses given by those arrested for gambling and prostitution in the labor camps show that all of the laborers were considered ripe fruit by representatives of the local black underworld.[69]

There was a trade-off, then, for unskilled black men in the late 19th and early 20th century. While some of the best domestic and personal service jobs were lost, new fields were opened for heavy labor. By comparison with the 1870s and 1880s, the heavy work of the 1890s and 1900s was more available, more secure, and often open nearly all year-round, enabling the community to absorb growing numbers of southern migrants. It was clearly preferable to have to fight Italians on relatively even terms than to be shut out entirely by the Irish. But the work paid no more, with prevailing wages still averaging between $300 and $350 a year. And while many southerners stayed on to settle in Philadelphia, the conditions of gang work and barracks living combined to introduce them to the city through its underside.

The increased migration of Afro-American women, meanwhile, seems to have changed conditions only for the worse. There is perhaps an element of nostalgia in many newspaper reports, such as the piece in the *Times* which, in 1893, recalled a bygone era when masters and servants had been bound in mutual fidelity. But the statement that it was no longer customary even to attend the funerals of household employees suggests a chilling lapse not only in the traditions of noblesse oblige but in simple civility. Similarly an increase in the number of stories involving the misery and exploitation suffered by young women migrating alone into a strange big city might be explained by changing tastes in journalism. But the black press, too, clearly believed that too many new arrivals were depressing wages and getting into trouble. And the bare records which record birth, death, and disease back up the impression that their situation was getting worse.[70]

Not everything was going badly, however, and there is a suggestion that some of the perceived problems arose, ironically, from the success of Philadelphia's black women in asserting their basic civil rights. As part of the new effort to upgrade the standards of service, a group of prominent white citizens formed, in 1890, a "Fidelity Servants' Reform Association." And as a beginning, its members voiced their complaints in a list that indirectly suggests some of the ways in which the city's Afro-Americans made their own adjustments to the new world opened by the Civil War.[71]

Employers generally agreed, as Eaton found later, that black servants did not usually steal money, or, unlike the Irish, liquor, although they did help themselves and others to food, and occasionally "borrowed" a gown to go dancing. This was all part of an ancient game; more troublesome was the fact that "colored girls" were often of "a migratory turn of mind," and in the springtime simply up and left for the Jersey shore or other vacation spots.

Freedom for many obviously meant freedom to move and change. A reporter noted that for much the same reason "the question of company or no company and the question of their entertainment is another rock upon which most contracts split," just as Eaton found that black women were more insistent than white on free time off. And while most found no protection, other than quitting, from sexual "insult," there were new kinds of redress for other indignities. "Having to stand a lawsuit" had cured many employers of making unsupported claims of theft, and payment of damages was now the penalty for the old practice of opening a servant's mail.[72]

Given the continuing demand for domestic help, those who could not put up with this kind of uppity behavior had only two choices. The richer ones could go abroad, as they did to get uniformed men. But the majority, looking both for cheaper help and for what Eaton called the "docility which is a recognized part of the negro character," looked to the South. There, tradition had it, the docility had been bred in by slavery, and there they hoped it might still be found, uncorrupted by big-city life in the North. In good years such as 1903, the *North American* reported with some exaggeration, the result was the arrival of as many as 500 southern women a month.[73]

This migration was not much welcomed by more-established members of the local Afro-American community. Both sexes increased competition in a limited job market, but while southern men at least added to the voting rolls, young women brought a special kind of trouble. During 1899 a group of black ministers in New York issued a warning against the moral dangers involved in the importation of unmarried females. Christopher Perry noted that the appeal only mirrored a longstanding concern of the *Tribune;* "the personnel of the colored servants has so changed lately," he argued, that "the demand . . . is steadily growing less." The reason was that, preyed upon by those who recruited them, "many servants are debauched before coming here, or become so before securing employment," and so damaged the reputations of the more respectable women already in the city. The same sentiment was echoed four years later by the *Afro-American Advance* of Minneapolis, which argued that the continued search for cheaper domestics only brought the "worst girls" north, and ironically echoed Booker T. Washington in urging employers to stay with the locals: "Cast down your buckets where you are."[74]

There is an element of myth-making in these complaints, as Old Phila-delphians or Minneapolitans countered the accusations of southern newcomers with social stereotypes of their own. Although studies of both 19th and 20th centuries have shown repeatedly that for Afro-Americans city life was un-healthier than rural, that migrants have been less liable to family disruption, imprisonment, or mental instability than those born in cities, established Philadelphians, New Yorkers, and Bostonians have never accepted this. But even with their attitudes discounted, concerns about the conditions of southern migration were by no means misplaced.[75]

The process of recruitment was in fact full of abuse. Isabel Eaton noted that servants avoided white employment agencies, and few dealt with newspaper advertisements. Carter Woodson found that the void was filled instead by black entrepreneurs, men and women who ran small agencies of a sort in connection with their own boarding houses. Some 50 of these operated in Philadelphia, on estimate, by 1904. The bigger ones did not wait for migrants but sent agents south to look for them, charging $12 to $20 in advance for the promise of jobs, then holding their bags hostage. In debt, then, before they even arrived, knowing no one in the city but the agent, these women were ripe for exploitation.[76]

In part because of the sexual imbalance among the newest European immigrants, many of whom customarily came to this country as single men, the business of prostitution flourished in the late 19th and early 20th century more than ever before or since. Philadelphia's Afro-Americans were already deeply involved in both of the main districts zoned, in effect, by police and politicians as the city's vice centers. Some worked in the generally fancier houses in the Tenth Ward, just north of the central business and entertainment district, others either as streetwalkers or in the cheaper places to the south, in the Fifth and Seventh Wards, which they shared with white immigrants. For many it was full-time work, but much was casual and sporadic, a way of picking up anywhere from 50 cents to a couple of dollars for a single sexual act, powerful attractions to women who could otherwise earn not much more than that for a week's drudgery.[77]

Many and perhaps most of these women found little wrong with the business, given the limited alternatives available. Contemporary surveys consistently confounded the stereotypes of the pious reformers who ran them by showing that the majority of prostitutes had chosen their way of living more or less freely, and moved on more or less unharmed within a few years. But the business was at best risky, and the records available to establish the proportion of blacks among those in Philadelphia, during the late 19th century, are among the most miserable of official statistics. The number of criminal arrests for keeping bawdy or disorderly houses, heavily weighted against blacks, are of course unreliable, often products of complex political maneuverings and calculations. But the harder and more objective indices, the numbers of deaths from venereal disease and abortion, prosecutions for infanticide, newborns found unburied in the streets, all fit together with the one contemporary survey from 1912. Taken together they suggest that Afro-American women, by the end of the 1890s, comprised about a quarter of the city's several thousand full- and part-time prostitutes, close to five times their proportion of the population.[78]

Newcomers could be recruited in a number of ways. They might find on arrival that the term "lodging" house as represented by their agent was in fact a misnomer, and had nowhere else to go. Others might be referred to jobs only

with "club houses and employers of doubtful reputation and immoral pro-
clivities." Finally any who had or were expecting a child were in an especially
vulnerable position. They soon found that, perhaps unlike employers' households in the rural South, those in the urban North had no live-in room for small
children, and that the cost of boarding an infant, usually $2 to $4 a week, was
almost precisely the wages of a female domestic. These usually deadly little
"baby farms" were then impossibly expensive for any but prostitutes.[79]

The darkest side of domestic migration is represented by the women new to
the city who were fired or unable to find work, especially those with children;
their stories are generally the most painful in the Dorsey Collection. Victoria
Washington, 21 years old, given notice within a week of her arrival from
Virginia in the summer of 1898, died from inhaling gas in her little room on
South 47th Street. One year later Betty Williams, 24, insane and nearly
starving, was found crooning a lullaby to her two-year-old in a patch of woods
near Fifth and Bristol; for the previous three weeks she had been kept alive with
handouts from nearby black residents. That same spring Mrs. Julia Gracey,
fired from a domestic's job, was found walking the streets at night with her
dying seven-year-old Emma. William Dorsey, who added only a few dozen
marginal comments in more than 30,000 pages of scrapbooks, made his own
feelings clear: the note by Emma's name reads, "Child weighed only 30
pounds. Reduced by circumstances—coroner."[80]

Desperate stories from the migration are only extreme examples of the hardships faced by the majority of Afro-American men and women. For those
trapped in dead-end jobs with low wages it was especially hard to raise families
in neighborhoods swelling with vice and crime. But the great majority managed
somehow to cope, to find ways of fighting back, not only to survive but to
succeed.

The problem of child rearing was especially acute. Live-in servants, whose
employers were not usually gladdened by the sounds of little feet, suffered
from obvious handicaps as parents; so did prostitutes, who while virtually
ignored by the census made up the next biggest category of working women.
Both problems were added to the basic poverty which meant that even when
the wages of the average black man were combined with those of the average
black woman the total did not reach the level required of the "minimum
adequacy" family budget. But there were other and less immediately obvious
obstacles which also helped to hold the black marriage rate in the city well
below the white. Unlike working-class whites, for whom marriage meant the
establishment of a joint household economic unit, taking women out of the
wage economy and putting them to work in the home, there were no economic
advantages for blacks. The overwhelming majority of Afro-American women
worked after marriage as before. Those who lived in cities typically married
late, and had very few children.[81]

Most urban immigrants, whatever their color or ethnicity, had smaller families than they had been used to on the farm or in peasant households, for the classic reason that youngsters in the country were extra hands from a very early age, and long remained only extra mouths in the city. But most foreign immigrants were able to counter this, in some degree, by putting children to work in factories at ten or twelve years of age; however much we now deplore child labor, they thought it essential to keep up the family income. But Afro-Americans had no choices in Philadelphia; while their children had worked very young in the fields back in South Carolina, no one would hire them in the city, and they tended to leave home early and so, unlike Irish, Jewish, or Italian children, did not help the family to meet expenses. It was partly in reflection of this that the official fertility statistics for blacks were so extreme across the country. As a group, the figures dominated by those from the rural South, they had more than 50 percent more children than the national average. In Philadelphia, a typical city in that all groups tended to have smaller families than average, black women in 1890 had nearly 20 percent fewer children than white. And the situation was growing worse, as by 1900 the figure had dropped to nearly 30 percent fewer.[82]

Not all of the reluctance or inability to bear children in Philadelphia was the result of personal poverty or disease; many of the best-situated men and women in the city also chose to stay single, or have few children or none. Part of the reason was surely that in contrast to their white counterparts they could not choose roomy households in safe neighborhoods. Residential segregation instead kept them trapped in the increasingly crowded, dangerous, and crime-infested neighborhoods of the black city.[83]

The best addresses among blacks were traditionally defined by two considerations. They should first be on open streets, such as Rodman, Locust, or Addison, rather than alleys; and second, they should be as far west as possible, that is, toward the Dorseys' 1200 block and beyond, away from the lower numbers closer to the Fifth Ward and the Delaware. While some residents were able by the 1890s to move out to new black clusters in other sections of the city, these were soon segregated too. And the economic need to locate near available work combined with other reasons, social and political, to keep many of the community's leading citizens in the historically central Seventh Ward.

Despite the crowding that was filling up the few available backyards of the area with new tenements, Du Bois noted that physical conditions were not worse but better than they had been fifty or even twenty-five years earlier, when many actually lived underground in cellars. What was growing worse was criminal behavior; while white gang invasion and assault were easing during the late 19th century, blacks were more often victimized by theft and especially violence from within their own neighborhoods.[84]

It is hard to confirm contemporary impressions about worsening theft from the official records. Those which survive deal only with actual jailings, figures which depend on many things besides the actual incidence of larcenies and burglaries, notably the victims' will and ability to prosecute for small-dollar losses. For what they are worth, they suggest a modest but ragged rise over time. More striking is the fact that the black rate of jailings ranged between a low of 5.5 and a high of 9.5 times the rate for whites, with a somewhat surer upward trend. Whatever the problems with the figures on which these estimates are based, they cannot be blamed on a racist justice system, since conviction rates and sentences for blacks and whites remained much the same, and above all because the great majority of black thefts were committed against other blacks, and it was these victims who brought the cases to court.[85]

The official figures for violence, as based on indictments for murder, are relatively more trustworthy than those for theft, since criminal deaths were always taken seriously by the justice system, and whatever the proportion of actual killings which eventually ended in indictment it was of course far higher than for acts of drunkenness, gambling, petty theft, or assault. And the homicide figures show two clear and opposite racial trends.

The first of these was that in the largely white city as a whole, the overall murder rate was going down as part of the general improvement in the state of public order and sobriety. The trend was national, even international, during the period of advancing industrial revolution in the Western World. The new economic order, formal schooling, increased employment in factory and bureaucracy, demanded sober, disciplined, even regimented behavior. For those included in that economic order, these changes in social psychology combined with greater prosperity to push the annual white rate of homicide indictment in Philadelphia down from its peak of 3.6 per 100,000 just before the Civil War to just 2.1 in the 1890s.[86]

The second trend, among blacks, meanwhile moved the other way. As the result of exclusion from the new economic order, Philadelphia's Afro-Americans felt its effects mostly in the form of cheaper prices for manufactured items, including handguns. The traditional fear of white assault and even invasion, nurtured in the mid-century decades of Irish violence, had created a long-felt need to carry weapons. The evident decision to zone black neighborhoods as centers of vice, robbing them of the benefits of the wider decline in drunkenness and filling them with nervous strangers looking for excitement, only added to that need. And the frustrations felt as white foreigners moved up and past them; the conditions that pushed strangers, lodgers, and families tight together in crowded rooms; the fact that guns were increasingly more likely than knives to be at hand in kitchens, bedrooms, purses, and pockets—all of these combined to push up the murder rate. The result was that the annual rate of homicide indictments per 100,000 in the Afro-American population climbed from 6.4 in the 1860s to 11.4 in the 1890s. And because the white rate was falling during the same period, the gap between the two was growing even faster, as the black rate rose from about twice to more than five times the white. [87]

Like the great majority of these homicides, black theft was also overwhelmingly contained within the bounds of race. Except for those involved in a series of highly publicized purse-snatchings that began to break out during the 1890s, black men in particular were no threat to white property. The more profitable kinds of professional crime, including forgery, counterfeiting, and embezzlement, safe-burglary, bank and hotel robbery, were all closed for much the same reason as with skilled legitimate employment. Members of the underworld of theft, recruited mostly from the same class and ethnic groups as skilled blue-collar workers, were no more willing to cooperate with Afro-Americans than their legitimate brothers were. Black men, always conspicuous and often in danger when in white neighborhoods, were then mostly confined to their own, and to stealing the small items, typically clothes and blankets, which dominated detectives' lists of stolen goods. With rare exceptions, frauds too were contained within the community, often exploiting traditions of mutual help by begging money for the burial of nonexistent mothers, or charging uniform expenses for nonexistent Pullman or hotel jobs. [88]

Successful theft from whites was more likely to be engineered by women. Domestics, as a result of easy access, could steal large amounts from rich white households, sometimes in cooperation with white professionals. Prostitutes added to their more routine earnings by preying on the other end of the social scale, sometimes with the aid of black pimps or confederates. Just the kinds of men who were the most frequent visitors, sailors, immigrants, and other itinerants, were also the kinds most likely to carry wages, even life savings, to be plucked from their persons. [89]

As a result of all this activity, the streets of black Philadelphia were dangerously full of temptation for youngsters with working parents and no jobs themselves. The Reverend Henry L. Phillips, rector of the Church of the Crucifixion, was the most extreme local spokesman for the forces of respectability toward century's end, an advocate of forced labor for petty thieves and gamblers, and of the whipping post for pimps and others who lived off money earned by women. He was especially upset, in sworn testimony before a special legislative investigative committee, about the effect of their insistent presence on neighborhood children, who saw so many prosperous criminals and honest victims that it was often hard for them to tell right from wrong. The burden of his homily is in fact borne out by the hard statistics from Philadelphia's House of Refuge, or juvenile reformatory. The reformatory was a testament to the difficulties of raising children, its inmates sometimes under court sentence but more often referred by parents or other relatives as "incorrigible." And despite the fact that the city's own blacks had fewer children than either whites, or, especially, rural blacks, the House of Refuge had a higher ratio of Afro-

American inmates than any other institution in the city, boys and girls overwhelmingly native to Philadelphia rather than the southern states.[90]

But black neighborhoods were neither passive nor helpless in the face of criminal activity. And while there were complaints, like those of the Reverend Henry Phillips, about some of the often hypocritical ways in which the city's criminal justice system dealt with vice, residents normally welcomed and in fact invited and joined in efforts to fight against theft and violence.

One unique set of complaints about the handling of vice in the Fifth and Seventh Wards arose in 1899, when the reforming Law and Order Society joined with the evangelical Christian League to clean up the immediate vicinity of Seventh and Lombard streets, historic center of black Philadelphia. The first priority was to round up prostitutes, which they hoped to accomplish by the simple method of having the League's white Christian innocents loiter about until accosted, and then, on the basis of their descriptions alone, swear out warrants before a sympathetic magistrate from outside the district. This effort was undermined by their own ineptness, and perhaps sabotage by the cops. Clara Fountain, for example, a tall dark woman weighing 200 pounds, was brought in on a warrant specifying a short "yellow" woman weighing 140 pounds, while her lawyer alleged that the whole scheme was simply part of a conspiracy to raise local property values. The police simply refused to execute some warrants, as against one pregnant woman whose husband objected vigorously and physically. And the whole plan seems to have collapsed when Secretary Griffith of the Christian League attempted to force his way into a "disorderly" house in an alley off Seventh Street, only to discover that the noise he had heard was the sound not of debauchery but of religious ecstasy. The place was home in fact to another evangelical society, locally more famous than his own, the one known to cops and neighbors as Brother Brown's "Monkey Mission," whose congregants assaulted Griffith and threatened to sue him.[91]

But while unique, the episode illustrates some of the classic elements of vice enforcement: the police sometimes moved on their own, but more often on the basis of complaints, while the magistrates, local residents, and politicians engaged in elaborate maneuvers aimed somehow at squaring the circle, or reconciling the demands of absolutely antagonistic groups. In general the authorities were able to keep both sides sullen but not mutinous, making enough arrests to keep moral indignation within bounds and certainly to keep gamblers and prostitutes out of neighborhoods strong and united enough to insist on it, while tolerating enough vice to satisfy illegal entrepreneurs and their customers, and pocketing some bribe money to boot.[92]

Black Philadelphians, like white, were deeply divided about vice. At one end of the spectrum were the single men in labor camps, far from the main residential centers, who resented police interference and set up a special cry, like the traditional circusmen's "Hey Rube!," on spotting cops, and often surrounded and attacked any who tried to make an arrest. In settled black areas, where illegal activity was an important economic resource to many beyond the actual gamblers, prostitutes, and speakeasy proprietors involved, there was much individual grumbling, since the arrest process was so obviously a kind of political lottery. But with the exception of the interesting suggestion about real estate values from Clara Fountain's lawyer—and most of those arrested in Law and Order raids did have lawyers, sometimes supplied by local politicians—there were no objections to vice enforcement on principle, and no cooperative resistance. By far the most eloquent black voices were those of men and women like the Reverend Henry Phillips, who wanted more police activity, resented the whole process which had zoned their communities as vice centers, and complained that the easy relationships between cops and streetwalkers were helping to erode the moral sense of neighborhood children.[93]

No group objected to police enforcement of the common law prohibitions against theft and violence, although by modern standards there were obvious grounds for resenting their methods. In an era, and a city, where the long historic drive against public disorder was conducted with open and sometimes illegal brutality, the police were all too ready to fill the air with bullets. The popular black officer William "Pop" Frey lost no more than two days' pay for emptying his revolver into an after-theater crowd on Walnut Street, in the spring of 1899, while trying to arrest a man for begging in public. There was no recorded reprimand in the case of the 10 cops who shot a combined total of 52 rounds at a single unarmed would-be mugger, in the course of a late-night pursuit along the edges of the Fifth and Seventh wards in September of 1894. Nor was there reprimand, just one week later, for the zealous officer who fired several times at a young man who jumped a fence to flee a breach of promise warrant sworn by his girlfriend.[94]

While this kind of exuberance could and did sometimes wound or even kill innocent bystanders, black Philadelphians were used to gunfire, and while there were a few demonstrations against police violence in other cities, there were none locally. There were complaints, sometimes, about class bias in law enforcement, as when a British visitor remarked on the different treatment given black suspects with or without a lawyer. But there is only one example in the Dorsey Collection of a protest directly alleging racial bias in any northern state; the *Tribune*'s correspondent "Ferguson" complained in 1898 when three women broke into a deserted New Jersey hotel and only the black was indicted. Otherwise, aside from vice enforcement, black Philadelphians did not complain about the justice system so much as use it, and did not complain about the cops so much as take over the arrest process on their own.[95]

The decentralized, often direct 19th-century system of justice was not heavily dependent on police or court bureaucracy. The great majority of cases began when people swore out warrants against those they accused of wronging them, and called the cops only to execute them. They might then pursue the case through arraignment, indictment, and trial—or not, if they so chose. This could become in practice an elaborate game, played between the man or woman who had sworn the warrant and the one named in it, a game which the city's blacks had mastered long before the Civil War. Sometimes it could be played for revenge, or even blackmail, as when a man who lost $67 shooting craps complained against the manager of the place. Sometimes it could be played as a kind of endurance contest, in which the aim on the victim's part was apology, chagrin, or restitution short of an actual jail term. The accuser had to invest time and energy in every stage of the process, but sometimes dropped the case after the embarrassing walk to the magistrate's court, sometimes after the accused, if unable to make bail, spent a night in the cells. The accused, meanwhile, could bluff it out in his turn or hers, hoping to be released at some point and turn embarrassment on the accuser. The most serious cases were of course taken over by the county or state, and often, especially in vice cases where no individual had been injured, the police or others pursued the matter from the beginning. But for the routine cases that made up most of the court statistics, the thefts of shirts and shoes, the domestic and neighborhood fights, the system of direct prosecution was usually in force. When "free warrants" were issued out of City Hall in the fall of 1897 the corridors were filled with Afro-Americans, the *Bulletin* reported, scrambling to get what were in effect blank forms for use the next time they wanted to invoke the system. It was a system obviously open to abuse, but it was democratic and accessible, and it essentially guaranteed that black Philadelphia got the kind of justice it wanted.[96]

The cops, then, walking their beats, mostly dealt on their own initiative with drunks and others against whom no one else was interested in complaining, and reacted to immediate disturbances. But they were not the only ones who stepped in to break up fights or answer calls for help; the police force was not big, by modern standards, and most citizens were not yet used to thinking it the first line of defense against crime. When there was trouble in public, people took action directly, and in the city as in the countryside criminals were chased and often caught by informal posses aroused by a kind of hue and cry.

Thus when at high noon of October 12, 1898, Mrs. Margaret O'Brien discovered a short, powerfully built black man under her bed he was pursued from 20th and Dickinson down to 18th and Morris by what the *Times* described as 200 men on foot, 8 to 10 more on bicycles, and a single cop, who of course vainly emptied his revolver before the quarry finally collapsed of exhaustion. These crowds, depending on the neighborhood, might be white, black, or both. Black men caught others who had snatched purses from white women, and there is in the Dorsey Collection no record of racial differences among pursuers based on the color of either the victim or the accused. And although many criminals were armed, few men seemed afraid to join the chase on that account, perhaps because the revolvers of the day were typically small, and their ammunition notoriously underpowered. There are accounts of one pursuer who in the course of facing "scores" of bullets was "staggered, but only for an instant," by a hit in the forehead; of a policeman whose matchbox deflected a bullet harmlessly around his body, where it left only a semicircular abrasion; of a shooting victim who found "the second bullet fell into [his] pocket," apparently after bouncing off and rolling around his clothing.[97]

The capture of William Allen's killer on Kater Street is especially revealing. Allen was just up from Georgia, in the summer of 1894, and the *Times* treated his story as one in which a country-bred innocent met a more experienced "town buck" from Philadelphia. Although matched by various nearby "courts," "runs," "rows," or alleys, Kater was as tough an address in the city wide enough to be called a street, and Allen's cousin, "The Graveyard Kid," had specifically warned him to stay away from its corner with 12th. Nonetheless the young stranger was there one night at number 1209, drinking at Charley Dean's place, where one of the regulars, a big stevedore named Isaac Sturgis, was standing treat on his twenty-eighth birthday. When Sturgis and Allen got into an argument about who was the better wrestler, they took it to the backyard. It was a short fight. Sturgis, the local man, struck out with his left hand, Allen ducked, and then Sturgis stabbed him four inches to the heart with a knive in his right. He then ran off into the local labyrinth. "But men were after him who knew the locality as well as he," led by Dean and George Pinckney, both familiar names to readers of the crime news. These two, with the help of a man known only as "The Neat Nigger," caught up with Sturgis near St. Alban's Court, and then turned him over to four policemen, summoned from the Second District, who arrived "huffing and blowing" behind them. The final comment in the *Times* was that "Kater Street will stand a fracas, but it will not protect murderers."[98]

Cooperation with established authority was striking in this case but not unusual. Many Afro-Americans must have harbored deep resentments against "the dominants," and some doubtless believed in or practiced a double standard which allowed either theft or unprovoked violence against whites. But no such belief surfaced in the hundreds of crime stories that Dorsey clipped out, and the practice must have been relatively rare. With respect to the basic moral values and prohibitions involved, the evidence is that with some allowance for differences in sexual morality and behavior, both blacks and whites in similar classes or occupations shared essentially the same codes.

Shared attitudes toward law and public behavior are only one indication that even the poor and unskilled black Philadelphians of William Dorsey's generation did not make up what has come to be called an "underclass."

According to Du Bois, to begin with, the overwhelming majority of those in the Seventh Ward, some 85 percent, showed their allegiance to traditional attitudes and institutions by "habitually" attending church, most of them not merely visitors but members. There and everywhere far more worked in the wage economy than whites, if only because the great majority of Afro-American women stayed on the job throughout their married lives, in contrast to a small minority of whites. Neither cocaine nor heroin had reached Philadelphia by the turn of the century, although in 1898 there were lurid stories about drugs among troops returning from Cuba after the Spanish-American War, and a story from Paducah, Kentucky, in the same year, reported that "hundreds of negroes are dying by inches in this city from the use of cocaine," mostly inhaled in snuff. Through the 19th century the prevailing drug problem was with alcohol, which blacks abused rather less than whites. Beyond that there was morphine, mostly afflicting middle-class white women "hooked" by their doctors, and finally opium, largely confined to ethnic Chinese and members of the white underworld. While some black Philadelphians did choose to practice illegal occupations, such as gambling and prostitution, others were driven into them out of desperation. The words "choose" and "driven" are both significant. Virtually all in good health—an important qualification—had the ability to work in the dominant economy, if given a chance, and many could exercise skills well above those required for the jobs they actually got.[99]

Despite the enormous obstacles posed by poverty and other handicaps, a considerable majority, too, tried to establish stable families. Du Bois's count for the Seventh Ward, which both reveals and tries to correct some of the errors in the census, suggests that nearly 70 percent of those over 15 were or had been married. And while that may be an exaggeration, as he adds that many single prostitutes claimed to be married, the very claim shows a stubborn belief in marriage as an institution. Even among domestic servants, who in England had historically had to live in legal celibacy, Isabel Eaton found that only a minority of men and women remained single.[100]

In raising children, as in other ways, they turned to each other for help in coping. Only the most desperate presumably had to lock little ones in rooms or closets, or to drug them, in order to keep them out of trouble during the long days, or nights, when parents were at work. Unemployment and crowding meant that there was usually someone about to deal with immediate needs; when a single domestic had to move out to the suburbs she might find someone else to adopt an infant. At the other end of the life cycle contributions might be raised, even benefit amusements held, to get up the admissions fee to the privately managed Home for Aged and Infirm Colored Persons. In between, the great majority had enough thrift and foresight to join in the array of benefit societies organized to deal with sickness or perhaps death. Single black men, if sometimes homeless as the result of an uncertain job market, were generally sensitive to that market, and moved back and forth either to where work might be had or to the old home which might take them in. And if most work was shut off, some found consolation even in deprivation; black people, a writer in the

Freeman pointed out, did not suffer as much as whites in bad times since they had no factory jobs to lose.[101]

Above all, finally, even the poorest of Afro-Americans in the city were as a class neither hopeless nor isolated from others better off. The Horatio Alger myth of the late 19th century was, among whites, truly a myth, as the great majority on top of the social and economic ladder had come from the upper-middle or at worst the middle classes. But it was a living reality among blacks, partly because the rise from rags to (comparative) riches was relatively short, partly because so many truly skilled and able men and women were stuck artificially in the unskilled category. Not only most of the entrepreneurs described in the following chapter but many of the other leaders described in the next several had spent some time doing either common labor or domestic and personal service. Southern birth was no real handicap either; despite the hardships of migration, more than half of those on the list of Philadelphia's leading black citizens had either been born on the other side of the Mason-Dixon line or lived some time below it. And in many other ways too, the lives and fortunes of the relatively successful remained linked to those of the great majority.[102]

Chapter 4

Owners, Artisans, and Entrepreneurs

The problems of Philadelphia's Afro-American businessmen in the decades following the Civil War were related to those which plagued the majority. They too had to face racism and conquer poverty. But the reasons why so few entrepreneurs were able to succeed were more complicated than these alone.

The explanations offered by Afro-American contemporaries themselves ranged from lack of entrepreneurial talent or interest to lack of capital. But the first of these is belied by the biographies of many black Philadelphians; and the second, a handicap shared with other groups, had earlier been conquered by many of them. And neither is enough to explain not only why the community's businesses remained small in number and size but why the relative resources and influence of their owners were actually shrinking. The situation was in fact complex, as different enterprises experienced different histories, not all were in trouble, and ingenious individuals found a variety of ways of making money. The community's entrepreneurial history may best be explained through looking at the specific problems and attitudes illustrated by the lives of some of its more notable businessmen, together with the stories of some of its leading businesses, from cemetery management and catering through the manufacturing trades, barbering, and others, including illegal enterprises of several kinds. Some of the lesser reasons for decline include an apparently widespread distaste for the self-denying, even miserly life-style of some local "success" stories, changing fashions and technology, and simple bad luck. But the most important were related to racism, and to the situation of the black majority, as shown in the last chapter.

Very simply, as the black population grew, and the crime rate rose with it, the old white patronage sank. And because the potential new customers, however numerous, were so very poor, they were largely unable to make up the difference, leaving most businessmen caught with no truly reliable markets at all.

It seems at first a paradox that urban blacks should lose entrepreneurial strength during the first decades of freedom and formal citizenship, especially during the great greasy Gilded Age of freebooting enterprise. But contemporaries were sure it was happening. In 1879 a reporter's detailed survey of Philadelphia's "colored citizens" concluded that "numerically the race has advanced, but in all other respects they have lost ground and gone backward." Much of this resulted from a shrinkage in "comparative wealth," because of failure to make gains in business.[1]

This charge, sometimes coupled with an elegiac backward look at "the palmy days of the colored haut ton," was familiar to and among the city's own Afro-American spokesman. In practice hard figures are hard to come by, whether in terms of numbers or real worth. W. E. B. Du Bois, using different definitions, suggested that there were in the late 1890s 45 or 200 black business enterprises in the city, and the census of 1900 counted somewhere between 300 and 500 "owners or executives." But whatever the real numbers, contemporary testimony agrees on the simple fact of relative decline. A closer look at the real people who made up the class of owners and businessmen suggests some reasons why.[2]

Whatever the direction of their fortunes, enterprising Philadelphians were heavily represented on the list of 36 men and women most often mentioned in news stories from the Dorsey Collection. Some of them earned these notices because of their businesses, others because of related or even unrelated civic, religious, political, or more rarely scandalous activity. Their collective variety makes it perhaps appropriate to begin with an owner-entrepreneur, of a sort, who allows no generalization at all.[3]

Robert Purvis was the one Afro-American who qualified, in late-19th-century Philadelphia, as a landed aristocrat, a type rare in the white community and unique in his own. Born in South Carolina, son of a rich white cotton broker and a free woman of mixed descent, Purvis was sent to the city in 1819, to begin his formal education at the age of nine. He inherited a reported $120,000 at 16. The money bought among other things some time at Amherst College and then a country estate in Byberry, in the far northeastern corner of Philadelphia County. There Purvis and his first wife Harriet Forten, daughter of the leading black manufacturer James Forten, raised prize animals, apples, and eight children. The estate was in effect a retreat in his later years, but before the Civil War Purvis had retreated from nothing and instead joined his father-in-law as an active abolitionist, philanthropist, and leader of the often embattled little Afro-American community of his adopted city. He ranks sixth in the total number of references in William Dorsey's collection, although most of his activity had occurred long before it was effectively begun.[4]

Tall, handsome, and articulate, a great favorite with the press once abolition was no longer in controversy, Robert Purvis in news accounts was often given the courtesy title "Esquire"; most others, black and white, called him "gentleman"; the census more prosaically listed him as "farmer." By whatever name his occupational history was irrelevant to the wider black experience. Most entrepreneurial leaders in the Afro-American community were more properly classified as shop owners, investors, or artisans.

The biographies of two men listed at different times as the "richest" in the community, although neither was a leader like Purvis, offer a better perspective on what was happening to black businesses, especially when their stories are compared with other and earlier successes. In the 1879 survey mentioned above, the Reverend Joshua Provine Bond Eddy was listed first, with an estimated total worth of $100,000, and Colonel John McKee, a younger man, still active, was thought to come in second at very near that sum. The fact that William Dorsey devoted a short scrapbook to the controversies surrounding each man's death helps to underline the wider significance of the similarities between them.[5]

The Reverend Joshua Eddy's life may be fairly divided in two, the first half a kind of success story not uncommon among his peers. Born to slave parents in Virginia in 1797, he was "thrown in" to the bargain by which his father bought freedom for himself and his wife. The family then moved to Pennsylvania, where as a young man Joshua experienced conversion at a camp meeting, and was afterward successively ordained a traveling preacher, then deacon, then elder by Bishop Richard Allen, founder of the AME church and the most revered single figure in the history of the Afro-American community. His rising clerical career was boosted further by marriage to Allen's daughter; the new family then settled in the town of Columbia, where Eddy supplemented his ministry by opening a barber shop and restaurant. In 1835 he and much of his congregation were driven out by a white mob; Eddy fled to Philadelphia, not much more secure during the riotous 1830s, and re-established himself. During the 1830s and early '40s he opened three barber shops, blacked boots, cleaned clothes, and traded in jewelry until his life was derailed by an event more damaging than the earlier Columbia Riots of 1835.[6]

What reportedly threw him off the tracks was the discovery of his wife's unfaithfulness, leading shortly to divorce. She remarried twice, her evident happiness the second time only aggravating his own turn into misanthropy. He retained some largely unwelcome influence in the church, by one account almost single-handedly blocking the union of the AME and AME Zion denominations, in the exciting period just after the Civil War, simply by threatening to persuade local congregations to secede if the merger went through. But what he did mostly was retire into a hermit's shanty at 511 South Street, using his business talents to speculate in real estate until his death in

September of 1882, and becoming in the process what the Reverend Theodore Gould, at the funeral, called the most eccentric man he had ever met.[7]

For a miser almost wholly without friends, the turnout at Bethel was enormous, heavily attended by brother ministers of the gospel. Dr. B. T. Tanner diplomatically took his text from St. Paul—"judge not"—but the "extraordinary gloom and depression that characterized the services" was lightened only by the relief of Eddy's longsuffering tenants, one of whom reportedly summed up the mood by saying, "If Joshua Eddy and men like him were to be in heaven, she didn't want to go there nohow."[8]

Later that afternoon the surviving grandchildren were further depressed at the reading of the will. Clara Eddy was cut off with a legacy of $100, Frank with $300, while after a few other specific bequests the rest, in a surprise codicil, was given to the old man's septuagenarian brother Josiah and to his nephew Isaiah Wears, reportedly the only man who had spoken to him in some years. The grandchildren sued on the grounds of mental incapacity and undue influence, lost, appealed, and lost again in 1884. After all the ballyhoo about great wealth, the whole of the estate, finally, was valued at just over $16,000.[9]

Something of the same story was played out, with its own baroque variations, on the death of Colonel McKee, just twenty years after. McKee, also born in Virginia, had been apprenticed to a bricklayer before arriving in Philadelphia at the age of 21, early in the 1840s. After a time as a stable boy he became a waiter for James Prosser, one of the leading black restaurateurs of the antebellum period, and then married Prosser's daughter. After some years the couple bought a solid but modest house on 1030 Lombard Street, then a prestigious address, while McKee got out of the restaurant business and into real estate. Although his wife died in the 1880s he continued to live and work out of the old place, while the neighborhood deteriorated around him until he died, at 80, in April of 1902.[10]

McKee was not as spectacularly mean as Eddy, and rather enjoyed playing Santa Claus for the children of his tenants each year, dressing up and pulling a wagonload of little gifts. His pallbearers, William Potter, Levi Cromwell, Robert Jones, Henry Allen, Alfred S. Cassey, J. B. Matthews, and his longtime secretary Raymond J. Burr, represented some of the best of local black society. And he had once been active enough in local affairs to have helped organize the segregated 13th Regiment of the Pennsylvania National Guard, under its white general, Louis Wagner, in the years just after the Civil War. At the same time it is clear that, like Eddy, he had for some decades before dying withdrawn from the civil, social, and political life of the community. The newspapers made much of the fact that his shabby office, or "den," had not been changed in fifty years and looked it. And despite the annual Christmastime charade, his property manager claimed that he had not spent as much as $50 a year on repairs to his houses, while another associate noted that "he viewed life and individuals from only one standpoint, and that was what it and they were worth to him personally."[11]

The question of personal worth was a subject of some titillation in the press. The *Evening Telegraph* believed him "the richest colored man in America," with a fortune estimated at $1,500,000, comprised of 300 to 400 properties in Philadelphia, 4500 acres in "McKee City," near Cape May, New Jersey, plus perhaps 300,000 acres of coal and oil land in the Appalachians. A few days later Raymond Burr upped that to $4,000,000, based in part on the late colonel's alleged rejection of an offer of $3,500,000, from a J. P. Morgan syndicate, for the West Virginia properties alone.[12]

By the time of Burr's allegation, however, the issue of the size of the estate had been eclipsed by the battle over its disposition. McKee had had two daughters; the eldest, who died some years before him, had married the lawyer T. J. Minton, and left a single child, Henry McKee Minton, while the other, Mrs. Abbie P. Syphax of Washington, had helped produce five more grandchildren. The will, handwritten on thirty-two pages of foolscap, granted Mrs. Syphax what one paper called "the very meanest house in Col. McKee's possession," together with a legacy of $300. The grandchildren were to get $50 each, half the amount given Burr, a clerk, a barber, and a cook. The remainder of the estate, in a truly astonishing development, was given to the Roman Catholic church, to use for building "Colonel John McKee College," with a curriculum modeled on that of the U.S. Naval Academy at Annapolis. The students were all to be orphans, but in contrast to the provision through which the notorious Philadelphia eccentric Stephen Girard, three generations earlier, had limited his orphan's "college" to "white males only," those at McKee might be of any race. As a final provision—the Santa Claus business was perhaps a clue—the Colonel provided that the entrance to this institution was to be graced by an equestrian statue of himself, for which he provided a sedentary photograph in what appears to be a Napoleonic hat from the previous century. The executors named were McKee's lawyer Joseph P. McCullen and John P. Ryan, Archbishop of Philadelphia.[13]

Whatever McCullen's role in this, the Archbishop, who could not be made to comment, was evidently embarrassed. McKee had been nominally a Presbyterian most of his life, although his interest in the church had fallen notably at the death of his pious father-in-law. While the will called for a Catholic burial there was no evidence that the old man had ever met a priest. A representative from yet a third denomination, the Reverend George McGuire of St. Thomas P.E., apparently sounded the sentiments of much of the black community by preaching from I Timothy 5:8: "If any provide not for his own, and especially for those of his own house, he hath denied the faith and is worse than an infidel." No self-respecting church, McGuire went on to say, would take the money.[14]

The whole affair was eventually compromised; the Colonel was buried a

Protestant after all and the relatives withdrew their objections to probate in exchange for "bountiful" settlements. The Archbishop's reluctance to fight harder may be explained in part by a preliminary accounting, made public two years after, which put the value of the estate at less than $72,000. Henry M. Minton had already gotten $25,000 of this, and Mrs. Syphax $26,500. The latter sum, plus whatever she may have won from suing her five children for cheating her, in 1903, qualified her at remarriage late in 1904 as reportedly "the richest colored woman in this city, and perhaps in the world."[15]

Had they been white, both Eddy and McKee could be simply classified as colorful versions of a familiar 19th-century type: the rising young man who marries the boss's daughter but then takes a turn into an increasingly embittered, eccentric, and miserly private life, speculating in secret and finally dying rich but unpopular. But theirs are not white biographies, and the fact that both evidently reached the topmost rung of the economic ladder in black Philadelphia suggests something more important about the ladder itself, and what was happening to it.

When the two young men arrived in the city, the title "richest colored man in Philadelphia" had belonged to James Forten, Sr., sailmaker and abolitionist, who ranks close to Richard Allen in the pantheon of local heroes. After Forten's death in 1842 it passed to the lumber dealer Stephen Smith, an exact contemporary of the Reverend Joshua Eddy. Smith, like Eddy an AME minister who had fled the Columbia Riots of 1835 to resettle in the larger city, was like Forten also an active abolitionist and philanthropist. Forten had employed some forty men, black and white, in his sailworks, and sold the product to merchants and shipowners. Smith, taking advantage of the expansive construction of the mid-century decades, dealt in millions of board feet of lumber, running his own railcars, buying bridge and bank stock, dealing on even terms with white businessmen up to his death in 1873.[16]

The contrast needs no belaboring. If the Afro-American economy of Philadelphia is considered as a whole, it could expand largely by taking in money from the white city and then spending it in the black; its leaders could contribute to this partly by offering employment, partly by active support of civic projects. Forten and Smith, with fortunes fairly reliably estimated at $100,000 or better, did all of these things, on a reasonably large scale. Even apart from the difference in actual worth, Eddy and McKee did not.

The Reverend Joshua Eddy, after retirement from the barbering business, apparently employed no one but his white lawyer, John Burton; while it is not entirely clear who rented his properties it appears that they were mostly or entirely located in black neighborhoods, and his profits taken from black tenants. Colonel McKee, who seems to have done much the same thing on a larger scale, did hire a black secretary and clerk, but despite one daughter's marriage to the most experienced black lawyer in the city entrusted his legal business, too, to a white man.[17]

Beyond that, much of the eulogy that B. T. Tanner preached over Joshua Eddy might apply to John McKee as well: "His life was a living protest against the life and manners of his race." The comment may partly have referred to the evident rejection of the Afro-American community which was part of both men's misanthropy. But the burden of the talk was directly economic; Tanner argued that Eddy might be seen—this was after all a eulogy—as something of a "reformer" by example, battling the charge, too often justified, that "we are an improvident and shiftless race." The protest of course went too far, he concluded, and there was after all something to be said for those who "give without question," if less for those "who live beyond our means."[18]

But the will, or ability, to "give without question" was itself in question, and during the postwar decades Philadelphia's shortage of rich and generous businessmen was not unique. T. Thomas Fortune, in 1889, rhetorically asked his readers, "Where Are the Colored Philanthropists?"; several weeks later he had collected just two nominations, one an ex-slave from Austin, Texas, who had left $25,000, the other the pioneer shipowner Paul Cuffee, who had died three generations earlier. In Philadelphia itself, twenty years after Eddy's death and a few days after warning Archbishop Ryan not to accept Colonel McKee's bequest, the Reverend George McGuire had some second thoughts. Mindful of his own pastoral problems, he suggested that philanthropic giving was in itself a good thing, after all, and "people of color are commonly negligent in this matter." All too few members of his own church "have bequeathed it even a few dollars."[19]

It was obvious why Eddy and McKee could not fulfill the community's ideal of open-handed leadership, but the case of William Still, most famous of local black entrepreneurs in the decades after the Civil War, was more complicated. Still was born in 1821, the same year as John McKee, arrived in Philadelphia at roughly the same time, and died later in the same year, 1902. Despite his absence from the census of 1870 he was by that time already one of the leading businessmen and philanthropists in the Afro-American community, and eventually succeeded Smith, and perhaps Smith's partner William Whipper, who died in 1876, at the very top. But while he clearly followed in the footsteps left by Forten and these others, he was never quite able to fill them.[20]

Still's story is again the stuff of 19th-century legend. The youngest of eighteen children born to an ex-slave couple in rural South Jersey, young William had left farm work for Philadelphia in the 1840s. Self-taught, hard-working, and ambitious, after a few years at odd jobs he caught the attention of local abolitionists. From working in the office of the Pennsylvania Society for the Abolition of Slavery he went on to a leading role in the Underground Railroad; the historian Benjamin Quarles ranks Still second only to Harriet Tubman in the work of rescuing fugitives from the South. From the beginning, too, he supplemented his wages by buying and selling land, ice, coal, and stoves. During the war years, perhaps with influential help from well-placed friends, he got a profitable contract as supplier to Camp William Penn, just outside the city, where black troops were stationed for training. Afterward, on suggestion of officers of the abolition society, he wrote a still useful and then popular *History of the Underground Railroad*, which he promoted through agents all over the country. In Dorsey's collection, although again his busiest years were behind him, he is tied for third in number of references, just ahead of his old friend Robert Purvis.[21]

Still was always an active member of the community. He and his wife Letitia George raised four children: Caroline, the eldest, was the second Afro-American to earn a medical degree in the city, and then married the Reverend Matthew Anderson, one of its leading ministers; Ella taught school; William W. went to Lincoln and to business college before becoming a lawyer; Robert was a reformer, newspaper editor, and finally head of the "Afro-American" section of the Democratic National Committee. William himself kept his ties with the former Pennsylvania Society for the Abolition of Slavery, which stayed alive after Emancipation by expanding its philanthropies and adding "and for Improving the Condition of the African Race" to its title. Treasurer of a number of black organizations, he gave not only to worthy causes but to people such as the abolitionist heroine Sojourner Truth when she was old and ailing. A pillar of his son-in-law's Berean Presbyterian Church, finally, Still was in many respects a worthy successor to Forten and Smith; he in fact succeeded Smith directly, taking a place as the leading spirit behind the Home for Aged and Infirm Colored Persons, an important local institution which Smith had founded before his death in 1873.[22]

His actual business, though, was rather more modest. His principal enterprise was a coal and ice yard on South Broad Street; unlike Stephen Smith he sold no lumber but only these consumer goods, presumably to small retailers in grocery stores, and even individual customers with buckets. And he was never rich, secure, or otherwise busy enough to turn down a salary for his work as secretary to the Pennsylvania Society.[23]

Most troubling, Still was continually plagued by criticism from within his own community, mostly over issues that seem too small, a century later, to explain their persistence. William Dorsey was one of those who evidently did not like the man, a near neighbor for most of his life. One story, reported in the New York *Globe* twenty-five years later, was that John Brown's widow had stayed with William and Letitia Still while awaiting her husband's hanging in Virginia, following his failed raid at Harper's Ferry in 1859; Dorsey noted in the margin that "This Is All Wrong"; Mrs. Brown had been the guest instead of "Mr. and Mrs. Thomas J. Dorsey," his own parents. But if Still had made an unfounded claim it seems uncharacteristic. He was not a vain man; one reporter in the New York *Globe* called him "quiet and unassuming," and the *History of the Underground Railroad* has been cited as a notably modest book, with its emphasis on the fugitives themselves rather than their rescuers. Some blacks complained that he took white money to help sustain his good works. But this was a charge that in that era might apply to many others, and Still himself pointed to the "fat salary" which Frederick Douglass enjoyed, from a patronage job in Washington, essentially to continue his dual work as spokesman for the race and for the Republican party. If his politics differed from those of Douglass and the majority of his peers, so did those of several leading Philadelphians. While Robert Purvis, among others, joined him in speaking out against the incumbent Republican mayor in 1874, it was Still who almost literally drew fire: an anomymous threat to bomb his coal yard, although presumably written by a black man angry at Still's betrayal of the GOP, was addressed to "Mr. Nigger."[24]

Still's supporters agreed that his opponents were simply "jealous." But he himself provided what may be a better clue in an extended public talk in 1867, later published as a pamphlet. The occasion should have been a celebration; the common battle to integrate the city's streetcars, a battle he had begun some years before, had finally ended in victory. But Still chose instead to go back over tactical differences with younger and more militant members of the community, first defending himself and then characteristically lecturing them. Too few, he argued, were following him into business, and so were doubly weakening the race, both by failing to win respect from whites and by spending the grocery and dress money in white stores. Both of these problems, he went on, had a common root in moral failure; in contrast to his own "hard labor, strict temperance habits, rigid economy, and . . . unimpeachable character," they chose to spend their time in "idle and frivolous society."[25]

It is quite true that the names of William and Letitia Still were never listed among those who gave, played at, or attended the balls and ballgames, concerts and club meetings, that occupied other members of the local elite. No one so visible was so conspicuously absent except for Robert Purvis, but Purvis lived some miles from the center of town, and may have won the indulgence often given natural aristocrats. Still lived rather at 1243 South 12th Street, in the heart of the community, and played not the aristocrat but the Protestant bourgeois, perhaps uncomfortably like the Presbyterian and Quaker associates who served on the boards of the Pennsylvania Society and the old people's home. Black men and women had in general no objection to riches and success, and admired those who earned them. But few wanted to follow, and certainly not to be lectured about, the classic early capitalist route involving thrifty self-denial. Philadelphia's ordinary Afro-Americans believed in good times as well as good causes, and it was Still's personal austerity, it seems, the implied rebuke, like Joshua Eddy's, to the more customary manners and mores, which played so poorly in his community, and not business enterprise per se.

A more congenial type of entrepreneur was Jacob White, Jr., secretary and manager of the Lebanon Cemetery, which ranked with or next to Olive

Cemetery as the biggest single enterprise run by blacks in Philadelphia. White was one of the young men who had defied the more conservative approach both of his own father and of William Still, in the course of the streetcar battle of the 1860s, in urging that the issue be taken directly to the streets. He had also had the satisfaction of giving Still a sharp written slap two years after that issue was settled. Popular and outgoing, White was the secretary of the Pythians Baseball Club, an organization composed of the community's young athletes plus some older supporters, many of whom, like William Still, were solicited to support the club as a matter of civic pride. When Still wrote to resign his membership, in the spring of 1869, citing the many less "frivolous" demands upon his hard-earned money, White replied that the resignation was moot since the older man had yet to pay his annual dollar in dues; beyond that, "neither the acquisition nor the disposition of your means is of interest to us as an organization." But whatever their other differences—and in terms of purely social activities they lived very different lives—Still could not fairly accuse White of lacking the spirit of enterprise.[26]

White's biography in many ways looks much like William Dorsey's. Both men were born in the city, in 1837, to successful businessmen; both attended the Institute for Colored Youth; both were named as consultants to W. E. B. Du Bois in the late 1890s and then helped found the American Negro Historical Society. Both men, too, shared the pack rat's passion for collecting. But while Dorsey clipped newspaper and journal items, supplemented with occasional reports, programs, posters, and broadsides, White—tied for twenty-second place in the collection—simply found it hard to throw away any of his personal papers, due bills, or ticket stubs, and so left a far fuller record than any of his peers, and one that makes it possible to re-create many of his ventures in business.[27]

Within the community White's most important role was educational. As the first black principal appointed by any of the city's local school boards, in 1864, he managed apparently to bargain himself into an initial salary of $625 a year, far higher than the $450 commanded by the other, white, principals in the district where his school was located. As the school continually grew in size, and its principal in influence, White expanded his role as the leading black in Philadelphia's public school system throughout the 1870s and 1880s until his retirement in 1896.[28]

His concurrent interest in business was a heritage from his father, a barber, sometimes unlicensed physician, and successful speculator in real estate. The father had founded the Lebanon Cemetery Company; the son became its secretary-manager while still a schoolboy, in the 1850s, and used its offices to found or run a number of other enterprises. During the early 1860s he served as the Philadelphia agent for two black weeklies, the *Anglo-African* and *Pine and Palm*, selling several hundred issues in good months for a gross annual profit of perhaps $100 to $200. (In 1860 White told publisher Thomas Hamilton of the

Anglo-African, ironically, that he might move 50 extra copies one week if the issue included a letter from William Still.) Perhaps as an outgrowth of his interest in *Pine and Palm,* which advertised opportunities for Afro-Americans in the independent state of Haiti, he also served in 1861 as an agent for the Haitian Bureau of Emigration. But while the papers were a means of harnessing his principles to profit, neither lasted very long. And above all, like his father, Stephen Smith, Joshua Eddy, John McKee, William Still, and many others, White was interested in real property.[29]

The attractions of real estate were obvious; money could be made without having to deal with white customers in number; housing was a necessity for even the poorest members of the black community; and much depended on an insider's knowledge of movement and prospects within that community. The senior White had owned rental property in Providence, Rhode Island, which sometimes returned $20 to $30 a year to his son and heir. The son presumably did better with the Benezet Joint Stock Association, which he founded as an enterprising teenager in 1854; stock sold initially for $25, which was converted into several homes in the black district and Benezet Hall, and returned dividends into 1885.[30]

In terms of the black economy, it is clear that Afro-American management of Lebanon, Olive, and later Merion cemeteries served two important functions. Contemporaries agreed that blacks, like European peasants, were deeply concerned about proper burial, one reason why mutual benefit associations, which among other things guaranteed funeral expenses, were the commonest type of Afro-American organization, and undertaking always a major business. In later years it was part of the fearful anti-urban folklore of southern migrants to the city that they might be kidnapped and sent "to the colleges," that is, to join the hanged killers and anonymous accident victims in medical school dissecting rooms. In the 19th century that chilling threat was sometimes a kind of curse, uttered for example by a pimp who refused to take responsibility for one of his dead women, and sometimes the focus of cruel practical joking by white hospital interns. And if one way that the Afro-American economy might expand was by taking in money from whites, the other, equally essential, was that it keep black spending within the community. Proper burials were the largest single expenditures that most families ever made, and while not all of them were entrusted to the specifically black companies it is clear that most were, and so stopped a potential drain of dollars out of black hands and into white. At the same time the Lebanon records make it clear that buying, selling, and indeed speculating in lots—Harriet Duterte, one of the two leading Afro-American undertakers, was an especially active dealer—was an important and relatively safe form of investment in real estate.[31]

The surviving records are a hodgepodge that allow no real estimate of profits. Lots sold for prices ranging between $3 and $30, the differences varying with the location as well as, presumably, the business cycle and the personal condition of the dealers. But it is clear that Jacob White, Sr., had chosen shrewdly; the five and one-half acres he bought in the far south of Philadelphia County, incorporated into the city proper only in 1854, were continually appreciating in value as the result of sheer growth. When the municipal authorities finally bought the cemetery in order to straighten the roads at the corner of 19th and Passyunk, the price was fixed at $90,000. But the last years of the Lebanon Company, which nearly coincided with those of Jacob White, Jr., who died in 1902, just prior to the final sale, could not have been happy ones for its manager.[32]

W. E. B. Du Bois, in discussing Afro-American enterprise in the city, twice cited the three cemetery companies as "fairly well-conducted." But this seems an example of the young scholar's walking the tight line that runs throughout *The Philadelphia Negro*. Du Bois wanted on the one hand to describe problems in the black community with enough force to call attention to them, and above all to the pervasive racism that was at their root. On the other hand neither he nor his advisers wanted to publicize problems in terms so bleak as to discourage hope, either in the community itself or in potential readers, and possibly benefactors, in the outside white world. And in fact, while there is little evidence about the Merion company, newest and smallest of the three, it is quite clear that both Olive and Lebanon were not well but wretchedly conducted.[33]

The most spectacular event in Lebanon's history was unraveled beginning in the spring of 1882, as the result of the investigative reporting and derring-do of Louis Megargee, a white reporter for the *Press*. In the course of doing a feature on anatomical research, Megargee noticed that far more bodies were being supplied to the students of Jefferson Medical College than they could possibly have got through the limited legal channels then available. Some midnight detective work revealed that in fact the college was being visited, in the wee hours, by a team of men with a wagon full of "dark" corpses, which were then unloaded inside. Of the two possible sources of properly colored bodies, it turned out that it was Lebanon, not Olive, where the wagon was first loaded. But just at that point the traffic stopped; the term was ending, "the pickling vats . . . filled to the brim," and no hard evidence was at hand.[34]

There was nothing to do but wait until the fall, sitting on the story; Megargee's first concern, such was the nature of journalistic ethics, was that "the discovery would leak into some other newspaper office." The new term finally came, but no new activity through a frustrating September and October, until finally in November the reporter again witnessed a delivery and was able to trace the wagon, identify the men involved, and manage secretly to swear out an arrest warrant. Finally on the night of December 4, Megargee, hidden on the grounds, saw the wagon pull up to a row of freshly dug corpses, then called in four other men from the *Press*, and with their help intercepted the wagon on Passyunk Avenue and captured the three wagoneers at gunpoint.

The next day, as the black community heard the news, was full of furious excitement. Guy Burton, a leading undertaker and president of Lebanon's board of trustees, had to battle at graveside with the journalist H. Price Williams, while uptown the three prisoners were nearly mobbed. When the whole business was sorted out it appeared that the superintendent of the cemetery, Robert Chew, appointed by manager Jacob White, had been involved in the business for eleven years, at the instigation of a black undertaker. He and his younger brother Levi split three dollars for each of an estimated several hundred bodies delivered over the period. All of these men, and several white confederates, were sent to prison the next spring. But after an especially bitter trial Jefferson's Dr. W. S. Forbes successfully pleaded ignorance of the source of his specimens, with the help of a battery of fellow physicians.

Olive's troubles, as brought to light later in the same decade, seem almost anticlimactic next to Lebanon's. Its eight acres at Belmont and Girard in West Philadelphia made it a little bigger, its property valued at a little more; it was however little better run. In the spring of 1887 the Philadelphia *Tribune,* in an early example of muckraking reportage, called it "a disgrace to the Board of Managers." William Henry Dorsey, "our special artist," was engaged to illustrate some of the problems cited in the piece: neglected grounds, falling stones and fences, and frequent flooding. Several years later, in 1894, a group of stockholders battled the board in a stormy session over the issues of salaries and the rights of those who held lots.

One problem was that while both companies had early bought what were then fairly small and essentially rural tracts, when the land filled up and space got tight their managers resorted to practices no longer acceptable in an urban environment; in 1898 the board of health enjoined both of them from burying more than one body in the same spot. Lack of the capital needed to expand by buying more land elsewhere was compounded by the lack of management skills shown in the accusations of disrepair and the loose rein allowed Superintendent Chew; Lebanon's directors further refused an offer from the more forward-looking new board of Merion. The next year the police, after a complaint, found Lebanon's superintendent prowling the ground with a shotgun, evidently paranoid, looking for grave robbers and "enemies." That fall, November of 1899, the board of health finally condemned it outright as a noisome health hazard, to the *Tribune's* great satisfaction. The $90,000 purchase price paid out in 1903 was simply provided to move the existing bodies to various suburban sites. When Olive died a little later there was no longer any place in the city in which blacks in number could be buried at all.[35]

While the death of the cemetery business in the city yields an easy postmortem explanation, with failure, despite some special circumstances, mostly the result of the familar problems facing most small businesses, the decline in the special

Afro-American business of catering had a special Afro-American flavor. Despite an entirely different market, catering ranked with the cemetery business as the most important in black Philadelphia. But the problems it encountered, mostly but not entirely the result of racism, were faced by a number of other enterprises as well, from barbering and the skilled trades to William Dorsey's own profession as "artist."

When an observer in 1879 noted that "years ago there used to be a good deal of colored aristocracy in Philadelphia," or when Du Bois nearly twenty years later recalled the day when "the triumverate Jones, Dorsey, and Minton . . . ruled the fashionable world," they were both invoking the same kind of nostalgia. The catering and to a lesser extent the allied restaurant business were at the forefront of a number of parallel enterprises, such as cabinetmaking, barbering, and upholstering, through which black businessmen had historically served, in Du Bois's phrase, as "purveyors to the rich."[36]

Du Bois gave especial prominence to the generation dominated above all by William Dorsey's father Thomas. But the caterers do not figure as strongly in the Dorsey scrapbooks, mostly concerned with the 1870s and after, as they might have earlier. The one mentioned most often was Levi Cromwell, tied for thirteenth place. But if Cromwell did not stand out, he does stand for a whole class of solid bourgeois whose support was essential to Afro-American organizations of all kinds.[37]

Perhaps the most important single businessman's contribution to the community in the postwar era was the purchase of Liberty Hall in 1866, a movement mostly and significantly led by the older generation. The war had ended slavery, but there was still much to do. Pennsylvania's Afro-Americans had yet to win the vote, and with it several other basic civil rights. Philadelphians were still in the thick of the long-running battle to desegregate the streetcars; soldiers, sailors, and nurses had been denied the right to ride even in wartime, and young militants just afterward were testing the rules with their bodies while their elders petitioned the all-white state legislature. It had always been hard for blacks to hold big meetings. The charter of the Musical Fund Hall not only forbade Afro-Americans from renting but reportedly from sitting in it, while the sight of blacks and whites mixing together to discuss the abolition of slavery had inspired a mob to burn down Pennsylvania Hall in 1838. While the war had helped to settle some issues, it had also raised expectations, and there was still a clear need for a community forum, which could not be denied.[38]

The answer was provided by William Still and William Whipper, Stephen Smith's partner in the lumbering business. When its Quaker managers proposed to move the Institute for Colored Youth a few blocks south and west of its location near Seventh and Lombard, the very crossroads of the black city, the old building became available. Still and Whipper bought it, and the Reverend Elisha Weaver of the AME Book Concern published an appeal for support; these three and seven others then put up $1000 each to buy and then renovate the building, turning it into a three-story structure with places for stores on the ground level and above all a meeting hall 40 by 80 feet on top. The purpose was twofold: to provide a place for the community to gather, and— Still's continuing project—to encourage business. "We MUST change the course of our patronage," the Reverend Elisha Weaver wrote, too much of which was going to white tradesmen. But if young men would "enter the channels of trade, and if they are polite, honest, industrious, and economical, their success will be morally certain."[39]

No white philanthropists were involved in the project; the ten black stockholders eventually had to put up a total not of $10,000 but $23,000. They included Still, Whipper, Weaver, and of course Stephen Smith; another clergyman, from a denomination usually thought rival to Weaver's, Bishop J. J. Clinton of AME Zion; Robert Adger, who located his furniture store on the ground floor; a barber, William Warrick; a teamster, Colonel Jacob Purnell; and two caterers, Henry Jones and Robert Allen. In the early years the dividends sometimes reached 12 percent. But as blacks were admitted elsewhere the need declined and so did profits; some of the original investors then looked to get out. Still was the first to sell his stock; Levi Cromwell bought it.[40]

Cromwell, like most of his small business colleagues, did not challenge the community's ministers or growing group of professionals as a public speaker or club president; he simply ran his restaurant and paid his dues. He appears, typically, in Dorsey's collection, at civil rights rallies; as an adjutant in the Grey Invincibles, the local militia company; as patron of a new black school in Virginia; at the annual celebration of Stephen Smith's birthday at the Home for Aged and Infirm Colored Persons; at the 50th anniversary celebration of the Pennsylvania Society for the Abolition of Slavery; as treasurer of a meeting to protest southern injustice. Other members of the Caterers' Association were almost equally involved; but the business as a whole was fading in importance.[41]

Du Bois once fixed the heyday of Philadelphia catering between 1845 and 1870, then pushed the date back to accommodate the deaths of T. J. Dorsey in 1876 and Henry Minton in 1883. In any case, the business remained vital for some time. Levi Cromwell's worth was estimated, with the usual reliability, at about $50,000 in 1879. That was the same amount credited to his fellow restaurateur P. J. Augustine, whose place at 1105 Walnut enjoyed a reputation as "the Delmonico's of Philadelphia." In fact the Augustines ran what was probably the oldest continuously managed black family business in the city. Peter Augustine, a refugee from Haiti, had started the place back in 1818; his heirs later joined with another West Indian restaurant and catering family, the Baptistes, to run a place on South 15th Street described in 1910 as bigger and, at $60,000 for the premises alone, more valuable than ever.[42]

At worst, then, the catering and restaurant business was a long time dying, and in some ways it may be argued that it reached its peak some time after Du Bois's terminal date, or dates. The Caterers' Association was formally organized only in 1866, the Caterers' Supply Company, a cooperative venture in wholesale buying, in 1894. Andrew F. Stevens, often president of the Association, the social leader of the Afro-American elite from the late 1870s, became in 1894 the sixth black man ever to win a seat on Philadelphia's enormous Common Council, serving until his death in 1898. And finally it was a caterer, John Trower, who as late as 1912 held the elusive title, lately surrendered by Colonel John McKee, as the "richest colored man in the city."[43]

Still whether in terms of numbers, wealth, or social standing, Du Bois's elegy for the caterers was not misplaced. Before the war, he wrote, this "remarkable trade guild" had taken "complete leadership" of the little community, and "led them steadily on to a degree of affluence, culture, and respect such as has probably never been surpassed in the history of the Negro in America." There was in this, as in the similar assessments of white observers, more than a touch of snobbery. To rich whites, caterers were among the most visible, and flattering, of black entrepreneurs; their business was service, as Du Bois pointed out, and it had evolved naturally among people who had themselves been servants, or waiters, men who knew the best in dress and manners. Often, too, like many house servants, they knew how to act imperiously and demand respect. Frederick Douglass credited Louise Dorsey, at his side, with giving him the social courage to face down hostility and attend President Lincoln's inauguration in 1865. Thomas Dorsey himself, when denied entrance to a ball in honor of the Russian Grand Duke Alexis, wrote the Duke an angry letter in December of 1871 which concluded by telling the future czar of all the Russias that "I regard you a much better republican than those Americans who have, in my person, insulted a man on account of the accident of his complexion. The act would not be tolerated in Russia, and I believe you despise it as [I do]."[44]

Within the black community itself the caterers' purely social leadership was equally natural; they brought the panache of professional party givers to their role as private hosts, and in the era of "Commodore" Andrew Stevens no social event was reported more often in the black press than the regular banquets of the Ugly Fishing Club, with a membership dominated by members of the catering fraternity. But there seems no question that the caterers were in decline toward century's end. Du Bois found only about ten men carrying on the old tradition successfully enough to do $3000 to $5000 worth of business in a year. In 1899 the 23rd annual meeting of the Caterers' Association was attended by relative unknowns, men who with the exception of Jerome Baptiste were almost entirely without the organizational memberships and community standing that their predecessors had enjoyed a generation or even a decade earlier.[45]

There were particular reasons for this decline. Du Bois cites changing fads in food and fashion, notably a new taste for French cuisine; perhaps this explains the continued success of the Augustines, Baptistes, and Dutrieulles among the survivors. Certainly the others seem to have specialized in the familiar dishes of the Middle Atlantic states; lobsters from New England, crab, oysters, and terrapins from the estuaries of the Chesapeake Bay, an unvarying cuisine that came out of the ice house as much as the oven. But for his puritanism, too, Du Bois might have added the effects of the new liquor licensing law adopted in 1888. In the continual, sometimes two-faced, 19th-century battle against sin and alcohol, Pennsylvania followed many other states in dramatically raising its license fees, so that a permit that used to take no more than $50 and a letter from a politician now legally required a $2000 bond and an annual $500 fee, shortly raised to $900. That was simply too high for all but a handful of black saloon keepers even to attempt. It was ruled further that licenses were granted only for specific and permanent locations, so that Andrew Stevens, for example, could not use one to sell wine while catering an affair at the Academy of Music. Given the lack of capital that plagued all Afro-American enterprises, no caterers or even restaurateurs even bothered to apply; they either gave up the substantial profits from liquor sales or, like thousands of others, white and black, continued to operate outside of the law.[46]

But these specific problems, while real enough, do not explain the fact that catering was only one of several kinds of business in decline. W. Carl Bolivar, the community's unofficial historian, one of the advisers to Du Bois and tied for fifteenth place in the Dorsey Collection, wrote a regular column for the *Tribune*. He himself was a rarity, the only black in the city who worked for a private commercial bank, spending a lifetime as clerk without promotion. In any case he took an interest in the economic condition of his race, the subject of several of his historical pieces. The only surviving examples of these "Pencil Pusher's Points" were written in the two years before Bolivar's death in 1914, and clearly reflect the attitudes of a man by then in his sixties. Like most of the contemporary elite, he believed in the progress of race relations as a matter of faith, almost as a psychological necessity, and thought the latter-day city in many ways a better place than the one in which he had grown up. At the same time, and allowing for some nostalgia, he also insisted, with much documentation, that black business was not then what it had been in the 1860s and '70s.[47]

The same period that William Still had seen as losing enterprise looked to Carl Bolivar, in retrospect, like a kind of golden age. Despite his own white-collar status he did not believe that "business" need involve formal offices or furnished premises; among those which he remembered that blacks in the 1860s had virtually monopolized were chimney sweeping, household cleaning, and whitewashing; furniture moving was not monopolized but "dominated." All of these, like catering, were natural outgrowths of domestic service, and perhaps took shrewd advantage of domestic connections, a mutually profitable friendship with the head maid or butler who arranged these homely matters.

Any of them, too, could be entered easily, like trucking, with little capital beyond perhaps a rented wagon. The public markets on Market, South, North Second, Callowhill, Spring Garden, and South 11th streets also gave many an opportunity to start small; "in all the economics of market industry the colored man had a part and parcel from time immemorial." Just a step up was secondhand clothing, another business dominated by blacks, who owned several stores on Second Street between Vine and Pine. The manufacture and sale of ice cream, too, once a virtual monopoly, was still important in the 1860s, with two parlors on South Street among those supplied by Jackson's manufactory on Walnut above Tenth. Above all, blacks predominated in the barbering business, in terms of the numbers involved by far the most important of the Afro-American trades.[48]

Fifty or even thirty years afterward, although the proportion of blacks in the population had grown greatly, there was no mention of their domination in any of these enterprises. As with catering there were special circumstances in some cases. The closing of all open markets but the one on South Street was hard on small-provision dealers of every kind. Chimney sweeping was still in the early 1880s conducted by just two entrepreneurs, both black; one of them, John Davis, an old sailor who had reportedly lost an eye in Lieutenant Franklin's Arctic expedition some decades before, employed 28 youngsters, indentured from the Guardians of the Poor, out of a headquarters in an alley off Walnut Street. But time and change were already eroding the business; the use of anthracite coal, wider chimneys, and grates had virtually extinguished it by century's end. The more typical case, in which decline can be traced to no unique or technological change, was barbering.[49]

The barbering business is one of those which confounds the census categories. Like other tradesmen such as masons or carpenters, barbers could be classified as either skilled workingmen, if they worked for others, or as small capitalist entrepreneurs if they were in business for themselves. The line between the two was slight and often artificial; given the prejudice against them on union jobs, it is appropriate to think of black tradesmen more as real or potential entrepreneurs than as wage-earners. During the 19th century there were so many barbers among them that they dominate whatever category they can be put into, accounting in one study for about one-third of all "artisans." In fact, however, neither the craft nor the capital required of the great majority made them at all comparable with the skilled members of the building trades, or with more-established shopkeepers.[50]

A survey of Philadelphia's barbers in 1885 estimated that there were about 1500 in the city; 500 of them were black, a smaller proportion than earlier, and 300 of these ran their own shops. Although they cut and shampooed hair as well, shaving beards was the backbone of the trade, at the modal price of a dime, although the range went from a nickel up to a quarter. In general the black employees aimed high; few worked in the nickel places, which were mostly "uptown"—that is, out of the central city where most blacks lived and worked. A handful, to illustrate the rule that there were few ironclad rules governing race relations, worked in integrated shops. Most, like those in the better shops generally, insisted on working for shares rather than straight wages. The best employees could generally make $8 to $10 a week, a few up to $15. And a man like William Warrick could do very well, with twelve chairs at the Hotel Commodore on Broad Street, and a branch in Atlantic City, for not only his own but his wife's business as beautician. Warrick, known as a "tonsorial artist," was one of the investors who put up the money for Liberty Hall, and successfully raised and educated one of the most accomplished families in the community; one son became a leading doctor, while a daughter won international fame for her sculpture.[51]

But competition was fierce; there were eight black barbershops on Locust between Eighth and 12th streets alone. And one of the rules that stayed unbroken was that no given shop, even if its personnel were all black, could deal with both white and black customers, but must specialize in one or the other. Only a third of the 300 shops run by Afro-Americans were able to attract white customers, and so bring white money back into the community; the other 200 had to split the modest business brought in by perhaps 15,000 adult black males, most of whom had few dimes to spare. Without licensing or apprenticing standards, barbering was the kind of enterprise set up by "a young colored man too lazy to work." The majority rented rooms for $3 a week, and grossed for their legitimate activities perhaps $1 a day after a total capital expenditure of perhaps $15.[52]

The occupational histories of the community's leaders suggest that barbering was often a kind of episodic phase, a business to move into, or better out of, in the course of a career. The orator Isaiah Wears, whose heavy political involvement made him the single person most often mentioned in the Dorsey Collection, is listed as "barber" in the 1870 census. This however was twelve years before he won the inheritance from J. P. B. Eddy and began to call himself a "notary public"; contemporaries believed that he lived mostly off a subsidy from the Republican party. The Reverend Joshua Eddy himself began as a barber; the journalist H. P. Williams, tied for third in the collection, sometimes took up the razor. So did David Bustill Bowser, tied for seventeenth, "portrait painter" in the census. Bowser's most important work, between the 1860s and a few years before his death in 1900, was as head of the United Order of Odd Fellows. As a young man, however, before this salaried position freed him to pursue his artistic talents, he had followed other native Philadelphians south, touring the Mississippi and Red rivers as a steamboat barber. But the man who best illustrates the tentative nature of the trade, and the protean character of much black enterprise generally, is James H. Teagle, tied for eighteenth place.[53]

Teagle's first appearance in the Dorsey Collection was in one of the "colored" columns in the *Times*, in the spring of 1878, in which he announced that following a trip to California he would return to petition Harrisburg for a charter to open a bank. That would have been the first such venture since the collapse of the local branch of the Freedman's Bank earlier in the decade, but neither this nor any other black bank was established during the rest of the century. At some time prior to 1880 Teagle failed in an expensive bid to win nomination for the Pennsylvania House of Representatives; the fact he went broke in this abortive effort, thirty years before any black man made it, did not discourage his interest in politics. Nor did the collapse of a restaurant on South 12th discourage his interest in business, and he went on to open a barbershop in the American Hotel, working with several assistants. It was there that the census apparently found him in July of 1880.[54]

On the other hand "The Majah," as he was universally known to the press, may have already dropped out of barbering, without being entirely candid with the man from the census. Early in August, the month after the count, the *Press* found him in the summer resort of Long Branch, New Jersey, working for the white gambler Phil Dailey as majordomo of a "gorgeous sporting house where the tiger claws from morn 'til every eve and then 'til morn again." At the same time he was engaged in a suit, under the still-operative Civil Rights Act of 1875, to recover $50,000 from a local saloon keeper who had refused him a drink.[55]

Nothing came of that suit, but Teagle was more successful ten years later. A big, broad-shouldered, gregarious man, the Majah was fully at home in the sporting demimonde, most integrated of the period's milieux. In the spring of 1890 he entered a suit against a white man, Harry G. Moore, for the sum of $1200 in back pay and bills due. Moore was an oddly innocent young 19th-century type, a privileged wastrel, supported entirely by his father on condition he stay away from home. Teagle alleged that he had served officially as Moore's valet, between October of 1887 and June of 1889, and unofficially as his guide through various gambling and bawdy houses all over the Northeast. He was able to produce bills and receipts from these establishments—Moore's naïveté suggests he truly needed experienced help—and collected the full amount in April of 1891.[56]

In the spring of 1892 Teagle was involved in at least two different ventures. First, from his oyster stand at the racetrack at Gloucester, New Jersey, he was accused of fixing races in collaboration with his cousin, a Captain Hitchen, who owned several horses. During the same spring season he also served as the "colored Chesterfield" or impresario for an all-black production of *Richard III* at the Academy of Music. At some time, too, he evidently got back into the restaurant business near Seventh and Lombard. He was arrested there in 1894 for serving liquor without a license; five years later an employee was arrested for threatening him with a knife and gun. In 1904, grown grayer and perhaps more respectable, he was recorded as an active member of the elite Quaker City Association, serving on the banquet committee under Chairman Jerome Baptiste.[57]

The Majah's experience, different only in spicy detail from those of many others, shows among other things that there was no lack of entrepreneurial talent in the city's Afro-American community. And yet by 1912, while the official Afro-American population count was more than twice that of 1885, the number of barbershops had been reduced from an estimated 300 to a carefully enumerated 116. And Teagle's story again may indicate the reason for the loss, specifically the central role played by white racial attitudes.[58]

Even if Afro-American barbers had been technically inferior to their immigrant competitors, and there is no such evidence, barbering was clearly not a business in which success, as in, say, cabinetmaking, was a matter of technical skill. Lack of capital was a handicap, as in any other enterprise, but black barbers had been around longer than others, and the competition also found it hard to start. But a barbershop was, and is, a kind of men's club, where a customer above all must feel at home. Each has its own character, and a good barber must be sensitive to moods and tastes, whether and when to swap jokes and ball scores, or, as a piece on the Majah's American Hotel experience put it, to tell "of their amours and quarrels of the night before." In the mid-century city, white patrons had felt comfortable with black barbers. In the late-century decades increasingly they did not.[59]

The relationship between customers and barbers was essentially the same as between customers and caterers, or customers and small businessmen generally. To be successful it must involve some familiarity on both sides. Racial prejudice alone need not hurt the relationship; white patrons were rarely free of that at any time, and some sense of superiority—literally, "patronage"—may have helped them feel at ease. But genuine dislike was obviously fatal, and in the late 19th century hostility and suspicion hurt black business enterprise in several distinct ways.

There is a paradox here. In many ways relations between blacks and whites in the city were growing better after 1870 rather than worse, and not merely in terms of formal civil rights. But in economic matters the tide was running in the other direction. Before the war, a reporter recalled years later, the great musician and bandleader Frank Johnson had been in demand at all the major white society affairs. The man Alain Locke called his successor, in the late 19th century, was F. J. R. Jones. Jones called himself a "musician" in the 1880 census; the *Public Ledger* the next year identified him as a "saloon keeper." There is no question about his skills, and it was the popularity of his band, 23 and even 60 pieces for the bigger occasions, that mostly accounts for his ranking ninth in the Dorsey Collection. But while he played for many Afro-American clubs and organizations, neither he nor any other black musician of the period was hired to play for whites. Without white patronage he was simply unable to make a living at his chosen profession, and in addition to tending bar he also worked successively, perhaps desperately, for the city, county, and national governments, moving in and out of jobs as watchman, messenger, special officer, and bail clerk.[60]

One of the problems which makes the census so dubious a source of Afro-American economic data is the number of those who, like Jones, identified themselves in terms of occupations that did not in fact support them, or were conversely listed as "laborer" only because no one would pay them to use their real skills. This was probably most true of building tradesmen, among the best-paid of all manual workers but a group whose history is especially hard to trace. The requisite skills were there and before the war, the *Times* recalled, rich white Philadelphians often demanded "colored" workingmen exclusively. But afterward the demand seems limited to black customers, and very few of them. Henry Minton, who had himself made shoes before a job as hotel waiter led on to catering, tried to open opportunities of several kinds before his death in 1883. Like many of his fellows he invested much of his profits in real estate; at one point he experimented with growing cotton in South Jersey, and at another he was able successfully to use none but blacks on a brick building project in Camden. The Union Baptist Church, in 1888, used only blacks in building a new church; two years later Union AME, moving nine blocks west to the 1500 block of Lombard Street, remodeled the old Howard Hospital into a new Grace American AME under the direction of the carpenter F. P. Main. But by the time that the Reverend J. B. Randolph pledged an all-black policy in the construction of his new Bethsaida Baptist in 1899 the gesture was cited as exceptional. While several other churches were built or rebuilt during the period, and a number of Building and Loan Associations helped individuals to construct their own homes, there is no other mention of black skilled work. Men identified as "contractors," such as Elias Chase, were doubtless foremen of labor gangs. Joshua D. Kelley was sometimes but not always called a "mason," the only one in the period and the leader in building Union Baptist; he is listed as "janitor" in the census of 1880. And two counts of the community's carpenters and cabinetmakers, in 1861 and 1883, came up with precisely the same totals, five and one, despite an official population increase of roughly 50 percent, while the four prewar plumbers disappeared entirely.[61]

Apprenticeship was the best way to learn a trade, but for young black men the prospects were virtually nonexistent. Racism in the period's unions meant that, as the *Evening Telegraph* put it, blacks could "no more find entrance into the skilled handicrafts than they can fly into the upper air." Although the *Age*, in 1891, did locate an Irish blacksmith willing to defy his fellows and teach his (doomed) profession to a young black man, that route was all but dead. On the other hand, those Afro-American craftsmen who were able to carry on were not employed fully enough, it seems, to require regular help, and thus young apprentices of any kind.[62]

The result was an apparent erosion of traditional skills among those few blacks who tried their hands at all. These skills were put on exhibit at several "industrial" fairs in the 1880s and 1890s, typified by the one in October of 1891 designed to show off the "Industry, Mechanism, and Artistic Skill of the Colored People" at Allen Chapel on Lombard Street. In fact the great majority of the displays featured the household arts, millinery and dressmaking, cakes and jellies; only one of the sixteen departments was of "manufactured articles," none of which was described in the several articles devoted to the fair as a whole. Perhaps the most distinguished department was the "artistic," which included works by Carl Bolivar, William Dorsey, and Robert Adger, together with a pair of busts by the well-known sculptor Edmonia Lewis, who had married a Philadelphian and was possibly living in the city at the time. Despite his own involvement, however, Bolivar later wrote that the best of all exhibitions was not this but the one put on in 1850. He cannot in fact have remembered that one directly, having been born just the previous year, and his praise for the good old apprenticeship rules that made it all possible was doubtless mixed with some nostalgia. But the bare list of items then turned out by the hands of black craftsmen, including canvas sails, brass and iron instruments, leather goods, and dental equipment, was much more ambitious than anything displayed during his adult lifetime.[63]

Some of the same problems that affected the artisans, including difficulties both in acquiring skills and then in selling their products, affected the handful who, like William Dorsey, identified themselves as "artists." Excluding the Sunday painters such as Bolivar and Adger, the *Times* in 1890 counted five, a group of slight socioeconomic but considerable symbolic significance. The oldest of these, Robert Douglass, Jr., born in 1809, had died three years before. Douglass was a member of the elite Bustill clan, who had studied both at the School of Design and the Pennsylvania Academy of Fine Arts, supplementing his education with travel to Europe. At least in the antebellum era he had enjoyed some important white patronage, and several of his oil portraits were reportedly "prized" by "prominent families" in the city. A man of several talents, he had also been one of the first daguerretypists in the city, but despite some attempts no Afro-American during the century was able to make a living as a photographer. Douglass supported himself in part through private short-hand lessons, but mostly, together with his sister Sarah, as a teacher at the Institute for Colored Youth.[64]

His cousin David Bowser took a different route. Bowser, born in 1820, studied for a time with Douglass. But while he did landscapes and especially portraits, his commercial talent was for flamboyant decorative banners, caps, and clothes. Before the war he had done these for a number of white organizations, indeed some of the most bigoted in the city, the Native American Party, later the Know-Nothings, and the often riotously violent volunteer fire companies. With the replacement of the volunteers by professional fire companies in 1871 he lost his near monopoly. But increasingly he was able to make the transition from white to black patronage, as he did much the same work for the proliferating "secret societies," like the Odd Fellows, for whom he worked on salary. A younger man, Alfred Stidum, had followed Douglass first to the School of Design and then the Academy, partly paying for his education by doing portrait sketches in crayon, one of them of President Garfield. But the most interesting story was that of Henry Ossawa Tanner.[65]

Henry Tanner is to all but historians perhaps the best-known black Philadelphian of the later 19th century, although in the Dorsey Collection he does not rank nearly as high as his father, Bishop Benjamin Tucker Tanner of the AME church. Born in Pittsburgh in 1859, young Henry was moved to Philadelphia seven years later when his father was called to Mother Bethel. On graduating from Jacob White's Vaux School, in 1877, Tanner pursued his artistic interests very largely on his own, despite two years, beginning in 1880, with Thomas Eakins at the Academy of Fine Arts. After some moderate recognition he sailed for Europe early in 1891, studying mainly in Paris until he returned home in the fall of 1893 to raise the money to carry on. The standard account is that after re-introduction to Philadelphia he "found the racial restrictions of life in America no longer tolerable," and simply auctioned off all of his pictures for a few hundred dollars, leaving for Europe in the early summer of 1894. This version, however, overlooks the significant experiment in marketing which occupied those final months in the city.[66]

Henry Tanner, in the years just before and after his first trip abroad, was neither wholly obscure nor quite famous. He had had several showings, in good places, and made some sales. But in an age when most American artists were struggling, so was he, and except for the fact that some of his sales were to black friends of his father, his financial history was not much different from that of contemporary whites in the same profession. He tried teaching and failed at commercial photography in Atlanta, sold a few illustrations to popular magazines for about $40, and found an occasional $80 buyer in the wider public. All this, and the patronage of a generous admirer, the white Methodist Bishop Joseph Crane Hartzell, was enough for survival but not for security. Paris, in the early 1890s, was instructive but more a drain than a source of funds. What was distinctive about the early Tanner was not his moderately hard battle to realize his ambitions but the sheer fact of his race, coupled with occasional use of specifically Afro-American genre subjects, done in his characteristically romantic-realist style. And it was this which led to a unique proposal by the Philadelphia *Item*, offered during the spring of 1894, just when he needed the money to return abroad.[67]

The *Item* claimed that "with the fairness that has ever characterized its actions" it was the first to have rated Tanner with the best of "his white brother professionals." What it proposed was to link black and local pride together by buying *The Bagpipe Lesson* to hang permanently at the Academy of Fine Arts.

The price, suggested by Tanner himself, would be $1000, many times what he had previously commanded, and enough to finance nearly three years in Paris. The actual buyer, approached through the lawyer John Stephen Durham and the Episcopal Reverend Henry L. Phillips, would be the local Board of Ministers of Bishop Tanner's AME Church, which would then present the picture to the Academy "on behalf of the colored people of Philadelphia."[68]

Most significant is the way in which the Board of Ministers proposed to recoup its $1000. Tanner was obviously unable to sell his work, at the needed rate, to the usual American market. The idea then was to capitalize on the young man's distinction, and the honor reflected on his race, by boldly creating another, this one a mass Afro-American market. The Board of Ministers would reproduce the painting in "levytype," and sell copies to blacks all over the country; perhaps the participation of the *Item*, and the two black Episcopalians who had first broached the scheme, would neutralize any thought that this was merely a sectarian or, worse, a family affair.[69]

In June of 1894, in any case, the *Item* proudly announced that the plan was in place, the money pledged, the sales campaign scheduled for the fall. But then it all fell through; the Board of Ministers could not raise any more than $300. Disappointed, perhaps embarrassed, Tanner apparently did not accept the money. He sailed for Europe, then, with only the proceeds from his hurried auction, forever leaving not only Philadelphia and the United States but Afro-American–genre painting as well, as his later European successes centered almost wholly around traditional religious themes.[70]

William Henry Dorsey, meanwhile, the last of the black painters celebrated by the *Times*, resembled Henry Tanner only in his determination to stay with his art, against even greater odds. Unlike the younger man, Dorsey lacked any formal school training at all, although an article in 1903 noted that he had studied under Azeno Schindler, "an Austrian of no mean degree of merit." Certainly he enjoyed no patron, and won no prizes; his work remains as obscure as Tanner's is famous. But in his own stubborn way he earned the right to list himself in the city's directories as an "artist" for nearly fifty years.[71]

Dorsey himself wrote about some of his early problems in an exchange carried by the Washington *People's Advocate* in the winter of 1877. The correspondence was initiated by two letters from "Blackibus" of Richmond, who complained about the lack of black portraits and black subjects in general. Whites were incapable of filling the void; "their hearts are not in it." Their pictures of light-complexioned subjects, at one end of the spectrum, tended to rob them of all distinctively Afro-American features, while those at the darker end they could see only in caricature. Speaking as one who took "glory in the term 'black,' as the white man glories in the term 'white,'" he wanted more for his children. "Pictures are powerful teachers," and young blacks should have the chance to see that not all biblical figures, historical heroes, and statesmen were white. But despite a wealth of potential subjects there were no appropriate pictures, and despite the Afro-American love of art no painters to do them justice.[72]

Editor J. W. Cromwell, himself a graduate of the Institute for Colored Youth, simply called in response upon a well-known collector and fellow alumnus: "Mr. William H. Dorsey, of Philadelphia, might give Blackibus some valuable information on this point."[73]

Dorsey's graceful reply did not address the issue of white portraits or caricature. But he did respond at length to the point about black pictures and subjects. While there were, indeed, no satisfactory portrayals of Crispus Attucks, his friend Robert Douglass had a number of portraits, copies, and originals of Haitian generals and Liberian statesmen; he himself owned one of Toussaint L'Overture, by John G. Chaplin of Huntingdon, a former Douglass student, and his mother had another, historical Chaplin, titled *The Death of Hannibal.* As for contemporary Afro-American artists, in addition to Chaplin he sketched the careers of Douglass and Bowser, Patrick Henry Reason, Robert S. Duncanson, and Edwin Bannister, who, with Edmonia Lewis, had won a prize just the year before at Philadelphia's Centennial Exhibition.[74]

Still, Dorsey admitted implicitly, this list was all too short. Blacks in general, he wrote, found that "it requires much taste, and still more means to be a patron of Art," and perhaps Blackibus did not appreciate "the obstacles a painter or sculptor has to contend with." Anyone who attempted to conquer them found that he had the "unending prejudice of the dominant race to buffet him from place to place, for only a few years have elapsed since we have been admitted, even as visitors, to . . . art exhibitions," and many galleries were still closed.[75]

While Dorsey had omitted his own name from the list of artists, there is no doubt that his list of obstacles reflected hard personal experience. Included in the items he left his alma mater is an instruction book, *The Miniature Painter's Manual,* dated 1844, its pages copied out by hand evidently because the young copyist could not afford to buy it, its exercises in perspective all carefully executed in pen. In addition to the many enumerated scrapbooks dealing with subjects such as Indian and African art, the Venus de Milo, the Flemish Masters, flags, coins, and stamps, there are a number of uncatalogued others filled with pasted black-and-white reproductions from every period. Most poignant are the over 700 catalogues from collections of art, rugs, vases, and jewelry, some of exhibitions, others of gallery sales or auctions. It is clear that even the son of a man prosperous by contemporary Afro-American standards could afford to buy few of the items described; it is not clear how many he was able, or allowed, even to look at.[76]

The result, in terms of the quality of his own work, is hard to judge directly. The only known examples extant are the youthful sketches-by-instruction, the two drawings done for the *Tribune's* cemetery exposé, and a few technically expert but not very original watercolors kept in the family. The *Times*, in 1890, made him sound dated at 53, noting that some of his oils and watercolors "are still to be found among the older families in the city." But even that may be too generous. The scattered correspondence about the fine arts in his own files refers to his passion for collection—he got Edmonia Lewis's autograph when she was only 23—rather than to his own work. His subjects, and methods, were evidently conventional, with titles such as "The Sentinel (after Salvator Rosa)," "Coast Scene (original)," "After the Bath," and "La Coucher." Most telling is the list of portraits presented to the American Negro History Society toward century's end: 22 of the 40 were Dorsey's, including several of local clergymen of all faiths, historical figures such as Henri Christophe, the 18th-century poet Phyllis Wheatley, and the contemporary singer Flora Batson. None, obviously, had been sold.[77]

The highest compliment he ever got was perhaps the one accorded by the Quaker City correspondent of the New York *Globe*, in November of 1884, who in connection with an upcoming Exposition in New Orleans suggested that Philadelphia boasted two artists "whose paintings have secured them almost national fame. I refer to William H. Dorsey and Henry O. Tanner." There is in fact no record of Dorsey's ever showing his work out of town, or at any but segregated local affairs. He did exhibit several pieces at the Progressive Workingman's Fair in 1884, but a recollection of that show, seven years after, mentioned Stidum and Tanner but not him, just as the *Times* piece in 1890 pictured Stidum, Douglass, and Bowser but not him. Dorsey contributed fully 56 pieces to the Ladies' Quaker City Association Exhibition of 1889; the *North American* reported that these included the best watercolors in the show, but attributed them to Philadelphia-born Professor Charles Dorsey, then a Brooklyn school principal; the *Sentinel* praised his crayons and oils, which he had to correct to "watercolors" in the margin. The same pattern seems evident in his relations with Du Bois, who wrote to Jacob White and then to Carl Bolivar while checking materials for *The Philadelphia Negro*, with only an afterthought for the man whom he identified as "W. M. Dorsey" in his acknowledgments.[78]

As an artist, then, the suspicion is that William Dorsey had to contend not merely with white prejudice or late-19th-century American Philistinism but with a certain merited indifference; since neither the white nor the black market would support him, it is fortunate that he had other sources of income. There is some mystery as to precisely what he did during the first twenty years of his married life. But between 1879 and 1881 the mayor of Philadelphia, GOP stalwart Bill Stokley, recognized the importance of his family and community by appointing him his own "personal messenger"; if the job sometimes involved such menial chores as cleaning the office, it paid a regular salary, apparently the first and only one in his life, of perhaps $700 a year. More important in the long term was the fact that T. J. Dorsey had established a trust whose income, after his own death in 1876 and his wife's just three years later, was split in equal shares between William, his sister Mary Louise Harlan, and the two sons of his dead sister Sarah Seville. One-third of the money, at first almost wholly from rental income on several Eighth Ward properties, was worth about $500 a year; by 1904 William seems to have been able to supplement this with profits from other places acquired on his own, which brought in something rather less. While the total, well less than $900 annually, was not enough to qualify as "middle-class" by white standards, it was handsome enough by black, and with a certain frugality would allow him to indulge both his historical and artistic passions.[79]

The experience of most of the city's black artists, perhaps excluding William Dorsey himself, is an example in miniature of the major problem which afflicted all black entrepreneurs in the period. Even those who had the requisite skills or useful goods to sell found themselves caught between two markets, neither of which they could command with confidence. They might profit both themselves and the black economy as a whole either, like the caterers, by bringing in white money or, like the cemetery owners, by preventing dollars from leaving the community. But in fact they were in the process of losing whatever hold they had once had on the first and by far the richer of these markets, and only a few were in position to capture the second and more limited.

There were apparently only two attempts to break out of this dilemma entirely, to transcend the natural limits of retail enterprise. The first was made during the 1870s, when a group of hopeful businessmen—their ranks full of janitors and waiters as well as men with some entrepreneurial experience—founded the Century Cotton and Woolen Manufacturing Company, Ltd. The founders planned to raise $50,000 by selling 10,000 shares at $5 each, with widespread participation encouraged by allowing buyers to put as little as 25 cents down. The mixture of motives, the appeal both to race and to private profit—the prospectus emphasized the need "to create a new labor field for the COLORED PEOPLE in the northern and middle states of America"—was reminiscent of the earlier appeal of Liberty Hall. And indeed two of the Liberty Hall investors, the barber Robert Jones as secretary and restaurateur Levi Cromwell as treasurer, joined president Fielding Ford, a "foundry hand" in the 1870 census, on the board of directors. But nothing came of this. Despite living in one of the world's great manufacturing cities, Philadelphia's blacks made nothing but the products of individual artisans, and there is no record of any of these employing, full-time, more than the four hands who worked for the upholsterer Warley Bascom.[80]

The caterer John Trower, nearly a generation later, was more successful in breaking out, by winning a contract to provide food services for Cramp's Shipyard, on the Delaware. Cramp's was a huge corporation, one of the largest shipbuilders in the world, and although it hired no blacks on its work force, the service contract was a great prize. No longer a retailer dependent on the whims of rich white individuals, Trower became a relatively rich man. But the transformation of his own business did not extend to others. Trower never married, and had no heirs, no imitators, and no successors; catering in general was unable to break out of the old mold, and continued its decline. Most retail entrepreneurs, in an age of increasing residential segregation, had still to face the old issue of whether they were aiming at white customers or black.[81]

The two kinds of business which could traditionally count on a monopoly of the black trade were undertaking and barbering, or hairdressing. Afro-American undertakers were in fact able to take advantage, more permanently than the cemetery companies, of the growing size of the black community. William Allmond, for example, had been a cabinetmaker, James LeCount a carpenter; even if unable to practice these skills profitably, both men could turn to the basic task of coffin making, and to join Harriet Duterte, Guy Burton, and other members of the growing undertaking fraternity. Beauticians did not make the news very often, but presumably they benefited from the two related late-century fads which created a demand for straightened hair and for wigs, the latter selling for $5 to $50 apiece. The barbering business, on the other hand, was already so oversaturated that it declined absolutely, as shown above, in the generation after 1885.[82]

Several other enterprises benefited from sheer growth in the size of the Afro-American population. Among these were those sometimes shady employment agencies, described in the previous chapter, mostly dealing in domestic help; Du Bois listed several, often attached to boarding houses for southern newcomers. As the ownership of real estate increased so also did opportunities for selling insurance. Life insurance was out; applicants were charged between one-third and twice as much as whites for the same coverage, as the major companies cited the alleged mulatto susceptibility to lung disease; one firm in Philadelphia reported in 1889 that it had granted just three policies to black applicants during the previous six years. But all who owned property in crowded neighborhoods needed protection from fire. William Scott was an especially active agent of the Chicago-based Globe Insurance Company; originally from Alabama, with no formal schooling, he became a trustee of Wilberforce University through his association with Bethel Church, among other local institutions. And with a reported worth of $75,000 to $100,000 at his death in 1878, he briefly succeeded, between Stephen Smith and J. P. B. Eddy, to the title of "richest colored man in Philadelphia."[83]

Others, like the long-term political associates Gil Ball and George Sharper, exercised their own expertise in their own ways. Ball, born in 1850 and tied for twenty-second place in the Dorsey Collection, had come to the city from Virginia as a child, and was unusual among those raised in Philadelphia in his utter lack of schooling. After working as a hodcarrier at 14, then as waiter in a New York political club, Ball found ways of using his youth and strength at the polls back home, and his connections with Republican chieftains enabled him to open a successful saloon in 1877. He had to close down in 1890, under the stricter licensing law of 1887, when the dance floor, piano, and "disreputable women" who enlivened his place near Seventh and Lombard offended the license commissioners. But he was not yet defeated. With years of experience on the fringes of the entertainment business, he was at the time of his rejection already planning to put on an all-black production of *The Merchant of Venice* in Atlantic City. The project gave him some verbal ammunition with which to lash back at Judge Gordon, his principal opponent on the commission:

> He hath disgraced me and hindered me half a million; laughed at my losses, mocked at my gains, scorned my nation, thwarted my bargains, cooled my friends, heated mine enemies; and what's his reason?

Ball told reporters, however, that the theater was only a stopgap; he planned in the longer term to fill an important niche in the real estate business that had apparently been occupied before his generation largely by whites.[84]

While Afro-American businessmen had many reasons to invest in property, they had some unique problems in collecting rent, especially during the era before the 1870s, when they enjoyed few of the rights of citizenship and tenants may have thought it possible to ignore them with impunity. There was in fact throughout the period a special reluctance to grant blacks any job that would give them authority over whites, even as streetcar conductors. As of 1879 several elite black landlords, including the estates of Stephen Smith and T. J. Dorsey, whose tenants seem to have been at least half white, had for some time employed a single agent, one William Whitesides. One reason was surely that Whitesides enjoyed some status with members of both races as a former uniformed constable; his power to stare down reluctant rent-payers could only have been enhanced by an 1870 manslaughter conviction for mistakenly killing a black man while on duty. It was then perhaps an ironic form of racial progress when some time later Gil Ball, after years of strong-arm work at the palls, was thought ready to take a similar position as "A Terror to Colored Delinquents."[85]

George Sharper, Ball's long-term aide, was an even better exemplar of black resilience. Five years older than Ball, equally unfamiliar with the classroom, Sharper had begun his working life as a barber before enlisting, as a teenager, in the Union army; when his father retrieved him and sent him into the mines he ran off into the army again. After the war he found work as a Pullman porter, then a police station turnkey, before opening a cigar store. In 1877 he was able to visit and tour Europe, presumably working his way across, before returning again to find work as Pullman porter, then successively yet again as turnkey, laborer, cop, and employee of the city's water department. Finally, in March of 1888, Sharper put his knowledge of the world to work by opening a private detective agency.[86]

But ingenuity alone could not overcome the fact that the local Afro-American community was simply too small, too poor, and too disunited to support much enterprise. Gertrude Mossell reported that the newspaper business as of 1889 employed perhaps 100 people, but few of these could have worked full-time. Jonathan Harris, managing editor of the *Tribune,* seems to have hung on to his barbering business after the paper was founded in 1883, and Christopher Perry, its publisher, held for decades a supplemental political job as clerk in City Hall. And the *Tribune* was the only secular paper of the period which survived; all of the others went down after a few issues or years, each competing with the others and with out-of-town black papers also for a few pennies their potential readers could afford.[87]

The geography of black Philadelphia was another and ironic obstacle to enterprise. While its Afro-American population led those in other northern cities in many ways, the very fact of its early lead meant that despite considerable concentration in the old southeast quadrant of the city it was more spread out than those in New York's Harlem, later on, or Chicago's South Side. Dispersed settlement meant dispersed buying power; while black merchants were located mostly in or near the Seventh Ward, small colonies elsewhere had no alternative but to buy their modest necessaries from white grocers, coal dealers, and tobacconists. And even in more concentrated areas, despite continual exhortations to "buy colored," the impoverished majority apparently felt no obligation to support local enterprises on the basis of racial identity alone.

In fact black business was caught in a double bind. While continual growth in the Afro-American population was not enough to create a solid black market, it was clearly enough to weaken the older and more profitable white market. It was after all those who dealt with rich white customers who were responsible for the New York *Freeman*'s statement, as late as 1885, that Philadelphia led all black cities in business success. It was their decline, conversely, that led to the sense of loss in so many reports from the late 1870s on. The explanation seems simple, if hard to demonstrate with hard numbers: just as white men were increasingly unwilling to patronize black barbers, white housewives were increasingly unwilling to visit the upholsterers, carpenters, secondhand dealers, caterers, and others whom they had once visited with confidence. If the Seventh Ward was not big and black enough to support much black enterprise, in short, it was getting big and black enough to scare off white women.[88]

Some of the growing reluctance to visit black Philadelphia was simply prejudice, and needed no reinforcement. But some of it resulted from one of the fruits of prejudice, that is, the growth of criminal enterprise downtown. And this in turn was fanned by the same daily newspapers that were at the same time exploiting the lynching phenomenon for profit. During the 1880s and 1890s, when most literate Philadelphians began their days with headlined stories of "black fiends," "black brutes," and "black beasts" down South, the papers inevitably found, or manufactured, other scare stories closer to home, and black businessmen fell indirect victim to publicity about black criminals.

In fact the relationship of Afro-American entrepreneurs and criminals was complicated; criminal enterprise had always cast a kind of shadow over legitimate enterprise of all kinds. In Philadelphia, as elsewhere across the country, the city's leadership had decided in effect to "zone" the leading black district as the red-light or vice district. Given the push and pull between groups and customers who enjoyed gambling, patronized prostitutes, and resented interference with their drinking habits, local authorities generally compromised. Vice could not be eradicated, they reasoned, but it could be contained, kept out of some places while allowed in others. Subject to just enough harassment to keep its operators off-balance and dependent, and its operations discreet, it might also be profitably taxed, through bribes, for profit. Its location was determined in part by geography and in part by politics. It should ideally be close to downtown hotels and theaters, docks and rail terminals, where both locals and transients could conveniently seek excitement late at night. It should also be located among people too weak or dependent to protest effectively. Almost everywhere that description fit the black district; in Philadelphia specifically it fit a corridor running on either side of South Street, starting near the Delaware and pushing west with time.[89]

It was equally inevitable that many inhabitants of this and similar neighborhoods, with more legitimate sources of income blocked off, should take what was offered. If the word "entrepreneur" is defined to include the several hundred black Philadelphians who ran or wrote slips for "policy" bankers, operated gambling rooms, sold liquor illegally, or profited from prostitution, then there were far more of them than legitimate businesspeople. The two groups in fact overlapped; the enormous oversupply of barbering establishments may have resulted from their use as fronts for the policy game, ancestor of the modern numbers racket and the most common form of gambling among urban blacks; the dramatic shrinkage noted by the early 20th century may have resulted simply from the stepped-up harassment characteristic of the reforming Progressive era. Secondhand shops, similarly, were sometimes outlets for stolen goods, cigar and grocery stores the kinds of places where a man might find an illegal game or drink.[90]

Some of those who ran these and other more obviously illegal enterprises made money, and their flamboyant habits made that obvious, too, to everyone in black Philadelphia. Given the growing trend toward residential segregation, the most respectable inhabitants of the Seventh and even Eighth wards found criminal neighbors inescapable. William Dorsey, as example, lived sometimes at 206 Dean Street (now Camac). But just across the way at 205 Dean was a political clubhouse, denounced by the reforming *North American* in 1899 as the home of eight fictitious voters and in practice, like most such clubs, a speakeasy and gambling resort. In the era before air conditioning, when the only defense against Philadephia's infamous summer climate was to open windows, the distance between Dorsey's and these neighbors' was just twenty feet, and there was no protection against excited noises late at night.[91]

From a strictly economic point of view, moreover, the profits taken by individual criminals did little to enrich the wider community, and if a balance sheet could be drawn, most illegal enterprise cost black Philadelphia more than it brought in. Black gamblers played with, or preyed on, their fellows. The game of policy was ultimately controlled by white bankers, with Afro-Americans only middlemen, so that the biggest share of the daily profits was taken out of the neighborhood. Blacks drank in white-owned bars as well as their own, and none of them went into the profitable wholesaling business. Only prostitution, then, as it catered to sailors, immigrants, transients, and others, routinely transferred money from white pockets into black.[92]

And if the direct costs of criminal enterprise were paid only by those who gambled, drank, and whored themselves, the indirect costs were borne by those who were struggling in the midst of all this to attract legitimate customers. Actual danger, like direct cost, was experienced only by nighttime visitors who courted it. Patrons of the red-light district were easy marks for robbery, found often with their trousers off and their attentions otherwise engaged, while anyone robbed in Soapfat Alley found it hard the next morning to tell it to the judge. Arguments led sometimes to violence, even murder, without attracting much attention; judges and juries did not sympathize with white men whom they thought recklessly sinful, and residents of the vice district itself had every reason to keep things as quiet as possible. But daytime visitors, while safe, could not have relished picking their way through the morning's evidence of the night before, their unease compounded by the "sullen" looks that whites routinely reported in black neighborhoods.[93]

In the 1890s another kind of activity, newly publicized, offered a more direct threat. During the late 19th century, people in cities came to enjoy increasing safety from physical violence, and to take it for granted. The growth of manufacturing industry, soaking up the underemployed and miserable immigrants of the mid-century decades, was closely tied to several other developments which tended literally to "civilize" public behavior: campaigns against drunkenness, the spread of public schooling, and the growth of regular police patrol. By the end of the 1870s Philadelphia's cops, like their counterparts elsewhere, had essentially won the older battle for the streets, and put down the kind of riots that had marked the pre–Civil War decades. At the same time the city's white murder rate began a long, slow decline which would last well into the 20th century. All of this, at the same time, raised late-Victorian standards of propriety, magnifying the impact, in and near the Seventh Ward, of an apparent epidemic of purse-snatching.[94]

W. E. B. Du Bois reported in the late 1890s that this was "a crime for which Negroes of a certain class have become notorious." But the notoriety was recent. Black crime was mostly confined within the boundaries of race, and whites, especially middle-class whites, traditionally had little to fear; it was possible as late as 1890 for a local newspaper to write that "there is no large crime element" among the city's growing Afro-American population. The outbreak of purse-snatching, late in the decade, helped to change all that. By the standards of the late 20th century, or the mid-19th, these were not noteworthy crimes. Weapons were not used, and women rarely hurt, as typically a young man simply grabbed a pocketbook from a shopper on Spruce or Walnut streets, certainly Locust or South, and fled into the twisted maze of alleys nearby. To the newspapers, however, these were the acts of "Bold Highwaymen," and "Daring Robbers." A single incident in the spring of 1899, when an elderly woman was struck at the corner of 12th and Spruce, was headlined "HIGHWAY ROBBERY!" in the *Item*, and a follow-up story rated 60 column inches.[95]

By that time a heightened concern about black violence was beginning to affect the city's justice system. Historically in Philadelphia, as in other northern cities, the pervasive racism of the wider society had not much affected the courts. No significant difference can be found in the sentences given Afro-Americans and others during the 19th century, and in the thirty years after the Civil War blacks convicted of homicide, even those whose crimes involved white victims, were less likely than whites to be sent to the gallows. The prevailing stereotype, as voiced by Judge Gordon in quarter sessions during 1893, was still derived from a mixture of southern nostalgia and contemporary minstrel shows. Having submitted gracefully to centuries of subordination, the judge observed, "their tendencies are most gentle," and he expressed a genuine puzzlement at the growing number brought in for acts of violence. But within a few years the constant publicity given the newer, more vicious stereotype took hold when black men, for the first time, were accused of attacking middle-class whites in the city.[96]

The routine administration of justice, it should be emphasized, was not affected, and the change in attitudes was not immediate. As late as 1898, as noted, both Frank Monroe and Scott Irwin were found not guilty of murder when defending themselves against attack by white laborers. But when alleged victims were from higher in the social scale than the white gang members, lovers, fellow workmen, and drinking companions typically involved in interracial violence, the standards changed accordingly. And in Philadelphia the escalation of fear and prejudice was neatly progressive.

There was little but racial prejudice to account for the 1897 arrest and indictment of Marion Stuyvesant in the unsolved killing of his employer, the book collector Henry Wilson; energetic protests helped to dismiss the case short of trial. In 1898 "Face" Epps was convicted of the felony-murder of a shopkeeper, Mary Ann Lawlor, as a result of a bungled robbery, but the sheriff himself led a drive for commutation of the death penalty. The turning point was reached instead in May of 1900, when a popular young lawyer, on his way home from work, was robbed and bludgeoned to death near the 30th Street Station. While the local bar mounted a volunteer defense team strong enough to defeat any suspicion of legal lynching, Henry Ivory, Charles Perry, and Amos Sterling were all hanged, the first execution for interracial murder in generations. In 1901, next, on the basis of evidence no stronger than that against Marion Stuyvesant four years earlier, the female domestic Mary Wright this time went to trial for the unlikely axe-murder of her mistress. And the new era was decisively signaled the following April when the butler William Lane shot and killed Ellen Furbush, his employer, together with her two small daughters. Although he was obviously insane there was this time no rallying by the legal community. The killing occurred on April 1; Lane was indicted on the 2nd, tried and convicted the next day, and hanged the next month, a speed record that still stands.[97]

It is possible roughly to measure the effect of white fear on the justice system. Although, as always, most homicides and other acts of violence were committed within rather than across the bounds of race, the first three decades of the 20th century reversed the pattern set in the last three of the 19th, as black convicts were not less but more likely than white to go to the gallows, or after 1913 to the chair. It is not so easy to measure the way in which fear slowed white visits to black areas of the city. But it is hard to avoid the conclusion that wide publicity given the new and violent stereotype, in combination with the natural growth of the Afro-American population, was the last and perhaps the biggest handicap faced by black enterprise in the period.[98]

What is most striking about contemporary descriptions of Afro-American businesses is less their relatively small number than their fragility. W. E. B. Du Bois, in listing 31 common grocery, cigar, and notions stores in the Seventh Ward, found that less than half were as much as a year old; the list given by R. R. Wright, half a generation later, suggests that only about 6 percent of the 212 black business establishments in the whole city had been around for thirty years, or one working lifetime. No one familiar with the histories of the period's businessmen, Still and White, Eddy and McKee, Teagle, Cromwell, Scott, Ball, and others, can properly accuse them of lacking the spirit of enterprise. But few of them were able to establish companies that would last. While Robert M. Adger, Sr., had operated what was described as the biggest secondhand furniture store in the city, as of the 1860s, his onetime location and investment property, Liberty Hall, had by 1912 gone over to Jewish storekeepers "on the edge of the Ghetto." His son Robert Adger, Jr., who had followed him into the business, gave it all up to spend the last twenty-one years of his life working as a postal clerk. William Dorsey was hardly alone in choosing to abandon the family business; only a handful of long-lived firms, the ones managed by the Augustines and Baptistes in the restaurant or catering business, William and Thomas Allmond in undertaking, stand out as exceptions to the general rule.[99]

Insecurity had many sources, some of them simply bad management, bad luck, or changing tastes and fashions. But the thread of racial prejudice runs through most. Sometimes it operated directly, as in the refusal to hire black musicians or to allow young men to practice the skilled trades. At other times it worked indirectly, as in the "zoning" decisions which pushed much black entrepreneurial talent into illegal enterprise. This in turn, combined with growing geographic segregation, helped to blight the chances of legitimate neighbors, especially in an atmosphere filled with widely publicized stereotypes that frightened off potential customers. At the same time, the various ways in which prejudice affected the wage-earning majority kept them too poor to support any substantial enterprise.

The result was that, with many full and partial exceptions, it was clear to ambitious young people that, barring crime, the route up was not through business but through education, subject of the following chapter.

Chapter 5

Education and Educators

The progress made in education at every level is the leading Afro-American success story of the late 19th century, in Philadelphia as throughout the country. It was a limited success, not easily won, and there was much confusion at the end of the period, as at the beginning, about where to go and how. But by 1900 the most obvious results, in terms of mass literacy, cannot be denied: in the North and the cities, even in the South and in the countryside, the majority of younger black citizens could read and write.

In Philadelphia, however, as elsewhere, it was not so clear what beyond simple literacy an education should provide, or how to spend limited resources. One of the things that gave the city a unique leadership role was the existence of a strong private school, the Institute for Colored Youth, William Dorsey's alma mater, which flourished especially during the period covered by his collection. But while the ICY both attracted and sent out an unusually able group of people, it was different only in its distinction. It stayed close to the main currents in elite black education, and it was always linked, in particular, to the city's public schools. The histories of both will be woven together through this chapter, as between the middle 1860s and 1903, both within the ICY and the public system, Philadelphians had to deal with the same issues as their fellows across the country: integration and segregation, academic versus manual training, the price of accommodation to white control, and finally how to translate education into jobs.

The institutions and personalities which would most affect the black educational experience until century's end were all put in place about the close of the Civil War. One key event in the public system was the appointment in 1864 of Jacob C. White, Jr., then a teacher at the still-young Quaker-run Institute for Colored Youth, to a job at the public Roberts Vaux elementary school, where he served as the city's only black principal and indeed teacher. For the ICY itself the even more decisive event was the hiring of Fanny M. Jackson, just out of Oberlin College. Jackson was made the head of the girls' department in 1866, joining Octavius V. Catto, her male counterpart, under the overall direction of principal Ebenezer Bassett, just as the institute moved to a new building on Bainbridge Street. By that time, too, the issues that all of these people would face had already been sketched out.[1]

Philadelphia's Afro-Americans before the Civil War had been educated in a number of public and private institutions. The Quakers had begun to establish small schools for blacks beginning in the 18th century, and the city itself was prodded in 1822, four years after the establishment of a public school system, into providing some of its own. But attendance was not compulsory, and by 1856, when the Afro-American school-aged population was about 4000, less than 60 percent were even theoretically enrolled. About half of these went either to the nine "colored" public schools or the two run by the reformatory and almshouse, the other half to a variety of "charity" or "private" schools, some 15 in all, mostly under Quaker auspices. All, public or private, were segregated. The Institute for Colored Youth gave the equivalent of a high-school education; otherwise only two public and two very small private places went beyond the three primary grades, and by one survey only about 19 percent of the city's black adults were fully literate.[2]

From the beginning the city's public "colored" schools had lagged behind in every way. The first of them in 1822 had opened with a single teacher for the 199 enrolled, at varying levels of skill; as of 1856 the average teacher-pupil ratio at the best of them, the so-called "Bird" school on Lombard Street, was still worse than 60 to 1. Attendance, perhaps fortunately, was ragged, in part because the children were; throughout the 19th century much truancy was blamed on the shame and misery felt by black youngsters without proper or warm clothing.[3]

Beyond the obvious problems caused by poor funding, a major issue was the lack of black teachers, as Philadelphians were convinced that the whites assigned to their schools were the worst in the system, and with the notable exception of James M. Bird neglected and even despised their pupils. Up to the Civil War there were no blacks at all. In 1862, the year when the Emancipation Proclamation was drafted, the white directors of the district which contained the little Banneker Colored School broke the line by hiring John Quincy Allen, a graduate of the ICY. But when Jacob White left his own post at the Institute to take the job at Vaux the two men in effect simply switched, as Allen quit the public job to replace him. There was then still only one public school teacher as of 1864, when Pennsylvania's Afro-Americans formed an active branch of the new national Equal Rights League. The next year, hoping for wider opportunities with the end of the Civil War, the Philadelphia delegation of the ERL opened a significant discussion of the whole issue at its October Convention.[4]

The first proposed resolution accepted Pennsylvania's school segregation law, but insisted that it was then "our incumbent duty, as lovers of the advancement of our race, to see to it, that our schools are under the charge of colored teachers." John Quincy Allen urged instead a "no discrimination" statement, as more in line with the theme of equal rights. His suggestion, fiercely opposed by those who insisted that the white teachers were hopeless, and that only blacks could properly teach blacks, was voted down. But some of its merits were rescued by Allen's ICY superior Octavius V. Catto, a major figure in the ERL. Perhaps because of his experience at the Institute, Catto agreed that Afro-American youngsters were best taught by those who "had the welfare of the race more at heart, knowing that they rose or fell together." But Allen's point about discrimination might be met by a different wording: "colored persons, their literary qualifications being sufficient, should receive the preference, not by reason of their complexion, but because they are better qualified by conventional circumstances outside of the schoolhouse."[5]

The compromise was accepted unanimously. And as Catto's old schoolmate, former colleague, and best friend "Jake" White took over as the "principal," indeed only, teacher at the Vaux school, the Afro-American agenda for the public schools was established for some years to come.[6]

The prewar history of the Institute itself was more varied but equally important in prefiguring the major issues of the future. The school had been inspired by the will of Richard Humphreys, who died in 1832. Humphreys, an ex-slaveowning Quaker from the West Indies, left $10,000 for "instructing the descendants of the African Race in school learning, in the various branches of the mechanical arts and trades and in agriculture: in order to prepare . . . them to act as teachers. . . ." For the Quaker executors who tried to follow them over the next three generations, those instructions turned out to be a complex and sometimes self-contradictory legacy.[7]

The executors first bought a property some miles out of the city, and tried to combine farming and such "arts and trades" as broom-making with book-learning and Bible study. Between 1839 and 1846 the place was put in charge of a succession of whites, but the executors discovered predictably that farmers couldn't teach and teachers couldn't farm, and that boys brought out from the city rebelled against all of them. By 1848 they had moved back to town, and wisely consulted with several Afro-American craftsmen about apprenticing youngsters either to them or to whites during the day, while teaching academic subjects at night. That plan, administered by Ishmael Locke, himself black, worked a little better than the farm, and as of 1849 Locke reported that the school was irregularly attended by 4 apprentice cabinetmakers, 6 carpenters, 1 turner, 2 tailors, 4 bootmakers, 4 barbers, and one who had "something to do with painting," perhaps William Henry Dorsey, then 12 years old. But in fact the Afro-American community could not sustain that many apprentices, and the plan foundered mostly on the unwillingness of white masters to accept them. The whole project was nearly abandoned in 1851, kept alive only on petition from the pupils themselves. Then it was turned around entirely when the board of managers decided to build a substantial school near Seventh and Lombard, and to reorganize it, to educate girls as well as boys, and to stress neither farm nor manual labor but the first and last of Humphreys's instructions, the ones about "school learning" and training teachers.[8]

Following the precedent set with Ishmael Locke—and not that pursued in the older, primary, "colored schools," which were taught by women members of the Society of Friends itself—the board next looked for a strong black man to run the proposed new Institute for Colored Youth. They found Professor Charles L. Reason, a graduate of McGrawville College in New York, and were able to open a boys' department with six students in September of 1852. Two months later Reason was joined by Grace A. Mapps, also of McGrawville and apparently the first Afro-American woman to win a degree from a four-year college in America. These two were joined by Mapps's cousin, the abolitionist Sarah Douglass, whose small private school was then annexed to the Institute as a preparatory school for girls. Over the next several years, as the number of pupils grew and a night school was added, the teaching staff expanded largely through the addition of recent graduates, young men such as Allen, White, and Catto. Ebenezer Bassett of New Haven, a Connecticut Normal School graduate who had spent some time at Yale, succeeded Reason as principal and head of the boys' department in 1855.[9]

Progress over the next ten years, however, was slowed by conditions at the Lombard Street site, which were not only cramped but in the opinion of the managers located in a neighborhood where crime and vice were "offensive to modesty" in the students. The last years of the Civil War, too, seem to have set things back, perhaps because the decision to admit blacks to the army combined with other newly opened opportunities to drain away potential students: there was no graduating class in 1865. The twin decisions, then, at war's end, to hire Fanny Jackson as replacement for the ineffective Grace Mapps, and to build a new and bigger building on Bainbridge Street, represented a bold effort to get things moving again.[10]

When Jackson arrived at the new site in 1866 she found a small but lively school, with a firm academic program and an equally firm mission: to train, under Quaker auspices, black teachers through other black teachers, and to supply a growing market for their services in Philadelphia and elsewhere. The managers believed that "at no time since its foundation, has there been more to encourage its friends." The optimism was well founded; over the next several decades the school more than fulfilled its mission in the surrounding community and across the country. The promise was interrupted, but not ended, when a series of dramatic events between 1869 and 1871 pushed Jackson herself into the lead.[11]

The school's new building at Ninth and Bainbridge was built in three stories, with exercise space, a library and reading room, classrooms, and laboratories. The whole was designed for up to 400 students; as of 1866 there were some 181 actually enrolled, with girls outnumbering boys by 80 to 40 in the high school itself.[12]

The highly pyramidal structure of the classes—only four students graduated in 1855—and the increasing disproportion of girls in the upper grades resulted from a combination of school policy and conditions in the black community. Admission was open to young people at least 11 years old, based on examination in the "3 Rs," with arithmetic through simple division. Those not ready for the high school were assigned a year in the preparatory department, with "good moral character and orderly habits" required at every level. As a result of higher expenses the managers began requiring tuition with the move to Bainbridge Street, $5 for the preparatory year, $10 for each of the three—next year increased to four—years in high school. But promotion to higher grades depended on passing strict examinations administered from outside, usually by teachers at the white Quaker schools, or Haverford College, none of which themselves admitted Afro-Americans. Many did not pass, and others were expelled for a variety of failings, so that the graduates were a surviving elite within an elite, those who could not only pass the tests, academic and moral, but afford the fees and the time out from work to support themselves and their families. The pupils were no richer than the community from which they came, and a survey in 1867 showed that there were more orphans, or the children of widows, 36 in all, than the 26 who came from the families of caterers, merchants, carpenters, and upholsterers combined. As the boys among them had more job opportunities than the girls, and perhaps because parents and guardians were more reluctant to let the girls into the wider world, the sex ratio was increasingly skewed in the upper grades.[13]

But dropping out before graduation was not a serious handicap for future teachers. Most black schools in the North as well as the South were simple institutions, and jobs did not require diplomas. The prewar "charity" and public schools, certainly those for Philadelphia's blacks, had long been dominated by the "Lancastrian system," which depended on older pupils teaching younger ones, with much oral roaring and recitation by rote. And it still seemed natural, and was often effective, to have literate teenagers teach the fundamentals to poor children who would go no further.[14]

But those who went through the full course at the ICY were exposed to a truly rigorous classical curriculum. By 1868 the Manager's Annual Report included a truncated version of the Humphreys will which omitted all reference to either "the mechanical arts" or agriculture, and official lists of graduates began only with those, starting in the 1850s, who unlike William Dorsey had passed through the academic course only. The second year of high school by then required a "critical reading of Milton" in English classes, algebra through quadratic equations in math, ancient and medieval history, geography, composition, Latin, and map drawing. Science in the next year included anatomy and physiology, with chemistry in the laboratory; math added geometry and bookkeeping to algebra; Greek grammar—Principal Bassett was insistent on this—was added to the Latin classics. The senior class continued along earlier lines: moral science, among several other subjects, trigonometry, Greek through the New Testament and Xenophon. [15]

The ratio of teachers to students, not much more than 20 to 1, was far beyond the reach of any public school in the era, black or white. The staff was exceptional; Mary J. Patterson, for example, brought with Jackson from Oberlin as her assistant, is usually cited instead of Grace Mapps as the first Afro-American woman to graduate from any four-year college. And the pay was by contemporary standards very high: Principal Bassett earned $1200 in 1867, and was given a nearby house rent-free. Jackson earned $1000 as head of the girls' department; Octavius Catto, without a collegiate degree, $700 as head of the boys'; other pay ranged from the $60 given a pair of undergraduate assistants who helped with the lower grades on to $400 given James Field Needham, a recent graduate. While the Society of Friends was not notable for its financial generosity, and raises followed only on specific petitions, the managers during the rest of the inflationary war decade did usually grant these requests—Catto was pushed up to $1000 by 1868—or met them with bonuses or loans instead. [16]

In these early years, especially, it would be hard to exaggerate the enthusiasm for the Institute in black Philadelphia and well beyond. The library, of several thousand volumes, was open to the community from the first; some 3,066 books were loaned out in 1870. An active body of alumni sponsored a series of outside Afro-American speakers, such as Frederick Douglass and the Reverend Henry Highland Garnet, while the regular course of instruction was supplemented by scientific lectures open to the public, some eleven of these in 1868 alone. The number of graduates, just one each in the years 1856, 1857, and 1858, reached eighteen by 1869, the first class to enter the new building and to enjoy Fanny Jackson's evidently inspired teaching. And from the first the annual graduation exercises, at which the young women read and the young men declaimed their specially prepared essays, were events whose importance reached far past the school. Usually about half of the graduates were from out of town, and in the absence of dormitories boarded with local families or relatives. But in an era, and among a people, as hungry for education as Afro-Americans after the Civil War, for graduation purposes the definition of "family" included much of the community: at a time when the city's black population was officially about 20,000 men, women, and children, nearly 3000 turned out at Concert Hall to watch just nine young people graduate in December of 1868.[17]

The Institute's reputation was not confined to blacks. The Quakers, who had every reason to be satisfied with its progress, invited guests, many of them southern whites, to the classrooms and annual public examinations; the Governor of Pennsylvania had attended the first graduation in 1856, at a time when the Commonwealth's Afro-Americans had no right to vote. The school's very first academic graduate, Jesse Glasgow, had gone on to the University of Edinburgh, taking a prize in every classical and scientific class he attended before succumbing to the Scots' climate and consumption in 1861. And a list of the graduates in the annual report for 1871 showed that, as intended, 50 of the 82 alumni then living were teaching, many in the South, not counting an untold and possibly greater number who had dropped out short of getting their diplomas.[18]

Ebenezer Bassett, too, tied for thirty-first in number of mentions in the Dorsey Collection, had impressed more than the Friends or his students. But it was still a surprise when incoming President U. S. Grant appointed him the first black diplomat in our history, as Minister to Haiti and the Dominican Republic. The Institute's managers were again proud; the job, announced in March of 1869, was formally the highest government post to which any black could aspire for generations to come. And although the timing was awkward and Bassett would be missed, they had no trouble in finding a successor; Fanny Jackson had earned the job. The only dissent came from Octavius Catto, who clearly believed that despite Jackson's collegiate credentials his longer service, and sex, should have given him preference.[19]

It is perhaps a sign of the relative, and in some ways selective, tolerance of the Society of Friends that relations with Catto and other members of the local black community had gone so well until then. The Institute was the only Quaker school not staffed by members of the Society, and there were indeed no black Quakers in Philadelphia. While Sarah Douglass had attended the Arch Street Meeting for a time, Quaker views about women, however advanced by contemporary white standards, did not live up to those among elite blacks, and she had quit over the issue of sex-segregated seating. But while the managers could assume that the Institute's teachers were all firm Christians, the Afro-American attitude toward the issues of the Civil War, pitted against the traditional pacifism of the Society, created some strains.[20]

In the late 1850s, when the North-South conflict was already physically under way in "Bloody Kansas," and through John Brown's raid on Harper's Ferry, the managers had felt some unease about student orations which smacked of "war, hatred, and revenge." Once the Civil War broke out they did suggest that a visiting speaker such as Frederick Douglass try to confine himself to "the peaceable principles of Friends." But as the war became in many eyes a crusade against slavery many Quakers themselves felt ambivalent; Catto at one point marched the entire graduating class up to the state capital in Harrisburg, trying vainly to break the bars against black enlistment, and toward the end of the war the Institute itself was, astonishingly, opened to military recruiters without any recorded objection.[21]

A handsome, athletic, and poetic young bachelor, as well as a strong public speaker, Catto at the age of 25 was from the first a major figure in the new Equal Rights League formed in 1864. The Friends shared the League's objection to streetcar segregation, the leading local grievance in the middle 1860s, and they were perhaps pleased with the tactics adopted by Catto and other militants. Anticipating campaigns waged against the same foe a century later, men and women used their bodies nonviolently to block the cars, fill them up, force cops and conductors to throw them off, while the leaders used the publicity generated when Christian ministers, sick children, pregnant women, and wounded war veterans were denied rides. When after helping win the right to ride in 1867 the League turned to the right to vote, the Quakers, although themselves largely apolitical, were generally supportive. But they must have been uneasy about black support for armed confrontation in the South during Reconstruction, and specifically about Octavius Catto's acceptance of a commission in the Pennsylvania State Militia.[22]

To mollify the young man after Fanny Jackson was placed over him in 1869, the board gave him a salary, $1200, equal to hers, although without the free housing. But the next two years were strained. Richard T. Greener, a former ICY student, was brought in 1870 to serve ostensibly as assistant in the boys' department. But it must have been hard for his immediate superior to see the move as anything but a threat; Greener had spent some time at Oberlin in Jackson's day, and came fresh from winning the first Harvard degree ever granted an Afro-American, together with prizes in oratory and writing.[23]

Octavius Catto was then looking for a new job, perhaps in Washington, when the strain at the Institute was unexpectedly and tragically resolved from the outside. When blacks stepped up to the polls in October of 1871, the first significant city election since they had won the vote, they were attacked by mobs of Irish Democrats downtown. Two men had already been shot and one axed to death when a young white man reached the most obvious target; Major Catto, leader of the local voting campaign, was responding to the governor's emergency call for troops by going home to get his uniform. He was shot point-blank in front of his house, at 814 South Street, and died almost immediately in the arms of one of the several policemen who were never able later to identify his killer.[24]

The riot, Catto's murder, and the Republican victory at the polls that day were all of great symbolic and actual importance in the political history of black Philadelphia, subject of a later chapter. In terms of its educational history, what it meant, once peace was restored, was that Fanny Jackson was indisputably in charge of the Institute for Colored Youth.

Over the next two decades the Institute managed both to consolidate its place in the community and to open new paths. The initiatives, in contrast to the earlier period, were virtually all taken by the principal. Fanny Jackson, by this time perhaps the most dominant personality in black Philadelphia, ranking number two in the Dorsey Collection, developed a number of interests beyond the walls of her school while continuing to work for educational innovation. But she had also to struggle continually with an increasingly conservative board of managers to make the Institute's program relevant to black needs as she came to understand them.[25]

Jackson's power was based less on her formal position as the first black woman to head a major educational institution than on the character and energy that had won her the job to begin with. She had been born in 1837 to a slave named Lucy Orr and an unknown father. Her freedom bought by relatives around 1850, she moved from Washington to Newport, Rhode Island, to work as a domestic in a rich white household. But while her employers were kindly and the mistress helped teach her the domestic arts, they did not otherwise encourage her education. She had then to manage somehow to pay for a private tutor, on her own, for an hour each week, while sneaking out for music lessons as practice for later dealings with the Quakers. She recalled years after that she had always wanted to be a teacher for the benefit of her race; after enrolling at the Rhode Island Normal School in 1859, characteristically paying for extra-curricular lessons in French, she transferred to Oberlin the next year.[26]

Oberlin College in 1860 was still headed by the veteran abolitionist minister Charles Grandison Finney, who inspired Fanny among other things to experience a genuine religious conversion. The college provided perhaps the most supportive interracial experience that could then be enjoyed in the United States. The atmosphere was not ideal; during Jackson's tenure the sculptor and free spirit Edmonia Lewis was beaten by local whites, and narrowly acquitted of the criminal offense of slipping an aphrodisiac into the drinks of two coed friends. Richard Greener at the same time believed that he had been denied the chance to be valedictorian of his pre-collegiate class. But Fanny Jackson, always driven to prove herself as a representative of her race, had a nearly idyllic time, welcomed into the Ladies Literary Society, invited to teach in the preparatory department, singing in church, giving music lessons, excelling in her studies.[27]

Pious, accomplished, and brilliant, the genteel Miss Jackson was all that the Institute for Colored Youth could have ordered when she was hired on graduation. What she showed the managers, on beginning four years later as principal, was that she also had a strong mind of her own.

Philadelphia's Orthodox Quakers in the late 19th century were suffering from a kind of crisis, losing members and influence as the result of narrowly rigid policies, devoted more to withdrawal than active involvement. Proud of their practicality and their historic benevolence, they were in fact often intensely impractical, increasingly out of touch with the world of affairs and notably with those urban blacks who had so often benefited from their earlier activities. But Fanny Jackson soon developed her own roots in the local community, and brought back ideas that were often in conflict with the Friends'.[28]

Jackson had played the organ for a black congregation in Newport; in Philadelphia during the 1870s she not only sang soprano in the St. Thomas choir but appeared on the stage in benefit church performances. Her church activities were not confined among elite Episcopalians; she began writing for the AME *Christian Recorder* as early as 1870, contributing a regular woman's column beginning in 1878. To cap increasing involvement with the city's largest Afro-American denomination she married the Reverend Levi Coppin in 1881, a middle-aged union that would last through his elevation to a bishopric in 1900 and until her death in 1913.[29]

T. Thomas Fortune in 1891 wrote that Fanny Jackson Coppin was one of the two most powerful Afro-American women orators in the country, and she would be heard. She continued, through the 1880s, to sing at St. Thomas, while joining the featured speakers at the semi-centennial of the Central Presbyterian Church, and helping Mother Bethel establish a Home for Fallen Women. She also helped to manage the interdenominational Home for Aged and Infirm Colored Persons. Her purely secular or political involvement led her to speak out jointly with the anti-lynching crusader Ida Wells Barnett, and to either speak or appear on the dais together with Frederick Douglass, the southern white author and reformer George Washington Cable, and fellow educator General Samuel Armstrong of Hampton Institute.[30]

Her concern with women's condition embraced both the job situation and issues directly related to gender. In part because of her firsthand view of the fact that teaching was virtually the only acceptable job for educated black women, she used her nationally distributed column in the *Christian Recorder* to suggest medicine, library work, and business as alternatives. And it was clearly her support that led the aging Sarah Mapps Douglass, in the 1870s, to give an adult course on "Women's Physiology" in her own home. Douglass, sister of the artist Robert, a veteran of the abolitionist and the early feminist movements, was given a special award for this in 1879. The citation, signed by 32 of the city's leading Afro-American women, read:

> Resolved: That women owe it not only to themselves but to their posterity,
> to study intimately their structures and those natural laws pertaining to
> their bodily and mental well-being.

The fact that Douglass's course was not given at the Institute, where she had taught for so many years, suggests that it was part of Fanny Jackson Coppin's continual if usually muted duel with her Quaker board of managers. She believed, justly enough, that she knew the needs of the community and her pupils better than they, and perhaps because they were unused to doing battle usually found ways of outflanking them.[31]

Her first move as principal had been to abolish corporal punishment, over the objections of Octavius Catto, among others. While herself a strict disciplinarian, who insisted on her right to expel unruly students without consultation, she believed that good teaching should rely more on mutual respect than the traditional rod. In order to keep an open channel with the parents, too, she began sending monthly written reports on each child's progress. While not challenging Quaker insistence on punctuality and, usually, attendance, she argued that allowance had to be made for poor students who left before the end of the spring term to work at various summer resorts. Such students had to miss the annual public examinations, a kind of showcase for the school; but the ritual was unduly stressful anyway, she thought, partly because of its public nature, partly because it covered a full year, up to perhaps sixteen courses. The system was then changed to privately conducted half-year examinations. And after a long campaign she succeeded, in 1877, in abolishing tuition. The Quakers characteristically believed that the $5 or $10 fee encouraged thrift; she thought it a hardship, quietly refused to collect or do the needed accounting, and encouraged what amounted in the end to a successful parental boycott. (Perhaps it was a coincidence that the next year, the last of the prevailing economic depression, the board of managers cut staff salaries by 10 percent, including the $1800 granted Jackson Coppin herself earlier in the decade.)[32]

Some staff turnover might be laid to managerial conservatism. Richard Greener left in 1873, and the board's hesitation killed two potentially outstanding appointments, of the black nationalist Alexander Crummell and the poet Charlotte Forten, granddaughter of the old abolitionist and shipbuilder. On the other hand the personal intervention of Alfred Cope, most supportive of the managers, led to a real coup in 1875. Following negotiations begun when he was still a senior at Yale, and after subsidizing his graduate education and guaranteeing him $1500 a year, the Institute was able to hire the first Afro-American to win a Ph.D, the physicist Edward Bouchet, who would remain throughout the history of the school.[33]

Meanwhile Jackson Coppin and the board continued sometimes to agree and sometimes to battle over curriculum. She was able immediately to convince the managers in 1869–70 that the Institute needed a specific "normal school" or teacher training program, which was begun the next year. To add these courses others would have to go; on consultation with outside experts Jackson Coppin, despite her own proficiency in five languages including Sanskrit, decided to drop the much-admired but impractical Greek studies brought in by Ebenezer Bassett. When several graduates, the next year, failed the Philadelphia examinations for teachers' certificates, she was ready with a nine-point program to bring the Institute's curriculum more in line with the requirements, with for example more stress on the United States Constitution, and there was no such trouble thereafter.[34]

But while the managers still thought of the Institute as a classical high school only, Jackson Coppin believed it could serve wider educational needs, and while the board threatened to eliminate the preparatory school entirely she managed slowly to extend it downward into the primary grades, so that by 1890 the school provided a start-to-finish education in just nine years, given its advantages over the twelve-year public system. The official reasons for the primary school expansion were that the public schools did not provide good training, and that the normal school students needed little ones to practice with—an idea that would also save expense. But Jackson Coppin was also concerned, together with Mrs. Gertrude Mossell and others, about the need for a kindergarten, in large part because working mothers needed what we would now call quality day care. When the board drew the line, in 1879, three ICY graduates opened their own kindergarten the next year, the first of several such efforts over the next two decades.[35]

Drawing the line was not usually a winning tactic in the managers' continuing duel with Fanny Jackson Coppin. They opposed the teaching of German; she favored it. After they finally agreed to an after-school program in 1878 they discovered, a year later, that she had quietly moved the language into school hours. Given the special Quaker emphasis on the spiritual value of silence—a religious position poles apart from her own—they were unanimously opposed, despite her pleas, to teaching music, even though music theory was included on the city's teacher examinations. Jackson Coppin, herself accomplished on the guitar and piano as well as the organ, simply took ICY students to lessons at a nearby church. As strict Protestants the managers opposed poetry in the curriculum; she encouraged rhyme and verse in everything from Bible study to grammar:

> "With all thy heart love God above
> and as thyself thy neighbor love"

and:

> "A noun is the name of anything
> As school or garden, hoop or swing."

They also opposed the teaching of fiction: she insisted on the moral value of such children's classics as the stories of Hans Christian Anderson. Another apparent contest was settled, too, when after the death of Sarah Douglass ICY graduate Dr. Rebecca Cole, first black to win a degree from the city's Women's Medical College, moved a version of Douglass's course on physiology, preventive medicine, and hygiene into the regular curriculum during the early 1880s.[36]

But by far the longest and most significant battle was fought over the issue of "industrial education." That was a phrase that meant many things to different people in the post–Civil War decades. Jackson Coppin got her special vision during Philadelphia's great Centennial Exhibition of 1876, when she and other American educators were impressed by the sophisticated techniques of the Moscow Imperial Technical School. Each trade, at the Russian Exhibit, was broken into a series of graded exercises involving drawings, models, and tools, so that the process combined intellectual with "hands-on" education. To the board of managers of the Institute for Colored Youth, however, her suggestion that industrial training be added to the curriculum clearly clashed with their own idea of what an elite high school should be and do. So she went instead on a lecture tour on behalf of what she called her "industrial crusade," reaching past the managers to the Afro-Americans of Philadelphia and beyond.[37]

Fanny Jackson Coppin, although she got on it earlier than most, was in fact riding a wave. The idea of "industrial education," in part because of its very flexibility, could be sold on a number of grounds. Speakers might sing one song while listeners nodded to their own beat; the phrase could suggest both moral and material ends, a thrifty self-help and technical mastery, old-fashioned virtues and newfangled trades, the opportunity to rise in the world and the need for a skilled labor force. Philadelphians were especially enthusiastic, or vulnerable, because of the great success of industrial exhibits at the Centennial, and just as black leaders were looking about for new ways to break into the labor market the Board of Education invited Fanny Jackson Coppin to hearings on the status of industrial education in the local public schools. She told them, forthrightly, that the only places where young black men could learn trades were the reformatory and prison, where the education was limited to making cane chairs and brooms.[38]

In 1879 she had an opportunity to realize a part of her own idea by organizing the first Afro-American "industrial exhibition" held in Philadelphia since before the Civil War. The intent was threefold: the fair would publicize the educational idea, and show what blacks could do, while the profits would go to *Christian Recorder*, then deep in debt. A fourth dividend was pure serendipity; in the course of planning the event she met the Reverend Levi Coppin, whom she would marry within two years.[39]

The exhibition, despite articles contributed from a number of different states, was in practice a modest affair, and sales netted only about $300 of the $7000 needed by the *Christian Recorder*. But it did succeed in publicizing the industrial idea, and Colonel Forney of the *Press* pledged $500 toward "an institution in this city" devoted to science, culture, and learning. Jackson Coppin continued to speak in and out of the city on the need for Afro-American self-help and job opportunities, raising racial consciousness and funds at the same time.[40]

She also used her prestige and powers of persuasion in an unremitting campaign directed at the ICY board of managers, who turned her down several times but were finally turned around in 1884. Even then the board was reluctant: the funds were not all there, plans would have to be modest. Jackson Coppin pushed on: since many of the students came from outside the city, often from faraway places in the South, there was a real need for a girls' dormitory, although "if the managers . . . intend this Institute to be purely local in its usefulness, the argument is closed." When they pleaded poverty again, she simply rented the house next door, beginning in 1884. Four years later, when visiting London on behalf of the AME's Woman's Home Foreign Missionary Society, she was still raising money for the proposed "industrial department"—and specifically for a dormitory.[41]

But while it took five fitful years, the managers finally raised some $40,000, including about $2600 from the principal's subscription campaign and a most un-Quakerly gala, benefit performance of Afro-American musicians, singers, and comedians held at the Academy of Music in 1887. Final plans were not all that Jackson Coppin had wanted, in some crucial ways. But as her own silver anniversary at the Institute approached, a solid three-story brick building was erected during 1888, right next to the main structure on Bainbridge Street. Rising community interest was reflected in over 400 applications for places in the new "industrial department." And as the first class in carpentry opened in January of 1889, the principal had every reason to be proud and hopeful.[42]

Progress in public education between 1864 and 1889 meanwhile kept pace with progress at the Institute for Colored Youth. Although Jacob White, Jr., at Roberts Vaux was an unquestioned leader, the public schools boasted no single person or institution to match Fanny Jackson Coppin and the ICY. Most of their black teachers, like White himself, were in fact graduates of the private Quaker high school. Afro-Americans in the city's schools, too, had to face white authority, and white constraints, far more restrictive than those imposed by a Quaker board of managers, a condition most dramatically evident when they had to deal directly with the emotional issues of integration and white competition from which the Institute was sheltered. Still the growing number of public schools could deal with far more students than the ICY, and provide at least some flexibility for parents and students when toward the end of the 1880s the Philadelphia Board of Education proposed its own version of "industrial education" for blacks.

When Jacob White began his work at Vaux the little primary school was located in the basement of the "Zoar Methodist Church (colored)," as it was usually identified, in a pocket of Afro-American settlement northeast of and divided from the major population center in the Seventh Ward. In 1864 he was the only teacher for all of his students, whatever their level, as well as the only black teacher in the system. But he apparently used the entrepreneurial ability practiced in his newspaper and cemetery businesses to negotiate a starting salary of $625, far more than the average of $450 for the experienced white principals of the section. Within his first year he had pushed the enrollment from 49 to nearly 200, evidently forcing a move out of the close, wet, and low Zoar basement, and helping also to force an expansion in the number of black teachers as well.[43]

In the course of this expansion he and his colleagues had to deal with central authority only in times of major change or crisis; Philadelphia's public schools, in keeping with the general decentralization of local government in the 19th century, were normally run at the ward level. The state, in return for about a third of the budget, set few standards beyond the mandate, beginning in 1834, that each district must provide some public education, and that once the number of black students reached twenty they might segregate them. The city had anticipated both of these provisions years before. Its Board of Education, elected by ward, directly administered the Central High School for Boys and the Normal School for Girls, setting citywide policy with respect to promotional examinations and teachers' certification, and letting all major contracts. But there was no superintendent to administer these matters until 1883, and the locally elected ward or sectional boards enjoyed the kind of power that they were most concerned with: the right to oversee every school in the section, to let small contracts, and in their own turn "elect" janitors, teachers, and principals.[44]

In terms of later debate the system combined the best and worst of two worlds. Decentralization made it sensitive to the needs of locally elected officials, but locally elected officials showed much less interest in educational innovation than in corruption and patronage, in the form of contracts under $100 and jobs for their supporters. The strict standards set by the central Board of Education guaranteed an approach to learning that culminated at Central High—the Normal School, or Girls' High, was less rigorous—which in 1880 demanded three years each of Latin and physics, two of German, mathematics through trigonometry and calculus, and an occasional course in elocution as the closest thing to a soft spot. But the price was high. Many children did not go to school at all; the first, weakly enforced, compulsory attendance law was not passed until 1895, and required only that those between 8 and 13 go 16 weeks a year. Meanwhile examinations or the need to work drove children out of the system at every stage, creating a pyramid like that at the ICY. It is hard to compare grade levels directly with those of modern schools. But the figures for 1880 show that fewer than half of the "primary" pupils, roughly equivalent to modern grades one and two, went on to the next stage, now the third and fourth grades; only a little more than half of the secondary pupils went to the four-year "grammar" school, modern middle school; and only a small fraction of grammar school pupils went to the high schools. It was easy to demand much at Central or the Normal School then simply because those who won diplomas were an educational elite, usually from privileged backgrounds. Having survived physically unhealthy buildings, notoriously indifferent instruction, per-pupil expenditures of about $20 a year and a pupil to teacher ratio of more than 50 to 1, they represented, in 1880, less than 1 percent of the 105,541 registered in the system as a whole.[45]

In some ways this system could be made to work to blacks' advantage. Teaching was a notoriously unrewarding job for whites; over 95 percent of those teaching in Philadelphia throughout the period were women, who typically entered the profession as teenagers, lived with their parents, and quit as soon as they got married. But there was no recorded racial discrimination in salaries, which averaged about $490 around 1880. And if that seemed low to most it was attractive to Afro-American women, who were less likely either to marry or to quit work if married than their white counterparts. And right on the heels of Jacob White, in the middle of the 1860s, they began to move in.[46]

One route, encouraged by the local boards' hunger for power and patronage, was simply to get an existing private school of 30 or more pupils accepted as part of the system. In the absence of regulations of any kind, it was not unusual for blacks to take on pupils of their own. Rebecca Cole did that with her brother William in Germantown, apparently in the 1860s; several others followed by 1875. And just as Sarah Douglass had converted her little school into the preparatory department of the ICY in the 1860s, Cordelia Jennings, an ICY graduate, converted hers into a public institution a few years later. Quite apart from their racial attitudes it was always in the interest of a sectional school board to encourage such a move. Whatever it meant in terms of education it always brought opportunities both for patronage and for building renovations; the latter, to bypass the Board of Education, broken neatly into $99 units.[47]

For parallel reasons, too, it could be good business to hire black teachers. Students might enroll in schools anywhere in the city, if accepted as qualified by principals. This simply encouraged the sectional boards to operate much like nation-states in the age of mercantilist economics, trying to maximize their own attendance, and thus the jobs and buildings at their disposal, by keeping local youngsters inside their boundaries and attracting others from outside. Able black women, certainly ICY graduates, must have helped bring in children who might not otherwise have enrolled.

The most successful of these women was Caroline V. LeCount, ICY '63. LeCount played an active role in the battle to integrate the streetcars shortly after her graduation, partly as activist colleague, companion, perhaps even fiancée to Octavius Catto. It was in fact her physical expulsion from one of the cars in 1867 which resulted in the successful court suit that helped to push the matter toward final settlement. Member of a prominent local family whose father, the cabinetmaker-turned-undertaker James LeCount, Sr., sent three children to the Institute, she began to teach at the Ohio Street School in 1865, and became its principal just three years later. A lively member of St. Thomas

Church, she sang and did dramatic and comic readings both for her peers, at the Bethel Literary and Historical Association, and at public fundraisers. Some of the same talents used in teaching may account for the number of pupils she attracted. During the 1870s, as the Republican party sought black support, her school was officially renamed in honor of her old friend the martyred Catto, just as the one on Lombard Street was renamed for James Forten. And as a secondary was added to its primary school in 1880, the 200 children enrolled by then required three assistants in addition to LeCount herself.[48]

In 1877 a newly opened primary school on Warnock Street, in the Twentieth section joined Catto in the Seventh, Forten in the Fifth, and a small primary school in the First among the black institutions. But the flagship was still the Roberts Vaux School. The great growth in Jacob White's first year was continued afterward, and as attendance expanded new grades were added, making Vaux, together with Forten, the only black grammar school in the system. Under legal segregation this meant that choices were extremely restricted: of the roughly 500 schools in the system, only five were open to black students, three beyond the primary grades, two beyond secondary. The only alternatives were the ICY, with its rigid entrance examinations and, before 1878, tuition, or the Roman Catholic schools, which were then "open without discrimination of color," although few apparently wanted or could afford a Catholic education.[49]

Given the 19th-century pattern of dispersed black settlement, school segregation was a special hardship for those who did not live near the crowded Fifth and Seventh wards. Years later Carl Bolivar remembered long, cold walks, through hostile Irish territory, to reach the old "Bird" school on Lombard Street, in an era when public transport was an impossible alternative; streetcar segregation meant that blacks had either to wait for every fifth or tenth car or, sometimes, to sit on the platforms or roof, exposed to the weather. And while segregation ended in 1867, the streetcars were still too expensive for most, and blacks were often absent or tardy because of the problems posed by traveling great distances.[50]

Roberts Vaux itself however flourished, partly as a result of its near-monopoly. In an unprecedented move the Board of Education in 1875 decreed that the school move west out of the Twelfth and into the Fourteenth section, where there were more black students; the new quarters were officially opened early in 1876. From the little place in Zoar's basement, where classes had to be interrupted for funerals in the grave site that doubled as schoolyard, Vaux had become a "consolidated" school, containing all grades through grammar. Since the James Forten School, while more convenient to black settlement, had an all-white teaching staff, Vaux was by far the most important open to the city's Afro-Americans, serving for many years as a magnet for elite children who did not go to the ICY. W. E. B. Du Bois, as a Harvard Ph.D. fresh from study in Heidelberg, later noted with a touch of condescension that the city's Afro-

American leadership typically "are mostly grammar school graduates." But an official semi-annual examination at Vaux involved among other things the ability to take the cube root of 0.000529475129, while Philadelphia until 1878 and other places for long afterward required no more than a grammar school diploma for schoolteachers. Only a small minority of any race went farther, and among a people with a newly awakened hunger for education, for Gertrude Bustill Mossell, Henry O. Tanner, and many others, a degree from Vaux was a genuine distinction.[51]

Certainly Jacob White enjoyed his central role in the school and community, as a social leader as well as educational and business entrepreneur. Within the black community the affairs of the First African Presbyterian Church, the ICY Alumni Association, the Pythians Baseball Club, the Douglass Hospital, the Equal Rights League, and the Progressive Workingman's Club all, at various times, vied for his attention; on retirement he founded the "Bird Association" for alumni of the old school. The first Afro-American, in 1870, admitted to the Teacher's Institute of Philadelphia, he became in time secretary of the Male Principal's Association, invited to a host of largely white school occasions, lectures, and graduations. The Baltimore superintendent of schools asked him for principals; the county superintendent in Salem, New Jersey, had any number of jobs at $33.33 a month. And in a political-educational atmosphere in which public debate about teachers' jobs centered on the fact that, for example, Mary Patterson was an orphan while Mary Durham was a resident of the section, he got teachers' recommendations from Fanny Jackson Coppin and janitors' recommendations from churchwomen, all of which he had then to negotiate with his own boards.[52]

Some of the differences between the public system and the Institute for Colored Youth were evident at graduation and other exercises. Because the preparatory school at the ICY was more intense, and the grades fewer, there was little difference in the ages of Institute or Vaux graduates. And Vaux exercises, like those at the private school, were enormously important community events. But otherwise the two were quite different. Public ceremonies at Vaux were held more often, at Christmas as well as graduation, and commencement was much livelier. The class of 1877, six boys and four girls—the sex ratio tended to be more even than at the ICY, as there was no preference given future teachers—graduated in front of an "overflowing crowd." Proceedings opened with a prayer from AME Bishop B. T. Tanner, father of the valedictorian; little concession was made, in 19th-century public education, to the sensibilities of non-Protestant parents. After that, the morning was dominated by music; of the 16 program events involving students, 4 featured the school's justly noted orchestra, 2 the ensemble chorus, 5 a series of solos, duets, and trios. While a reporter praised the music, he felt that some of the recitations "lacked animation"; it was perhaps hard to get excited about Miss R. Armistead's reading of "The Angels of Buena Vista" or Raphael Bowser's oration on "The Character of Napoleon Bonaparte"; Henry O. Tanner's valedictory address on "Compulsory Education" was the closest anyone came to a matter of topical importance.[53]

There was of course no music at the ICY graduation the previous spring, and Fanny Jackson Coppin was known to frown on fancy dress. But every one of the thirteen graduates was on the program, delivering earnest addresses on "The Politics of the Negro," "The Civilization of Africa," and "Tenement Houses and Public Baths." While Vaux graduates year after year paid tribute to "Truth" and "Constancy," their cousins downtown grappled with "Industrial Education," "The Negro in Business," even "Intermarriage—Is It To Be Encouraged?" The principal, her biographer suggests, may even have prompted seniors to "educate" the Quakers in the audience; a powerful 1879 address on "The Slaughter of the Innocents" was in fact a plea for kindergarten education, a proposal then before the board.[54]

It is not clear how far the politics of public education muted Jacob White's behavior. He had been secretary of the Pennsylvania Equal Rights League when first hired, in 1864, but he was not militant by nature, and his name does not afterward appear among those engaged in partisan politics, or on the front lines of protest. In some ways Roberts Vaux benefited from school segregation, and the issue of integration remained dormant during the period of its greatest growth. There was a mild protest in 1869 against the Board of Education's refusal to grant a music teaching certificate to Alice Gordon, at a time when in the absence of music instruction in the "colored" schools she would have qualified to teach whites. But despite some objections from the Equal Rights League, by then far from active, the Board in 1874 explicitly ruled that "colored" persons (although not whites) must be confined to educating children of their own race. Otherwise there was no real attack on the system until the late 1870s.[55]

The new outbreak of Afro-American protest over the schools may have been prepared, on the national level, by the early successes of the federal Civil Rights Act of 1875, which worked to open a number of public places, although not schools, before its death at the hands of the Supreme Court. Local stirrings may have been precipitated by the Board of Education, which in 1878 passed a reform which required two years of Normal School or its equivalent for all Philadelphians seeking teaching certificates, making an education at Vaux no longer good enough. But perhaps it was simply inevitable that as more young Afro-Americans climbed the educational ladder three of them should present themselves, in the same year, for the high-school entrance examinations. Edward Green, son of a "janitress" whose building tenants encouraged his application, was the only Forten student ever to express an interest, according to his principal, who predicted he would pass easily. Jacob White noted that one of his boys wanted to try, but that his parents could not afford it. The first two from Vaux were then Amanda Bustill and Miranda C. Venning; the *Record* noted that they were both "very ladylike in manner and deportment." Although a sour note was struck when the controller for the Fifth Sectional school board refused to sign Green's application, the objection was overruled; the real noise broke when they all failed.[56]

There were obvious reasons why blacks, in general, did not normally go as far up the school ladder as whites. One ironic by-product of economic discrimination worked in their favor; while white youngsters, especially immigrant boys, often dropped out early to take factory jobs, blacks had far fewer opportunities to work until they were big enough to do common labor or domestic service. Otherwise everything conspired toward high rates of absenteeism and failure: the travel problem, the diseases of poverty, the fact that few had nonworking parents to monitor them. Another handicap in these early years was that, despite the gains made among black teachers, there were still only eleven of them in 1878. Most schoolchildren were taught by whites, often Irish Catholics. These people, hostile to a "Protestant" public education to begin with, were stuck into what they thought the worst assignments in the system, among people they often despised.[57]

But the problems of black children in general did not apply to Green, Bustill, and Venning in particular, who had the confident support of parents and principals. Unlike the ICY graduates who, until their curriculum was adjusted, had had trouble with the certifying examinations for teachers, very similar to those for entrance into the high schools, all three had gone through the standard course and textbooks. And most of their peers did not find the tests too hard. The reason for the steep falloff in numbers between the grammar and high schools was not academic but economic; the great majority of those whose parents felt they could afford the four additional years passed the qualifying examinations, some 307 of the 380 trying for places in the Normal School in 1878. But in this case, since there was no possibility of establishing separate high schools for just three young people, what was riding on the examinations was nothing less than school integration in Philadelphia. And it is hard to avoid the suspicion voiced by Edward Green himself: "I think that my failure . . . was part of a scheme to keep me out of the school."[58]

The Equal Rights League, although in hibernation for some years, was roused to agree, and bestirred itself to demand a proper investigation. The Fifth Sectional board censured its own controller for his role, and promised to look into the whole matter, although it lacked authority to examine the examinations. Fanny Jackson Coppin wrote an eloquent and bitter letter complaining that while white youngsters had "all the world before them, where to choose," the failure of the two girls who aspired to be teachers denied them the only opportunity open to educated black women. The *Christian Recorder*, over the next several years, intensified its campaign against the use of white teachers in black schools. And although young Green was too discouraged to try again,

L. P. Gordon, from Vaux, was quietly admitted to Central in February of 1879, while Bustill and Venning passed the Normal School examinations that June.[59]

During 1880 the employment issue continued to simmer, as in September 150 parents from West Philadelphia signed a petition demanding black teachers in a new school at 42nd and Ludlow. Mrs. Josephine Herbert, the leader, argued that they paid taxes, that white parents would not allow their youngsters to be taught by people of another race, and that they wanted no more than the same: "White people do not understand our race as well as we do ourselves, and do not take the same interest in our children." The Board of Education lamely insisted that it could find no Afro-American teachers, although the 14th Sectional board had turned down two in favor of white applicants at Vaux the year before—ironically and no doubt uncomfortably to serve under Jacob White. And by that time it had even bigger troubles on its hands, in the form of a suit, announced just two weeks earlier, that challenged the whole segregated system on the grounds that it violated the Fourteenth Amendment to the Constitution of the United States.[60]

The petitioner, Benjamin Chew, a barber with four children, simply insisted that they ought to be able to go to the "nearest convenient school." He would be happy to take them to either Forten or Catto but it was simply too long a walk for the younger ones. After failing to make this case to the Third Sectional board he went on to the Board of Education. Failing there he went to the Court of Common Pleas, which granted him in December the first step toward a writ of mandamus, requiring the Board to show cause why it could not relieve the petitioner. The Board had tried, all along, to turn him off quietly. Whatever its case in law it was losing in the public press; even the Democratic *Record* argued that there were too few blacks in Philadelphia for them to outnumber white children in any given school. The Board's position was simply that it did not assign pupils on the basis of race and never had; the question of admission to individual schools was up to the sectional boards, or perhaps the principals. But just after the Equal Rights League petitioned the state legislature in April of 1881, the whole matter was rendered moot by a Democratic judge in rural Crawford County, who ruled in May that school segregation was indeed unconstitutional in Pennsylvania, to the relief of most of those involved. The state law which followed, in June, was almost an anticlimax.[61]

In fact, following the usual rule, the rules in the city's system had never been airtight. The walls at Central and the Normal School had already been breached, and the Board of Education was probably right in arguing that local boards, on their own, had sometimes admitted Afro-American—doubtless light-skinned—children to individual schools. Given the attitudes in the city's newspapers, together with the growing black insistence on teachers from their own race, and thus pride in Catto and Vaux especially, there would probably have been little trouble in the city were it not for Henry Halliwell, secretary of the Board of Education. In July, after school was out, Halliwell noted that the Misses Bustill and Venning had dropped out of the Normal School. And he went on gratuitously to insist that because of inferior black teachers, easier examinations, high absenteeism, and the unruly behavior tolerated in their own schools, "I think it very doubtful that there are many colored children who can submit to the course of studies and discipline of the regular public schools."[62]

Halliwell drew an immediate and detailed reply from Caroline LeCount, who was, the *Sunday Republic* noted, "a match for all the officers and members of the Board of Education combined." After making the obvious point that school examinations were the same for all, she went on to note that the "colored principals" (she and Jacob White) had never had to have their bureaucratic reports corrected, unlike many of the others. One of the two girls at Normal had had to drop out for financial reasons, while the other had moved with her family to West Chester. The black teachers, finally, had had to pass their certification examinations with a minimum average of 70, compared with the 65 required of others. Every single Afro-American in the system then signed a protest letter to Halliwell, led by Jacob White, Caroline and Ada LeCount, Dora Cole, sister of Dr. Rebecca, John S. Durham, future diplomat and novelist, and Florence Lewis, future journalist. The group as a whole was obviously more distinguished than the citywide average, and the *Press* joined the *Republic* in agreeing that their argument was "conclusive," and the case closed.[63]

But the schools had to reopen in September, and the stand taken by Halliwell, Simon Gratz, and others on the board must have contributed to the troubles which broke out when blacks enrolled in new places. The *Times* blamed adult intransigence for violence in Catherine Street, in what was then an immigrant, largely Irish, section of South Philadelphia, and a "squad of Ninth District policemen" had to be called to quell white youngsters at the Thaddeus Stevens School, ironically named for the author of Pennsylvania's public education law, later the champion of black Reconstruction in the South.[64]

There were few such violent incidents after the first month, however, and the situation stabilized into the familiar pattern of partial, de facto segregation. Several schools remained semi-officially "colored"; otherwise black children went to largely white schools with varying degrees of trouble, as local principals retained much control over admissions. Highly uneven treatment, as in other areas of race relations, was the rule. An investigation of the Seventh Section's U. S. Grant School revealed in 1887 that on account of complaints that Afro-American girls stole things and smelled bad, the girls', but not the boys', seats and cloakrooms were separated. Nine years later the boys at the Manual Training School balked when a black student was chosen, by the faculty, as class orator. But the first two to graduate from Central High, in 1888, were largely accepted by their peers. John Henry Harris was described as quiet but "well-liked." The more outgoing William Herbert Jones, a reporter for the *Sentinel,* was elected to several class offices, and perhaps coincidentally was thought "the finest second baseman in the C.H.S. League."[65]

By that time attention had shifted away from pupil integration to its companion issue: the hiring of black teachers. One reason perhaps why school integration was so long a dormant concern was that the city's Afro-American leaders were afraid, like their southern counterparts nearly a century later, that it would cost them teaching jobs. That note of caution had been sounded in the first, 1864, debates in the Equal Rights League, in the late 1870s campaign by the *Christian Recorder,* down through the municipal election campaign of 1880. The press clearly sided with children faced with discrimination, and most whites could accept "the mixing of colors" among pupils. But to have black adults teach white children, with an authority to discipline which then included the use of rod or whip, was another matter. And in the late 1880s as Vaux, in the shadow of a noisy new elevated streetcar system, lost students and teachers, and the westward movement of black population lowered attendance at Forten, the threat to jobs was real. While several Afro-Americans were elected to the Fifth and Seventh sectional school boards, they controlled neither, and the employment question was subject to fierce infighting.[66]

At Forten, at the very end of the decade, there was both a breakthrough and a setback. Located in the city's worst neighborhood, with Italian and Jewish immigrants moving in from the river to replace more respectable blacks, Forten was chronically troubled. It was clearly a victory when the Fifth Sectional board replaced the longtime white principal with Thomas Murray in 1888; valedictorian of his ICY class of 1876, highly respected among his peers, Murray had had to go to rural Maryland to teach years before, despite an outstanding score on the certification examination. But within months the Board of Education, citing falling attendance, stripped away the grammar school and lowered Murray's salary, then at $700 a year. And despite a mass indignation meeting held by the city's leading Afro-American politicians, newspapermen, and professionals, things got worse. In July the Board appointed a committee to investigate charges of "gross immorality" at the school. In fact that allegation involved nothing worse than chronic use of "bad language" by children raised in the slums, and the investigation seems little more than an excuse to embarrass the newly appointed Murray. That was, as it turned out, only half of the hidden agenda; the other half involved the growing vogue for "industrial education."[67]

The city's education establishment during the 1880s was in fact caught up in the same wave as Fanny Jackson Coppin, and was less naturally conservative than the board of managers of the Institute for Colored Youth. The history of enthusiasm for industrial education in the public system and the ICY in many respects ran parallel. Just as with Fanny Jackson Coppin, it was the Centennial Exhibition of 1876 which first inspired public educators. There were attempts in 1880 to convert Central High into a "technical or scientific school," and the next year to introduce the use of tools and sewing into the public schools generally. The first objective was approximated, with enthusiastic backing from city council, with the establishment of the Philadelphia Manual Training School in 1885. The new school, it was hoped, would supplement a regular academic course for students 14 and older with mechanical drawing, forging, welding, molding, casting, and a host of other technical subjects; the idea was so popular that another, Northeast Manual Training School, was opened in 1890. And the second object—that tools and sewing should be part of an elementary curriculum—was not forgotten either. Especially when paired with notions of teaching thrift and discipline, it seemed worth a trial. Perhaps inspired by the infighting over Thomas Murray in the racially divided Fifth Section, the Board of Education decided that the best place for such a trial would be the James Forten School. And in 1890, just a year after the Institute for Colored Youth opened its new "industrial department," the Board in a truly unprecedented move took direct control of Forten, fired Murray, and put the school in charge of a white Quaker, Hannah Fox, whose ideal it was that "every boy will eventually become a first-class cook, with the ability to make his own shirt."[68]

The experiments in Afro-American "industrial education" begun almost simultaneously at James Forten and the Institute for Colored Youth both turned out disastrously in the 1890s. The story at Forten was relatively simple, and the public school system was big and flexible enough to allow both blacks and industrial education to recover from its failure. But the story at the ICY, involving all of the elements of the contemporary debate over the issue, was much more complicated, and failure there was a small tragedy for the city's black community.

The Forten experiment was doomed from the first by local hostility. Blacks were enthusiastic about their own visions of industrial education, but these visions did not involve education in cooking and sewing from the first grade onward, with the implication that their children were doomed to a life in domestic service, incapable from the very beginning of mastering an academic curriculum. The leadership was furious at the firing of Thomas Murray; Murray himself spent his last bitter days in office signing transfer slips, encouraging students to leave the school and present themselves elsewhere, to the chagrin of white principals in and out of the section. The all-white Fifth Sectional board was assured that the old teachers, excepting Murray, would be placed elsewhere, but it remained unhappy that Forten had been taken from its control.[69]

Hannah Fox, from Massachusetts, was an outsider to everyone but the Quakers, who had invited her just two years before to evaluate the program, then still academic only, at the ICY. But there were few Quakers in the Fifth

Ward. As black students transferred, she began her stay at Forten by admitting the children of immigrants, Italian and especially Jewish. She continued bravely on, aided by her cousin Agnes Fox, and consoled perhaps by a salary of $1200, far bigger than usual and nearly double what Murray had earned during his brief stay. By 1896 the school was only 22 percent black. Two years later a local councilman, perhaps alerted by parents, "mostly Russian Jews" who had learned enough English to realize what was going on, complained that the curriculum was "of a kindergarten sort," and "by no means adapted to the needs of the scholars." Those blacks interested in industrial education had by then a number of alternatives.[70]

The most exciting of these alternatives was the one offered at the Institute for Colored Youth, which opened its industrial department early in 1889 under Joseph Hill, a graduate and teacher since 1877. The department from the first was not all that Fanny Jackson Coppin had hoped. Hill himself had graduated from the Spring Garden Institute, the oldest technical school in the country, and systematically studied the Russian technical system through visits to other places where it had been adopted. But the ICY board of managers did not want and could not afford to train scientists, architects, or draughtsmen. There were no machines at the ICY either, no access to the modern industrial skills that the public manual training schools hoped to provide. And despite Jackson Coppin's pleas, there would be no full-time or daytime instruction: male students would visit the new building three evenings a week, while females would study in the old one on afternoons. The emphasis was on the traditional practical trades: carpentry, bricklaying, plastering, shoemaking, sewing, and printing; later tailoring, typewriting and stenography, millinery work, and cooking.[71]

The hunger for these trades, the trust in Fanny Jackson Coppin, and the excitement of the black community are all shown in one of the most revealing, and poignant, of the historical documents housed with the Dorsey Collection: the rollbooks from the first years of the industrial department. The managers had expected young people coming in after school; what they got was a cross-section of the community, people between the ages of 12 and 57 looking to better their condition. They signed in with their names and addresses, occupations, and ages; Joseph Hill then transcribed the key information in his own draughtsman's hand with a final column, "Trade Desired," to record, in effect, their ambitions. Hodcarriers came in clusters, sometimes over the river from Camden, looking to be bricklayers; middle-aged waiters wanted to be carpenters, errand boys and grade-school students cabinet-makers; housewives and laundresses signed up for "fancy-work" and dressmaking, for a grand total the first year alone of 604 registrants.[72]

The great majority had to be disappointed. Much of what they wanted was not offered, either in the first year or afterward: engineering, plumbing, blacksmithing, upholstering. As testimony to the need, despite the best efforts of board and principal no blacks could be found to teach any of the courses except for Ida Burrell's sewing class and Joseph Sweeney's tailoring, so that for the first time since the old farm days the Institute had to hire white instructors. The shortage of instructors, and perhaps material expenses, restricted class size; just four aspiring plasterers were actually enrolled the first year, and only the coeducational shorthand classes ever consistently got above 25.[73]

But black Philadelphia was still enthusiastic. Another benefit concert was held at the Academy of Music in October of 1890, this one for Jackson Coppin's girls' dormitory project. Beginning in 1890 it was decided to grant certificates to graduates of the industrial department, and at the same time to show off their projects in public exhibitions. Through the 1890s the press coverage given these annual shows rivaled those of the ICY graduations themselves, as students displayed model walls, stairways, samples of printing, hats, and dresses made in class. Enrollments continued to grow at the same time, so that by 1900 the Industrial School had actually grown bigger than the academic Institute itself.[74]

But that last statistic hinted at one aspect of the quiet and highly civil war between principal and board which threatened the whole institution by the end of the decade. The rivalry between the "industrial education" associated with Booker T. Washington and the academic demands of the "talented tenth" later championed by W. E. B. Du Bois is one of the best-known stories in all of Afro-American history. In purely educational terms, stripped of the other attitudes represented by the two men, there was no incompatibility between their approaches: blacks needed to enter both "the common occupations" and the professions, and required the schooling appropriate to each. But it was hard to separate the purely educational from the other positions taken by Washington in the 1890s, when Du Bois was neither yet the public figure nor the militant he later became. It was not strictly necessary that the gospel of industrial education be tinged with a kind of anti-intellectualism, but in the competition for white dollars and attention it was politically inevitable. An emphasis on the ordinary occupations need not imply that those were all that blacks could hope for, but in the racist atmosphere of the 1890s that too was inevitable. Washington's version of the gospel, based on his long experience in an increasingly restrictive South, was also bound up with ideas of thrift, self-help, and practicality, the avoidance of politics and protest, and deference to white philanthropists. It would be hard to imagine a message more appealing to Philadelphia's Quakers or one which on several key points clashed more directly with Fanny Jackson Coppin's proud vision of the mission of the Institute for Colored Youth.

The board and the principal agreed on several points. Both believed in building character through work, and the Industrial School had rules about promptness, good order, respect, and cleanliness as strict as those in the academic department. There could be no disagreement about the need to learn trades. And in her eagerness to sell the still ill-defined industrial education idea in the 1880s Jackson Coppin had herself sent messages that were easily twisted into whatever the listener wanted to hear: the *Public Ledger*, in 1881, agreeing that "education is the one answer" to poverty and crime, also noted that "the marked distaste of . . . school boys to be skilled artisans and mechanics is one of the worst signs of the times. . . ." But however she believed in extending the mission of the ICY to help ordinary working people, Jackson Coppin had hoped to upgrade industrial education rather than compromise academic: in a speech at the Chicago World's Fair in 1893 she argued that educated black women "wanted to know how to calculate an eclipse, to know that Hesiod and Livy thought; we wished to know the best thoughts of the best minds that lived with us."[75]

The Quakers had once shared that vision. Historians differ about how much racial condescension marked the early years of Fanny Jackson Coppin's tenure at the Institute. But much of the failure to understand black aspirations was not so much racist as simply cultural. The insularity of the Society of Friends, their objections to music and art, their distrust of the power of language and the uses of power all put them out of sympathy with what the staff at the ICY believed in. Back in 1874, in the course of opposing the extension of language study, the managers had warned the principal that "a fine voice and a free manner of speaking often captivates the popular ear," but "a political life is far from desirable on many accounts, and is often corrupting to those who engage in it." This was not welcome advice during the era of Reconstruction, when Afro-Americans were excited about entering politics for the first time, but it was consistent with what Quakers told their own children. And at the same time they entertained no apparent doubts about the sheer intellectual power of young Afro-Americans. They had presided over the introduction of Greek into the curriculum, and much like Jackson Coppin herself seemed to delight in confounding visitors, especially white southerners, with demonstrations of the superior mathematical quickness and other mental powers of the Institute's students; the principal liked purposely to choose "the darkest boys" for these exhibitions.[76]

But the Quakers of the 1890s were different from their predecessors, and at the same time less different from their white peers in elite Philadelphia. Disheartened by the failure of Reconstruction, tired of putting money into black educational and other enterprises, they were easy converts to the doctrines of Booker T. Washington. Washington came to Philadelphia several times beginning in 1894; Fanny Jackson Coppin, the city's leading black educator, never appeared on the dais with him, and unlike Frederick Douglass he never appeared at the Institute. But just after Washington's first appearance in the city the managers told the principal she must "tone down" the academic program, that it was "pitched too high" for the students. This was spelled out in 1896; the higher classical and mathematics courses must be eliminated. Next year the code words "manual training" were used for the first time; the year after that, in 1898, as the managers proclaimed, "We are more and more inclined to give a larger place to the Industrial Department," they cut the salary of Edward Bouchet, the Institute's Ph.D.-holding scientist.[77]

There is no hint, during this time, that the academic department was failing in any way, except that instead of 300 or more students it shrank, in competition with the industrial department, to about 250. In terms of credentials its staff was stronger than ever; Charlotte Bassett, daughter of the ex-principal, was a graduate of the University of Pennsylvania, and other teachers either held college degrees or took extension courses at the university and a variety of other places. Despite constant skirmishing over salaries there was little turnover, and none at all after 1894, as graduates continued to go out, as always, primarily to teach.[78]

At the same time, ironically, it seems that the industrial department had at best reached its limits. It is hard to imagine that the white instructors were inspired: given the money available to skilled workingmen, as compared certainly with part-time teachers, the old adage that "those who can, do," has always been the curse of trade-school education in the United States. The press was captivated by the notion of industrial education, and always polite about the annual exhibits. But by 1899 these were being held in the school library; the model brick walls could not have been imposing, and the whole show was heavily mixed in with watercolors, drawings, and handmade articles that had little directly to do with education in the trades.[79]

The most important of the brick walls encountered in the industrial department was in fact the one built of white racism. At the ICY as elsewhere the central problem with the idea of "industrial education" was that while it made sense in principle it was not addressed to the most important problem, which was less that blacks lacked manual skills than the fact that no one would hire them. Many hodcarriers had always learned somehow to lay bricks, and there were generally more Afro-Americans who could practice the traditional trades for them, with or without school certificates. There is no evidence that ICY graduates were any more successful than others in finding work. Perhaps as a sign of the limited education and experience they got, none of them in more than ten years of "certification" was hired at the Institute itself, in strong contrast to the academic department, where all but Bouchet were loyal alumni. The principal hoped that the training "would be of great service . . . to them in their homes."[80]

Increasingly barred from the older trades, never admitted into the new blue-collar industrial army, the city's blacks were also barred from the even newer ranks of white-collar sales clerks, bureaucrats, secretaries, and phone operators. The most telling statistic is that despite the fact that typing and shorthand could indeed be mastered in the classroom, and certainly in three years of evening coursework, as of 1896 only one of 90 graduates had been hired anywhere. Outside of the public education system and government service, virtually no whites, including the members of the ICY's own board, several of whom had firms or offices of their own, would take Afro-Americans in jobs that involved literate skills.[81]

What the board somehow concluded from all of this was that the Institute's academic program be downgraded and that not less but more "industrial education" was required. Events moved swiftly after the turn of the century. Fanny Jackson Coppin's resignation was secretly announced at a board meeting in 1901; her biographer believes that she was fired. Hugh Browne, a disciple of Booker T. Washington, was hired to replace her, and promptly announced the "suspension" of the academic department; the teachers were fired in 1902, with Edward Bouchet denied the usual courtesy of three months' salary. The black community of Philadelphia responded by in effect boycotting the Institute; enrollments fell off sharply during 1902, and first several courses, then the entire school had to be suspended.[82]

The final step was taken in 1903. Unhappy with the crime-ridden location at 12th and Bainbridge, as half a century before their predecessors had been with Seventh and Lombard, evidently tired of their larger involvement with the city's Afro-Americans, the board of managers bought a property in rural Cheyney, Pennsylvania, 25 miles out of the city. Hugh Browne would have a chance there to implement a new program, still designed specifically to train teachers, but stressing less the "school learning" than "the mechanical arts and . . . agriculture" specified in the original Humphreys will of 1832. As Fanny Jackson Coppin sailed for Africa to do missionary work with her husband, the Quakers after nearly three generations in the city prepared to move her old school back to the farm.[83]

The effective death of the Institute for Colored Youth was obviously a blow to the black community. But the loss was not so immediately important as it would have been earlier, as the educational patterns and prospects for Afro-Americans had already been set by the turn of the century.

There was no shortage of places, private or public, for those who wanted industrial education. In 1903 the ICY turned over its remaining pupils to the Reverend Matthew Anderson's newly formed and, within the constraints set by the employment situation, successful Berean Manual Training Institute. That same year the Reverend L. G. Jordan opened the Pennsylvania Institute for Domestic Science, specifically to "lessen the miseries of this nation of dyspeptics" while at the same time helping to "elevate the colored help to a higher plane" by teaching them French cookery. The regular public manual training schools had long since been opened by then.[84]

Within the public system Roberts Vaux had lost much of its appeal. During 1890 Dora Cole, longtime assistant principal, had quit to take a job as clerk in the government pension office, and Julia Jones, the primary principal, left to head her own school in Kansas City. Jacob White, Jr., whose educational career lasted almost as long as Fanny Jackson Coppin's, retired finally in 1896. Otherwise things continued much as before. The year after White's retirement, Henrietta Farrelly, the new principal at Vaux, introduced a special Parents' Night to help get them involved in the battle against absenteeism. School transfers remained always difficult, never quite impossible, for Afro-American youngsters. In 1890 a group of Germantown property owners, led by General Louis Wagner, long considered a special "friend of the race," successfully blocked construction of a much needed black school in their neighborhood. And in 1899 Garrison B. Trusty, principal of what was still called the "Number 10 Grammar and Primary Colored School," eighteen years after legal deseg-regation, joined with other black teachers and parents to form the "Eureka Educational and Charitable Association" to help find clothes for children unable to come to class in cold weather.[85]

Whatever the problems with the system, by the time that Du Bois surveyed the Seventh Ward he found that the amount of total illiteracy had been cut to a little over 12 percent, a truly striking improvement over the figures from forty years before. As ever, the key to learning was the appetite for it, and many had always picked up the ability to read, write, and figure from parents, friends, and other informal mentors. But the role of free public education is undeniable. Night school was an important part of the system in Philadelphia, and working adults, hundreds in any given term, had gone after hours to Forten, Catto, and other available schools, often with immigrant neighbors, when their children were still separated. More than any other set of mass statistics relating to blacks in Philadelphia, the literacy figures show an undeniable progressive trend, with total inability concentrated in the oldest generation, and very rare among the young.[86]

There were still problems. The Reverend C. A. Tindley, presiding elder of the AME's Philadelphia district, born a slave in Maryland, had like so many of his generation painfully taught himself to read, and was severely impatient with those who sometimes wasted their own chances, so much better than his own. Tindley, at a graduation ceremony in 1899, complained:

> I see two public schools—one for white, the other for colored children. When the bells ring, the white children run towards their institution of learning, the black children run from theirs and scamper off into the woods. Would to God I may live to see my people running towards the light.[87]

The explanation for the apparent paradox, a hunger for learning among many combined with high rates of absenteeism and dropping out among others, goes beyond the issues of poverty and segregation. Literacy was perhaps its own reward, and for many a badge of racial progress as well. But school itself was usually overcrowded and dirty, full of alien rules and sometimes hostile people. The need to sit still, take turns, hold your water, mind the teacher, and listen for the bell has always been hard to impose on active young people. The promise of long-term reward can make it tolerable, but once past bare literacy there was no reward for the overwhelming majority of black children. They needed no learning to serve as domestics or laborers. For educated women there were few jobs outside of a highly contested handful in teaching. The situation for young men was only marginally better; twelve years of often fruitless work trying to find jobs through the industrial department of the Institute for Colored Youth could only have nurtured a conviction, growing stronger with every year of deprivation, that education gets you nowhere—if you're black.

Only at the highest levels was it possible for what Du Bois called the "talented tenth" to defy that conclusion, and enjoy at least some rewards for climbing to the top of the educational pyramid. Part of the importance of the academic department of the ICY had been its continuous role as inspiration, with its long list of "firsts," Mapps and Patterson, Greener, Bassett, and Bouchet, together with all the graduates sent out, especially in the early years, before such great crowds of spectators. That could not be replaced entirely. But there was some compensation in the growing numbers who could make it through the Philadelphia public system.

The number of public school teachers had nearly doubled in the fifteen years before W. E. B. Du Bois's arrival, reaching 28 all told with more coming along. Thirteen years after Bustill and Venning had failed the entrance examinations, Carrie Compton and Marie Dutton graduated from the Normal School, generations before grade inflation, with scholastic averages over 90, and shortly after that Jesse Fauset led her class. Five young Afro-American women were included in the class of '99; one of them, Clara Sadler, not yet 16 years old, had her prize essay read at commencement. This flawlessly crafted discourse imagined "The World's Art Palace" open, free, to anyone who cared to visit:

> No crumbling pile is this, the world's art palace, but a structure raised in
> fair symmetry by the geniuses of all the world; the dramatist, the novelist,
> the sage, and the poet. . . ."

In less than 1300 words the essay managed to include 6 references to various nations or civilizations, 21 to the Greek and Latin classics, 5 to William Shakespeare, 1 each to the Bible, Milton, Dante, Coleridge, Scott, and Uncle Remus, together with whole lines or couplets from Chaucer, Tennyson, Bryant, and Gray.[88]

What it represents, from this distance, seems almost equally various. Certainly it was the ideal product of a classical 19th-century education, a stinging rebuke to Booker T. Washington, and a tribute to learning for its own sake. It was not nearly so certain that it would help win its author a job. But in fact it did, at first at an integrated school, with an integrated staff, and later as one of a powerfully inspiring group at the public Joseph E. Hill School, named for the longtime teacher at the Institute for Colored Youth. Despite shadows and setbacks in other areas, then, around the turn of the century the careers of young people like Sadler represented a vindication of the academic ideals pioneered by the ICY and the others who worked to open the highest levels of the public system to hopeful blacks.[89]

Chapter 6

The Learned Occupations

For many of those who, in Reverend Mr. Tindley's phrase, were "running towards the light" of ideas and education, late 19th-century Philadelphia was a natural destination. The Quaker City was a lively intellectual as well as educational center, home not only to the Institute for Colored Youth and several white professional schools but to a number of outspoken black newspapers. All this helped to swell the number of those in learned occupations which, even excluding the teachers, already discussed, and the ministers, to be discussed later, grew proportionately much faster than the population. At the time of the Civil War there had been only a single trained doctor in the Afro-American community, no educated dentists, no nurses or lawyers, no secular journalists or lecturers; by the end of the century there were in most of these catagories more educated men and women than could comfortably make a living.

The limits were set by the community they served. Unlike the entrepreneurs who had enjoyed some white patronage before falling back on black Philadelphia, the professionals and semi-professionals had to rely on the black community from the first. That community needed their services, often badly, but it was not only poor and small but often unwilling to patronize fellow Afro-Americans in novel positions of authority. The very advantages of the city made it hard to make a living, since Philadelphia as an intellectual, educational, and religious center appealed to more professionals than it could support. Lawyers and journalists had to compete with each other as well as with established whites; so did doctors, who also faced additional problems posed by illegal or unlicensed practitioners. The result for those who stayed in the city itself was then a qualified success story; many lived and worked in ways that made it misleading to include them in the "professional" category in the census, for example. But for the race as a whole there were fewer qualifications: many of those who were attracted by the bright lights, even those raised in Philadelphia itself, found that they could serve, or survive, better by moving away from it, to places where the light was needed more.

No professional group in the city had a harder time getting established than the lawyers. For many years, even decades, Philadelphia in fact produced more lawyers for export than for local use. The key to this imbalance was Reconstruction politics, the irony that once the Civil War was over, the backward South leapfrogged over the North in terms of opportunities open to the ambitious. Southern blacks won the vote state by state beginning in 1865, Pennsylvanians only with the Fifteenth Amendment in 1870. Unlike teachers, then, who went south knowing that they would find relatively primitive and badly paid situations, lawyers or would-be lawyers could go to the reconstruction states or to Washington in the hope of finding more power, prestige, or security than they could win at home. The result of this and other handicaps was that Philadelphia's lawyers remained few and isolated. One of them, John D. Lewis, had some role in guiding a kind of popular civil rights movement in the late 1870s and 1880s; otherwise, with some exceptions, his colleagues and successors were largely confined to marginal cases and the darker corners of the profession.

The first Afro-American admitted to the Pennsylvania bar, in 1866, set the pattern. J. Jaspar Wright, while not a resident, was well known in Philadelphia as the first president of the Pennsylvania Equal Rights League. While Octavius Catto, the League's secretary and his de facto successor, stayed home to wrangle over his schoolteacher's salary, Wright moved permanently to South Carolina in 1867 and was elected to that state's supreme court just three years later, an eminence reached by no black Pennsylvanian for another century. Young Theophilus Minton followed Wright to Columbia in 1869, shortly after his graduation from the Institute for Colored Youth. And even after Reconstruction was over, in the 1880s, another equally well-connected Philadelphian, W. Wilbur Still, son of the leading businessman, judged that his chances for a successful legal career were better in the Palmetto State than in his native city.[1]

The South Carolina connection was not unique. During the 1860s and 1870s, when most American lawyers did not go to law school or indeed college, a legal education usually meant apprenticeship to an established member of the bar. While there was a total lack of successful black mentors in Philadelphia, and the law schools were still unwilling to accept them, young Afro-Americans could find white lawyers in the South, some of them northern-born, who for political or idealistic reasons were willing to take them on. The best alternate route also ran south, to Washington and the Howard Law School under Dean John Mercer Langston. Especially between its founding in 1868 and 1877, when its requirements were lengthened and admissions greatly restricted,

Howard was attractive to Philadelphians and others looking for bureaucratic careers in the capital.[2]

While the census, incorrectly, listed several lawyers earlier, it was not until 1876 that the first two blacks in Philadelphia were actually admitted to the bar. The way was led by John D. Lewis, who came originally from Toronto, went to Yale Law School, and practiced three years in Boston before moving to the city; he was followed shortly by J. Howard Scott, son of the successful local insurance salesman William Scott. But Scott soon dropped his attempt at a legal career, and so Lewis for most of the fifteen years between his arrival and his death in 1891 was the only practicing Afro-American attorney in the city.[3]

He was a complicated man with an unusual career. In view of his credentials the Pennsylvania Supreme Court unanimously waived the usual residency requirements before admitting him to practice almost immediately on his arrival. As a young widower with two small daughters he soon established local roots through marriage to Mary E. Jones, the caterer's daughter. Lewis came also to play the expected role in the social and organizational activities of his adopted community, joining Dorseys and Mintons on committee, visiting with Mrs. Andrew Stevens on New York's Day, planning receptions for visiting militia companies, going to graduations at the Institute for Colored Youth, marching with the Temperance Templars. But despite tieing for twenty-fourth place in the Dorsey Collection, Lewis had political and perhaps private differences with local Afro-Americans that kept him out of the top position his profession might have earned him.[4]

The young lawyer was elected, with William Still, as a Pennsylvania delegate to the Nashville Convention of Colored Men in 1879, one of several national conferences held by black leaders during the 1870s. Most of these simply stressed the need for economic self-help and racial solidarity, political and civil rights. John Lewis, always outspoken, promised instead to raise the less popular issue of "caste within the race." More important, in an era of nearly solid Republican bloc voting he became an "independent," in practice a Democrat, as a result of disillusion with the famous compromise through which, contemporaries believed, President Rutherford B. Hayes had bought the disputed election of 1876 by abandoning black Republicans and withdrawing the last federal troops from the South. While not a wholly isolated position, this did put Lewis in a distinct minority among his peers. References to his social activities thinned out notably after the late 1870s, and his politics may have affected his legal practice.[5]

To be the only black lawyer in Philadelphia was bound to be uncomfortable in any case. While the city's Afro-Americans were often eager to go to court, they were in the early years still unused to the concept of the attorney as impersonal agent, and some of Lewis's cases had a distinctly personal and bitter flavor. He made history in 1880 when he was chosen by the Philadelphia District Attorney as the first of his race to prosecute a criminal case in the name of the Commonwealth. But the case of course pitted two more blacks against each other, in a suit for criminal libel. The dispute arose out of an election, the year before, for president of the prestigious Bethel Literary and Historical Society, in which Robert Holland had run against the journalist H. Price Williams. Holland, the plaintiff, charged that Williams had falsely accused him of having been convicted of larceny in New York City. Lewis won the case, but with it the enmity of the most popular, and scurrilous, Afro-American newpaperman in the city.[6]

He was tried himself in 1881, for allegedly overcharging a client. The plaintiffs argued that Lewis had successfully pressed a claim on the United States Pension Office on behalf of their mother, Nettie Wilburn, who was owed $780.39 as a Civil War widow, but that he had kept $130.39 for himself. Much of the testimony centered around the lawyer's allegedly grasping reputation among blacks in Philadelphia. But the leading witnesses were the Republican leaders Isaiah Wears and "Majah" James Teagle, backed by two clergymen, Josiah and his rich eccentric brother J. P. B. Eddy, not a notably generous man himself. Cross-examination revealed that J. P. B. Eddy had been convicted of forgery and Josiah tried by an ecclesiastical tribunal for "gross immorality." It was a small community, however, and that embarrassment was revenged in turn next year when the Rev. J. P. B. Eddy died. The will went to court, as noted in Chapter 4, when the old man's younger relatives unsuccessfully disputed the award of most of his estate to his brother Josiah and nephew Wears; John Lewis was the losing attorney.[7]

Whatever his politics, however, Lewis was a leader on the desegregation issue, working from his arrival in the city to repeal the "offensive statute" which called for separate schools. His aim was always to balance the community's needs. In contrast to both those who wanted more "colored" schools and those who would disband them he would preserve places like Vaux and Catto, with their all-black staffs as well as students, while insisting that new buildings be integrated from the first. The repeal of legal segregation in 1881 was just a start; he called on organizations as different as the Equal Rights League and "Bethel Lit" to monitor events at the ward level to ensure that both students and teachers be more evenly distributed through the city.[8]

Lewis's legal practice followed his principles, reportedly centering mostly on civil-rights cases. And he came to Philadelphia just in time to capitalize on a genuinely popular push toward the desegregation of public accommodations. No single piece of legislation in the period was more popular in the black community than Senator Charles Sumner's 1875 federal Civil Rights Act; the newly formed Sumner Club organized great rallies before and after passage, with Thomas J. Dorsey serving as one of the vice presidents and William as secretary. And although it is impossible to identify the lawyers in most cases, the act was followed by a rash of suits which successfully opened much of the city that had earlier been closed to its Afro-American residents.[9]

One of the most emotional cases followed the death of Henry Jones in the fall of 1875. Jones's biography reads much like those of T. J. Dorsey and Henry Minton, the other members of the city's "big three" caterers in his day: born in Virginia, he had come to Philadelphia penniless in the 1830s, working his way up from domestic service to a position of leadership in St. Thomas's and other leading organizations. A big crowd of mourners, including his widow and five children, had begun to gather in funeral procession on the afternoon of September 27 when Mrs. Jones got a note from the manager of the Mount Moriah Cemetery Association which claimed that there was no record of her ownership of the lot. The cortege had to be diverted at the last minute to Mount Lebanon, its members furious and humiliated. But Mrs. Jones was not helpless; the newspapers were strongly on her side, and at least equally important her fellow blacks, under the provisions of the new federal Civil Rights Act, had been bringing successful suits since the previous spring. She then filed one herself, and eventually won a judgment before the Pennsylvania Supreme Court; perhaps it is no coincidence that her daughter married Lewis, the civil rights lawyer. [10]

Black men and women developed a variety of tactics for dealing with discrimination throughout the period. Some were elementary: Gil Ball raised a ruckus in public when the Girard House overcharged him in 1887; Charles Johnson, in 1903, simply skulled an Irish bartender who refused him a drink. Some were more refined: Charles Taylor, told that a cup of coffee and a piece of pie would cost him a dollar, took them both, scattered toothpicks on the floor, left a dime and told the manager to sue him for the balance. The law did work, evidently; it seems no coincidence that all of these defiant stories, as well as the suits, are dated after passage of the Civil Rights Act. [11]

The testing of Philadelphia's customary segregation began in March of 1875, when a pair of "dusky damsels" drew no more than stares in the dining room of the Continental Hotel. But it was not all so easy. The next month Mr. and Mrs. Pusey A. Peer were refused admission to the Arch Street Theater, when Louisa Drew, doyenne of the celebrated Drew-Barrymore acting family, reportedly urged her manager to "get those niggers out of the line"; Mrs. Peer was then hurt in the crush. At about the same time the Reverend Alexander Cook, of Virginia, in town to hear the celebrated revivalist team of Moody and Sankey, was denied permission to stay at the Bingham House. Both the Peers and Cook sued and won, with Mrs. Peer awarded $1100; Cook, $500. [12]

Such victories had a real impact on the public treatment of Afro-Americans, at least in the North. Other cases followed: in the same month in which the Puseys were denied entrance to the Arch Street Theater, William R. Davis challenged the Booth, for keeping him out of the parquet circle; some years later he brought a parallel case in New York. For people as poor as most blacks the monetary rewards of victory ensured a continual flow of suits, and by 1880 it was reported that despite much private grumbling most public places in

Philadelphia were prepared to obey the law. The death of the Civil Rights Act just three years later, at the hands of a Republican Supreme Court, was then thought a serious betrayal, and greeted with an indignant rally in Philadelphia almost as big as those which had celebrated its passage eight years before.[13]

The clock could not be turned back at once. While the Bingham House immediately announced that it would no longer take black guests, most local establishments were more cautious, and promised to shut their doors only after specific white objections. The city's largest newspaper believed that "progressive public opinion" would no longer support exclusion, and the Commonwealth of Pennsylvania, four years after the Supreme Court's decision, passed another, milder, Civil Rights Act of its own, again banning discrimination in hotels, theaters, restaurants, railroads, and other places of public accommodation or amusement.[14]

Whether it was "progressive public opinion" or the state law that kept places open thereafter is not fully clear. But a survey taken by a "colored reporter" for the Philadelphia *Press* in 1888 suggested that things were better in the Quaker City than in New York. The reporter was uniformly denied first-class theater seats on Broadway and rooms in West Side hotels; locally there was no trouble in any restaurant or theater, and the Continental, Lafayette, and Columbia found him rooms, while only the Girard House and Bellevue turned him away, a result generally confirmed by the *Freeman* the following year.[15]

One side-effect of these developments was that, as the heyday of civil rights suits faded, John D. Lewis's legal speciality was no longer as profitable as it had been. Pennsylvania's 1887 law put the ceiling on damages at just $100, far less than plaintiffs had won under the federal statute, making the expense of a suit more risky. And it is not clear that Lewis had ever really made a living from the law in any case. In the course of defending himself during his 1881 trial for overcharging a client he had claimed a "substantial" practice, in addition to an income of $3500 from properties in Toronto and $1500 more from nine others in Philadelphia. His committment is clear; on his death ten years later he left a fund to help pay for further civil rights prosecutions. But his obituary in the *Freeman* suggested gently that an "independent fortune" had kept him from expanding his practice, or perhaps depending on it.[16]

What is clear is that the several lawyers who followed Lewis toward the end of the century had a very hard time, and that civil rights was no longer a significant item in their caseloads. In the absence of strong law a "progressive public opinion" proved a weak reed in the 1890s when conditions deteriorated in the South and elsewhere. It is perhaps symbolically important that the first losing case reported in the Dorsey Collection occurred in 1890, when an elderly potential patron at the Blue Anchor Inn failed to disprove, in the opinion of the court, that he had been seated in the kitchen only because it was the lunch hour, and crowded. A doctor writing to the New York *Age* in 1895 believed that a confident bearing was all that was needed to command service. But that confidence must often have been hard to summon. By 1897 the *Bulletin* conceded that "There is no city in the union which for many years has had a worse reputation than Philadelphia for its beastly treatment of the negro." Next year Pulitizer's *World* reported that one restaurant in the City of Brotherly Love discouraged Afro-American customers by deliberately breaking their dishes, in front of their eyes, instead of taking them back to be washed. By 1903, in New York and perhaps in Pennsylvania, a summons for civil rights violation was regarded as no more than a nuisance, or form of blackmail; usually it was enough to signal that "their patronage is not desired."[17]

It was perhaps fortunate that Theodore Minton, who returned from South Carolina in 1887, via tours in Indiana and Washington, was both the scion of a wealthy family in his own right and married to the daughter of the "richest colored man in Philadelphia." While he was clearly able and well connected, aside from the battle over his father-in-law's will in 1902 his only recorded case in the Dorsey Collection involved a state law of 1885, passed as the result of lobbying by the Society for the Protection of Children from Cruelty. The society was concerned about conditions in the city's "baby farms," places which it had located and identified by questioning inmates of the Midnight Mission, a refuge for prostitutes. While it was impossible to save many of the infants, the worst abuses might be curbed if the proprietors were licensed. Minton is recorded as helping a woman get such a license, in 1889, which would enable her to take out burial insurance on her charges, a practice which some advocates of children's rights believed was an encouragement to infanticide. As for civil rights, he was unable to prevent his own eviction from the Witherspoon Building in 1899, when fellow tenants complained about his color and his clients'.[18]

Minton was by then the dean of Afro-American lawyers in the city; for a short time after Lewis's death he had been the only one, but several others then arrived by a variety of routes. Dr. Nathan Mossell's younger brother Aaron, having started at Lincoln University, was the first to graduate from the University of Pennsylvania's law school, in 1888, and while it took him five years, he was admitted to practice in 1893. John Sparks also graduated from the university's law school; he and another black man, George Mitchell, then read law in the offices of the nationally famous municipal reformer Clinton Woodruff. Sparks first opened an office in 1896, working for a time with A. F. Murray, another Pennsylvania graduate, who had read with ex-District Attorney George Graham. When that collaboration failed he formed a partnership with Thomas Wheeler, from the Institute for Colored Youth and Howard Law School, who had spent sixteen years in South Carolina before following Minton's route home in 1897. Toward the turn of the century these five were followed by four more: G. Edward Dickerson, John C. Asbury, William Fuller, and Henry W. Bass.[19]

Wheeler and Murray did win much praise for their handling of the case of

Marion Stuyvesant in 1897. This was the first in the ominous late-century series, described earlier, in which blacks were accused of killing middle-class whites, as Stuyvesant, a janitor, was indicted for the murder of a well-known local book collector; it was a coup for his lawyers to have him released before trial. Two years later Wheeler and Sparks made history as the first two of their race to appear before the Pennsylvania Supreme Court, in a case involving an injured construction worker.[20]

But these cases were exceptional. If it had been hard for one black attorney to squeeze out a living in a city-within-a-city of perhaps 40,000 mostly impoverished black souls, it was utterly impossible for nine of them to survive even when the community expanded to an officially counted 65,000 or so. The more elite blacks hired whites for their important business, so that black lawyers mostly had to scramble for clients in the criminal courts. But while there was plenty of potential business there, few of the nine got much of it. Like their straight brothers and sisters, the richer criminal defendants, successful gamblers or prostitutes, got themselves well-connected white attorneys. The Republican party organization seems to have supplied J. F. K. Scott, in particular, to those with political connections; Scott also got some of the juicier civil cases in the Afro-American community, such as breach-of-promise suits. Some black men acted as "steerers" for confused defendants in the middle range, volunteering to find them lawyers, bail bondsmen, or other help, often hinting at the ability to fix cases for a fee. But with their own success hinging on suggested connections with authority, by definition white authority, they had no reason to steer anyone toward the city's obviously inexperienced black lawyers.[21]

The poorest criminal defendants, finally, got no counsel at all except in capital cases. But while judges did assign some of these to Mossell, Murray, Wheeler, and the others, they tended to be the simplest ones, such as infanticides. The whole system was embarrassed by these cases, in which desperate single women, usually without friends or connections, typically strangled their newborns, or drowned them in privies. Most such killings were given no newspaper coverage at all, and the defendants were either found to have been temporarily insane or given a few months in jail; this involved only the briefest of court appearances, and so the barest of fees for their lawyers.[22]

One of the problems in these court assignments was summed up in the humiliation dealt Edward Dickerson in the Cornelius Bush case of 1903. Sent to prison for attempting to murder his stepfather, Bush had then proceeded to murder his cellmate. The case was assigned to Dickerson, and looked easy enough; the *Telegraph* thought it might break the speedy trial record set the previous year, in the legal lynching of the butler William Lane. When it turned more complex, and Bush entered a plea of insanity, the young black lawyer was demoted to "associate" status, as the judge appointed an experienced white man to take over.[23]

Some of the desperate atmosphere in criminal court is shown by A. F. Murray's 1897 conviction for assaulting a cop, in open court, when accused of trying to intimidate a witness. Aaron Mossell was sued the next year by Charles Robinson, one of his own clients, who was accused of ramming an umbrella into another man's eye. Bail was set at $1000; Mossell at first took the money for the bond, itself a violation of court rules, and when the judge waived bail he was accused by Robinson's family of keeping it.[24]

There seemed, too, no way out of the circle of competition. The southern alternative was not entirely closed off, and as late as the 1890s a young graduate of the ICY won a judge's job in Florida. But the return of Minton and Wheeler was a further sign that the opportunities had mostly disappeared with Reconstruction. And in Philadelphia itself, progress measured by numbers admitted to the bar was ironic and self-limiting progress at best.[25]

The wider situation toward century's end was outlined by Josephine Bruce, widow of the Reconstruction senator from Mississippi, in an 1899 speech to the National Convention of Colored Women. "Negroes," Mrs. Bruce suggested, ". . . have entered the learned professions in disproportionate numbers, and have failed because there is no great industrial class to employ [them]." Locally the civil rights business had effectively ended by the 1890s, just at the time, ironically, that the number of lawyers began to grow. Without access to the more profitable areas of the law, unable to win white clients, few of the city's black lawyers, perhaps none, could make a professional's livelihood out of their legal practices alone. Further progress was stalled then by the unwillingness of Afro-American entrepreneurs, legal or illegal, to trust them with important business, and as with so much else by the poverty of the majority, who were simply unable to afford them.[26]

Dr. Nathan Mossell, shortly after beginning practice in 1881, was optimistic about the future of Afro-American physicians in Philadelphia. It was true, he told an interviewer for T. T. Fortune's New York *Globe*, that the city was a center of medical education and practice, with nearly 1700 white doctors, and that many of the younger ones could spend weeks in waiting for patients to call. But for the blacks the situation was brighter than for most. Well educated themselves, they were in position to take advantage of increasing education in the Afro-American community, the decline of superstition and of illegitimate or "voodoo" medicine. While some might have trouble winning acceptance from white colleagues, Mossell himself, as the first black graduate of the Medical School of the University of Pennsylvania, had been welcomed to practice at Pennsylvania Hospital, and he expected that others would follow.[27]

In fact neither the past nor the future of Afro-American doctors in the city was quite as Mossell imagined it. He himself was just then beginning a distinguished career that would last nearly half a century; tied for thirteenth in the Dorsey Collection, despite the lack of references before 1880, he would come to dominate black medical practice nearly as strongly as Fanny Jackson Coppin dominated education, and would also come to be nearly as important to the wider community in many other areas. The city's educational strength would mean that even more than lawyers Philadelphia would export Afro-American doctors, especially women. Mossell's own Frederick Douglass Clinic, later Hospital, was the first such institution in the North to be staffed wholly by blacks, an important training center not only for doctors but for nurses and pharmacists from its founding in 1895. But at the same time, like lawyers, individual mainstream or "regular" physicians found old prejudices powerful and competition strong, not only from whites and each other but from a host of irregulars whose success belied Mossell's confidence about the triumph over "superstition."[28]

In the twenty years before Mossell's 1881 interview, Philadelphia's Afro-Americans had been served by graduates of the best of universities, perhaps because only the best of universities were confident enough to admit them. Dr. David Rossell, with a degree from Heidelberg, was apparently the only educated black physician in the city between 1864 and his early death in 1871; he was succeeded by Edwin C. Howard, from Harvard. The first two to graduate from any local institution were Rebecca Cole and Caroline Still, daughter of the abolitionist and businessman, who won degrees from Women's Medical College in 1869 and 1871. Neither of these women practiced medicine with any regularity, at least until Still married the Reverend Matthew Anderson and began work in the dispensary set up in his Berean Presbyterian Church during the 1880s. But James Potter and Thomas G. Ives did set up practice in the city before Mossell, although neither they nor any of the others was able to win hospital or county medical society affiliation as he did.[29]

The real problem, however, was that while Dr. Mossell counted just 5 in 1881, the census as early as 1870 had found 11 Afro-American men and women who called themselves "physicians," in addition to 4 "doctors," 3 "medical doctors," and 4 "herb doctors," a total of 22. Some of these extra people may have practiced their various arts as effectively as Mossell and his colleagues. Regular physicians, through most of the later 19th century, were not yet able to cure most patients, and still tempted to prescribe quantities of morphine to deal with a suffering that left them professionally impotent. But the period marked a great advance in combining medicine and science; the germ theory of disease was quickly incorporated into the practice of surgery and public health, and in combination with a renewed emphasis on empirical investigation improved the quality of diagnosis. Medical school curricula were tightened at the same time; one elementary change involved longer terms and the substitution of a three- for a two-year course, reforms begun at Harvard shortly after Howard's graduation, and at the University of Pennsylvania shortly before Mossell's arrival. Armed with higher standards, leather bags full of impressive new instruments such as the stethoscope, and above all the authority of science, mainstream practitioners sought successfully to distinguish themselves from the many others who had earlier hung out their shingles with equal confidence.[30]

The two keys to their new position were educated opinion and state law, specifically the 1877 Pennsylvania statute that required a reputable medical diploma to practice in the state. But the earlier era of democratic free competition, in which essentially anyone a patient believed in could function as a doctor, did not disappear at once. The law allowed longstanding practitioners who met the other requirements—good moral character, "a sound elementary education," knowledge of anatomy, physiology, chemistry, and *materia medica*—to operate without diplomas. Many people had educated themselves, done apprenticeships, or gotten degrees from places not recognized in the mainstream; there was a real difference between those who continued to believe in schools of medicine that had lost out, simple eccentrics, and outright charlatans. The only thing they had in common was a stubborn refusal to go away.[31]

In 1913 Carl Bolivar, musing over a copy of the *Christian Recorder* nearly half a century old, noted that there were advertisements in the 1860s for "Dr. James Clark, Eclectic; Mrs. M. Bennett, herb doctor; Nathaniel I. Durham, 911 Christian Street, cupper, bleeder and leecher . . . ." The three offered quite different alternatives to potential consumers. Durham was practicing an outmoded and mildly dangerous art long past its prime. Mrs. Bennett's harmless brand of "Thomsonian" medicine had been fairly respectable and quite popular thirty years earlier, and still had important adherents. It is less certain what the word "Eclectic" advertised in the case of Dr. Clarke. Sometimes it was a label that meant simply what it suggested: a mixture combining botanic, mainstream, and other approaches. But if it meant that he had a degree from Philadelphia's Eclectic College of Medicine he was simply a fraud. The "college" was a notorious diploma mill, whose "students," black or white, paid a fee, sometimes attended a few lectures, and got a degree that looked good on the wall; as early as 1869 its "graduates" were barred from signing death certificates in the City of Baltimore.[32]

The difference made by law, opinion, and perhaps personal ethics was shown in the quite different careers of Drs. James Still and James Littleton Teagle. Both men were self-educated Afro-American doctors, but Still operated quite legally across the river in New Jersey, while Teagle had to flee from a conviction in Philadelphia.

The Still family was equally remarkable on either side of the Delaware. James, one of the seventeen siblings of the abolitionist William, enjoyed a success that matched his brother's. The two men shared an utter lack of formal schooling, but James stayed on the farm, picked up herbal medicine from books, and combining it with local tradition and his own gift for healing won a reputation as "the cancer doctor" that spread beyond South Jersey. The year before his death in 1882 the state moved to require a formal diploma; his friends, including one well-known white cleric from New York, managed to win an exception for all who had practiced in the same locality for twenty or more years. His elder son, James C., born in 1840, graduated from Harvard in 1871 and, after marrying Elizabeth Handy of Philadelphia, set up a practice in Boston. The other son, Joseph, born in 1842, enjoyed a more complicated career. The only one of his five siblings to resist formal schooling, he followed his uncle William to Philadelphia, originally to study art. But as with so many of his peers young Joseph was caught up in the wanderlust created by Civil War, staying for awhile in Cuba and then Charleston before returning to the city to apply to Jefferson Medical College. Rejected on account of his color, he took a job as college janitor, reportedly read the books, did anatomical sketches and dissections, and went back to inherit his father's practice near Mount Holly. While the authorities made no trouble about the fact that he had no license, Joseph added a drugstore and a $20,000 house to the old office and farm, drove a carriage and lived in high style until, after reportedly voting Democratic in 1892, he went on to die drunk and broke.[33]

The law was stricter in the big city where J. Littleton Teagle set up shop. Born a slave about 1812, Teagle migrated to Philadelphia and went into business as a herbalist and fortune-teller, successfully enough to be recalled, years later, as "the most notorious and most wealthy 'voodoo' ever . . . in the state." Jailed in 1880, the doctor fled the city for West Chester after transferring all of his money to his wife's name. Catherine Teagle died in 1888, leaving a will which specified a $1000 coffin to be modeled exactly on the one which held Samuel G. Tilden, late Governor of New York and onetime Democratic presidential candidate; otherwise bequests went to Wilberforce and Lincoln universities and the Home for Aged and Infirm Colored Persons. These terms were disputed, in a bizzarre footnote, by Robert Clayton, a scapegrace graduate of the Institute for Colored Youth who claimed to be her son until doctors somehow determined, on exhumation, that she had died childless. Although the sum involved was reported, with presumably no more than the usual accuracy, as up to $100,000, Dr. Teagle himself was left only a modest annuity, and lived quietly until killed by a freight train while walking the tracks in the summer of 1891.[34]

Some unlicensed doctors, often fresh from the rural South, were simply unaware that they were outside of the law until they innocently signed death certificates; caught and reprimanded by the coroner, they were rarely punished. But most of them knew enough to combine medicine with other ways of taking money from the unwary. When the Baptist pastor L. G. Jordan told a visiting clergymen's convention in 1903 that "the voodoo doctor, the fortune-teller, and the policy shop keeper have too great a hold on all the people in this community," he was making often unneeded distinctions. What the papers and others loosely called "voodoo" was often no more than unorthodox medicine of several kinds. But however harmless the treatment its effectiveness basically depended on a client's simple faith in the authority of the practitioner, and practitioners found it easy to exploit that faith by claiming special powers that went beyond curing warts or tuberculosis.[35]

Those who got in trouble with the law were uniformly brought in by clients who had lost the faith. William Mackerow charged a modest $3 a bottle— perhaps two or three days' pay—for restoring lost youth and hair, but it took more for him to align nine pins in a way that would restore a lost lover. "Professor" David Bruce was willing to bargain, but wanted $10 for a lucky stone, and about $1 for tips on the daily policy numbers. Lizzie Sydnay got $15 for ridding the stomach of harmful snakes and centipedes, but Joseph Hill extorted fees ranging from $125 to $175 from people who wanted relatives cured of blindness or paralysis; the recipe for restoring sight reportedly involved splitting a chicken and placing the two halves on the eye sockets.[36]

The difference between men and women that Nathan Mossell would recognize as colleagues and "doctors" of this kind was clear to more than the licensed physicians themselves. Only one of those outside the mainstream, Edwin Still, a Philadelphian of the Mt. Holly Still clan, was accepted in local black society. Still, who kept offices on both sides of the river, advertised that through "Electricity and Will Power" he could cure "Paralysis, Trance, Epilepsy, Hysteria, Vertigo" and several other ills including pimples, with "no charges for failures, because there are none." William Dorsey, carrying on an old family feud in the margins, branded him "a fraud," but Still was one of the two main sponsors of one of the elite Quaker City Club's events in 1898. Usually, in contrast to the regular doctors, the names of the unorthodox do not appear on the lists of those at the political rallies, Odd Fellows Balls, or church events that make up much of the Dorsey Collection. But the regulars must have found this little comfort.[37]

Only three of the men who practiced before the 1890s stand out from the others: E. C. Howard, Mossell, and Charles Shadd, a Harvard and Howard graduate whose chronic alcoholism once led to an arrest at the insistence of his own father. The rest remain indistinct: unlike their illicit competitors their names did appear on the boards and occasions where respectability was important, but none of them took a position of leadership. Several, like Shadd, were graduates of the Howard Medical School, which whites considered inferior and so further reason to exclude them from genuinely collegial relations and the hospitals. The blacks at the upper end of the income scale went to white doctors; at the lower end, either to the charity wards of the hospitals or to the ecletics, herb doctors, and fortune-tellers. Most galling perhaps was that the unorthodox, by most accounts, attracted a number of white believers, much like the "conjure men" in the rural South, while the regulars were almost entirely shut out of white patronage. Morally unable to promise much more than their still limited profession could produce, they were hopelessly disadvantaged in competition with others whose imaginations were not so restrained.[38]

The result as with lawyers was real ecomomic strain. Even the Harvard-educated Dr. Howard, a throat specialist, seems to have had trouble maintaining a practice. Howard was a "handsome" and convivial bachelor, president of the Music Association at St. Thomas's, who appeared often at the community's social events, sometimes leading the figure at a dance. But it is hard to tell how he met expenses. Together with Dr. Henry Longfellow he ran successfully for a position on the Seventh Sectional school board in 1888; he was consistently opposed by school reformers, perhaps for tight adherence to the Republican party line, perhaps because of his interest, with other board members, in the extralegal perquisites of the unpaid office. The *Freeman* suggested gently that he had "ample leisure" to devote to politics. And perhaps to other pursuits as well: fortunately his life did not revolve around his purely professional resources, and in the summer of 1891 he was seen sailing for Paris "together with" Madame Roberts, the presumably wealthy widow of an ex-President of Liberia.[39]

Nathan Mossell, like his brother Aaron, was sued by his clients at least twice, and the resulting cases offer some glimpses into his practice and finances. In 1896 he lost a suit in which Charles Key accused him of keeping $75 of a $100 check he had cashed on Key's behalf; Mossell argued unsuccessfully that the amount was a fee for operating on Key's brother-in-law, who had left town. Much more revealing was the case in which Ella C. Brown, a 23-year-old domestic, accused him of attempting an abortion on her.[40]

The undisputed facts were that Brown had come to the doctor's Lombard Street office, weak and tired, and told him that she was "in trouble." He had answered that "this was not in his line of business, but because I was a poor girl and young he would do it"; the fee would be $35. After several internal probings or operations Mossell then recommended that she go to the City Hospital, where she had a premature infant. At that point the accounts differed; Mossell, at a preliminary hearing, stated that he had been treating her for a fibroid tumor, and had sent her to the hospital as soon as he realized that her real complaint was pregnancy.[41]

Several white doctors rallied to him. Abortion was then illegal, and had been since 1861, but older physicians remembered when it was commonly acceptable, and everyone was familiar with the results of the legal ban. Prosecutions then averaged six or eight a year, almost always initiated when a woman had either died or suffered damage to her reproductive system at the hands of an unlicensed practitioner. Given the high incidence of prostitution in black Philadelphia, and the disastrous economic consequences of motherhood to domestics like Ella Brown, whether or not it was in their "line of business" the city's licensed as well as unlicensed Afro-Americans must often have been asked for abortions. After testimony that indicated that fibroid tumors might indeed be mistaken for "delicacy," and noting that Brown, having been sent to the hospital by Mossell himself, was then suffering from nothing more than exhaustion, the judge dismissed her complaint.[42]

Whatever the social significance of the case its economic implications are clear. Mossell's bail had been set at $3000, of which only a fraction had to be given to a bondsman. The doctor evidently could not come up with the money, which was advanced instead by the politician and saloonkeeper Gil Ball. Although it was testified that Mossell had "a large and lucrative practice," neither he nor any other mainstream black doctor could match the incomes earned by the unorthodox Stills and Teagles.[43]

But Nathan Mossell's standing in the Afro-American community was not measured in dollars. Born in Canada in 1856, Mossell had come to town in 1873, and shortly entered Lincoln University to earn a bachelor's degree. When next admitted to the University of Pennsylvania's Medical School, one later account suggests, he was surrounded for a time by a screen in the lecture hall, lest the sight of him upset his classmates; when he graduated, three years after, with highest honors, the ceremonies were interrupted by an unusual and prolonged applause. The fact that along the way he had turned down scholarship money from the American Colonization Society, on account of its racist associations, was an indication of his views and later career. The fact that he was the first of his race to graduate from any department of the city's leading university was even more significant to black Philadelphia. And his connection was further solidified by marriage in the 1880s to Gertrude Bustill, daughter of a prominent family, author, reporter, and teacher, graduate of the ICY and Roberts Vaux school.[44]

Lincoln University, located in Oxford, Pennsylvania, played a role among elite Philadelphians second only to the Institute for Colored Youth. In 1878, about the time when Mossell was an undergraduate, Princeton's legendary President Joshua M'Cosh told the students that they equaled any at his own institution or at Queen's College, Ireland, where he had recently visited. Its loyal all-male alumni included some of the city's most distinguished blacks: Wilbur and Robert Still, the Mossell brothers, the politician Stephen Gipson, Dr. James Potter, newspaperman Andrew Jones, and in keeping with its Presbyterian connection several ministers of the Gospel. Lincoln's six professors were all white, however, mostly Princeton graduates. The Philadelphia alumni tried to challenge the color line in 1886 by demanding that an empty chair in mathematics be filled with one of their own; the proposal was vetoed by more conservative southerners, afraid of losing rich white support. But Nathan Mossell was appointed chairman of a committee to push the matter, in 1888, and two years later the alumni stepped up their demands. They resolved not only in favor of federal aid to education, a matter then before Congress, and the hiring of the Reverend Francis Grimke, son-in-law of James Forten, as professor of psychology, but—rightly anticipating that they would be blocked by the trustees—proposed election of William Wilbur Still '74 as a member of the board.[45]

Mossell's role among Lincoln alumni was only a part of his growing leadership in matters involving race. During the series of anti-lynching meetings which marked the fearful 1890s he stood next to the city's traditional clerical spokesmen, serving at the end of the decade as chair of the Afro-American League's advisory board. And in 1906 he seized the lead himself. That spring, over the objections of a number of clergymen of both races, Thomas Dixon's incendiary play *The Clansman,* precursor to the movie *Birth of a Nation,* opened in Philadelphia. While the newspapers gave it mixed reviews, both as racial commentary and as melodrama, it was an enormous popular success, and the manager of the Walnut Street Theater proposed to bring it back in the fall. With still fresh memories of the fiery lynching in nearby Wilmington, the Afro-American community had had enough. Dr. Mossell led a call to protest: on opening night, October 22, two thousand blacks converged peacefully in the street outside the theater, joined by one thousand largely curious whites. While several inside threw eggs at the stage, Mossell was called, by the director of public safety, to help quell what was becoming a riot outside. The next day the ministers stepped aside to let him be spokesman in a meeting with Mayor Weaver, at which the mayor reluctantly agreed to follow the lead of several southern cities and cancel the run.[46]

But while he exercised it in several areas, Nathan Mossell's authority was based above all on his role in founding and running the Frederick Douglass Hospital. By the early 1890s it was clear that the Afro-American community required some kind of medical facility of its own. The need was threefold, given the death rate in the city, the shortage all over the country of places in which to train nurses and other personnel, and the refusal of white hospitals to accept Mossell's colleagues as affiliated doctors. Mossell's determination was fueled by a long visit to London, where he was able to further his own specialized training. He and Gertrude began to raise money, mostly among blacks, soon after his return; even the notoriously tight-fisted Colonel John McKee gave $5, on condition that the gift remain a secret. The building actually opened in 1895, but was so heavily mortgaged that fundraising continued for some years, reaching a peak in an 1897 concert and ball at the Academy of Music which featured a poetry reading by Paul Lawrence Dunbar and the presentation of a bust by Edmonia Lewis.[47]

The board was dominated by the community's leading blacks; Jacob White, Jr., following retirement from Vaux, served as chairman. This was in itself a break with tradition; rich white supporters usually took the lead in not only funding but chairing black philanthropies. But at Douglass they were a minority, and took no position higher than treasurer. There was in any case no doubt as to who was in charge, as Mossell's crisp notes to the chair were more nearly orders than requests. The hospital at 1512 Lombard was just a block from the Mossells' own home, and within two years was treating over one thousand patients annually. Susan Patterson, the matron, was the first Afro-American nurse to graduate from the Philadelphia City Hospital, and Douglass soon won an annual state subsidy of $5000 to train its own. [48]

The hospital not only graduated three or four nurses each year, about half of them from out of state, but also served as a training ground for pharmacists and doctors. A dozen physicians, and one dentist, were listed as attending staff by 1900. While Mossell had had to use white lawyers in his own 1890 criminal case, Douglass employed his brother Aaron as solicitor on its letterhead, and gave further legal business to other black attorneys. And partly because of its leadership, the 1890s witnessed a great surge in the number of trained Afro-American health professionals of several kinds. [49]

Women's Medical College continued to be an important resource; if competition was hard in the city, there were many other places that needed its graduates more. During the 1890s Bishop Tanner's daughter Hattie Tanner Dillon, settling in Tuskegee, became the first woman of any race admitted to practice in the state of Alabama; Mrs. L. Hughes-Brown won the same honor in both North and South Carolina. The string of distinctions was continued in 1897 by Clizo Ann Grier, first in Georgia. Grier, a native of Atlanta, had watched white doctors in her hometown reaping the rewards of "accouchements" at which black midwives were in charge, and simply decided, "Why should I not get the fees for myself?" [50]

The story of Lulu Fleming, in 1899, was a sobering reminder that opportunity was not the whole of the Philadelphia story. Fleming, originally from Florida, was educated at Woman's Medical before leaving as a missionary to the Congo. When stricken with a fatal sleeping sickness at 35 she asked to come back to the city and die. The newspapers were impressed with her loyalty to her race, her church, and her adopted home. But while accepted as the only Afro-American member of the Baptist Temple, and the only such patient at the hospital the Temple maintained, acceptance ended with her death in July. Although the church owned her lot in a cemetery managed by the Knights of Pythias, the little cortege was turned away at the last minute and sent off to Merion. A generation after the parallel experience of Henry Jones, there was this time no strong civil rights act and no legal recourse; the *Tribune* could only rail at the fact that in Philadelphia "citizenship and religion count for nothing— race everything." [51]

But by that time it was hard to discourage young black doctors and pharmacists. Julia Hughes, at Douglass, was one of just two practicing women druggists in the city. William H. Warrick, son of the barber, one of the first to graduate from both the undergraduate and medical schools of the University of Pennsylvania, thought for a time that he might avoid competition by moving west. He decided however to stay in Germantown, and did well enough to buy a $23,000 house and maintain a carriage. While Warrick was unusual in his ability to beat white competitors in practice, others had little trouble in winning strictly scholastic honors: Benjamin Sayres, at the university's dental school, finished fourth in a class of 89 men; John Allen McFall, working for a doctorate at the Philadelphia College of Pharmacy, was one of seven, out of 127, to win an "excellent" distinction in his first examinations. Above all Robert Abele, an ICY graduate from an old local family, set a state record on the qualifying physicians' examination of 1895. Once past the point where only merit counted, however, he was denied any positions at the mainstream hospitals, and took a job on the staff of Hahnemann, whose osteopathic founders were perhaps less prejudiced.[52]

It was never easy to make a living, and in 1903 one young man, a licensed physician in the state of West Virginia, was found working locally as a bellhop at the Hotel Walton, hoping to earn enough money to get married. The great majority of blacks still dealt either with whites or with irregulars. Contemporary doctors could in any case do little about the appalling death statistics, concentrated especially among infants, which cut short black lives in Philadelphia as in other major cities. The problems were economic and municipal: poverty, bad water, and poor sanitation generally. The Afro-American diagnosis, rejecting the argument about "constitutional weakness," was quite correct that the need was for more work and more washing. Improvements in public health would make a greater difference than individual doctoring, and in this sense the labor gangs working on Philadelphia's reservoirs and filtration system were doing more for longevity than most of the medical establishment.[53]

But within these and other limits the city was becoming a real center of black as well as white medical education and practice. The seal was set with Henry Minton's establishment of Mercy Hospital in 1907. Minton, first of his race at Phillips Exeter Academy, where he was both an athlete and editor of the literary magazine, had been on the Douglass staff as a pharmacist, and his father the lawyer T. J. was on the board. It seems it was the reluctant legacy of his grandfather, Colonel McKee, which after 1902 gave him the means to get his own medical degree, and afterward the courage to lead several young colleagues in what was in effect a revolt against the imperious Nathan Mossell. A dozen years earlier there had been no black hospital in the northern states; to have two in the city of Philadelphia was not easy on either, but it was an ironically healthy sign of growing pains.[54]

But while medicine was the most prestigious of the learned occupations in Philadelphia, journalism was the biggest and liveliest. If progress in literacy during the period was not matched by equal progress in job opportunities, it did create a growing class of readers, and writers, all across black America. And while only a few authors could make a living through the word, the business of writing was sometimes a source of income and always an important means of expression. This was especially true for women, and perhaps nothing more distinguished black Philadelphia, considered as a small city-within-a-city, than the number and ability of its learned women, as celebrated by Gertrude Bustill Mossell.

Among the younger generation, those who came of age after the Civil War, Mossell was as important a journalist as her husband was a doctor. Born to one of the city's leading families in 1856, educated in its leading schools, young Gertrude Bustill caught the attention of Bishop Tanner when she was still a student at Vaux. With his encouragement she began contributing early to the *A.M.E. Review* and the *Christian Recorder,* and went on to write for several papers, in and out of Philadelphia, as well as for the magazines *Our Women and Children* and *The Ladies' Home Journal.* Active in community affairs and as reporter, poet, and later author of a children's novel, most important she was both exemplar and historian of *The Work of the Afro-American Women,* first published in 1894.[55]

That work did not always go easily, and there was one incident, relatively early in her long career, that illustrates some of the special vulnerabilities of a black woman in a largely white male profession. Beginning in the 1870s, some of the local dailies began to employ Afro-Americans to cover events in their own community; Bustill Mossell was one of the most successful contributors in the *Press, Times,* and *Inquirer.* But one piece for the *Times,* which she wrote only in draft, created enough of a stir that she felt compelled to explain and apologize.

The apology was inspired by one of the rare pieces in which a Philadelphia paper treated locally respectable blacks in clearly offensive fashion, in a review of what was billed in 1886 as the first amateur Afro-American production of Gilbert and Sullivan's *Mikado.* A benefit for the Church of the Crucifixion, the performance packed Horticultural Hall with some 1500 spectators, what the writer called a "kaleidoscopic congregation" of black and white together. He gave the company the backhanded compliment of a mixed review instead of the indiscriminate praise usually dealt to nonprofessionals; the music was judged better than the acting. But the insistent emphasis on the physical, on this one's baggy tights and that one's careless makeup, above all the almost compulsive attention paid to the complexions of audience and cast alike—"black," "mulatto," and "quadroon"—made the whole piece obviously obnoxious.[56]

The apology followed in Bustill Mossell's regular column in the weekly New York *Freeman.* Journalism for her was a way of learning the writer's craft, and after that of airing matters "most creditable to my race." But for both white editors and herself it was first a means of making money; what was printed was simply what would sell. The objectionable article had been rewritten by a colleague and submitted over her objection. She had warned that her community was sensitive to the issue of skin color, but she could not veto the final product.[57]

The incident remained isolated, and the apology was in effect accepted; however powerless in a white newsroom, Bustill Mossell was as securely a member of the national Afro-American intelligentsia as of the local community. Her contributions to the nationally circulated *A.M.E. Review,* the Richmond *Rankin Institute,* the Indianapolis *Freeman,* as well as the New York *Freeman* and *Age* assured her a wide audience. And the variety of her writings ensured that she would touch on most of the issues and reflect most of the moods that affected her race.

One poem, written in 1889, celebrated a famous incident which had occurred in Georgia twenty-one years before, when a group of schoolchildren was asked by General O. O. Howard, Jr., what message he should bring back north about them. The answer, provided by 13-year-old Richard R. Wright, himself a leading Philadelphian in later years, was "Tell the North That We Are Rising":

> Tell the North that we are rising
> Tell this truth throughout the land
> Tell the North that we are rising
> Rising at our God's command.[58]

But within months the triumphant note in this piece was countered by a different one, prompted by yet another national magazine article which suggested "extermination" as the eventual fate of the country's nearly eight million Afro-Americans. Mrs. Mossell's indignation, even fury, led her so far as to question the Christian commitment which inspired her and so many of her peers: given the hypocrisy of professed white "Christians" in the United States, "The black man says give me Mohammedanism, paganism, or any other ism but the one that leads to this result."[59]

But her characteristic voice was not political but feminist, and well expressed in her "Woman's Department" columns in the *Freeman.* Some of these sounded such traditional themes as the need for thrift, for black domestics to imitate Irish in saving money for an eventual marriage. Many championed chastity, and readers joined an especially lively debate about why so many Afro-American women defied the usual standards of sexual modesty: ". . . and who is bringing them down?" Some laid the blame on white men, others on black mothers, black men, and the young women themselves. In Bustill Mossell's own view the culprits were ignorance and lack of communication: "Don't be afraid to speak to your daughter about such matters as are possibly discussed by . . . her schoolmates."[60]

But her favorite subject was "the value of woman's work." She was not entirely sure whether women needed special protective legislation in the work force, an issue that would continue to divide feminists for generations. But she did know that "to claim that women were never intended to be breadwinners, while at the same time it must be admitted that all over the world she [sic] furnishes one-half the workers in this line, seems to cast a reflection on somebody's management." Both seven years a schoolteacher and the mother of two children, she knew how hard it was to handle two careers: it might be possible to write, say, a cookbook on one knee while balancing a six-week-old infant on the other, but the act was no longer possible when the child reached six months. And she wanted to hear no more about the century's most famous author and mother: "Mrs. Harriet Beecher Stowe may have written *Uncle Tom's Cabin* in the midst of household duties, but there has been but one Mrs. Stowe, and, also, she has not surpassed *Uncle Tom's Cabin.*"[61]

Bustill Mossell's concern reflects the paradoxical situation of educated Afro-American women, an exaggeration of the patterns found among both women and blacks generally. All women, in the first place, tended to stay in school longer than men during the late 19th century, but the gap between the sexes was much greater among blacks, although for different reasons. White boys often dropped out early to take relatively good jobs in the trades and factories, while young women needed more education for the literate skills to work in stores and offices as sales clerks, typists, and the like. But this does not explain why the majority of ICY graduates, in some years the entire senior class, was female. Young black men could not get good blue-collar jobs; they simply quit when it became clear that they had no vocation that required grammar or high school. Young black women had even less chance to win good jobs, but they tended to stay the course because barring prolonged professional training their only hope outside of domestic work was schoolteaching, which required a degree.[62]

In the second place, while more blacks than whites of both sexes were employed in the money economy, the gap between women was especially marked, even though black women were squeezed into so few possible jobs; in 1900 only 4 percent of married white women were officially counted in the national labor force, as opposed to 25 percent of blacks, the latter figure much higher in urban areas. For most this was simple necessity, but for the more educated there were both special opportunities and special problems. On the one hand, unlike pioneering white doctors such as Elizabeth Blackwell, who had to make the deliberate decision to remain celibate, blacks such as Hattie Tanner Johnson, Lucy Hughes Brown, and Caroline Still Anderson seem to have had little trouble combining medicine and marriage. On the other hand, at a time when medicine was virtually the only advanced profession open, many could not make it that far. And for the large class of literate women who wanted to exercise their educations in some way besides teaching, Gertrude Bustill Mossell was both an example and champion.[63]

In Philadelphia she was not alone. Virtually all the privileged young women of her generation had met Fanny Jackson Coppin, Grace Mapps, Sarah Douglass, or Caroline LeCount in the classroom, and newcomers to the community met them in church, at fairs, in concerts, and sometimes at political rallies. An especial inspiration to Bustill Mossell, most heavily featured in her book on Afro-American women, was Frances Ellen Watkins Harper, who although bypassed by the 1880 census is tied for eleventh place in the Dorsey Collection.[64]

Mrs. Harper, born in Baltimore of free parents in 1825, became the dean of the city's Afro-American career women on the death of Sarah Douglass in 1882. She had come to Pennsylvania first as a schoolteacher, in 1851, but soon decided to give up the classroom for a wider public career fighting slavery. William Still, a friend of her father's, took her into his household and introduced her into the abolitionist network, where her poetry and especially her platform oratory won her an important place; more than thirty years later T. T. Fortune ranked her with Fanny Jackson Coppin as one of the two most powerful black women speakers in the country. The Pennsylvania Anti-slavery Society, Still's employers, hired her as an agent for a time, but mostly she organized her own lecture tours. Shortly after Abraham Lincoln's election, in 1860, she quit touring to marry Fenton Harper, an often struggling Ohio farmer, and spent most of the war years quietly near Columbus. The quiet ended with Harper's death in 1864. Although she had bought the farm with her own money, under Ohio law she was responsible for his personal debts, and the experience of being turned out, penniless and nearly 40 with a small daughter to support, helped convert her to a new cause, women's rights.[65]

Several new causes in fact engaged her after the war: peace, the women's movement, and finally temperance. But her immediate focus was Reconstruction in the South. After moving from Ohio back to Philadelphia and the Stills, during the late 1860s she was continually touring the ex-slave states. While several black women from the city went south to teach, she, like the men, went to rouse the freemen politically, living off lecture fees and sales of her poetry. She did well enough to be able to buy a house, in 1870, at 1006 Bainbridge Street, less than a block from the Institute for Colored Youth and little more than around the corner from Fanny Jackson.

Harper may have earned something for a time as assistant superintendent of a YMCA Sunday school, and beginning in the late 1880s as head of the Negro Section of the Women's Christian Temperance Union. But both Bustill Mossell and her most recent biographer believe that she supported herself essentially from her writings and speaking—the only Afro-American to do so until Langston Hughes in the 20th century. Her several volumes of poetry dealt mostly with slavery and women, as seen through the reigning religious sentimentality of the age; one epic narrative, *Moses*, went through thirty-one editions in ten years. *Sketches of Southern Life*, based on her own tours, ran through four editions, and a Philadelphia publisher brought out a novel, *Iola*

LeRoy, or The Shadows Uplifted, which in 1892 anticipated one of Hughes's favorite themes in telling the story of a woman, able to pass for white, who discovers and then deliberately chooses a black identity.[66]

But despite her national reputation, Harper remained a Philadelphian. Her daughter Mary, who stayed with her mother until her death in 1911, graduated from the city's National School of Elocution and Oratory in 1884, in order to follow her along the lecture circuit. Like Gertrude Mossell, Mrs. Harper contributed to the *A.M.E. Review* and the *Tribune* as well as other black and white journals across the country. Her local interests included Bethel's Mite Missionary Society—although she was herself a Unitarian—the Home for Aged and Infirm Colored Persons, and St. Michael's Home for Crippled Children, whose boards or directing committees also included Dr. Rebecca Cole, Mrs. Josephine Heard, Fanny Jackson Coppin, and other black women.[67]

While none of these, or their male contemporaries, was as successful a speaker or writer as Harper, Gertrude Bustill Mossell's celebration of Afro-American women included all of them, and several other Philadelphians. Dr. Cole, she noted, was a German scholar as well as a teacher and pioneering physician. Frazelia Campbell, a good friend who like Harper helped prepare the volume, also did translations from the German while teaching at the ICY. Josephine Heard, wife of AME Bishop W. H. Heard, wrote a volume of poetry, *Morning Glories,* which was well represented in the Dorsey Collection. Mary E. Lee, married to the Reverend B. F. Lee, sometime editor of the *Christian Recorder,* was also a poet, whose "America" celebrated the need to remember African origins in the New World.[68]

Mrs. Mossell approved of motherhood and marriage; she signed her columns "Mrs. N. F. Mossell," and the frontispiece to her book pictures her with her children. She was proud to cite her husband's efforts as a Lincoln alumnus, too, in a long chapter on the need to use black teachers in black schools and colleges. But she emphatically did not see matrimony as an end in itself; Heard and Lee were among the few married but non-working women included in her study, and she was patronizing, at best, toward those who devoted full time to house and home, observing that "men tire of sweet women more quickly than even of scolds." Teaching was the profession best represented, but inclusion required some distinction beyond the classroom, as with Campbell's German translations, Julia Jones's paintings, or Grace Mapps's poetry. Otherwise it was administrators who made her list, Mollie Durham and Annie Marriott, who joined Caroline LeCount as public school principals, Fanny Cozzens and Fanny Somerville, who established kindergartens. Her sister-in-law Ella Mossell, who had gone to Haiti with her missionary husband Charles, was cited as a composer, "The Black Swan" as singer, Inez Cassey as pianist, Ida Bowser as first black graduate of "the musical department of the University of Pennsylvania." In her own field she was especially generous to

Florence Lewis, the ICY graduate who had quit grammar-school teaching to work full-time as a reporter, becoming editorial head of a department of the *Press,* and winning appointment to Pennyslvania's committee at the great Chicago World's Fair of 1893.[69]

Frances Harper was surely thinking of her own nearly unique situation when, in speaking to a largely white woman's convention in 1895, she suggested that natural ability alone would win "colored women [their] true position in the world, not as paupers but as sisters, in the front rank of wage earners in the nineteenth century." Mrs. Mossell was more cautious. She believed that women journalists had one single advantage, in that they could more easily get interviews from subjects of either sex, counting on female sisterhood and male gallantry. Beyond that she never forgot the double disabilities of race and gender—or the fact that both were imposed, rather than natural. Even marriage and motherhood, although hard to combine with a career, were in themselves no more a barrier than blackness. The success of her own friends in Philadelphia was testimony that "we believe in [woman's] place being at home and in other places also."[70]

Many of the reasons which led black women to write for publication also inspired black men. But there were others as well, political, institutional, economic, and perhaps personal, that led to the establishment, in the late 19th-century city, of fully twenty-three journals of various kinds. Most of these were short-lived weeklies, some traceable only through the memories of Carl Bolivar years after they had died; others are well represented in the Dorsey Collection, and one, the *Tribune,* remains the oldest Afro-American secular newspaper still published. Editorially these journals were variously Republican, Democratic, Independent, and apolitical; AME, Baptist, Methodist, and irreverent. Their editors, publishers, and reporters included some of the city's most important citizens, and collectively they provided a mixture of insight, color, and personal invective that their white peers rarely brought to the coverage of Afro-American affairs.[71]

Personal invective was the hallmark especially of H. Price Williams, the first of the secular journalists in the period and one of the most wide-ranging. In the later 1870s and early 1880s Williams, tied for third place in the Dorsey Collection, published and edited at least two weeklies of his own, and contributed at various times to the AME's *Christian Recorder,* the *Tribune,* and T. Thomas Fortune's New York *Globe.* Most important he was the pioneer in writing a regular weekly feature for the white *Sunday Mercury,* and it was the success of his "Items on the Wing" which opened the way for Gertrude Mossell and other Afro-American columnists to cover social, lodge, church, and other community events of interest.[72]

Most of these columns were routine enough, but some of the flavor of Williams unchained may be conveyed through an early piece in the *Mercury,* dated October of 1873, which while not bylined seems unmistakably his own. The subject is William Dorsey's own St. Thomas Episcopal Church and its elite congregation, the "colored four hundred." And the approach to this eminently respectable institution is almost unimaginable in a white reporter, with its curiously involuted style and heavily ironic tone: "What has been done by this beloved people, we fear, few of us white churchmen little know." (Although Williams himself was described as "light-skinned," the last note was perhaps deliberately designed to preserve his anonymity.) Following a few observations about the congregation as a whole—"In quite good taste the sisters dress. Refinement everywhere observable"—the piece is devoted to a list and description of the vestry and other officers of the church. The skin colors of several men and women are noted, and in parentheses the occupations of all, presumably to provide an implicit contrast between the pretensions and the relatively modest jobs of these caterers, coal dealers, upholsterers, and "tonsors." The litany is interrupted only by ad hominem excursions into the affairs of a few notable members such as James Field Needham, son of a prominent family, ICY graduate, and ex-schoolteacher who had recently won a job in City Hall: "Brother Needham once needed Ham. Ham he no longer needs."[73]

The sheer maliciousness of the piece suggests that it was born of social rejection. When some years later Williams lost not only the presidency of the elite Bethel Historical and Literary Society but, as noted earlier, a criminal libel suit to boot, he reacted in much the same way. Tasting sour grapes, he took his revenge on that occasion by comparing the locally revered "Bethel Lit" to the "Limekiln Club," a fictitious fraternity whose proceedings served the white papers of the day much as Amos 'n' Andy later served radio, as a vehicle for satirizing black dialect and pretensions. It was Williams, too, who coined the term "Gutsocracy" to describe the well-fed caterers who dominated much of the social scene. It seems unlikely that this and other spoofs of the local leadership were born of a genuine populism. Williams did embrace the Greenback-Labor party when it endorsed his bid for local political office in 1879, but the affair was a brief one, and he went back to the Republicans before going on in turn to the Democrats.[74]

In any case the "Chameleon Statesman" got as good as he gave. He did win election to the presidency of the National Colored Press Association in 1884, but in general he earned more bruises than honors. A small man, despite his big orator's voice, he was assaulted once by the giant William Teagle, brother to "the Majah," and again by Captain James Junior of the Grey Invincibles, both times for misrepresenting their political positions, and Guy Burton severely manhandled him, at graveside, when he tried to walk off with a souvenir from the Mount Lebanon bodysnatching scandal, a woman's slipper hastily grabbed from a corpse. Despite working as sometime columnist for the *Globe* he was also a favorite if merely verbal target of T. Thomas Fortune, who called him a "demagogue and blatherskate," among other things, on occasion of his election

William Henry Dorsey (1837–1923) as custodian of the American Negro
Historical Society, 1903 (*from* Colored American Magazine)

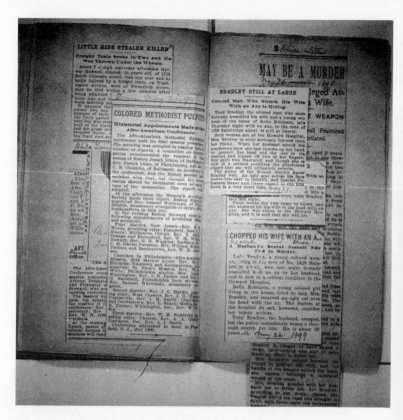

Page from one of the 388 surviving Dorsey scrapbooks, with a few of the tens of thousands of items dealing with contemporary African-Americana (see pp. 1–3). (*from Dorsey scrapbooks*)

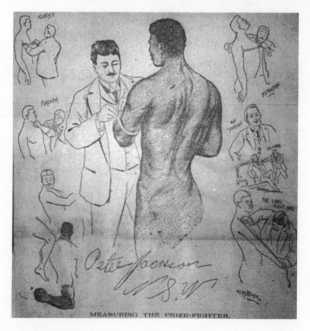

Sketch of Peter Jackson, most popular black heavyweight of the 1890s, 1890 (see pp. 15–17, 322). (*from Dorsey scrapbooks*)

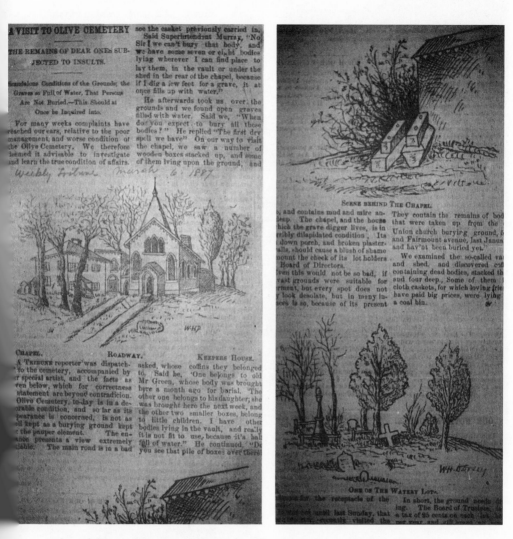

A few of the surviving Dorsey artworks: illustrations for muckraking attack on management of Olive Cemetery in Philadelphia Tribune, 1887 (see pp. 4, 110, 122–25). *(from Dorsey scrapbooks)*

Dorsey note on portrait of Francis Lingo, accused of sex-murder of a white woman in two celebrated New Jersey trials, 1892 (see pp. 46–48). (*from Dorsey scrapbooks*)

Dorsey poster about Francis Lingo's vaudeville appearance following Lingo's acquittal, 1892 (see pp. 46–48). (*from Dorsey scrapbooks*)

Editorial cartoon denouncing the Reverend Robert P. Elwood, who helped incite a fiery lynching and race riots in Wilmington, Delaware, 1903 (see pp. 49–51). (*from Dorsey scrapbooks*)

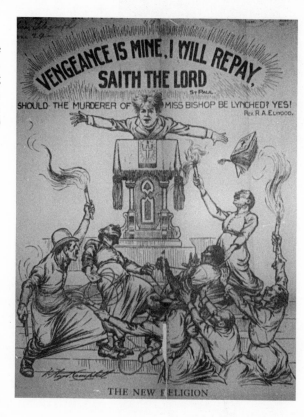

The *Philadelphia Item* covers an attempted interracial elopement, 1899 (see pp. 25–37). (*from Dorsey scrapbooks*)

An Eighth Ward Stronghold.

This is the Patterson Club, at 206 Camac street, the place of registration of eight voters, none of whom live there. It is a gambling and drinking resort of negro idlers who regard Senator Penrose as their patron saint.

In Senator Penrose's division, as well as in other parts of the Eighth ward, there is some anxiety, which all the eloquence of "Buck" Devlin is powerless to allay. The negro politicians and workers in that ward are ready to go a long way, especially when there is a political office in sight, by way of reward.

Now, however, that they feel that the inwardness of the Penrose-Henson-Moore political strategy is understood, they are seeking shelter, and obeying orders only when they get them in very plain language.

Picture and story about a boisterous establishment (now the Franklin Inn Club) less than twenty feet across the way from Dorsey's home at 206 Camac St. (see pp. 129–30). *(from Dorsey scrapbooks)*

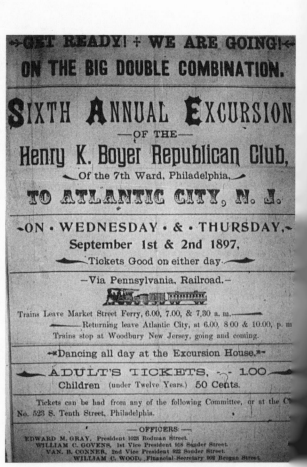

Poster advertising political club excursion to Atlantic City, open to all paying guests, 1897 (see pp. 318–20). *(from Dorsey scrapbooks)*

Poster advertising Alantic City excursion sponsored by Hod Carriers Union, 1890 (see pp. 318–20). (*from Dorsey scrapbooks*)

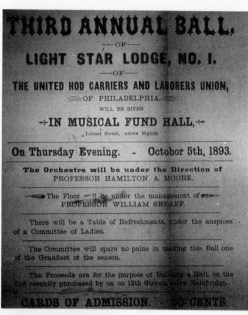

Poster advertising traveling all-black concert and variety program for benefit of "Mother Bethel" A.M.E. church, with performances by local and national entertainment stars, 1894 (see pp. 312–13). (*from Dorsey scrapbooks*)

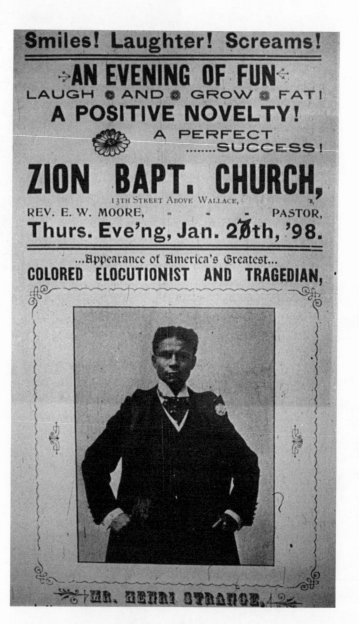

Poster advertising local church appearance by Reverend Henri Strange of Philadelphia, leading African-American actor of the day, 1898 (see pp. 314–15). (*from Dorsey scrapbooks*)

to the Press Association post. Fortune was generally pleased by his competitors' ill-fortune, such as the collapse of William's short-lived weekly, the Philadelphia *Gazette*, in 1883. And he was especially delighted when the *Pilot* followed it down the next year; on that occasion Williams, who was often in court and sometimes in jail, was sued by a disgruntled subscriber in New Jersey, and had to skip bail and then town in order to go on with his career.[75]

That career, while a significant contribution to local black journalism, was hardly typical; nothing and no one was. In fact the leading male writer of the period just after Williams was almost everything he was not. John Stephen Durham despite his late start is tied for thirty-first place in the Dorsey Collection, and his own career was probably the most publicly honored, and certainly the most varied, of any black Philadelphian in the period. While like Frances Harper he might fit into any of several categories, "writer" or "journalist" seems as good as any.[76]

Born in 1861 into one of the city's elite families, cited in the New York *Age* as "noted for the rare personal beauty of its members," Durham graduated from the ICY in 1878, and worked as a schoolteacher, supporting his widowed mother and sisters, before entering the University of Pennsylvania's Towne Scientific School in 1881. He finished the undergraduate curriculum in 1886, winning an advance degree in civil engineering two years later. To pay his way he also worked as a night clerk in the post office and as a reporter for the Philadelphia *Times* and New York *World*. His undergraduate years seem to have been nearly as idyllic as Fanny Jackson's at Oberlin, and even more energetic. Although first rejected he was later accepted by the Philomathean College Society, elected German class orator and moderator of the German Society's debates; he found time also to box on the university's team and play four years of intramural football. Most important, he served as editor in chief of the school paper, a job that led directly to work with the *Bulletin*, eventually as associate editor.

But for all his apparent acceptance at the university, no one would hire him as engineer, and Durham was never able to put his hard-won degree to work, and so decided to study law, privately, while working for the *Bulletin*. His real ambitions were political, and given fluency in French and Spanish as well as German he seemed to Secretary of State James Blaine a natural successor to Frederick Douglass in the dual post of Minister to Haiti and chargé-d'affaires to the Dominican Republic in 1890. He stayed there until the election of a Democratic President, Grover Cleveland, in the fall of 1892, an event that clearly doomed his patronage appointment. The election returns came in while he was visiting the offices of the New York *Age;* it is impossible to imagine any other Afro-American of that era greeting such news with a reported, "Oh, well, I guess I'll go up to the Polo Grounds and see the football game between . . . Pennsylvania and Yale."[77]

After resigning his diplomatic post Durham came back home and was admitted to the Philadelphia bar. Over the next ten years he practiced law and sometimes international law in his hometown, while writing for a number of journals. He also found time to run a sugar refinery in the Dominican Republic, to serve again on a diplomatic commission in Cuba, and to write two books, one an account of the giant volcanic explosion in Martinique, the other a short novel, *Diana, Priestess of Haiti*. In 1897 he married a kindergarten director, Constance MacKenzie, daughter of a white associate on the *Bulletin*. Only one other notable Philadelphian of the period had married outside of the race. But unlike Robert Purvis, who as a widower married a Quaker late in life, Durham was evidently a sociable man, and local reaction to the match forced him eventually to move to Paris. Until that time, however, despite his successes in the wider white world he never left his own.

During the 1890s Durham wrote a column for the *Tribune*, served as Quartermaster of the Grey Invincibles, and joined both the Citizens' Republican Club and the Quaker City Association. T. J. Minton, who did the young man's biography for the *Age* in 1890, wrote that his chief interest "has been the higher employment of colored young men and women." The statement was based in part on a series of articles in the *Bulletin*, which sketched the "socio-economic problems of the colored people," and in part on his service as president of the Progressive Workingmen's Club, a self-help and improvement organization that tried among other things to place young men and women in white-collar jobs. In later years he also continued to raise the issue of blue-collar employment, as in a piece on "Labor Unions and the Negro" in the *Atlantic Monthly* of January, 1898.[78]

The other major concern that runs through his writings is the need to recognize and promote a distinctively Afro-American history and culture. As a practical guide he published, in 1895, a small book based on a series of lectures to Tuskegee and Hampton, *To Teach the Negro History*. But the earliest and most dramatic forum for his views was provided by the AME church, which invited him, as an Episcopal layman, to deliver a major address at the great Centennial Celebration held at Mother Bethel in December of 1887: "The A.M.E. Church as Seen from Without."[79]

As Durham saw it, the church, by far the biggest of black organizations, had special responsibilities and opportunities, not all of which it was fulfilling. He was especially disappointed in the *Christian Recorder*, whose great potential and sometimes brilliant editorials were too often buried in "the meanderings of presiding elders and the doings of parishioners who want to see their names in print." But the denomination's Wilberforce University, still then new, had a real mission. Howard, and notably Lincoln, whose alumni were just beginning to protest the matter, were run by white philanthropists and teachers. And although he had himself just graduated from Penn, he believed that, as a result of the lack of black teachers, "there are today more good men spoiled by Lincoln and Howard Universities than there are strong men who succeed in spite of the influences brought to bear upon them." The *A.M.E. Review* was a strong publication, he went on, but although northern magazines were generally fair the newspapers were often biased in favor of southern whites, and both the *Review* and the *Recorder* had to train journalists to fight that tendency. Above all they had to search for and encourage black novelists, people who could portray the Afro-American experience in ways that no whites could do, getting past the charming fictions of Uncle Remus to tell the real story of the newer, post-slavery generation.

But if by John Durham's standards the real black story was not being told, there were dozens of fellow journalists eager to give their own versions. In addition to himself, Francis Harper, Gertrude Mossell, and Florence Lewis, at least twelve others, including Daniel Adger, Alexander Caldwell, Alexander Davis, Henry Griffin, Robert Holland, Philip Holmes, Eleanor Ketchum, Randolph Lewis, William Dorsey's son-in-law William Ramsey, and Wallace Swan, followed H. P. Williams in writing for the city's white dailies. The surviving columns of those with bylines do not much differ from the ones contributed by other Philadelphians to the out-of-town black papers. Six different people wrote the "Quaker City" column for the New York *Globe* during 1883–84 alone: "Olga," "Bouse" (probably David Bowser), "Carl" (Bolivar), H. P. Snowden, Claude Duval, and C. M. Minnie, one of the early black cadets at West Point. While the *Globe* or *People's Advocate* columnists in particular could not have made much money from what Bolivar called their "penny-a-line" contributions, they were otherwise following Gertrude Mossell in learning the craft. They had their own definitions of what was "most creditable" for potential white or out-of-town readers, but the natural concern was generally with the activities of the leadership, their peers, as members of social clubs and churches, the Odd Fellows and Grey Invincibles, or as outstanding lecturers, students, jobholders, or politicians.[80]

The regulars were not the only ones who used the dominant dailies, moreover. Most community leaders, including John D. Lewis, Fanny Jackson Coppin, and Dr. Nathan Mossell, wrote letters to explain or defend their positions on current issues, or express their outrage at events from Philadelphia to Mississippi. Still others wrote to criticize the leadership. And some journalists, such as Mrs. Mossell, if not regularly published in a given paper, took advantage of the letters column to remind readers of the achievements, for example, of black women doctors.

But the most important and varied outlet for airing opinions was the Afro-American press itself. The fact that the city was a regional center and indeed national headquarters for much of black America helps to account for the simultaneous existence of some eight different journals as of 1890, each with a distinctive voice. The weekly *Christian Recorder* was the oldest, founded in 1849, and published a great deal of secular news and comment, much like the newer, Baptist *Christian Standard.* The *A.M.E. Church Review,* as John Durham suggested, was not really a denominational organ so much as a quarterly vehicle for literature and commentary on a range of issues. The quiet weekly *Echo,* founded just a decade earlier, was the oldest secular paper, while the *Traveller* and the *State Journal* were both less than a year old. The *Journal* was unique in the city, and rare among black papers anywhere, in being avowedly Democratic in politics. More characteristic, and important, were the seven-year-old *Tribune,* founded and edited by the Republican Christopher Perry, and George Gardiner's *Sentinel,* a year younger, which insisted on its political independence.[81]

All of these journals, excepting the magazine *Review,* were weekly newspapers, six to eight pages long. Buyers usually paid $1.50 a year, 3 cents or 5 cents an issue, not only in cigar stores or barbershops but wherever race-conscious people gathered, in Gil Ball's saloon or Dr. Mossell's office. What they lacked was neither liveliness nor variety but a strong economic base; the problem with journalism, as with much else, was that there were simply too many talented and ambitious people for the Afro-American community to support. The modern city, with perhaps fifteen or twenty times as many black residents as in 1890, has not eight commercially sold weeklies but just one. Far more people read the papers than paid for them, the *Recorder* complained, and its secular counterparts were doubtless passed about pool-rooms and street corners just as the *Standard* and *Recorder* itself circulated at choir practice. Despite its own national circulation the paper was chronically in debt, while most of its competitors for the available pennies folded quietly after a few weeks or months.[82]

Political independence did not generally play well, or long, in the world of black publishing, and neither the *Sentinel* nor the *State Journal* survived the depression of the middle 1890s, during the Democratic administration of President Grover Cleveland. But resilience was as characteristic as fragility, and they were soon replaced by two others. The *Journal,* national organ of the Odd Fellows, was edited by the politically ambitious lawyer J. C. Asbury. And the *Germantown Astonisher* picked up the tradition of irreverent self-criticism. After surveying the political landscape toward the end of 1897 the *Astonisher* announced, "There are no discontented Afro-Americans except a few who have been too highly educated and who want offices they can't get." The major problem with the race, it went on, was with those who, "eternally shooting off their bazoos," were failing to "settle down and *do* something, with emphasis on the *do.*"[83]

But the death of two papers and the birth of two others during the middle 1890s does not begin to measure the amount of ambition, and frustration, represented by the history of black journalism in Philadelphia. One optimistic publisher attempted a daily, the *Advocate,* during the centennial year of 1876, when the Afro-American population of the city had yet to reach 30,000 by official count. Some of the other efforts, by date of first publication, include the two failures by H. P. Williams, the *Pilot* and *Gazette,* in the early 1880s, the weekly *Times,* beginning in 1883, the *Public Director,* 1886, the *Sunday Mirror,* uniquely selling at one cent in 1889, the *Sun* and *Weekly Standard* (later merged with the *Echo*), both in 1891, the Philadelphia *Methodist* and *Sunday Journal* in 1895, the *Sunday Herald* in 1896, and the *Defender* and *Messenger* in 1898.[84]

What did all of these hopeful editors, publishers, and reporters hope to get out of all of these projects? Few of them could expect to make a living; for many the opportunity for expression was an end in itself. Even Christopher Perry did not live off the *Tribune* alone. Born in Baltimore before the war, Perry had moved to Philadelphia at age 10, and wrote for the *Times* and *Mirror* after graduation from the Institute for Colored Youth. But he also worked as a printer and caterer as well, and long after establishing the *Tribune* held a series of theoretically full-time jobs at City Hall.[85]

The officially declared aims of new journals range from the modest claims of the *Sunday Mirror,* whose collection of jokes, clippings from other papers, and society news was simply "Devoted to the Social, Educational, and Religious Interests of the Colored People of Philadelphia," on to the fierce manifesto of the *Messenger:* "We Propose to Wage Relentless War upon the Rotten Political Conditions Which Make the Negro in Pennsylvania 10,000 Times Worse than a Chattel." The church and lodge papers had institutional purposes to advance. But the commonest reason for putting out a paper was, broadly speaking, political.[86]

The "political" character of the black press had two dimensions, public and personal. Everyone involved was devoted in some way to the advancement of the race, pointing up achievements, indulging in self-criticism, contributing to a series of lively debates about what to do about lynching, how to vote, how to relate to the wider white world. At the same time many were devoted to the advancement of their own editors or publishers. If journalism was not a means of self-support it was at least a vehicle for self-promotion. As white politicians looked to win black voters they looked for influential leaders to round them up, and in the absence of better information tended to accept newspaper editors as "influential" by definition. H. P. Williams, the "Chameleon Statesman," was notorious for trying to use his columns and papers as stepping-stones to office, whether as jailhouse turnkey or candidate for city commissioner; Christopher Perry surely earned his bail clerk's salary as much for his work on the *Tribune* as for the county sheriff. For both men, and many others, it was in any case hard to distinguish politics from publishing.[87]

The situation of Philadelphia's black journalists, then, was in many ways like the situation of its doctors and lawyers. The black city was brutally competitive, and many more failed to make a living than succeeded. On the other hand it was also headquarters to a large hinterland; while doctors and lawyers, sometimes reluctantly, left Philadelphia for other places, many of the journalists were able to do much the same thing by reaching beyond it to lodge brothers and co-religionists across the country. Whatever their individual success, they served collectively to make the city a major intellectual center.

The growth of the learned professions then was rightly taken as a sign of racial progress, a light and inspiration for the ambitious. But the growth was two-edged, as competition for the meager fees or pennies available in the Afro-American community meant that a "progress" measured by numbers in any given occupational group meant failure or hardship for many of the people who made it up. And so for many professionals, together with entrepreneurs, laborers, educators, and others, both the effort to win individual security and the effort to raise the race as a whole led finally to political action, and government jobs.

Chapter 7

Politics, Politicians, and Civil Servants

At the close of the Civil War, Pennsylvania's blacks, while free, were not yet clearly citizens, had no right to vote, held no political offices, and just one single government job, as a menial messenger for the city's health department. Citizenship was granted officially by the Fourteenth Amendment in 1868, but its meaning, in a still racist and segregated society, would not be clear for generations. The Fifteenth Amendment, passed two years later, was in contrast short and simple. Its first section read:

> The right of citizens of the United States to vote shall not be abridged on account of race, color, or previous condition of servitude.

And in Philadelphia that was enough to inspire a profound change in the behavior and prospects of the local black elite.

For Afro-Americans after the Civil War the purposes of government were reduced to their simplest: physical safety and jobs. The first of these, while not secured to the south, was essentially won in Philadelphia and other northern cities. The second was important everywhere, and in the thirty years after 1870 no occupational opportunity grew as fast as government service, or matched its significance for the black community as a whole.

But there was, as always, a price. Government jobs offered more security and better pay than any others available, but they had to be won through politics. And while the high politics of racial solidarity and protest, inspired largely by events to the south, were important in binding the community together, the low politics of Philadelphia divided it. Political organization encouraged the already serious problem of crime. And continual battles had to be fought to preserve individual and racial dignity in the face of political dependence on a single, white-dominated, Republican party, a dependence that was continually debated, and even fought, against the odds.

Politics was deadly serious business for Philadelphia's new black voters. The local community, with its thick web of southern associations, was sharply aware of the brutality which marked Reconstruction. At the same time, the murderous "Election Riot" which killed Octavius Catto and others in 1871 reminded them that racial violence had long been as much a part of Philadelphia's tradition as of South Carolina's. Through the pivotal year 1877, Republican politicians continually, and successfully, reminded members of the local community that it was Republican administrations which had freed the slaves, enfranchised the freedmen, and protected blacks from Democratic killers on both sides of the Mason-Dixon line. But afterward, as disillusion grew, the nature of interracial and political violence turned in different directions in the South and in the city.

In the South, as black voters lost ground and were largely abandoned by the national Republicans, the directly political battles of the 1870s were succeeded by the lynchings of the later 1880s and 1890s. As lynchings moved north to lap around them in Delaware, New Jersey, and Pennsylvania itself, fear and anger helped to unite the local Afro-American community in an outrage that crossed all other bounds.

In the city itself, meanwhile, black neighborhoods after 1871 were no longer subject to recurrent white invasions. As they organized politically they were able, encouraged, indeed used to fight back. But as time went on, and earlier memories faded, so did the clearly racial nature of electoral violence, so that the city's black warriors simply blended into the general tradition of fighting at the polls, striking out at competitors regardless of color.

This kind of fighting, in Philadelphia as in other cities, had gone on for decades before the Fifteenth Amendment, and required no blacks to push it sometimes into murder. Six men were killed in the local election of 1868, when all the players were white. In contrast the fall election of 1870, the first in which blacks were eligible to vote, passed in relative quiet.[1]

The fact is that none of the parties, not Republicans, Democrats, or blacks, was fully prepared for that historic occasion. The Fifteenth Amendment, when it finally came, was the result neither of the hard efforts of the Pennsylvania Equal Rights League nor of the local Republican party. It was designed by the national leadership to benefit the party in the North, southern blacks having won the right to vote years earlier, under reconstructed state constitutions. But northern Republicans, as in Pennsylvania, were not enthusiastic, and not yet ready to move in and use this new bloc of voters. Democrats, again across the North, were not sure whether to woo it or fight it. And the city's own Afro-Americans, with many of their most politically conscious leaders off to try their ambitions in the South, had no experience in political organization.[2]

The passage of the amendment was greeted in April with bonfires, banners, and a series of parades through downtown neighborhoods, with marchers carefully instructed in a uniform dress code, black hats and coats, white gloves, and blue sashes. But symbolic celebration was no substitute for systematic organization over the six months between passage and the next general election in October. The stakes were not high, with the local congressional outcomes assured and only two county offices on the ballot. When the great day came, on October 11, Afro-American voters were lined up in the Fifth, Seventh, and Eighth wards at four in the morning, partly out of excitement and partly to steal a march on the Democratic opposition and avoid the usual gauntlet of flying bricks, or "Irish Confetti," that they would have to run at any later hour. But the turnout was slight, and so was the trouble. There was fraud and fighting as always, especially in the Fifth Ward, domain of the Irish Democrat "Squire" William McMullin. But the local U.S. marshall was able under a Reconstruction statute to call in the Marines to quiet things down, a development relegated to the second page of the *Inquirer*'s special post-election issue.[3]

All this changed dramatically the next year. The scheduled 1871 election of a mayor and city council would decide who controlled the city, the cops, and the machinery of election itself. The incumbent Democrat, Daniel Fox, had followed tradition in using "his" police to discourage Republicans at the polls, and the officers often sided against black men in the little affrays that were part of the daily fabric of city life. The Republican challenger, Bill Stokley, promised not only to turn the cops around but to promote "law and order" in other ways as well, notably by scrapping the city's volunteer firefighters. The fire companies, mostly made up of combative young men organized along neighborhood and ethnic lines, seemed to the city's "better element" little more than street gangsters cloaked in official authority; Afro-Americans especially feared them as leaders of race-riots past. The issues were then as clear as black and white, with the blacks ready this time to vote in number, while Irish Democrats, according to one elite political veteran, "devoted themselves wholly to inflaming the prejudices of the ignorant."[4]

Politics always involves more than control of civil government, or even the spoils of office. In 19th-century cities it was often an expression of clashing value systems, religious and ethnic, revolving around drink, sport, sex, and other forms of sin; Daniel Fox had in fact won his 1868 election in large part on account of his freethinking opponent's position on the divinity of Jesus Christ. In the early 1870s it was easy for the city's Democrats to use the dominant national issue to garnish a purely local contest, to add racial hatred to the usual issues of power and morality, and to ask whether this was to be "a white man's government" after all. The result in October was to transform the usual election battles into a classic "race riot."[5]

The term "race riot" itself has meant very different things at different times. In strong contrast to the 1960s, or the 1990s, in 19th-century cities it traditionally translated into something like "pogrom," in which white mobs invaded black neighborhoods to punish and sometimes burn out the inhabitants. The 1871 riots in Philadelphia differed only in the seeking out and apparent assassination of Octavius Catto, a special target on account of his leadership of the Equal Rights League, and perhaps because his education and bearing were especially aggravating to those "prejudices of the ignorant."

Interracial fighting broke out in fact during the Sunday and Monday before the election; Jacob Gordon was shot by Officer Ed McNulty on October 9, and died on the 11th. On the day itself, October 10, white mobs ranged far from the polls, surging all about between Sixth and 11th streets, Lombard and South, the west end of the Fifth Ward and the east end of the Seventh. Shops were closed as "the colored population was frantic with terror, and many bundling up their wardrobes started . . . for some more secure portion of the city." One group of rioters in the early afternoon broke down several doors and into locked yards in hot pursuit of Isaac Chase, who was shot to death and then mutilated with an axe on the steps of his home at 811 Emeline Street. At least twenty other blacks were treated for gunshot and other wounds at the Pennsylvania Hospital alone. Catto himself spent most of the day quietly at the Institute for Colored Youth, leaving not to vote but, following the governor's emergency proclamation, to take his place as Major of the Fifth Brigade of the Pennsylvania State Militia. He was going home to get his uniform when he was spotted near his house at 814 South Street, pursued, and deliberately shot by a young man with a bandaged head.[6]

The social significance of this event was that it was in fact the last riot of its kind in Philadelphia, very nearly the last in any major northern city. The fundamental reason, evident all over the Western World, was that the new industrial city demanded order, rationality, and sobriety as the old commercial city never had. The discipline demanded in factory and bureaucracy was increasingly enforced by police and prisons, above all by highly regimented public schools, whose real function was to prepare young people for all the frustrations and boredom which they would later find in office or industry. Regular, repetitive, carefully supervised work was simply incompatible with the old free-swinging habits, above all the drinking habits, of a pre-industrial population. And one important by-product of the increasing demand for public order, and the more inhibited, rational, social psychology it encouraged, was a dramatic drop in the amount of violent behavior in cities across the world. Among Philadelphia's Irish Catholics, notably, historic enemies of the black population, the effects of the new discipline of school and work was to cut the rate of indictments for murder from 4.7 per 100,000 in the 1860s and early 1870s, the time of the Catto riot, to 1.8 per 100,000 in the late 1880s and 1890s.[7]

The end of the mid-century era of interracial riot, rout, and tumult was then mostly the result of economic change as embodied in social psychology. But if this is now evident to historians, what was more evident to contemporaries was that Bill Stokley won his election the day that Octavius Catto lost his life, and that he won it with black votes. In historical perspective, again, "Martinet"

Stokley's tough and even brutally illegal campaign against riot, first as mayor and then as police commissioner, may be seen as part of an increasing national and even international insistence on public order. It was most notably directed against labor organization. But to black Philadelphians what mattered most was that Stokley, first in a long line of Republican mayors, was apparently making good on his promise to protect them from mob violence.[8]

What gave point to the promise, year in and out, was that corruption and violence were so woven into local politics that blacks and whites did find themselves fighting continually. The machinery of election was built on two clashing concepts of government, both of which, embodied in the city's charter, demanded that individual voters be bound together in larger organizations. The first and by far the oldest envisioned the city, like the larger state or nation, as a kind of great public corporation or "commonwealth," managed by what were in effect elected directors; the vote should then be restricted to property owners, taxpayers, responsible men who held a "stake" in municipal affairs. The second, legacy of the Jacksonian era, held that public officials must answer as closely and often as possible to all male citizens. The first concept bred corruption, the second violence.

Corruption began with the fact that in Philadelphia as in many cities only taxpayers could vote. If many poorer citizens, largely indifferent to the matters which occupied City Hall, did not want to pay for the privilege, there were hundreds of businessmen, contractors, and candidates eager not only to provide these reluctant citizens with 25-cent poll-tax receipts but with $2, $5, and even $10 additional for their votes. Violence began with the fact that rampant democracy created hundreds of elective offices, in city, county, school district, and ward, all of them nominated in rowdy conventions whose delegates were in turn selected by popular vote, making the electoral process nearly a year-round business, involving literally thousands of separate contests. All this activity nurtured extreme parochialism, verging on anarchy, with each of the city's scores of common councilors or hundreds of district school directors pursuing his own local or personal agenda. The only way of combating this tendency was through party organization, designed to unify all these separate people across the lines of neighborhood and office, so that a majority coalition of city and county officials, mayors and councilmen, commissioners and constables could somehow work together. Party members were often united around common principles; after these the major weapons of organization were first money, supplied by the same businessmen, contractors, and candidates who bought voters, and then muscle, supplied by the more aggressive voters they bought.[9]

New black citizens were easily incorporated into the system when militant Republicans began to recruit them, after that first confused election in 1870, and help them organize their own political clubs. From the beginning these segregated clubs, like Afro-American politics generally, operated on different levels. Some members made political decisions largely in terms of broad racial purposes, including the demand for a fair share of legitimate government jobs. The Charles Sumner Club, for example, founded in 1873, was named after the Massachusetts senator most conspicuous for his stand on civil rights. Carl Bolivar and William Dorsey both served as secretaries; President James F. Needham was a former teacher at the Institute for Colored Youth, one of the first blacks named to a white-collar job in city government; while the membership included many other elite citizens, called to organize for "literary, social, and political purposes." On the other hand most new voters were very poor, and many illiterate, and so eager to take tax receipts, dollars, and directions from above. Large numbers, too, were willing and able to use their muscles at every stage of the electoral process, helping to keep opposing voters from the polls, or to silence them in convention. Their clubs, typically named after local politicians or in later years their own officers, were often used in effect as small mercenary armies.[10]

In the early years there was little conflict between the different purposes of these clubs. Whatever the complexities of the highly factionalized convention system, after all, by election time virtually all could unite against the Democrats. There were complaints about the meager share of patronage jobs the Republicans granted their black supporters. And the old abolitionists William Still and Robert Purvis went further to denounce the whole system. Perhaps influenced by their long association with Quakers and other elite whites, the two men were offended by the corruption which went with the Stokley Regime, which was hardly immune from the post–Civil War political venality associated at the same time with Boss Tweed's New York and General Grant's Washington. But neither set of complaints made any serious dent in black support for Stokley and the Republicans. If the job situation was not good there was no assurance that the opposition would be more generous. And in the atmosphere of the 1870s, to vote for anyone but Stokley and the Republicans was "desertion in the face of the enemy." The much revered Purvis was simply shrugged off, but Still was threatened with lynching, and his business with firebombs. As the Sumner Club put it, after helping beat off one challenge in 1874, they had "showed that the colored men of Philadelphia have not forgotten Catto, and do not mean to bring his murderers back into power"— "and property," William Dorsey added in a pointed marginal note.[11]

But two events in early 1877 helped crack this nearly solid front. At the national level, this was the year in which the disputed election of 1876 was decided by the famous compromise which led Republican President Rutherford B. Hayes to withdraw the last of the federal troops from the old Confederate states. At the local level, Mayor Stokley's police managed after six years of Afro-American complaints to track the man indicted for Octavius Catto's death to Chicago. But the arrest was made just three weeks before the mayor narrowly beat off another reform challenge at the polls, and once the election was over the young man, Frank Kelly, was unanimously declared not guilty in two separate trails for the murders of Catto and Chase.[12]

To historians, again in retrospect, some version of the national "Compromise of 1877" seems nearly inevitable by that date. The chance for real Reconstruction had come much earlier; few U.S. troops were left in the South by then, and Washington already had all but abandoned black Republicans in the face of white intransigence. The Kelly verdicts were almost equally predictable. Few men were ever convicted of murder in riots, whatever the color of the participants. Given all the smoke and confusion, the number of witnesses, and the passage of time, this case was especially difficult. While identification at the inquest had been fairly firm, six years had given Kelly much time to change his appearance, and people of all colors on both sides to change their testimony. In a hotly political atmosphere, with attorneys accused of tampering and witnesses of perjury, it proved impossible to return a verdict of guilty beyond a readonable doubt.[13]

But whatever the reasons for these setbacks, both of them infuriated local blacks. Still and Purvis had already expressed their unhappiness with the Republican party; John D. Lewis and Nathan Mossell, the first lawyer and leading doctor in the community, both said later that the "Compromise of 1877" had broken their allegiance, while a long list of notables wrote a respectful but emphatic challenge to Isaiah Wears, the city's leading Republican apologist, to demand an explanation for it. As for the Kelly verdicts, Fanny Jackson Coppin, Redmond Faucett, Robert Adger, Henry Minton, and other community leaders had all personally appeared for the prosecution. And the *Times*, owned by Stokley's most recent mayoral opponent, taunted the Republicans for mishandling the whole affair, with its editor still insisting nearly thirty years later that it was a "blistering reproach" that they had been unable to convict anyone for the riots of 1871.[14]

During the presidential campaign of 1880 Afro-Americans were urged to remain "Faithful in the Cornfield, Brave on the Battlefield, Solid for Garfield." But it was three years too late to count on the old faithfulness and solidity for the GOP, and many of the braver souls in the community were making that clear. Among the leaders, disillusion may be measured by a notable change in the spirit and occasions which, after 1877, drew out big crowds and fresh emotions.[15]

Early in the postwar period black Philadelphians had joined others across the country in establishing two traditional anniversary celebrations: of the Emancipation Proclamation in January and the Fifteenth Amendment in April. Both occasions easily lent themselves to Republican self-congratulation, and were honored not only by black ministers and old abolitionists of both races but by ambitious white politicians. The events of 1877 killed neither celebration outright, but they quickly lost their old luster. The committee established in February of 1879 to honor the Fifteenth Amendment, composed of William

Still, J. D. Kelly, Colonel McKee, David Bowser, the Reverend Tanner, and other notables suggested, with due respect, that passage had been "carried through as a political necessity rather than as a question of right," a touch of heresy which William Forten, the old warhorse of the Equal Rights League, found it politically necessary to denounce the next day. By 1889 the Pennsylvania Abolition Society's grand 25th Anniversary of Freedom celebration was worse than an anti-climax, despite the presence of many dignitaries, from Frederick Douglass, Booker T. Washington, and General Armstrong through Frances Harper and William Still. The small audience at Association Hall was two-thirds white; they were further embarrassed when Robert Purvis, throwing away the traditional script, denounced General Louis Wagner, Republican head of the Philadelphia Department of Public Works, for his treatment of a black job applicant, closing the meeting "amid considerable confusion."[16]

By that time the only political events which drew impressive crowds were protest meetings, held not to celebrate historic landmarks but to denounce the current state of violence in the South. The first of these, called by the Afro-American League to denounce events in Carrolton, Mississippi, in the spring of 1886, attracted a thousand people; the handful of politicians in attendance were pointedly kept off the dais, in company with the few other whites. Chairman Robert Purvis, "in a full, rich, round voice," declared, "My blood boils when I see the gingerly, mealy-mouthed way in which the press of my country has treated the subject." The only reference to the Republican party was made by editor T. Thomas Fortune, who lumped it with the Democrats and others in declaring that "there is not an existing party in the United States that has not outlived its usefulness so far as the colored man is concerned."[17]

Southern violence inspired a number of other meetings throughout the 1880s and '90s, all following the same formula: overflow crowds, representing an impressive percentage of the city's Afro-American population, whites generally relegated to seats in the audience, no support for partisan politics of any kind. When Ida B. Wells brought her whirlwind anti-lynching campaign to Philadelphia in the fall of 1894, she spoke to associations of white ministers, Baptist and Methodist, both of which passed favorable resolutions. But her primary audiences were at black churches, typically "filled to the doors," while the major meeting at Association Hall, composed "almost exclusively of colored persons," featured officers or speakers from both sexes, all professions and churches: Nathan and Aaron Mossell, Bishop Wayman, Reverend Henry L. Phillips, Frances Harper, Levi Cromwell, Fanny Jackson Coppin, Harriet Duterte, and dozens of others.[18]

Four years later, following the "race war" in Wilmington, South Carolina, there were mass protests at five different churches, each carefully involving people from other denominations. An angry "pandemonium" greeted the Reverend E. W. Moore's suggestion, at a preliminary meeting of the Afro-American League, that hiring the Academy of Music might be too expensive. In fact the Academy on December 1 was "crowded from top to bottom," with hundreds more on stage. And while coroner Samuel Ashbridge was there, as part of his campaign for mayor, he was not allowed to address the meeting. The nation, as usual throughout the period, was governed by a Republican administration, and the Reverend William Phillips suggested that just as President McKinley had intervened in Spanish Cuba the previous summer, "for humanity's sake," Afro-Americans might make the same appeal to the European powers, urging them to protect the basic rights of U.S. citizens.[19]

But at the same time that racial violence in the South was a matter of growing concern, it was becoming impossible any longer to cast political violence in Philadelphia in terms of black and white. Members of both races continued to fight in bar-rooms and on street corners as well as at construction sites. They argued, within as well as across the line of color, about the Giants and the Phillies, steam engines and playing cards. Other kinds of provocation were more fundamentally racial, including who belonged where, and when, and wearing what kinds of clothing or attitudes. But neither kind of masculine aggression had much directly to do with government. Justice in the courts, as noted earlier, as distinct from punishment inflicted by cops on the streets, was rarely discriminatory. Political leverage may have helped in some cases, as in getting a white cop fired for beating a black man in 1898, just as racism affected some extreme cases such as the legal lynching of butler William Lane. But statistically, the relatively evenhanded way in which Philadelphia judges and juries handled interracial violence, and, as in New York and Boston, the essential equality of criminal sentencing, were largely unrelated to partisan politics. And there could be no pretense, as the Catto riot receded, that the routine violence of clubhouse, convention, and polling place was primarily a matter of defending or advancing the race.[20]

Black political clubs continued to operate on varying levels, although all of them shared some features. Almost none had a constituency bigger than a single ward, and many were organized around precincts, or "divisions," within wards. While a few included "honorary" white members, usually local politicians, active membership was all black. For those who belonged, the larger ones provided a variety of legitimate activities, excursions to the Jersey shore, picnics and dances, which shaded into illegitimate activities such as unlawful drinking and gambling. For the mainly white Republicans who claimed their allegiance, their legitimate function was to parade, in uniform, during election rallies, set bonfires, light firecrackers, and get out the vote. They rarely canvassed door to door; the usual means of drawing a crowd to a meeting was to entice it with a brass band and line of marchers. Their major illegitimate function was to register their own illegal voters, often from the bawdy and boarding houses which served sailors or southerners, and conversely to challenge the ones, illegal or otherwise, who came out for the opposition.[21]

While many black political clubs insisted on their respectability, the pull was always in the other direction. Success was measured ultimately not by the quality but by the quantity of voters, or at least votes, that they were able by whatever means to produce, and they often had to compete with others for members. The results may be measured by the history of the two leading elite clubs, the Charles Sumner and the Citizens' Republican, both of them in this period based in the Seventh Ward, where the number of black voters was greatest.

The Citizens Republican Club was originally begun in 1884 by Andrew Stevens, Carl Bolivar, and others unwilling to join, for example, the Matthew S. Quay Club, founded the same year in the same ward by the veteran knife-fighter and saloonkeeper Gil Ball. Their rules showed what they objected to: there would be no drink or gaming on the premises, no office-seekers among the leadership, no money spent on music or other entertainment. But within a few years Stevens was elected to the Philadelphia Common Council, and the club began to put on a series of lavish annual receptions. At the third of these, in 1894, President Stevens presided over a company comprised of 52 male guests, including Sam Houseman and Israel Durham, white leaders of the ward, together with Nathan Mossell, Christopher Perry, Carl Bolivar, Richard Warrick, and other community notables, none of them with their wives. The other sex was represented by 19 married and 47 unmarried females: "nearly all disreputable women," according to William Dorsey's marginal note. [22]

The older Sumner Club, meanwhile, which Dorsey himself had helped to found, was no longer devoted to "literary" pursuits, although its members still played politics and other social games. Its premises on Rodman Street were raided in October of 1897, and several patrons arrested; many of these places provided card games, slot machines, and crap tables as well as liquor. When the club went back into business almost immediately, to Judge Gordon's annoyance, the cops pleaded that they couldn't get in. When he issued a warrant for another raid, a jury freed manager Littleton Gumby, although the proprietor, Thomas Spence, was found guilty of operating a speakeasy. [23]

Periodic police raids were part of the system, although meaningful convictions were rare. Sometimes a reform group, such as the Law and Order League, began the process by applying for a warrant, sometimes an aggrieved wife or mother, worried about gaming losses, sometimes a loser himself out of revenge. In any case the police, struggling to muster all the shock displayed by Claude Raines in *Casablanca,* went on with the game, knowing that most raids would prove fruitless. It was hard to find twelve Philadelphians willing to condemn gambling or liquor sales, whatever the law said, or to condone interference with what men chose to do in the privacy of their own "clubs." The real stumbling block was finding proof that those found inside were not members—annual dues at the Sumner were pegged at 25 cents—or their guests. [24]

The major disadvantage of these places was that they could not routinely serve women, or whites, without violating the "members only" fiction, which was perhaps why Gil Ball kept his saloon at 720 Lombard Street in addition to the Quay Club two blocks up. But the ironic result of the liquor licensing law of 1887 was that by multiplying the cost of serving spirits legally it also multiplied these illegal alternatives, so that by the middle of the 1890s there were twelve or fifteen of them in the Seventh Ward alone, and dozens more throughout the city.[25]

By then, too, the notion that these clubs somehow served the interests of the race was a patent fiction too. Once a year their members did face mostly white Democrats at the polls. But the general elections, in what increasingly approached a one-party city, state, and nation, were rarely climactic events, even in the 1870s when racial emotions still ran high. Of course there was trouble, but Stokley's cops were able to keep the "peace" with the aid of deputized federal marshals, many of them black, fully 773 of them in 1878 alone. While the political murder rate generally dropped as a result of the increasing pacification of the white majority, most of the six men killed outright in campaign infighting between 1871 and 1900 died at the hands of members of their own parties, in the factional battling which marked primaries or conventions.[26]

Lousiana's Governor Pinchbeck once suggested that the twin curse of black politics during Reconstruction was "thievish friends and brutal foes." The same might be said of black politics in Philadelphia, except that friends and foes were not so easily identified by either party or color. The inevitable result of combining extreme factionalism and limited rewards was violent competition. The inevitable result of organization by territory was to discourage thinking of the Afro-American community as a whole and to encourage the kind of parochialism expressed in 1897 by a new club, founded in the Twenty-fourth Division of the Twenty-sixth Ward, "for the political advancement of the colored voters *of the division*" (my italics). With "advancement" usually going to the strong, the inevitable result of recruiting tough young men was that many black clubs, like the old white fire companies, behaved much like neighborhood street gangs.[27]

Certainly by the 1890s most of the "political" violence recorded in the Dorsey Collection was fought among blacks rather than against whites. Most of it was routine enough so that Israel Loat, accused of stabbing H. K. Bruce in November of 1899, could offer the excuse, in court, that "it was only an election fight." Some of it was criminal enough so that when in February of 1898 a gang failed to wrest the ballot box from judge of elections James Butler, after storming the polls in the Sixteenth Division of the Third Ward, they settled for stealing his overcoat. And like all violence it had a way of perpetuating itself, or outgrowing its original aims, so that the ambush laid by thirty members of the Frank Harrison Club for a much larger contingent of picnickers sponsored by the Robert J. Moore Republican Club occurred at a park in Lakeside, New Jersey, in August of 1897, dozens of miles from the Fourth Ward and many weeks away from any possible confrontation at the polls.[28]

The contrast was then complete. By the end of the century, growing violence in the South helped to unite black Philadelphia across the lines of party and other divisions. But violence in the city itself helped to divide it. As battling at the polls became more of a problem, with the increasing size of the Afro-American electorate, it also became less of an issue. After 1877 especially, as the older forms of race rioting died, no one but the participants could tell why some black troopers were fighting for various, and usually white, candidates for council, commissioner, or constable, and why some were fighting against them. By then the major racial issue locally was no longer physical security but jobs.

The issue of jobs in government and related businesses was by far the most important political concern in late 19th-century black Philadelphia. Apart from early references to the Catto riot and others to segregation, usually in the schools, it was in fact the only local issue, as no political piece, speech, or candidate seems ever to have referred to the water supply, streets and sewers, trolley lines and gas prices, or any of the many other things that occupied white politicians and reformers. It was, too, an issue that concerned the leading men and women of the community, whether or not they were looking for work themselves. The outcome was mixed: while a growing number won jobs with the city or federal governments, that number was both disproportionately big, in relation to the professionals and businessmen who made up the rest of the local black elite, and disproportionately small, if measured against the whole number of black voters.

The case for more jobs was based on two arguments. The first, that blacks were entitled to something like proportional representation, was bitterly opposed by many of their own reforming allies. The second, for "color-blind" employment based on merit, was unanswerable, as no one denied that Afro-Americans generally tested better and were otherwise better qualified for the civil service than their white competitors. But neither argument won a fair share of jobs, and the fact, finally, that the greatest single breakthrough in the period was made by a Democratic mayor encouraged more disaffection from the original Republican alliance.

Political jobs were sometimes defined as including those with the gas company, the streetcars, or other private corporations dependent on government contracts. They were not defined to include wholly unskilled labor: with the exception of a single reference to street graders, in 1879, there was no campaign for the kind of pick-and-shovel work needed on the city's subway and reservoir systems. Established Philadelphians were willing to do hard work, but literally backbreaking labor, best done by young and healthy single men from the South, was no political prize. At the other end of the scale the diplomats appointed from the city did not figure in political debate either. E. D. Bassett, the pioneer appointment to Haiti, continued to make his home in the city; John Stephen Durham and the Reverends W. H. Heard and C. C. Astwood were also sent to Haiti, while John Smythe, another ICY graduate, served as minister to Liberia, and both Charles L. Moore and later Richard Greener took other diplomatic posts. But whether because these positions were more than most men could hope for, or because they were reserved for Afro-Americans in any case, they were rarely mentioned in arguments about whether the Republicans were doing enough for the race.[29]

The jobs at issue were rather as elected officials, or otherwise, in ascending order, as janitors in public buildings, messengers or watchmen, schoolteachers, firemen, and cops, finally clerks or other white-collar civil servants. The attractions were obvious. While some patronage jobs could be uncertain, many were not, especially with the introduction of early civil service rules, and to those who faced the continued decline in business opportunities, or the growing competition among professionals, a job with the government seemed an oasis of security. In addition they paid very well relative to the alternatives; the mayor's messenger, in the 1890s, earned over $700 a year, roughly as much as a well-placed janitor or policeman; teachers, as noted, were paid between $450 and $1000; postal workers got over $1000, and by the 1890s long-term clerks in City Hall up to $1500.[30]

With the partial exception of schoolteaching, all of these jobs were ordinarily restricted to loyal voters. As further evidence that few rules were absolute, one man, David Brown, held a menial job in the health department between the Mexican War and the late 1860s, a period when he and his fellows were all politically irrelevant, or neutered. Otherwise neither patronage nor elected office was open until passage of the Fifteenth Amendment. Progress from that point could be measured in either of two ways. Extreme Republican apologists simply pointed to any jobs at all as evidence of the party's goodwill, and using James Needham's tax office appointment in 1870 as a base it was easy to point, in later years, to improvements of several hundred percent. But most wanted more. Blacks were repeatedly told, often by Democratic papers such as the *Times* or *Record,* that they held the balance of power in the city as well as the nation. And during the 1870s, when their several thousand new votes, even if counted only one time apiece, were indeed Mayor Stokley's margin of victory in two close elections, the number of officeholders listed by his champions was an insult.[31]

The proportionate standard suggested several hundred jobs. As of 1875 the actual jobholders listed by *Our National Progress,* a black party organ published in Harrisburg, were Needham, John Smyth in "a U.S. Office in Philadelphia," Dan Adger and the Reverend James Underdue in the post office, William Forten's brother and a Mr. Demar as watchmen in the customs house, the undertaker Guy Burton as janitor in the Forten School, and William

Henry Dorsey as personal messenger to the mayor—the latter job often described by its critics as involving the cleaning of cuspidors and the shining of shoes. If the only elected officials were unpaid members of the Fifth Sectional school board, "nearly all the wards in the city, have had delegates of color in the voting conventions of the Republican Party."[32]

The number of postal employees did grow fairly steadily in the late 1870s and early 1880s. These men, like the others listed above, were members of the local elite: Alfred Cassey, Lewis Bedford, Edward Lewis, and John Durham. Others, such as Jacob Ballard, Clifton Moseley, and Pliny Locke, moved to the department's Washington headquarters. But following the rule that generally kept Afro-Americans out of jobs where they might have to deal with white citizens, especially from positions of authority, none of them was allowed during the 19th century actually to deliver the mail. The pioneer carriers were restricted to picking up letters from deposit boxes, while the others worked behind the scenes, often at night.[33]

Given this situation, and these prejudices, it was then an especially bold step for local leaders to center their employment complaints increasingly around the police department, Mayor Stokley's power base and the backbone of Republican electoral success. The call was sounded as early as 1873, when Robert Jones organized a "Republican Equity Club" as a sounding board for dissidents. After 1877 and the fiasco of the Kelly trials the mayor attempted to meet it by appointing twenty-one black men as "turnkeys," in effect janitors in charge of police station cellblocks. The new jobs were welcome, but few agreed with Stokley's argument that they were in some ways better, because sheltered from the elements, than actual appointments to the patrol force. With drunkenness by far the leading cause of arrest, and stations crowded nightly with aggressive, nauseated, often incontinent transients, "the stench from many of the cells, and the improper trapping of the water connections, rendered many of the houses simply untenantable," and the job of cleaning them no sinecure. But Stokley would go no further. Like Tweed in New York, the mayor was spokesman and representative of the skilled white workers and shopkeepers from which the police were drawn, and his stated objections to black cops reflected the bedrock racism of his constituencey. Under the reserve system the men often had to sleep in the stations after their daily tours, and although it would seem that a strong stomach was a prerequisite for police work of any kind, Stokley noted that "of course the white men would object to getting in a bed just vacated by a colored man."[34]

But the issue would not die, and became one of the keys to the extraordinarily complicated Philadelphia election season of 1880–81, in which a variety of groups, in and out of the GOP, sought for their own reasons to block the mayor's bid for a fourth straight term. His leading opponents, gentlemen-reformers organized as a "Committee of One Hundred," had little appeal for blacks. The "One Hundred" believed that local government was ideally conducted by civic-minded, nonpartisan amateurs, managing the city's affairs with an honest efficiency designed, perhaps above all, to hold down its tax rates. The city's leading Afro-Americans in contrast shared with Stokley, as with most active voters regardless of color, the idea that local politics was above all a source of jobs and other benefits, to be shared among those who helped win them at the polls. In effect Stokley and the Republican regulars counted on overcoming this expectation through the memory of Emancipation and the hope of other if less legitimate rewards. And if there were no blacks patrolling the city, there had been no race riots, either, under the current regime.[35]

What complicated black choices was that George Keim, one of Stokley's Republican rivals, promised that if nominated he would break the color line on the police force. The idea was then picked up by H. P. Williams. During 1878 Williams had been the first black nominated for major local office, as Greenback-Labor candidate for city commissioner. During 1879 he had served as one of Stokley's new turnkeys, while writing, for a campaign paper, a violently partisan article entitled "The Bloody Shirt," traditional symbol of Republican appeals based on the Civil War. During 1883 he would write secretly to Congressman Sam Randall, promising to help the Democrats if properly rewarded. As of the fall of 1880 he was an anti-Stokley dissident and supporter of George Keim, as he and Alexander Davis, another ambitious newspaper editor and publisher of the *Spectator*, used the police issue to help drum up interest, citing precedents in Chicago, Washington, and Newark.[36]

Keim had few credentials as a friend of the race, and Williams little credibility. But the police issue was older and it turned out stronger than their personal political campaigns, both of which collapsed early in the new year. Leading blacks, courted on all sides, did not forget it. Given slapstick ineptitude among the "Committee of One Hundred," and its almost total lack of communication with the Afro-American political community, the great majority finally decided, as before, to "Stick with Stokley" during the February elections. But the old fireman had more than ten years' worth of enemies, and despite the loyalty of his black troopers he was narrowly, and surprisingly, defeated by the opposing coalition of reformers, Democrats, Independents, and dissidents. The bigger surprise is that the new mayor, Samuel King, freely decided to follow up the police issue on his own.[37]

King's intention to court the Afro-American community was first signaled by his treatment of William Dorsey. Dorsey was of course fired as personal messenger when the new mayor was installed in April. At the same time King reportedly considered replacing him with Gil Ball, and chose instead an old white friend only when Ball failed "an investigation of his antecedents." Dorsey, with perhaps ironic political justice, was given instead a place as turnkey; in breaking the news King, apparently for the first time, "said to Dorsey, however, that he proposed considering the employment of some colored men in the police department." Four months later, in August, he made good by appointing Richard Caldwell, Charles Carroll, Alex Davis, and Charles Draper to the force.[38]

The move was of course controversial. Ex-mayor Dick Vaux, who had often physically joined the new police force, during the 1850s, in doing battle with street gangs and river pirates, spoke for the older "Bourbon" Democrats: "Darkies, uniformed as officers, and empowered to lay violent hands upon white men . . . is an insult too unpardonable to think of." Some black toughs reportedly claimed that they would not submit to the authority of others of their race, and a few white men quit the force. But there was no real trouble. The inevitable crowds which followed the new men on their downtown beats made jokes but threw nothing. The Sunday *Times* did print a satire in which "Majah" Teagle in a nightmare found himself, in uniform, patrolling Irish Port Richmond through a cloud of bricks. But in practice there was no effort to confine the officers to Afro-American neighborhoods, perhaps in part because residential segregation had not gone far enough to allow it. Four days after starting work Draper made the historic first arrest, of a drunken Irish-American, without incident.[39]

The newpapers, regardless of party, applauded the move. The four new cops were interviewed and investigated, and it seems clear that all, recommended by Robert Jones, had been chosen with the kind of care that went three generations later into selecting the first children to enter newly integrated southern schools. The four were settled married men, with families to support. At a time when there were still no formal requirements of any kind for police officers, Davis, the newspaperman, was an ex-slave, graduate of Lincoln University, and former law student at Howard. Draper was a Civil War veteran, secretary of the Equal Rights League, active Mason, music teacher, and longtime leader of his Presbyterian Choir. Carroll, who like many white cops had served an apprenticeship as turnkey, was a native Philadelphian, well-educated, and "of a studious disposition." Only Caldwell, a laborer, had no résumé to quote beyond the fact that he was a native of Chester County, 23 years old, "very dark . . . five feet 9½ inches tall . . . about 160 pounds."[40]

And if the press was pleased by the mayor's four choices, the Afro-American community was more excited than by any other event since the vote. Blacks of both sexes and all ages made up much of the crowd that followed them about during their first days in office. And on August 22 some 2000 people, or roughly one-third the total number of Afro-American voters, crowded into Liberty Hall for a great celebration called by the veterans Robert Purvis and William Still, and joined by several white abolitionists. The organizers did not include the usual Republican stalwarts, but most of them were there, and the occasion was so obviously joyous and nonpartisan, as Purvis and Robert Jones worked the audience by mocking Richard Vaux and the white cops who had quit, that even the subsidized Republican Isaiah Wears was called by popular demand to make a graceful and often humorous speech, in which he managed to speak no ill of the Democrats.[41]

The fact that a single act by a Democratic mayor was allowed to outshadow a generation's worth of alleged Republican blessings was a matter of concern to some newspapers and black politicians. But the only real dissent was inspired by a resolution praising King for honoring "the just and equal claims of colored men to appointments." The phrase was seized by otherwise congratulatory editorial writers for the *Press*, the *Ledger and Transcript*, and the *Sunday Dispatch*, all of whom agreed that the proper issue was merit, without regard to race or party; the mayor's action should be seen as a triumph over, rather than a triumph for, the "vile" claim that "the color of a man's skin" should count in his favor.[42]

To the city's white Republican leaders what mattered more than these high principles was the threat to their nearly exclusive hold on the black electorate. Their response was to allow a matching breakthough in elective office. Earlier black victories in primary elections had been overturned in convention, but in 1884 Colonel Jacob Purnell, former hero of the Underground Railroad and Civil War, was nominated and elected as one of four common councilmen from the Seventh Ward. The matter was of some symbolic importance, and Purnell was the first of a line of councilmen, highest local office which any of his race would win during the 19th century. But in contrast to the police appointments his election inspired no special excitement in the Afro-American community.[43]

This restrained reaction may have resulted from a general disillusion with elective politics by the 1880s. Perhaps it was a recognition that one councilman, even the two or three won by the early 1890s, could have no real impact on a complex city government whose common council, in every sense the lesser of two legislative branches, consisted of well over a hundred members. Like school directors they were unpaid, indeed barred from holding any paying job with the city; unlike school directors they had no direct patronage at their disposal. While the blacks elected in the 19th century, including Purnell, David Chester, George Wilson, Constantin Hubert, Andrew Stevens, and Christopher Perry, were distinctly more reputable than their white counterparts, they were not generally richer. Election to council was often only a means to the end of winning paying jobs in government; while some councilmen, such as Andrew Stevens, had relatively good incomes of their own, others, such as Christopher Perry and Stephen Gipson, were given jobs as clerks not technically paid by the City but the County of Philadelphia. But perhaps the major reason why Colonel Purnell's election was no reason for celebration is that his candidacy was part of the successful effort to defeat Samuel King for a second term as mayor.[44]

Black leaders had reason to mourn the passing of King's administration, and many otherwise fierce Republicans remembered him for years to come. By the end of his term the reform mayor had appointed 35 Afro-American policemen, a number then far bigger than the total number of schoolteachers, messengers, janitors, or clerks employed by the city. And while William Smith, his successor, could pointedly fire the ones who, like Davis and Carroll, were most obnoxious to partisan Republicans, the obvious success of King's initiative made it impossible for the GOP to turn back the clock. At the same time the movement for civil service reform, an important inspiration for the original "Committee of One Hundred" movement, gave black office-seekers unexpected new support.[45]

Civil service reform at the national level was won in part when President James Garfield, in the summer of 1881, was shot by an assassin then and always afterward labeled as "a disappointed office seeker." During August, bulletins on the dying Garfield's condition vied in the Philadelphia press with stories of King's police appointments, and helped to give emotional support to those reformers who objected to claims based on color, party, or any qualification other than merit. The resulting civil service commission began work in 1883, shortly before the election of President Grover Cleveland. Afro-Americans across the country were naturally anxious about Cleveland, the first Democratic President since the war. But both his willingness to conciliate and his genuine belief in civil service kept him from sweeping black Republicans out of federal jobs. Dan Adger was fired from the postal service, for "offensive partisanship," but most Philadelphians kept their jobs and some advanced. Pliny Locke, son of Ishmael, first black teacher at the ICY, and father of Alain, first black Rhodes scholar, made top score on a promotional examination, as did James Williams, and both were moved up into the money order department. And during Cleveland's first year, in 1885, the "Committee of One Hundred" was able to bring a version of civil service reform to Philadelphia.[46]

It was a soft version, compromised by legislators in Harrisburg and administered by partisans in Philadelphia, and it was hard even for students at the time to find out how it worked, or even who was covered. For the police it meant political "character references" and a background check, a set of minimum physical qualifications and an examination in basic reading and writing skills. For black applicants, given their generally good and growing record of literacy, it meant increasing success. By 1891 there were sixty Afro-Americans on the patrol force, a percentage reasonably close to the official black proportion of the city's population, although none of them had ever been promoted. Du Bois wrote a few years later that these men were "good average officers," a phrase he did not elaborate. At worst it could mean that, like their white peers, the black cops were notorious for politicking with their nightsticks at the polls; one was indicted, with a white colleague, for killing a white kid fleeing a petty larceny; a couple were accused of investing in bawdy houses. But on the whole the group was better than the general average on the force.[47]

The *Times,* in 1896, published a long piece on "The Colored Policemen" which emphasized their superior quality. About a third of the men were assigned to the Fifth and Nineteenth districts, heavily settled by blacks, but most were scattered throughout the city—always in even numbers, perhaps because of the problem of sharing beds. Most whose biographies were given had worked at the better blue-collar jobs open to them before appointment, as coachmen and butlers, cobblers and sailors. Several had been cited for heroism. "Pop" Frey was one of the most visible and popular officers in the city, assigned to the bicycle squad, where he wheeled about downtown and some-times arrested "scorchers" after spectacular chases down South Broad Street. Bart Page had once played first base for the famous "Cuban" Giants, and used his quick reflexes when "he risked his life to save people from being run over by trolleys." Charles Bolling had "the finest physique in the district"; "Deacon" Garnett was a student of serious secular literature as well as the Bible, and "there is no more intelligent man on the force." (The reporter felt obliged to explain that his other nickname, "Handsome George," was a joke, since he was "the darkest colored man on duty.") Taken all together, the piece went on, the men were "a credit to the force, and were it not for their color, many would be in high official positions." It was true that none had ever won promotion: "Most, however, are content with their lot, and do not aspire to distinction of rank."[48]

If they were indeed content, Councilman Constantin Hubert was not. Hubert, elected from the Fifth Ward in 1890, was the only black to make any kind of news while in office. One of his campaigns, in which he enlisted Nathan Mossell, was to try to break the will of Stephen Girard, once the city's richest merchant, who in 1831 had endowed Girard College for the free education of "white male orphans." The basic argument was simply that the provision was discriminatory. But it was embellished by a claim in effect for racial repara-tions: much of Girard's fortune had been won by cheating Toussaint L'Over-ture and the Haitian people, and the admission of black youngsters would help to right this historic wrong. The city council agreed at least to refer the matter to the city solicitor, who ruled against it, with the strong support of news-papers, in the name of the sanctity of private property generally and testaments in particular. Later the same year Hubert tried to win black representation on the state's World's Fair Committee, to help prepare for the great Columbian Exposition of 1893; while he lost in council the governor did eventually appoint Florence Lewis to the post. But his first and most important compaign, begun as he took office, was to reform the civil service. After noting that despite their qualifications none of the city's black cops had been promoted to sergeant or above, or to specialized jobs as in the Harbor Division, he moved that all city and county appointments should be made not only after examination but in strict "order of merit," that is, on the basis of the highest scores.[49]

Some black men, like James Davis, head draughtsman first in the water and then the gas department, had such valuable technical skills that they could win good jobs without ever involving themselves in politics at all. But most departments could get by despite passing over the best, as determined by test scores, in favor of the merely acceptable. Hubert's campaign was inspired by men like Lee Ransom, who had won the highest score on his patrolman's examination in 1888 but failed to win a job. Under the existing system appointment required only a passing score, and a department head could either choose or reject qualifiers without regard to whether they had earned the equivalent of an "A" or a "D." For higher jobs, promotions were given to any of the top five finishers in their respective examinations, but the tests were given so often, and so irregularly, that any man who consistently scored well could still be consistently passed over if his politics, race, or other characteristics were counted against him. And since "the highest percentage is usually achieved by Afro-Americans," strictly following the test results would benefit the race.[50]

Hubert first tried to pass a city ordinance to remedy the situation. But the move was blocked by the city solicitor's ruling that his draft covered the county as well, and was beyond the jurisdiction of the councils. The campaign then moved to the state legislature in Harrisburg; a great rally at the Academy of Music, in the spring of 1891, was chaired by Robert Purvis, who shared the dais with several influential white politicians. But the bill failed a second reading, and the system remained.[51]

A generation after winning the vote, then, the city's Afro-Americans had made impressive gains in government service. By the middle of the 1890s, in addition to the policemen, Du Bois counted 29 white-collar employees, not including Philadelphians in Washington: 17 in the post office, 11 in city government, one each in the customs house and navy yard, plus a number of messengers, turnkeys, and janitors. The total, well over a hundred people in relatively steady and well-paying jobs, was an important addition to the tiny black elite. But the fact that the percentage was still far less than the proportion of black Republican voters, that the glass if not empty was still less than half full, continued to inspire debate about the need for political leverage, and the value of continued fidelity to the GOP.[52]

During the height of Reconstruction only one black Philadelphian identified himself with the Democratic party; Joseph E. Williams, who had already distinguished himself by enduring three army courts-martial, attended the national nominating convention in 1868 as an obvious token, and never dared return to the political wars in his native city. By 1874 a few independent souls such as Robert Purvis and William Still, without political ambitions of their own, could challenge the Republicans' hold on the local black electorate. After 1877 the gates opened wider, and by the 1880s it was possible to challenge the GOP from within as well as without. Some questioned its record on local appointments, others its national and international policies. Local leaders were quite aware, and continually reminded, that their political potential depended on the leverage provided by a balance of power. And while some remained blindly loyal to the bone, a few even of the local club leaders and ward politicians were willing to challenge the city's white bosses in a series of test votes pitting black insurgents against endorsed white candidates.[53]

Some of the crucial events have already been sketched: the "Compromise of 1877" in Washington, the King administration in Philadelphia, a Republican Supreme Court's emasculation of the Civil Rights Act in 1883, the conciliatory attitude adopted by President Cleveland after his election in 1884. These and similar developments helped inspire a continual reassessment of the labels stuck to friends and foes. John D. Lewis, attacked as a Democrat, used his experience as a civil rights lawyer to argue that judicial fairness, regardless of party, was more important to his fellows than "class legislation in their favor," and cited local Democratic Judges Allinson, Briggs, Ludlow, and Thayer. Bishop Turner praised the ex-slaveholder John Marshall Harlan for his eloquent dissent in the Civil Rights cases, followed sixteen years later by the old man's lone objection to *Plessy v. Ferguson.* William Still's friend Allen Tarnage, in an open "Letter to . . . Colored Voters" in 1895, remembered New Jersey's Judge Wescott in the Lingo case, the Crawford County Democrat who had struck down school segregation in 1881, William Allinson's stand against streetcar segregation in 1865.[54]

It had always been clear that Republican support for Afro-Americans was less than skin deep, and there were continual reminders of the party's often callous past and racist present. Older leaders could remember when Pennsylvania Republicans had supported segregation and denied the vote; the selection of Attorney General Brewster recalled the day when he had worked to send fugitive slaves back south; when ex-Senator Donald Cameron was fined for viciously whipping a black man while quail hunting in South Carolina, William Dorsey noted that it was "great pity he was not shot. . . ." What was new after 1877 was that the Democrats were moving to exploit this disaffection. Robert Purvis in 1890 recalled that "the only man in Philadelphia who ever carried out those principles of equality which the Republican Party professed was Samuel G. King, a Democrat." The next year Governor Robert Pattison, another reform Democrat, was the only state official to attend the opening convention of the new Afro-American League. Even the old warrior and saloonkeeper "Squire" McMullin of the Fifth Ward was capable of making a gesture. While McMullin, his biographer believes, had ordered the killing of Octavius Catto in 1871, the distance traveled after may be measured by the fact that when Gil Ball, his Republican counterpart, died in December of 1890 the "Squire" visited the widow, as a kind of professional courtesy, with an elaborate funeral wreath.[55]

The city's blacks by then had discovered that Democrats as well as Republicans could supply jobs. Alexander Davis, fired as a cop by a Republican mayor, found a place in the customs house under the Cleveland administration. While William Still often anticipated the later position of Booker T. Washington by urging his fellows to forget politics and stick to business, Robert Still moved past his father's professed independence into avowed membership in the Democratic party. The young man, graduate of the ICY and Lincoln University, began by joining his brother Wilbur in supporting Cleveland in 1884, then founded the Democratic *State Journal* in 1890. After running for city council in 1891, the first black ever endorsed by Democrats in the state, he helped the Democratic State League to expand across the country and then shortly before his early death went to work for the National Committee, in 1892. At the topmost diplomatic level, finally, although Cleveland did fire John Durham, the Reverend C. C. Astwood found a place as consul to Santo Domingo.[56]

Some Afro-American leaders held to the old faith in every jot and tittle. The once aggressive Equal Rights League moved out of town after Catto's death; after losing some independent spirits such as the journalist William Howard Day, the League was left with what Isaiah Mayhugh contemptuously called "seven men," locally led by William Forten, who could not be persuaded to criticize the GOP. One of these loyalists, Isaiah Wears, could be kept in line partly by putting him on the campaign payroll and partly by playing on his vanity, appointing him to symbolic posts such as presidential elector, or the mayor's "Citizen's Advisory Committee." The party of course had a grip— although some would twist out of it—over its own officeholders. But once Reconstruction was history most others found reason to question its policies both at home and abroad.[57]

The major domestic issue centered around the tariff, historic centerpiece of Republican economics. John D. Lewis was an active member of an "Independent" Convention held in New York, during 1884, in effect to promote Grover Cleveland's candidacy without rousing the old emotions associated with the word "Democratic." Four years later, again in Cleveland's interest, he led young Robert Still, the newspapermen Andrew Jones and George Gardiner, and other disaffected blacks such as ex-patrolman Charles Draper into the Sentinel Tariff Reform Club, named after Gardiner's paper. The argument in 1888 as in 1884 was mostly economic: the Republican party, as representative of manufacturing interests and capital, had nothing to offer Afro-Americans. Most of his people, Lewis pointed out, were farm laborers or farmers, or in the city professionals, small tradesmen, and laborers. The tariff at best was designed to benefit those members of the working class who labored in factories protected behind its walls, but despite continual pleas the GOP had not persuaded manufacturers to hire black men and women. Tariff protection meant nothing then but higher consumer prices to a race slotted, apparently forever, to remain "hewers of wood and drawers of water" under Republican rule.[58]

This was a powerful argument, and even Republican journalists, if they mentioned it at all, had to apologize for the tariff. But while the issue did not go away it was overshadowed during the 1890s by the more complicated issue of American expansion abroad.[59]

Until the imperialist aftermath of the Spanish-American War of 1898, Philadelphia's Afro-Americans had found a variety of reasons for supporting an aggressive foreign policy. Lincoln's alumni, gathered for the 1890 graduation, began a declaration of principles by extending "sympathy for the struggling of all nations that are reaching for democracy, liberty, and freedom from oppression"; a sentiment which, unlike most of the others, would easily fit into a traditional party platform. The Reverend Mr. Astwood, after some years in the Caribbean, believed the United States a "paradise" next to most of the islands, where no one could vote. The war itself, undertaken ostensibly to free the Cubans from Spanish brutality, did not seem at first to offend him. He and his church may have believed that the expansionist "Mission of America" might aid in the expansion of their own more traditional mission; Protestants were not welcome in the colonies of Catholic nations, and Astwood himself opened the first AME mission in Cuba only after American troops had moved in. Christopher Perry, meanwhile, as editor of the *Tribune*, stretched hard to find another kind of opportunity when the war over Cuba led to invasion of the Philippines, suddenly opening visions of a tropical empire to match those of Great Britain and other European powers. After black troops had performed heroically in Cuba the *Literary Digest*, in the summer of 1898, suggested that the otherwise doomed race might have a future after all, as tropical troopers in our new empire. Perry thought there might be some merit in this, so long as they were allowed to fight under black officers.[60]

But while the Spanish War itself did not disturb Philadelphia's Afro-Americans, its imperialist aftermath did. Disillusion set in for C. C. Astwood shortly after his arrival in Cuba; writing from Santiago on August 30, 1898, he noted that "the color line is being fastly drawn by the whites here, and the Cubans abused as Negroes." All the romantic talk about "freeing" them had been based on simple ignorance of the fact that most were people of color; but "now that that fact has dawned upon the white brother, there is no longer a desire to have Cuban independence." Reverend Theodore Gould established a "General Relief Committee of Colored Citizens of Philadelphia and Vicinity" immediately after the victory, which pointedly included Cuban citizens as well as U.S. soldiers as objects of its charity. Bishop Turner noted that the Spanish were "far better friends to our race than the United States will ever be."[61]

It took little longer to disillusion Christopher Perry. In September of 1898, little more than a month after the fighting stopped, T. Thomas Fortune called a new "National Afro-American Council." The new group, a less ambitious version of the Afro-American League which had collapsed earlier in the decade—in Pennsylvania its name was appropriated by an organ of the

Republican party—made a clear connection between the treatment of colored peoples at home and abroad, and Fortune predicted that Cuba, Puerto Rico, and the Philippines would all revolt if subjected to American racism. Perry, as a member of the executive council, helped to call for "a liberal system in the treatment of the natives in the newly conquered possessions." The call was inspired in part by increasing Republican fascination with the idea of a special and perhaps God-given "Anglo-Saxon Mission," a form of racism which both fueled and was fueled by the prospect of colonial empire. Talk of the "White Man's Burden" inspired much black derision; Perry, in the spring of 1899, suggested that any drive to "uplift" backward peoples might begin in the mountains of white Appalachia. Conciliatory by nature, and generally careful not to criticize the local leadership, he was also a Republican officeholder, and it took much offense and some courage to lead him to describe President William McKinley as "the poorest apology for a statesman that Ohio has ever produced."[62]

Over the previous twenty years then a long line of leading black Philadelphians had shown that they could criticize and even break from the Republican party. Only a few would go so far as Robert Still in identifying as Democrats or sit with Robert Purvis and Alex Davis on the dais during a great rally for Benjamin Butler's Greenback-Labor party in the fall of 1884. But disaffection had begun with unrest about jobs in Philadelphia in the 1870s, moved on to economic policy in Washington, during the 1880s, and finally to foreign imperialism in the 1890s. The trouble was in translating it into actual votes, protests that would keep politicians from taking the race for granted.[63]

Most of the actual votes registered in Philadelphia's endless round of primary, convention, and general elections were racially irrelevant. The Seventh Ward was the only one in the city in which black voters held a potential majority, despite significant strength in the nearby Fifth or Eighth, so that they were usually asked to support various white men as candidates for prothonotary, coroner, or council for reasons that were hard to understand at that time and impossible to recapture at this one. But there were several key occasions which tested fidelity to race versus fidelity to orders, beginning with Samuel King's bid for re-election in 1884.

Shortly before the election the *Times* asked several community leaders how they intended to vote. All of them had good words for the mayor, although Bishop Tanner said he could not bring himself to vote for a Democrat and Gil Ball noted that he was after all a member of the Republican City Committee. But Robert Purvis and Nathan Mossell answered with an enthusiastic endorsement, and the Reverend Mr. Stephenson believed that all Afro-Americans would agree. Three businessmen, the real-estate dealer Andrew Jones, grocer Jacob Ramsey, and flour merchant Thomas Boling, although avowing that they were not politicians, declared for King, as did Alfred Bettencourt, a saloonkeeper identified as a (Republican) "Seventh Ward politician." Three weeks later the Seventh Ward brought in its usual and overwhelming Republican majority, prompting "Silenus" to conclude, in the New York *Globe,* that it was "the colored voters" who had done in the mayor.[64]

King was, however, a white Democrat, and a clearer test was offered in 1886 when Stephen Gipson campaigned in the Republican primary for nomination to the state assembly from the Seventh Ward. Despite the confidence of Gil Ball, "the real leader of the colored people in the ward," Gipson was counted out, the result, according to "Possum" in the *Sunday Mercury,* of the fact that "so many unprincipled 'niggers' sold their votes" for $1.50. While a number of divisional leaders had followed Ball in defying the white ward bosses, others deserted their man in convention. But Ball, predicting that "our people are ripe for a bolt," joined with Dr. Mossell and others in a great meeting at Liberty Hall, threatening to run Gipson as an Independent. "Possum" noted that the primary had been a farce and the convention a tragedy, but predicted high drama in the general election, going on to say, "The white leaders laughed over the farce, were participants in the tragedy, and may learn a lesson from the drama."[65]

In fact the drama had just begun: when Gipson withdrew early in October, his supporters turned to a third party entirely: Gil Ball, the city's leading black saloonkeeper, led a special meeting which called for a split ticket comprised of the usual Republicans plus two black men running as Prohibitionists, the Reverend John R. Palmer for congressman-at-large and John W. Jones in Gipson's place for assemblyman. Once again the *Times* surveyed the leadership, and found the clergy—this time including Tanner—was solidly Prohibitionist, together with Mossell, Jones, and others; even David Bowser, although opposed as "staunch Republican" to third parties in general, believed that the Seventh Ward should go for Jones. On November 2 Palmer won just 216 votes out of 5,165 counted; what the white leaders had learned from the drama, *pace* "Possum," was expressed with an ironic verbal flourish: "The same old coon still on top!"[66]

Independence after that fared progressively worse. Stephen Gipson, perhaps as reward for dropping out, was eventually elected to join George Wilson as one of the Seventh Ward's four councilmen in 1890, winning by a handsome 2000 votes at the same time that Constantin Hubert was elected by an even more impressive 3000 in the Fifth. That brought the Afro-American total to three, the most for a long time to come. But it was still two less than their proportional share of the population, and in a heavily Republican city less than half what their 10 percent of the party's vote might have earned. Neither of the new men was grateful; just as Hubert was pushing for civil service reform, Gipson, a veteran of the politics of South Carolina, noted that "in southern cities the Democrats take far better political care of the colored man than the Republicans do in Philadelphia," citing the fifty black firemen in New Orleans as contrast to the one in his own city. His frankness cost him two years later, when with Gil Ball dead the leadership denied him renomination in favor of the older and less outspoken Andrew Stevens. Hubert, in the same 1892 election, was deserted in favor of a white Democrat. The nadir was reached in 1898 when the popular young lawyer and Lincoln graduate Henry Bass repeated Gipson's challenge by running against a white man in the primary for the State Assembly. He failed to win a single division in the Seventh Ward, losing by nearly 10 to 1 in some of them.[67]

Republican domination was then complete. It obviously owed little to the memory of Emancipation: dissent had flourished more in the late 1870s and 1880s than in the 1890s, when the Civil War, the Catto riot, and Reconstruction had long faded, and the economic and imperialist policies of the GOP pulled it farther and farther from the interests of the articulate leadership. Toward the end of the century, despite continued growth in the number and proportion of black voters, the Afro-American councilmen were cut back from three to one. There was continued disaffection among intellectuals, but the city's white leadership had little to fear from the kind of rebellion once represented by Purvis, Lewis, Mossell, and Still, the *State Journal* and the *Sentinel*, Gipson and Hubert, even Bettencourt and Ball. There had been great gains over the period, clearly, but while most leaders tried to battle for independence they could not finally win it against a party that had as many strings to pull as the GOP in Philadelphia.

The right to vote in the late 19th century was unquestionably a benefit to Philadelphia's blacks, but political activity was not as rewarding as for the Irish and others. Historically other groups played much the same role as newcomers to politics, winning legitimate and illegitimate rewards in return for the number of legitimate and illegitimate votes they produced or suppressed. The problem was that the unique economic situation of the Afro-American community, its exclusion from the wider rewards of the urban-industrial revolution, combined with racism and dependence on a single party to make it uniquely vulnerable to political exploitation. The result was to make the legitimate rewards of politics relatively few, despite their great importance, and the illegitimate rewards all too common. In general the jobs went directly to the elite, usually reinforcing respectability, while the illegitimate payoffs and protection went to the rest, often encouraging crime. But neither the respectable nor the disreputable had power enough to combat political dependence, and both had to battle to maintain dignity and integrity in the face of pressure from white politicians.

Neither of the two reasons for growing dependence on the Republican party can be blamed on the city's black leadership. The first was simply the fact that the Democrats, for reasons having nothing to do with the Afro-American vote, grew weaker in the city, state, and nation as the century progressed. In Philadelphia, during the 1870s and 1880s, the minority party could count on about 40 percent of the vote, enough in a decentralized system to win a number of offices; by the later 1890s it had sunk closer to 30 percent, and was generally shut out. The doubly paradoxical result was that while the black vote grew progressively bigger it was progressively less crucial to the GOP, and still had nowhere else to go.[68]

The other reason for dependence was the central fact of exclusion from industrial and other good jobs, and the failure to win them through legitimate politics. This was decidedly not the result of neglecting the issue. Politically articulate Afro-Americans of every persuasion continually stressed the need for better opportunities. Robert Jones in 1878 called for jobs not only in government but in the gas company, notoriously close to the city's Republican "Ring." Alexander Davis and H. P. Williams, at their very first anti-Stokley meeting in December of 1880, talked about opening factory gates as well as the doors to civil service. Many thought the police appointments important because they might help to conquer the wider prejudice against blacks in uniformed authority, the usual reason given for refusing to hire them as, for example, streetcar conductors; Isaiah Wears, in August of 1881, expected the four cops to be followed by five men on the cars, as the beginning of an upward spiral. Christopher Perry, not yet a councilman but always a politician, was one of the men involved in negotiations to open the garment business, during the Blum brothers strike in 1890. Seven years later the "Colored Men's Republican Association of the 29th Ward" appointed a committee headed by the Reverend Matthew Anderson to plead for jobs with the Union Traction Company. Both Robert Purvis and John Durham publicly and continually sounded the same call. But of the city's Republican employers only John Wanamaker, motivated perhaps as much by his Christian beliefs as his political ambitions, defied prevailing custom by hiring Afro-Americans in his department store, mostly but not entirely in the stock room.[69]

The result of this failure, and the fact that the limited number of government jobs went mostly to members of the educated elite, was that there was nothing legitimate to offer the hundreds of men who enrolled in all those political clubs to march, burn, and fight for the GOP. Ordinary members, unable to win real jobs, were perhaps satisfied with the several annual occasions when they might sell their votes, sometimes for a week's wages. The fact that the clubs themselves welcomed southern newcomers, and offered semi-protected opportunities to drink and gamble illegally, was itself a reward for joining or even visiting. For the officers the clubs could be not just a reward but a living; there was often little distinction between clubs and speakeasies, gambling "parlors" and bawdy houses, and one of the things they all shared was the need to pay off police and politicians in one coin or another in order to stay in business.

Votes and vice were often entangled, as reformers found when in 1894 they brought fraud charges against several of the divisional assessors in charge of keeping the voting lists. The move was part of an attempt to purge the names of dogs, cats, and ghosts from the rolls, but it uncovered other irregularities as well, as in the case of James Briscoe. Briscoe, elected assessor of the Twelfth Division, Fifth Ward, was, it appeared, able to support himself entirely as unsalaried "night clerk" of the Carleton "Hotel" on South Street by making double use of its 17 rooms, charging "guests" for renting them for short periods and registering 50 voters from the address.[70]

Both vice and politics could of course be dangerous. Any one of the ingredients of life in the vice district could cause trouble of a kind beyond the reach of law. And alcohol, weapons, cards, dice, and sex were especially volatile when mixed together, often stirred by people of two races, in an atmosphere heated by fear and sometimes guilt. The underside of politics, too, could involve not only strong-arm work at the polls but bundles of cash off the books. Senator Matthew Quay, "The Kingmaker," often used Gil Ball's lieutenant Warren Jackson, of the Quay Club, to perform various "trusted" errands around the country, involving "political secrecy" and "considerable sums of money." In the summer of 1890, as Quay's influence in Washington neared its peak, Jackson's body was fished out of a canal near Harrisburg, clothing in place but pockets emptied.[71]

Those who played this kind of politics, such as Jackson, took physical risks, much like periodic arrests and jailings, as the price of profit. The problem was that they victimized many others as well. The fact that in terms of sheer voting power black politics was dominated by club members with a strong stake in illegal activity had far-reaching effects. The whole of the black community, parents, workingmen, churchgoers, and businessmen, paid for the series of political decisions that resulted in the fact that much of the Fifth, Seventh, and Eighth wards served as a vice or "red-light" district. And political dependence, the fact that the troopers continued to turn out for the Republican party regardless of its treatment of blacks, had several other kinds of impact on many not usually found in the back rooms of clubhouses.

Some of the politicians simply gave in. Henry Bass, for example, after his disastrous attempt to beat the organization in 1898, finally realized, in 1910, his ambition to become Pennsylvania's first black state representative, but at a price. When taxed with neglecting the interests of the Afro-American community, he reportedly insisted that, on the contrary, "I am in perfect accord with my constituents. I have consulted both of them"—naming the two white bosses of the Seventh Ward.[72]

Gil Ball was a stronger man, able to defy his mentor Matt Quay during the first attempt, by Stephen Gipson, to win the seat that Bass won a quarter-century later. But when Quay pulled hard enough on his strings, Ball too had to jump, even if it killed him. During the same August of 1890 that Warren Jackson was scragged outside of Harrisburg, Senator Quay was involved in making the key decision that took the Republican party down one of the several forks in the road that led away from its anti-slavery origins to its identification with manufacturing capital. The Senate than faced a choice: to take up the liberal Republicans' so called "Force Bill," aimed at using federal power to protect southern blacks at the polls—in effect the last echo of the policies of Reconstruction—or to take up the McKinley Tariff. Quay moved for the tariff in August—with the full endorsement of the Matthew S. Quay Club of the Seventh Ward. Both decisions, by the senator and by the troopers, outraged Afro-Americans all over the country, and there is good evidence that the Quay club's own officers, intelligent men who had originally joined the party of Abraham Lincoln and Charles Sumner, had agonized over theirs. The abuse they earned for their loyalty may have contibuted to the fact that Jackson, a family man, had reportedly plunged into a "protracted spree" just before his murder, and it certainly helped bury Gil Ball well before a heart attack, in December, at the age of 40.[73]

Black dependence was not usually displayed so dramatically. Most of the routine humiliations daily compounded of arrogance and racism are hidden from historians, but a lawsuit in 1898 offers a rare look at some of the atmosphere in City Hall, and the ingenuity with which one black man struck back. For nearly a quarter-century Isaac Holland, a longtime messenger for the Bureau of Surveys, had to put up with racial harassment from Edwin A. Pue, an auditor in the City Controller's office. It was Pue's custom to run his fingers over Holland's head, in passing, while treating observers to his own parody of the jargon of phrenology:

> A splendid development of cephalophia, approaching cephalopteridae, which fully proved a myocephalic condition, from which one could only obtain—complete mental oblivion, or supering insanity.[74]

The longsuffering Holland finally replied with a newpaper ad in the name of his tormentor, a lifelong bachelor, who allegedly wanted:

> A neat, tidy, pleasant-looking young colored girl for child's nurse, and for cook, and another for chambermaid. Apply to Edwin A. Pue, City Controller's Office.

The response was overwhelming—some fifty young women, "neat, tidy, and, withal, pleasant looking" crowded the office and out into the corridors. City Hall was amused; Pue was not, and sued Holland for defaming his character.[75]

The legal calendar was shorter in the late 19th century than today, and the courtroom the next week was packed with civil servants struggling unsuccessfully to keep their faces straight. Holland was a popular man, active in Jackson Post No.27 of the Grand Army of the Republic, and his case was taken gratis by Colonel John Frazier, a white fellow veteran. Frazier granted the facts of the case, including the hurt done Pue. His defense was based in part on extenuation: he asked the judge to imagine how he would feel if, at the club, Senators Penrose or Quay were in the habit of grabbing his head "and diagnosing it as Mr. Pue did Mr. Holland's." But the basic defense was insanity. His client was obviously not responsible for his actions, the Colonel noted, the result, as "dear, proud, Pue" himself had noticed, of "an increasing ruyoeephalic carditian" which had resulted in "mental oblivion." With the room on the verge of eruption Judge Devlin dismissed the case, while the spectators scrambled forward to pay Holland's $4.85 in court costs.[76]

Holland's case was of course unusual, and he was lucky that Pue lacked real authority as well as any sense of humor. Usually messengers were simply fired when, much like secretaries in more recent times, they complained about shoe-shining and other menial duties not included in their job descriptions. William Lee, a successor to William Dorsey who served as personal messenger to four mayors, was dismissed on demand of William English, campaign manager to Mayor Sam Ashbridge, because he was overheard calling English "a warm baby"—a term that he claimed, unsuccessfully, meant simply "stylishly dressed." Such low-level patronage employees were vulnerable by definition, but while those in better jobs were less so they were also careful not to offend. People like the school principal Jacob White and the tax office clerk James Needham were not forced to play clubhouse politics, but despite their promi-nence in the community they and other civil servants were not found on the dais during political protests either, whether those which involved hiring cops, running Afro-American candidates, or protesting lynch law in the South.[77]

Political dependence also reached beyond officeholders: even in an era of relatively minimal government the party had a number of strings to pull when it felt the need. Henry Minton, for example, was embarrassed, or threatened, during his testimony at the Catto trial, by references to his "saloon"; like most caterers he had no liquor license, and was able to operate a step outside the law only on sufferance. When local blacks complained about a white-owned bar-room in the Fifth Ward, whose patrons' indecencies threatened girls on the way to Forten School, several trustees of nearby Bethel Church were pulled in to join the blacks on the sectional school board in testifying to the good character of the place. The precise reasons are no more clear than those which persuaded Dr. Mossell, four years after Gil Ball made his bail in the abortion case, to testify to the good character of saloonkeeper Al Bettencourt; license was denied, and Bettencourt stabbed in his own place the day it closed. Within a few years, too, the once avowedly Democratic physician found himself lobbying the state's Republicans to win the subsidy needed to make a reality out of his dream for Douglass Hospital.[78]

Politics, then, was full of problems of many kinds for Philadelphia's new black citizens. But in terms of the two issues which most concerned them, jobs and safety, the leadership at least could look back, from about 1900, with much satisfaction at the progress made locally. In strong contrast to their fellows in the South they were safe from racial violence, as the older kind of riot-pogrom grew rare, although never quite extinct, in northern cities generally. And while never proportionate to their overall voting strength the number of government jobs was enormously important, and growing. Their significance must be considered in terms of the entire economic situation described throughout this Part II.

Despite all its drawbacks government work was more desirable than almost any other kind. The majority of urban blacks in the late 19th century were very poor, shut out of the industrial revolution and increasingly of the skilled trades, losing even the better male servants' jobs, with only a more dependable supply of laboring work as consolation. Business opportunities, at best in transition, were apparently shrinking as the century progressed, the result partly of racism and partly of white fears of the vice and crime in growing black neighborhoods. While the professions, in contrast, were opening, they offered little real independence. Teaching, with the death of the Institute for Colored Youth and the decline of "charity" schools, was itself a form of civil service. While the city's doctors, lawyers, and newspapermen multiplied severalfold few were able to support themselves in professional style; both journalism and the law were often thought simply stepping-stones toward jobs in government, and even doctors found themselves, one way or another, involved in politics.

No more than a few dozen men, then, enjoyed legitimate jobs that they would not gladly have traded for a place in the post office. Given perhaps a dozen lawyers, a few more doctors, and probably less than a hundred truly stable small businessmen, civil servants loomed very large among the securely employed elite. The number of those hired by the city did stall at the end of the century, as the result of political weakness, so that W. E. B. Du Bois found no more on a return visit in 1905 than he had in the middle of the 1890s. But while local patronage jobs were not reliable, and local civil service rules did not protect blacks against whites with lower examination scores, the slack was more than taken up by the federal government. At that level, where Afro-Americans could generally use their growing literacy to outperform others on tests truly graded in order of merit, progress was steady and undeniable; while Du Bois, not counting those in Washington, had listed 17 postal workers during his first stay in the city, Carl Bolivar by 1914 found 200.[79]

For those who held these jobs, and for others on political strings, the price as measured in dependence was real but not overwhelming. Many remained outside and above the reach of the Republican party, from Robert Purvis to the bishops of the AME church. Those within reach did not always go where they were pulled; Henry Minton, whatever the legal status of his catering business, joined with Robert Jones to keep the Catto case alive during the six years between his murder and the Kelly trial, and Nathan Mossell, in later years, gave up his state subsidy rather than acquiesce in the medical segregation that his hospital and training school were designed to combat. Of those black Philadelphians who in effect surrendered unconditionally to the GOP many were older men, like William Forten and Isaiah Wears, who perhaps saw voting more as privilege than right, remaining grateful to the GOP for the great victory over slavery, or the freedom from race riot they associated, however wrongly, with Bill Stokley and his cops. Others, even with strong strings attached, were able to defy the party some or indeed most of the time, whether voicing their opinions on American imperialism, like Christopher Perry, or taking on the leadership over racial candidates and jobs, like Gil Ball, Steven Gipson, and Con Hubert.

More important than direct dependence were two other results of political weakness. One was the inability, and on the part of many clubhouse politicians the unwillingness, to fight back against the "zoning" of the black district as the red-light district, a condition which affected everyone in the community. The other, and even more fundamental, was the inability to use political power to crack the color line in private employment, and improve the opportunities for the majority.

The ultimate importance of politics was social as well as economic, and in both cases tended sometimes to unite and sometimes to divide the community's experience. Protest against lynching helped to pull black Philadelphians together across the other lines which divided them, just as the uneven course of segregation and integration in theory affected them all. While most shared the same crime-ridden neighborhoods, political protection for vice, in contrast, sharply separated those who benefited from those who did not. And political or civil service jobs tended to reinforce the many other tendencies which worked to separate an educated elite from the rest. Over the period as a whole, the highly visible successes of a relative few tended to obscure the eroding position of the less visible majority, just as, conversely, the poverty of the majority set limits to the successes of the few.

Part III

THE WEB OF ORGANIZATION: RELIGION, RACE, CLASS, AND RECREATION

The most powerful contrast in late 19th-century black Philadelphia is the one between the weakness of its economic base, the poverty of its occupational opportunities, and the great strength and variety of its religious, associational, and social life. And there was another contrast embedded in this one. Differing economic opportunities tended to divide Afro-Americans, as some groups and individuals did relatively well, and others, including the great majority of wage-earners, were left behind. In contrast many of the most important forms of associational life tended to pull people together, as the leadership needed the numbers provided by the majority.

The numbers were needed, as example, in the churches, as the city's Afro-Americans by 1897 supported some fifty-five different mainstream churches alone, almost as many as those maintained by the Roman Catholic Archdiocese in the city, although the Catholic population was then six or eight times bigger than the black. Beyond its purely religious functions each of these churches also housed or hosted a number of other organizations, racial, fraternal, and social, while still more, hundreds more, of purely secular organizations, bands, ball clubs, and dancing schools, flourished outside of their walls.[1]

The variety of these groups, and the links between them, make it in some ways artificial to draw the lines which divide the chapters in Part III from each other or from those earlier, in Part II. Economic conditions had implications for virtually all Afro-American activities; the church was the center of much secular social life; and there were obvious connections among race pride, politics, and recreation. What should emerge from the chapters which follow is some sense of the great web of associations which shaped the life of the city's blacks. It was a web of many seams, clearly, made of very different and even competing groups and activities. But ultimately it was a single web, one whose very existence helped to define most of Philadelphia's Afro-American residents as members of a single community.

Chapter 8

The Churches

Philadelphia's historic importance as a center of Afro-American life rests in large part on its role as site of the nation's first black churches. During the late 19th century, hard work and sheer population growth multiplied the number of these churches, while shifting the earlier denominational configuration among them. But nothing could make them more important to the community than they already were. The church in Philadelphia as elsewhere helped to shape identity in terms of race and class, was both an expense and a source of professional employment, and served as a forum for discussion and the focus of much social, intellectual, and recreational life.

It is paradoxically easier to describe the secular role of these black churches than the purely spiritual. Journalists obeyed an unwritten rule by stopping outside the doors of mainstream churches on Sundays, printing only authorized versions or excerpts from sermons. They described the actual conduct of worship or worshippers only at camp meetings, or more rarely among marginal congregations, mostly as folk behavior or as foolishness. Established ministers, while willing to discuss doctrine and belief, provide little insight into the ways in which religion affected the lives of their followers. And W. E. B. Du Bois, less conventionally respectful than the journalists, had his own strict standards of morality and progress that made him unsympathetic in discussing the conduct of the major churches and especially hostile to traces of "primitive" worship or behavior among the others.

But within this limit it is still possible to trace the histories of the city's major black churches as they struggled with the two kinds of tension, within and without, that generally marked black history in the period. First they had to define their relationship with the surrounding world of white Christianity, balancing the felt need for independence against their own poverty, and the advantages of financial and other support. Second, within the black group they had to work out ways of competing within a framework of racial cooperation. In some ways all had much in common while in others "The Black Church" did not exist at all, as in practice there were several denominations and dozens of congregations competing for the attentions of potential members, each with a distinctive message and personality.

The *Christian Recorder* in 1887 published a story about three little girls, two Irish-American and one black, curious about Philadelphia's evident plans for a great historical celebration. One of the white girls, perhaps dimly remembering the events of the previous decade, thought it had something to do with the Declaration of Independence. The other, a better student, recalled that the Constitutional Convention had met in the city a hundred years earlier. The last girl was however confident that everything was being prepared for the centennial of her own AME church, the uniquely black denomination founded on a kind of Afro-American Revolution of its own.[1]

The church had chosen 1787 as the key date in the series of events which led to the founding of not only one but three distinct black congregations, first in this country. Late in the 18th century a number of Philadelphia's blacks had come to worship at St. George's Methodist Episcopal Church, but the more who came the less they were made welcome. When publicly and physically threatened with segregation, finally, a delegation led by Richard Allen and Absalom Jones declared their independence simply by walking out. Jones and Allen together helped form a Free African Society which carried on a number of activities, notably responding to the city's need for willing nurses and workers during the great yellow-fever epidemic of 1792. On purely religious issues the two leaders however split apart, Jones establishing St. Thomas Church, which maintained a kind of independence within the confines of Episcopalianism, Allen founding a separate African Methodist Episcopal denomination based in his own church, the original "Mother Bethel." Meanwhile a group of those who had stayed at St. George's during the original walkout successfully petitioned in 1794 for formal permission to meet at their own place. This third black church, built with some white help, also established a third pattern of relations with white ecclesiastical authority, remaining formally within St. George's denomination, first as the African Zoar Methodist Episcopal Church and later simply as Zoar M.E.[2]

During the late 19th century as earlier, Zoar remained a less historically noteworthy church than either of the other originals. It was located from the first in a small black settlement north of what was then the city proper, and farther yet from the larger black center where both Bethel and St. Thomas were built. With no such charismatic leader as Jones or Allen the little congregation met in a single room, wholly dependent on visiting white ministers until it built its own plain brick building in 1838, closely modeled after St. George's, and began hiring its own preacher. But despite these modest and dependent beginnings Zoar and Methodism generally kept a significant place among the city's black churches, managing to achieve a distinct identity while keeping some of the advantages of the white connection.[3]

The recognition of Zoar's black identity, beyond the simple segregation of its worshippers, began when the Methodist General Conference of 1864, like the Episcopalians and others, recognized that wartime Emancipation was creating an enormous demand for black preachers. Pushed in part by Afro-American communicants, the response was to create whole new regional conferences, segregated de facto, within the denomination. Given this new autonomy, delegates to Zoar's Delaware Conference, by the 1890s, were routinely meeting not only with other Methodists but with representatives from the African Methodist Episcopal Church, and indeed from Union Baptist and First African Presbyterian; the bond of color was able to unite them all across the formal divisions of doctrine and denomination.[4]

In the meantime, too, parishioners from Zoar, following the general westward movement of Philadelphia's Afro-Americans, served as outriders for several other missions or churches, most importantly Bainbridge St. Methodist, founded in 1840. The advantages of the connection were clear enough; among other things white Methodists, whether out of piety or a desire to maintain segregation, were always willing to help black Methodists build separate churches. Haven was built in Germantown, in 1882, with white help; the next year the Bainbridge Street Church was moved from below Eighth to 12th Street and a generous philanthropist helped Zoar itself move from Fourth and Brown to a new building at 12th and Melon. By 1897 these three and two smaller missions, in Frankford and on Waterloo Street, accounted rather quietly for over 1200 black Methodists.[5]

St. Thomas's, meanwhile, by the late 19th century not as big as Zoar, was not a quiet church despite its powerful respectability. Absalom Jones, in a dispute with Richard Allen, had led his group of secessionists from St. George's into an uneven relation with the established Episcopal denomination in 1794. The Episcopalians agreed to ordain Jones, despite his lack of Greek and Latin. They also agreed to accept his new St. Thomas Church, at Fifth and Adelphi, as one of their own, provided only that the congregation have no voice in the wider governing conventions. The issues involved in all of these decisions, to join a white denomination, to insist on a black pastor, and to accept a kind of "wardship" status, would continue to concern St. Thomas's through much of the 19th century.[6]

Acceptance of the Episcopalian connection meant acceptance of what the historian of the early years at St. Thomas Church has described as a "restrained European" style of worship from the first, in contrast to the enthusiastic "theology of the heart" which marked the equally European Methodists. It also involved a commitment over the years to an elaborate exterior and interior architecture, the traditional soaring Gothic outside, inside an ornate altar and high pulpit, eventually an orchestra pit, the first pipe organ in any black church, pews, and pew rents. At the same time the communicants explicitly limited their numbers to people of "African descent," and although they at first accepted their second-class status they began to protest in 1848, demanding full recognition from the Episcopal Convention. The Episcopalians, like their Methodist cousins, were moved to action finally by the Civil War; delegates from St. Thomas's were granted voting rights in 1863, while the church at the same time dropped its own rules barring whites from holding office within the congregation.[7]

In the decades following the war the church continued to enjoy its reputation as the home of the city's black elite: Du Bois sometimes stereotyped local congregations in a sentence or two, but few could object to his description of those at St. Thomas's as "the most cultured and wealthiest of the Negro population." Octavius Catto had been a parishioner, although his father was a Presbyterian minister; Fanny Jackson belonged until her marriage to the Reverend Coppin of the AME. Others included James Field Needham, Warley Bascom, Carl Bolivar, Edward Bouchet, the Bowers, Browns, Casseys, Coles, Dorseys, Gordons, Mintons, Vennings, Vidals, and Warricks. But the very distinction of its membership seems to have limited its reach.[8]

Finding and holding appropriate ministers was one persistent problem. Following Absalom Jones himself there were no more waivers of the strict language and other educational requirements required for Episcopal ordination, and given the denomination's limited appeal to Afro-Americans generally there were, as late as 1892, no more than thirty black priests in the United States. The usual solution was to have white pastors serve as interim "priests in charge," sometimes for years, until a black man could be installed properly as rector. It took sixteen years after Jones's death in 1818 to find the Reverend William Douglass in 1834. Douglass then settled in for nearly thirty years, marrying Sarah Mapps Douglass, and was succeeded on his death in 1862 by another black man, William Alston. But after Alston's resignation ten years later it took another decade, several interim priests, and protests against a white lay reader until J. Pullam Williams was installed in 1882. When Williams in turn resigned after a decade he was succeeded for three years by the Reverend Owen Waller, whose resignation in 1896 was followed by an interregnum until George A. McGuire was called to the rectorship in 1902.[9]

Although some of these were distinguished men—Waller was in fact the second black Oxford graduate in the country—they did not generally become leaders in black Philadelphia. Alston, who played a prominent role in the battle to desegregate the streetcars, was the single postwar exception, but he and every one of his successors quit rather than died in office. The reason seems to lie within the nature of the congregation or vestry itself. Politics, as in other black churches, was taken seriously: candidates for the vestry sometimes ran together, like members of a political party, with printed ballots. But Episcopal vestrymen, unlike politicians, did not always try to recruit new voters; St. Thomas's hardly welcomed poor strangers to the city. As the Reverend Mr. Williams put it, on his way out, "The masses of the colored people feel that the . . . church is too high-class for them"; and a century after its founding the membership, at a little less than four hundred souls, was smaller than it had been in 1795. The result was that, since even the most prominent blacks had relatively low incomes and little capital, the church was chronically in debt. [10]

All churches were familiar with mortgage debt, but even without new building, maintaining standards at St. Thomas's was expensive. In the late 1870s one group of vestrymen, reportedly ashamed that the city's richest congregation carried a $3000 debt for renovations and operations, worked hard to retire it and was rewarded by being voted out of office. But the real battle came when another, in 1891, decided to move the church seven blocks west to a new and "more fashionable" part of town. Without consultation with either the congregation or the bishop they undertook to build a $65,000 church at 12th and Walnut. The new place was unquestionably impressive by the standards of the day, a two-story English Gothic structure of limestone and granite, 45' by 105', with its 70' tower soaring above anything boasted by its competitors, even those with two or three times as many members. It also carried a debt of nearly $20,000. The Reverend Mr. Williams, meanwhile, was earning just $874 after ten years of service, well below the average. When he asked for a raise he was turned down, and heard the call of another parish out of town. [11]

The church survived the new debt burden; it may have helped that the young Reverend Mr. Waller, just 23 years old at the time of his appointment to succeed Williams, was married to reportedly the richest black woman of the day. But throughout the later half of the 19th century the burdens of pretension kept St. Thomas's turning inward. During the Civil War, William's mother Louise Dorsey had served as treasurer of a women's committee which raised an impressive $1,240 in cash, food, and blankets for black soldiers and others in need. But in later years the charitable instinct at St. Thomas's seems to have withered. The church, like virtually all others, maintained a "Dorcas Society" to help its own indigent, and had been a pioneer in establishing a mutual benefit association, "The Sons of St. Thomas." But in its case the sexton's job, traditionally given to worthy men in need, went to people like Morris Brown, owner of a shoe store, and the schoolteacher James F. Needham, shortly before Needham won his tax office job. It maintained a Sunday school and a variety of clubs and organizations. But in strong contrast to its younger and smaller cousin, the Church of the Crucifixion, founded in 1847 near Eighth and Bainbridge, it carried on no educational or community activities which reached beyond the membership. And unlike Zoar it did not send its people out to help found new churches: both the Church of the Crucifixion and St. Michael's and All Angels, established in West Philadelphia in 1894, were built as missions by

Philadelphia's Episcopal diocese. As of 1897 the three together counted about 800 members.[12]

The third of the late 18th-century secessionist churches meanwhile reached the peak of its influence about the time of its 1887 centennial. At the time of their split during the early 1790s Richard Allen had led a smaller group than Absalom Jones, and he took a harder road. From the beginning Allen had helpful white friends, notably the civic leader Dr. Benjamin Rush, and black and white worked together, symbolically ate together, and took turns serving each other when they joined to raise the roof on Allen's new church in 1793. Bethel, too, made no doctrinal break with white Methodism. But it was a fully independent church and beginning in 1816 headquarters of a separate African Methodist Episcopal denomination, which while willing to cooperate with whites was historically very conscious of its origins in protesting racism. And it enjoyed very little outside support as it built an international organization over the next several generations.[13]

Bishop Allen left several important legacies at his death in 1831. A skilled craftsman, successful businessman, educator, and abolitionist, he was deeply involved in his community. As head of the only major black-run organization in the country he was naturally a spokesman for the race on all matters, assuring that his church would remain in the broad sense political, drawing no hard line between the sacred and the secular. Despite the inevitable squabbling he maintained generally good relations with other black churchmen, such as his old friend Absalom Jones, and with white Methodists as well. His own charisma and organizational skills assured that the AME would enjoy firm Episcopal authority. But while it spread through much of the Northeast and West during his lifetime the AME was still a relatively modest denomination at the time of the Civil War, with no more than about 20,000 adherents.[14]

But if the war reawakened white Methodists and Episcopalians to their duties toward the freedmen and Afro-Americans generally, it was the AME church which was in best position to seize the opportunities. The biographies of its ministers are full of stories about young men, often free southerners or escaped slaves, who like Henry McNeal Turner were raised in some other faith and then attracted to a truly black church. After education and ordination in the North these men were more than ready to turn around and join the more than seventy missionary-organizers the AME sent south in the middle 1860s, where like Turner himself, tenth in the Dorsey Collection, they founded schools, organized voters, ran for office, and helped create a truly explosive growth in denominational membership, a reported twentyfold increase between 1860 and 1880 to a total of 400,000.[15]

But if Turner represents one side of the AME story in those exciting years, as populist orator, fiery but pragmatic politician and organizer, the other side was shaped by his older colleague, the scholarly Bishop Daniel Payne. Payne, like Turner, was a free-born South Carolinian, but he came north early, and was teaching school in Philadelphia when he left the Methodist connection for the AME in 1841. His election as bishop in 1852 has been called the most important in the history of the denomination next to Allen's in 1818, largely because of his lifelong campaign, often in the face of serious anti-intellectual resistance, to maintain an educated ministry. It was Payne who in 1863 bought Wilberforce College, in Xenia, Ohio, from the white Methodists, becoming the nation's first black college president while founding the first of several AME institutions of higher learning. It was Payne who put Turner in charge of the missions in Georgia after the war, as it was Payne who had assured that the young minister, just before the war, would be well grounded in theology and the biblical languages.[16]

In the late 1890s W. E. B. Du Bois described the descendants of Allen's original congregation: "at Bethel may be seen the best of the great laboring class—steady, honest people, well dressed and well fed, with church and family traditions." But while this may be an accurate sketch of the membership of Bethel itself, it does no justice to the rich traditions represented in the wider denomination. Philadelphia in the late 19th century had room for both Turner's enthusiasm and Payne's scholarship, and more besides.[17]

Nearly a century later an observer at Mother Bethel witnessed the parishioners routinely "shouting"—that is, singing and moving rhythmically in a way that dates back to well before the Civil War; she guessed that this was an innovation brought by recent southern immigrants. But while the church was founded in Philadelphia, the word "African" had appeared in its title from the first, and Bethel was never isolated from the forms which shaped black religion all over the New World. A correspondent of the *People's Advocate* in 1880, describing himself as a "rational" believer, complained that worship at Bethel was too frenzied and emotional, with much "clappin' pattin' juber." Beyond that, the church regularly sponsored camp meetings which must have seemed as familiar to the most recent arrivals from rural South Carolina as to its older members.[18]

The most important was held at a campsite outside of Ocean Grove, New Jersey, where Bishop Jabez Campbell had founded an "Annual Missionary Jubilee" as a kind of religious summer holiday. Perhaps no other black church could have organized so big an event, which required bishops from both New York and Philadelphia to confer with the local authorities as well as with officials of the Pennsylvania Railroad to coordinate special excursion trains full of celebrants, together with singers, bands, and provisions to last for several days of evangelism. But there were other places more convenient to city-dwellers. Summertime camp meetings held in West Philadelphia's Titlow's Grove or Eastwick's Woods were open to black preachers of other denominations but organized by the AME. Wherever held, the meetings offered much joyful noise: evangelism, singing, and spontaneous response. One special advantage was the opportunity offered women preachers: Sisters Emma How-

ard of Bethel, Rachel Vernain of Zion Wesley, and Rachel Woolford of Union
AME were joined by others from out of town during "Women's Day" at
Titlow's Grove in 1897, while Amanda Smith, "The World Famous Evange-
list," was the major attraction at Ocean Grove the next year.[19]

At the same time, Philadelphia was home not only to the *Christian
Recorder,* founded in the 1840s, but its own publishing house, the AME Book
Concern, and beginning in the 1880s the AME *Quarterly Review.* While the
book concern published mostly religious literature the two journals included
secular articles of interest to the race as whole; Fanny Jackson had not yet met
her future husband nor presumably left St. Thomas Church when she first
began to raise money to help the publications. Bishop Payne's insistence on
education, too, is reflected in the fact that work with the journals was often a
stepping-stone to the episcopacy: Jabez Campbell had edited the *Recorder* in
the 1850s; Henry Turner was called to the city in 1876 to help with its business
end; while Bishops B. T. Tanner, B. F. Lee, and Levi Coppin all served as
editors during the 1880s before their elections.[20]

Education itself was provided in a complex of institutions. Sunday schools
were attached to virtually every church, while Wilberforce University, like
many contemporary black colleges, was able to educate those eager to learn at
any level. The Reverend William Yeocum, for example, Kentucky-born ex-
slave, came to Xenia after the war as a wounded veteran, unable either to read or
write; he earned a doctorate in divinity within seven years, and during the
1880s, while working for the *Recorder* and then as pastor at Union, won a local
reputation as a classical scholar with an especial interest in Hebrew. By 1884
Wilberforce itself was joined by five other colleges, four normal schools, and a
mission school in Haiti.[21]

During the late 1880s, when Bishop Turner was installed as head of the
missionary department, the denomination formally extended its work past
Haiti to Africa. Parishioners at Mother Bethel meanwhile reached out closer to
home. As the black population grew in the Fifth and Seventh wards the church
at Sixth and Pine found itself surrounded by a growing vice district; Eddy's
Row, just behind the building, was an especially notorious home to "badger
thieves," often violently larcenous prostitutes. But unlike St. Thomas's, Bethel
had too strong a sense of its own history to move. When time came to replace
the old church, late in the decade, it was done at the old site despite the
inconvenience; the Reverend William H. Heard conducted services at Horticultural Hall while supervising $50,000 worth of work on a new Gothic
structure and two other buildings. The women of the church meanwhile met
the prostitution issue head-on. Since blacks were generally barred from the
Midnight Mission and other reforming Protestant institutions, the pastor's
wife Josie joined with Frances E. W. Harper, Fanny Jackson Coppin, and
several representatives from other denominations to establish the Bethel Home

for Fallen Women in a three-story building near the church, with Nathan
Mossell as visiting physician. Heard himself may have been looking for another
way to fight local vice and corruption when he continued the denominational
tradition of political involvement, running for city council as an Independent in
1891.[22]

Heard's defeat at the hands of the Republican regulars in February may be
taken as a kind of symbol of the fact that the expansion of his church, and
denomination, was slowing by the 1890s. Some part of this may have resulted
from divisions at the top, as the other bishops were unhappy about Henry
Turner's increasing fascination with Africa. But much, one suspects, was the
price of success and independence itself. To maintain high ministerial standards
throughout the explosive expansion of the 1860s, '70s, and '80s was a strain,
and Bishop Payne refused to compromise, declaring in 1890 that fully two-
thirds of the black Baptist and Methodist preachers in the South were either
morally or educationally unqualified. AME bishops themselves often lived
lives nearly as modest as they had begun them; Alexander Wayman, senior
bishop between Payne and Turner, having arrived in Philadelphia as a coach-
man, left only his household furniture and $1000 in life insurance at his death in
1895. But it was still enormously expensive to build schools, colleges, and
missions, aimed at people from the sidewalks of the Fifth Ward to the villages of
Sierra Leone, all the while renouncing white influence, and so much white help.
Bethel's congregation of "steady, honest" laborers simply had more to bear
than the parishioners at Zoar, St. Thomas's, or any other black church in the
city.[23]

Both the problem of discipline and the need for funds were evident in the
conduct of camp meetings, aimed partly at conversions but also at collections.
The great summer jubilee at Ocean Grove, well isolated from any but the
faithful, was carefully managed and relatively easy to control, but not those
nearer the city. In lonely wooded areas there were occasional assaults by
toughs, and in the summer of 1898 one camp meeting site in Delaware was
twice turned into a battlefield by rival Afro-American gangs. Picnic groves,
too, were public space, and black preaching and especially singing were a form
of free entertainment that often drew crowds of whites (including reporters),
partly curious and partly mocking. Sometimes the religious participants were
greatly outnumbered, surrounded by rings of perambulating spectators of both
races, the whites to gawk, the blacks to see and be seen, men in their Saturday
best, women "dressed to paralyze," all of them buying souvenirs, hot food,
and soft drinks from hawkers. Given the competition for pocket money the
collections were often painfully small; it took four or five separate pleas to net
$8.27 from a mixed crowd of six hundred at Titlow's Grove in July of 1896. The
following year a committee of elders understandably declared that most of
these events were "a disgrace to the Christian Church," and tried to impose a

series of rules, including no loud talking, no drinking, no flirting, no sales of watermelon, drinks, or ballads, all of them as impossible to enforce as the suggested nickel charge for admission.[24]

But more important than any of the internal problems of the AME church was the simple fact that especially in a sophisticated big city there were so many others to choose from. Somewhat shaky statistics suggest that in 1867, shortly after the war, the city's five AME churches counted over 2000 members, led by Bethel's 1100, or close to half of the black city's formal communicants. By 1879 there were six churches, still more than those of any other denomination, and in 1892 eleven. But despite this absolute growth the AME was losing ground relative to others, its perhaps 3000 members in 1897 accounting for less than a quarter of the black total. By 1899 Bethel had been replaced by Zion Wesley, more centrally located at 15th and Lombard, as the biggest single Afro-American congregation in Philadelphia, a circumstance perhaps especially galling because Zion was the flagship of the AME's bitterest rival, the schismatic AME Zion denomination. In fact a little more than a century after their different declarations of independence from white St. George's, all three denominations represented in those original walkouts had been numerically overshadowed, the result of the continuing expansive vitality of the wider "black church."[25]

Next to change, variety was perhaps the leading characteristic of Afro-American religion in late 19th-century Philadelphia. Some white churches lost black congregants as others gained, while almost all the purely black denominations prospered, offering newcomers more choice than was possible in any smaller place or earlier time.

Apart from the Methodists and Episcopalians several of the white churches which had attracted black members in the 18th and early 19th centuries tended to lose them as the black community got bigger and its own churches beckoned. A survey in 1813 included, for example, a number of Lutherans and Quakers. But the strongly ethnic North European flavor of Lutheranism perhaps alienated its Afro-American communicants, as did the austerity of the increasingly inward-turning Society of Friends. Sarah Douglass was apparently the last black to quit the Quakers, and by 1879 there were few if any black Lutherans left in the city.[26]

The Presbyterians had a stronger hold. First African Presbyterian, founded at Seventh and Bainbridge by the ex-slave evangelist John Gloucester in 1811, was the fifth black church in the city, following the original three and First African Baptist. The founder's son Steven led a split in 1844 which resulted in the establishment of Central, on Lombard below Ninth. With the arrival of John B. Reeve, in 1861, Central soon outstripped its parent. Reeve, educated at Union Theological Seminary, remained in Philadelphia for more than forty years, with some time out for missionary work in Tennessee during Reconstruction, and four years of teaching theology at Howard. While Du Bois in the late 1890s believed that the Presbyterians were showing "some desire to be rid of blacks," Berean was founded in Germantown in 1884 with much white help, and its pastor, William Still's son-in-law Matthew Anderson, early established himself as one of the most active churchmen in the city. With support provided by nearness both to Princeton Theological Seminary, where Anderson got his degree, and Lincoln University, where Reeve won a doctorate in divinity, the city's Afro-American Presbyterians remained influential beyond their modest numbers, as Central, First African, and Berean accounted for something over 600 members in 1897.[27]

The descendants of Haitian and other French West Indian émigrés meanwhile gave Philadelphia a small but economically important nucleus of black Catholics, led by the Augustins, Baptistes, and Dutrieulles. In the postwar decades, too, following earlier support for the institution of slavery, the American hierarchy took a real interest in adding Afro-American converts to these pioneers. Journalists agreed that the Roman church had many advantages over those Protestants who stressed silence and simplicity: editor J. W. Cromwell of the *People's Advocate*, himself a graduate of the Quaker Institute for Colored Youth, wrote in 1879 that the church had taken special note of "the developing Negro, his love for pomp, display, for music." Writing at the close of Reconstruction, Cromwell also noted that the church had led in feeding and clothing the freedmen "as no other single denomination had dared to do," a fact which might shame the rest into better treatment. Philadelphians, sometimes including Protestant ministers, continued through the century to stress the universal character of the Catholic church, its open schools and opposition to segregation.[28]

Within this generally open framework the Archdiocese did however help provide the city's black Catholics with a place of their own. Movement began with a special convention of Afro-American communicants, held in Washington late in 1888, which resulted the following spring in formation of a Philadelphia Catholic Union led by P. A. Dutrieulle, Jerome Baptiste, M. J. Lehman, Mr. and Mrs. Frank Dorsey, and Mary Thomas. The following year Archbishop Ryan announced that the church was building a mission at Ninth and Pine to be named for St. Peter Clavers, the first modern missionary to Africa. The archbishop believed that "the Negro story and unjust treatment of the Indians are the two great blots upon American Civilization," and in a rare admission of fallibility suggested that the Roman church had "reasonable cause to regret" its own earlier policies. He also noted that Philadelphia's most famous convert, the heiress Katherine Drexel, although then still a novice, would take a special interest in the work. A couple of months later T. Thomas Fortune, longtime champion of rapprochement with Irish-Americans, was invited to speak at a benefit spring bazaar. The bazaar's $6000 in profits, in an era when even the most successful black fundraisers typically netted no more than a few hundred, helped to underline the importance of outside help, and St. Peter's was shortly established at 12th and Lombard as a regular parish church. The pastor was of course white, given the virtual absence of black priests in this country, and a few whites were scattered among the parishioners, just as most of Philadelphia's four or five hundred black Catholic communicants remained scattered across the city.[29]

These successes remained small, however, next to those recorded by several black churches in the same period, including three small Methodist bodies, the Baptists, the Holiness, and those wholly unaffiliated.

The schismatic tendencies of white Methodists, themselves an 18th-century outgrowth of the parent Anglican or Episcopal church, were easily matched by their 19th-century black brethren. The AME Zion connection, which had early held apart from Bishop Allen's church, remained in many ways a smaller, looser version of the original. While like the AME itself the AME Zion was galvanized by Civil War and won some success among freedman it was largely confined to the Northeast and upper South. In Allen's own city it had only three churches by the late 1890s, although as reported one of these, Wesley Union, had become the single largest black congregation in Philadelphia. Meanwhile, virtually across the street on Lombard above 15th, stood another although smaller monument to Methodist particularism: the Grace Union, once AME Zion, later affiliated with the African Union Methodist Episcopal denomination. Out in West Philadelphia, finally, the Methodist Protestants boasted a single Church of St. Matthew, making a total of more than two dozen Afro-American churches or missions as of 1897 representing five different denominations within the greater Methodist family.[30]

This variety was meanwhile outdone by the Baptists, who in the city as in the nation came to outnumber the Methodists during the same period. Differing sources yield differing numbers of churches at different times: while Du Bois listed 17 in 1897, more conservative sources count 4 in 1867, 5 in 1879, 6 in 1892, and, to show the great growth toward century's end, 17 in 1903, including 5 established after Du Bois left the city. All of these, unlike some which belonged to more hierarchical denominations, were by definition self-sustaining, and the *Tribune* suggested their total membership had surpassed the Methodists' by 1898 at the latest.[31]

Philadelphia's first Afro-American Baptists went through much the same experience as the Presbyterians and Methodists. At first welcomed by "liberal" white members of the First Baptist Church, they decided in 1809 that they had enough souls to found their own, and then left amicably to found the First African Baptist Church at 11th and Cherry. When James Underdue, its Oberlin-educated pastor at the time of the Civil War, left to serve as a chaplain in the Union army, the church in 1864 called the Reverend Theodore Doughty Miller, a former Episcopalian and missionary to Sierra Leone. Over the next thirty-six years Miller carried on the tradition of the Cherry Street "Mother

Church." While the congregation, according to Du Bois, grew "staid and respectable," its scholarly pastor helped to found several smaller Baptist congregations in the city, rebuilt First African itself, and served as one of the leading black clergymen in the city.[32]

But if Cherry Street was the oldest and in some ways the strongest of the Afro-American Baptist churches in the city, the biggest by century's end was Union. And Union's quite different history illustrates the range of alternatives within the loosely structured denomination.

Union was an old church, established on Minster below Seventh in the 1830s, and the natural place for James Underdue to go when he returned to Philadelphia in 1865 and found Miller in his old post at Cherry Street. Trouble began, however, when after Underdue's death in 1876 he was succeeded by the combative William Wallace, who inspired a murky but instructive battle among deacons and trustees over issues of sin, authority, and brotherhood.[33]

Problems at Union surfaced in the summer of 1884, when a delegation of twelve deacons, not fully freed from paternalist tradition, brought a complaint to Mayor William Smith. The twelve represented a faction, probably a majority of the congregation, opposed to Reverend Mr. Wallace and most of the trustees, who controlled the church and its property. In the absence of a bishop or other authority they wanted advice from the city's highest elected official. The mayor, on hearing that one of the deacons and Trustee George Gardiner had fought over a Bible, simply urged that they take out a warrant for assault, advice perhaps helped by Gardiner's Democratic politics as editor of the *Sentinel.* This satisfied the twelve but gave another issue to the Wallace faction, who cited I Corinthians 6:2: "Dare any of you, having a matter against another, go to law before the unjust and not before the saints." Wallace himself had suggested that the dispute be arbitrated by the eight pastors of the city's other Afro-American Baptist churches. But that proposal was foiled the next day when the realtor Andrew Jones, Union's sexton and the only anti-Wallacite on the Board of Trustees, refused to unlock the church.[34]

The problem, according to both groups, was rooted in sin, specifically the universally familiar trio represented by "rum," "policy," and "bigamy." While no one officially favored any of them there was still room for difference. Baptists as well as Methodists urged abstinence from liquor. But pastors differed in the vigor with which they attacked this and other kinds of sin, or their willingness to point the finger. The Reverend William Creditt, for example, T. D. Miller's successor at First African, and tied for twenty-seventh in the Dorsey Collection, denied in 1899 that policy was a problem among his parishioners, while the Reverend Levi Coppin complained that the game was worse than the saloon, since women and children would be ashamed to enter a bar-room while policy was played by people of all ages and sexes, including some of Bethel's best. Bigamy, finally, could be a poignant personal problem for Afro-Americans as for other poor and migrant peoples.[35]

In July of 1890 the *Times* printed a sympathetic story about the plight of Carrie Beals, a 28-year-old domestic who was turned away at City Hall, denied a marriage license because she was still locked into union, for practical purposes unbreakable, with a man serving a life sentence back in Virginia. Both marriage and divorce were often problematic, beginning with the fact that slave marriages, however honored by the parties, were not binding under law. The *Christian Recorder* was often filled with personal advertisements looking for spouses and other relatives lost in the turmoil of emigration or flight. For many, not literate enough to write and unused to legal forms, it was at best hard to produce valid evidence of divorce in some distant jurisdiction.[36]

Whatever the problems, the Reverend Mr. Wallace at Union took pride in his reputation as a plain-talking man who confronted sin whenever he smelled it. Others may have believed that he was stiff, even un-Christian, in denying the sacraments to those who asked in all sincerity. In any case his congregation pushed him out by early 1885, and found a more flexible successor in the Reverend C. C. Stumm. Stumm proceeded to admit new members, among them the veteran sinner Gil Ball, within four years built a new Church at 12th and Mt. Vernon, and in a little over a decade pushed the membership over a thousand. Wallace, meanwhile, had simply founded his own church, Ebenezer Baptist, on South Street above 11th. But there the same scenario was again played out within the year, and the founder exiled once more. Ebenezer was saved only by a charismatic young man, who took the lead in welcoming six controversial converts whom Wallace had denied, although their actual baptism into membership had to wait for two years until he was ordained himself.[37]

The whole story is doubly significant. It points first to sharp disagreement among Baptist and presumably other congregations over standards of respectability. There is no evidence of a double standard or alternative morality in principle. But while some were eager to cast stones, the majority at both Union and Ebenezer were if not more tolerant of sin more charitable toward sinners. At the same time the resulting changes illustrate Baptist weaknesses and strengths: the lack of higher authority to settle disputes, the power of individual preachers, the ease of winning ordination and establishing new congregations.

Sometimes, as with Holy Trinity, founded by the Reverend D. D. Evans in 1892, the local Baptist Association denied formal recognition to a new church for some time. But for those with strong convictions the difference between recognition and non-recognition need not be crucial in any case. If either Evans at Holy Trinity or the anonymous young savior at Ebenezer had failed to earn regular Baptist credentials they might simply have joined the ranks of the unaffiliated charismatics who, like Brother Isaiah Brown of the "Pleasant Valley Mission," simply set up shop on their own, preaching to their little congregations in rented halls or rooms.[38]

It is hard to find out much about these unaffiliated preachers and places because the press, the established ministers, and W. E. B. Du Bois all patronized or even despised them. For the newspapers, many "church" stories began with a building, a place with concrete dimensions and specific address, whose founding date and cornerstone, stained-glass windows, pointed arches, and mortgage could all be compared with others. The Church of God in Christ was established in the city during 1895, as the largest of the Holiness churches, independent congregations usually in the Baptist or Methodist tradition, which tended to appeal to the poor and uneducated, with a strong emphasis on revivalism. But it got no mentions in the Dorsey Collection except for those dealing with its spectacular cold-weather riverine baptisms in 1903. The regular ministers also had their own reasons to ignore, or distrust, these informal operations, joining cops and neighbors in labeling the Pleasant Valley Mission as "Monkey's Paradise" during the 1890s. When a bitter dispute broke out between the founder, Brother Isaiah Brown, and a rival, Brother John Diggs, the popular press was of course delighted, and imagined razors being stropped all up and down Lombard Street; the Episcopalian Dorsey, in a unique venture into dialect, indexed the story as "Br'er Brown vs. Br'er Diggs."[39]

Du Bois's attitude, finally, was shaped partly by his New England morality, partly by his Harvard exposure to the white liberal elite, and partly by the prevailing doctrines of social science, with their emphasis on progress through evolution. His own Congregational experience was long over, but it left him unsympathetic with the emotional "heart theology" of most black churches. While he had loved his time at Fisk, supported largely by northern Congregationalists, he had been unhappy as a young teacher at pious Wilberforce, flagship of the AME educational system. By the time he reached Philadelphia he had lost any lingering faith in organized religion while saving a vision of what a church ought ideally to be, one best exemplified by the contemporary "Social Gospel" movement. A black church especially ought to aid in uplifting a race beset with problems by concentrating on rational morality and education in self-help, fostered through a variety of secular services. None of the black denominations lived up to this standard. Even in the larger churches, in place of sober morality "noise and excitement attend the services, especially at the time of revival or in prayer meetings." And the unaffiliated missions were to Du Bois the worst offenders of all.[40]

His account of a service in the Fifth Ward is taken from a white observer, although he had witnessed similar scenes himself. It sounds much like descriptions of the Pleasant Valley Mission, and with some modifications like those of the camp meetings held by more established denominations. Its emphasis is on the illiteracy of preacher and flock, with their musical "repetitions of senseless sentiment and exciting cadences," culminating when all join in a recognizable "ring shout," singing and moving rhythmically into a state of exultation that lasted for some hours. Du Bois, in a footnote, noted that "the writer hardly does justice to the weird witchery of those hymns sung thus rudely." But he found consolation in his Social Darwinist belief in inevitable progress. The missions were only "survivals of the methods of worship in Africa and the West Indies." And "for the most part . . . these customs are dying away."[41]

While it is impossible to guess how many little rented churches there had been in the 1860s, Du Bois estimated that there were dozens scattered through the city by the mid-1890s. According to his accounts of religious preferences in the Seventh Ward, in which well over 80 percent of families "habitually" attended church, 70 percent as regular members of established denominations, the non-traditional churches attracted only a small proportion of Philadelphia's Afro-Americans. But they were hardly "dying away"; charismatic churches in the city would flourish far more in the 20th century than in the 19th. And already in the 1890s they were contributing, together with the traditional denominations, to the rich variety of alternatives offered to southern migrants and established Philadelphians alike.[42]

To join a church is to join a community, at times isolated but at others part of a series of wider or overlapping communities. Given their racial and denominational differences there were, apart from Christmas or Easter, no occasions or institutions that encouraged all of the city's Christians, black and white, to think of themselves in common. Pastors instead often seemed to think in terms not of cooperation but of competition for members and dollars, fighting to increase the size of their own churches at the expense of others. On the other hand the bonds of denominational membership sometimes united black churchmen across the lines of race with helpful whites. More often cooperation ran along the other axis, uniting the race across the lines of denomination. As in politics, so in religion, clerical and lay leaders found symbolic occasions at least to affirm a racial kinship that transcended the differences that usually divided them.

Some of the differences occurred within churches, where as at St. Thomas's the custom of electing trustees prompted rivalries that the *Tribune* reported with some relish. Strong-minded pastors such as William Wallace, or the Reverend Mr. Christian at Shiloh Baptist, could create real crises; Christian, not long after his intervention in the cloakmakers' strike of 1890, was involved in a battle that got him briefly deposed from the Baptist ministry. Church politics on at least two occasions other than the Union quarrel of 1884 were serious enough to get some of the parties arrested on warrants sworn by others. Ministers were sometimes found in bawdy houses, or embarrassed poor families at funerals, or called each other names in public. But in general, given more than thirty years and the size of Philadelphia's Afro-American population, the city seems remarkably free of the truly scandalous affairs that led William Dorsey's old friend and fellow collector Joseph Cathcart to label one of his clipping scrapbooks "The Crimes of Ministers."[43]

Denominational rivalries, like those in Darwin's animal kingdom, were generally strongest among closely related connections, notably the AME and AME Zion. The formal differences between them were purely organizational, with Zion generally favoring a stronger laity, and the two tried three times to reunite, in 1868, 1885, and 1892. The first attempt was reportedly disrupted by Philadelphia's eccentric Reverend J. P. B. Eddy. The second may have foundered in part on politics; the *Tribune* accused Zion's bishops of slavish Republicanism at a time when former Bethel pastor W. H. Heard accepted a diplomatic post under Grover Cleveland, and the highly visible Bishop Turner, Heard's mentor and fellow veteran of southern politics, was an often violent critic of GOP policies and sometime friend of Democrats. In any case the two groups soon reverted to their normal state of sibling rivalry, mostly carried on between the *Christian Recorder* and the *Star of Zion*.[44]

But neither the rivalries within congregations nor between denominations was as important as the competition between churches. Du Bois's major criticism of black clergymen, the fact that they were less moral or intellectual leaders than businessmen, was equally applicable to their white counterparts, and in fact built into the structure of American Protestantism. In the absence of tax support, reliance on voluntary contributions dictated that building a church was wholly dependent on a pastor's success as fundraiser. But two conditions made the financing problem especially acute among Afro-Americans.[45]

One of course was the poverty which ensured that each dime in the collection plate was missed by the giver. And with ministerial salaries the highest non-capital expense in the budget, each dime also widened the gap between the pastor and his flock. Ministers often took outside jobs to add to their incomes: James Underdue of Union Baptist as one of the city's first black postmen for example, others as upholsterers or even newspaper vendors. But the regular salaries of those in established churches, according to Du Bois, ranged up to $1500 a year, far more than most other black professionals. Given special testimonial collections, in effect bonuses, to add to this base, and with parsonages thrown in, Bethel's Levi Coppin and his peers at places like Cherry Street and Wesley Zion were the only salaried black men in the city whose total compensation challenged the $1800 earned by Coppin's wife Fanny at the Institute for Colored Youth, and all probably earned more than T. J. Minton or Nathan Mossell, the city's most successful lawyer and doctor.[46]

Growth in numbers, second, and the general movement westward, meant that black churches were continually being bought, built, or rebuilt. No major groups in the city were growing faster than the blacks. And as they moved in a relatively narrow corridor across the Schuylkill, and in more scattered fashion north into Germantown, the churches both led and followed. Some new-comers came in chain migrations, bearing letters for example from a former Baptist pastor in Washington to a new one in Philadelphia, while the AME seems deliberately to have established outposts a step or two ahead of migration, with the Allen Chapel, notably, in 1873, a pioneer in the movement west of the Schuylkill. The 1880s, especially, witnessed great capital expenditures on building, and by the turn of the century a black population officially measured at something over sixty thousand supported roughly sixty different stone churches and uncounted numbers of smaller ones in rented halls. Historic Mother Bethel, meanwhile, was the only major institution left in a Fifth Ward increasingly abandoned to Italians, Jews, and other European immigrants.[47]

What hurt most was that the capital spent was usually lost to the black community. A few routine budget items, other than ministerial salaries, were kept within: the money paid to sextons, a little spent on advertising various affairs in black papers, perhaps flowers and the coal bill. But as Carl Bolivar noted years later, the expansion of such events as plays and concerts beyond the sponsoring churches meant that halls must be hired from white landlords, thus putting "money into the pockets of the dominants." And with the exceptions of Union Baptist in 1888, the smaller Union American Methodist in 1890, and Bethsaida Baptist in 1899, all noted in Chapter 4, the building money went almost entirely to white contractors who refused to hire black workingmen. With virtually all of them elaborately Gothic, costing between $7000 and perhaps $40,000 in construction, this amounted to a huge loss to the Afro-American community.[48]

At the same time the press both reflected and encouraged a competitive atmosphere in which size of membership, buildings, and funds collected were the measure of a congregation, or more pointedly a preacher. Reporters could not attempt to describe the spiritual qualities of a ministry. Instead the routine occasions for a story were anniversaries of a church or pastor, the announcement of a fund drive, or the retirement of a debt. All of these invited an emphasis on growth and size, the number of converts won since the Reverend —— was called to the church, the cost and dimensions of his building project. The *Globe,* in 1883, rated the Reverend C. T. Shaeffer the "leading" pastor in the city for having raised $10,000 in three years out of a congregation not much over 200 souls; six years later the *Age* noted that after promotion to Bethel he was given that year's biggest Easter testimonial at $200. Shaeffer, tied for sixteenth in the Dorsey Collection, actually had a medical doctor's degree, but clearly found the ministry more profitable.[49]

The *Tribune,* meanwhile, when the Pennsylvania State Baptist Convention met at Zion, in 1898, noted that the denomination by then had "distanced all the rest of its competitors." And the Methodists at Zoar made it clear that under pressure of debt fundraising was a form of war. For the special collection to celebrate its 103rd anniversary, in 1897, the church was divided into five "regiments," each commanded by a colonel and assisted by a captain, plus a special "Infant's Brigade" for the Sunday scholars; the amounts were then published in the *Tribune,* with Colonel W. F. Simmons's First Regiment winning top honors by raising $604.24 out of the grand total of $1790.71.[50]

The money collected in most black churches usually went to the most necessary expenses: salaries, housekeeping, and building. Virtually all maintained Sunday schools, very important in encouraging literacy, and most had Dorcas Societies, run by women members, to assist the needy in their own congregations. Few seem to have joined the AME in supporting foreign missions. And only two attempted to mount the kind of institutional services associated with the late 19th-century Social Gospel. These were run by the local clergymen most often mentioned in the Dorsey Collection, the Reverend H. L. Phillips of the Church of the Crucifixion, who ranks eighth, and the Reverend Matthew Anderson of Berean Presbyterian, tied with Shaeffer (and William Dorsey himself), for sixteenth place. Both of these men significantly belonged to white denominations, and got much white help.[51]

Phillips's Church of the Crucifixion had a very different history from St. Thomas Church, the other major black Episcopal congregation. Established by the diocese in 1847, close to the worst slums in the city on Bainbridge above Eighth Street, it was intended, Carl Bolivar recalled, "to reach out to those whose poverty made them hesitate to go to other churches," and its first pastor approached them "with the Bible in one hand and succor of clothes, food, and fuel in the other." The neighborhood was dangerous for Afro-Americans, who were sometimes beaten on the way to church, and it was not always attractive to white priests either, whose quality was varied at best. But it did have a pipe organ, built as well as played by Joseph Carter, and although it never lost its sense of mission to the poor, some of the "better element" among the city's blacks gradually took an interest in it, notably the musical Adger family. And in 1877, fresh from a short stay at St. Thomas's, the Reverend Henry L. Phillips, like many of his faith a native of the British West Indies, was called to take over as its first black rector.[52]

The vestry, teachers, and other church workers were then still white, but Afro-Americans followed Phillips into all these offices. The building, with too little ventilation and too many rats, was replaced by a "pretty little" Gothic Revival structure in 1884, fully paid for by 1890. Most important, Phillips managed to encourage his now mixed vestry, led by the white philanthropist Theodore Starr, to get involved in the local community in a number of unprecedented ways.[53]

The first charitable organization attached to the parish seems to be the Progressive Workingmen's Club, organized in 1878, and headquartered in a three-story building on South 11th Street, with a gymnasium, baths, lecture room, and games: Phillips served as president, Starr as treasurer, while Levi Cromwell and Thomas Murray joined two white men on the board. By the middle of the 1880s the club was reported in decline, perhaps for the usual reason that it appealed more to the ambitious and educated, "the leading young men" such as John Durham, rather than to the truly disadvantaged it was designed to reach. But some of its offshoots such as a Penny Savings Bank, later a Dime Savings Bank, continued at least into the 1890s, with Phillips and Cromwell still on the board. At the same time the church sponsored a Coal Club and Free Ice Fund for the neighborhood poor. Its Home for the Homeless, Du Bois reported in the mid-1890s, had an annual income of about $500, "supported largely by whites but not entirely," which supplied thousands of meals and nights' worth of lodgings to transients and invalids. There was a parish kindergarten, too, in line with the concern of Gertrude Bustill Mossell and Fanny Jackson Coppin for working mothers. Phillips was also involved, in the 1890s, in establishing a home for crippled children in connection with St. Michael's and All Angels, a new West Philadelphia mission for Afro-Americans, and again supported in part by the community. He reached, too, into Moyamensing Jail and the Eastern State Penitentiary through a Penitentiary Service which brought the consolations of religion to at least some killers condemned to the gallows.[54]

Meanwhile the Reverend Matthew Anderson was following and expanding on the kind of activism that Phillips had pioneered. Although Berean was founded thirty years later, it grew, like the Church of the Crucifixion, out of a mission established by whites for blacks. Originally named in 1878 for John Gloucester, the city's pioneering Afro-American Presbyterian, Berean became a full-fledged church in 1884. Anderson, the first pastor, supervised its blue-marble Gothic construction, at a cost of $32,000, on South College Avenue above 19th and Ridge. The basement, in addition to the usual reading rooms, boasted a gymnasium, one of the characteristic features of churches involved in the Social Gospel, but the heart of the ministry was the minister himself.[55]

Beginning in 1888 the church began to sponsor a Berean Building and Loan Association, the biggest of several such black enterprises in the city. Within four years it had issued a second series of shares and listed twenty people whom it had helped to buy homes. William Still, Anderson's father-in-law, served as president, his son Wilbur as treasurer until replaced by the leading white stockholder; Still's established contacts among the city's philanthropists may have helped bring in several white directors, including Michael Brown, editor of the building department of the *Press,* who wrote the constitution and bylaws. Although Anderson himself, the association's secretary, had first believed that "it would be a difficult matter to sufficiently interest our people to save money," the first series, worth a total of $90,000, was paid off in 1899, with an average interest rate of a then unusually high 7.81 percent. While the biggest stockholders were white, the majority, as of the board, were black men and women.[56]

Meanwhile in 1890, several years before Nathan Mossell began to work on the Douglass Clinic, Anderson opened a medical dispensary at the parish house, largely operated by his wife, Dr. Caroline, with help from the dentist James Brister. By 1903, in addition to the more usual groups such as a Mother's Meeting, a Temperance Society, and a Young People's Society of Christian

Endeavor, Berean housed its own employment bureau, and, like the Church of the Crucifixion, a kindergarten. But its most visible educational venture was the Berean Manual Training School, founded in 1899. Anderson was the principal, and H. L. Phillips, who had once thought himself of opening a small industrial training school for young women, served as secretary. Given their joint reputations and the contemporary vogue for industrial education, they had little trouble finding white men to fill the board. The definition of "industrial training" was as loose as usual, and Berean seems at first to have concentrated on cooking, sewing, and the other domestic arts. But it also taught carpentry, and when the Institute for Colored Youth was closed down in 1902, and its Quaker managers referred stranded pupils to Berean, the younger school, with financial support from people like John Wanamaker, was able to add shorthand, tailoring, printing, and bookkeeping to its curriculum. In 1903 it won state funding as the biggest black training school in Philadelphia.[57]

Matthew Anderson was honored the same year when his fellow Presbyterians elected him to represent the city at the denomination's general assembly in Los Angeles. But while years of successful cooperation with white laymen made him an especially obvious candidate, the recognition was unusual only in degree; within the wider framework of segregated religious institutions white and black did sometimes find common ground. William Still had been chosen to a parallel lay convention nearly twenty years before his son-in-law; and clergymen, who had often gone to the same divinity schools, were for obvious reasons more likely to reach out to each other than most. Episcopalians shared the same priestly offices, and in his last official act as Bishop of Philadelphia, Phillips Brooks, in August of 1869, had called in the Reverend William Alston of St. Thomas's to assist in the sacred ceremony of ordaining new priests, two white and one black. The citywide associations of Methodists and Baptists were both interracial and sometimes rallied around their black members, as at the anti-lynching meetings with Ida Wells in 1894; perhaps it was no coincidence that the Reverend T. D. Miller was elected president of the local Baptist Association that year.[58]

But while shared denomination and similar purposes occasionally brought them together, most of the time black and white lived in different worlds, certainly on Sundays. And in practice the denominational ties that bound some of them together were not nearly as strong as the racial ties which united most of the city's black ministers and laymen across the formal lines that divided them into Baptist, Methodist, Presbyterian, or Episcopalian.

Sometimes it was practical matters, shared ends, that brought them together, as with Matthew Anderson and H. L. Phillips on the Berean Industrial Training School Board. As early as 1857 the musician Addison W. Lively, of Shiloh Baptist, had begun organizing "Grand Union" concerts of Sunday schools, with programs combining all of the young people's choirs except those of the very largest churches; while Bethel, for example, put on its own concert most of the AME churches joined with the rest. Projects too big for a single church often brought people together; Mrs. Phillips was among the several original founders of the Bethel Home for Fallen Women, and the Women's Union Missionary Society, which sponsored a Paul Dunbar poetry reading to benefit a day nursery in 1897, was composed of "colored women, representing the different religious denominations throughout the city." Simple courtesy, and perhaps the expense of hiring secular halls, seems to have dictated that a conference of the African-American Methodist Episcopal Church, a denomination still new to Philadelphia in 1899, should meet at First African Presbyterian. The Methodists' Delaware Conference, as noted, brought black Methodists and others together despite their different connections. In practice, then, much of the sound and fury between the AME and Zion, for example, seems a kind of verbal ritual, with no evidence outside of newspaper squabbling of real local hostility, and much of cooperation.[59]

Competition for members and dollars was certainly real, but it was carried out within a framework of formal professional courtesy. At the major public occasions when a minister celebrated an anniversary or a church was dedicated, white pastors typically came to represent the relevant denomination, but they were greatly outnumbered by Afro-Americans from outside it. When First African Baptist retired its latest debt in 1898 the long list of speakers included not only ministers from other persuasions but such lay persons as Fanny Jackson Coppin of Bethel and T. J. Minton and Carl Bolivar from St. Thomas's. The *Christian Recorder*, in one of its two principal anniversary issues in 1887, devoted an entire front page to the remarks of the Episcopalian J. S. Durham, while every denomination in the city turned out to welcome the 1903 assembly of the National Baptist Convention, to which most of the local black Baptists belonged.[60]

But it was, above all, the racial occasions, the meetings of outrage and protest, which united them. Sometimes, as in the series of different church meetings held for Ida B. Wells in 1894, there are hints of separateness or jealousy. But usually the events were too big for individual churches, and held in great secular halls. While the programs included laymen, and women, sometimes in prominent roles, the dais was always dominated by men in clerical uniform. The rotating arrangements were clearly designed to demonstrate cooperation: one minister typically convened the meeting, then turned it over to another as chair, while a third was elected president of the committee called to draw up a memorial or petition, the rest serving as vice presidents, secretaries, or treasurers. Despite all their different buildings, and doubtless clashing pastoral egos, these meetings before hundreds and even thousands of the city's Afro-Americans served at least ceremonially to make a reality of the abstract "black church," reminding everyone present that it was the most important institution that the race possessed.

Chapter 9

Race Pride and Race Relations

Black Americans have always had to wrestle with the issue of race, but in a series of changing historical contexts. The major questions have been much the same: what to call themselves, how to think of Africa, how to relate to other disadvantaged or minority groups, and how, in a society dominated by whites, to deal with their own blackness. Philadelphians, like others across the country, expressed a variety of answers in a variety of ways, dealing with some of the issues directly and formally, others indirectly and even unconsciously. What made the late 19th century distinctive is the historical background, as the end of slavery, changing white attitudes, and the challenge of other groups made new choices both possible and necessary.

The descendants of Africans were never agreed about what they should call themselves, and between the Civil War and the turn of the century the choices widened rather than narrowed. Among the acceptable alternatives "colored" was clearly dominant at the beginning. But it seems to have remained so at the end only because there were not one but two major alternatives: "Negro"— with blacks beginning to insist on the initial capital—and "Afro-American," both gaining ground.

There were other possibilities. The term "black" was used by editors and reporters of both races, as in "Give the Black Man a Chance," but it was never widely popular, perhaps partly because in a color-conscious era it was often used to distinguish some from others, as "blacks" from "mulattoes." The *Anglo-African* was one of the weeklies which young Jacob White, Jr., used to sell during the early 1860s, and the same term was used by a white Presbyterian minister in 1881, but that is the last year in which this compound noun appears in the Dorsey Collection. The simple unmodified "African" was almost equally rare. One extreme position, urged by Isaiah Wears in 1878 and often implied by Robert Purvis, was that ideally there should be no racial names at all; individual human beings were the reality, race an unimportant abstraction, and using labels such as "Negro" tended to distract attention from individual accomplishment.[1]

No black leader championed the word "colored," which seems to have survived mostly through inertia. T. Thomas Fortune in 1890 claimed that he was partly responsible for the name he used for the "Afro-American League," and a debate between that and "Negro" had in fact surfaced in his New York *Globe* in 1883, the first year for which any issues survive. A decade later a group of southern black editors formally declared its choice of "Negro," which the white New Orleans *Times-Democrat* implied it would honor. While white papers were not usually so sensitive, Philadelphia's *Evening Telegraph,* which carried the story, announced later the same year that it would abandon the use of "colored" entirely in favor of either of the alternatives that the race itself seemed to favor.[2]

The debate stayed low-key. The proponents of "Afro-" and its variants such as "Africo-American" simply argued that all peoples were somehow "colored," making that too vague a term, while on the other hand by no means all the descendants of Africans were colored black, as "Negro" implied. Fortune did feel it necessary to deny that "Afro-American" was favored principally by those with light skins, and when looking to score points against John Lewis, the Democratic lawyer, the devout Republican John Stephen Durham urged that "American Negro" was a more appropriate term than "African." But most seem to have used one or the other without much thought for their ideological or other possibilities; Ida B. Wells combined both "Colored" and "Afro-American" in a single pamphlet title, and brought "Negro" into the text. For a generation, in short, that had to wrestle, often for the first time, with the issues that they suggested, the names themselves were not a high priority.[3]

None of the issues which faced black Americans in the period was more emotionally divisive than colonization, especially colonization in Africa. It was inevitable that many should dream of escape to some other place, and equally inevitable that others should see this as a betrayal of the long fight for full inclusion as citizens of the United States. But citizenship was only one of the many complicating aspects of the colonization movement, which also involved religion, politics, and profit, alternatively providential and evolutionary views of history, and a variety of purely practical and personal concerns. Partly because Bishop Henry McNeal Turner, the leading champion of African emigration, was a sometime Philadelphian and frequent visitor, the Afro-Americans of the Quaker City were deeply concerned in the debate. And despite the fervor with which positions were held several of them seem to have felt ambivalent, and changed their minds toward the end of the century.

Urban blacks were used to travel and resettlement, and the military and southern adventuring of Civil War and Reconstruction seem especially to have inspired many young people to go west. One result was to tempt even the sedentary William Henry Dorsey, whose personal history includes no known trips out of his native city apart from the wedding journey of 1859, to join in a plan to settle the then largely empty Territory of Montana with Afro-American emigrants.

The Montana Agricultural Emigrant Aid Association was organized in Philadelphia on January 17, 1871. David Bustill Bowser, a veteran of steam-boating the Missouri, was one of the organizing vice presidents; so was Dorsey, as corresponding secretary, together with fellow Philadelphians Joseph Bustill, Dr. David Rossell, and general superintendent J. Lambert Dutrieulle, stationed out in Helena. The rest of the seventeen officers and directors included president William Nesbit, of Altoona, longtime head of the Pennsylvania Equal Rights League, with seven others from upstate; three men from Delaware, led by William Howard Day; and New York's most distinguished clergyman, the Reverend Henry Highland Garnet. Although the Association was a nonprofit organization, it included none of the usual philanthropic whites, indeed no whites at all.[4]

Its objects, as outlined in a flyer entitled "HO! FOR THE WEST: Farms for the Farmless! Homes for the Homeless!," was to assist "worthy but poor men and their families to emigrate" along the proposed route of the Northern Pacific Railroad. Taking advantage of, and in some ways modeled on, the Homestead Act of 1862, it promised small farms to men who would cultivate them—their "twenty to sixty acres" recalling the fabled "forty acres and a mule" which so many freedmen had once dreamed of. Assistance would take the form of seeds, cuttings, and tools; the public was invited to contribute, and it was hoped that fifty people could be outfitted by spring.[5]

While nothing further is known of the project, which was doubtless doomed in the absence of outside money, its very existence is significant. The swirling migrations of the postwar period had been dominated numerically by freedmen, uprooted, rebellious, or simply hopeful, who had little sense of where to go and mostly remained in the South. The Association's founders were scarcely about to take up the plow and join them; with the exception perhaps of Dutrieulle, who seems to have had a personal stake in the venture, they were aiming their appeal at others. But wanderlust was widely shared across the bounds of class and education; leading northerners were moved by the same range of motives, from ambition to desperation, which drove their poorer fellows. Talk of alternatives, opportunities, and migration, whether for themselves or others, clearly reached into the highest circles. Even in 1871, when Reconstruction was still alive and the obvious routes ran north and south, there were no geographic boundaries to their hopes.

But while individuals or small groups might move anywhere, those concerned about the future of the race had to think about the fate of the great majority who still lived in the South. And just as after the war it was the South which had fueled hopes for transformation through Reconstruction, when Reconstruction ended in the late 1870s new events fueled hopes for transformation through migration. Throughout the decade small groups of freedmen had been moving out of nearby border states into Kansas, the kind of emigration that perhaps inspired the Montana Association. But then at the very end the troubled blacks of the Deep South states seized on distant news of free land on the plains, and the trickle threatened to become a human flood, moving up against the course of the Mississippi. To many at the time it seemed in fact that the flow of these "Exodusters" out of the South might wholly transform the economic and political future of Afro-Americans and indeed much of the nation. But there were several different versions of what should or would happen, and the actual course of events fit no one's expectations.

The movement's historian has outlined its causes in just two words: "terrorism and poverty." Neither was new, but southern white terrorism worsened once the threat of federal force was gone, and without the hope of battling exploitation through politics the burden of poverty seemed heavier than ever. Calls for help reached Washington throughout the late 1870s, as many were struck by "Kansas Fever," an almost millennial belief that the government would provide money, farms, and tools for those who wanted to resettle. Pushed by desperation, pulled by hope and rumors, many simply set out upriver in the early spring of 1879, looking for help west once they got to the port of St. Louis.[6]

Another point had been raised that January by Minnesota Senator William Windom, who urged that since southern blacks were being denied the vote the federal government might help them resettle "into such Territory or Territories . . . as may be provided for their use or occupation." A group of Washington's Afro-Americans elected Richard T. Greener, then a Howard law professor, to head a delegation including Congressmen Cain, Small, and Rainey to meet with Windom. What most intrigued them was the promise of a special black territory, perhaps eventually a state, "to be governed by them," an idea endorsed by every man there.[7]

The actual migrants who began reaching St. Louis in March were overwhelmingly poor and illiterate refugees from Louisiana, Texas, and Mississippi, few of whom had ever heard of Windom's resolution, by then already rejected in the Senate. There were never as many as ten thousand of them, but widespread exaggeration of their potential numbers was only one of the many mistaken points in the contemporary national debate. Black observers hoped not only that they would find better lives out west but that the depopulation of the plantation South would improve the bargaining position of the tenants and laborers remaining. Panicky white Southerners feared just that. The blacks who visited them saw the "Exodusters" primarily as desperate refugees. White southerners, pointing to examples of fraud, insisted that they had no real complaints but had been stirred up by "outside agitators" selling bogus tickets or titles. All sides believed that mass migration would strengthen Republican voting power in Kansas and elsewhere. But Frederick Douglass broke with Greener by insisting that the races must learn to live together, and warned that segregation in the West, as in a separate territory, might pit black and white against each other in race war, and that Afro-Americans would go the way of the Indians.[8]

Philadelphians reacted in characteristic ways. William Dorsey's interest is shown in the amount of space he devoted to the movement. H. P. Williams, incapable of shame, insisted that all should remain at home "and cultivate the fields of the white man." "It is he," Williams wrote without irony, "who is our great employer, and it was his blood, money and acts that clothed us with citizenship. We cannot afford to say one unkind word against him." William Still more quietly opposed the exodus on the grounds that blacks should "eschew politics," concentrating on economic self-help and trusting in the power of education. Most blacks in contrast supported the movement, in the city as elsewhere. They tended in the early weeks, like many at some distance, to think less of the desperate plight of the actual migrants than of the political potential they might represent. Gil Ball thought Douglass was over the hill, and that the younger men would follow Greener; Mayor Stokley was persuaded by a group of "representative colored men," perhaps including his personal messenger William Dorsey, to establish a citizens' committee to "encourage the movement." Most of the newspapers, too, even those not specifically Republican, were equally enthusiastic.[9]

Neither the blacks nor the papers ever officially changed their minds, but the emphasis shifted with mounting news of desperation and hunger among those stranded in St. Louis. It was hard to disagree with those who urged more planning and caution. The city's Quakers characteristically investigated the situation and then sent aid. The Bethel Historical and Literary Society forwarded $107 in late April not to "encourage" the movement but to offer relief to those already uprooted, the same position taken by Mayor Stokley's committee in May. And at the national level Richard Greener joined Senator Windom and others not in encouraging a separate black territory or state but simply in trying to feed and clothe those already in Missouri.[10]

But while the Kansas exodus petered out within a few months, it set most of the themes for many less publicized ventures over the next two decades. The idea of a separate state continued to appeal, sometimes to Afro-Americans, sometimes to segregationist whites, so long as there seemed to be empty land in Montana, Washington, or Oklahoma. During 1893 such a proposal by John Temple Graves, a white Georgian, inspired a debate among AME ministers in and near Philadelphia; only one man favored the scheme, however, which Isaiah Wears denounced as "the verdict of a coroner's inquest" over the race as a whole. White politicians continued sometimes to suggest that the Republican party might gain voters through migration northward, while depopulation of the Democratic South would cut into that section's congressional representation. But while in favor of migration in principle, Philadelphia's leading Afro-Americans were in practice generally hostile to southern newcomers, convenient scapegoats for the host of social ills that plagued their neighborhoods. The Reverend H. L. Phillips in particular, while dedicated to the "worthy poor" that his Church of the Crucifixion was founded to help, believed that "of late years our northern cities have been overrun with a lot of scum that is rapidly affecting the status of the colored people of this section," and called for a revival of the Elizabethan Statute of Laborers, which would in effect enable the city either to drive out unemployed migrants or arrest them and sell their labor. For Afro-Americans, then, the least controversial hopes centered on small black communities outside the South, which would at the same time involve self-government, escape from peonage, and avoidance of urban problems. These schemes, much favored by real estate promoters, ranged from a proposed "Blacktown" in Chavez County, New Mexico, to "Whitesboro" in South Jersey, the latter named for an ex-congressman from South Carolina and inspired, in part, by the success of the nearby Jewish settlement founded by Baron Hirsch.[11]

Despite all this activity, none of these alternatives within the United States generated as much emotion as proposals for colonization outside. There was some local interest in Haiti, although generally discouraged by men like ex-Minister Ebenezer Bassett. The papers reported attempts to establish colonies in Mexico or Central America, always plagued by heat, fraud, greedy men, and hungry insects. None of these schemes could rival the long and tangled relationship between Afro-Americans and Africa itself.[12]

One of the ironies that helped to tangle the relationship was the fact that emigration to Africa appealed to two directly opposite constituencies. The American Colonization Society had been founded by frankly racist whites in 1816 to ship freed blacks back "home" on the grounds that they were both unwelcome and doomed on this continent; its Pennsylvania branch, headquartered in Philadelphia, remained active throughout the 19th century. During the 1890s, too, as Social Darwinists continued to predict the extinction of American blacks, both Senators Matthew Butler of South Carolina and John T. Morgan of Alabama urged that the federal government subsidize emigration simply to get rid of them. At the same time a long list of distinguished Afro-Americans, including Martin Delany, the leading intellectual churchmen Henry Highland Garnet and Alexander Crummell, above all Bishop Henry McNeal Turner, identified themselves with the emigration idea in protest against American racism, with Turner, in 1876, accepting a post as vice president of the American Colonization Society.[13]

But its ability to attract strange bedfellows was only one of the multiple complications of the African idea. In an age when most respectable black activity was centered in the church and every black leader was identified as Christian, the champions of emigration had to repudiate the United States, and sometimes "white civilization," without repudiating Christianity. Bishop Turner managed this with an elaborate theology which suggested that the enslavement of Africans and their transportation to the New World was part of a still unfolding Providential Plan. Agreeing with many others, of both races, that slavery in itself was a blessing insofar as it had brought Christianity to black pagans, he went on to argue that white Americans, through their cruelty and racism, had subverted its purpose. That was an insult to God, a collective sin for which they had paid through Civil War. Given a last chance at redemption through Reconstruction, the nation had failed again. What remained then was for blacks to leave this accursed place and bring the best of Western civilization and Christianity back home. Few contemporary Afro-Americans were able to find a less convoluted way out of the apparent conflict between their racial and their religious heritage; one of them was H. M. Joseph, a correspondent of the New York *Freeman,* whose front-page article on "Negrodom vs. Christianity" in 1887 arrived at the nearly unthinkable conclusion that African missions did more harm than good, and compared Christian racism unfavorably with Muslim tolerance.[14]

Any statement, such as Joseph's, that suggested the superiority of African ways ran directly counter to the reigning American belief in progress. For some, like the young Du Bois, that belief was bolstered by a Social Darwinism which thought African "survivals" doomed by civilization. Others found hope in glossing American history through optimistic lenses, measuring the great advances made in the short time since the race had moved up from slavery, shrugging off problems as due to laggard white opinion and the backwardness of rural southerners, themselves still close to African barbarism. From any progressive viewpoint the Dark Continent represented not the future but the past, and even the most sympathetic missionaries, colonizers, and visitors felt themselves superior to the natives. Neither black nor white Philadelphians liked to stress what we still call cultural "survivals" from Africa, whether in language, art, or custom, and the Dorsey Collection is almost barren of such references. But for all the obstacles, the African continent remained a place of fascination for a wide variety of black Philadelphians.

William Henry Dorsey, for one, filled more than twenty scrapbooks with Africana. The items represent the range of what was then available through the press, mainly stories of colonial battles, missionary work, exotic peoples and customs: "Muley Hassan and the Riffs," "Wild Women Warriors," "African Superstition," "Kaffir Beauties," "Funny Foods," "Slavery's Horrors," "Emigration to Liberia." His own interests were reflected in the number of illustrations, in proportion to text far higher in these than in most of the scrapbooks, sketches and then photographs of pyramids, warriors, or native peoples in costume. [15]

Two occasions especially brought parts of the continent home. Both the Orange Free State and the Republic of Liberia sent objects for display at Philadelphia's Centennial Exhibition of 1876, with some man-made robes, weapons, and canoes included among the exotic animal skins from the Free State, coffee bags and jars of palm oil from Liberia. Far more interesting was the Liberian Exhibition at the Chicago World's Fair of 1893. One of the country's two commissioners, the Hon. William E. Rothery, was a native of Philadelphia, and partly responsible for bringing most of the 430 catalogued items back for a lengthy stay at the Pennsylvania Museum and School of Industrial Art. Instead of agricultural products and exotic fauna this was mainly an "ethnological collection . . . from the back country tribes, such as the Mandingo, Golahs, Veys, and Grebas." The reviewers were delighted with the illustrated Islamic manuscripts, ornate etchings, and varicolored clothing, together with the "hideously carved" spears. Relatively little space in the papers, although many square feet of the museum, was devoted to the two model homes, a bamboo hut representing pre-colonial primitivism contrasting with a wooden, tin-roofed, contemporary dwelling looking "very much like a comfortable, capacious, seaside villa along the Jersey coast." [16]

Interest in the continent took many forms. In the late 18th and early 19th century blacks in Philadelphia and elsewhere clearly thought of themselves as African. Perhaps because of distaste for deportation schemes their descendants by the time of the Civil War did not commonly use the adjecive to identify "Cherry Street Baptist" or "First Presbyterian," and ironically the young Henry Turner, for one, had proposed dropping it from the name of his AME denomination. But it was still part of the formal titles of most of the churches founded in the early years. Whites as well as blacks sometimes cited the glories of Egyptian or Carthaginian civilization, the Episcopalians noting at the beginning of Reconstruction that "there have been eras in which the African exhibited, while our own ancestors gave no trace of, these very capacities for intelligence, self-support, and industry, to which we now appeal." Papers like the *Freeman* routinely carried features such as "King Cetowayo, Ruler of Eululand" as well as missionaries' and travelers' accounts. The city had its own more direct contacts; aged people took pride in their Ebo or other tribal roots; Lincoln University welcomed occasional African students; some leaders had at least visited Liberia, where Richard Greener picked up an honorary Lld. at the college in Monrovia. [17]

Western interest in Africa was never greater than in the late 19th century. On the one hand it was still "dark" and mysterious, with big animals and geographic landmarks continually being "discovered" for the first time; on the other the Western powers were pulling the continent into the global political and economic system, busily carving out territorial bounds, fighting native tribesmen and threatening to fight each other. The same period witnessed a great expansion in Afro-American religious activity abroad as well as at home. In Africa as elsewhere, there was no hard line to separate the secular and the sacred, and in part to advertise their missions churchmen routinely praised the beauties of the landscape, the richness of the soil, the potential profits in trade or investment. Liberian coffee was advertised in Philadelphia's black weeklies during the 1890s; the cornerstone of the rebuilt St. Thomas Church, no hotbed of missionary fever, was filled with samples from thirty-two bags of it, "the first ever shipped to this port to a colored man." None of this sort of interest raised hackles in itself, but there was bitter conflict when it led to calls for emigration.[18]

These calls were most seductive during periods of disillusion with the promise of America. One was widely heard just before the Civil War, with the government firmly in proslavery hands. "Almost every Negro leader of consequence," one historian has noted ". . . was at least open to the idea of colonization in Africa or one of the Caribbean lands," at the time when young Jacob White, Jr., was recruited to act as an agent for Haitian emigration. The call was muted during the 1860s and early 1870s, but grew louder as Reconstruction faded later in the decade, appealing especially to the same embattled freedmen who were subject, at the same time and for the same reasons, to "Kansas Fever."[19]

Black Philadelphians, with one exception, showed no interest in emigration during the 1870s. The emigrationists' goal was almost always Liberia, originally founded by the American Colonization Society under an American protectorate, and still supported by the Pennsylvania branch. But while the Society after Emancipation tended to stress its missionary and civilizing purposes, advertising the republic as a Christian gateway to a heathen continent, it got no local recruits. As the *Times* discovered, "The colored people of this city, strange as it may seem, look upon the society with disfavor. They have always distrusted its intentions and think its purpose is simply to thin out the Negro population of this country." A survey in April of 1878 found no one with plans for African trade, missions, or emigration except for Dr. Henry M. Turner, just up from South Carolina to take charge of the AME Book Concern.[20]

Turner was in fact already central to plans to ship southerners to Liberia. During the previous year, bypassing the white Colonization Society, which he formally served as vice president, he and two other AME clerics from Charleston, Congressman R. H. Cain and Professor B. F. Porter, had formed a "Liberian Exodus Association," which bought a ship, the *Azor*, and proposed to transport several hundred blacks across the Atlantic for about $35 apiece. Shrugging off a resolution of censure by the New Jersey Conference of his church, Turner insisted that a million more were ready to go, and that he would join them "as soon as I can educate my children." His optimism survived a disastrous, death-ridden voyage by the *Azor,* accusations of fraud, and the opposition of virtually every newspaper in Philadelphia, far more hostile to Liberian than Kansas emigration. A little congregation organized on board the unfortunate vessel seems to have made it ashore, but the ground in the "civilized" areas of Liberia was already thick with white missionaries of several denominations, and it is not clear that any of the communicants survived for long with their connection intact. This failure, coupled with discouraging reports from ex-Liberian Minister J. Milton Turner, dampened interest in Africa for a while. But it remained too strong to go away.[21]

One continuing source of that interest was southern misery, the eagerness of battered tenants and sharecroppers to welcome plans for migration almost anywhere. Another was the natural pride of Afro-American leaders, their eagerness if not to go to Liberia at least to see it succeed as a black-run republic. Henry McNeal Turner was in position to fuel both. One later biographer describes him as a big man, although contemporary reports suggest that he was only 5'5"; the difference may result from the fact that all agree on adjectives like "thunderous." Du Bois, on his death in 1906, called him a "charging bull," last of a clan of "mighty men, physically and mentally, who had started at the bottom and hammered their way to the top. . . ." Although born free he had paid his dues by working the cotton fields in his native South Carolina; his direct and earthy manner always gave him a special rapport with southern audiences. At the same time he had earned the right, as author and publicist, to talk just as directly to Afro-American intellectuals, and a combination of persuasiveness and fighting spirit made him an especially powerful force within the church he served so long.[22]

Black objections to African colonization were based partly on principle, partly on practicality. Robert Purvis was the fiercest of Philadelphia's spokesmen for principle; while proud of his African connections—a portrait of the chieftain Cinque, who had led a slave-ship mutiny in the 1830s, was reportedly his most prized possession—Purvis was deeply opposed to segregation in any form. He had refused in 1867 to join the elite Civil, Social and Statistical Association simply because membership in any all-black organization might prejudice his right to demand full citizenship, just as he refused in later years to be known as an "Afro-American," as distinct from "American" without hyphen or qualification. In 1886, at a mass meeting to protest a massacre in Mississippi, he chose to use his position as chair to issue his most pointed attack on colonization. "There is not a single African in the United States," he told ex-Mayor Samuel King, T. T. Fortune, South Carolina Congressman Robert Smalls, and a thousand other listeners at Musical Fund Hall: "We are to the manner born; we are native Americans." A white minister, praising the work of the Colonization Society, had claimed that "colored men are waiting and watching to be wafted to Liberia." Using words that his audience might be tempted to apply to others, Purvis thundered, "This clerical wolf, who has stolen the livery of heaven to serve the devil in, tells a lie." The remarks were "cheered to the echo."[23]

T. Thomas Fortune, the second speaker that night, was as the leading Afro-American editor in the country the most effective opponent of colonization on practical grounds. Turner and other emigrationists were never precise about how many should leave, but virtually every commentator remarked that the cost of transporting any significant fraction of the eight million blacks in the United States was simply prohibitive. Fortune denounced Edward Blyden, longtime Liberian publicist, as "a hireling spy of the American Colonization Society." The movement was plagued by fraudulent playing on false hopes, and while the Colonization Society sent out several dozens from Philadelphia each year, the newspapers continually reported on Arkansans and others who arrived in eastern ports, hungry and homeless, to be bailed out by local charities. Above all Fortune and others hammered at the issue of viability; Liberia was a poor and miserable country, and despite individual success stories the death rate among émigrés was appalling. Malaria and other more exotic diseases took their toll even among the most privileged. When following Grover Cleveland's election in 1892 Bethel's Pastor W. H. Heard was angling for a job as minister to Liberia, one of the two most prestigious diplomatic appointments to which a black man might aspire, Fortune pointed out that beginning with Ebenezer Bassett every former Haitian minister was still alive, while every former Liberian had died, several of them in office.[24]

But Turner had great reservoirs of hope and emotion to draw on, and on elevation to bishop in charge of missionary work he had also the resources of the biggest Afro-American organization in the world. While a few AME churchmen had gone to and died in Africa from the early 19th century, generally supported by white Methodists, the denomination's own meager budget did not then allow for any independent missions. During the great expansionist period of Reconstruction the church was devoted to struggles in the South, and the freedmen themselves provided a missionary field vast enough to absorb all its energies. But interest picked up quickly afterward; while there are few accounts of missionary action by black Philadelphians of any persuasion before the 1880s there were many thereafter, with the AME especially prominent. While the major white denominations sent most missionaries to Africa, and especially to Liberia, the only country where Americans were clearly welcome, they made surprisingly little use of Afro-American ministers, and none of them was interested in promoting either racial pride or emigration. And since neither of the other major black churches, AME Zion or the National Baptist Convention, was able to mount effective African missions until early in the 20th century, the AME in practice had a monopoly on the ground.[25]

Turner's biographer suggests that he was especially affective in recognizing the role of churchwomen, who were involved from the beginnings in the Mite

Missionary Society, organized in 1874. And in Philadelphia he had some exceptional women to work with; his tenure as head of the missionary department began about the time when Fanny Jackson married into the church through his younger colleague Levi Coppin. The bishop founded the Women's Home and Foreign Mission Society, but Jackson Coppin was at least partly responsible for its growth, and fundraising took her as far as London in 1888. Bishop Jabez Campbell founded the annual Ocean Grove Conference, with its missionary appeal, during the same decade. And in 1882 Dr. B. T. Tanner, then editor of the *Christian Recorder,* called for the establishment of a regular semi-monthly packet to Liberia, announcing that he had pledges of $10,000 from a pair of "capitalists" provided $80,000 more could be raised elsewhere for a colonization project.[26]

There was an understandable lag in time, as clerical rhetoric exceeded the AME's reach and reach exceeded grasp. It was not until 1891 that Turner himself visited Africa. But he impressed his hosts everywhere, including white clerics, with whom he generally got along very well. After establishing conferences in Sierra Leone and Liberia he was appointed Bishop of Africa, began publishing his own *Voice of Missions,* and visited again in 1893, ordaining and appointing local officers of the church. He was in place then to take advantage of a renewed interest in colonization, as in the 1890s an odd combination of depression, growing imperialist interest in the tropics, and worsening race relations inspired deportation sentiment among southern whites and emigrationist fever among southern blacks.[27]

The interest still failed to move a majority, especially in the urban North. Bishop Turner called for a national conference of Afro-Americans in Cincinnati, late in 1893, but Baltimore's AME ministers refused to send a single delegate, and the African side in a debate held by the Bishop Payne Historical and Literary Society of Philadelphia's Union Church was weakened when the first speaker, to a roar of laughter, admitted that he would never go himself. The Cincinnati Conference was well attended, and Turner well received, but the members were more concerned at that date with violence than emigration, passing resolutions denouncing both rape and lynching while rejecting any call for an African exodus.[28]

While Turner's growing obsession reportedly created some friction with his fellow bishops, as he returned twice more, to Liberia in 1895 and notably to South Africa in 1898, he was still powerfuly persuasive. The Rev. Mr. Heard, having won the post of Minister to Liberia, when visiting back in Philadelphia during 1896 would say only that things were not as bad as pictured. Three years later, returned to his pastorate, he insisted that "its mineral and other resources are boundless," and that investments would return a full 100 percent. Bishop Abram Grant in early 1899 called for the establishment of an emigrant's information bureau in Washington, urging intervention before the European powers gobbled up the continent, which he went on to visit later that year. At the same time the Hon. C. C. Astwood, as the new superintendent of missions, echoed Turner and exceeded Alabama Senator Morgan in calling for a congressional grant of $100 million to assist in deportation/emigration. By 1903 the enthusiasm had spread to the National Baptists, meeting in Philadelphia, where the Reverend S. E. Griggs of Nashville proposed his own version of Turner's emigrationist theology. The purpose of African missions, he suggested to the several thousand delegates, was not simply to bring the Gospel to the natives but to civilize them to the level of the more advanced Afro-Americans who might soon be forced into exodus. Without this preparation the returning colonizers would otherwise "look down upon their own people in South Africa just . . . as the white people of the South look down upon the negro of to-day."[29]

Actual emigration plans, during the 1890s, were meanwhile advanced by several different societies. The International Migration Company, headquartered in Birmingham, proposed in 1894 to inaugurate a "White Star Line," with a capital of $300,000, to transport homesteaders to Liberia at an average cost of $41 a head. In September of that year a company ship did leave the Port of Philadelphia carrying the Liberian consul, 170 southerners, a load of tools, and a giant ice-making machine. Many of its passengers, complaining of horror, death, and hardship, returned within two years; this and a sister voyage helped decisively to kill potential mass emigration to Liberia. The old gray American Colonization Society, meanwhile, its original rationale long gone with the end of slavery, continued each year to "thin out" the Afro-American population by a few dozen souls, blaming failures on unscrupulous profit-making ventures like the Migration Company.[30]

As of 1897 these two societies were joined by two others which proposed alternatives to Liberia. The Philafrican League, led by the French explorer Heli Chatelaine, was composed of white adventurers who planned to buy up land in the interior. Much more ambitious was the African Colonial Enterprise promoted by a black West Indian, J. Albert Thorne, who proposed to settle 10,000 acres in British Central Africa. Thorne's scheme, like many others, was supposed to be nonprofit. He came to the United States from Edinburgh with letters from a number of distinguished Britons, including Lord Bryce. These had already contributed toward the $120,000 he thought was needed, over the following three years, to start a colony with a balanced mix of artisans, doctors, and farmers. All would be given homesteads in exchange for labor, beginning with one hundred "carefully screened" families or three hundred people.[31]

While every leading Afro-American interviewed in Philadelphia had joined the otherwise distrusted Colonization Society in condemning the International Migration Company, with only Bishop Turner keeping the faith, Dr. Thorne was much more persuasive. Thorne visited the city in the fall of 1897, preaching not mass emigration but simply the advantages of opportunity for those unable to realize their ambitions in the United States. He spoke at Union Baptist and, after staying as the overnight guest of the Reverend Matthew Anderson, at Berean Presbyterian reminded his Afro-American audiences of the "cheap competition" they faced from European immigrants, suggesting that those of African ancestry might thrive near the Zambesi while white men died. At Lincoln University, a student audience unanimously passed four resolutions in favor of his proposed new state. Promising to recruit a substantial expedition to Nyasaland the following March, he did recruit a Philadelphia executive board to help him solicit funds and settlers, with the Reverend Levi Coppin as president, Dr. Nathan Mossell as vice president, T. J. Minton as solicitor, the Reverend Alexander Gordon as secretary, and Dr. T. C. Imes as treasurer.[32]

The expedition was postponed a year, to March of 1899. On the eve of his leaving, a host of leading Philadelphians attended Dr. Thorne's farewell reception at the AME's Bainbridge St. Church, not only the executive board and several prominent whites but also Isaiah Wears, E. D. Bassett, Christopher Perry, Dr. E. C. Howard, and ministers from most of the leading churches. By then the project was much scaled down; toward the end Thorne was asking for no more than $5000 and just ten good men to start. No one went from the city, although three years later the Reverend Levi Coppin, by then elevated to bishop, took his wife on a missionary voyage to South Africa, following her resignation from the Institute for Colored Youth. The couple returned after a year which much taxed Fanny's health, forcing her to spend most of the rest of her life confined to their home on Bainbridge Street.[33]

In the end then few ever personally acted on the African idea. But those who did included the most famous Afro-American clergyman to live in Philadelphia during the late 19th century, together with the city's most respected educator and citizen. And for other leaders, those without the same compelling sense of Christian mission, the lack of personal commitment did not mean lack of interest. Even those who were comfortable themselves had sometimes to think of the future of the race as a whole. The only alternatives that many contemporaries could imagine, whether white racists or African nationalists, were continued subordination, extinction, amalgamation, or exodus. Given these choices, in an atmosphere of unpredictable hostility, the list of those willing to work for the Central African Enterprise included the city's leading black doctor and lawyer, while the leading orator, diplomat, and publisher all turned out to honor its founder. For all of them Africa was obviously a source of some pride, and African enterprise of any kind a means of keeping options open.

Whatever their attitudes toward further emigration, most blacks in late 19th-century Philadelphia had made at least one major move already: into the city itself. And one of the conditions that made their lives more complicated than they had been in the South or elsewhere was the variety of the other peoples they found there. Their lives were framed in the most important respects by a white Protestant male elite, who in the city and nation as in the old South still dominated business, politics, and the press. But any big city also contained other groups with their own disabilities or grievances: Irish, Italian, and Jewish immigrants from Europe, Asians from China, the outspoken wives and daughters of the dominant elite. The relations between these other groups and Afro-Americans were different in each case, shaped sometimes by a need to live together, sometimes by a sense of alliance, often by the mutual hostility that came with life toward the bottom, the desperate need to struggle in the same arena for limited rewards.

Poor, Protestant, and Republican, victimized for years by Irish toughs, the city's blacks began with a natural distrust of foreigners. And it was naturally tempting for some Afro-Americans to identify with the powerful men who shared their Protestant and Republican identity against the immigrants with whom they shared only their poverty. Gil Ball and many others joined the American Protestant Association, one of the several anti-Catholic or anti-foreign groups which flourished in the late 1880s and 1890s. And Councilman Stephen A. Gipson served as president of George Washington Camp No. 579 of the Patriotic Sons of America, which in a special ceremony in October of 1891 presented an American flag to Principal Caroline LeCount and the students of the Octavius V. Catto School. With Mayor William Smith joining a black delegation including Isaiah Wears, the Reverend John B. Reeve, and James Field Needham, Gipson described his group as "Dedicated to the maintenance of our public school system against all its foes, to the keeping from our shores of all immigrants, incapable of development into good American citizens."[34]

But there was no real comfort in a bigotry which was far more likely to turn on Afro-Americans than to welcome them. Gipson's Washington Camp No. 579 was in fact not recognized by the constitution of the Patriotic Sons, which contained an "anti-colored" clause, while later in the decade the American Protestant Association of Philadelphia insisted that its segregated affiliates identify themselves with the prefix "Colored." And during the same period many leading blacks and Irish Catholics were seeking mutual rapprochement rather than continued hostility.[35]

Some of this has been outlined earlier, notably the exchanges between T. Thomas Fortune and his Irish counterpart, the nationalist and Catholic editor John Boyle O'Reilly, the aid given Home Rule by Richard Greener, the establishment of St. Peter Clavers and other efforts under Archbishop Ryan. Du Bois had some faith in these efforts: "The Catholic Church can do more than any other agency in humanizing the intense prejudice of many of the working-class against the Negro." For Fortune at least the attempted Irish alliance anticipated later efforts by Southern Populist leaders to transcend racial hostility in the name of the common economic problems of poor blacks and whites, with the added fillip of a common battle against prejudice.[36]

A decade later many Irish and blacks were united in distrust of a United

States imperialism based in part on the British model, and urged in part because of an alleged racial identity between Americans and Englishmen that gave both a special genius for governing themselves and dominating lesser breeds. This particular form of racism was denied by those of Celtic as well as African descent, and William Dorsey in 1899 saved a selection from the *Irish World* attacking the then-fashionable "Anglo-Saxon Humbug."[37]

But old habits die hard, real differences remained, and despite T. T. Fortune it was not the recognition of common economic problems so much as growing economic differences that moderated the earlier ferocity of Irish confrontations with blacks. During the 19th century, with few governmental programs at any level designed to help the whole of the working class, the existence of two groups working in the same areas, or even hoping to, created more mutual hostility than cooperation. Insofar as it has an economic explanation, the mellowing of Irish attitudes toward Afro-Americans resulted from their continual late-century movement out of unskilled and into skilled factory or white-collar jobs. This meant among other things that Irish-Americans were subjected to the regimenting discipline of the urban-industrial revolution. As they learned in time to moderate their behavior, to stop spitting in each other's drinks and settling all arguments with fists, feet, teeth, and bricks, their overall murder rate, as noted, fell by a factor of three over the late 19th century. At the same time, increasingly secure behind union walls that protected them from direct competition, better educated and less desperate than before, they could afford to be more generous toward blacks they had once seen as threatening.[38]

The importance of all this may be shown by the contrasting behavior of the city's new Italian immigrants. Blacks and Italians, as shown in Chapter 3, were still pitted against each other in labor gangs competing for pick-and-shovel work. Without, as yet, the economic security or the new social psychology brought by the urban-industrial revolution, the city's Italians in the late 19th and early 20th century succeeded the mid-century Irish as the most violent people in Philadelphia, their murder rate for some time far exceeding the blacks'. Partly as a result there were no local stories involving Afro-Americans and Italians in any relations other than fights; the only reason why these stopped short of the riotously deadly attacks mounted earlier by the Irish was, as suggested, the fact that the Italians had no numerical advantage strong enough to tempt them into invading growing black neighborhoods.[39]

The city's Chinese, meanwhile, far fewer in the 19th century than the Italians or any other major ethnic group, posed a different threat entirely. When addressing a Republican rally in 1884, some years before they had actually encountered Afro-Americans in the East, Richard Greener "strongly approved" the total exclusion of Asian immigrants. But perhaps influenced by his Irish-American connections he was then presumably thinking of competition in heavy labor. In practice the few Chinese who drifted all the way into the urban Northeast during the late 1880s and 1890s were not the common laborers who had built western railroads twenty years earlier but small businessmen. Most of them settled into a little "Chinatown" occupying a few blocks of Race Street, then part of a "red-light" district located north of the densest Afro-American neighborhoods, where their restaurants were "patronized largely by disorderly women," more of them white than black.[40]

Virtually the only evidence in the Dorsey Collection of any sense of identity based on the common experience of color discrimination is provided by its author. Dorsey himself did collect some art catalogues which featured Oriental rugs and other objects of art, and indeed handcopied, in March of 1882, eighty-nine pages of text from *China Painting: A Practical Manual*, published two years earlier by M. Louise McLaughlin. But while his scrapbooks indicate a wide interest in Native Americans, Pacific Islanders, and other peoples of color, none was devoted to either Chinese or Japanese subjects. Perhaps because of their small numbers and poor English the local Chinese seem to have had no significant contact with the leaders of the Afro-American community, so that relations in Philadelphia were confined to the largely inarticulate on both sides.[41]

As the Chinese brought even fewer women than the Italians they sometimes patronized black prostitutes, while blacks ate at Chinese restaurants, sometimes worked there, and occasionally experimented with opium. But otherwise recorded contacts were mostly hostile. The laundry business, among the legitimate occupations which employed black women, ranked only second to and indeed overlapped with general domestic work. The great majority of these women worked at home, in crowded tenements with little specialized equipment and no running water. And perhaps partly because of the growing sense of fear and insecurity which increasingly limited white women's visits to Afro-American neighborhoods during the 1890s, customers came to prefer Chinese. Isabel Eaton noted that the Afro-Americans of the Seventh Ward were "justly resentful of the work given to Chinamen." While one group was famous for generally pacific behavior the other increasingly was not, and every local account of violent behavior involves Afro-American aggression against Chinese, women throwing acid in their faces, men beating, mugging, and robbing them.[42]

Relations with Philadelphia's Jewish community were more complex. The city had an older group of German and Sephardic Jews who doubtless seemed, to its black residents, much like other whites. But East European Jews, like the Italians and Chinese, began to arrive in the 1880s and 1890s, settling in the Fifth Ward and moving into the Seventh, where their closeness to established blacks sometimes grated on both groups.

One source of hostility was Christian evangelism among the mostly Orthodox newcomers. The police were continually called to deal especially with one small but noisy band of two blacks and three whites who sang and paraded through the crowded streets of the Delaware River wards. The blacks of the Seventh Ward, in turn, were unhappy with the incursions of the Presbyterian convert Moses Greenberg, whose campaign to clean up the area, in cooperation with the Law and Order League, resulted, as described in Chapter 3, in a number of false arrests and a major confrontation with the congregants of the Pleasant Valley Mission. But these conflicts were over-shadowed by the daily friction resulting from living patterns not yet fully segregated, so that Jews and Afro-Americans were crowded together along almost impassably narrow streets, such as Addison, on the border of the Fifth and Seventh wards, where it was reported with little exaggeration that "neighbors can shake hands . . . across it from third story windows." One tragicomic illustration of the problem occurred when two funerals were scheduled for the same 3 o'clock hour on a stifling August Sunday in 1898.[43]

On one side of the street William Allmond's undertaking parlor was filled with an unusually tough band of mourners for William Allen, the young southerner who had been stabbed to death the week before in the yard outside of Charley Dean's Kater Street speakeasy. On the other side, a little to the east, Isaac Slabonski, who had just died in the Jewish Hospital, was laid out in the little Synagogue of Rubin. Both sets of funeral carriages were late. The first to arrive, turning west from Sixth Street, was the one Allmond had ordered for Allen, but on reaching the synagogue it was commandeered by the Slabonski mourners, who assumed it was theirs, packed the body into the lead wagon, themselves into the others, and ordered the driver on toward Frankford. The lead black driver, however, refused to be moved by Yiddish curses, and the commotion attracted the crowd at Allmond's, less than a block away. When Allen's friends discovered that, as they saw it, their cortege was being hijacked, they began pulling out the astonished Jews, and the resultant "international complications," as the *Tribune* put it, were quelled only by the Third District Police and the fortunate arrival of Slabonski's cortege.[44]

During the 1890s both Jews and blacks meanwhile shared the Forten School for a time, and also the services of the settlement house near Seventh and Lombard where young William E. B. Du Bois and his wife lived during their stay in the city. The settlement house, its purposes continually evolving and its location later changed, had been founded in the late 1880s by women interested primarily in working with blacks. The college women and early social work professionals who staffed the enterprise variously stressed the doctrines of home improvement, thrift, temperance, sexual morality, hygiene, and self-help. But as their clientele, like nearby Forten's, changed with time and the composition of the neighborhood, blacks had some reason to feel victims of discrimination even by these most well-disposed-of whites.[45]

From the beginning the deeply Christian women who ventured into the Seventh Ward had been upset by the public drinking, sexual freedom, and to their eyes casual family arrangements that they found in black Philadelphia.

During the first decade of the 20th century, finding the attitudes and behavior of the Jews and Italians much more congenial, they gradually cut back their work among Afro-Americans in favor of these more pliable immigrants. As early as 1895, a visiting reporter discovered that the Jewish and black boys were organized into different drill teams. Both groups seemed to take proudly to the parading, the main difference being that the former, as "Davis Cadets," were rehearsing in smart blue and gold uniforms, while the "Dudley Pioneer Corps" had no uniforms at all.[46]

The city's Afro-American leaders had some contact with the Jews, as with the Irish and unlike the Chinese or Italians, but their relations were uneven. Even the same observations could cut in two directions. The traditional identification with the oppressed Hebrews of the Old Testament was reinforced in the late 19th century by the addition of two new ritual celebrations to the calendar, of Emancipation and Enfranchisement: "The Jews have always followed this custom," one minister noted, of honoring God as the author of secular deliverence. On the other hand Carl Bolivar, one of the founders of the American Negro Historical Society, viewed the teaching of history as a kind of competition for credit, attention, and textbook space, noting with a mixture of jealousy and admiration that in contrast to his own "the Jewish people and the Catholic contend for a square deal whenever they are left out of the general consideration."[47]

But Bolivar seems the only explicit anti-Semite among the city's black leaders. In attempting to explain the decline in Afro-American businesses in the Seventh and Eighth wards, he wrote in 1912 that "the Jew is a parasite, and if segregated would starve. The Jew thrives on others, and he followed the colored people, opening up haberdasheries, shoe shops, lodging and eating houses, barber shops and the like." Bolivar's opinions probably reflected attitudes picked up in a lifetime of clerking for the small white banking house of John Ashurst & Co. The *Standard-Echo*, in 1892, did sound an obliquely bitter note in complaining that the white Protestant ministry was far more likely to sympathize with the victims of pogroms in faraway Russia than of lynchings in the South, but there are no similar statements anywhere else in the Dorsey Collection. In terms of routine interaction, too, there is no indication in its voluminous crime reports of any disproportionate aggression toward Jews, as there is toward Chinese.[48]

Otherwise the relatively few reports of black-Jewish interaction are all favorable. When T. T. Fortune, for example, early in the 1890s, carried on a brief campaign to test enforcement of the civil rights laws in New York's restaurants and theaters his white witnesses were all Jewish. And in 1896, the Hon. Oscar Strauss, ex-minister to Turkey, apparently invited local Afro-Americans to a meeting of the American Jewish Historical Society to hear a paper on "Slavery Days: The Part Taken by American Hebrews."[49]

But none of the relations between Philadelphia's blacks and the city's other ethnic groups was as complex as those with middle-class white women. White women in general shared the racial attitudes of men, but not all of the advantages, and for better and worse they had different experiences with those on the other side of the color line.

Through childhood, first, and for the more privileged, high school and college, white girls and young women had less direct experience with Afro-American playmates or friends than their brothers. Boys could be cruel and even brutal in their treatment of black peers, and taunted black adults with sticks and stones as well as names still alien to well-bred girls. But the newspapers of the day are also full of stories of mixed groups of boys at play, fishing or horsing about the docks, playing ball and duelling, daring each other to throw "crackers," and otherwise attracting attention. Some of these grew out of the obvious fact that this kind of boyishness did indeed attract attention, in a way that playing with dolls or jacks did not. But they also grew out of the differing ways in which pre-adolescents behaved.[50]

Boys, then as now, tended to play in larger groups than girls, sometimes with relative strangers whose daring, strength, or speed won admiration as well as jealousy. The sheer physical ability to play various roles successfully was enough at least to win entry and a certain impersonal respect. Girls, in contrast, then perhaps more than now, joined in smaller circles, mostly confined to established confidantes, playing at activities which had no impersonal standards of success. One historian has noted that through the 19th century middle- and upper-class white girls began at an early age to establish intensely emotional "sororial" relationships that often lasted a lifetime, excluding outsiders.[51]

Differing gender roles carried over into high school and then college. During the late 19th century so few blacks went to either that except at segregated places they had virtually no classmates of their own race. Since both high school and college with rare exceptions were sexually segregated in addition, the formal rules reinforced by the fact that interracial friendships across sexual lines were virtually unthinkable, their social contacts were almost wholly confined to whites of the same sex. And while the experience was surely difficult for all, the evidence is that young black men had a better time adjusting than their sisters.

During the late 19th century, girls of both races, and especially Afro-Americans, were more likely than boys to graduate from high school. The very reverse was true of college, however, with fewer young women and especially black women even attending. While there were many reasons for this imbalance, one of them was surely the difference in their social or extracurricular lives. It was possible for men to have experiences as miserable as Arthur Whittaker's at West Point. But perhaps in part because of the ways in which the students were screened, virtually every story about black males at white institutions stresses their popularity or at least success among their classmates. For the pioneers at Central and manual training high schools, young Minton at Exeter, Durham and Warrick at Penn, indeed all but Greener at Harvard, the common thread is success at team sports, usually leading to other if limited forms of acceptance.

There are simply no such stories in the Dorsey Collection about the more numerous young women who went to Girls' High, and no evidence that any went to white private schools of any kind. Several, as noted, successfully completed the professional training at Women's Medical College, which like its contemporaries required no prior bachelor's degree. But Fanny Jackson, Mary Patterson, and the retiring Grace Mapps are the only local women recorded as having gone to college at all, and Jackson's happy years at interracial Oberlin seem to have been exceptional. The elite women's colleges were far slower than their male counterparts to open even token places for blacks, with M. Carey Thomas, longtime president of nearby Bryn Mawr, an especially notorious racist. Anita Hemmings, the first at Vassar, was a light-skinned woman who revealed her racial identity only on graduation in 1897, to the intense delight of the sensational journals and the equally intense "dismay" of the college's administration, while Booker T. Washington's daughter Portia had a highly publicized and miserably brief time at Wellesley, during 1901–2, where she suffered from exclusion and loneliness.[52]

The paradox is that for educated men genuine interracial contacts essentially stopped at graduation, and educated women's began. Among the working classes, although the near-horror inspired by interracial sex presumably inhibited friendships at puberty, the men of both races routinely continued to meet and mingle, however warily, at all male sporting events and in some bar-rooms, where they took various sides in arguments about boxers, ball clubs, and horses. But there were no such settings where middle-class men could continue to meet their black classmates, rare in any case. There is no evidence that white professionals enjoyed any real intimacy even with the privileged Durhams, Greeners, and Warricks once graduation broke up the teams or clubs they had briefly shared. But their sisters, meanwhile, began at the same point in their lives to experience close if lopsided relations with black women.[53]

Middle-class white women who "only married," as M. Carey Thomas put it, were the largest single employers of domestic servants, in turn the largest single class of black workers. Whatever the extent of real intimacy involved in the mistress/maid relation, it was closer than those between subway magnates and gang laborers. Employers liked to believe that they thoroughly understood their "girls," while their very differences were a continual source of gossipy speculation. Given the number of black businesses that essentially catered to household needs, too, white women were heavily represented as customers, at least until the changing atmosphere of the 1890s scared them off. But the most interesting relations were those enjoyed not by white housewives and maids but by "advanced" women and their black peers.

An "advanced woman" in the late 19th century was one who championed the cause of women's rights, including the right to work outside the home and enter the public or political area. Historically the cause of women's rights had grown out of involvement in other reforms which because of their clearly moral nature were thought appropriate objects of women's attention. Anti-slavery, before the Civil War, headed the list of those which gave many women their first experience of public life, and the arguments for racial equality often led naturally to arguments for sexual equality. But after the war there was a falloff of interest in the black cause. Many of the most uncompromising women were unhappy that the Fifteenth Amendment granted suffrage to blacks and not to them. And what was a betrayal to the more radical was an insult to the socially conservative, who argued increasingly that granting votes to ignorant and illiterate Afro-American or immigrant men while denying it to educated and responsible white women was worse than illogical.[54]

The estrangement between champions of blacks and women's rights was fueled by some practical consequences in employment, when for example an incoming Republican administration in 1897 fired all the women attendants at the Smithsonian Institution in favor of black men; the given reason, that the job involved contact with dust and the curious questions of the visiting public, only fueled more "indignation . . . among friends of advanced women." But these real differences in interest were relatively minor, and do not in any case explain the growing postwar estrangement not between black men and white women but among the women themselves. Leading women, black and white, generally agreed on a host of issues rooted in a common religious morality, notably the need to protect the family and battle intemperance. But while Frances Harper worked as an agent for the Women's Christian Temperance Union, the biggest woman's organization of the period, the militants Ida B. Wells attacked the WCTU for its racist policies and propaganda. And while Susan B. Anthony spoke at the organizational meeting of T. T. Fortune's Afro-American Council in 1898, her Women's Suffrage Association the following year refused to condemn Jim Crow legislation and other assaults on black rights.[55]

On the controversial issue of outside jobs or careers Philadelphia's Afro-American women were well out front. The high proportion of educated women in the black community has already been noted. Unlike their white peers, too, who typically either chose celibacy or quit working once married, Afro-American teachers, doctors, and journalists continued matter-of-factly to combine family and career.

Black men sometimes took a conservative stance: Anne E. M'Dowell of Philadelphia wrote to the *Sunday Republic,* in answer to a little homily on marriage by the Reverend Alexander Crummell, that "there is no tyrant like an enfranchised slave." But few at any level challenged women's right to work or otherwise play active public roles. On the negative side the Reverend H. L. Phillips, among others, complained on the contrary that too many men at the lower end of the economic scale enjoyed living off the earnings of wives and girlfriends. On the upper end there is much evidence of acceptance and encouragement. The Reverend W. A. Lynch of First Presbyterian could sound as militant in urging the right to work as any of his listeners at a Women's Quaker City Club banquet in 1898. The Berean Savings and Loan Association was only recognizing social reality in specifically noting in 1892 that "women can take shares in their own right." So were the many other organizations in which women took responsibility; it is impossible to imagine a major white church in which, like Allen AME in 1898, a woman served as treasurer.[56]

Gertrude Bustill Mossell, as the city's leading writer on women and marriage, is an especially interesting case. No one reading her advice columns or her book on Afro-American women could doubt her devotion to home, family, and conventional morality. But her chapter on "The Opposite Point of View" made it clear that she was a mother with no use for the conventional Victorian view of home as "a haven in a heartless world," a refuge where sweetly nurturing women brought tired men their pipes and slippers by the fireside nights. Her ideal instead was involvement in the wider world, committee meetings, late hours, and shared activity. Her advice to young people was to fight the tradition that while "courting is mighty pretty business, . . . courting is no more like marrying than chalk is like cheese." Courting instead should be a time for sizing up partners and getting things straight. "The man who used when single to kiss the babies, pet the cat, and fail to kick the dog when they visited are the men who remain home most when married." Properly ambitious men, too, could take only so much sweetness from their wives: "most of us could eat a greater quantity of pepper hash than of sugar after all."[57]

None of Philadelphia's remarkable black women expressed hostility to any major women's organization, as Ida B. Wells did toward the WCTU. But despite lives and writings that might have served as models for Charlotte Perkins Gilman and other contemporary feminists, none of them, except for Frances Harper, joined such organizations either, or indeed had any known contact with white peers. Among women, as with ethnic groups, in the atmosphere of the late 19th century occasional recognition of common problems was simply not enough to make genuine alliances.

Whatever their relations with other groups, their attitudes toward colonization, or the name they chose to call themselves, the simple fact of color itself was the most obvious badge of racial identity worn by every Afro-American every day. Legally and socially their world was starkly divided into "white" and "colored," but the intense color consciousness of the period encouraged specific identification along the whole human spectrum from ivory to black. Afro-Americans were as aware of these distinctions as any others, and many adopted the dominant attitudes toward them. One history suggests that Afro-American color-consciousness was at its height during the late 19th century, while elderly Philadelphians interviewed in the 1980s recalled, sometimes bitterly, that it was still powerful early in the 20th. But the mixed evidence from the Dorsey Collection suggests that attitudes toward blackness were by no means simple, and often positive.[58]

One sampling of the city's Afro-American organizations reveals that the leadership was more often "mulatto" than "black"; mulattoes have also been found richer, on average, and better off in most of the other ways associated with leadership, such as literacy rates. One practical problem however is that all of these figures are taken from the census, which is no more reliable on the issue of color than others: William Dorsey is only one of many who were listed some years as "B" for black and others as "M" for mulatto, the general word used for all people who looked, to the enumerator's unpracticed eye, as though they had some white ancestry.[59]

It does make sense that light-skinned blacks should have advantages. Mulattoes made up a disproportionate number of free blacks in the prewar South, in large part because slave masters often freed and sometimes educated or otherwise helped their own children by black slaves. These people typically flocked to cities, where despite their often miserable status the relative sophistication and complexity of life offered still more opportunities for them to add to the differences between themselves and their darker cousins back on the plantation. The real question is whether there was yet a third kind of advantage based simply on appearance, the fact that they were in various ways favored by whites, or a fourth, that they were also favored by other Afro-Americans.

The irrationalities of contemporary racism led whites into sometimes contradictory attitudes toward blackness. One set, which neatly fit the general abhorrence of miscegenation, stressed the vitality of those of unmixed heritage, and it was common for newspapers to use terms otherwise reserved for prize animals in describing, for example, First Presbyterian's Reverend John B. Reeve as a "fine specimen of a man," "of pure African stock." Beyond that the *Press* reported in 1885 that "the prettiest model in New York" was "a pure type of Afric's golden sands." Jet black but "most attractive in appearance, with a figure that is statuesquely superb," she was able to command the extraordinary sum of $2.50 an hour when posing nude; a young woman of "exemplary propriety," she reportedly took it all straight home to her aged parents and crippled younger sister.[60]

But for all the anomalies there is no denying that whites decidedly preferred light-skinned Afro-Americans to dark. Racist doctrine suggested that the gifts of distinguished leaders resulted from their white ancestry, although this weakened their constitutions in the longer run. Doctrine apart, a purely aesthetic bias was reflected in the tendency to describe sympathetic victims of prejudice as light colored, so that white readers could more easily identify with their plight. The same bias was reflected in male sexual preferences: the single noun "mulatto" covered all Afro-American men of mixed ancestry, while "quadroon" and "octaroom" were reserved always for women and almost always in a sexual context, or coupled with adjectives such as "attractive" or "flirtatious."

It is harder to find evidence of color prejudice among Afro-Americans themselves. For some women the growing popularity of straight wigs and hair-straightening devices during the 1890s doubtless represented an attempt to live up to Caucasian standards of beauty. But while some ministers immediately denounced the fad as vanity other leaders saw it as no more than an episode in the age-old practice of cosmetic experiment, and pointed out that all the while white women were struggling with rolls, cremes, and curlers.[61]

There are in fact only five direct references in the Dorsey Collection to color prejudice within the group. The *Press* in 1877 reported that some South Carolina blacks had formally complained to the Hayes administration that a majority of government jobs were being given to mulattoes, a small minority, as they saw it, of the state's Afro-American population. Whatever the merits of their case a white reporter described longtime Congressman Robert Smalls, the onetime Philadelphian, as decidedly black in color. In 1878 the Baltimore *American* published a frank and detailed article on the state of black Baltimore, reprinted in the *People's Advocate*, which directly denied that shades of color had any recognized social importance. The following year, on the eve of the National Colored Convention in Nashville, the outspoken lawyer John D. Lewis suggested that he might raise the issue of "caste within the race," presumably based on color prejudice. The *Record*, in 1889, described a New Jersey church as being split between "black" and "yellow" factions, although it is not clear that the issue was color as distinct from the social and economic differences often associated with it. In 1903, finally, the *Bulletin* carried the story of a complicated quarrel between Mrs. Lulu Lee, wife of the pastor at Monumental Baptist, and James Skipworth, a deacon, which began when Lee called Skipworth's cousin Bernard "black"; among hundreds of assault cases pasted into the Dorsey Collection, however, with sparks provided by a rich gamut of provocations running from cold dinners to hot glances, this one is unique.[62]

If in fact light skin was an asset among Philadelphia's Afro-Americans, the advantage was muted, more tendency than rule, perhaps more important among women than men. Contemporary reports, sketches, and photographs suggest that it would take the whole palette to represent the city's most active citizens. Above all there was no link between color and racial philosophy. William Still, perhaps the most conservative of Philadelphia's late 19th-century leaders, the community's major link to the world of white philanthropy, was clearly a black man. Bishop Henry M. Turner, in contrast, the most radical of separatists, fiercely proud of what he believed was his own descent from African royalty, was described as "copper-colored" in the *Freeman,* itself two or three shades darker than he appears to the untutored eye in an Episcopal portrait of 1895.[63]

If color prejudice was an issue in practice, no black leader embraced it in principle, and except for J. W. Cromwell's reprint of the piece on Baltimore and Gertrude Mossell's apology about the *Mikado* review, no reporter or editor even commented on it. With all the criticism of Bishop Turner none attacked his continual and deliberate insistence that Adam was black, and so perhaps was God. And the call for a self-conscious black aesthetic sounded by "Blackibus" in his public correspondence with William Dorsey in 1878 was eloquently elaborated by the Reverend H. L. Kealing, editor of the *A.M.E. Review,* in 1899. Kealing was perhaps rising to the challenge outlined three years earlier by Howard's Professor Kelly Miller, who had pointed out that "history, anthropology, ethnology, and the whole range of the inexact sciences . . . have been ransacked for testimony against the African," and that blacks needed to fight back on the same ground. In any case Kealing, himself light-skinned, called his talk to Union's Bishop Payne Historical and Literary Society "A Human Black Beauty," a title perhaps taken from the observation that "white has no real aesthetic advantage over black in people more than horses." "The greatest bane of slavery to the American negro," he went on to argue, "is that it robbed him of his own standard and replaced it with the Grecian," an act of despoilation it was then time to restore.[64]

Kealing's plea was an implicit admission that too many had internalized the values of the master, that what John Lewis had called "caste within the race" was in fact a problem. But there is no evidence that it was a major problem. The Philadelphia community was divided along many lines, as Baptist, Methodist, and Presbyterian; Republican, Democratic, and Independent; southern-born and city-born. All of these other lines generated more argument than shades of color; none of them was nearly as important as the one which united Afro-Americans by dividing them from the rest.

Chapter 10

Organization and Social Class

Few things about late-19th-century black Philadelphia are more striking than the richness of its web of clubs, organizations, and associations, all of them, like politics, religion, and color itself serving at the same time to divide and unite the larger community. There were organizations for every purpose: fellowship and mutual insurance, charity and prestige, education and the celebration of common origins and experience. Given a population of only a few tens of thousands, collectively they represented a truly astonishing amount of energy and sometimes expense.

Many of these groups competed for members; some were designed to set people apart from others, to draw lines based on social class, place of birth, or other differences. But it was hard in practice to establish a stable class system in a community so poor. The income difference between top and bottom was always narrow, and the many clubs and associations themselves often demanded a conspicuous consumption that combined with the uncertainties of economic life to make personal security hard to win and even harder to transmit across the generations. And despite efforts to reinforce class lines through selective association, the need to unite for religious, political, and other purposes prevented any group of Afro-Americans from truly isolating themselves from the rest.

The biggest of Afro-American secular organizations in Philadelphia were "secret" fraternal orders, Masons, Odd Fellows, and others. Even more than other associations these all had several functions, economic and social, moral and religious. All competed to attract members and attention in ways that strictly limited their secrecy. At the same time they all shared much the same historical ancestry, structure, aims, problems, and many of the same members, so that they were in practice not much more competitive than secret.

Black or "Prince Hall" Freemasonry was in this country an ironic outgrowth of the American Revolution. Prince Hall himself, a free black, was
initiated into its mysteries in 1775, by British soldiers stationed in Boston.
After failing, despite encouragement from some local whites, to win a charter
from the Grand Lodge of Massachusetts, Hall successfully applied in 1787
directly to the Mother Lodge in England itself. His counterparts in Philadelphia went through much the same experience a little later, overcoming white
American rejection by winning their degrees or charters elsewhere and establishing their own segregated lodges.[1]

The importance of Freemasonry in the early black community, and some of
its tone, may be shown by the fact that both the Reverends Richard Allen and
Absalom Jones were leaders, with Jones winning a position as Grand Master of
Pennsylvania. Although each state's Grand Lodge was formally sovereign and
independent, chartering local lodges as it chose, the fraternity was spread by
men, many of them ordained clerics, who paralleled their religious vocations
by acting in effect as missionaries to the South and West. Pennsylvania and
Philadelphia, during the James Forten era, in fact took the lead once enjoyed by
Boston and Massachusetts, always bringing the secular gospel emphasized by
Prince Hall from the beginning. Much like Allen and Jones, Hall had preached
dignity and called for an end to discrimination, meanwhile urging virtues that
would both prove useful in themselves and help win white respect, including
"promptness, regularity, and reliability," the avoidance of vice, the giving of
brotherly aid and advice, and the need to "secure jobs for the unemployed."[2]

The Masons flourished powerfully after the Civil War, moving south with
the churches to harvest the freedmen. Afro-Americans continued to stay in
touch with their white counterparts, keeping up with the rituals, organizing
Demolay for the young men, the Order of the Eastern Star for the women, the
Knights Templars for some committed initiates. Toward the end of the century
William Dorsey's nephew Dorsey F. Seville, a Washington resident cited as a
member of the "celebrated Dorsey family of Pennsylvania, which is known all
over the country," was credited with organizing some 150 lodges in the middle
Atlantic states from his base in the postal service. The last of the white
auxiliaries to catch on was the Order of the Mystic Shrine, whose antic and
sometimes alcoholic shenanigans were hardest to reconcile with the earnestly
quasi-religious character of Prince Hall Masonry.[3]

Philadelphia's lodges were often on display. In a typical performance
during August of 1877 the presentation of a standard by the Ladies of Queen
Esther's Court, No. 1, to Demolay Consistory, 32 degrees, Sublime Princes of
the Royal Secret, was followed by an exhibition of drill formations by both
Demolay and the Knights Templars, then by a ball at the Assembly buildings
with grand march and countermarch at midnight, and finally by a banquet
furnished "with all the festive and floral trophies of the season." Two years
later six fully uniformed Commanderies of Templars, three from out of town,

following Grand Captain General Eminent Sir William Powell and three marching bands, paraded the whole way from Independence Hall to the Centennial Building in Fairmount Park, the route reportedly lined by applauding citizens of both races.[4]

The appeal of titles, uniforms, and pageantry to insecure people is obvious, and by the later 1890s Philadelphia boasted some nineteen lodges, and probably several thousand members. Like other fraternities the Masons made a point from the first of owning their lodge headquarters, and Du Bois noted that they owned two buildings worth some $50,000. Bishop Levi Coppin in 1902 agreed to serve as Grand Chaplain of the Most Worshipful Grand Lodge of Pennsylvania, in keeping with his church's tradition: the rebuilt Mother Bethel boasted windows dedicated to the Masons on its Lombard Street side and the Order of the Eastern Star on Pine Street. But for all of that the Masons, locally, could not match the organization and popularity of the Grand and United Order of Odd Fellows.[5]

Part of the problem was internal to the order. With power and prestige at stake, the lack of a central national organization made the Freemasons subject to argument and schism: Dorsey's nephew, for example, was continually harassed by jealous fraternal rivals who tried to get him fired from the civil service. And Philadelphia's leading Masons, with a few exceptions, were generally not chosen from among the truly elite members of the community. Only Bishop Coppin, tied for thirteenth, ranks among those most often mentioned in the Dorsey Collection, while the florist Claudius Bisand, Deputy Grand Master of Philadelphia County in 1902, was in fact a convicted thief.[6]

The Masons' real problem was, however, less their own weakness than the competitive strength of the Odd Fellows in the City. The Odd Fellows, among whites an imitative and far less prestigious order, was similar in many respects but ritually simpler, with only four or seven degrees instead of thirty-two. For a long time, too, it lacked the military dash provided the Freemasons by the uniformed Knights Templars. But it had one clear advantage for blacks in that, perhaps as reflection of its relatively plebian 18th-century origins, it provided explicitly for sick and death insurance benefits, with the rules spelled out rather than left to gentlemanly but vague exhortations to mutual help. Above all the Masons, however important elsewhere, could not locally compete with the fact that Philadelphia was the American headquarters of the Grand and United Order of Odd Fellows, with a unique claim to international legitimacy.[7]

The white Odd Fellows had been imported into the United States early in the 19th century. The black branch was formed in 1842 by a ship's steward, Peter Ogden, initiated into the mysteries by British fellow workers. When the white Americans indignantly turned down his request for a charter he simply went directly to headquarters in Liverpool, which honored it. A group of Philadelphians in turn went to Ogden in New York for their own charter, in 1844, and national headquarters were removed to the Quaker City six years later. When the white Americans meanwhile broke their ties with England, precisely over the issue of racial admissions, the Afro-Americans were left the sole true heirs of the British tradition, with Philadelphia the conduit to the international Mother Lodge.[8]

The leaders of the Odd Fellows were truly prestigious men. Philadelphia's national Grand Masters between 1849 and 1875 included James Gordon, J. C. McCrummell, D. B. Bowser, Robert Jones, R. Emery Burr, and Redmond Faucett, while the Grand Secretaries, who by the later 19th century ran the permanent national organization out of a four-story building at Sixth and Spruce, were James Needham between 1849 and 1870, D. B. Bowser between 1870 and 1892, and Charles H. Brooks beginning in 1892. Bowser and Burr were among the group which instituted the fancy-dress semi-military Patriarchie, in 1873, on the model of the Knights Templars, in order to compete with the Masons for the attentions of young men.[9]

Their success may be measured by the show put on in October of 1886, on the occasion of the order's third biennial convention in Philadelphia. By that time, with a reputed 37,000 members and total assets of $343,197.60 it was already the biggest Afro-American fraternity in the country, and some 400 of the 1000 lodges nationwide sent delegates to the Quaker City. Festivities began Tuesday the 5th with a reception and concert given by the local Household of Ruth at the Musical Fund Hall, Eighth and Locust. At the business meeting on Wednesday the delegates were greeted by dignitaries including Mayor William Smith. The grand parade next morning was led by Patriarchs on horseback, each of them wearing the uniform which the artistic Bowser had modeled after a British admiral's, minus only the ostrich plume. To accompany the several hundred marchers, some carrying battle axes, others banners, a few leading goats, the city's own lodges supplied the U.S. Cornet Band, the Philadelphia Drum Corps, the Metropolitan Band, the Liberty Drum Corps, and the Philadelphia Independent Fife and Drum, which accompanied other bands from New York, Washington, Wilmington, Camden, West Chester, and Atlantic City on a long tour from Spring Garden Street up Broad to Girard Avenue and back down again to the Musical Fund Hall, where the whole throng was treated to an oration by William Howard Day. That night's entertainment at the Academy of Music began with a drill competition between Patriarchies from Boston and Washington, with the Bostonians winning the $100 grand prize. Five thousand people jammed into the Academy either to dance, for $1.50 a head, or simply to watch from the galleries at 50 cents. Most of the city's leading blacks were there, including William Dorsey's two daughters, many with guests from out of town. H. P. Williams's breathless descriptions of the ball gowns mentioned silk 32 times and diamonds 18.[10]

That occasion was topped by at least one other, held in the summer of 1894 to honor Richard Hill-Male, Grand Master of England and so head of all lodges the world over. The British connection was of course crucial to the prestige of the Grand and United Order of Odd Fellows; it would be hard to overestimate their pride in the international recognition given them and at the same time denied to the white Americans in the "Independent" order. Hill-Male, arriving in New York late in June, was escorted on a triumphal tour of the major cities of the United States stretching south to New Orleans, north to Boston, and west to Chicago, with Philadelphia the final stop. The city then boasted an estimated 5000 to 6000 members, roughly a third of its officially counted population of black male adults. All of them were in effect ordered to turn out, wearing the standard uniform of claw-hammer coat with the society's rosette and badge, to hear the welcoming address by the mayor and the historical oration by James Field Needham of the tax office, son of one of the Philadelphia founders. This and other ceremonies were free for all members, but the organizers charged $1.50 for the concluding banquet at Musical Fund Hall, with places set for 2000.[11]

Toward the end of the decade, still growing strongly, the total number of American lodges reportedly reached well over 2000, while the membership had more than quadrupled, between 1886 and 1898, to close to 156,000 men. In nation, state, and city the order was financially strong, often investing more than it paid out and continually adding to its total assets. Benefits paid out averaged something more than $2 per member, each year, half or more going to relief from sickness, most of the rest to funeral expenses, with some modest relief to widows and some other charities.[12]

But with all its impressive statistics the Odd Fellows was not a jealously exclusive order; many of its ambitious members joined other societies as well, with Bowser himself a thirty-second-degree Mason. Despite some competition, then, there were no truly heated rivalries. In Philadelphia the most important of the other orders, next to the Masons, was the Knights of Pythias. An Afro-American lodge of Knights was formed in Richmond a few years after the order itself, during the Civil War. It was introduced into the Quaker City in 1882; seven years later, at the biennial convention encompassing all Supreme Lodges of both the "Eastern and Western hemispheres," Philadelphia's Dr. Henry W. Longfellow was elected Supreme Chancellor and Dr. Nathan Mossell Supreme Medical Director. By 1899 the city reportedly boasted 32 lodges and 3000 members.[13]

John Durham, and later Du Bois, wrote that the secret orders ranked second only to the church in their importance to the black community. There were practical differences betweeen church and fraternity; major funerals could tie up individual churches for hours, ministers complained, as important people belonged to two or more different orders, each of which insisted on bringing uniformed officers to perform its own mystic funerary rites, often upstaging the pastor. But the parallels are more striking than the differences: hierarchical organization within an overarching order or denomination; problematic relations with white counterparts; much emphasis on ceremony and ritual; competition for members based in part on competitive display; a range of social, economic, and broadly speaking political functions. Above all the role of the fraternities' ministers and chaplains was a reminder of the overlapping aims and functions of the two kinds of association. [14]

At the same time these societies were social clubs, and for ordinary members their loftier aims were often less important than the balls and out-of-town trips they sponsored. The excursions sometimes involved hundreds and even thousands of people on specially chartered trains or boats. And the combination of long rides, alcohol, and the sense of holiday release made them lively occasions, as when several leaders of the Knights of Pythias were arrested after a long afternoon of "couchie-couchie" dancing, drinking, and fighting in Reading. That kind of gap between theory and practice was familiar to fraternities everywhere; so was the fact that, as Du Bois put it, leadership provided "a field for ambition and intrigue."[15]

In practice it seems that the reason why the chief officers of Philadelphia's Odd Fellows were generally more distinguished than others is simply that leadership of a national organization was a field big enough to challenge them, just as it was for Doctors Mossell and Longfellow of the Knights of Pythias. Grand Secretary David Bowser, for example, had the chance to perform an important public service during the yellow-fever epidemic which hit parts of the South during 1878, as his long experience with leading black southerners helped him guide white philanthropic efforts from the North. Charles Brooks, his successor, was able in 1899 to return the trans-Atlantic visit made by Richard Hill-Male four years earlier; just two years before Booker T. Washington and President Theodore Roosevelt created a political firestorm by violating American social custom through the simple act of dining together, Brooks was treated to a grand banquet held in his honor by his white British brothers in the old medieval city of York.[16]

But short of that, while prominent men such as Carl Bolivar, John Durham, and Christopher Perry belonged to various fraternal orders they seem to have taken little part; leadership of a neighborhood lodge was a "field for ambition" but a narrow one, and lists of officers below the very top levels show that almost none of them were well known for other memberships or accomplishments. The fact that money was involved provided a special temptation, and both business sessions and the criminal courts were called to deal with petty cheating and embezzlement, $6 here and $17 there. A more revealing incident was uncovered in August of 1890 with the arrest of John Diton, a high official in both the United Order of Odd Fellows and the Masonic fraternity.[17]

Diton served as president of all the Philadelphia lodges of Odd Fellows in 1889, presiding over the annual Grand Ball. That year and the next he was also a member of the committee in charge of a September excursion to Atlantic City jointly sponsored by six Masonic lodges. The brothers authorized a printing of 5500 round-trip tickets; Diton took one to duplicate 500 copies to sell on his own, a scheme discovered the second time around only because he took the job to a suspicious printer, who had worked on the original contract. Throwing himself on the mercy of the court, he described himself as a man who "does odd jobs for anyone," frequently unemployed, currently working as a janitor to support his family. He had been sick, he told the judge, and there had been a death in the family; he had wrestled hard with his conscience, turning to crime only after "he had applied to his brother members for assistance and . . . had been refused."[18]

Diton's self-serving and not wholly believable tale was designed to tell the court something about the gap between the ideals of brotherhood and the often harsher reality. It does reveal, without embellishment, something of the hardship resulting from the fact that Afro-Americans were ordinarily denied commercial insurance; modest fraternal sick and death benefits, however helpful in modest crises, were no real buffer against the times when the chill winds of economic insecurity turned really bitter. But Diton's story also suggests another kind of commentary on the social and political nature of the fraternal orders.

Despite formal admissions requirements which invoked many of the values that we have come to call "middle-class," the actual membership of both Masons and Odd Fellows was overwhelmingly composed of men who, like John Diton, were economically members of the working class at best. Even the most distinguished of the officers were all elected, with power and prestige coming to those who successfully mingled with and appealed to the majority. A heavy emphasis on membership statistics, the prestige which came from signing up newcomers, the evident need to impress and even sell tickets to the public at large all reinforced this ultimately democratic calculus. Sick and death payments, moral reinforcement, and mutual aid were all real benefits, however weak or flawed in practice. But none of these was unique to the secret societies, whose real service to the community as a whole was both wider and not so clearly spelled out in their charters. All of them provided occasions for janitors or "odd-jobs" men to organize and preside over gatherings of hundreds and even thousands of people, their names printed on elaborate programs and sometimes cheered to the echo. The societies' drills, parades, and banquets served both as public entertainment and as source of pride. Above all, although they were designed in theory to exclude, to separate initiates from all others, their broad and overlapping memberships in practice served as wide networks which united Philadelphia's Afro-Americans far more than they divided them.

The significance of the many functions served by the secret orders may be shown by comparison with two other and narrower kinds of association. Parade and display, important to the fraternities, were central to the purpose of the city's Afro-American veterans' clubs and militia company. Both the Grand Army of the Republic and the Grey Invincibles played highly visible social roles in the community. But no American military adventure after the Civil War really appealed to black Philadelphians, and given restrictive membership in one case and significant requirements in the other, neither the GAR nor the Invincibles ever grew to involve large numbers of men.

The Afro-American community's interest in the military began with its heavy participation in the Civil War. Philadelphians began to enlist once the Emancipation Proclamation, formally issued on January 1, 1863, made it clear that they had a real stake in the outcome. Racial prejudice and a longstanding fear of black men in arms kept them out of the Union army before then, and Pennsylvania's procrastination pushed many men north, early in 1863, to join the famous 54th Massachusetts. But the response grew truly enormous once the threat to Gettysburg scared the Pennsylvania authorities into calling for help in the summer of 1863, and Camp William Penn was set up outside the city to train black regiments. There is no way of knowing exactly how many Philadelphians signed up, since the camp welcomed men from a wide area, but fully eleven regiments were raised, or over 8600 soldiers, three or four times the officially counted number of Afro-American males in the city between the ages of 19 and 35. Several regiments, notably the 6th, 8th, and 22nd, saw unusually distinguished service; although they began organizing only when the war was more than half over, the combined total of 2,492 dead, wounded, captured or missing amounted to 29 percent of the whole number enrolled. All of these men were volunteers, not draftees. And despite discrimination, low pay, and high death rates, the biographies of individual soldiers suggest that the war was a proud and liberating experience for many of them.[19]

Part of that emotion was carried over after the war when several veterans, notably Colonel Jacob Purnell, John W. Simpson, and Isaiah Mayhugh, opened a course of drill instruction at the Philadelphia Institute, 717 Lombard Street. The men were confident that "parents will consider the advantages to be gained by . . . this innocent and profitable source of amusement, for a youth develops precaution in business and promptitude in active life." The continued fascination with precision drilling was an important part of the postwar appeal of the Templars, Patriarchs, and other quasi-military orders within the fraternities, just as drill teams were used to attract slum youngsters, toward the end of the century, to the College Settlement around the corner from Purnell's instruction school. And drill was one key as well to the community's enthusiasm for the Grey Invincibles.[20]

The Invincibles were black Philadelphia's company of infantry militiamen, organized after the Civil War and later incorporated into the Pennsylvania National Guard. Much of their annual appropriation, fixed in 1878 at $500 a company per year, went into trig uniforms, and they were best known for parading. Most public celebrations, as of the Fifteenth Amendment, brought out the Greys, who were sometimes called to other cities to celebrate the anniversary of West Indian Emancipation, for example, one of the older holidays on the special Afro-American calendar.[21]

The Greys had their own celebrations, receptions, and banquets, but the group was most socially visible when it was called to host its visiting counterparts from other cities, and Philadelphia's leading black citizens were asked to subscribe. Thousands reportedly turned out to watch Boston's Shaw Guards in June of 1878; Cheston's Excelsior Band led the Greys all the way from their armory at Fifth and Chestnut out to West Philadelphia to greet the train. That night the visitors beat their hosts at the inevitable drill contest, although both groups were awarded crystal and silver punch services. The next day they visited Jacob White's Roberts Vaux School and listened to its orchestra before going on to see Fanny Jackson at the Institute for Colored Youth, finishing their stay with a reception at the Hotel de Storms. Portsmouth's Virginia Guards, arriving in August the next year, were treated even more elaborately, as after their stay in the city the Greys took them along on their own annual five-day excursion to Cape May.[22]

The "Citizens' Reception Committee" in both of these cases, as in others from the same era, was made up of men such as David Bowser, Levi Cromwell, Andrew Stevens, William Dorsey, John D. Lewis, Dr. E. C. Howard, and other notables. But the Greys themselves were not so distinguished. Their longtime Captain Oscar Jones, a messenger in City Hall, never appears in the Dorsey Collection in any other context. Two other officers, George T. Burrell and James Junior, were active in various political clubs, and also held city jobs as messengers or janitors; the combative Junior succeeded Gil Ball for a time as president of the Quay Club until his manner sparked a revolt. But membership in the Greys obviously took more training time than most of the community's busy leadership had to spare, and perhaps few were willing to compete with, or worse under, the single-minded Captain Jones for the three officers' jobs, all of which required some technical expertise in teaching marksmanship and drill.[23]

For veterans, membership in the Grand Army of the Republic was a more relaxed means of keeping old memories alive. The GAR was segregated locally, as the Union army had been, although the Afro-American posts joined the rest on holiday encampments, and their officers were sometimes elected to state-wide positions. They made the news mostly on Memorial Day, when they marched out to Olive, Lebanon, and Merion cemeteries to lead crowds of mourners in honoring the war veterans buried there, a total of well over 600 by 1898.[24]

Relative indifference to the postwar military was briefly broken during the mid-1890s, when it was proposed that the Greys expand fourfold, from company to battalion size, or 260 men, and the great increase in available positions inspired a younger generation of leaders to turn out. In addition to four line Captains and eight lieutenants, the proposed battalion-level officers included Major Andrew F. Stevens, Jr., son of the councilman, caterer, and social leader; Adjutant William H. Jones; Surgeon Dr. William H. Warrick; Quartermaster John S. Durham, then studying law after dismissal from the diplomatic corps; Chaplain Owen S. Waller, the Oxford graduate; Inspector of Rifle Practice Christopher Perry; Ordnance Office Jonathan Harris, Perry's brother-in-law and managing editor; plus a long list of Mintons, Cowdreys, Prices, and Jacksons to serve above the line as sergeant majors, hospital stewards, stable sergeants, and the like.[25]

There is no obvious reason for the timing of this explosion in martial sentiment. The Pennsylvania Guard was famous for its use against striking workmen, and Afro-Americans, who had no reason to sympathize with labor unions, had sometimes been sent out to challenge them. But the Greys had never seen such action, and despite the increase in labor troubles during the depression of 1893 there was no increase in the authorized stength or payment of Guard units. Probably no motive beyond the increased availability of titles, and payment, is needed to explain the planned expansion. Privates in the Guard got $1.75 a day for their two-week summer encampments and other assignments (such as acting as honor guards), a good deal more than most Afro-Americans could ordinarily make, while first sergeants got $3 and officers were paid as much as those of the regular army. Expansion would create at least thirty jobs over the grade of first sergeant.[26]

The first task was however to recruit enough privates, 55 per company, to support the proposed number of superior officers. Despite its hierarchical structure the Guard was not the regular army after all but closer in democratic spirit to the fraternal orders. Some of its tone is suggested by a contest, sponsored by the *Evening Telegraph* in 1895, to select the most popular officer in the Greys, the winner to be presented with a ceremonial sword. Carl Bolivar, years later, when the younger Stevens had succeeded his father as community leader, took a certain delight in recalling that he had lost out to Lieutenant James H. Davis, despite "heroic efforts" by his friends.[27]

In any case the officers were able to sign up the privates, and the Greys reached 260 by 1896. By that time, however, some of the proposed officers had failed to make the grade; it took much extra work to bring the company up to the Guard's marksmanship standards, and the whole expansion scheme foundered on the next hurdle when the Commonwealth refused to accept it.[28]

The defeat of the Invincibles, the only Afro-American unit left in Pennsylvania by that time, meant reversion to company size and status. And there was little further enthusiasm for anything military beyond the occasional parade. Black regiments fought with Native Americans out west throughout the period, but while they were a source of pride, and their maintenance an issue for Afro-American congressmen, there is no evidence that they inspired Philadelphians to enlist. Some signed up to fight the Spanish in the summer of 1898, but the community's leadership was ambivalent about that war, and in contrast to 1863 there was little publicity and apparently few recruits. By century's end, as Civil War memories faded and the GAR thinned out, it was clearer than ever that the Grey Invincibles were not central to the social life of the community but simply a kind of colorful accessory to it.[29]

Far more important than the military in the life of Philadelphia's black community were the economic organizations, or the social and economic, of two types. Both called for the kind of mutual aid which also marked the fraternal orders, but they were individually smaller and more specialized. One was the building and loan association, which offered either profit or the promise of homeownership to those who subscribed. The other type was simply a club which, like the fraternities, offered mutual insurance; highly varied in membership, purpose, and size, collectively these clubs probably enrolled more people than the ritual orders, ranking them second in numbers to any kind of association outside of the church.

Philadelphia's 19th-century reputation as "The City of Homes" was largely built on the comparative ease with which, using small building and loan associations, skilled or steadily employed workingmen could get the capital needed to finance the brick row houses which radiated across the city. Based on neighborhood or ethnic group, these societies, somewhere between bank and club, were naturally attractive to many of the more prosperous members of the closely knit black community.

The success of the Berean Building and Loan Association, built in part on white investments and expertise, has already been sketched. But the Berean, although apparently bigger than any of the four others which served the Afro-American community, was not the first but on its organization in 1888 the last, and so able to draw on successful earlier experience earned in institutions run entirely by black men.

William Still, president and driving spirit behind the Berean, was also involved in the first of these, the Philadelphia Building and Loan Association organized in the fall of 1869. The officers, president John H. Thomas, Vice President Isaiah Wears, Treasurer William Whipper, and Secretary Thomas Boling, were all successful businessmen; they and the directors, who included Still, Robert Jones, Robert Adger, and Francis P. Main, overlapped with the group that had recently invested also in Liberty Hall. The original idea was to raise capital by selling shares monthly at a modest $1 apiece, and then auction the total to the highest bidder, with each member allowed to borrow up to $200 apiece. Not long afterward the group apparently decided to follow more conventional building and loan procedures, and it was claimed that before its dissolution in the 1880s the Philadelphia had paid off nine series in fourteen years without loss of a single dollar and only three foreclosures.[30]

That claim was made by the Century Building and Loan Association, organized in 1886 from headquarters in Shiloh Baptist Church. Many of these men had gotten their experience originally with the Philadelphia B & L, and aimed to succeed it. Although the flour merchant Thomas Boling and the used-furniture dealer Robert Adger were by that date the only two from the original group, the Century's roster of officers and directors was almost equally distinguished, including Bishop Benjamin T. Tanner, the upholsterer Warley Bascom, restaurateur Levi Cromwell, and schoolteachers Joseph Hill, Alexander Lively, and Daniel T. Masten. Over the years as some members dropped out and others were added, the Yale Ph.D. Edward Bouchet, civil servant James Field Needham, politician and schoolteacher Stephen Gipson, and undertaker William P. Allmond were among those who joined the board.[31]

The Pioneer Building and Loan was established in 1888, the same year as the Berean; by the time it issued its own seventh series its officers included the provision dealer Walter Hall as president, the restaurateur P. Albert Dutrieulle as treasurer, and T. J. Minton as solicitor. The Enterprise Savings and Loan, founded in 1882 with a less well-known group of officers and directors, issued 52,000 shares, according to a review of its first Annual Report, and had a modest $122.89 on hand. Nothing else survives, and indeed among the few records available from any of these associations only the Berean and the Century include balance sheets.[32]

But these, and occasional newspaper articles, indicate that with the possible exception of the Enterprise, which varied the customary pattern by investing in coal, among other things, they were all basically sound institutions. Many Afro-Americans across the country had had a disastrous experience with banking during the 1870s, when the Freedman's Bank, which had appealed to many of them, collapsed and lost their savings. Any significant failure by any of the local building and loans, on top of that, would surely have killed the chances of all the others. But this clearly did not happen. Their strength lay perhaps in their ability to draw on the knowledge of local real estate that was the traditional strong point of Afro-American businessmen. The Century reported annual receipts and disbursements in 1896 of over $10,000, while the Berean reported almost $33,000 two years later. All together the four associations seem to have returned good interest on their investments and helped several dozen families, by the end of the century, to buy their own homes.[33]

Far more people were involved meanwhile in the hundreds of mutual benefit societies which crisscrossed the community. In the great majority of cases even their names have failed to survive; in others it is not always clear that they were indeed benefit societies, and not simply social clubs. But there is enough information to suggest that they were varied in almost every way, and involved almost every possible principle of association.

Some of the occupational societies, of barbers and waiters, hotel workers, saloonkeepers, caterers, and others, have already been described. In general the bigger groups reached out the furthest. During the 1880s at least the Saloonkeepers' Association met every fourth Friday with each other, but apparently no one else. The Caterers' Association held an occasional reception for limited numbers of guests. The others, Coachmen, Private Waiters, Hotel Workers, and Barbers, all threw annual fancy dress balls.[34]

Around 1910 the eminent economist and clergyman R. R. Wright, Jr., recently from South Carolina, was told that "thirty-five years ago" these balls had been exclusive, with admission by invitation only, instead of commercial money-making affairs. This piece of nostalgia, or retrospective snobbery, was however just a part of the long process of building a fictitious past on which some of these Old Philadelphians could rest their claims to social superiority. Only the Coachmens' Association, founded in 1869, had in fact existed during the time "remembered," that is, the middle of the 1870s. And from the first their annual balls, like the others, had been open occasions which pushed their members, much like those who belonged to political clubs or the fraternities, to reach out to a wider public to sell tickets. They were indeed spectacular events, which people then young might well remember for a lifetime: a columnist for the New York *Globe* estimated that in 1883 the total cost of the Private Waiters' Association Ball, including hall rental, musicians, decorations, tuxedos, gowns, flowers, perhaps cab fare amounted to some $50,000 all told. But it was open to any who could afford a ticket, usually $1.50, and keep up the customary standards of dress and appearance; the fact that a reported 200 cabs were parked outside of Horticultural Hall suggests that many managed somehow to make it.[35]

One of the first signs of division between the "O.P.s" and newer residents, during the 1880s, was reflected in a local uproar over another kind of association, directly based on place of birth. But in this case it was, at first, the native Philadelphians who were stung by rejection. When a local graduate of the Institute for Colored Youth died untimely in 1886, drunk, broke, and uninsured, his old friends, mostly fellow natives, took up the customary burial collection. But one potential giver hit F. J. R. Jones with the response: "Why don't you bury your own dead?" Jones, a popular saloonkeeper, politician, and musician, then began to organize the "Quaker City Association," a benefit society for those born in Philadelphia.[36]

In later years the Q.C. and its companion Ladies' Quaker City Association were important elite organizations, genuinely exclusive, which held not open annual balls but closed banquets. At the eighteenth of these affairs, in 1904, which according to William Dorsey's notes seated 90 members and guests, the traditional program involved a series of toasts and short speeches in reply. The Reverend J. B. Stansbury, as toastmaster, called for responses on the subjects of "History" by W. C. Bolivar, "The Ladies" by Hans Shadd, Sr., "Guests" by J. H. L. Smythe, "The Stage" by R. Henri Strange, "The Bar" by T. J. Minton, "The Race Problem" by Constantin Hubert, "Diplomacy" by the

Hon. J. S. Durham, and "The Medical Fraternity" by Dr. James Potter. But while other clubs like this, the Standard or Crescent, inspired no overt resentment, the Quaker City was born in controversy.[37]

The principle of association by origin was not itself a problem. The Ottawa Club, founded in 1855, held a reception for 200 in 1888; its membership of about 40 was presumably open only to the Canadian-born such as John D. Lewis and Nathan Mossell. A West Indian Union was organized in 1892, with a set of rooms and abortive plans to start a newspaper. The Fraternal Association of ex-Charlestonians, founded by P. A. Dutrieulle, threw what Christopher Perry thought the ball of the season in November of 1894. But there seemed something a little chilling from the first about the Q.C., an exclusive ssociation of men or women born in the host city, and a reporter, denied admission, claimed that it was hostile to southerners. There was an obvious irony in this, given the large number of leading Philadelphians born in the South, and the fact that the majority of the rest were only a generation or so removed: the real issue then and later seems to have been less geography than class: rural southerners, fresh up, were different from such freeborn Charlestonians as, say, Robert Purvis.[38]

In any case Stephen Gipson, running for the legislature in 1886, the year of its founding, had to send out a flyer denying that he was a member of the Quaker City. Having after all paid his dues in Reconstruction South Carolina, Gipson declared that he stood for unity and not division. And three years later an ambitious Industrial Exposition reportedly "caused more of a sensation in this city than any other event for years," opposed by the majority of the community simply because it was sponsored by the Ladies' Q.C. While the division was perhaps too deep for permanent closure, it was sutured in revealing fashion: the day after the Exposition closed, on May 28, 65 men got together to form the "Southern League Beneficial Association." Most of the officers were little-known—except for Financial Secretary F. J. R. Jones, not only Philadelphia born and bred but founder of the offending Q.C. Jones was after all among other things a politician, and more than that the most popular of the three bandleaders who usually played at major social functions, with a real professional stake in harmony.[39]

None of the other beneficial associations made much news. The oldest surviving was the Sons of St. Thomas, organized in 1813, but Du Bois suggested that by the late 1890s "nearly every church is beginning to organize one or more such societies." The churches were not alone, either in their interest or in the somewhat checkered conduct of those which they had managed in the past. The *Tribune* in 1898 praised the Cosmopolitan Relief Association, just seven years old, for its just dealings—"unlike some others in our midst"—and listed some 70 of the "hundreds" who had benefited the year before, mostly for $10 or $15, but with a couple at $60 or more. Virginians brought the United Order of True Reformers north with them, and in 1899 claimed 5000 local members on the occasion of dedicating a new hall at 1134 Pine Street. William Harvey, before his death in 1897, had spent thirty years in the city, fifteen of them as Grand Master, establishing the Sons and Daughters of Moses. There was an Old Men's Beneficial Association, its name the only clue to its principles, and others gathered around notable individuals, such as the Friends of J. P. B. Eddy, who in fact benefited from the old miser's otherwise notorious will, and the Bishop Campbell Association.[40]

Every account suggests that there were hundreds of these societies, a number far beyond anyone's ability to name or even count. The better ones, like the Quaker City, with 280 members in the late 1890s, distributed over $5 a member per year on average, more than twice as much as the Odd Fellows. In terms of their soundness, or ratio between what was paid in and out, they all ranked somewhere between the good commercial insurance that Afro-Americans were denied and the predatory commerical insurance that they took out by default. But beyond the purely fiscal there was a social dimension, the creation of an overlapping network that bound virtually every more or less usually employed Afro-American in the city to others who shared some of the same origins or interests.[41]

But while the mutual benefit societies helped deal with some of the need for fellowship and insurance, the problems growing out of the poverty of the Afro-American community created a continuous need for help of many kinds. Given an estimate that fully half of the whole city's 1880 population was "very poor," the majority of Philadelphians in fact, white as well as black, required public or private charity at some time. But while the city did not discriminate, the public institutions with the exception of the hospitals were truly bleak places of last resort, police stations for lodgers on cold nights, or the dreaded almshouse for truly helpless paupers. The private alternatives ran a much broader spectrum, but except for institutions such as soup kitchens, the more ambitious ones, such as summer camps, did not welcome black residents. The Quakers had long offered some help, and notably kept two homes for poor or orphaned children. But as the Afro-American population expanded and Quaker charity did not, there was a felt need for organizations in which blacks themselves had more voice in dealing with their community's problems.[42]

The first and most impressive of these organizations, a bridge between white charity and self-help, was the Home for Aged and Infirm Colored Persons. Founded right after the Civil War as a small institution run mostly by Quakers, the home was transformed in 1871, moving into spacious grounds at the corner of Belmont and Girard avenues as the result of a gift from the leading black businessman Stephen Smith. Smith served briefly as president, and left most of his sizable estate to the institution. The city's Quakers together with some other philanthropists continued to take an active interest, periodically giving enough so that the Home was able to expand with the need. But William

Still succeeded Smith as president, and unlike the Institute for Colored Youth, the Shelter for Colored Orphans, or the home for Destitute Colored Children, the HAICP was managed not by the Quakers alone but in cooperation with leading blacks.[43]

This kind of interracial cooperation was at first unique, although later imitated by, for example, the Episcopalians involved in the Church of the Crucifixion and the Presbyterians at Berean. What remained entirely distinctive was that the practical management of the Home's affairs was dominated by women, in reflection of their traditionally active role in both the Afro-American community and the Society of Friends. By 1894 although the board was chaired by the AME pastor and M.D. Cornelius T. Shaeffer, and the treasurer was the devoted Quaker Henry S. Laing, only 9 of its 25 members were men. The two key executive committees, on management and on cooperation, were entirely made up of women, with Fanny Jackson Coppin, Thomas Boling's wife Margaret, and the undertaker Harriette Duterte the best known among the blacks.[44]

The Home was in many respects a model institution. There was by the middle of the 1890s an initial fee of some $150 for admission, at a minimum age of 60, before a resident was guaranteed a lifetime of free care. The residents were continually visited by patrons, pastors, and guests. Baptists, Methodists, Episcopalians, Presbyterians, and Quakers conducted services on alternate Sundays, and the city's leading Afro-American ministers were all there on special occasions. No one was patronized; Fanny Case, a woman in her nineties, was encouraged to give two sermons on Founder's Day in 1882. In general the residents were encouraged to vote and keep abreast of news of interest to the race, bad as well as good. Although it was doubtless for the benefit of white sponsors that concerts sometimes featured "plantation songs," otherwise never part of Afro-American programs in the city, William Still, Fanny Jackson Coppin, and the Reverend Horace Wayland, editor of the *Christian Banner,* all spoke about the lynching phenomenon in 1892.[45]

There is no question of the institution's popularity among benefited and benefactors both. Some elderly people seem to have come to the city expressly to move in; the friends of Eliza Grant threw a benefit ball at the Grey Invincibles' Armory in 1892, charging 50 cents a couple in order to raise the necessary admissions fee. Blacks left considerable sums to the Home in their wills, whites substantial to enormous ones. The total annual budget was $9000 in 1882, enough to house 88 women and 22 men in little dormitories of five to six beds each. Ten years later the budget had reached $25,000; as of 1894 the number of inmates had reached 200, and the following year the legacy of a white benefactor from New Jersey, John Cooper, survived a contest by his other heirs and left fully $600,000 to the Home, making it by far the richest black institution in Philadelphia.[46]

No such sums were available to the Women's Union Christian Association, organized without white support in 1873 mainly to extend "the same kind of fellowship and assistance that is available to white women." While the Association took on a range of problems, helping a group of Arkansans, for example, stranded in the city during 1877 by one of the fraudulent Liberian expeditions, it was especially concerned about women "who are dependent on their own exertions for support." On formal incorporation in 1878 Miss Harriet Smith, president, Dr. Rebecca Cole, secretary, and Treasurer Letitia Still, wife of William, answered to a board composed of 10 Baptists, 11 Methodists, 4 Episcopalians, and 4 Presbyterians, some of them elite wives such as Martha Minton, Sarah Page, and Rachel Thomas, but including also Mrs. Abigail White, of First Presbyterian, whose address was given simply as "Currant Alley," one of the worst in Philadelphia. If the term "elite" as applied to Afro-Americans of that generation means artisans, entrepreneurs, white-collar workers or their wives, the adjective does not apply to many of these women. Of the 24, not including those mentioned above, whose addresses are given, 11 are not listed in the Philadelphia City Directory at all, generally a sure sign of low economic standing. While all but three of these women were or had been themselves married, they had a clear sense of what was needed, if little money to realize the need.[47]

The Association collected some $346.20 that year through a concert, an entertainment given by the treasurer, and several collections, together with used clothing donated by Mrs. William Warrick and others. Some of this was spent on an employment office operated by Lucy Davis out of her home at 407 South Seventh Street, some on two small "industrial schools," where groceries and other necessities were sold at half-price at Mothers' Meetings. During the 1890s, with the schoolteacher Julia Jones as president and the two Still daughters, Miss Ella and Dr. Caroline Still Anderson, as secretaries, the group worked to establish a badly needed day nursery, and sponsored among other things a poetry reading by Paul Dunbar to help raise funds.[48]

The problems of young women in the city were in fact a growing concern to many groups. One of them was created by the ironic fact that while black and white prostitutes often worked together in brothels, they were not welcome to live together in church-sponsored reformatory institutions; the Bethel Home for Fallen Women was the response, already mentioned, from the Afro-American community. It was followed by Germantown's St. Magdalen's Asylum for Colored Girls, a particular interest of Katherine Drexel founded in 1892, and three years later by one of the national string of Florence Crittenden Homes, established without regard to creed or color in what had been a notorious local bawdy house at 531 Lombard Street. But none of these places was very successful, to judge by the experience of the Magdalen and Midnight Mission societies, in effect often jails to which "inmates" were sometimes sentenced by the courts, and who constantly struggled to escape. Although the Magdalen reported that it had 175 residents in 1903, learning to read, write, and sew, the Crittenden had only a handful, and the Bethel had been abandoned entirely.[49]

The somewhat more promising approach of the Women's Union Christian Association, with its stress on job placement, guidance, day care, and groceries was the one usually adopted by other black groups. One of them, in 1894, was the United Southern League of Philadelphia, its name and some of its purposes changed since F. J. R. Jones had helped to found it six years earlier. With several clergymen on the board, the League then proposed to establish an information service to help find migrants for their friends and families. More ambitiously it hoped to offer lodging and employment services and in general "the protection of a friend" to save some of the "many young girls" whose predecessors, coming to the city without it, had "never attained to true and perfect womanhood." Three years later five more clergymen in Germantown planned to open a ten-room house, with a restaurant, employment agency, newsletter, and reading rooms for the same clientele, but were unable to fund it.[50]

The need that all recognized for young women was the one which the Young Men's Christian Association tried to meet for their brothers. A "Colored" YMCA, funded by the national organization, opened at 12th and Lombard in 1889, under the leadership of the energetic President William Still, two ministers, Methodist and Presbyterian, and Secretary L. B. Moore. It was at first successful enough to seek larger quarters during the next year. But just as the Progressive Workingman's Association, earlier, had wound up as a kind of club for aspiring members of the black middle class, the "Y" seems to have appealed not to those southern newcomers most likely to fall in with evil companions but to earnestly pious young men in little need of help. The members seem mostly, and literally, to have preached to the choir, taking turns in the pulpit at Union AME, for example. Du Bois, who believed in the need for a really attractive club to reach out to the young men, was obviously offended by the pious dinginess of the segregated YMCA, and had no regrets when it temporarily suspended operations late in the 1890s.[51]

The major reform organizations largely or partly run by members of the Afro-American community themselves had then a checkered history. The ideal combination, as shown in a number of institutions, was obviously to combine white money and in some cases technical expertise with black knowledge of local needs and people. But this was no simple or automatic formula: William Still, backed by white philanthropy, was a key man both in the Home for Aged and Infirm Colored Persons, an unqualified success, and the YMCA, a barely qualified disaster. And the experience of the Women's Union Christian Association also showed that despite the fact that day care, for example, was not on the major philanthropic agenda, a local experience with felt needs could sometimes make a little money go precisely where it was needed. The one thing clear was that black Philadelphians had a long experience not only with charity but with self-help, and that charitable reform was one of the several purposes that brought them together across the lines of religious denomination and, sometimes, of social class.

It is clear that the great majority of adult black Philadelphians belonged to some kind of organization, church, lodge, benefit association, or political club. At the same time it is impossible even to estimate how many such groups there were, or how many members were truly active, as distinct from those who simply joined the church or paid their club dues. But before suggesting what organization meant in terms of social class, family, and personal life, there are at least some numerical clues to offer.

The New York *Globe* mentioned over sixty clubs and organizations in the twenty-six "Letter from the Quaker City" columns which have survived for the year 1883. Although mutual benefit societies or lodges were included, and some charities, the great majority were devoted simply to good times. Literary clubs led the list with ten, followed by bands or choirs with eight, while others were devoted to athletics, whist, and whatever occupied the Steamboat Association and the Mysterious Social Club. The list, as a sample, omits whole categories, such as the "race" organizations, represented at various times by the Equal Rights League, the Africo-American Protective Association, the Afro-American League and later Council. It scarcely touches on the political clubs, or the half-dozen organizations common to all of the large churches, King's Daughters, choir, Sunday school, Dorcas, and Mite societies. And no mere listing of titles can do justice to the fact that the lodges or clubs themselves generated subcommittees to organize each of their dinners, balls, and excursions, or the fact that the bigger organizations growing out of ad hoc meetings all began with presiding officers who then turned matters over to a permanent chair, executive committee, and small army of vice presidents, secretaries, and board members, with only the treasurer usually facing his or her responsibilities alone.[52]

One clue to the number of active members is offered by Dorsey scrapbook number 70, a collection of flyers, posters, tickets, and invitations to various events sponsored by lodges, churches, clubs, and other organizations. For the four years 1890–93, when the officially counted adult black population of the city averaged perhaps 30,000 people gathered into about 9,000 households, this one book lists about 700 people, eliminating duplications, who had their names printed on official announcements as active in some 44 events, as organizers, ticket sellers, or performers. Some of these represented combined groups: five Masonic lodges joined for an excursion, or a benefit for the AME denomination rather than a single church. But even with some allowance for this, the list still represents no more than 3 of the perhaps 60 political clubs in the city, 10 of an equal number of lodges—not counting the women's auxiliaries—6 of the 40 churches, 20 of the innumerable other societies and institutions.[53]

A more ambitious numerical estimate for the churches might start with William Dorsey's own St. Thomas Church, the only one for which there is a complete list of officers in the first half of the 1890s. Apart from the pastor, St. Thomas's in 1894 boasted 48 different men and women seving as officers, not counting the members of the men's and women's choirs (the women's alone had 24 members in 1891), the Sunday school teachers (the Church of the Crucifixion had 18 in 1889), or the ordinary members of the Mite Society, King's Daughters, and other groups. St. Thomas's was a proud old church, but of medium size; conservatively perhaps 100 to 150 of its 340 communicants at that time were active members. For the rest of the 50 or so mainstream churches then in the city perhaps 75 to 100 apiece would be an equally conservative guess.[54]

There are even fewer clues for the other groups, but an estimate may start with the fact that each of the 60 or so political clubs typically required some 12 officers: 6 directors, 1 president, 2 vice presidents, 2 secretaries, and a treasurer. However farcical these bylaws, about that many would be required to plan battles or picnics. The same number, perhaps, was active in each of the 40 lodges. The minimum requirement for the hundreds of beneficial societies was someone to act as secretary-treasurer, and the larger ones had their own slates of officers and directors; there is simply no way of making even the most fearless guess as to the numbers involved in the purely recreational or social clubs, or of accounting for all of the overlap. But together it all suggests that just as the great majority of adults fit somewhere into the organizational web that covered the black city, the majority of households contributed at least one member who was truly active somewhere in that network. And that fact had important implications for the nature of social class.[55]

The very purpose of social clubs is to exclude by including, and black Philadelphia had a number of these. There seems to be only one, however, which had no purpose beyond its snob appeal to the city's male elite: the Ugly Fishing Club, or more formally the Philadelphia Annex to the Ugly Fishing Club of Newport and New York, locally organized in 1880. The Uglies occasionally held a dance or reception, but through the early 1890s the dozen members, dominated by "Commodore" Andrew Stevens and other caterers, mostly took turns throwing monthly banquets for each other and a few select guests, their twelve-course menus lovingly reproduced in the society columns. But given its essentially bibulous purpose, the Club did not include the more notably serious-minded professionals, J. D. Lewis or Nathan Mossell, and of course no clergymen. And while there were other elite clubs in practice, none of them was so exclusively self-indulgent. The Bird Association, for example, organized in the 1890s, was composed mostly of leading citizens from Philadelphia, Washington, and New York, but open to any man who had attended James Bird's Lombard Street School half a century earlier. Henry Minton, as a medical student in 1904, met with several doctors at his house to found the first national Afro-American Greek letter fraternity, Sigma Pi Phi, which he served as Grand Sire Archon. But while exclusive by definition, Sigma Pi shared with most other black groups in the city a common interest in "the elevation of the race," and like them held events whose proceeds went at least in part to some good cause.[56]

Many upper-class whites during the late 19th century were able to segregate themselves away from contact with the rest of the city through a truly exclusive network of private associations. Some black men and women may have wanted to imitate them, to be rid of the stigma associated with what T. Thomas Fortune called "V.C.N.s," or Very Common Negroes, the kind of people whose public behavior was thought to pull down their own reputations. But while leading blacks could join elite clubs it was impossible for them to live truly isolated from the majority of the race.[57]

Virtually all, to begin with, were active in church, and their churches tended to scatter the leadership rather than unite it. While St. Thomas's basked in its elite reputation its communicants comprised only a small minority of the community's most distinguished residents. Bethel may indeed have been made up mostly of the "great laboring class," but in the 1870s it was also the mother church of the two "richest" Philadelphians, the Reverends Stephen Smith and J. P. B. Eddy, and in the 1880s of its two most distinguished families, the Mossells and Coppins, while "Bethel Lit" and the two AME journals made it the center of intellectual life. Andrew Stevens and John Trower, the two most successful caterers in the post-Dorsey era, were both active Baptist laymen; Christopher Perry, Robert Jones, Colonel McKee, and the Stills were all Presbyterian. Of the 36 leading people in the Dorsey Collection, the 31 whose religious affiliation is known were scattered through at least 9 different churches—the several AME congregations cannot be separated from each other—and communicants of St. Thomas's, although heavily represented, do not outnumber those who belonged to the AME.[58]

Politics, too, like lodge and fraternity, by definition demanded the common touch, and unlike the white upper class, few blacks were able to ignore the needs of political organization. The two most elite of political organizations were the statewide Equal Rights League, which issued careful pronouncements without getting involved in the grimier work at the polls, and the local Citizens Republican Club. ERL members engaged in "considerable discussion" about admitting Gil Ball in August of 1882—within a year, apparently, of the raffish saloonkeeper's assault, at the Quay Club, on their scholarly, bespectacled colleague James F. Needham. But Ball was finally elected. And while the married men mostly left their wives at home, John Durham, Nathan Mossell, Carl Bolivar, Chris Perry, Dr. E. C. Howard, Richard Warrick, and a host of other leading citizens did attend the Third Annual Ball of the Citizens Republican Club, as already noted, in company with the usual bullyboys and a crowd of what William Dorsey labeled "nearly all disreputable women."[59]

The breadth of the organizational network, then, when added to residential segregation, pulled the community together from two opposite directions. On the one hand those toward the bottom of the social ladder had easy access to those toward the top, people who went to the same churches, belonged to the same political clubs and societies, appealed to them in meeting for support, memberships, contributions, dues, and votes. On the other hand most of those at the top were forced to live in the same high-crime red-light district as the rest.

The result of both pulls was to create, for better and for worse, an unstable social situation which combined much downward with its upward mobility. It is not hard for a historian to establish who were the community's most active and distinguished residents, simply by counting the number of times an individual name appears in the Dorsey Collection, with the most mentions typically going to the church trustees, authors, club officers, letter writers, and award winners. Many of them, as noted, had worked their way up from the bottom, as unskilled workers or even slaves. But the term "elite status," implying family continuity as well as individual success, is harder for a historian to define, and was harder yet for contemporaries to secure.

Certain families were heavily represented in responsible social positions, even if no individual members were truly outstanding, among them Joneses, Hintons, Hollands and Cowdreys, Mintons and Mintesses, Pages, Ramseys, Gordons, Vennings, Chews, and Moores. A writer for the *Freeman* in 1886 explained this by suggesting that Philadelphia's young men "are recognized more by ability and previous social status than by money." Given the limited resources of even professional and entrepreneurial families, the relatively narrow income gap between the community's top and bottom, it is obvious that social differences could not be measured primarily in terms of income. But from the point of view of the more distinguished families, the cruel fact was that in the absence of much capital to pass on and the presence of illegitimate temptations nearby, prestigious status and occupations could easily slip away, a condition vividly illustrated by the story of the Dorsey family itself.[60]

Philadelphia was actually full of Afro-American Dorseys, some 43 officially counted in the census of 1850, 66 in 1880. A majority of the adults in the earlier year, were listed, like Thomas, as natives of Maryland, but it is impossible to establish the network of relationships among them. Over the decades the group made the news in ways typical of the community as a whole. Augustus, in the oldest generation, was an entrepreneur like Thomas, dealing in secondhand clothes and finally real estate. One of the two Charles Dorseys of William's age, either or both of them possibly cousins, became the first black school principal in the City of Brooklyn; the other, a coatroom attendant active in Zoar United Methodist Church, founded the National Negro Church Ushers Association in the 1890s. William made a number of marginal corrections in the accounts of

Eve Dorsey, about his own children's age, who bungled the robbery of a small immigrants' bank in 1899. But as illustration of the special obstacles to the transmission of elite status, the most instructive stories are those of William himself, his sisters, and their children.[61]

Thomas J. and Louise Dorsey lived in the handsome style appropriate to his position, with household servants to help entertain Senator Charles Sumner, their good friend Frederick Douglass, and other notables of both races at their private table. His will, drawn in 1867, established a trust to run through two more generations. At his death in 1876 Louise was given the household furniture, officially appraised at nearly $1300, together with the income from several nearby properties and continued use of the big house at 1231 Locust. Even without his earnings, the annual rents of about $1500 were enough to maintain her securely as a member of what in the wider white world would be the middle class. But when she died three years later, and the income was split three ways, it afforded William, Mary Louise, and Sarah's orphaned boys no more than a working-class income apiece. And it proved to be a troublesome legacy, in many ways.

Trouble immediately developed between Mary and William. The will had been drawn at a time when the black community still had no lawyers, and the white attorney Thomas had named as trustee begged off on Louise's death in 1879. Mary, although a woman and thirteen years younger than her brother, at 29, had more power than he in the choice of a successor. The extra cards had been dealt her when her older sister Sarah, married to John Seville in 1858, had returned home a widow and then died herself under the parental roof, in 1871. William, it was perhaps judged, was not an exemplary father, and either Sarah or perhaps later their mother designated Mary as legal guardian of young John C. and Dorsey Seville. Mary then controlled, in effect, her own share of the entrusted inheritance and the boys'.

Mary was by then a married woman and mother in her own right, having sometime during the 1870s married Robert Harlan, Jr., a native of Cincinnati three years younger than she. Harlan himself was the acknowledged half-nephew of John Marshall Harlan, of Kentucky, a former slaveowner and then justice of the Supreme Court of the United States, who would be widely hailed within the black community for his lone dissent in the segregation case of *Plessy v. Ferguson*. But despite his distinguished connections the young man apparently brought little money of his own to the marriage. His own father was the son of old Judge James Harlan, a plantation owner who had taken up with a "colored" woman on the death of his first wife. But "Colonel" Robert Harlan, Sr., was a colorful high-liver who lost most of what had once been a considerable fortune during the 1860s, partly because of devastation in the South, partly because his racing stable had done poorly in England. In any case during 1879 the younger Harlans and their two daughters were living in the elder Dorsey's old Locust Street home, and William in a less desirable place on Erie Avenue, when Mary petitioned the court for her own choice as trustee of the family estate.

Her nomination was another white man, her father's rental agent: ex-constable William Whitesides. Her brother filed a formal objection to this on the grounds that Whitesides, having after all killed a black man in 1870, was distrusted in the community, had no experience as a trustee, and had been known to let properties to "persons of ill-fame." Mary in her turn filed another petition dismissing these objections: the man was widely used as an agent by other Afro-Americans, the manslaughter conviction had been a mistake, and he tried as hard as possible to police the character of all tenants. But Whitesides withdrew his candidacy in any case, as William held some cards of his own.

During 1880 William Dorsey was in the midst of his tenure as personal messenger to the law-and-order mayor of Philadelphia, William Stokley, whose power, like those of all mayors of the era, was built on control of the police force. Stokley had been known to manipulate vice raids for political advantage, and perhaps for other reasons: in any case on June 5 Mary L. Dorsey was arrested at 1033 Locust Street for running a "disorderly house," and given a summary sentence of three months in the House of Correction. The address was not the one where Robert Harlan, their girls, and the Seville boys had lived and were probably still living, but another one located next to one of the family properties at 1035, where she apparently kept a separate household of a different character. One of the other things she kept there was an informally adopted white daughter, Nellie, just 12 years old, who was taken in charge, after the raid, by Philadelphia's Society for the Protection of Children from Cruelty. On Mary's release in September she went looking for the child. But in a special hearing remarkable among other things for the total absence of any reference to race she agreed that, given the nature of her profession, her place was no place for a carefully reared girl just entering puberty. Perhaps in the lack of an appropriate Episcopal placement, Nellie was then sent to the West Philadelphia Industrial School of the Immaculate Conception, and there disappears from the historical record.

Early the following year, however, Mary Dorsey Harlan sent one more petition to the court, this one from Washington. In view of their recent move to that city, where Robert, Jr., had just won a job in the postal service, she suggested that she could no longer properly serve as legal guardian to the Seville boys, who had stayed in Philadelphia. She had a candidate all ready however in William Whitesides, who then assumed that responsibility.

Over the following two decades her personal history is harder to trace. Robert Harlan, Jr., stayed in the Capital City at least through 1884, where family legend has it that he and his famous uncle routinely greeted one another on the streets. He eventually returned home, however, to Cincinnati, where he took another patronage job with the city. Whether his marriage to Mary remained intact is not clear. She died back in Washington in 1901, of heart trouble related to hypertension; her death certificate states that she had lived in the city for only 23 months previously, subtracts five years from her true age, and lists no next of kin. While the family took her back to Philadelphia for burial, knowledge of her very existence was later shielded from its younger members.

If there was any gossip about their mother, however, it had no serious effects on her daughters, who had by then moved back to Philadelphia to be raised in the household of their cousin Sarah Dorsey Ramsey, William's second daughter. Both of them lived active social lives and married well, Caroline to Albert Curry, of a catering family, Louise to William Bascom, son of the leading upholsterer and pillar of St. Thomas Church.

Dorsey Seville meanwhile had followed his aunt to Washington and his uncle Robert into the postal service, where he enjoyed a successful career, incidentally maintaining good relations with "Uncle Bill," to whom he occasionally sent bundles of local newspapers. John C. Seville is harder to trace. His name appears just once in the Philadelphia City Directory, as a "waiter," in 1885, and then reappears only in the last of the documents relating to the family estate, when it was finally dissolved; in a final Dickensian twist, it turns out that his share was "assigned" to the heirs of William Whitesides, his legal guardian, who had managed somehow to diddle him out of his inheritance.

The story of William Henry and his own children, if less melodramatic, is equally revealing. Following a brief stint as a turnkey, after being fired as messenger by Mayor Stokley's Democratic successor Samuel King, Dorsey apparently earned no income other than what little he might have gotten from his artwork, plus his share of his father's trust and his own real-estate investments. Given the expenses involved in raising six children, his wife's earnings as dressmaker were essential to the family. Finances grew even tighter after 1892, when the parents separated and let out the big place on Locust Street to take up two separate households of their own. There was no question of divorce in that day and in that class, and William moved back to the 206 Dean Street address where the young couple had lived early in their marriage. He continued to send Virginia checks from the estate over the remaining years of her life, as she moved several times, eventually joining her Harlan nieces in her daughter Sarah's house. But the estate itself was constantly subject to litigation as the result of apparent mismanagement by a series of white trustees. Certainly Virginia was never able to quit her work as dressmaker, and neither one of them had any real capital to pass on to the children other than their connections, education, and manner.

For their two daughters, Virginia and Sarah, much like their Harlan cousins, these and their own persons were enough. Both were continually in the social news, although in 1889 "Sadie," the younger, was married at 19 to William Ramsey, a printer and sometime journalist. Virginia, or "Jenny," a schoolteacher still remembered by family and other Old Philadelphians as a striking woman, later married Frederick Doll, a barber from Cincinnati. The wedding was a major event of the Christmas season of 1890, with Blanche Warrick as her maid of honor, and her younger brother Thomas J. as best man; Mamie Minton, Ida Bowser, William Warrick, Benjamin Sayres, and Andrew Stevens, Jr., served as a most elite group of bridesmaids and ushers. Just as Sarah's six children and their descendants generally went on to successful careers in business and the professions, Jenny's nine reportedly did much the same across Ohio.[62]

The sons turned out more variously. Ira, born in 1867, reportedly quarreled with his father and left home at an early age, returning occasionally from upstate New York as a kind of "boulevardier," living close to the edge of respectability. John, the youngest, born in 1881, stayed with his mother, occasionally making the news either by dancing at a debutante ball or getting caught shooting craps. The census of 1900 lists him as "janitor," the city directory as "clerk"; the certificate registering his early death from pneumonia, in 1907, has him a "dental student." Van Dyke, the eldest, left home sometime after 1880 but returned as a 48-year-old "laborer" in 1909. Even more than Ira he enjoys, in family memory, a raffish reputation; periodically living with his mother or at various other addresses over the next decade he appears occasionally in the city's directories as a "bartender," and after the onset of national Prohibition in 1919 as a "chemist," to the further confusion of later occupational analyses. Only Thomas, then, who in classic shirtsleeves-to-shirtsleeves fashion reverted to his grandfather's earlier occupation as a waiter, remained a stable member of local society. He and his wife, Blanche Bradford of Baltimore, had a single daughter, Helen, a promising young woman who, however, died in her twenties, the last of the Thomas J.'s descendants to bear the Dorsey name in Philadelphia.

William himself apparently lived alone during his later years, a gruff and very occasional visitor to his nearby grandchildren. Sometimes he was visited himself, by William Ramsey or Thomas, when the support checks were late, and Thomas and Blanche reportedly nursed him through the last three years before his death in 1923. He left no will of his own; when his father's estate was liquidated five years later most of the originally intended beneficiaries had either died or somehow "assigned" their shares to strangers. None of either Sarah or Mary's children or heirs had any part, although Sarah Ramsey, Virginia Doll, Thomas and Ira Dorsey each got one-twelfth of the total, appraised at a little over $6000 apiece in the relatively inflated currency circulating on the eve of the Great Crash of 1929.

The combination of trouble and success in this family saga was unusual in degree, but the situation of the city's black elite ensured that there were skeletons in other closets too, and no family could be held socially responsible for the behavior of all of its members. What was nearly unique about William and Virginia's family was its size: six grown children. While the biographical annals are full of southern or rural families like the New Jersey Stills, with eighteen children born to a single mother, those who made it to the city had radically different patterns of fertility. The urban figures are dominated by the poverty of the majority, low rates of marriage, high rates of both infant mortality and diseases resulting from prostitution. But it seems also that the most distinguished Philadelphians, too, had small families, not as the result of disease or desperation but of decision. Although some of the leading 36 men and women listed in Appendix III had quite a number of children, the average was only 2.4, and the median less than 2.

One reason for limiting family size was that it was a classic response to the financial burden of elite status, as children were more expensive than most material goods. Part of the problem was that, as Du Bois pointed out, whites with incomes of $1500 knew they were poor and lived accordingly, while blacks with the same incomes were at the top of the Afro-American scale, and felt compelled to live up to the ranking. There was no problem finding the appropriate style; everything from charitable balls through silver table settings was modeled on the life-styles of the elite whites whom so many of them knew well as patrons, customers, and employers. No one complained about the expense of church building, for example, but toward purely conspicuous consumption the journalistic attitude was more ambivalent. H. P. Williams, in the New York *Globe,* denounced the money spent on balls and then in the *Sunday Mercury* devoted whole pages to the description of ball gowns. T. T. Fortune both complained about high living among Washington's civil servants and gave front-page coverage to the menu for a going-away banquet for the Reverend C. C. Astwood, on the occasion of his leaving to take up the post of Dominican consul. That affair, to compound the irony, honored a minister whose church often preached total abstinence, and by the account in the *Age* featured a wine list that ran from Sauterne through sherry, claret, Niersteiner, Macon, and champagne on to after-dinner liqueurs with cigars.[63]

Some of the resulting strains may be shown through the financial histories of the three people who earned the highest salaries in black Philadelphia during the 1860s and early 1870s. Octavius Catto, Fanny Jackson, and Ebenezer Bassett had little personally in common except that they all worked for the Institute for Colored Youth, and they all had trouble making ends meet.

Catto's tenure at the ICY was marked by continual squabbles over salary; a threat to go elsewhere, his "standard tactic," was not always but generally enough to win the needed raise, and by his death in 1871 he was earning some $1400 a year. In the late 1860s his expenses included much travel in connection with two rather different organizations, the Pennsylvania Equal Rights League, which he served as secretary and de facto leader, and the Pythians Baseball Club, which he served as captain and shortstop, playing teams in

Washington, New England, and New York. He was also perhaps the town's most eligible bachelor, a gallant who wrote poetry to a young woman in Washington and often escorted Caroline LeCount around Philadelphia; his correspondence with "Jake" White, Jr., his best friend, is much concerned with fashions in trousers, and his own tailoring bill at Wanamakers' ran well over $100 for just two months.[64]

Fanny Jackson, like many of her peers, was in contrast something of a Puritan, and especially opposed to the pretensions of fashion. But she was also, her biographer points out, a very generous woman, especially to needy students and probably to the church as well. The result was that she had continually to ask for advances in pay, and when in 1871 the total was raised to $1800 she owed outside creditors some $300, and her Quaker Board of Managers in essence took over management of her finances, giving her an allowance and taking on the burden of repayment, interest, and investment for themselves. Bassett, a family man, was in even worse straits, "having to borrow from the board time and time again." When interest charges of 6 percent did not cure what the managers clearly viewed as his irresponsibilities, they devised a characteristically Quaker solution. Beginning in 1866 the principal was also appointed school janitor, to earn an added $200 a year. "Spelling out his duties carefully," the Board insisted among other things that Bassett, shortly to join the white-tie circuit as Minister to Liberia, should clean all toilets twice a week.[65]

But it was not only the obvious expenses of life toward the top of black Philadelphia that worked to limit family size, but also another and less obvious effect of its thick round of obligations and association. Du Bois, morally a model late Victorian, was greatly concerned about the quality of family life at all levels, and found that even among "the best" there was "a tendency to let communal church and society life trespass upon the home." His solution was less activity—even, or perhaps especially, less religious activity. Gertrude Bustill Mossell, on the contrary, through book and columns the community's professional advisor on family matters, shared his concern with sexual morality but rejected his premises about a home life built around pipe, slippers, children, and fireside. She wanted a man, as noted earlier, who would not pat but kick the family dog on his way out nights, and a woman not saccharine but peppery; for her a marriage would join two people who led not primarily private but active public lives.[66]

Both the material condition and the social values of her own class encouraged the realization of this ideal. The homes of even the richest of black Philadelphians could not have been furnished as impressively as their owners were dressed, and none were as spacious as the churches and halls where most events were held. Mrs. Andrew Stevens was the ony woman in the city's elite who won much attention in the role of traditional hostess, known exclusively for her New Year's receptions and private dinners. Her three sisters chose more characteristic lives: Rebecca Cole as a teacher and physician, Dora as school principal and civil servant, Mrs. H. L. Phillips as an active contributor to her own as well as her husband's philanthropies. In fact her own daughter Helen shared management of the catering business with Andrew Jr. after their father died in 1898.[67]

In terms of social class, the fact that the lives of leading citizens centered less around home and children than around church, club, and community reinforced the fragility that went with the general inability to amass and transmit capital. And it is possible broadly to measure the combined effects of having relatively few direct heirs and little money to pass on to them by comparing an elite list from one generation with a matched list from another.[68]

A representative if by no means complete roster of some 130 of the most distinguished black male citizens of the 1860s may be made up simply by combining three smaller lists of those engaged in various leadership or elite club activities: an 1860 petition to the singer Mary Brown, an 1863 "Call to Arms," and the first four Pythian baseball teams of 1869. Another and matching list of 137 may be drawn by the same criteria for the 1890s: the Douglass charity ball of 1898, the American Negro Historical Society in 1897, and the DECAGON ball of 1899. But however carefully matched in terms of distinction, the two composite lists from the two decades match up very little in terms of direct inheritance. Just four men from the 1890s, all members of the Historical Society, are known sons of others from the 1860s: James F. Needham, William Dorsey, Robert M. Adger, and T. J. Minton. The John Dorsey who helped organize DECAGON was William's son as well, and Minton's son Henry, then a pharmacist, was active in the Douglass ball, extending the list to three generations. But there are only 10 possibilities to add to the four families known for certain to have produced a second locally distinguished generation, as there are only 10 surnames in the 1890s list which match others from the 1860s: Allen, Ash(e), Brown, Burrell, Davis, Hall, Johnson, Thomas, Williams, and Wilson. Of this group, some members of the later generation are doubtless descendants of those from the first, but the names are so common that this cannot be shown. It is in fact the commonness of so many Afro-American surnames which makes the discontinuity so striking: there are actually more duplicate surnames within the generations—16 in each case—than the 14 across them.

The problem of sustaining family position was then one of the major features of the Afro-American class system, one of the indications that the social situation pulled many down as well as up. And together with poverty and segregation the web of associations was a major contributor to the community's social structure, not only by binding the classes close together but by helping to define them. More important than the pretensions of a few exclusive societies was the simple fact that there was an extraordinary amount of work to do in black Philadelphia, defending the race, fighting for the party, supporting church, lodge, and club. Given the relative lack of other distinctions, such as income, social class was in part a matter of reputation, and it seems that those who could do the work won the right to do more of it. But the right was not easily heritable; those who did or could not join in slipped into obscurity or worse, making the whole concept of "elite family" problematic. For those who dropped out of respectability, and stayed whole and healthy, there may have been some consolation in the fact that the community's web of associations was too big to be ever wholly out of reach, making it possible to climb back after a fall from solvency or grace.

Chapter 11

Recreation, Entertainment, and Postscriptum to William Henry Dorsey

William Henry Dorsey's collection is full of evidence of every kind about the most exciting period in Afro-American history. In 1860 thousands of his fellow Philadelphians had once been slaves; almost all of them, slave or free, found the Civil War a liberating experience. By the end of the century even more had witnessed the ups and downs of southern Reconstruction, where early hopes for genuine political and economic inclusion were largely defeated by white southern intransigence. Historians of the South have often told the story of how the systematic denial of the vote and the spread of an officially sanctioned segregation eroded many of the gains of the late 1860s and 1870s, with help from the quasi-sanctioned practice of lynching. But the more paradoxical and in the long run equally significant history experienced by Dorsey's own community in the same era is less familiar.

The urban North already represented the future, marked by less dramatic but more complicated developments than those to the south. There were in Philadelphia few absolute triumphs, in an era in which pseudo-scientific racism infected the whole of the country, and many small victories for civility were matched or followed by defeats. But Afro-American contemporaries were more inclined to emphasize progress than pain. A major gain in personal security from white violence helped to balance the dangerous rise in vice and crime which blighted economic and personal life in growing black neighborhoods. Desegregation, however incomplete, advanced on several fronts, and there were undeniable advances in education and the professions to set against the systematic discrimination which shut the majority out of the industrial revolution. However shadowed by a subservient and even criminal politics the right to vote brought dignity to many and jobs for some, adding an important new layer to the black leadership class.

To a reader a century later, too, the evidence of vitality, based in part on the strength of church, lodge, and club, is more striking than the evidence of the fundamental economic weakness which would lead to further trouble ahead. And at the risk of stereotype, the most striking material in all of the Dorsey Collection is the evidence about good times, the great variety of ways in which members of a small, poor, and threatened community managed to enjoy life.

Enjoyment can be analyzed in many ways. Its forms offer clues to class and culture. Like many other aspects of black life the pursuit of fun involved competition within a wider framework of cooperation, or community. It is possible, especially in music, to trace development over time, the growth away from white forms on the one hand and southern roots on the other toward something distinctively urban, black, and contemporary. But the records in the Dorsey Collection remind a reader at the same time that while it provided no full escape from the sometimes tragic poverty and racism that limited black lives, full-throated enjoyment, even joy, often soared above these limits, and was at last its own end.

One of the great differences between Afro-American and many white religions was the fact that the black church was not uniformly opposed to the joy provided by music and theater but an important source of both. Philadelphia's black churches not only encouraged but nurtured the talents of the city's professional or semi-professional performers who appeared at functions of many different kinds across the city.

The tradition began with the fact that the church was among other things a place to have fun, starting with the youngest parishioners. Only a few cities had begun to build playgrounds by the very end of the century, blacks were specifically barred from the contemporary equivalent of fresh-air camps, and public schooling was in general a grimly serious business. Sunday schools were then almost the only place which provided organized recreation. The giant picnic sponsored by five AME churches in late July of 1889 was unusual only in its size: several special trains took eight thousand people to a popular resort at Neshaminy Falls, in nearby Montgomery County, which the churches had contracted for the day. The proprietor hired a small army of extra hands to cope with "this remarkable influx," but most of them, and the donkeys, could not make it through the day; even the inanimate swings, boats, coasters, and merry-go-rounds were reportedly exhausted. "The picnickers alone never grew weary," and given 19th-century rules and field conditions an epic ball game between "two mission nines," begun in the morning, was called in the seventh inning only on account of advancing darkness.[1]

Church activities routinely mixed the serious with the entertaining. A major benefit for an AME chapel, held in the Academy of Music of 1890, featured a talk on "The Duty of the Hour" by the Hon. John R. Lynch, former Philadelphian and ex-Reconstruction congressman from Mississippi. For 50 cents the audience was also treated to Miller's Quartette and four other local musicians. Miller's group appeared again the next month as part of an evening at Concert Hall for the Africo-American Young Men's Association of the Church of the Crucifixion, following the Reverend J. H. Hector's lecture on "The Race Problem." Bishop Jacob F. Ramsey failed even to win top billing when he visited Grace Union in 1903. The headline event on the posters was "A Tag Social and Baby Contest"; Ramsey and his talk on "My Trip South: What I Saw and What We Need" was listed lower down.[2]

Music was of course an integral part of religious service; indeed together with dance, in the form of the ring shout, singing *was* the service for many smaller congregations outside the major denominations. Sometimes, as with Samuel Adger, one suspects that the quality of the music was in fact the key to the choice of denomination. Adger, evidently a restless as well as a gifted man, had spent some time as a youth searching for gold in Australia and California, followed by several years playing the organ first at Cherry Street Baptist and then at Central Presbyterian. But when he encountered the magnificent new instrument at the Episcopal Church of the Crucifixion he exclaimed, "I have come to my bride," and remained happily wedded to it for the rest of his life.[3]

But music in church was a means of reaching to God, no more entertainment in purpose than the silence observed by the Society of Friends. What was truly distinctive about black churches, and musicians, was the way in which they so easily combined the secular and sacred.

Elizabeth Greenfield, the "Black Swan" raised and tutored by a Philadelphia Quaker woman, returned to the city in the 1860s after her years on the international concert stage. Reunited with Addison W. Lively, her original accompanist, she took an especial interest in Lively's Shiloh Baptist Choir, and seems to have spent her last years helping coach it as well as giving occasional recitals of her own. Their joint efforts helped make Shiloh a major musical center, and when just the year after her death in 1876 the stately Academy of Music agreed for the first time to open its stage to an all-black performance, the pioneers were youngsters from the church's Sabbath school, perhaps groomed for the occasion as carefully as those who, with help from the NAACP, were chosen to integrate southern schools three generations later. The affair was in any event a great financial success, as three thousand people of both races turned out to hear a young organist play "The Roman March," as well as soloists, quartettes, and the ensemble chorus sing "Faded Leaves," "The Old Gate on the Hill," and other sentimental favorites.[4]

Even the sober Presbyterians, their white counterparts not known for dramatic flair, put on performances at every level, mostly in the churches themselves. In 1868 guests at First African, come for a performance of "Aunt Polly Bassett's Singin' Skewl" were assured that "Ye women folke will be found goodly places to see and hear by certyne discreete young men of ye parish." A generation later, in 1891, a single Sunday school combined boys' and girls' drill team exhibitions, a Tom Thumb wedding, some humorous skits, tableaux vivants, and of course musical selections. The Reverend Matthew Anderson, at Berean, put on one of his own "unique, entertaining, and wonderful photographic exhibitions" in 1894. Central had enough talent, including Samuel Adger, Gertrude Bustill, Carrie LeCount, and Christopher Perry, so that its Literary and Musical Entertainments in 1873, 1875, and 1877 featured substantially different casts and singers each time. The next odd year, 1879, its Young People's Association staged the scriptural cantata "Esther," moving out of the church to Musical Fund Hall, with the help of the Vaux School Orchestra; as usual with these entertainments there was a competition for most tickets sold, top prize a gold watch.[5]

Bigger churches were able to do more ambitious things. In 1898, 10 cents for Mother Bethel's building fund won admission to a program at the church which included a review by the Allen Guards, the church's drill team, a talk by Bishop Grant, the elocutionist Mae Jones, the prize-winning soprano Sarah Masten Lewis with her sister-in-law, the journalist Florence, and the choir's rendition of the anthem "Land of Ham," by Dr. J. Albert Thorne, the African colonizer just then preparing to lead an expedition to Nyasaland.[6]

But the most ambitious programs were those which featured touring professionals with national and even international reputations. Dessaria Plato was the featured singer, for example, at the celebration held for the dedication of Shiloh's new organ, in 1892, in which John A. Lively, Addison's son, played a series of dance numbers and the fifty-voice choir of the Church of the Crucifixion sang hymns. Both Madame Selika and Blind Tom appeared at the great 1887 100th anniversary celebration of the AME church. Flora Batson sang at the Academy in 1894, at a Bergen Star Concert to benefit Bethel's New Building Fund, with tickets ranging from 25 to 75 cents, balcony and pro-scenium boxes for $5 and $8; instead of the usual competitive prizes everyone who sold sixty 50-cent tickets won a barrel of flour for either themselves or a favorite charity.[7]

These Star Concerts, organized by J. G. Bergen, of Florida Street in Philadelphia, were the most important of those which specialized in giving one-night church benefit performances in major halls across the country. Bergen generally netted between $350 and $500 for the sponsoring institution, with up to $100 in competitive prizes going to local ticket sellers. The bill always mixed touring stars with local talent; lead singers, usually doing operatic selections, alternated with dramatic readings, quartettes singing popular harmonic airs, and comic skits. The recipe ensured both that Philadelphia audiences, black and white, were continually exposed to the best black performers from across the country and that Philadelphia artists were given a chance to show their stuff in the best company.[8]

At the time of Batson's 1894 visit to the Academy, for example, two of the other four featured performers were Philadelphians. Together with a tenor from Boston and a violinist from New York, the two were W. I. Powell, "The

Celebrated Baritone and King of Fun," and R. Henri Strange, "America's Greatest Colored Tragedian." Both had worked their way through various local churches and halls to become professionals, or semi-professionals; Strange was a regular member of the Bergen troupe for four years by then.[9]

While the churches were the major nurseries of local talent, they were neither jealous nor exclusive. Some benefit productions were put on by Sunday schools or young people's associations which belonged to the sponsoring institution. But others, although the proceeds went to a specific building, missionary, or organ fund, routinely combined people from different denominations, as with the organ dedication described above. Shiloh was host in fact to an open citywide competition, in 1893, in which prizes of up to $5 were given to the winning tenors, sopranos, baritones, and comedians. The same people, or groups, also appeared at secular affairs, balls, and musical competitions, at least partly for the money as well as for the fun of it, without reference of course to denominational lines or to the one which separated amateurs from professionals.[10]

The Dorsey Collection also contains several programs or notices which refer to local productions of Gilbert and Sullivan, Shakespeare, and other major plays or operettas, some of the references so glancing or casual as to suggest that they were fairly routine: an 1887 *Richard III* appears only in the obituary of a New York impresario; another in 1892, plus an *Othello*, is mentioned in the story of the arrest, on a minor charge, of the lead actor's brother. Here too some were commerical, some amateur benefits, others mixed. *H.M.S. Pinafore* was put on as part of a purely commercial variety bill, with other performers black and white, at Fox's American Theater in 1879: Dorsey noted on the program that "all of this troupe are colored people of Philadelphia." The *Mikado* which sparked the row over coverage in the *Times* in 1886 was done mostly by young amateurs of the Church of the Crucifixion, but the musical director, identified as "a special officer of the 5th District," was among many other things the city's leading Afro-American bandleader, F. J. R. Jones.[11]

Shakespearean performances were unique in that all references to adult productions involve aspiring professionals. When the New York actor J. C. Arneaux brought *Richard III* to the Academy in 1887, local management was in the hands of ex-policeman and politician Alexander Davis, whose Philadelphia Standard Dramatic Company produced R. Henri Strange as Richmond, plus others in more modest secondary roles. Five years later Strange was playing the lead in "Majah" Teagle's commercial productions of the same play and *Othello*.[12]

The smell of greasepaint in concentration evidently had an intoxicating effect: once gathered together an ensemble was naturally tempted to try its hand at going professional. In the spring of 1894 the success of the operetta *Pauline*, put on by organist Samuel Adger's Shepard Colored Opera Company, led to plans to tour Baltimore and Washington, and to form a permanent organization. But in practice the Shepard Company seems not to have lasted longer than Davis's Standard Dramatic Company during the previous decade, and nothing further was heard either of Strange's "new theater for colored actors," for which he had performed *The Merchant of Venice,* in 1891, or the troupes organized by Gil Ball and "Majah" Teagle in the years before and after.[13]

Most commerical black productions in fact played no more than one-night stands, and it seems clear that despite these brief successes there was not enough support for a real professional theater. The more typical story was of Alina Bright, of North 15th Street, whose hopeful career as prima donna of the Afro-American Specialty Company was cut short in 1899 when the company went broke and left her stranded in the Midwest, an event which lost her custody of her child to a disgusted husband. Even the Bergen concerts, which earned about $25 a night for a major star like Flora Batson, were only occasional events; Philadelphia had the biggest black population in the North, and Bergen came to town no more than once a year or so, and could not have toured continuously for long. The situation for those who were not singers, people like R. Henri Strange, or the elocutionist Hattie Q. Brown, was even more uncertain.[14]

While contemporary black leaders despised white minstrel shows— featuring people, T. T. Fortune said, who "blackened their faces to hide their gall"—black variety shows did play in Philadelphia. In 1895 Strange appeared at the Academy for the Afro-American Amusement Company, whose bill was typically as varied, and democratic, as anything on the Elizabethan stage: featured as "The Black Booth," he gave Shakespearean recitals, and Bessie Lee sang operatic selections, while the audience was invited to join in pie-eating, tug-of-war, sack-racing, buck-and-wing dancing, whistling, and cakewalking contests, "all for substantial gold prizes." But this too was a one-night affair, and most black troupes were reportedly confined to lesser halls and theaters, their jobs never really secure.[15]

One of the things which stood in the way of further commercial development was paradoxically the very wealth of talent in the city that enabled its entertainers to go as far as they did. Billy Farrell and his wife were billed as stars of the Afro-American Amusement Company program noted above, having come fresh from winning a cakewalk contest in Madison Square Garden. But Philadelphians were not easily impressed; two of their own, Frank Johnson and Elizabeth Greenfield, had played before the Queen of England, and the city was still full of that tradition and their pupils. Just a month before Farrell's company came to the Academy, managed by a white impresario, local theatergoers might have seen their friends and neighbors in *East Lynne,* sponsored by Zion Wesley at the New Odd Fellows Hall, directed by Johnson's successor F. J. R. Jones. Nothing that the Afro-American Company put on, including the cakewalk contest, could not have been seen, and done, at a local church benefit. For those who really wanted to hear R. Henri Strange there was no need to pay Academy prices: a few years later, together with three sopranos, two tenors, one contralto, and two comedians, he was back at Zion itself, reading from Paul Lawrence Dunbar, under the irresistible heading "Smiles! Laughter! Screams! An Evening of Fun! Laugh and Grow Fat!," and all for just 20 cents. [16]

In addition to going to, perhaps acting in, the theater, black Philadelphians of an intellectual or creative bent enjoyed a number of outlets for their interests. There were clubs for those with literary or historical tastes, platforms and publications for poets and authors, fairs for hobbyists and painters. Even those who like William Henry Dorsey were afflicted with the essentially solitary collector's passion could find others to abet and even share it.

Most of the city's Afro-American authors have already been noted: the New York *Age,* in 1894, in listing the nation's twenty leading poets, counted four Philadelphians among them: Frances Harper, Josie Heard, the Reverend B. T. Tanner, and Mrs. B. F. Lee, wife of Tanner's ministerial colleague. Mrs. Harper, the best known, was in effect the community's laureate, who declaimed her occasional pieces at many major observances. But the list leaves out a number of others, like Gertrude Bustill Mossell, who published serious verse, and there were still more whose newfound literacy and love of words led them to express themselves in rhyme. [17]

There is no counting these authors, since many in the Dorsey Collection are not identified by full name or place. But during 1877–78 alone at least three Philadelphians and one former resident not otherwise known as writers published poems, verse, or bits of doggerel in four different causes. Two short religious pieces, entitled "Onward" and "Upward," dated October of 1877 and signed by J. F. N., appeared probably in the *People's Advocate;* Dorsey identified the author as James Field Needham. John W. Rhodes, one of the city's first black turnkeys, put out a broadside, probably in the same year, to celebrate his own and other appointments by Mayor Stokley: "The Chief and Captains of Police / They visited each of the districts / The men was reviewed and then inspected / They all proved worthy to be selected." Daniel Adger, of the post office, put out a campaign broadside for postmaster John Bingham the next year: "With heart and hand united / Come start the ballot ball / To see our nation righted / Shout BINGHAM one and all." And later that fall Harvard-educated Richard Greener, then living in Washington, published a sentimental piece about a captive medieval warrior: "Les Hirondelles," which he identified as "(From the French of Berengar)." [18]

Each major church, and some secular clubs, like the Hannibal, encouraged appreciation of the written word and other broadly intellectual subjects. The Henry Highland Garnet Literary Society of Lincoln Alumni was a prestigious organization which appears to have organized the school's graduation exercises, but the Bethel Literary and Historical Society was most often in the news. "Bethel Lit" was broader than its title in terms of both membership, not confined to the church or even denomination, and the matters which engaged it. Organized with a board of directors and slate of executive officers, its elections, as shown in the Holland-Williams battle of 1879, were taken very seriously. During 1883–84, under the presidency of Dr. Mossell, the members heard among other things original poetry by Gertrude Bustill Mossell together with lectures by her husband; the lawyer J. D. Lewis; the artist Alfred Stidum; the Reverend J. Pullam Williams; and W. Wilbur Still. At least one of these occasions reportedly drew an audience of four hundred people; not, presumably, the one by Still, true son of his father, who chose to talk about "Debtor and Creditor."[19]

One of the society's officers was a chorister, and at least during the early 1880s, its season, which began in September, traditionally ended with a concert in May. One of its offshoots in fact was a chorus, the Amphion Singing Society, born in 1881. Its twenty-six members in 1887 included much of the social elite, Stidum, Still, and Carl Bolivar, Richard Warrick, Samuel Adger, Joseph Hill, Dr. E. C. Howard, and James G. Davis. Membership in the Society was confined to those with "an unblemished character, a passable voice, and a clear sense of music," but despite the faint praise implied in the second qualification the Amphions were good enough to sing at the Bergen Star Concerts, by invitation in New York, and at least once, on a notable occasion, as part of an otherwise all-white program at the Academy.[20]

The Society's emphasis on public performance—dramatic readings and dialect poetry as well as music—was clearly part of its attraction. But while the purely private pleasures were less publicized, and given cramped housing hard for most Afro-Americans to enjoy, the Dorsey Collection suggests some of their range. The "Philadelphia Quartette Club" appeared for the first time, as example, in 1876 during a concert given by the Amphion Choral Society, as elite as their near namesakes but mixed, with mostly women's voices. The Quartette was composed of first violinist F. J. R. Jones, cellist Augustus Capps Hazzard, second violinist J. D. Rollin, and violist Hamilton Moore. All of these men had studied under major masters of their instruments; Moore, later Jones's chief rival as the community's leading bandleader, had reportedly played in three different English orchestras over the course of thirteen years. The four agreed, apparently for sentimental reasons, to appear on this occasion only; normally they gathered privately, once or twice a week, to play chamber music for each other.[21]

The "industrial" fairs of 1884, 1889, and 1891 also pulled private recreation into the public eye. Of the more serious artists, Stidum and Henry O. Tanner showed their works at the small Progressive Workingman's Club Fair of 1884; Edmonia Lewis was represented by a bust at the Quaker City Exposition of 1889, and two at Allen Chapel in 1891; Meta Vaux Warrick, who won her first artistic prize in 1899, was still too young to exhibit at any. Dorsey however missed none of them, and he was joined in the last two at least by dozens of hobbyists of all kinds. Robert Adger, Jr., contributed paintings on glass in 1889; Carl Bolivar showed watercolors and the professional draughtsman James G. Davis drawings in 1891. They were joined by many others less familiar in elite circles, people who worked in every medium and brought out oils and watercolors, woodcarvings, photographs, clay sculpture, pastels and crayons, china painting, and illustrated manuscripts in Gothic, medieval German, and Old English scripts. And the "artistic" was only one of sixteen prize categories in 1891, most of which were devoted to the various domestic arts, baking, quilting, needlework, and lace-making. Edwin Hill and Samuel Adger showed off their original musical scores; others exhibited model ships and steam engines, or handmade clocks; Clara Williams, aged 11, had built a mechanical wind-up dancing dog.[22]

Dorsey's own contributions were purely artistic, including portraits of the bandleader Frank Johnson and the slave rebel Cinque. But Jacob White, Jr., in 1891 put his own anti-slavery memorabilia on exhibit, and Adger some of his collection of portraits and pamphlets. Both of these men joined Dorsey later in the decade as local advisers to W. E. B. Du Bois, and after that as founders of the American Negro Historical Society; the fact that they had collections of their own is reminder that Dorsey's passion, while distinctive, was unique only in its size and breadth.[23]

Dorsey in fact created a network of his own, men and women who contributed materials to the files, books, pictures, scrapbooks, catalogues, and artifacts that must have occupied much of his quarters on Locust and then Dean Street. At least three of his Philadelphia contemporaries also made their own collections of clippings. Dorsey himself apparently fell heir to a miscellaneous scrapbook compiled by Ira D. Cliff, locally a well-known musician, between 1862 and 1866, and by 1877 the janitor Joseph Cathcart had accumulated 90 of them, ranging from two pages to 600. Adger, whose interests more nearly matched Dorsey's, was also an artist of sorts and kept a notable collection of rare books and memorabilia as well as clippings. Dorsey wrote to all of them, and they to him.[24]

The Dorsey files are in fact full of inquiries back and forth. He wanted a biography of Edmonia Lewis when she was still in her early twenties, and searched for a portrait of Crispus Attucks, killed in the Boston Massacre, until satisfied that there was none. The U.S. Commissioner of Education sent a bibliography on black education and authors. Ebenezer Bassett wanted some material on Frederick Douglass after the latter's death in 1895; the Reverend Alexander Crummell, virtually on his deathbed in 1898, wanted to see the whole collection. Others sent him materials, the musician A. S. Cassey old concert programs, his nephew Dorsey Seville—pending the postage—bundles of Washington newspapers. Indeed while he surely subscribed to several on his own, the fact that there are well over a hundred newspapers and magazines represented in the scrapbooks, from virtually every northeastern and southern state plus a few from the Midwest and California, suggests that he had many correspondents all over the country.[25]

Dorsey was nearing 60 when in the summer of 1896 W. E. B. Du Bois moved into the College Settlement near Seventh and Lombard, under a grant from the University of Pennsylvania to study the Afro-American community. It was only natural that Du Bois should seek him out, together with the other native Philadelphia intellectuals of his generation; Robert Adger, Jr., Jacob White, Jr., and W. Carl Bolivar. All of them had a demonstrable interest in history, Bolivar as author of the retrospective columns of the *Tribune,* and White as president of the Bird Association, whose sole purpose seems to have been the retelling of stories about the old days. A young lawyer friend, George Mitchell, and the Reverend H. L. Phillips, doubtless introduced to Du Bois through mutual contacts in settlement work, completed the young sociologist's list of local informants, who seem to have stimulated each other as well as him.[26]

Their help in guiding the young man about their city's past and present culminated for Du Bois in the epic *Philadelphia Negro,* and for them, in the fall of 1897, in the formation of the American Negro Historical Society. The initial meeting was held at Phillips's Church of the Crucifixion; A. S. Cassey, in the chair, gave way to T. J. Minton, who in turn deferred to Adger, as president. The Reverend Matthew Anderson was elected vice president; Phillips, treasurer; Edward F. Harris, recording secretary; Thomas P. Ringgold, corresponding secretary; and William Henry Dorsey, custodian.[27]

The election crowned his career as collector. The first part of the Society's stated object—"to collect relics, literature, and historical facts in connection with the African race . . ."—fit perfectly with what Dorsey had been doing over much of his lifetime. The second and more didactic part, which suggested an interest confined to matters ". . . illustrative of their progress and development," was perhaps too narrow for his own wide and honest curiosity, but he doubtless shared its optimistic assumptions. The surviving records of the ANHS suggest that, with perhaps characteristic diffidence, he did not introduce motions or speak out in debate. But once its collection was opened it seems that he drew no line between his own Afro-Americana and the Society's. Certainly he donated all of the initial autographs, and most of the portraits and artwork. And with the massive collection of scrapbooks growing faster than ever, stimulated by an audience of his peers, the custodian's job seems more appropriate than any other.[28]

But the majority of the city's Afro-Americans, their lives already cramped and dusty, did not share the historian's passion for libraries and reading rooms, and unlike Du Bois understood that during the hot months Philadelphia was not a place to come to but to escape from. Between June and October, in fact, the most popular form of recreation for all classes was the summer excursion. Wherever and however they went, all shared the urge to escape from the heat and congestion of their steaming neighborhoods.

Any direction might do for those who simply took a train or trolley for a day trip to a nearby picnic grove. Direction, distance, other company—none mattered much to courting couples who enjoyed the cool breezes provided by moonlit trips along the Delaware, on steamboats specially chartered by a lodge or club. At the other extreme, the Masonic Knights Templars sponsored trips all the way from Washington to Boston, the prices confining the company to elite passengers picked up along the way in Baltimore, Wilmington, Phila-delphia, Trenton, and New York. Full fare for fifteen days in the late September of 1889 was $12 round trip from the capital, with the last leg provided by the Fall River Steamer; excursionists would follow the parade-and-banquet route of the Washington Cadets and National Brass Band. Two years later, the pro-rated price quoted by thirteen local commandaries for a similar "Grand Pilgrimage and Excursion" was $8.67 from the Chestnut Street Depot, one apparent object, again, to knit together the leadership of the different cities en route.[29]

But the easiest popular trips were simply across the Delaware into New Jersey. One important attraction was the amusement park at Gloucester City, which ran direct ferry service to Philadelphia and offered swimming, rides, illegal gambling, and Sunday beer until shut down in the middle 1890s. Stockton Grove, in the black section of Camden, remained after the closing, reached by a short trolley ride tacked onto the ferry that left from the foot of Market Street every fifteen minutes. Major J. A. Wright chartered the Grove for several years in the late 1890s, inviting not only individuals but "all prominent social and political clubs in a body." The attractions in 1897 included racing for everything from fat men to bicycles, a jig, clog, and buck-dancing contest, and a "scientific exhibition" which pitted the alleged mid-dleweight boxing champion of Pennsylvania against the Major himself, billed as "the Beer man and All-Around Athletic of Philadelphia." Dance music was provided "all day, rain or shine," by the People's Orchestra; admission was just 25 cents, 15 cents for children. The inducement for clubs to come together was a special prize, on exhibit for five weeks at 11th and Lombard, for the "best appearing organization"; the Crescent Club had won the year before with uniform white flannel suits, white duck shoes, and light Stetson hats.[30]

But while Gloucester or Stockton was a relatively routine diversion, by far the most important goal of Philadelphia's excursionists was the Jersey shore. Several members of the city's black elite owned their own summer homes in New Jersey, while employers complained that once the summer turned hot, domestics could not be kept from following the salt breezes to the east. Certain days, often Thursdays, the traditional maids' day off, were set aside as, for example, "Colored People's Salt Water Day" at resorts presumably segregated the rest of the week. Above all, Atlantic City, where many Philadelphians had family and other connections, offered an array of amusements regardless of weather. And while visitors flocked to the boardwalk at any time, it was recognized that September—a little past the season and so the monthly equivalent of Thursday—was special to Afro-Americans.[31]

The Atlantic City correspondent of the *Times* believed in September of 1894 that the horde who had begun to arrive "on Thursday last" represented the "colored aristocracy of Philadelphia, Wilmington, and points throughout New Jersey." But the "aristocracy" judgment was perhaps based on the style displayed on the boardwalk; the crowd was too big to represent any small elite. John Diton's scheme to sell 500 last-minute counterfeit tickets for a single Masonic lodge excursion (the previous year he had gone undetected) gives some idea of the magnitude of the annual migration. The crowd on "opening day" alone was estimated at 10,000 in 1895, and 10,000 or 11,000 in 1899.[32]

The local merchants loved it, and a delegation came out to present the keys to the city in 1895. The excursionists stayed largely in segregated places on the lower end of the boardwalk, surrounded by an array of outdoor cooking stoves, and whole sections of the city, it was reported, were in effect abandoned to them. But in general, and certainly during "their" unofficial season, white visitors seem to have treated them as part of the show. A "colored baby contest" drew 50 entrants in 1896, viewed by thousands who enjoyed much "mirth-provoking excitement." By the late 1890s the evening crowds grew even bigger, as after a day of splashing in the surf the waltzing of earlier years gave way to cakewalking contests. If there was much patronage in all this it was the same ocean for all, and equally important the same boardwalk for a promenade. Excursion tickets cost just $1, or something less than a man's daily wage, but with amusement fees and especially clothing, one correspondent noted that many couples "had no doubt saved up for several months" to be able good-naturedly to "elbow the white folks" in style. They had earned the feeling, the piece went on, "that, for one day at least, they are there in the capacity of visitors and pleasure-seekers, with 'money to burn.'" One day in the sun, certainly a week or month, was after all better than none before the season ended and the chill returned.[33]

While surf-bathing was confined to the summer months, there were other active pastimes which could be enjoyed the year around. Philadelphia's blacks, many of them fresh from rural backgrounds, fished, crabbed, and hunted rabbits. The Virginia opossum, in the course of its own historic migration northward, had also reached the northernmost of southern cities, and possum hunting in the outskirts was another source of fun and meat. Children of course skipped rope, wrestled, raced, and invented things to do with balls of every size and shape. But the late 19th century marked the real beginnings of organized team sports and other commercial athletics, and—together with the crap and poker games that sparked assaults and murders—it was these that most made the news.[34]

The two oldest of professional sports, the ones with which Afro-Americans were especially identified, were boxing and horse racing. Boxing especially was popular in Philadelphia. But neither of these sports involved large numbers of people. And although the prize money had a powerful appeal to some young men, both were heavily clouded with problems.

Black success in thoroughbred racing was capped by the triumphs of the ex-slave Isaac Murphy, described in Chapter 1, but Murphy's career was no model for young men to follow. His net worth was estimated at $75,000 in 1888, $200,000 just two years later, either sum truly enormous even with a discount for the usual hyperbole. But like many of his fellows he was trapped in the atmosphere of gambling and corruption that had always haunted the sport. Even as a young man he had a reputation for drinking, and at a major race in Long Branch, New Jersey, in May of 1890 he simply fell off his heavily favored mount, Firenzi. His only defense was that someone had slipped something into the champagne which he had taken just before the gun, apparently to get a head start on the expected victory celebration. The claim inspired little confidence, and Murphy was then suspended for the season, disgraced, and demoted in effect to lesser mounts. Six years later he died at 35, "unloved and unmourned," shortly after another scandal at a meet in Coney Island.[35]

The example perhaps made little impression in Philadelphia, which had no flat racing of its own. But together with "fixers" and gamblers like "Majah" Teagle, several local black jockeys did suffer from the roughly simultaneous closing of the Glouscester Track across the river. More important, the mid-1890s were also marked by an intensified and largely successful drive to bar them from horse racing altogether, following the precedents in baseball and bike racing.[36]

Afro-American boxers, in contrast, although facing some parallel problems with prejudice, not only remained in the ring but continued to move up. But while John Durham boxed at Penn during the 1880s, much like his contemporary Teddy Roosevelt at Harvard, there was reason to draw a firm line between gentlemen amateurs and professional pugilists. Professional boxing, never more than quasi-legal in most states, was even more deeply shadowed by corruption than horse racing. And although young black men were eager to enter the arena, one of the very few open routes to quick fame and big money, their elders had some right to worry about the examples set by leading boxers such as George Dixon and Peter Jackson.

Dixon, "Little Chocolate," having won the bantamweight crown in 1890 at the age of 20 and the featherweight the next year, held the lightweight title throughout the 1890s, mostly by giving up serious bouts in favor of vaudeville exhibitions. After squandering a lifetime's earnings reported at $100,000, he

finally lost his championship too, by a knockout to "Terrible Terry" Mc-
Govern in January of 1900. Eight years later, still well short of 40, he died in the
alcoholic ward of New York's Bellevue Hospital.[37]

Peter Jackson's case was even more tragic, the result not of any fault of his
own but of the very nature of the sport that he graced with his wit and bearing.
Contemporary sportswriters were clearly fond of the Australian-born con-
tender, and while they agreed that he was a charming and convivial man, none
suggested, during his career, that he was addicted to liquor or otherwise
afflicted with the high living and weak livers blamed for killing Murphy and
Dixon. Nonetheless by 1896, only a couple of years after he was still actively
seeking the title, a reporter visiting Jackson in London noted that "when he lifts
his glass, his hands shake a little, and there is a curious halt now and then in his
speech." The syndrome, result of repeated blows to the head, was as sadly
familiar to that generation as to this one.[38]

The route up in Philadelphia was hard and sometimes demeaning, and role
models toward the top even less attractive than George Dixon. White "sports-
men" at the Oxford Social Club hired five black men in 1899 to stage what was
called "an old Roman sport," the "battle royal" of all against all until a single
"winner" crawled out of the ring. The Ariel Club, in 1892, staged a tournament
for Afro-American hopefuls in which the top prize was a janitorial job at the
club itself—far richer, in fact, than most available purses. Meanwhile Joe
Butler, the city's leading heavyweight and sometime Republican party bul-
lyboy, was repeatedly arrested for assault, threats, and larceny; in 1899 the
police officially labeled him "a dangerous professional thief." And his older
contemporary, Walter Edgerton, "De Kentucky Rosebud," lived out still
another of the hazards of a boxing career.[39]

Edgerton continually challenged Dixon to meet him for the lightweight title
during the middle 1890s, and fought professionally at various other weights.
But like many boxers his reputation had been based first and foremost on his
status as the toughest kid in the neighborhood, and under pressure he was more
concerned with the championship of Lombard Street than of the world at large.
During the spring of 1894 he heard a lot of talk from John Henry Johnson, who
wanted that title for himself. On June 10 Johnson finally confronted Edgerton
in Weaver's cigar store, and "De Rosebud" put up his fists. But when the challenger invoked his own rules by backing his claim with a pool cue Edgerton
topped that with a pistol and shot him in the face. The wound was only superficial, but "De Rosebud" left too quickly to discover that, and fled to Atlantic
City where, obviously unnerved, he nearly drowned the next day in the surf.[40]

The only saving grace in fighting was that it was always a democratic sport,
open to any young man tough enough to draw attention to himself. In the
absence of playgrounds, gymnasia, and space, many Afro-Americans could
not easily exercise their athletic potential, and most sports were played by
teams organized as clubs.

The most important of these were the Pythians, the pioneering baseball team which flourished during the 1860s. The main problem in the early days was finding a field. More heavily concentrated in the densely settled downtown area than later, black men in the 1860s could not safely enjoy the green pastures of nearby South Philadelphia on account of the "deadline" set up along Bainbridge Street by hostile Irish-Americans. They had then to cross the Delaware into Camden, or the Schuylkill into Fairmount Park. Perhaps one reason why the Pythians emerged as a single club of several nines, absorbing earlier rivals, was simply that there was safety in numbers.[41]

The game as they played it was relatively expensive, beginning with club dues of $5 for active members and $1 for inactive supporters. This initial outlay, and the need to buy equipment, was compounded by the expenses involved in visiting and then entertaining in return other Afro-American teams from Washington to Chicago and back again to New England, and ensured that the Pythians remained essentially an elite organization. But they were serious about their level of play, and in the time-honored manner of athletic clubs both discouraged inferior players, shaming poor Daniel Adger into resignation, and recruited good ones from out of town, doubtless finding ways of paying their dues. By 1867 Captain Catto noted that "the white fraternity"—presumably including the national champion Philadelphia Athletics, whose facilities they amicably shared—were showing "considerable interest, and not a little anxiety" about their prowess. They could not settle the matter on the field, however, and two years later they were officially barred from playing the organized white teams in the state, a prelude to the later color bar in professional baseball. Perhaps it was this blow, perhaps Catto's murder, that killed the club, but there are few records of the Pythians after 1870.[42]

Baseball itself, however, did not die but grew in popularity. As racial hostilities eased enough to allow them onto playing fields, more and more young Philadelphians learned to play the game. At the purely amateur level, where enthusiasm was more important than technique, ball games of one sort or another were a regular feature of the picnicking excursions that filled the summer months. Beyond that, matches between organized teams were advertised attractions at amusement parks, and by the 1880s several men from the city were involved in the success of the professional "Cuban" Giants.[43]

One result of the great growth of spectator sports during the late 19th century, and the parallel growth of newspaper sports reporting, was that the more informal games were ignored in favor of those which pitted formally organized teams against each other. Football is an example, a game impossible to play without the kind of equipment and coaching sponsored by a school or club. Afro-Americans did play football by the late 19th century; Lincoln University, although small in size, went undefeated in 1898, finishing its season by beating a town club, the Media Volunteers, which had not previously lost a match in eight years. But there were apparently no black clubs in Philadelphia itself; instead young Afro-Americans were accepted early onto mostly white school and college teams. Some, too, for better and worse, were not only accepted but actively recruited.[44]

During the 1880s a student-athlete like John Durham simply played games for fun. Philadelphia's Crescent Club provided some expert training in track as well as boxing, and in 1890 William H. Warrick, while an undergraduate at Penn, won the gold medal in the 440-yard dash at the state college championship meet. However Warrick earned his way through college, he was a strong student, on his way to a useful career in medicine. But during the 1890s, as college athletics became a business, the business of purely athletic scholarships was born, and from then on many of the young men involved, amateurs only in theory, got college educations only in theory. By 1903 one such youngster, still in school, was described as a "wonderful colored sprinter whom the colleges covet," while in 1899 another at Central Manual Training, already shunted off the usual, and in that era highly demanding, academic high-school track was nonetheless ticketed for Penn simply because of his talents as a football player. Once there, as illustration of the irrational patterns of racial prejudice in its heyday, he and other black players could expect to mix blood and sweat with young white gentlemen in a physical closeness matched only by boxers, with the significant variation that half the players were teammates who left the arena together, sharing either the ectasy of victory or the agony of defeat, and then, presumably, the showers.[45]

But football was not really a city game, and while some local schools were beginning to play basketball there were still no playgrounds to play it on, and no record of black participation. None of the big team sports then, excepting the more informal versions of baseball, could have involved more than a tiny minority of poor people in Philadelphia. But during the 1890s fairly large numbers of Afro-Americans, long familar with club and competition, managed to turn the new pastime of bicycle riding into a team sport.

Whites as well as blacks of course joined in the new fad for bike riding, and established clubs of their own. While in 1894 the American League of Wheelmen voted to bar Afro-American members they could not bar them from the sport, and in Philadelphia it was in fact heavily identified with blacks. There was no need for open fields; much of the downtown was newly paved, and straight and level city streets were ideal places on which to race and to attract spectators. Black men dominated the police department's "bicycle squad," established it seems both to chase fleeing criminals and to enforce the speed laws. The papers were intrigued especially by the fact that Afro-American women, characteristically and uniquely, had by 1894 established a racing club of their own, the Stars of Hope, whose "waving skirts of various hues" were a familiar sight on Lombard, Locust, Chestnut, and Broad streets.[46]

As of 1892 there were only three black clubs in the city, beginning with the Ebon, founded by the bicycling cops. But the sport was growing in popularity, and while many could not afford their own bikes to take on long jaunts through the countryside, large groups could rent two or three for the day and race each other in relays. And by October 1898, when the Germantown Colored Wheel Club held an open meet, it drew others from all over the city. Races were held at three different distances, the third-of-a-mile and mile for both novices and experts, the five-mile for experts only, with some events handicapped, each with prizes for win, place, and show. Not only the numbers but the status of the participants suggests that the sport was far more democratic than baseball had been thirty years earlier. Of the nineteen men who finished among the top three in one or more heats, only three, Harry Anderson, C. C. Morgan, and Albert Smith, had surnames which matched those of the city's male elite in either the 1860s or 1890s, as described in the previous chapter.[47]

However hard it is to define "social class" in black Philadelphia, respectability was one of its elements, and respectabililty, in turn, was defined in part by the way in which people enjoyed themselves, the games they played, the music they listened to, the way they danced. Some of the elements of respectability were universal, matters in part of association and in part of economics: shooting craps or pool was less reputable than playing whist or billiards, just as champagne and oysters were preferred over hoecakes and beer. But among Afro-Americans there was another and unique dimension to respectability, even identity. This was the one which ran along a cultural spectrum with white European forms at one end and rural black at the other. The more articulate, at the beginning of the period, clearly favored the former, but attitudes toward both of them changed over time. In dance and music, most obviously, the men and women who lived in black Philadelphia increasingly adopted a style of their own which redefined, in some ways defiantly, their historic relationship to the dominant culture. The new style inevitably owed much both to America's European heritage and to their own southern and perhaps ultimately African origins. But it was more contemporary than either, distinctively urban, and definitely black.

The new style was not intended to drive out all others, and some Philadelphians clung to older traditions throughout. At one end of the social scale there were migrants who held tight to earlier southern forms, in religion and speech as in music, people like the worshippers at the Pleasant Valley Mission. At the other there were people like Fanny Jackson Coppin, the elder William Still, and many ministers of the Gospel, who simply never appeared at balls, plays, concerts, or musicals, and gave no clues to their tastes in secular entertainment.

But the simpler forms of rural music, with instruments limited to percussion and perhaps banjo, were continually being complicated by life in the city. As noted earlier, the fact that urban blacks turned their backs on this part of their past was not directly a repudiation of African roots but, contemporaries

reported, because the South represented slavery and subservience, everything
they hoped to put behind them. There was no need to add that as in every
incoming group younger migrants, or their children, were easily attracted to
the varieties of big-city entertainment.

At the other end of the social spectrum, while some may have held aloof
from the new urban style, it was easy for others to make the transition because,
excluding the purely rural forms, class differences in musical taste were no
greater than the differences in income.

Easy movement among styles and genres was shared by the dominant
society, in which the now familiar gulf between popular and patrician tastes
was just beginning to widen irrevocably toward the very end of the century.
Before the Civil War, while folk music was sung at home and at work (and
collected by some intellectuals), and while minstrel shows spread popular tunes
across the country, the greatest theatrical applause was reserved for foreign
artists like Jenny Lind, who performed in what we now consider the "classical"
European tradition. While a kind of cultural conflict grew after the war, it was
conducted not so much between devotees of Tin Pan Alley and the classics but
between those whose programs featured or at least mixed in "light" works,
such as Strauss waltzes or the more accessible Italian arias, and those purists
who increasingly insisted on uncompromising standards, full operas, and
highly trained symphonic orchestras. Meanwhile across most of the country
Shakespeare alternated with *Uncle Tom's Cabin* at local "Opera Houses," or
the two were cheerfully mixed together in bits and pieces, while patrons in beer
gardens drank and chatted indiscriminately to operatic selections and barbershop harmonies.[48]

For most of the late 19th century, Philadelphia's blacks were distinguished
only by two extreme developments. One was the degree of audience participation, a custom which reached self-parody in those mixed bills which alternated
dramatic recitations, violin solos, and various comic contests. The other was
the degree to which a few tens of thousands of people generated so many
musicians who were able to master the classical European canon, an achievement especially remarkable given the practical handicaps imposed by poverty.
Frank Johnson had been above all a bandleader, at a time when serious
composers were equally at home with band and orchestra, in part one suspects
because cornets were cheaper than cellos. While churches built organs privately
owned pianos were expensive, and as late as the 1860s Carl Bolivar remembered
that despite the wealth of local singing talent white pianists were hired to play
the more important concerts. In fact one event used in part to define the city's
Afro-American elite in Chapter 10, the grand complimentary concert held for
Madame Mary L. Brown in 1860, featured solo and classical duets by Brown
and Elizabeth Greenfield accompanied by a (white) Professor Keonig on an
instrument, the program notes, "kindly loaned" by a nearby white merchant.[49]

Both of these traditions—audience participation and mastery of the standard classical repertoire—were combined in concert balls, the most characteristic secular entertainments recorded in the Dorsey Collection. It would be hard to exaggerate either the number of balls held or the number of musicians who played them between the Civil War and the turn of the century. Every major club and lodge held its own affair, from the Pythians in the 1860s to the Ebon Wheelmen in the 1890s, some of them more than once a year; Van Dyke Dorsey, during 1879, served as secretary of the Apollo Social Club, which held dances every month. But no formal organization was required, and ad hoc balls or parties were held at every social level. Some of William Still's young elite tormentors took over Liberty Hall in 1869 for a Grand Valentine's Day Ball Masque to celebrate "the patron saint of billing and cooing": the entertainment was led by the hosts, "Bob Madger," "Billy Minty," "Davy Bowserup," and "Prof. Ogeessee de Cattoguttee." Twenty-one years later Laura Shepard promoted a more modest affair at her own place on Davis Court for just a dime; "rent parties," to help meet the bills, were routine events at least by 1902. Even prostitutes apparently advertised. Unless the sponsors were naïvely ignorant of the term "calico dance," as applied to "disorderly" occasions which mixed blacks and whites, that was surely the meaning of the "Grand Calico Leap Year Reception" held at Natatorium Hall in March of 1884.[50]

Prices varied. The most expensive quoted in the Dorsey Collection was for an 1870 ball and reception sponsored by the Union Beneficial Association, headed by James Field Needham; a ticket cost $3, but that included all refreshments and perhaps admitted not one but two. Usually 50 cents, sometimes 25 cents, children always half-price, was enough to get Benjamin Oliver's Orchestra, for example, in a swinging garden hung from the ceiling, plus several other entertainments. A dollar was extraordinary, the price of a special musicale and reception sponsored by the Hotel Brotherhood in 1892 for which F. J. R. Jones brought in an orchestra of sixty pieces; before the dancing seriously began the audience was treated to a military band, Miller's and Guinn's Quartettes, humorous and Shakespearean recitations, and assorted duos and soloists. But these extras aside, through the middle of the 1890s the formula for the major events was essentially the same for the Hod Carriers' Ball as for the Pennsylvania Beneficial Association and others with more elite membership lists.[51]

The big balls were always held on week nights, usually Thursday, perhaps because weekend rentals were more expensive. They ran from 9 or 10 usually until 4 in the morning, and newspaper accounts suggest that the ballgoers did in fact "dance until dawn," with no thought for the fact that work would begin again shortly after. Food and drink were either continuously available or included as part of a banquet, with band or string music and singers alternating with formal dance sets, and many people for reduced prices admitted to the galleries as spectators, without access to the floor. At every social level the women listed as present, married, widowed, or single greatly outnumbered the men; even at the highly elite Douglas Hospital ball in 1897, excluding the patrons and patronesses and people from out of town, those mentioned in the papers included 13 married couples, 6 single men, 10 unescorted wives or widows, and 10 single women. In some settings, Du Bois agreed with William Dorsey, many of the extra women were prostitutes. More generally the imbalance, much bigger than the modest female edge in the census figures, was simply another sign of the independence enjoyed by black women, who needed no escorts to go dancing. And as the *People's Advocate* observed of an 1878 reception for Ebenezer Bassett, held by his former students at the Institute for Colored Youth, when having a good time they were "not held back by those restraints common to a mixed company," in the late Victorian era.[52]

A concert ball required a master of ceremonies, but after the orchestra leader the most important person advertised in the bills was the floor manager, often one of the community's several dancing masters, who might employ two or even six assistants to help organize one or more grand marches in the course of the evening. Together with the sergeant-at-arms he was also responsible for keeping the standard promise: "Good Order Will Be Strictly Maintained." Violence, even murder, occasionally resulted from arguments over who should lead the figure at the more raffish events, and the obituary of frequent floor manager James Augustus, at his death in 1890, stressed that he was both "magnetic and brave."[53]

Most of these customs, with some special variations, were directly derived from the formal dances held by the city's white elite in the same era. Most striking, too, so were the music and the dances. While some of the quartette singing or instrumental entertainment featured popular American favorites, the actual dance music, and the dances themselves, were always European in origin. The dancing academies all taught these: the one run by Mrs. F. J. R. Jones charged admission for its closing exercises in 1890, where at Natatorium Hall the "little misses" performed the "Spanish Cachucha" and the "young masters" the "Sailor's Hornpipe."[54]

But while the social dances listed on concert-ball programs were always polka, mazurka, schottische, waltz, and later two-step, there is no question that despite the common names these were simply not the same steps or done in the same way as at the white assembly balls. Those spectator galleries at big events were filled not only with blacks who chose to sit out the dances but dozens and even hundreds of white observers. Some of these perhaps came to pick out prostitutes, others to titter at maids in borrowed finery. But a major motive was surely the simple fact that the show on the floor was not available anywhere else, especially as the "waltz, plain" gave way later in the evening to the "waltz, glide," the "waltz, gallop," and the "waltz, polka."

These and other unnameable Afro-American variations on the basic forms doubtless grew out of others continually being practiced in parlors, hallways, and the back rooms of speakeasies, at private parties and on street corners. Jigs and clogs, the buck-and-wing, were done not by couples but by single performers, often in a highly competitive spirit. The next step was simply to translate the same kind of competition into the bigger social events. By January of 1891 the Young Men's Social Club, inviting all others to attend their regular monthly "in full regalia," advertised Professor Samuel Grubb's exhibition of "one of his old Scotch dances." But the major attraction was that prizes would be awarded to the two couples who best showed off the new "mirror waltz." And the step after that, taken for the first time later that year, was to bring out the cakewalk, taking it to Horticultural Hall for its first public performance in the city.[55]

The cakewalk, most characteristic dance of the century's last decade, was distinguished by two things from the start. One was that the element of contest was built into it, that it was never performed at major events except in competition. The other, more important, was that it was undeniably Afro-American in origin. Contemporaries traced it back to Louisiana; the *Press* first found it in Philadelphia late in 1876. At that time it simply involved couples with linked arms, sometimes of the same sex, stepping in time to unaccompanied singing around a table laden with two iced cakes. The pairs judged the "most graceful" and the "most eccentric" then took the cakes. Unlike directly commercial forms of entertainment its geographical movement was evidently slow; the New York *Times* reported it a novelty in both the big city and rural Georgia as late as 1884. But by December of 1892, sometime after the historic debut at Horticultural Hall, the contestants were fully into the spirit. A newspaper piece reported on favorites and contenders preparing as though they were racehorses, with dancing masters cast as trainers, and all couples handicapped equally by the fact that the parlors of Lombard Street were too small to maneuver in, while public practice, on the street itself, might tip competitors to their routines. The real craze for the cakewalk only arrived, however, when it was linked to another and parallel development in music.[56]

In music as in dance, the big public performances tended to lag behind what was done in more intimate settings. One key was the versatility and experimental opportunities offered by privately owned pianos, which however rare in the 1860s were widely advertised in Afro-American newspapers by the 1880s. Gil Ball's insistence on providing piano music for "calico" dancing upstairs was the major offense in the list which cost him his saloonkeeper's license in the summer of 1890, and precisely the same issue plagued the other licensed blacks as most of them, too, were legally pushed out of the business later in the decade. White as well as black denizens of the city's vice districts clearly believed that Afro-Americans were doing something distinctive on the piano by that time; it was as customary in Philadelphia's Tenth Ward as along Bourbon or Beale Street to hire black men to play in bawdy houses staffed mainly with white prostitutes.[57]

All this was background to the emergence of the "coon songs" of the late

1890s. Scholars may trace some of the elements of the new genre to "pseudo-Negro" sources as early as the 1880s, but its real popularity with both races, all over the country, may be dated from the immense success enjoyed by Ernest Hogan's 1896 hit "All Coons Look Alike to Me." Musically an early version of ragtime, the coon songs introduced Americans to a new kind of syncopated rhythm, a device then wholly novel. This in turn, as it happened, fit perfectly with the already established cakewalk. And as the two together reinforced each other's popularity they also posed a dilemma for Philadelphia's Afro-American elite, and the musicians who customarily played for them. On the one hand there was much pride in Hogan, a man "without a drop of white blood in his veins," who reportedly earned $25,000 in just three months from singing and selling his song. On the other hand the rhythms of the new music were strange, its origins suspect, and its words potentially as offensive as the name of the genre as a whole.[58]

The great affair of the 1897 season, the first after the coon songs began to take off, was not calculated to introduce them to ballgoers at the Academy. A benefit for the new Douglass Clinic, its organizing committee composed of doctors, lawyers, and pharmacists and its list of patrons studded with white well-wishers, the ball brought out a number of people who did not ordinarily dance at all. With all that, the program was still less rigid than those of the previous decade. For the Odd Fellows in 1889, for example, Oliver's Orchestra had provided three sets of eight dances each, with "Waltz, plain" followed by "Waltz, Redowa," "Quadrille, Lanciers," and so on through the evening. For the Douglass affair, in contrast, following a musicale and presentations, F. J. R. Jones played a number of the newer two-steps by American composers, including John Phillip Sousa, to vary the more traditional promenades by Bach and Verdi, a Hill gavotte, and waltzes by Strauss and Waldteufel. But with 1500 guests and a distinguished gallery of whites and blacks, including Police Chief Francis Linden in a purely social-philanthropic capacity, it was no time to bring out the coon songs.[59]

The next April however, with neither white patrons nor the more strait-laced Afro-Americans to worry about, the Hotel Brotherhood pulled out the stops. The guest list was not identical to that for the Douglass ball; the Mossells, the Stills, and many others who had come out for charity would not normally go to the Brotherhood's or any other ordinary ball. But there was a good deal of overlap, and John Washington was floor leader for both. The orchestra was led not by the veteran Jones but by Benjamin Oliver, a younger associate who sometimes played cornet with Jones and Hamilton Moore in the classical Philadelphia Octette. And the program was full of coon songs, the audience reveling in an old tradition of self-mockery with "The Black Four Hundred Ball," "Hesitate, Mr. Nigger, Hesitate," and "I Don't Care If You Nebber Comes Back." The *Tribune*, nostalgically reviewing fourteen years of Brotherhood balls, declared this one "the premier of them all."[60]

The cakewalk by that time had long been established as a fixture at Afro-American entertainments, rivaling and sometimes replacing the grand march as the high point of balls. In Atlantic City contests were often held nightly, sometimes featuring contestants from ten different states. The "most eccentric" category, translated as best or most extravagantly dressed, fit easily into the more informal competitions held continuously on the boardwalk. Even the kimono-clad inhabitants of the Japanese Teahouse were tempted to enter the fray. Most important, the addition of the seductive new rhythm of the coon songs helped pull formerly passive white spectators onto the floor.[61]

The contagious combination of song and dance swept both into wholly new places. The rage was not confined to Atlantic City; beginning in 1897, it conquered Saratoga, Newport, and Tuxedo Park, where society matrons hired black instructors to help them master the moves. The New York *Journal*, in the interests of democracy, enlisted the great Afro-American minstrel team of Williams and Walker to pose for step-by-step photographs to benefit those who wanted to learn "the real old darkey style" without the aid of private tutors. Philadelphia socialites, inevitably, put on a full-dress parody of a black contest, with winners taking the cake while second and third place finishers had to settle for a possum and chicken respectively.[62]

But the significance of the fad went beyond the obvious opportunities for mockery, too often seized by white songwriters and publishers. It went beyond, too, the popularity of the music, or the cakewalk, both passing phenomena. What was really important were the attitudes embodied in the lyrics, which have stayed with us ever since, both as the stuff of stereotype and as part of our popular culture.

The theme of Hogan's original hit was familiar enough in real life, but up to then not in popular song. The lyrics of "All Coons Look Alike to Me" are voiced by a woman who tells a lover essentially that he can be exchanged for anyone else who can afford her. Variations of the same sentiment were suggested by many and maybe most of the songs. The lyrics might be sung by a woman to an admirer: "If you haven't any money / You needn't come around." They might turn it around and suggest the very opposite relationship between the sexes: "She must follow with the 'dough' / When he's high on 'tick.'" And the woman in one song, having gotten a sealskin coat from one impulsive suitor the day after they met, made it quite clear that she was not interested in the bonds of matrimony: "What's the use of being in a hurry with a man, / When you know that you have got him 'dead'?"[63]

Some of the impact of all this may be seen through a hostile piece written by an anxious mother, Winifred Black, which suggests that white reaction was composed of elements more complicated than either simple admiration or condescension. Published in the *Journal* during 1898, the title was "SONGS THAT NEED LYNCHING: And Yet We Let Our Daughters Sing Them." The author was willing to tolerate May Irwin's (white) renditions in an appropriate or music-hall setting. But she was appalled to learn that the Band of Hope at a local YWCA not only planned to put on its own show but had turned down such relatively innocent pieces as "My Gal's a High Born Lady" for genuine hardcore material: "Get Your Money's Worth," and "I'se de Hottest Baby in de Bunch." And that was only the beginning: the music was everywhere, at church socials and girls' boarding schools; her own young daughter had been to a birthday party where one little blue-eyed blonde—this was still the era of live performance in the parlor—had belted out the lyrics to "Take Your Clothes and Go."[64]

The coon songs, then, not only changed the nature of the Afro-American influence on popular culture but began the process of changing the nature of the culture itself. Unlike the earlier minstrel songs they were undeniably authentic, contemporary products, like the increasing use of the word "coon" itself, of the post–Civil War era. This was distinctly city music, piano music. Neither derived from a distant source nor diluted, it was simply itself, written out of immediate experience with a commercial audience in mind. Almost two decades before Bessie Smith it expressed a toughly unsentimental, characteristically urban attitude toward life and sexuality. In an age that had thought "Annie Laurie" deathless, its widespread acceptance amounted to a mini-revolution in popular culture. At the same time its reception was conflicted, real white admiration balanced not only with the usual condescension but with other and more troubled overtones.

Philadelphia's Afro-American community, despite its small size and limited resources, was culturally and socially complicated, and by no means all of its members were enthusiastic about the new musical fad. But it was widely accepted, and together with other developments may be taken to mark the beginning of a new age.

By the early 20th century, blacks all over the country had survived what one historian has called "the nadir," the period from 1877 to 1901 marked by growing racism all over, tightening segregation in many places, and in the South disenfranchisement and lynching. But even for the southern majority, second-class citizenship was better than none at all, and these setbacks could not erase the undeniable advances made since the Civil War, the continued progress of literacy, and the achievement of such basic civil rights as legal marriage and property ownership. In Philadelphia and other northern cities, meanwhile, despite many setbacks and in particular the continued exclusion from the modern industrial sector of the economy, the multiplication of cultural, educational, and political achievements made the same years undeniably the most hopeful in the Afro-American urban experience.

In the early years, the 1860s and 1870s, men like Robert Purvis and Isaiah Wears had rejected the very notion of race, even of a group name which would distinguish those of African descent from other Americans. But the failure of

Reconstruction had made it clear that while progress would continue it would be slower than previously hoped, and that the end of prejudice and stereotyping, in particular, was nowhere on the horizon. By the 1890s, finally, the coon songs, in their own way, represented the recognition and even defiant acceptance of a separate group identity. This was the same cultural acceptance represented at the same time at other levels by a reawakened if still limited interest in an African homeland, the enormous growth of distinctively black organizations, the very word "Afro-American."

Cultural ties to the dominant civilization, and the need for material white help, were too important to be rejected. But as southerners kept moving north into the urban future, creating what we now call "ghettos" out of more mixed and scattered settlements, it was clear that the old patterns would have to give way to a new stress on economic and cultural self-reliance. The new message was not as optimistic as the older faith in deliverance through some combination of divine intervention, white politics, and philanthropy. But it was more realistic than either that or the dominant contemporary predictions of racial extinction. And it gave at least some ground for believing in the familiar funeral epitaph, that "Morning was ever the daughter of night."

Postscriptum

William Henry Dorsey lived through the first two decades of the twentieth century, still at 206 Dean Street, still an "artist" in the city directories, still as alone as when Virginia and their remaining children moved out during the 1890s. For the city's Afro-American community as a whole these were years of accelerated population growth, and of continued social development along lines already laid out. But for Dorsey himself, and his beloved American Negro Historical Society, they were years of decline.

The society, like its custodian, lasted into 1923. But while it acquired the papers of some of its own leading members, Jacob White, Jr., Isaiah Wears, and William Still, all of whom died between its founding and 1903, the surviving records indicate little activity beyond that date. That is the same year in which almost all of Dorsey's own scrapbook clippings end, and suggests a link. The link cannot be proven, but while there is no way of showing conclusively just why he stopped most work so long before his death, there is at least a clue among his effects.[65]

A little "rent-book" found among the other Dorsey materials at Cheyney State University, and dated 1904, was used mostly to record not collections but "Thoughts," in a shaky hand. Whether or not consciously modeled on the "Pensées" of Blaise Pascal, these consist of 30 short numbered observations or aphorisms, most of them religious in spirit: "I am a part of the 'All'"; "Any man with the breath of God in him is a master, not a slave"; "Si vis amari, ama (Sin)." A number of them deal with the conquest of physical infirmity, one twice repeated, as numbers 6 and 24: "I possess health because I possess God. 'I am.'" Several deal with images of light, one with a metaphor involving the optic nerve. Number 15 reads:

> If you want to get well
> Strongly enough to believe
> That you are well
> No power in the universe
> Can keep you from being well. (Eyes)[66]

Progressive blindness, in an artist and voracious reader, would account for the apparent and tragic inactivity of the last twenty years of Dorsey's life. For a time he still recorded some events of importance. The short book entirely devoted to the local protest against *The Clansman*, for example, is dated 1906, and there are a few other scattered items, in other books, with datelines after 1903. But the last series of clippings, of the tens of thousands which survive, is in a small scrapbook with the handwritten title "Horner Murder Case, Camden, N.J. 1907."[67]

This final book deals with the robbery-murder, on August 20, of a white farmwife, Mrs. Frances Horner, in her isolated home just east of Cooper's Creek. Two young black men were arrested. One, an ex-hand on the Horner place, confessed to the crime; the other denied it. A jury convicted both after an hour's deliberation on September 2. The last clipping in the collection deals with their execution on the morning of December 17, an event which helped rate an extra edition of the *Bulletin* only because it marked the inauguration of the state's new electric chair. Both men went calmly, after prayer. The historic first victim was Charles Gibson, the one who confessed. The second, having spent much of his jail time reading, continued to profess his innocence to the end, after writing a series of last letters "in a remarkably good hand." His name was Steven Dorsey, but he told the authorities nothing about his background, and the relationship, if any, is impossible to establish.[68]

Part IV

WILLIAM DORSEY'S CITY
AND OURS

Historians write about the past, but they and their readers live in the present, and especially when facing issues of such contemporary importance as black city life they cannot escape the connections between the two. In my case I have found it impossible to research, read about, and especially in their own words to hear the people of William Henry Dorsey's world without seeing shadows, hearing echoes, and being forced to look at both past and future from the perspective of my own time. And my intention in this final part is to use less of the impersonal historian's voice and more of my own to suggest some observations about the relation between Dorsey's world and ours.

I was born a century after he was, but the late 19th-century city has been the focus of most of my career as writer and scholar. Equally important, late 20th-century Philadelphia is the place in and near which I have spent most of my working life, and as a white observer and sometimes participant have most directly seen, felt, and otherwise encountered the modern black struggle for full inclusion. Writing this book has given me a fuller appreciation of the black city and its landmarks, both physical and intangible. It has also made me reflect on the history which stretches between the late 19th and the late 20th centuries and on projections for the future of the great majority of Afro-Americans who now live in cities. These reflections are partly based on some of the same kinds of sources collected by William Dorsey, beginning with the newspapers and other journals. But in this part, finally, my understanding of the city and the African-American condition is also based, as his was, on personal history and observation, on walking and talking and experiencing the city. I am not an insider, as he was, and other people, with other backgrounds, may hear different echoes from the past, and have different visions of the present and future. There is no pretending that my own are free from subjective bias, and every historian knows the dangers involved in trying to predict the course of future events. But much of what follows is based on solid information, from people whose direct experience is wider than mine, and all of it is a serious effort to understand a set of serious issues.[1]

Chapter 12

Survivals and Evolution: The Black City Today

The African-American population of this country is now officially counted at about 12 percent of the whole, almost precisely what it was in 1870, the first census following the Civil War and emancipation from slavery. But its geographical setting since then has changed dramatically, as result of the movement out of southern and rural areas into cities across the country. In Philadelphia, during these six generations, the black percentage has risen from perhaps 3 to about 40 percent of the whole. But the old city, once in the forefront, is now less a leading than a representative metropolis, as except perhaps for the severity of its current fiscal plight it ranks not at the top but toward the middle of a host of statistical indices used to compare the bigger cities with each other.[1]

More than a century's worth of history has of course brought great changes in the nature and context of the black experience. Here as elsewhere the two most obvious developments have been the growth of local political power and the move from an industrial to a service-based economy. Both of these present great future challenges, but they can be understood only after a look at some of the other aspects of black city life. One way to begin is to look at some of the direct and evolutionary survivals from the previous century, the way in which they fit into the wider city and indeed nation, as prelude to the history which has brought us to this point.

The current state of William Dorsey's city, the places where he and his neighbors went to school and church, the less tangible culture that they helped to develop and share, represents much of the wider history of the black city over the past three generations. Despite all the great national and international changes wrought over that time, and closer to home a black population perhaps fifteen times bigger than it had been, physically and institutionally Philadelphia is still recognizably the same place in which he helped form the American Negro Historical Society in 1897. The city then had officially about 1,200,000 residents, not much smaller than the 1,600,000 entering the 1990s, and many of its major landmarks, beginning with City Hall, are still in place. So, too, are many of the features of the specifically black city of the 19th century, although often changed with time.

In some ways the fate of the historical materials collected by Dorsey and his contemporaries represents much of what has happened to black history in general, with decades of neglect, some of it irreparable, followed by a more recent burst of interest, still uneven and not fully secure. The American Negro Historical Society, after many years of slow decay, finally died in obscurity when he did, in 1923. While some of the Society's original collection has been saved by the Historical Society of Pennsylvania, and Wellesley College now owns many of the books once kept by its first president Robert Adger, Adger's scrapbooks, much of Jacob White, Jr.'s collection, and Carl Bolivar's entire library have all been lost. Dorsey's own collection, meanwhile, after having disappeared for decades, has experienced a kind of partial and precarious resurrection.[2]

What remains of the collection was accidentally rediscovered at Cheyney State University, successor to Dorsey's alma mater, the Institute for Colored Youth, among the effects of longtime President Dr. Leslie Pinckney Hill. The timing was good; when, in 1976, the whole dusty pile was rescued from a drastic office cleaning, years after Hill's own death, the long moribund interest in African-American history was riding high. The university, after some delay, was able in 1980–81 to get a federal grant of more than $50,000 to preserve the materials for use. For much it was too late; the physical objects described by contemporaries, bricks and regalia, many scrapbooks, and, above all, the African-American portraits and other pictures bought or painted by Dorsey himself cannot be found. The remaining books and catalogues were however catalogued themselves, and biographical clippings saved; above all, most of the now brittle and yellowing scrapbooks, including all but a few of those dealing with black subjects, were skillfully preserved on microfilm. But while interest in black history beginning in the 1960s and 1970s was big enough to inspire the establishment of several local institutions and many books, financial support by the 1980s was running low, and the grant money ran out before either the microfilming or cataloguing was finished.[3]

Family legend has it that the collection was carted off and dumped on Hill by William's son Thomas, for whose generation it was simply a messy hobby which consumed space, and time, better devoted to other things. And Hill himself was properly concerned with not preserving but breaking with the past. Beginning in 1913 as successor to Hugh Browne, the Booker T. Washington disciple who had presided over the removal of the ICY from the city itself, Dr. Hill took the Institute one step further by guiding it out of management by the

Society of Friends into sponsorship by the Commonwealth of Pennsylvania. Renamed Cheyney State College after its new location, it served as an unofficially segregated school inside the state teachers' college system for several decades, somehow surviving as a virtually all-black institution even when the rest of the system, after Hill's retirement in 1951, was at least formally desegregated during the 1950s and 1960s. During the late 1980s it fell on hard times, the result in part of financial mismanagement, some of it related to an overemphasis on athletic teams, and lost its formal accreditation. After its expenses were cut back, however, and its academic program strengthened, Cheyney regained its accreditation in the spring of 1989. It then enters the last decade of the 20th century, in a climate which again encourages African-American self-help, with a student body of about 1200 and a good chance to survive.[4]

Lincoln University, meanwhile, the other nearby black institution which had flourished during the late 19th century, is in an even stronger position. As a private institution it was never pressed to change its black student body, although like Cheyney these days it does have a few white students. The historic issue at Lincoln, first raised in the 1880s by the Mossell and Still brothers, Stephen Gipson, and other Philadelphia graduates, was rather the hiring of black faculty and administrators. The first African-American professor was hired finally in 1931, the first president, Horace Mann Bond, in 1945. William Dorsey's great-grandson, Professor William Johnson, served until the mid-1980s as chair of the Chemistry Department. Always attractive to students from all over the United States and Africa, Lincoln's impressive roster of 20th-century graduates includes Langston Hughes, Thurgood Marshall, and the first presidents of the independent states of Nigeria and Ghana. While in even better position than Cheyney to take advantage of the renewed interest in black collegiate education, its current president, first woman to hold the post, has been warned by undergraduates to stress not past glories but present needs.[5]

Most recently Lincoln was in effect given control over one of the world's great private art collections, one which follows Dorsey's once rare interest in works by both African-Americans and Africans. The provision was included in the will of Albert Barnes, which gave Lincoln the right, beginning in the spring of 1989, to name the majority of trustees of the foundation which controls the collection. The friendship between Barnes and Horace Bond, which led to this result, was begun when the two met in 1946 at the funeral of Dr. Nathan Mossell, at 90 the last survivor of the leading black Philadelphians of the late 19th century.[6]

One of Mossell's own educational crusades was won some twenty years after that meeting. When I arrived in the Philadelphia area in the mid-1960s the local NAACP, under its combative and colorful president, the criminal lawyer Cecil B. Moore, was successfully fighting two major campaigns left over from the previous century. One was to eliminate from the annual Mummer's Parade the caricature, by white mummers, of black characters in the old minstrel style. They are still allowed however to strum James Bland's signature "(Oh Dem) Golden Slippers" on banjo, as a kind of nostalgic gesture to the past. The other of Moore's projects, first voiced by Mossell and Councilman Constantin Hubert in 1890, was to break the will of Stephen Girard, who had restricted the school he founded in the 1830s to "white male orphans." Girard College now, in North Philadelphia, reflects the contemporary need in admitting children of single parents, its enrollment mostly black. Farther west on Girard Avenue, still at the old site, the former Home for Aged and Infirm Colored People, since renamed, after its founder, the Stephen Smith Home for the Aged, continues to take care of people at the other end of life's cycle.

Both Roberts Vaux and Octavius V. Catto, meanwhile, most important of the public schools headed by African-Americans a century ago, still survive as parts of the Philadelphia system. Vaux is a junior high school, but Catto is now reserved for delinquent students only. And like most of the institutions which once served the black population of the Seventh and adjoining wards it has followed the geographic movement already evident in the 1890s by relocating to the west, at 42nd and Ludlow.

Three of the most important of the old churches have, however, stayed in the old neighborhood. Wesley Union, of Zion AME, which had the largest African-American congregation in the city at the turn of the century, still stands at 15th and Lombard; like many other churches of the era it was built to last, although the vicinity is no longer black. In fact the old downtown corridor once occupied by African-Americans has suffered from a squeeze at both ends. But whereas the newcomers pushing in from the river wards were once Italian and Jewish immigrants they are now members of the urban gentry, and what was the most slum-ridden section of Philadelphia is now "Society Hill." Through the early 1980s, South Street on the other or west side of Broad was still a run-down black business district of small shops, bars, fortune-tellers, and dealers in medicinal herbs, but it too is now becoming fashionably residential.

The Church of the Crucifixion remains near Eighth and Bainbridge, but in a modest new building which replaced the 1884 structure after a fire; while the majority of its 67 active communicants, as of 1990, are still African-American, its Australian-born pastor expects that the racial composition will change to reflect its largely white neighborhood. The Starr Park, now a playground a little to the east, is still visited by African-American youngsters these days playing basketball. And just beyond that, a few blocks farther to the east, at Sixth and Pine, "Mother Bethel" still stands and will remain. Although already left largely behind when rebuilt in the 1890s on the site first chosen a century before that, the most ancient of African-American churches was declared a National Historic Landmark in 1974. A full-length study in the 1980s found it functioning in part as a house of worship, largely supported by migrants from

South Carolina who often traveled long distances to come every Sunday, and in part as a kind of museum.[7]

Berean Presbyterian, with the Episcopal Church of the Crucifixion the most socially "progressive" of the churches of Dorsey's day, has followed another route, to the north. Together with Berean Community Center, a logical outgrowth of its earlier work, it stands now more imposing than ever on the corner of Broad and Diamond. The Berean Building and Loan Society, now in West Philadelphia, celebrated its 100th anniversary in 1988, and the Berean Institute is still at the original site near 19th and Girard, graduating about sixty students a year in cosmetology and various office skills, its well-kept grounds a green oasis in a now blasted neighborhood.

The Dorseys' own St. Thomas Church has moved too, to 52nd and Parrish in West Philadelphia, giving up the old building in 1938; its main meeting room is dominated by a portrait of William Bascom, husband of William's niece Louise Harlan and a major benefactor. But while its history has been recognized with a plaque back at Fifth and Adelphia, and 52nd Street bears signs which call it "Absalom Jones Way," it is no museum. While the old rivalry between "O.P.s" and more recent southern migrants is not yet dead, St. Thomas's is no longer at its center. Longtime Pastor Jesse F. Anderson, who served from 1944 to 1975, "fought tooth and nail" against its traditionally snobbish reputation during his tenure, and worked to make everyone in the neighborhood feel comfortable. Mildly fortified today, like many urban churches, with an electronic alarm system, St. Thomas's is still home to many professional families and businessmen, and it is today bigger than ever, with more than 2000 active congregants and a far larger list of sponsored organizations than ever, including several which involve various forms of outreach to the local community.

The building earlier occupied by St. Thomas's, built at 12th and Walnut in the 1890s, is still there, in part, but in 1989 it was converted to wholly new uses. The destruction of that immediate neighborhood, the Dorseys' own, has resulted not from the westward creep of gentrification which is threatening to surround Bethel and the Church of the Crucifixion but from the southward creep of high-rise office buildings, symbols of another kind of change, the city's conversion from a center of manufacturing to a center of banking, insurance, and other service industries.

William Dorsey's last house, at 206 Camac, is now a painted concrete-block building long used as a storehouse. The whole area near 13th and Locust had an unsavory reputation dating from the 1960s at the latest, frequented during the day by myself and other historians come to visit the surviving records of the American Negro Historical Society and other collections at the nearby Historical Society of Pennsylvania, and at night, as a reminder of Mary Dorsey Harlan's profession, by others come to visit prostitutes of both sexes. The three-story Dorsey ancestral home, at 1231 Locust, was last occupied by the "Bag O'Nails," an especially notorious hangout, before being torn down, in the summer of 1989, to make way for new construction.

Even if there were no physical destruction in the area, the old neighborhood in and near the historic Seventh Ward would no longer be the vital center of the black community. In fact black Philadelphia cannot now be considered a community in the older sense; it is simply impossible to imagine any occasion that would attract so big a proportion of the whole population as used to turn out for graduations at the ICY or Vaux, in the 1860s and '70s, or the one that Dr. Mossell and the ministers mustered to protest the showing of *The Clansman* in 1906. But much of this is simply the result of sheer population growth and movement. Black Philadelphians, over 40 percent of all residents of the city in 1990, are no longer a self-consciously embattled minority, with fresh memories of violent persecution. And the fact that they are in many ways unavoidably integrated into the wider affairs of city and nation means that some, although by no means all, of the community institutions that flourished a century ago are no longer needed in the same way.

One of the most obvious changes brought by time and numbers is that African-Americans are no longer peripheral but central to the city's politics. As the culmination of the long drive for power and recognition, Philadelphia in the 1980s joined many other cities in electing its first black mayor, and entered the 1990s with a black school superintendent and police chief as well. Race, indeed, is now the dominant issue in local politics, here as elsewhere. The importance of this development in terms of jobs belongs in another chapter, but it should be noted here that the recognition that comes to numbers and influence reaches well beyond politics as narrowly conceived.

Recognition, for example, was extended to Virginia Ramsey Chew, William Dorsey's granddaughter, when during the 1976 Bicentennial Celebration she was honored as a descendant of one of the "First Families of Philadelphia." For parallel reasons not only African-American politicians but beauty queens, community organizers, and scholars are now thought worthy of headlines in the dominant press. But the influence of all this on the old sense of community is in some ways ironic: the very increase in recognition in the dominant media has helped to dilute the once powerful role of the black press: instead of the 23 commercially sold newspapers, up to 8 at a time, which once served a population of a few tens of thousands, only one now serves a population of several hundred thousand.

A biweekly now, proud of being the oldest continuously published black paper in the country, the Philadelphia *Tribune* has a circulation estimated at about 100,000. It has over the past quarter-century veered between sensationalism and a heavy sense of its responsibility to report, as Gertrude Mossell once put it, on what is "most creditable to [the] race." Perhaps because much of its circulation goes directly to the classroom, in effect supported by the school district, it now tends to stress the uplifting more than the lurid. There are other papers, which serve individual neighborhoods or deal with special interests, such as night life, but they are modest operations, not sold but distributed free. And as one veteran observer puts it, echoing an old tradition, they are usually put out by "people who want to call attention to themselves."

The relative decline in the black newspaper business is not fully balanced by representation in the other media. The five journalists who regularly contribute columns to the *Inquirer* and *Daily News* represent a range of opinions and styles, and they include some award-winning and locally powerful people. But proportionately, perhaps because there are now so many other outlets for literate black men and women, these five are far fewer than the numbers who used to write for the white papers a century ago, when Florence Lewis ran an entire department for the *Press,* and Gertrude Bustill Mossell, John Durham, and so many others contributed articles and columns for the dominant journals. There are radio stations that serve mostly black audiences, with gospel and popular music, talk shows, and some syndicated national features of special interest to African-Americans. But most Philadelphians, of whatever race, get their news and entertainment from television; none of the local television stations is black-owned, and although the number of black "personalities" who relay news and features is proportionately greater than in the newspapers, it falls far short of 40 percent.

The net result of all of this is that despite the great increase in black power and population the routine events of presumed interest to the community, graduations and ordinations, anniversaries and special holidays, are now less often reported in major news sources than they used to be. Beyond these there are as always whole areas of African-American life that remain beyond the reach of routine reportage.

Perhaps the most important of these, as a century ago, is religion outside of the mainstream. With far more, proportionally, than in the 1890s, Philadelphia is home to many little storefront churches. The best estimate is that there may be 1500 such congregations, each containing 15, 30, or 50 members. These are all testaments to the power of individual charismatics and the felt need for the intense support of small neighborhood subcommunities. But they are not part of any truly larger community, their part-time ministers, for example, not members of the organized Black Clergy of Philadelphia and Vicinity. And they simply do not make the news, unless, as with the battle between Brothers Brown and Diggs in 1894, they erupt into serious disputes.

Part of this neglect may reflect the fact that religion of any sort is far less important now than in William Dorsey's day, among black Philadelphians as well as white. During 1987 the Urban League published an article which was to have been based, in part, on a mail survey of 225 pastors, taken with the cooperation of the Black Clergy of Philadelphia. Partly because of the minuscule response to the survey itself, the regnant word in the article was "apathy," and the collective portrait was one of churches which had largely lost their young people, and were currently dominated by women, many of them elderly, and disproportionately from the South.[8]

That piece is not widely endorsed by working clergymen, and there are other ways of looking at the black church. But there is no denying that there has been some loss of membership over the past generation, and that African-Americans have not been wholly immune to the secularization of the wider society over the past century. The replacement of the highly organized AME with Baptist and other less tightly bound denominations, a development already evident in the 1890s, has weakened the place of the church in the wider web that once helped join black Philadelphians to each other. And even without this loss, the existence of alternatives has cut into some of the secular uses of the church; just as there are now ways of following the news about leading local African-Americans outside of the black press, or the "black" columns of white papers, the modern city offers a number of places to meet, socialize, organize clubs, and do business that did not exist when the church virtually defined the community.

Alternatives, too, have eliminated or weakened the mutual insurance clubs and fraternal orders which supplemented the church as parts of the wider web of community association. The national headquarters of the Grand and United Order of Odd Fellows is still here near 12th and Spruce, but its membership across the country is now only a few thousand, and its offices have shrunk; the largest tenant in the old building, as of 1990, was a video store, and a historian who mentions the Order to contemporary African-Americans draws no more recognition than he might with reference to the Society of the Cincinnati. The Masons are still active in a variety of good causes, such as raising scholarship money, but they too have proportionally fewer members than in their heyday; many of the older all-male associations have declined in part because the elimination of Sunday "blue laws" has cost them their monopoly as holiday and after-hours drinking clubs. But more important, as with the mutual insurance societies, decline has resulted simply from the fact that the wider society, in this case the state, has picked up some of their most important functions. The financial crises which used to call for mutual support are now met instead—for those regularly employed—by social security, workmen's and unemployment compensation, and a variety of health benefits. And even for those not so employed, the intangible benefits of community cooperation have been replaced in some ways by the financial benefits of the welfare state, a tradeoff impossible to measure and weigh.

But if many of the features of William Dorsey's Philadelphia no longer exist in the same way, historical continuity is no more a question of unchanged survival than of physical landmarks frozen in time. The only law of history is that things will change, and continuity is a matter of finding cultural and institutional links between past and present. And just as it is still possible to see some of their older roots in institutions like St. Thomas Church or Lincoln University, many of the forms, if not always the content, of African-American culture in the city are still around to remind us of their origins, even as some of them have spread into the wider society.

The black church, to begin with, however weakened with time, remains far livelier than its white counterparts, its forms and institutions continually changing, as it offers an even greater variety than ever to potential members. Some religious developments belong wholly to the 20th century; despite the occasionally sympathetic view of Mohammedism offered by 19th-century stories from the African continent the Muslim movement is perhaps the most important of these. And if the Muslims lost much of their black nationalist distinctiveness during the 1980s, as they moved closer toward the multi-racial Islamic mainstream, the African appeal itself is far from dead, and 1990 opened with plans to establish a schismatic African-American Catholic Congregation in the city, Kuumba Temple, to appeal to the 40,000 black communicants in the Archdiocese of Philadelphia.

Black women evangelists meanwhile remain strong among Protestants, on the radio and in politics now as well as in revival meetings, and in two predominantly white denominations the tradition of strong black women reached two important milestones at the end of the 1980s. The first ordinations of Episcopal women as priests took place in Philadelphia during 1974, in what a reluctant bishop called "valid but irregular" ceremonies sponsored by an activist black pastor. In the fall of 1988 this breakthrough was followed by the fully sanctioned consecration of a black woman from the city as America's first female Episcopal bishop. Perhaps as part of the American Catholic hierarchy's renewed interest in black communicants, itself an echo of the 1890s, the event was celebrated in the Roman Catholic Cathedral of Saints Peter and Paul. It was also followed within days by the installation of a black man as Episcopal bishop of Pennsylvania. And in the spring of 1989, following the steps first taken by the Reverend Matthew Anderson, the nation's Presbyterians elected another black woman, from nearby West Chester, to their own highest office.

In terms of social involvement Anderson's tradition was followed most famously, beginning in the 1960s, by the Opportunities Industrialization Center. Established by an energetic Baptist minister and supported by the majority of mainstream black pastors from several other faiths, the OIC's work in job training has now spread across the country and indeed into Africa. Other churches meanwhile have developed other ways of doing secular work, sponsoring for example modest efforts to preserve or restore housing in their own neighborhoods.

Above all, and as always, the social as well as the spiritual lives of many communicants may still be met almost entirely through the church. Many, large and small, continue to offer a constant round of programs, reunions, celebrations, entertainments, and classes that may occupy much of a free weekday and all of a weekend.

As sites for larger secular or even spiritual events, apart from the venerable Academy of Music, one of the great stone monuments from the 19th century which still graces the city, the neighborhood halls which once held community concert balls and other events sponsored by various occupational associations have all gone. But others have succeeded them to the north and west. And although Horticultural Hall out in Fairmount Park has burned down, its successor on the old site, the Horticultural Center, may still serve for example as host to a reception, dinner, and dance sponsored by the city's Minority Business Enterprise Council.

The Elks and American Legion, 20th-century successors to the Odd Fellows and GAR, have faded with similar organizations, and remain visible mostly on parade days, when following on old tradition their young people's drill teams march. In some ways, in the course of historical evolution, their places have been taken by Greek-letter fraternities, greatly grown since Henry Minton and his friends founded the first of them out of his home on Lombard Street. If its import as headquarters of the Odd Fellows is no longer significant, Philadelphia has long been a regional center for collegians. Traditionally the springtime "Penn Relays" track meet was a time for those who could not comfortably visit a segregated Florida during the Easter holidays to come to party instead on the grassy banks of the Schuylkill. Since the early 1970s Fairmount Park has become home to a second tradition, with "Greeks," 60,000 men and women in July of 1989, coming from several nearby states to hold barbecues, reunions, and of course formal and informal competitions.

The traditional African-American flair for turning virtually anything into a contest is dramatically on display during these reunions. The most notable of formal competitions is in "steppin'," a kind of choreographed, athletic set of rhythmic group maneuvers. Obvious descendants of the drill-team competitions once sponsored by Patriarchies, Knights Templars, and churches, mixed in with the cakewalk contests of the 1890s, these exercises in "steppin'" now draw Greeks and others to the Spectrum, the city's biggest indoor auditorium, to watch uniformed young men and women strut their stuff for several thousand dollars in prize money.[9]

Later the same month another echo of William Dorsey's generation was heard when the National United Church Ushers Association met for its regular decennial convention, always held in Philadelphia since the organization was founded here by Charles Dorsey nearly a century before. Some 2000 ushers, representing some 38,000 nationwide of all major Protestant faiths, met in the Wyndham Franklin Plaza. The convention climaxed with a drill competition among several uniformed teams responding to a set of silent hand signals.[10]

Ever since Philadelphia's Reverend C. A. Tindley essentially invented gospel music, early in the twentieth century, informal contests among gospel groups have always taken place in church, their rivalry in what cultural anthropologists call "performance style" muted by the fact that all, brought together to celebrate an anniversary or other shared event, are formally devoted to a common worship. More open competitions, like those once held at Shiloh Baptist, for example, have now grown far too large for any single church. The fast-food companies instead now sponsor concerts at the Mann Music Center, the great outdoor amphitheater, where the best gospel choruses in the Philadelphia area are officially chosen each July. (The interdominational group of which I am an honorary member, lacking a single church to act as claque, has several times just missed first place.)[11]

The movement from church to amphitheater, like the earlier movement from church to theater, is of course only one symbol of the fact that African-American music has long moved out of restricted surroundings and into the wider popular culture. The cultural conquest begun in dilute form with minstrelsy and stepped up with the more direct, authentic, and undiluted "coon song" and cakewalk craze of the 1890s has long since been won. A purist elite may complain that cultural compromise is necessary for commercial success, that the "Philadelphia Sound" of the 1970s was even further removed from its original roots than the "Motown" of the 1960s. But this is no more true for black artists than for others, and ordinary African-Americans have accepted the products of recording studio and record company as joyfully as any. Educated whites in fact seem more ready than blacks to follow contemporary jazz down its increasingly esoteric journey away from its beginnings. But the more usual track of popular music in this century, and even more of social dancing, from Charleston to disco, is still in place, running from black origins through wider acceptance on to either evolution or abandonment.

There seems in any case no danger that either inventiveness or "roots" will be lost. The black musical culture of the American city is more and more popular in Africa itself, and a look at the entertainment pages of any metropolitan newspaper suggests that in return sounds from both Africa and the West Indies routinely echo through the United States, while kids on street corners are continually experimenting with new forms of their own.

In other forms of professional entertainment, meanwhile, popular and serious, African-American contributions have been recognized at an accelerating pace between the 1960s and the 1990s. Black comedians have a long record of success with white or mixed audiences; those now popular work in a variety of styles, some relying heavily and others scarcely touching on directly racial material, and while important, it is not surprising that no one in recent years has dominated the supremely lucrative field of television comedy more than Philadelphia's Bill Cosby. At another artistic level the increasing and indeed now dominant role of women writers, too, has its own precedents in the generation of Frances E. W. Harper and others. The real break from the restraints of the previous century and most of this one is that there is now simply no medium of entertainment or artistic genre in which black men and women have not won both popular and critical applause.

And of course the campaign for recognition in sports begun a century ago in professional boxing, collegiate racing, and football has also long since resulted in triumph. Young black men train in ex-heavyweight champion Joe Frazier's North Philadelphia gym, hoping to earn millions in the ring; and with collegiate scholarships, grown from their modest 19th-century beginnings, now a highly publicized route to fame and possible fortune, far more are continually practicing basketball moves on public playgrounds. The success of a tiny fraction of these hopefuls may be measured by the fact that the track and basketball teams of nearby Villanova, together with the professional Philadelphia Seventy-Sixers and Phillies, won national titles in the 1980s, and the Eagles came close. All of these teams, like others in the same sports across the country, enjoyed disproportionate contributions from African-American athletes. Meanwhile middle-aged men of both races, in bar-rooms all over the city, are prepared to argue that Wilt Chamberlain, who before playing professional basketball had set track records at Overbrook High School in the 1950s, was the greatest athlete of all time. And Julius Erving, a couple of years after his retirement from the court, was officially named the city's most popular sports personality in a marketing test conducted in 1989.[12]

All of this both affects and reflects changing white attitudes. A century ago sportswriters were willing to concede that black men—there were then no female athletes of note—were as good as any in the ring or on the field. As an ironic twist today there is some quasi-serious debate about the possibility that people of African descent may be not merely equal but physically superior in several important ways. To compound the irony black athletes have tended to deny this, crediting their success not to stronger calves or quicker reflexes but to hard work, practice, and the intangible "desire" born of a desperate wish to rise out of impoverished obscurity.

The whole athletic debate—far too entertaining to go away, or to give way to hard data of any kind—is only one index to the changing nature of racism and race relations over the past century. The very term "racism," successor to the "racial prejudice" of my youth, has changed its popular meaning. No historian can deny that much of this is real progress; there are no more learned pieces on the sickliness of mulattoes, and it has been some time since doctors insisted that blacks did not sneeze, or that some of them had poison sacs behind their teeth. There are in fact only two areas of significant racial difference still discussed. And the talk-show argument about innate athletic ability—perhaps a more publicly acceptable version of the older one about sexual prowess and dimensions—is conducted in terms not of absolutes but of statistical generalizations, as no one denies that there are fast and slow members of all races. The same is true of the other, less publicly heard but far more widespread and dangerously misunderstood argument about the distribution of formal intelligence.

The term "racism" now means very different things to different people. It is in fact hard to get white Americans to admit to it, whatever it means. As one symptom of change the word "nigger," familiar in my youth, is one I hear nowadays almost entirely among blacks, mostly kids on playgrounds; I have not heard it used seriously for decades by my own white middle-class peers. Highly conscious that they are listening to African-American music, watching African-American entertainers, and rooting for African-American athletes, often admiring all three, only one person in four in a national survey taken in 1988 would agree that they themselves were even "somewhat" prejudiced. The nature of "prejudice" was not defined. But while ordinary citizens of both races are more willing than academics to talk about such issues as differences in the ability to dance with style, few whites—less than one in six—reportedly believed in the kind of inborn handicaps, such as lower intelligence, that were once widespread articles of faith. [13]

In public discourse, meanwhile, many prominent African-Americans have changed the terms of debate so that in Philadelphia, criticism of mayor, city council, or even basketball coaching techniques runs the risk of being labeled "racist." So too do simple statements of statistical generalization such as blacks have higher crime rates than whites, or different family structures, or even different voting patterns.

Differing viewpoints and definitions were evident in the newspaper coverage given a poll sponsored by the NAACP Legal Defense and Educational Fund and released early in 1989: the headlines over their respective stories about the same Louis Harris survey read "Poll Says Americans Favor Racial Equality" in the Philadelphia *Inquirer*, "Blacks and Whites Are Found 'Worlds Apart'" in the New York *Times*, and "Notion That America's Poor Don't Seek to Improve Status Is Refuted in Study" in the *Wall Street Journal*. [14]

Even the least sophisticated of both races further cloud the issue by either paying lip-service to formal ideals or actually using terms once confined to social scientists. When in the summer of 1989 the residents of an all-white neighborhood succeeded in driving out a black woman with hostile graffitti, anonymous threats, and rocks through the windows, one young man who applauded all this at the same time denied that he and the others were "bigots." Shortly afterward, in a far more peaceful—and ultimately unsuccessful— attempt by local blacks to block a white woman's appointment to head a neighborhood community center, the leaders insisted that their objections were not "racial" but "cultural." [15]

The one conclusion on which all can agree is that whatever else has persisted, evolved, changed, or disappeared in the course of a century, racial hostility, and, on a statistical basis, sharp social and economic differences, are still here. The change in racial attitudes since William Dorsey's day has been important, but it is obviously not enough, and troubling parallels remain between the situation in the 1890s and the 1990s.

One result of being professionally immersed in the black experience of the late 19th century while living through the late 20th is that I am continually struck by comparisons and parallels, the fact that the men and women of the earlier time anticipated almost all of the issues and many of the experiences of the later. William Dorsey's contemporaries as well as my own were concerned with the need for a black artistic aesthetic and a black literature; they debated the proper relation to a white society and nation they often saw as hostile, weighed the practical losses as well as the gains of legal integration, the costs as well as the benefits of outside philanthropic help. Intellectuals argued whether the group as a whole should be called "Negro," the Spanish word for "black," or "Afro-American"; W. E. B. Du Bois listed the three main internal problems in black Philadelphia, the ones most demanding self-help, as, in order: crime, family life, and work habits.[16]

Many suggested parallels, however striking, are merely curious, more coincidental than significant: Tawana Brawley and Charles Whittaker, found in similar circumstances a full century but only a few miles apart; black Philadelphians accused of selling black bodies to white doctors in both the 1880s and the 1980s; Peter Jackson and Mohammed Ali plummeting from public acclaim to public pity. But one class of comparative experience—the economic—is not merely coincidental but centrally important to the African-American experience. While there have been changes enough to remind us that change is not only possible but inevitable, the parallels are both dramatic and discouraging. The persistent failure of black Americans to win the same living standards as their white fellow citizens is of course the most obvious of these parallels between then and now. But there are others, too, which help to explain this central failure.

The figures from Philadelphia are a good if not quite perfect place to start. Two facts combine to make white Philadelphians significantly poorer and less educated, on average, than those elsewhere. Statistics drawn from the city itself do not include those from the surrounding suburbs, which benefit in many ways from its presence, and the fact that the city is an old one, with a once powerful manufacturing sector, means that the transition into a service economy has been unusually painful for all. But the statistics for the city's black population, as gathered by the local Urban League, show that as of 1988 it was all too typical of those trends across the nation which point toward the future: some 39 percent of young people between 15 and 24 were living in poverty; 34 percent of those over 15 had not graduated from high school; and while only a little less than 26 percent of men were married and living with spouses, almost 74 percent of all children were born to single mothers.[17]

These statistics, subject to change, sometimes shaky, always numbing, tell a familiar story. Another part of the story, not so familiar, impossible to measure but no less important, is the one told when the occupational situation today is compared with that of a century ago.

One difference is obvious: the old bars against factory and bureaucratic employment are down. Black men and women have worked for decades now in the city's manufacturing sector, now slowly dying. More visible in any visit downtown is the number of those in white-collar jobs in shops, stores, and corporate offices, working at every level from clerical to executive.

In absolute terms, too, great gains in the national standard of living have affected the black population, as was already apparent between the Civil War and 1900. However they trail whites, African-Americans now live longer and enjoy better health than they used to; no longer 90 percent but less than half across the country live below the contemporary "poverty line," and even those who do have more access to material goods, food, and medicine, than most of their more affluent ancestors. But despite these important gains, the differences within the African-American community in the 1990s are a kind of exaggeration of those in the 1890s, so that again the situation may be made to look good or bad depending on which group is looked at—with by far the largest group losing ground, at least relatively.

During the late 19th century black athletes and entertainers, George Dixon, Ernest Hogan, and Isaac Murphy, ranked at the very top of the African-American income scale across the country. If none in Philadephia was quite that successful, a few who took their talents on the road, such as the minstrel star Louis Brown or the concert singer Elizabeth Greenfield, were able to do very well while the opportunity lasted.

Capitalizing on the great educational gains begun during the era of Reconstruction, as black men and women went to school and took jobs as teachers, the 1880s and 1890s witnessed a dramatic relative increase in the number of licensed professionals, doctors and lawyers. During what was sometimes called "The Second Reconstruction," too, beginning in the 1960s, the later '60s and '70s also witnessed a surge in higher education and the professions. Both a century ago and today, however, the positions of these new professionals were for various reasons not fully secure.

Politics, or at least the civil service, has been more reliable. There had been virtually no political or civil jobs before the vote was won, in the South in the late 1860s, elsewhere with the Fifteenth Amendment of 1870. After that, despite later setbacks in the South, in northern cities like Philadelphia men and women with jobs in government made up an important layer of the late 19th-century black middle class. Today, as once again black voters in the South have won some leverage, as increasing numbers have empowered those in cities, still more have been added to the already important number of those working for city, state, and federal governments.

The state of independent black business, in contrast, is still unhealthy. William Still complained about lack of interest and support beginning in the 1860s; so did both W. E. B. Du Bois and Booker T. Washington later in the same century. Despite much talk there was still, entering the 1990s, no black bank in the city, and as of the middle 1980s only a little more than 8 businesses per 1000 inhabitants, while even the leading cities in this respect, most of them on the West Coast, average not much over 11. The research director of Philadelphia's Urban League, reporting in 1987, was then echoing an ancient complaint when, in surveying the economic situation of the city's African-Americans, he chose, uniquely and literally, to underline the consequences of the evident lack of entrepreneurship: *"To own wealth in property is to be among the potential directors of the social order. To be only a wage and salary earner is to be one who is largely directed and controlled by others."*[18]

To me however the more immediate problem is that those who "only" earn wages and salaries are threatened by those who do not. The most troubling comparison between William Dorsey's city and ours involves the condition of those toward the bottom of the social and economic scales.

Except for the entrepreneurs, the number and proportion of those who made up the top and middle layers of black society were growing faster between the Civil War and 1900 than at any later time. But the growth among clergymen and journalists, cops and teachers, postmen and government clerks, doctors, lawyers, boxers, jockeys, and musicians owed much to the fact that there had been so few to begin with, and their absolute numbers remained small. Most blacks, in contrast, members of the ordinary working class, were losing ground relative to the white majority, as in a time of economic transition they were deliberately shut out, by overt racism, of the blue- and white-collar jobs opened by the urban-industrial revolution. A century later a disturbing parallel has emerged. No matter how threatened, the upper and middle layers of black society today are currently doing well, and account for far more people, with more power and influence, than in the 1890s. But the urban economy is again in transition, and many of those who now hold solid wage-earning jobs, and certainly those who have none, are being left out of the new service revolution. The reason is not so simple as it was, and in many ways the people who make up what we have come to call the "underclass" have and create problems far worse than the domestics, laborers, or even criminals of the 1890s.

The number and proportion of those with severe family and personal difficulties of all kinds is far higher now. A century ago members of the "unskilled majority" were able to participate in the dominant economy whenever given a chance, and managed somehow to survive by their own resources, or with some mutual help. Members of the underclass today are increasingly unable to participate even when given a chance, and cannot survive on their own. Growing rates of crime, once committed by the desperate and by some ambitious men and women who profited from it, victimized neighborhood professionals, wage-earners, and businessmen in many ways. The same is true now, except that the level of violence, especially, has escalated dramatically, and the drug problem is wholly without precedent.

To understand why all this has occurred, why the undeniably impressive progress made since William Dorsey's day has been balanced and is now threatened by retrogression, is not an empty academic pursuit. The course of a century has helped us rule out truly racial—that is, genetic or biological—reasons for black problems of all kinds. But to deal with the situation now requires some understanding of how much of it is the result of new conditions and how much of old, how much of current discrimination and how much of the heritage of past discrimination as now rooted in black "underclass" behavior. This in turn requires a look, however brief, at what has happened between then and now.

Chapter 13

Transition: From There to Here

Urban black history in the 20th century has not moved along straight lines. Its three major themes for the purposes of this book are, first, the basic migration from farm to city; second, the assault on racism and move toward acceptance; and third, the change in economic opportunity and conditions, from those of wage-earners and the unemployed at the bottom to educated professionals at the top. The first two have proceeded unevenly, in fits and starts, but generally up; economic conditions have followed an even more complex path, sometimes up and sometimes down.

Americans in general were aware of the first two movements as they occurred, as African-Americans were ever more visible on city streets, and the milestones in their long battle for dignity and inclusion were visible in the daily papers, or later on television. Some of the social problems with economic roots, notably rising rates of crime, were also all too apparent. But in general the basic economic situation was not as clear as the more dramatic events which made the headlines, from the Great Migration and Harlem Renaissance of the 1910s and 1920s to the protests and later riots of the 1960s and 1970s. The muse of history, Minerva's owl, "flies at dusk," surveying the day only after its close, and it often took years to compile the dry statistics which trace economic and educational trends, and even more years for this historian, at least, to appreciate what they meant.

The events of the last years of William Dorsey's life followed mostly along the lines laid out during his prime, with some significant variations. If it was not already obvious between 1870 and 1900, the decade of the Great Migration, between 1910 and 1920, showed that the black future lay in the cities. The agricultural South, already weak, was further exhausted by the boll weevil's attack on the cotton crop. And the manpower needs of the World War I era briefly allowed African-Americans to work productively in the kind of factory employment from which they had been so long shut out. An estimated 170,000 men and women moved out of the South, mostly to northern cities, between 1900 and 1910, 454,000 more between 1910 and 1920. And while over the whole twenty years Philadelphia's black population officially leaped from 62,600, or 4.8 percent of the whole, to 134,200, or 7.4 percent, the magnetic power of New York, and the pipeline straight up the Mississippi to Chicago and other midwestern centers cost the city the numerical leadership it had held for so long in the North.[1]

The social problems which accompanied this huge population movement drew much attention. Meeting the wartime labor shortage by bringing up trainloads of all-male work crews from the road gangs and turpentine forests of the South created crime scares in northern cities, and migrants of all kinds strained housing and other facilities. Even before their arrival, black homicide rates, already high, had continued to climb slowly, while white rates dropped. In Philadelphia, typically, the tension between immigrants and "O.P.s" probably reached its peak in these years, as the easy habit of blaming new-comers for African-American urban problems of all kinds—"stickin' it to the Southerners"—was intensified; civic leaders of both races insisted, as they had before and would later, that "There was nothing wrong with Our Fair City"— or "constituents" or "parishioners"—until "they" arrived. Nationwide, building resentment among whites meanwhile broke out sometimes during the war, more usually in the months just after the Armistice late in 1918. As blacks were laid off from their newly won jobs in war industries, and proud veterans marched home, a new wave of lynchings in the South was matched by riots of varying size in several cities, including Philadelphia. But this time white invaders of black neighborhoods, briefly reverting to the tactics of the mid-19th century in trying to drive the newcomers away entirely, often ran into serious and sometimes armed resistance.[2]

The blacks then stayed, but the jobs stayed lost. As in earlier hard times, Africa beckoned to those losing faith in the United States. In Philadelphia the West Indian Reverend George McGuire, former pastor of St. Thomas Church, succeeded the AME's Reverend Henry M. Turner as an especially prominent supporter of colonization. But the real difference between the earlier appeal of men like Turner and the new one led nationally by the dynamic Marcus Garvey after World War I was that Garvey's United Negro Improvement Association attracted not simply southerners desperate to move but masses of those who had already reached Philadelphia and other northern cities. The urban North, clearly, had shown that it was not the promised land that many had hoped for, and migration out of the South was not in itself a solution to the triple problems of poverty, racism, and exclusion.[3]

There were hopeful signs in the period, as educated urban blacks, disdain-ing Garvey's popular appeal, took the lead in new organizations like the

National Association for the Advancement of Colored People and the Urban League. In the South the lynching phenomenon, despite the publicized resurgence just after the war, began slowly to recede from the peak reached in the 1890s, if only because blacks had successfully been denied the vote. Even less visibly, the anthropologist Franz Boas began about the turn of the century the long process of destroying the pseudo-scientific basis of racism, with his attack on some of the physical evidence long misused to support the idea of Caucasian superiority.

The most dramatic gains in professional sports were still in boxing, as Jack Johnson reigned as heavyweight champion between 1908 and 1915. In music the end of one era was signaled locally when the concert soprano Flora Batson retired to Philadelphia shortly after the turn of the century, and the old minstrel composer James Bland died broke in the city in 1911. But new forms were continually evolving. Southern migrants took joyfully to gospel music, which Chicago's Thomas Dorsey picked up from the great Philadelphia Baptist preacher Charles A. Tindley. The wider world was more aware of a more obviously urban and definitely secular music, the evolution, all across the country, from "coon songs" to ragtime to jazz.[4]

But despite these publicized cultural developments, truly solid economic gains were confined mostly, as before, to a privileged elite. In Philadelphia, while nothing really replaced the Institute for Colored Youth, the opportunities in public education continued to widen at the top. Jesse Fauset, after leading her class at Girls' High, was denied admission to nearby Bryn Mawr College but earned a Phi Beta Kappa key from Cornell in 1906. The next year Alain Locke, a graduate of Central High School and grandson of the man who had perhaps been William Dorsey's first black teacher, was appointed the first black Rhodes scholar in 1907. But while those toward the very bottom still managed more gains in basic literacy, by every available measure African-American children trailed well behind their white peers in school.[5]

If the educational record for most was discouraging, the root cause remained the same: despite some advance into blue-collar manufacturing between 1900 and 1920, the fact that the wartime breakthrough into factories was soon lost, and that above all white-collar employment was still closed off, meant that there was no way in which any but a handful could use any literate skills at work.

While the statistics for entrepreneurs are highly variable and suspect, varying from one count and one city to another, the basic movement was, as before, away from the kinds of businesses which catered to whites and into the more modest establishments, barber and beauty shops, undertaking parlors, small insurance and employment agencies, boarding houses and real estate, that could count on an African-American clientele. Philadelphia tended to fall behind New York and Chicago not in the relative number but in the size of those places which tried to catch and hold this growing market, largely because, it seems, of its historically different patterns of black residence. During the late 19th century and into the early 20th those in the old Quaker City were still consolidating their scattered settlements into different centers in South, West, and finally North Philadelphia. Those moving into the more newly populated cities in contrast settled into great segregated ghettos from the first, Harlem or the South Side, where buying power was concentrated. In any case the great majority of small businesses, grocers and tobacconists, which catered to blacks everywhere remained white.[6]

Growing numbers translated into political gains, as across the North hundreds of thousands of southern black men, and by 1919 women, were able for the first time to vote. In Philadelphia Henry Bass of the Seventh Ward was finally elected to the State Assembly in 1910. But politics was still corrupt, and everywhere the electorate was still largely managed by the white leaders of a racially insensitive Republican party. Most important, clubhouse politicians were still deeply involved in gambling, speakeasies, and prostitution, and black neighborhoods were still in effect zoned as centers of vice, dangerous for residents and frightening to outsiders.[7]

On the other side of the ledger, the underside of politics was balanced by governments' continuing and even growing importance as a source of jobs, as always more reliable than private employment. In Philadelphia the switch for example from private contractors to municipal trash and garbage collection, among other things, helped open new opportunities at the bottom. And toward the top the city still provided employment for a disproportionate number of the elite. By 1920 the census, which counted government workers more reliably than it did businessmen and women, listed 274 African-American policemen in the city, and 276 schoolteachers, all but 50 of them women. By that time too, within the more secure federal civil service, a modest breakthrough in the nature of postal work was recorded when 145 men were listed not merely as employees but "mail carriers."[8]

The situation among licensed professionals was more discouraging. Philadelphia's importance as a center of medical education, and the existence first of Douglass and then of Mercy Hospital, kept the number of physicians relatively high, and some 78 were counted in 1910. Over the next decade, however, as only a handful were taken into the white institutions, such as Women's Medical, which had earlier accepted them, the total reached just 95—far less than the number needed to keep pace with black population growth. Chicago in the same period had rather more doctors per capita, New York less, and although the figures were a little less stark in those cities, there too the number of physicians failed to keep up with the overall increase in African-American residents.[9]

For lawyers the situation was even more grim. The census of 1910 counted 13 black lawyers in Philadelphia. But none was able to make a living out of legal practice alone. And not a single new African-American was admitted to the

Philadelphia bar between 1910 and 1920, the decade when black migration reached heights it had never reached before.[10]

Among licensed professionals, then, the great late 19th-century gains won by those excited by new educational opportunities were beginning to erode. Since their numbers outstripped their ability to make a living, as they were shut out of white firms and hospitals, forced to compete for poor African-American clients with white professionals and black irregulars, the positions won could not be held. By the second decade of the 20th century earlier black enthusiasm for education had already been seriously dampened by the effects of racism. The lesson already learned by ordinary members of the working class was then spreading upward: the enormous amount of time, money, and energy required for higher education or professional training was rarely worth it—for blacks.

The years between 1920 and 1940, between the aftermath of World War I and the undeclared American entrance into World War II, were years of ups and downs for blacks as for other Americans. The movement toward equality and acceptance gained consistently, in politics and elsewhere. The economic situation was in contrast a kind of roller coaster, although less steeply graded than for whites, as always, simply because the good times of the 1920s were not so high for blacks, and the bad times of the Great Depression more nearly resembled the old familiar lows. But sensitivity to economic conditions in the city was reflected in the statistics of migration: 749,000 left the South during the 1920s, but just 347,000 during the 1930s. In Philadelphia, over the same twenty years, the number increased from 134,200 to 250,880 and from 7.4 to 13 percent of the whole population.[11]

The assault on racism in this era was inspired by several sources, including the work of white scientists and black artists. The appeal of Social Darwinism, with its emphasis on struggle and even war, had been killed by the reality of death in the trenches of France. As culmination to Franz Boas's destruction of the biological evidence for an alleged Anglo-Saxon superiority, disciples such as Margaret Mead and Ruth Benedict helped to create a new kind of anthropology, which stressed that differences among various groups of humans were rooted in culture rather than heredity. And just as the belief in human equality, long rooted in religious conviction and uncommon sense, was reinforced by a formerly hostile science, black men and women in several fields showed that they had to be taken seriously.

Millions of Americans followed F. Scott Fitzgerald in semi-officially christening the 1920s "The Jazz Age," and there was some local pride in the fact that Bessie Smith, its greatest black recording star, married a Philadelphia policeman and moved to the city in 1923, the same year in which William Dorsey finally died at the age of 86. But popular cultural acceptance by then was an old story; the new one was written by more serious artists, writers, and critics.

Their white peers were first impressed by the participants in the "Harlem Renaissance," nurtured in part by the expatriate Philadelphians Jesse Fauset and Alain Locke, and then by Richard Wright, Paul Robeson, and others whose careers flourished later. Recognition of this kind of black achievement, largely ignored until then, helped win the conversion of reform-minded white intellectuals to the black drive for dignity and inclusion. The opening of previously closed minds was symbolized locally when Dorsey's granddaughter Helen was admitted to Bryn Mawr in 1926 to do graduate work in French, apparently the first black student accepted at any level, just three years before her tragic early death.

But it was in the realm of politics that this new set of intellectual allies proved most important. During the first decades of the twentieth century American reformers, many of them southern agrarians or patrician Progressives, had been indifferent or even hostile to demands for equality, associating blacks with corruption and ignorance. The new urban "liberals," however, many of them intellectuals, some with connections to the labor movement, began to insist that equal treatment belonged again on the national reform agenda, together with the economic issues which had arisen out of the abuses of industrialism.

This new political "liberalism" was however only one of a rich mix of ideologies and possible tactics which competed for the attentions of African-Americans during the 1920s. Marcus Garvey's appeal to African pride among the urban masses was picked up and carried on by many intellectuals long after Garvey himself, and the United Negro Improvement Association, went down under the combined weight of mismanagement and government harassment. Following the death of Booker T. Washington in 1915 the more militant approach of the NAACP began to produce victories, for the first time, in cases concerning voting rights and segregation, together with others which involved individual injustice in the courts. As disenfranchised southerners moved to the urban North and voted in increasing numbers, Marxists as well as Democrats worked to undermine their traditional Republican allegiance.

As the 1920s gave way to the 1930s, prosperity to depression, while none of the other possibilities died entirely it was the NAACP and the Democrats who won out. Legal victories continued to accumulate. And while fifty years earlier the appeals of many leaders had failed to shake allegiance to the GOP, their descendants had more success; during the 1930s a historic voting shift took place as a significant urban black voting bloc joined a new and highly successful Democratic coalition. Franklin Roosevelt's New Deal, although still too dependent on southern whites to endorse federal anti-lynching laws, for example, gave more important jobs to African-Americans than they had enjoyed since Reconstruction. The new Congress of Industrial Organizations was far more receptive to organizing blacks than the older American Federation of Labor. The evident sympathy of the President's wife Eleanor was symbolically important, and the slowly rising wave of victories for civility reached a famous climax in 1939 when, after the conservative Daughters of the American Revolution refused the great Philadelphia contralto Marian Anderson the use of Washington's Constitution Hall, Mrs. Roosevelt quit the organization and arranged for a huge, emotional, outdoor concert on Easter Sunday, in which Anderson sang from the steps of the Lincoln Memorial.

But if African-Americans were visibly moving into the political main-stream, and more and more white Americans were moved by the injustices routinely dealt them, they were still shut out of the economic mainstream.

The 1920s were relatively good years, but only in the sense that, as the momentum of the Great Migration pushed on, southern newcomers found their usual, marginal, places in the urban economy. There were in most cities no real breakthroughs into the still vibrant manufacturing sector. Between 1920 and 1930, typically, the biggest job category in the census was still "domestic and personal service." Everywhere the "domestic" category was over-whelmingly the biggest among women, typically somewhere close to 60 or 80 percent of all legally employed, and edged up slightly in Chicago and New York, down in Philadelphia. A drop of two or three percentage points among men, to 20 percent in Philadelphia, 36 percent in New York, and 27 percent in Chicago, was equally meaningless, given that most of the rest were classified as "unskilled labor." As in the 19th century, many found refuge in crime and vice. And again as in the 19th century, the social-psychological effects of the inclusion of white immigrants into factory and office continued to lower white rates of murder and manslaughter, while the black stayed high. In Philadelphia the black rate, roughly five and a half times the white in 1900, reached fully sixteen times as high by 1930, further separating the experience of the races.[12]

One ironic result was that while the rate of southern lynchings declined sharply through the period, white fears of black crime rose in the North. As part of the new pattern evident in Philadelphia only at the very turn of the century, blacks sometimes attacked white strangers, killing police officers and robbery victims. But while as always most murderers and their victims were members of the same group, black killers, in contrast to the late 19th-century pattern, were not less but more likely to suffer execution than white.[13]

This fear of crime accelerated the long decay of businesses dependent on white patrons: by various counts the number of Philadelphia's caterers, pegged in 1908 and 1910 at 80 and 82, had dropped to 11 and 9 in 1923 and 1928. While this loss was balanced in part by evident gains in the segregated concerns best represented by barbers, beauticians, and undertakers, the gains were registered only on tiny scales. In 1929, just before the Great Crash, only 3.1 percent of all black custom went to black businessmen and women, an annual average of about $9 per capita.[14]

Among the highly educated, physicians continued to lose ground. All testimony suggests that doctors in this period ranked at the very top of the

African-American social scale across the country, regarded with enormous respect by their fellows, disproportionately represented in Philadelphia among the entries in such registers as *Who's Who in Colored America*. But in an age when the trend toward medical specialization was already accelerating, only six African-Americans practiced a speciality as of 1925. As both Douglass and Mercy, the small black hospitals, struggled to maintain funding and accreditation, only a fraction of medical school graduates were able to train as interns in these or the white institutions. And while the absolute number of doctors in the city rose to 143, the increase, as between 1910 and 1920, did not keep pace with population growth.[15]

Lawyers did better, numerically, during the 1920s, after the dead halt in the previous decade. Some of the young attorneys entering the profession during the period, such as Aaron Mossell's daughter Sadie and her later husband Raymond Pace Alexander, were beginning distinguished careers, and able to attract some business clientele and civil rights cases. But most black lawyers still worked with minor crininal cases, as the more successful illegal entrepreneurs in the black community still went to white attorneys; those new to the bar, according to Alexander, had to settle mostly for divorce suits. And while the numbers climbed substantially, from 13 to 30 between 1920 and 1930, they stayed far smaller than for doctors, and still never reached the proportion of the population held either locally or nationally in 1900 or 1910.[16]

And of course in the Great Depression of the 1930s the bottom dropped out. Blacks through the 1920s, as always previously, had higher rates of employment than whites in large part because proportionally far more black women worked for wages. But by 1933 over half the African-Americans in Philadelphia were out of work, and in a special survey taken in 1939 accounted for only 1 percent of all the young men employed in the city's factories.[17]

Even the government employees were unable to hold all of their ground, although they did better than most members of the middle class. By 1940 the number of cops had dropped to 174, and while teachers moved up to 452, some 360 of them women, this did not match population growth; only the mail carriers working for the federal government really advanced, to a total of 409. Among professionals, only 10 doctors were added to the totals between 1929 and 1938, 3 lawyers between 1930 and 1940, accelerating the long slide down in proportional representation, as the great majority of African-Americans were unable or unwilling to make the sacrifices required of professional education.[18]

In striking contrast to the depths plumbed in the 1930s, the 1940s and '50s were in many ways a golden age for blacks in Philadelphia and other cities, the most hopeful time since Reconstruction. For the first time in the 20th century all three of the trends followed in this chapter moved up together, as in-migration accelerated, striking victories were won in the continuing battles for civil rights and inclusion, and there were real breakthroughs on the economic front. The

African-American population of Philadelphia officially more than doubled in these twenty years, to reach 535,033, or 27 percent of the total. As before, the movement was part of a nationwide trend, and after the slowdown of the depression years there was a net gain of 1,081,000 in the North between 1940 and 1950, 1,037,000 more between 1950 and 1960. As in the 19th century the migrants, mostly southerners, were not the hapless ignorants of legend but typically ambitious young men and women, attracted by better opportunities, with stronger family systems, less liability to criminal arrest, and even better educations than those native to the cities they arrived in. With their help the 1960 census recorded a historic milestone, as after nearly a century of movement off largely southern farms proportionally more blacks than whites, 73 to 70 percent, were officially found living in urban areas.[19]

The events which touched off this progressive period occurred overseas, as German and Japanese aggression scared the United States into preparing for war. As a generation earlier, the need to supply the friendly powers abroad and then the actual entry into the fight opened up the doors to factories and even offices, as well as the armed services themselves. Segregation was still the rule in the military, as in much of the wider society, and rapid change, crowded housing, and other strains brought fights and riots to some cities—with blacks battling back, as they often had in 1919. But this time, given the earlier experience, African-American leaders pressured the government, more receptive under Franklin Roosevelt than Woodrow Wilson, into helping. Segregation was cracked in places, and troops were sent to Philadelphia in 1944 to counter white strikers, who had violently protested against the hiring of black men to help run the city's streetcars.[20]

This time, too, partly because of their growing importance to the Democratic party, African-Americans were not deserted when the fighting was over. Returning black veterans, as proud as their fathers had been, were not lynched but given the same benefits, including job preferences, as their white peers. And they came home to a truly different racial climate, one which the middle-aged of my own generation may still remember.

It was a time when the whole course of our national history, the conquest of polio, the harnessing of nuclear energy, the apparently painless (to the suburbs) process of urban "renewal," the slow expansion of the welfare state, all encouraged the idea of progress. Even for those who, like myself, had been raised to demand more "social justice" than contemporary politics would ever allow, that idea was still fundamental. All that blacks would need, it seemed to follow, was the end to formal exclusion and a chance to join us all on what seemed an escalator toward the better life.

Well before the dramatic days when southern blacks themselves so directly and courageously challenged the old order, the national mood and news were fundamentally encouraging. Eastern Republicans, still in charge of the GOP, were at least respectful to the demand for civil rights, and northern Democrats positively encouraging. The Supreme Court was clearly moving toward the position of the NAACP on segregation even before the critical 1954 decision in *Brown vs. Board of Education.* Across the world good news came from formerly colonial states in Africa, as graduates of Lincoln University took over as leaders of newly independent nations. And all the time, having been born into an atmosphere too racially restrictive for young people now even to imagine, we had innumerable little victories to celebrate in the battle to change dominant attitudes.

In a period when African-Americans were still widely thought to lack the cool courage and skills used to play team sports at the highest levels, Jackie Robinson's march through the National League in 1947 coincided with my own first awareness of the game of professional baseball. And this was only the first of a stream of such events. Between the late 1940s and the 1960s, when we were gripped by more profound matters, each sport, each team, had its own pioneer: Marion Motley on the old Cleveland Browns, "Sweetwater" Clifton on the New York Knicks, on to "Pumpsie" Green on the Boston Red Sox, last holdout in any major league. In the collegiate ranks, too, as southern coaches like "Bear" Bryant gave in to the need to stay competitive, every hit, touchdown, and basket seemed to prove a point.

In another but related world, beginning at a time when it was daring for a black man like Billy Eckstine to join Ella Fitzgerald and Lena Horne in singing love songs to us white teenagers over the radio, progress was equally continuous. Bigoted resistance, as in the white southern attack on "King" Cole in concert, was as self-defeating as in the world of school desegregation, where events in Little Rock or at the University of Georgia only reinforced the determination to change.

We didn't then read the economic statistics. But while blacks still lagged far behind, most of these numbers, too, were moving upward. The most striking were those in manufacturing and in office employment, the ones opened by the war. Between 1940 and 1960 the proportion of African-Americans in the skilled crafts doubled, from 3 to 6 percent, and in white-collar jobs more than doubled, from 6 to 13 percent. And the 1960 census recorded another historic first, as significant as the fact that proportionately more blacks than whites were living in cities. In Philadelphia, by 28 to 21 percent, across the United States by 25 to 20 percent, proportionately more blacks than whites were actually working as operatives in the factories from which they had so long been shut out.[21]

But if we didn't read the statistics we could still sense the palpable fact that this was a golden age not only for blacks but for ordinary urban Americans generally. The urban-industrial revolution had reached a takeoff point about three generations earlier, around 1870, or just as Willian Dorsey was beginning his scrapbook collection; it was the mid-20th century when it finally reached its height, in this country and in fact all over the Western World. The horrors of

World War II, and then a time of postwar deprivation, obscured this for Europeans until the 1950s. But in the United States these were, for older citizens of both races, "the good old days" of city living. One result of the maturation of the urban-industrial economy, the combination of relatively high and regular wages it now brought to the regularity and discipline it had always demanded, was that national homicide rates fell to the lowest levels recorded in our history. An important part of that pattern was that as blacks entered the mainstream economy, really for the first time, their rates dropped, also for the first time, to join the general decline that had marked the wider urban work force for decades.[22]

Several members of my family, with a rare assist from me, were then involved in community work in Harlem. We all ate routinely with local people at Frank's, on 125th Street; some of us went occasionally with my mother to her regular meetings, day or night, at the Morningside Community Center. In northern Manhattan, as in Chicago, Philadelphia, and indeed Paris and Stockholm, men and women at that time still found the age-old reasons to fight in bedrooms, bar-rooms, and kitchens; in this country the routine presence of handguns made more of them turn unexpectedly fatal. Harlem also had its local "youth gangs," of course, and they fought each other with sometimes murderous intensity. But their battles were not conducted on the same scale as those of young Irishmen, a century before, farther down the island. And we were not rival gangsters, after all, or targets of neighborhood or domestic frustrations. The streets themselves were dirty, and their inhabitants often shabby, but they menaced no one in the daytime. Drafted once into walking a bunch of small children down the twenty or so blocks from the St. Nicholas Housing Project to Morningside Heights, I was concerned only that everyone stop for the traffic lights.

The proportion of black civil servants in Philadelphia meanwhile grew far faster than the population, strengthening the middle class. By 1960 the census counted 836 policemen in the city and 1,101 mailmen. Most hopeful of all for the future of education was what must be described as an explosion in the number of schoolteachers of both sexes, which reached 3,345 by 1960, fully 903 of them men.[23]

There was some modest good news, too, on the professional front. In Philadelphia, during the twenty years after 1940, while the African-American population was doubling the number of lawyers more than tripled, from 21 to 66. The men and women who made up this group were unusually distinguished, many of them going on to careers as federal or state judges. But their distinction was in part a matter of survival, the fact that they had to be especially good just to jump the hurdles needed to get past the bar. Black parents, as had been the case for decades, were much less willing than white to encourage or pay for the needed education; in a 1959 survey the law in particular was thought "a starvation profession." And in Philadelphia, as surely elsewhere, there was through the 1950s real reason to suspect that actual cheating on the part of bar examiners resulted in a high rate of failure among African-American applicants, to further discourage any who dreamed of a legal career.[24]

The larger and more prestigious group of doctors meanwhile did less well. In Philadelphia the absolute increase was from 127 to 188, well below the proportionate standard. This was true, again, across the country as well— despite some improvement over the dismal 1930s, virtually every decade had witnessed some slippage from the census of 1910, which had measured 1 black doctor to every 2,883 black citizens, in Philadelphia 1 to 1,075.[25]

And none of us read the several other ominous if still slight signs which also marked the period. In general black women found somewhat better jobs to take the place of the domestic service which still occupied 60 percent of those employed in the money economy as of 1940. This went down to just 36 percent in 1960, as higher wages and expectations for black women elsewhere helped kill the ancient American middle-class expectation that every family should have at least a maid. But despite twenty years of relatively good times, longer life spans, and greater opportunities for both sexes, the official statistics for intact black families, those with both husbands and wives present, declined a fraction, from 77 to 74 percent, while the white rate edged up from 86 to 89 percent. The hunger for family life, as for education, had been strong in the decades after the Civil War. But here too it had been beaten out of many, so that even in good times those with long memories recalled all those decades of exclusion, when few men could support wives and children by themselves, and families were for other folks.[26]

And in fact the refusal to trust in good times and economic opportunity was well grounded. While African-Americans scored impressive gains in both urban population and factory work, it is clear now that all that time they were in effect being piped aboard a sinking ship, welcomed into the urban-industrial age only as it was beginning to die. While proportionately more blacks than whites were living in cities, older cities were beginning to lose population, as more whites left than blacks entered. Philadelphia itself, having peaked officially at over 2,071,000 residents in 1950, sank back to 2,003,000 in 1960. And the manufacturing jobs were beginning to leave, too. Across the country African-American unemployment rates reached a historic low of 4.5 percent during the Korean War, in 1953, but then started back up. By the end of the 1950s they had reached double digits, a condition especially marked among young men in cities. And in the very last year of the decade, 1959, the FBIs index of national homicide rates began its first sustained upward climb since the Bureau began to compile its figures in the early 1930s.[27]

The hints of contradiction in the 1940s and '50s, of progress won but trouble to come, were all realized during the exciting 1960s and '70s, and more besides. These twenty years, immediate background to the situation in the contemporary city, in some ways resemble the late 19th century more than any time in between. The political drama of the "Second Reconstruction" was followed by reaction, as the first had been a century earlier. Economically too, as in William Dorsey's day, a growing split developed between a highly visible occupational progress toward the top of African-American society and a more worrisome, for many years less visible, slippage toward the bottom. But history does not repeat itself exactly, and there were many gains not lost, as well as problems without precedent.

During these two decades the great population shift from south to north, country to city, although still strong, began to slow. Conditions in the South improved politically, lynchings were reduced to truly isolated events after the turbulence of the early and mid-1960s, and the urban North, visibly decaying, was no longer as attractive as it had been. In Philadelphia, as a fairly representative northern city, the African-American increase from 27 to nearly 38 percent of the whole population owed much more to white flight, as the city shrank down to a total of 1,688,000, than to the relative modest gain of 103,000 black residents. Here as elsewhere the growth brought with it a continuous slow advance in political influence, sometimes locally tipping the balance from white to black control.[28]

Far more than in the previous decades the politics of the 1960s were directly shaped by those affected, even those without the vote. Slow elective gains in local power did not move fast enough to satisfy long-felt needs—and in many areas, especially to the south, the lack of votes was itself an issue. The relevant events defy summary: even more than in the 1920s there was an enormous variety of leaders, organizations, and tactics for blacks to choose from, as the NAACP, the Southern Christian Leadership Conference, the Student Non-Violent Coordinating Committee, the Urban League, and the Congress of Racial Equality all differed among themselves, and certainly with the religious Black Muslims, the separatist Black Nationalists, and the (sometimes) Marxist Black Panthers. All had constituencies of varying size, but while some of them scared white Americans none but the NAACP had any significant dues-paying membership across the country, and none but the Muslims any large committed following in the cities. Certainly none was directly responsible for the periodic urban riots which marked the period. These began among other places in Philadelphia, during 1963 and 1964, the time of my own arrival in the area, sparked neither by ideology nor by plans for betterment but by specific incidents and inarticulate resentments.

There was much debate, during and after that eventful decade, about the respective recipes for success and failure, the kinds of action that won political and economic gains from governments and other white institutions, such as churches, universities, and corporations, and those which did not. And even in retrospect a historian cannot re-create winning and losing formulas with absolute confidence.

The need in every case was to appeal for action from the dominant majority, which had the money, places, jobs, or power which blacks did not have themselves but wanted to benefit from, take, or share. The central issue was whether the appeal was best made to conscience or to one of several varieties of fear. Most of these fears were not directly of violence but of economic loss through boycott, for example, of bad publicity (perhaps a variant of the appeal to conscience, in this case someone else's), or of intervention by some higher power. But the possibility of physical violence played a role, and—in the case of some relatively weak institutions, such as churches or colleges—so did the simple possibility of unpleasant confrontation in itself. Every one of these tactics won sometimes and lost at others.

The fear of actual violence, in the early stages, was not created but faced down by those blacks who, sometimes with a few white allies, confronted powerful whites in the South with unprecedented demands. The early victories, as in the Montgomery bus boycott taken over by Martin Luther King, Jr., or the student sit-ins in retail stores, were won by appeal to some combination of conscience and fear both of economic loss and of intervention from above. The national political victories which followed immediately after the brutal southern killings, beatings, and bombings of 1963 and 1964, and the massive March on Washington of 1963, resulted more simply from the appeal to conscience alone. With the intellectual basis of racism long dead, educated white Americans no longer had any support for the kind of racial prejudice which they had simply absorbed through the culture. If they had no real stake of their own in the practices and institutions being attacked, and if no other emotions were aroused, racial justice usually beat out bigotry in the internal battles waged in millions of hearts and minds. It was a growing national sense of indignation which after all pushed Presidents John Kennedy and then Lyndon Johnson into risking the traditional support of southern whites, who far outnumbered blacks, by calling for the congressional action which eventually resulted in the Civil Rights Act of 1964, and the Voting Rights Act of the following year.

These acts combined with earlier court decisions to ensure, at least on paper, the triumph of "non-economic liberalism," the end of publicly supported segregation and other forms of discrimination. But by the middle of the 1960s it was already clear that this was not enough. While the more eloquent speakers at the Washington Monument in 1963 had appealed to a general sense of justice and idealism, the one I most remember was a short, ineloquent, and angry young man, John Lewis, already a veteran of many battles to the south, who talked about the wages of laborers and maids. The next issues were not civil rights in the traditional sense, but access to education and economic opportunity, and a "War on Poverty" that would cost money.

President Johnson announced the opening of this War on Poverty in January of 1964, and within a few years the Congress enacted virtually all the legislation requested, together with the other measures that collectively made up the President's Great Society. Relatively easy passage was assured by the fact that many of these acts, such as Medicare and aid to higher education, were designed to help a range of Americans of all races. But many were understood to be directed mostly at blacks, especially in inner-city neighborhoods: programs such as Head Start, the Job Corps, the Neighborhood Youth Corps, the expansion of welfare aid to mothers with dependent children, school funding, and grant money for a great variety of community action programs.

Actual appropriation money for the War on Poverty was harder to find after 1965, however, as the tone and tenor of black activity shifted. Dramatic action and brutal reaction gave way in the South to the quiet business of registering new voters, and the well-dressed schoolchildren, college students, and ministers who had led the earlier movements faded from the television screens. Their places were taken by largely northern spokesmen for "Black Power" of several kinds, and by angry rioters in the cities, some of them chanting "Burn, Baby, Burn!"

One aspect of the new African-American awakening, the complex of cultural events and movements designed to underline the fact that "Black Is Beautiful," was and remains generally successful. I was skeptical at the time, as a young college professor, about all the Afro haircuts and dashikis worn to underline what seemed a purely symbolic and possibly distracting issue. But in perspective it is now possible to see that a frontal assault on the whole Indo-European "white" aesthetic, much like the one Professor Kealing, among others, had urged during the late 19th century, did help support group pride.

But other aspects of the awakening were not so successsful, in part because rising black assertiveness coincided with the wider ferment in American society during the middle and later 1960s. This was a time, after all, when radicals, liberals, and conservatives were battling simultaneously over the Vietnam War, the youthful "counterculture," and countless new ways of looking at everything from traditional American history to sexual practices and gender roles. In the midst of this, all too ready to be either scared or exhilarated, white Americans of all persuasions tended to exaggerate and misrepresent what blacks really wanted.

Conservatives, fearing social revolution, were scared by the rhetoric, itself often exaggerated, of the community activists sponsored by Johnson's War on Poverty. Radicals, even liberals like myself, hoped on the contrary that black energies could be enlisted in the battle to reform the whole of the society, to make it more nearly just, humane, and egalitarian. Martin Luther King's increasing concern about the Vietnam War, and conversely the adoption by restless white college students of several African-American demands, were among the signs which encouraged us, across the political spectrum, to believe that black restlesssness would lead to major structural changes.

But we were all wrong. Whatever was demanded by leaders at the very top, most black Americans, like their white immigrant predecessors, simply wanted inclusion into the benefits of American society as it was: like the early American Federation of Labor, what they were really asking for was "More. Here. Now." Their own values traditionally balanced the need for mutual help and cooperation with a strong streak of competitive individualism and stress on material consumption. One side of this fit perfectly with the idealized way in which the dominant majority viewed the American system as a whole, the other with some of the worst of its actual practice. Much of the community administration encouraged by the War on Poverty, and many of the neighborhood groups encouraged by the government and other sources, did produce modestly useful results. But the characteristic failing of those which did not was not the radical subversion feared by conservatives but simply corruption, with money siphoned off for big cars, fur coats, and other traditional symbols of material success.

And in politics the direct appeal to physical fear, through rhetorical or actual violence, was disastrous. The urban crime rate that began to rise around 1959 was becoming a political issue even before the escalation of urban riots brought the sight of looted stores, burning buildings, and armed confrontations to television screens. Entrenched local governments did not back down before violent threats, and, sometimes in combination with state and federal troops, successfully confined rioters to their own neighborhoods. A third definition of "race riot" emerged: neither the anti-black pogroms of the 19th century, nor the black-white conflict of the earlier 20th century, but eruptions within the ghetto, combining property destruction and some uneven battles with authority. White civilians simply stayed safely on the sidelines, watching the bulletins, rooting for the cops. And while local police, often brutally or illegally, crushed the Black Panthers, and other militant groups feuded and broke up, the dominant electorate in 1968 clearly sided with "law and order."

That 1968 election was one of the critical ones in American history. The issues framed by Robert Kennedy on one side and George Wallace on the other, picked up in more muted form by Hubert Humphrey and Richard Nixon, have lasted into the 1990s. They include domestic versus military spending, support for "progressive" versus "pro-American" Third World regimes, expansion versus curbing of the welfare state, acceptance versus rejection of what are viewed as African-American demands for special treatment. The political geography of the following quarter-century was another legacy of the same period, as the urban East and Midwest were pitted against the suburbs, South, and West. And in every presidential election except the one in which Jimmy Carter beat Gerald Ford in 1976, black Americans have lost, their agenda rejected.

But the lack of presidential leverage at the top, beginning in 1968, did not kill the advances of the 1960s. The Democratic party remained strong enough in Congress to continue existing programs, and President Richard Nixon actually added some new ones. The voting rights won under Lyndon Johnson ensured a steady growth in African-American officeholders and respect in the South, whose white elected representatives soon learned to curb the openly racist rhetoric of just a generation before. Continued in-migration meanwhile combined with white fear and flight to bring black mayors to power in northern cities of varying size. And through the later 1960s and 1970s, sometimes as a result of direct pressure and sometimes not, a host of private institutions also re-examined everything from educational curricula to hiring practices.

Much of this movement outside of politics resulted from the old appeal to conscience, but it is impossible to rule out the effect of the appeal to fear. After 1968 the riots faded. No city had more than one big one, as those who had lived through them remembered their futility, and the difficulty of finding shoes and groceries on burnt-out mornings after; in Philadelphia, what had been a thriving black business district along Columbia Avenue has never recovered from the destruction suffered back in 1964. But those who ran institutions which, unlike elected governments, were sensitive to the demands of relatively small numbers of table-pounding protesters or picketers could not have forgotten the more ferocious images which had so recently dominated the screen. Whatever the combination of motives which moved whites, they resulted in greatly improved opportunities for African-Americam men and women to win educations, and to use their degrees once they were earned.

The rate of college attendance for both blacks and whites soared during the 1960s, the result in large part of federal scholarship money, and the black rate continued to move up well into the 1970s, while rates for white men dropped. White-collar employment, a traditional if somewhat inaccurate measure of middle-class status, also shot up, even more dramatically, and far more for blacks than whites in the same period. While the proportion of employed white men in these jobs crept up from about 40 to 43 percent between 1960 and 1980, the proportion of nonwhite men more than doubled, from less than 15 to about 30 percent. Improvement among women was even more dramatic, as white women moved up slightly, from 60 to about 65 percent, while nonwhite women nearly tripled their white-collar employment, from about 18 to 52 percent.[29]

At the top or professional level, in Philadelphia as elsewhere, there was also a great leap forward, for the first time in decades. It was registered first in law- and medical-school enrollments, and then in the numbers admitted to practice as physicians and attorneys.

During the 1960s a series of anti-discrimination suits against white institutions such as Women's Medical College combined with changed attitudes to complete the process, already evident during the 1950s, of opening the city's medical schools and hospitals to black applicants. By the early 1970s, in fact, Mercy-Douglass, founded during William Dorsey's generation and merged during the 1950s, finally closed its doors, symbolizing the full formal integration of the medical establishment.[30]

The same period in law witnessed a truly enormous increase in numbers, especially among women. While changed census procedures make it hard to count more recent figures exactly, the 66 black lawyers of 1960 had grown to an estimated 400 by 1981. Most of these were of course young: the Philadelphia area's three law schools had less than 20 black students as late as 1968, but 185 ten years later. By 1980 over half these students were women. And while direct geographical comparison is also difficult, it appears that in terms of successful practice as of 1980, Philadelphia stood somewhere in the middle of sixteen big cities surveyed. While still trailing their white peers badly, and with public careers, as in the judiciary, far more open than partnerships in big private firms, the gap was at any rate closing.[31]

But these same twenty years that brought so much progress to professional and other educated African-Americans witnessed a precisely opposite movement at the other social pole. While black doctors, lawyers, and office workers gained on their white peers, millions of others moved back. And the two most disturbing and publicized social indicators among the whole group shot up with frightening and unprecedented speed, the murder rate by several hundred percent, and the number of black children born illegitimate from about 17 to well over 50 percent of the total.[32]

Meanwhile the explanation for these last two trends was long buried under a political fog created on the one hand by a still new and exaggerated deference to black sensibilities, and on the other by the fact that the most dramatic rises coincided roughly with the simultaneously conducted wars on poverty and in Vietnam. Liberals, in short, were simply reluctant even to acknowledge, certainly to confront, any black problems other than poverty itself. Conservatives railed about the permissive society, the contributions of peaceful protest to lawbreaking, and the effects of welfare in encouraging illegitimacy, going on to deny that all the money spent on the War on Poverty had any positive effect at all.[33]

Liberal refusal to recognize problems did not make them any less real, while the conservative diagnosis did not allow for the fact that both the decline in two-parent households and the rise in the murder rate had begun not during the Democratic administrations of the 1960s but, as noted, during the previous era. In fact the whole complex of legislation passed during the 1960s had a decidedly positive effect, moving many households out of poverty, helping young people into college, and removing discriminatory barriers to employment. But that legislation was in effect moving against a deeper tide in the American urban economy, the one already evident in the late 1950s, which was shifting the whole structure of that economy in a direction which made it increasingly inhospitable to poor blacks.

The Vietnam War, as well as the War on Poverty, helped obscure this shift. The unemployment rate moved down in the middle of the 1960s less as a result of legislation than of the war. Wars generally have this effect, and this one had an especially heavy impact on African-American men. The political need to pacify the middle class essentially kept educated white males out of Vietnam—my own students agonized about the draft but not one of them was caught in it—so that the war was disproportionately fought by uneducated black males. But while those looking for jobs—the ones measured by the unemployment statistics—could generally find them, the far more important but less publicized statistics of those wholly out of the labor force, those who had given up, or gone into illegal occupations, rose steadily higher. And after their short two years of duty the veterans returned to the same mean streets they had left.[34]

The fundamental problem then, the one which both helped those at the top of the scale and hurt those at the bottom, was the shift from an industrial to a post-industrial or service economy. The former type rewards a variety of abilities, with room for people who have little more than muscles to sell, or perhaps special skills with their hands. The latter rewards only those with formal educations, and frustrates those without.

The impact of the shift on both crime and family is evident. Young men who have no jobs and no prospects are liable to give in to impulsive acts of violence. If surrounded by other people and messages which flaunt ever higher standards of prosperity they are also likely to indulge in impulsive acts of theft. Young women are affected in parallel ways. Always liable to get pregnant, historically young women used simply to get married afterward. During the 1960s and 1970s soaring rates of illegitimacy did not result from the fact that more young women were having children; quite the contrary, the birth rate tended to fall over the period. But if for the most traditionally old-fashioned of reasons there is no one to marry—that is, no young man with a future and a job—then the rate of illegitimacy will rise. And when, as in the 1970s, less than half of young black men in cities met this traditional standard, the rate of illegitimacy rose dramatically.[35]

The contemporary city then is the product of several layers of history. Some of its patterns go back directly to William Dorsey's 19th century, others are more recent. The two most compelling are the latest fruits of historical trends that go back for generations. One is the achievement of local political control, culmination of the long trek to the city, more recently accelerated by white fear and flight. The other is the growth of the underclass, resulting from an economic change more fundamental than political action and largely ignored by it. Although shut out of the service economy for different reasons than its late 19th-century predecessors were originally shut out of the industrial economy, the condition of the underclass today is a direct heritage of that earlier injustice, and the decades of deprivation and frustration which followed from it.

The growth of the underclass confirms the final and most troubling parallel between the late 19th century and the late 20th, between William Dorsey's city and ours. It is now clear, with a historian's hindsight, that Dorsey's productive adult years, the ones which began with the Civil War and stretched to sometime after 1900, encompassed the most progressive period in African-American history. Its only rival, in terms of visible economic gains, was the one which began with World War II, when I was a small child. But it is becoming clearer that those good years, too, which lasted most of my lifetime, are now history. Just as the end of the first "golden age" may be marked, among other things, by a dropping proportion of educated professionals, the end of the second may be dated from the late 1970s, when the rate of black college attendance began to fall. Above all, just as the progress of the earlier period was eventually doomed by a fatal contradiction, with gains at the top undermined by weaknesses at the bottom, there is now a structurally different but effectively similar threat eating at the gains of the more recent one.

In any case the issue of how we got from there to here is important principally as it helps to suggest how we might get from here to someplace better, subject of the final chapter.

Chapter 14

A Common Destiny: Prospects for the Black City

Americans have always thought themselves a special people. In the late 20th century we must reject many of the ways in which earlier generations sometimes conceived this notion; for 17th-century Puritans it involved a religious, specifically Protestant, example to the world; for late 19th-century racists a mission of "Anglo-Saxon" conquest; in the post–World War II era a superiority based on "free enterprise," an economic system which proved we were best because we were richest. But there have been other and more attractive ways of expressing the central idea of special destiny, notably the idea that this country is a kind of "great experiment."

For its most eloquent earlier spokesmen, Thomas Jefferson and Abraham Lincoln, the experiment was political, as for generations after the United States was founded we were the only major nation in the world with a formally democratic government. This is of course no longer relevant: while the attractions of democracy—and some of its problems—are dramatically evident during the 1990s, many countries have constitutions at least as democratic as ours, and the United States can no longer claim the lead. But toward the end of the college year, with a little embarrassment—neither I nor today's students are comfortable with idealistic flights of fancy—I sometimes suggest that the idea of "experiment" may still be worth considering, in terms not of democracy but of race and ethnicity.

America was founded after all without any of the elements which defined a "nation" in the Old World: its people had no unique language, no common religion or culture or history. Three races, too, were already in place—the black fully one-fifth of the total—and innumerable separate ethnic groups, making it impossible for us to claim even a mythical common ancestry. From the start then, however reluctantly, we have had instead to learn to live with diversity. And if we are no longer pioneering in politics, we are after all still

374

pioneering in trying to make a truly multi-racial society work. All across the world, certainly in newly "democratic" states without our history, however painful, of learning to accommodate to others, wracking racial and ethnic conflict reminds us that ours is by far the longest, most visible, and most important such experiment in mutual living.

From this point of view, among others, the condition of the African-American population at the end of the 20th century is morally intolerable. The long move out of rural slavery into the cities has been marked by much progress, a decline in racism, the winning of political power by the traditional rules, the growth of a substantial middle and wage-earning class. But it would be a massive admission of failure if that movement should end, as is now threatened, not in progress but in retrogression, with the urban situation in many ways less hopeful for all of us than in William Dorsey's Philadelphia.

The problem which needs help is the condition not just of part but of all of urban black America. While the condition of the underclass most visibly cries for attention, for both good reasons and bad the future of all African-Americans is so bound together that whatever affects one social level affects all.

Only a few things about that future are fully clear, beginning with the fact that the race will not go away, as many expected during the previous century, as the result of either biological or cultural extinction. My own hope is that we will move toward a more truly plural society, in which racial identity and association are largely matters of individual choice. To the minority of blacks who would prefer instead simply to reject the dominant society and its institutions I would suggest a paraphrase, from an entirely different perspective, of the famous compromise offered by Booker T. Washington a century ago: "in all things purely cultural we can be as separate as the fingers, yet one as the hand in all things essential to mutual progress." Mutual respect is essential to any such progress, and so is the recognition that whatever may happen in other areas, the American economy is a single arena, and we are all in it together.

From this perspective, the immediate need is for fuller black inclusion in that economy more or less as it stands. One lesson of the 1960s is that we must all begin by accepting the hopes of most African-Americans rather than trying to impose our own. While I would prefer more ambitious restructuring in the long run, the felt need is for an opportunity to share in the jobs and rewards of competitive capitalism, and this final chapter is devoted only to matters relevant to that end.

The first step will be to define the interrelated problems of urban black America from underclass to middle class, with an assessment of their historic origins, both structural and "cultural." That in turn requires some rank ordering in terms of what is fundamental and what merely symptomatic, what may realistically be expected and what may not. The next step will be to assess the possible sources of help. Some traditional ones have reached their apparent limits, but there are others that may take their places. Some involve a reawakened sense of self-help, from within the black middle class; some, outside support, from government. None can be taken for granted: there are problems and contingencies in every area. But the fact that there are some new elements in the situation, from African-American political control of Philadelphia and other cities to an awakening sense of national economic needs and priorities, offers some ground for optimism. And the conclusion as a whole is offered in a spirit of both realism and hope, the notion that together both our national ideals and our economic needs may combine to remind us that we all share a common destiny.

The term "underclass" has no precise definition. Here it simply means people who have no legitimate jobs, not those usually counted in the "unemployment" statistics, who are actively trying to escape out of them, but those who are unable to connect with the world of work because of any one of a number of handicaps. These range from specific problems such as lack of transportation, the need to care for small children, or drug addiction, to more general or fundamental ones such as lack of education and ignorance of or indifference to the requirements of modern employers.[1]

Philadelphia's "labor force" as of 1989 consisted of some 660,000 men and women, with official unemployment very low and indeed competition for competent help so fierce that companies throughout the 1980s had routinely to interview seven or eight people to find one to fill a job. Meanwhile a careful survey by the city's prize-winning Private Industry Council found that there were about 300,000 residents living in poverty and of working age who were "unattractive to employers." Although many of these held marginal or temporary dead-end jobs, and so were counted as part of the "labor force," all were at risk of perhaps permanent unemployment if they should lose them. As a group they may then be defined as the city's "underclass."[2]

But while this economic definition is simple enough, it is meant to combat a great deal of confusion among both ordinary citizens and academic specialists as to who makes up the underclass, why it exists, what kind of threat it poses, and what may reasonably be expected of any assault upon it.

It must be noted, first, that while this class was and is very heavily black it also contains many Hispanics and indeed whites, as a reminder that the economic problems of the late 20th century are not confined to any one race. But what is most significant, in terms of the nature and future prospects of the class as a whole, and the structural problem which has helped to create it, is what makes them "unattractive" to begin with: these 300,000 people, however far they may have gone in school, do not have the equivalent of eighth-grade literate and "numerate" skills, at a time when the eighth-grade is now thought a minimum threshold for job training and employment even at the lowest levels.

The trend toward ever higher educational demands in the marketplace has been with us for decades. While an array of rapidly outdated statistics may paralyze a reader, a very few may suggest the outlines of the picture. It was already true in 1980 that in ten of the biggest eastern and midwestern cities the only growing job categories required not merely high school diplomas but some college training. By that date the percentage of current jobs held by those with some college experience ranged from an extreme high, in white-collar Washington, of 65 percent, to a low in blue-collar Baltimore of 38 percent. Philadelphia, a little farther up I-95, stood close to the lower pole at just 40 percent. That means that in Philadelphia it was and has been a little easier than in most places to win a job with no more than a high-school degree. But even here the number of openings for those without college has been shrinking rapidly, and since 1980 the average education required has gone up, by about one grade level as of 1990, and it is predicted that it will go up by another by the year 2000.[3]

The basic historical trend which has created this new kind of "lack of opportunity" is of course the shift from an urban-industrial to a service economy. With its greater stress on education, and devaluation of simple hard work with back or hands, this new economy has in effect stranded large numbers of people, especially young black men. Job-training experts point out that such men often come in eager for work. But what they want is blue-collar "macho" jobs—their word—of the sort which their fathers sometimes won but which rarely open during the 1990s. The "pussy" jobs which are available call for reading and writing skills that their sisters are more likely to have—which is why black women, certainly if not encumbered by young children, have far better access to the market than men.

But in addition to this structural problem which has created an "under-class" of people left behind by the educational demands of a service economy, there is another, even older, dating back to the 19th century, which applies specifically to its black members. Part II of this book detailed the way in which deliberate racism excluded the urban black population, in Philadelphia and elsewhere, from participation in the urban-industrial revolution which was then the dominant force in the economy.

In the early stages of this process, the decades immediately after the Civil War, I argued in Chapter 3 that despite deep poverty and—by that era's standards—high crime rates there was as yet nothing comparable to the modern underclass. The African-Americans of Philadelphia and other northern cities had higher rates of overall employment than whites, although in dead-end jobs; they had more skills than they were allowed to use; they had for most of the period an evident hunger for both academic and "industrial" education. Hope then still ran high that the barriers would crumble, and that it was possible to embrace the norms of the dominant society; as one index, despite the enormous obstacles posed not only by poverty but by the specific nature of the jobs they held—such as live-in domestic work—urban blacks also struggled hard to get married and raise families. Chapter 13, however, sketched the way in which the persistent deprivation which marked most of the 20th century killed these early hopes, as the experience of several generations bred a widespread skepticism about the possibility of winning good jobs through education, or establishing stable families.

Modern social scientists argue whether the stubborn persistence and indeed growth of the underclass is the result of structural conditions which simply deny its members the chance to work, or of other "cultural" factors within the group, which make its members unable or unwilling to take advantage of opportunities even when offered. The argument of this book is that both are involved, historically, as cause and effect, currently as a double set of handicaps, the proportion differing with each individual and situation.

The basic structural problem is compounded for poor blacks in Philadelphia and other cities by a number of other external handicaps. Two of the most obvious are the abysmal condition of most inner-city schools, and the lack of available transportation to those places, such as suburban malls and assembly plants, where jobs may still be had. Another, less obvious, is that in many ways the black underclass suffers from two different kinds of isolation.

The first of these is simply geographical: as housing and other opportunities opened for the black middle and wage-earning classes in the 1950s and after, they tended to move out, leaving the poorest areas and people behind. In a far more severe reprise of the situation suffered by Philadelphia's black businessmen during the late 19th century, those left behind have found themselves passed by simply because no one wants to visit their crime-ridden neighborhoods, or open new enterprises, or even provide transportation in and out to those places which may have jobs.[4]

But "social isolation" in this analysis is even more important than the merely geographical. The fact that professionals, civil servants, even the remaining factory hands have left the worst districts means that there are no "old heads," no role models, no one to help in any way. Many young people literally do not know a single adult with a job, while hustlers of many kinds have traditionally flaunted a number of other ways of making money.[5]

Certainly the old web or network of associations that once united black Philadelphians across the lines of status no longer reaches to the underclass. One symbolic change is the one noted in Chapter 12: the fact that today Greek-letter fraternities and sororities, with their requirement of collegiate experience, have in effect succeeded the far more democratic secret orders such as the Odd Fellows. Even more important is the marked decline in church membership, especially in the mainstream churches, which once tied social classes together; the myriad smaller churches may unite some of the very poor in fellowship, a contribution that must not be slighted, but they cannot function as economically useful networks of information, helping members to find jobs.

At this point the structural problem of isolation, in denying many members of the black underclass any contact with the more successful members and traditional institutions of their race, begins to merge into the second or "cultural" problem. Many academic sociologists, calling it an attempt to "blame the victims" for their condition, bristle at the suggestion that there is a "culture of poverty" which handicaps many poor people economically and distinguishes them from others. But for a historian, if "culture" is defined simply as a widely shared set not only of formal values but of attitudes, habits, and priorities, then to deny that a racist frustration of opportunity practiced over many generations has had no important impact on culture is to deny the importance of history itself.

Few members of the underclass in practice share a culture whose formal beliefs are radically different from those of middle-class or wage-earning blacks or whites. They watch the same television shows, listen to much of the same music, admire many of the same personalities. Certainly most will tell inquiring sociologists that they believe in work, education, family, and other "respectable" values. But when faced not with survey questionnaires but with choices in real life it is clear that these same people have habits, attitudes, and priorities which make it impossible to live up to these ideals. All those generations when it made sense to give in to impulsive self-gratification, when it was impossible to count on a job or support a family, have left their mark. The testimony of teachers, social workers, and employers is nearly unanimous: to excel in school is to "act white," and to invite derision and even violence on the playground; to persevere at any task is exceptional; even to apply for job training in the face of peer pressure is an "act of courage." In addition to poverty itself, then, the African-American experience has created a large number of people who are easily discouraged, unrealistic about the relation of ends to means, lacking pride in themselves and trust in others.

The very existence of this population is in several indirect ways, to be explored later, a threat first to the black middle class and second to the wider society. But the nature of that threat should not be misunderstood. Despite white nervousness, and leftover rhetoric about the choice between "ballots and bullets," the underclass clearly lacks the discipline or ideology needed to carry out any kind of successful social movement, certainly not a revolutionary one, and its members pose more of a direct threat to themselves and each other than to anyone else. The most publicized of the three social problems which afflict them, crime, drug addiction, and family instability, are all different. But all are related in two ways to the more fundamental job situation: all three tend statistically—which means by no means always—to be symptoms, or results, of long-term structural unemployment, and all three make it hard—which means by no means impossible—for those caught up in them to break out and get good jobs. But we tend to deal with each of the three separately from their statistically economic causes.

The problem with various forms of illegal hustling and crime is not of course exclusively or even primarily an African-American problem. Every western nation has shown a dramatic increase in criminal behavior beginning at some time after the middle of the 20th century, much of it built into the way that the international economy is structured. An economic system built on high levels of consumption and credit, and boasting a continual stream of skillfully crafted messages urging viewers to get and display temptingly expensive products, is one that will inevitably inspire illegal shortcuts. No class is immune to the temptations, and by far the largest illegal profits go to those who commit "white-collar" crimes. These include some of the most powerful politicians and richest businessmen in the country, who make huge sums with minimum effort through personal contacts. Their usual and basic defense, that it is hard in the modern economy to distinguish between illegal and legal practice, is hardly designed to promote the work ethic, honesty, or thrift among the rest. Young blacks—and whites—without access to bigger things will continue to commit burglaries and larcenies as a matter of relatively rational economic choice. If caught, however, as most eventually are, the resultant criminal record is more likely than for those higher on the social scale to cost them the chance to win good jobs.[6]

Crimes of violence, in contrast, notably homicide, are rarely committed as matters of rational choice. Murder and manslaughter are usually no more than extreme versions of thoughtless, often drunken or drug-induced aggression, their motives momentary, the odds of punishment high. Here again the historical evidence, stretching over a century and a half, suggests that violent crime is statistically related to the nature of long-term employment. Specifically the kinds of jobs provided by the urban-industrial revolution are clearly related to the long-term and international drop in violent behavior measured between the middle of the 19th century and the middle of the 20th. Jobs that demand regular, cooperative, and predictable behavior at work, ideally promising long-term rewards, at the least absorbing the energies of young men full-time, were once open to people with little prior education. The movement into a different economy has coincided, by no accident, with an international rise in violent crime, with the especially vulnerable African-American population the most visible but hardly unique victims.[7]

The drug trade obviously intensifies all this in many ways, and no discussion of crime among Philadelphians, whether on the air or in living or lecture rooms, gets very far without turning to it. But drugs, too, are a symptom. The long history of drug abuse in this country suggests that the recent surge in addiction has little to do with either supply or cost. While neither was yet much of a problem, both cocaine and heroin were known to the late 19th century, and both these and marijuana were cheap and available through much of the 20th. The more temporary physical effects of all drugs, including alcohol, affect all people equally, regardless of class or color. But incapacitating addiction, like disease, is by far most likely to strike the most vulnerable groups. For the purpose of fighting addiction the equivalent of a strong immune system is not physical but emotional or psychological; people with no stake in the future, family, work, and society are statistically more likely to fall victim than those who have such a stake.[8]

The only real successes of the decades-long "War on Drugs" in the United States have resulted from middle-class fears about the health effects of legal alcohol and nicotine, more recently illicit cocaine and marijauna. While this shows the potential effect of education, especially among those who have reason to hope for long and productive lives, the concurrent attempt to deal with illegal drugs by trying to stop imports at the border and punish domestic users is obviously bankrupt. It has long been a cliché that these policies have simply had the effect of keeping profits so high as to remain enormously lucrative for suppliers, while prices remain low enough so that they can reach even the poorest. The history is that the most costly of police efforts have had only a temporarily chilling effect on supply, while the cycles which periodically move different drugs into and out of fashion have responded more to the social experience and attitudes of users than to law enforcement. There is some hope that the currently devastating epidemic of "crack" cocaine may wane in its turn, but so long as there are people whose worlds seem too ugly to face straight, something else will take its place. And no border patrol can deal with the escalating ingenuity of those chemists who are producing artificial substances far more dangerous than the illegal vegetables we have grown used to.

But all this may change. Baltimore's courageous black mayor drew on his experience as a prosecutor when, in the spring of 1988, he became the first nationally visible politician to suggest that we explore truly radical new ways of attacking the problem. He was preceded, and has been followed, by a number of other social observers from both ends of the political spectrum. But black and white elected officials have been largely resistant to his call at least to debate alternatives. The whites, generally longer in power, simply fear the effects of abandoning established policies they have trumpeted for years; the blacks have worried that to soften the criminal approach is to make drugs too easy to get, and in affect to abandon millions of their own constituents to crippling addiction, a belief that at its far fringes embraces the notion that the whole problem is a deliberate "genocidal" plot. It was then an enormous breakthrough when early in 1990 one of Philadelphia's most streetwise politicians succeeded in persuading his fellow city councilors to call, at least, for a study of the effects of decriminalization. While real change seems by no means imminent, it does then look increasingly possible.[9]

Meanwhile family instability is the last and ultimately the most threatening of the personal problems which not only beset but reach past the underclass. At its most extreme level, when combined with severe drug addiction, it cripples two generations: not only the mothers but their babies. Around the time of

W. E. B. Du Bois's sojourn my grandmother, returning from volunteer work
in the Seventh Ward's Pennsylvania Hospital, used sometimes to cry about the
blind or syphilitic children, "misconceived and misbegotten," too often born
to the neighborhood's prostitutes. Modern medicine can deal with some of
those problems now, but delivery rooms are even more filled with despair over
infants addicted already in utero, whose rising numbers and multiple handicaps
threaten to swamp not only urban hospitals but many other institutions.
Entering the last decade of the 20th century, the still relatively young and
responsible grandmothers of these families have been able, sometimes, to
rescue some of their children's children. But as one observer in Philadelphia's
Family Court put it—"What will happen when all the grandmothers are
gone?" And while these are the most miserable stories of the age, an even bigger
problem is represented by the less extreme but more common situation posed
by illegitimacy itself.[10]

The growing number of female-headed families is the most obvious example of a growing, historically traceable, "cultural" handicap among the specifically African-American underclass. For nearly a generation now, scholarship
about slavery has shown that, despite an inevitable weakening under its regime,
the mass of its victims came out of it with workable family ties and a real
eagerness, even hunger, to marry and establish legal nuclear families. While life
in cities made this hard, as shown in earlier chapters of this book, virtually all
studies, and perhaps more important memories, testify that most blacks
continued to want and to practice nuclear family life through Willian Dorsey's
generation and well beyond. But again, all those decades of frustration, the
inability of fathers to support wives and children, left its mark. The proportion
of husband-wife families began to sink, as noted, even in the relatively
prosperous 1940s and 1950s, and has plummeted dramatically since.[11]

The effect may be seen through a study, made in 1986, which traced
marriage patterns among several ethnic groups. All the people involved lived in
desperately poor areas of Chicago, and presumably faced comparably bleak
opportunities for education and work. Among Mexicans, many from rural
backgrounds in which the family is still a useful economic unit, the proportion
of men who married before conceiving their first child was 64 percent, higher
than for non-Hispanic whites, at 62 percent. Among Puerto Ricans, many split
between earlier rural and urban experiences, the figure was 42 percent. Among
black men it was just 22 percent.[12]

During the excitement of the late 1960s and early 1970s it was sometimes
claimed, by blacks and others, that female-headed families were actually
superior to the suffocating, male-dominated, families of the middle class. But
while, like other aspects of the African-American culture of poverty, the
female-headed family may be a realistic way of adapting to or coping with the
harsh world of the ghetto, it offers no help with the very different problem of
escaping from it. There is no longer any doubt that children raised by single

mothers are not only far more likely statistically to be poor than those with two parents present but are further handicapped emotionally and psychologically in dealing with the wider world. If unable routinely to see adult men in positions of family responsibility, in tender and affectionate moments, their vision of the male role will be limited to what they see on the street: competitive, aggressive, sexually and otherwise exploitative.

Perhaps no single statistic is more pregnant with trouble for the African-American population as a whole than the one which indicates that more than half of all births occur out of wedlock. This is a figure which reaches far beyond the unemployable underclass, well into the ranks of wage-earners and even the middle class. No one who has watched a young woman with a secure and longheld job in day care struggle over a mile through the snow to open her center at 6 o'clock on a winter's morning can doubt her capacity for responsible hard work. But the fact that she is a single parent, pulling the younger of her two children on a sled, is more poignant yet, and suggests real trouble ahead.

Historically the fortunes of the black middle class have, with some exceptions, always been fundamentally dependent on those below it. If membership in the middle class today, as earlier, is defined to include steadily employed or skilled blue-collar as well as white-collar workers, together with professionals and entrepreneurs, then it is bigger than it was a century ago. More of its members, too, belong to large and mostly white organizations, insulated from any direct dependence on the inner-city underclass. But for most dependence is still real, and connects them in many ways to those they have left behind in the ghetto. The very word "underclass," with its ominous resonance with "undertow," suggests an ability to reach up and knock people off their feet, pulling them back down and in. And there is real danger in the fact that the gains of the African-American middle class are threatened by some of the same things which created the underclass, a few of them "cultural," in the sense defined above, more of them structural, the result of the same set of economic changes which have created the underclass.

Stereotyping, most obviously, as always lumps the race together. Whether prejudice or simply prudence, the fear of black crime in black neighborhoods has always handicapped entrepreneurs struggling to attract white customers. More recently the progressive conquest of legal and social barriers has allowed young African-Americans out of their own neighborhoods into others. The price of this hard-won freedom, however, is that fear of young black men has jumped over its traditional geographic bounds, and the nervous or myopic may attach it to college students, salesmen, or executives encountered anywhere, as well as to potential muggers. This is a genuine handicap: one reason why black women have a relatively easier time in winning white-collar employment than their brothers is not just that they often have better educational qualifications but simply that their physical presence inspires less unease. And so long as the television images generated by crime and drugs are likely to get worse rather than better, the illegitimate activities of some will continue to threaten the ambitions of others.

And drugs, second of the trio of underclass problems, pose an even more direct threat to individual black members of the middle class. While as a statistical generalization people with jobs and family are more likely to be immune than those without, addiction may sometimes strike them too, just as disease may strike the young and strong. This is a problem for whites as well, but African-Americans are more likely to live in or near neighborhoods where drugs are sold, to have old friends or schoolmates whose habits make them eager to win profits through conversion, to be subject to pressures and disillusionments they are eager to escape by any means. And there are few sadder sights than watching formerly "straight" friends or acquaintances lose weight, the ability to talk straight, and then all else, as more mothers give up, fewer little girls get their hair braided for Sundays, and more little boys stray out nights on the streets.

Far more common is the spread of illegitimacy as a norm. While the national rate for African-Americans was over 50 percent, by the late 1980s in Philadelphia it had soared to well over 70 percent. This is a figure that reaches far beyond the underclass: reluctance to take the risks involved in marriage is now well entrenched within the middle class, as fewer than 40 percent of the city's eligible black males had ever been married at all, and nearly half of those were currently separated or divorced. And while it is entirely possible for women to raise children successfully on their own, it is very hard to do, and there is a small army of single working mothers in the city, many with good jobs, who are living too close to the edge.[13]

The persistent problem of entrepreneurship, next, is as always mostly structural but partly cultural as well. A century ago the apparent decline in the number and influence of businessmen in black Philadelphia resulted in part from being caught, temporarily, between two markets. A combination of racism and the fear of visiting big and crime-ridden black neighborhoods was losing caterers, barbers, and tradesmen their traditional white customers, while the black market itself was not yet big and certainly not rich enough to provide alternatives as profitable. Since then the straight white customers have been lost entirely: during this century it has mostly been those looking for illegitimate services or substances who have made the trip into the ghetto, and still do. Meanwhile parts, but only parts, of the African-American market have been won, and while this is now big it is still not rich. The most characteristic opportunities are still those which depend on social segregation, hairdressers and undertakers, plus real estate and a few—too few—small neighborhood shops. None of these except real estate has much room to expand, and even real estate does not employ many people.

Current African-American efforts either to monopolize their own neighborhood businesses or to break into broader markets suffer from several handicaps. The biggest and oldest is of course the persistent poverty of potential consumers close to home, so that purely local successes remain modest at best. This in turn aggravates the second problem, lack of capital and the mistrust of dominant bankers. While other groups have been able to beat this, partly by establishing their own banks, Philadelphia's African-Americans have never had much success in banking. While the 19th-century city boasted a series of well-run if small building and loan societies, there has been no black-owned bank in the city since the Citizen's and Southern was merged into the Lincoln Bank during the 1950s. More broadly, there are obviously some elements of African-American "culture," not universally but widely shared, which turn young people away from successful commercial enterprise.

There is no clear explanation for this. Much like the 19th-century Irish, the most important city voters of their day, blacks have long enjoyed a reputation for colorful personal behavior that sits oddly with the fact that so much of their leadership has traditionally worked within the gray security of the civil service, their livelihoods dependent on waiting patiently in line for raises and promotions. Certainly there is no cultural prejudice against either risk-taking or competition, and the accomplishments of successful businesspeople are continually cited in the African-American media. Those, too, who favor more cultural autonomy, "Africanicity," distinctive dress, speech, behavior, or values, are most vividly aware that apart from some universities big white bureaucracies of any kind are essentially hostile to diversity, and salaried dependence is fatal. But repeated campaigns to get ordinary people to "buy black" flounder at least as often on the fact that there are so few to buy from as on any lack of racial solidarity.

Within the group itself, the oldest explanation for the relative lack of entrepreneurship is that an insistently conspicuous consumption eats up potential savings. In more recent times, the relative weakness of the African-American family has ruled out that classic route to small business success, most recently taken by immigrants from Asia, which is essentially built on the exploitation of family labor. A final explanation may be that much potential entrepreneurial talent, and capital, gets diverted to other directions. One is the ministry, and church building, both still highly competitive. Another is illegal hustling, which has historically been especially hurtful for two reasons, first, because of its blighting effect on legitimate local business, second, because the net effect of most illegal enterprise has been to drain money out of the community and into the hands of white and even foreign suppliers and wholesalers. And while illegal enterprise has been for some groups a significant if shadowy source of capital turned to more conventional purposes, most black hustlers have traditionally been unwilling either to save or transmit their profits across the generations; certainly in the late 20th century they have tended to live recklessly short and single lives, and are scarcely known for settling themselves down and setting their children up in business or the professions.

But the most ominous current threat to the black middle class is not the old problem of entrepreneurship but a new one, which runs parallel to the one which has created the underclass: the fact that the trajectory of black education is running precisely counter to the demands of the service economy, not only at the bottom but also at the top. The American Council on Education reported early in 1990 that college attendance among African-Americans, having peaked in 1976, had fallen by 10 percent, a decline even steeper in graduate and professional education. Most of this was due to drastic cuts in federally guaranteed scholarships and loans, but its impact was not confined to poorer families; the drop was especially sharp among those with "middle incomes," whose children's rate of attendance plunged from 53 to 36 percent over the same period.[14]

These figures of course threaten the hard-won economic gains of the 1960s and 1970s across the board. So does a separate but related development, one of the more puzzling in recent history: a persistent African-American failure to score well on written tests of all kinds. While law school enrollments, for example, roughly held steady through the 1980s, in contrast to declines in medical and other professional schools, that success was partially undermined by widespread inability to pass the bar examinations. Perhaps above all, the problem is now threatening access to the most traditional bastion of the black middle class: the civil service, where standardized tests have always served as gateways to government jobs and promotions.

This is a serious problem, which goes well beyond the issue of hiring in government. Low scores on standard examinations of all kinds helps keep alive the largely underground issue of African-American "intelligence," the only important vestige of popular racism still with us in the old sense. And one standard explanation for the results is no defense. After years of having black and other experts tinker with the tests, the claim that they are culturally or racially biased is wholly unconvincing, especially in light of dramatically higher scores recently won by other minorities with far less exposure to standard English.

There are several ironies here, resulting in part from ignorance of history as well as of the large body of evidence that has been accumulating, since Franz Boas, about "intelligence" testing. A century ago, after all, black men and women consistently scored not lower but higher than white competitors on civil service tests, and demanded that they be used more widely in hiring and promotion decisions. Evidence from the same era also undercuts the argument about culture; when Robert Abele set a state record on the Pennsylvania qualifying examination for physicians he was a century closer to his African roots than all but a handful of modern blacks, and like others at the highly successful Institute for Colored Youth educated wholly in a demanding but standard curriculum.

Clearly the problem of test scores reflects neither low intelligence nor, in the sense usually meant, "cultural" bias. What it does reflect is the abysmal condition of the schools from which too many young blacks graduate, coupled with a widespread ignorance of, or indifference to, the demands of formal written testing.

In terms of the future, perhaps the most worrisome test scores are those for teachers. In contrast to some other areas of civil service, the idea of standardized examinations for educators, perhaps even national standards, has been gaining ground since the middle 1980s. The argument that African-American children are best served by teachers of their own race is historically an old one, although the historic record in and near Philadelphia is mixed, with impressive results achieved both by the all-black staff of the Institute for Colored Youth and by the all-white staff of Lincoln University. But granted the strength of the argument, it may in practice prove irrelevant. In the summer of 1989 Pennsylvania's State Commissioner of Higher Education, himself black, announced the results of the latest round of tests, which are designed to be stiffened gradually each year. Overall, 3,426 young men and women took the semi-annual tests in November of 1988; the white pass rate was 93 percent, the black 68 percent—up from 57 percent in the previous or April round—the Hispanic 79 percent. Only 79 blacks and 29 Hispanics took the tests at all.[15]

Such results, together with the general dropoff in college attendance, suggest that, at a time when the need for "role models" and black self-help have become clichés, not only the proportion but the number of African-American teachers will shrink across the country. In Philadelphia, among the more desirable jobs in civil service, the percentage of blacks in the teachers' union was the only one which, at 39 percent in 1989, roughly matched their percentage in the city's population as a whole. The inevitable retreat from this peak represents only one of the enormous problems facing the middle class.[16]

What compounds all black problems across the nation is that while hostility toward African-Americans is likely to grow in the immediate future, for a variety of reasons, many of the traditional sources of favorable publicity, or help, are no longer as strong as in the past.

Realism suggests, first, that the role of achievement in the worlds of sports and entertainment has reached a kind of dead end. During 1989 it was announced that four of the top six money-earners in these fields were black: Michael Jackson topped the list, Bill Cosby was third, Eddie Murphy fifth, and Mike Tyson sixth, with only Stephen Spielberg and Charles Schultz breaking the string. There is still of course much room for improvement farther down the scale, in terms of entrepreneurial advancement, the ownership of teams and theaters, the promotion and marketing of talent. But in terms of their historic import in melting white racism, little further can be expected from athletes and performers.[17]

However over-optimistic, neither the black fans of Peter Jackson in the 1890s nor we young white sports fans of the 1950s were entirely wrongheaded in rooting for something more significant than immediate victory. And there is no doubt that the kind of adulation surrounding a Julius Erving or, in a parallel field, say, a Patti LaBelle, has changed attitudes. But by now there is nothing left to prove, and the resistance that remains is probably unshakable. Those whites who make up the audience for the more intellectual arts are rarely serious racists, but many young fans of "heavy metal" or country and western are more or less consciously identifying themselves as resistant to African-American influence on popular music. And of Philadelphia's four major professional teams, the most successful in terms of available tickets sold has been the hockey-playing Flyers, the least successful basketball's Seventy-Sixers. No one in the city plays serious hockey, while tens of thousands play basketball. But white customers and businessmen, who buy most tickets, complain about conditions during basketball games and go instead to the same arena to watch the Flyers, where both skaters and spectators behave with a bloodthirsty boorishness unmatched in any other sport.

Despite the genuine affection felt for Bill Cosby and other prominent blacks, meanwhile, the emotions are not transferable. White Americans, like the newspapers of the 19th century, still seem able in effect to segregate their perceptions, seeing African-Americans through different lenses in different arenas. And within the black community itself, while many leaders have called for more self-esteem through racial pride, the truly famous people, seen at a distance, have done about all that they can do. Well-publicized gifts by Cosby and Oprah Winfrey may help the revival of historically black colleges, locally Cheyney and Lincoln among them. Beyond that the current drive, much of it led by prominent men and women, to stimulate pride by reaching past the "African-American" to the specifically African roots seems less promising. Genuine trans-Atlantic cultural exchange is now far more common, and fruitful, than it was a generation ago. But while Nelson Mandela's visit in the summer of 1990 revived memories of the 1950s, when we had such hopes for all those young leaders educated in the States, the current economic and political prospects of the black African nations are not the stuff of inspiration, and there will be much pain yet before real equality comes to South Africa.

In terms of role-modeling and direct impact on behavior, too, there seems little left for television and movies to accomplish. The enormous popularity of the *Cosby Show* and other family-centered black programs during the 1980s was not enough to stem the deterioration of black family life over the same period. The guarantees of free speech, too, in an entertainment industry ultimately devoted to private profit, has meant in any case that "ba-aa-ad" images, exploiting white fears by stressing threatening behavior and posturing by black men on either side of the law, have been at least as successful as more positive ones.

The contributions of athletes meanwhile may have reached something worse than a dead end. Success in boxing in particular, the sport once first and now most heavily dominated by black champions, has always been at best double-edged. It is of course impossible to read about the sad later years of Peter Jackson without thinking of Muhammed Ali, while the descendants of George Dixon and "Rosebud" Edgerton are equally easy to recognize. In a climate which now encourages relentless publicity about the private lives, drug use, and sometimes criminal actions of famous athletes, there is inevitably more newsworthy bad behavior than good. As important, and worse, the business of granting collegiate scholarships to young athletes of any race, begun for blacks around the turn of the century, has long been an open scandal. Some tens of thousands of young men, and more recently some women, are in effect used and encouraged to gamble, against very long odds, on making it into a select circle of a few hundred extravagantly paid professional athletes. At the same time millions more are given a distorted view of what higher education is about, and how success is won.

The colleges and universities themselves, meanwhile, no longer offer the same kind of support that they once did. The purely scientific case against racism was originally built upon university research, but no one since has mapped a way to win further acceptance for that case in a resistant population. Generous college admissions policies and scholarship money—much of it federal—helped ambitious young African-Americans during the 1960s and 1970s to win entry into the middle class, but since then, as noted, the money has dried up and the rate of college attendance has plummeted. At least equally unfortunate is the evidently changing attitudes of young educated whites, the ironic result of some successes in the immediate past together with some of the deeper failures.

One of the most disturbing trends of the 1980s was the evidence of increased racial tension—almost wholly directed at blacks—on college campuses across the country. Education through most of the 20th century has been an impor-tant weapon against racist thinking, and middle-class white college students were important allies in the "Second Reconstruction" of the 1960s. But any historian knows that young memories are short, and those who have taught the high school and collegiate cohorts of the 1980s know that their students have had very different memories from their elders.

To a professional historian, the most discouraging thing about the reception given the televised version of *Roots,* in the late 1970s, was that it showed that few young people of any race could conceive of the horrors of slavery, what it meant to own the bodies of human beings, until it was all dramatized in color. A decade later the same thing was evident when the courage and suffering of the civil rights battles of the 1960s were re-created, more realistically, by *Eyes on the Prize.* Both times the lessons proved only short-lived exercises in ancient history, hard to conceive as parts of still-living memories with living conse-quences. The fact is that middle-class whites under 40, having typically grown up in segregated suburbs, have little experience with blacks in number. With no appreciation of historic handicaps, and a very lively sense of the impact of affirmative action, their restricted diet of television news has shown them little to make them sympathize with African-Americans and a great deal to make them hostile and suspicious. Conversely, smiling black faces, in the various never-never lands of advertising, situation comedies, and films combine to suggest that everything is essentially all right. Black classmates who do not live up to this image are seen then as sullen complainers demanding special favors.

And where there is a recognition of severe problems in the black commu-nity there is simply no hope for the concept of collective white responsibility for them. The very foundation of this book is that African-Americans were not simply brutalized by a handful of slaveowners, once upon a time, but system-atically denied dignity and opportunity by the majority of Americans, unions and employers, established Anglo-Saxons and recent immigrants, over many generations after Emancipation. Collegians now, although the best of them will acknowledge and even work to right these wrongs, will not—and properly—accept any personal blame for them. Very few are descended from southern whites, more and more from peoples who were somewhere else, in Ireland, Poland, Puerto Rico, or Vietnam when the most obvious racial injustices occurred. Many of these peoples have been uprooted by events not only in the Third World but in the old Russian empire, eastern Europe, and the British Isles, which remind us that every group—not least southern whites—has its own sense of historic grievances. And there are few uglier classroom debates, either among students or adult schoolteachers, than those which try to weigh the respective moral horrors of slavery, the Holocaust, and Hiroshima.

The effect of growing nonwhite immigration has in several ways not helped but further isolated African-Americans. Even unskilled Hmong refugees from Vietnam ran into trouble in West Philadelphia. And the Asian merchants who have filled up the entrepreneurial void in many areas have inspired class resentments in addition to racial hostility. Korean shopkeepers, in particular, often supply the poorest of neighborhoods with at least some retail outlets, but they have been greeted with even more aggression than the Chinese laundry-men of the 19th century, and unlike these distant predecessors have sometimes fought back, shooting to kill apparent robbers, for example. While some black leaders, at various levels, have worked to create bonds among "peoples of color," others have undercut them by moving in to exploit these tensions on the street. And all the while the white majority, finding the immigrants easier to accept than the natives, cites this acceptance as evidence to deny racial prejudice.

The picture is not entirely bleak in absolute terms. Idealism and generosity in the dominant population have not disappeared, nor has its sense of justice. All of these have historically been essential to black progress in the past, and have a big role yet to play. But history, too, has shown the limits of our sense of common humanity, a sense that in the 1990s as in the late 19th century is under a kind of assault. The old well of white idealism, however important, is not growing deeper with the need, and cannot be counted with the newer signs of hope.

In the course of interviewing Philadelphians for this book, I usually saved the hardest question for last: "Is there hope for the underclass? And if so, where?" The answers varied greatly, but black men and women tended to begin at least with the idea of self-help, one of the stronger traditions of the 19th century.

Self-help in this sense may mean either of two things. One is the ability to realize the American Dream by rising out of poverty through individual effort; successful African-Americans today, like those of a century ago, are more likely than their white counterparts to have lived out some version of the Horatio Alger myth, moving up with little financial help from their parents, climbing past less ambitious (or less fortunate) schoolfriends and neighbors "back in the projects." They are quick to remind me, quite properly, that no one person *must* do drugs or drop out, that character still counts, and that the problems of the present are not wholly different from those of the past.

But virtually all those with success stories had at least one strong parent to help in some way, relatively stronger neighborhoods, schools, and communities to support them. And while purely personal qualities may still lead some people out of the modern underclass, they are statistically exceptional, and the real need is not inspiration for a few but help for the majority. This must result from the second kind of self-help, the sort traditionally supplied by the wider African-American community. That sort of help, long weakened as an ironic by-product of the economic progress and civil rights gains of the mid-century decades, seems now to be staging a kind of comeback in different form.

Perhaps simply because it was, and rightly, seen as progress, the flight of the black middle class from the more depressed neighborhoods of the inner city was not viewed, until recently, from the perspective of those left behind. The price of residential segregation for the middle class was a long felt problem. The result of being squeezed together with criminals and prostitutes was dramatically evident among William Dorsey's generation and indeed family, with a raffish sprinkling of illegal entrepreneurs among its more respectable majority a testament to the perils of raising children in neighborhoods zoned as centers of vice. The relief at being able to escape—in Philadelphia during the 1950s and after to parts of Germantown and Mount Airy, for example—obscured the effect of the loss of role models and "old heads" for the ones who could not afford the move. In some ways the loss is irreparable: those who fled are not going to expose their own families to the environment from which they escaped, and there will be no re-creation of the old neighborhoods and natural networks. But some of the lack may be met through formal voluntary action.

The NAACP, for one, began as early as the 1970s to move beyond its traditional concern for civil rights to try to deal with economic and social problems, a position underlined at the 1990 annual convention. But the most promising efforts which might reach the underclass—or indeed shore up the middle or working class, as an alternative approach to the same problem—date largely from the 1980s.

The Greeks, as example, with their large and loyal body of alumni, have begun to shed their "School Daze" image and turn more seriously to deal with problems of the ghetto through tutoring and similar programs. One study of young black men and women at largely white colleges found that most, through the middle of the 1980s, felt that the example of their own career success was all that they owed to the race at large. But in the last few years others from my own elite suburban college have recently begun to join Greek organizations at the larger University of Pennsylvania, now an island in an African-American neighborhood, not for Saturday night binges, not wholly to join big "networks" on graduation, but in large part because of an appeal to their idealism and an ideology of racial self-help. One program, begun early in 1990, brought young men from the University of Pennsylvania and their sorority counterparts from Drexel and Villanova universities as well into the city's middle schools to talk about responsible sexual behavior and pregnancy. To watch these approachable athletes and students spend an entire and intensive school day with small groups of often worshipful children is to see what "role modeling" really means, and to feel some real hope that these attractive young messengers may have an impact their elders cannot match.[18]

But the most important of the new recruits have been the mainstream and some other churches. There is much lay skepticism, still, about the social commitment of black ministers, much of it a heritage of the relative apathy of decades past. The pastor with the longest and most visible record of social activism in the city, a man who hosted the Black Panthers in convention during 1968, and who pioneered in the ordination of women Episcopalians in 1973, has generally taken a tolerant view of that era. The church after all—and perhaps especially those churches which cater to those most in need—has historically been a place not to confront but to forget social problems; he himself lost half his established congregation when he began afflicting the comfortable in the mid-1960s. The traditional economics of the collection plate naturally encourages caution, and many of the problems of the late 20th century, growing rates of drug-related prostitution, teen-aged illegitimacy, perhaps above all AIDS, are the kind which many would prefer to deal with verbally, if at all, from the pulpit, rather than wrestle with directly on the streets. But the sheer weight of these problems has forced a historic shift away from that side of the ministerial tradition which emphasized personal charisma and back toward the other which emphasized social action.

The Black Clergy of Philadelphia and Vicinity was founded to deal with a specifically political problem in 1981, and no one has doubted its purely political influence. But it also began during the later 1980s to deal with social problems. While even to raise the issue of AIDS in the middle of that decade was to risk being laughed at—the disease was still associated with gay white men—a few funerals among parishioners helped raise consciousness. By the winter of 1989 some one hundred African-American pastors were willing to sign up for a special retreat dealing with that one previously taboo subject alone.[19]

There are still, after all, large and active churches even in the most devastated ghetto areas. Some pastors insist that middle-class members have come back, commuting even from the suburbs, with specifically social goals in mind. Certainly the major mainstream churches are proud of the largely recent energy that both ministers and congregants put into tutoring and scholarship programs, efforts to stop local housing from deteriorating, campaigns against drugs and drug dealers.

The range of activities broadly classifiable as racial self-help is in fact enormous. The Big Brothers have been around for years; Big Sisters now often concentrate on pregnant teens; while the Girl Scouts, late in 1989, began reaching into shelters for the homeless. Some of the other and even older organizations are moving out of their more traditional orbits, past college scholarships to grade school tutoring, for example. The Grand and United Order of Odd Fellows has in recent years begun to rebound across the country, its membership now overwhelmingly concentrated in its women's auxiliaries, mothers attracted by the promise of disciplined programs for young people. In place of the older male marching, drinking, and social clubs a newer generation is represented for example by the Concerned Black Men of Philadelphia, founded by a group of police officers late in the 1970s. The organization, now spread to several other cities, sponsors awards and events for schoolchildren, and raises money for everything from chess teams to music instruction. And on a single morning early in March 1990 it was joined, in an anti-crime rally at Broad and Girard, by representatives of many more: some local, such as the Glenwood Anti-Drug Committee; some institutional, such as the One Day at a Time treatment center, and the reformatory House of Umoja; some citywide, such as Eighteen Generations of African American Men, Parents Against Drugs, and Community Against Pushers; some national, such as Operation PUSH.[20]

It is still too early to say what all this may accomplish. Black leaders have many issues on their agendas, from raising pride in African origins to cleaning local streets, not all of which deal immediately with the looming economic threat of the underclass. But almost none of this can hurt, and much can help. And it it impossible to imagine any solutions to the problems of apathy, low self-esteem, and fear of failure that do not start within the race itself.

After the restoration of community action, the other obvious arena of self-help is local politics. The first of the two historic political issues—physical security from organized white attack—is long dead, and while black men may still be brutally murdered, in ad hoc fashion, in hostile white neighborhoods, the long-term trajectory of violent racial incidents has gone down with African-American influence with or even control over police. But jobs, the other issue, are as politically central as ever. Despite periods of relative neglect, and a persistent failure to grant jobs in proportion to number, government has been an unmatched source of black employment ever since the vote was won. Now that throughout the East and Midwest African-Americans are becoming almost as stereotypically identified with big-city politics as Irish-Americans a century before, they too may legitimately hope to parlay politics into a variety of opportunities. But black power has been won during a period of big-city decline, rather than expansion, and despite real promise, politics, unlike voluntary action, is full of possible wrong turns and bad choices, its potential easily misunderstood.

In city after city, in fact, including Philadelphia, the winning of political power typically symbolized by election of the first black mayor has been greeted with high hopes, and followed quickly by disillusion, as the condition of the African-American community has not improved in any comparably dramatic way, and instead, together with the condition of the city itself, has usually continued to slide. It is obvious to any observer with a long view—if not to many white residents—that the deterioration of urban life is far older than the achievement of black power, and due more to fundamental economic change than to the complexion of municipal politics. Philadelphia, typically, reached its peak in terms of both population and manufacturing jobs in the census of 1950, at a time when politics was still in the hands of unreconstructed Republicans; the most cynical way of looking at later developments is simply that white residents, in the course of abandoning it for the suburbs, simply tossed the keys to the city over their shoulders on the way out.

But while it may seem that newly empowered black politicians have been left little to do but preside over an inevitable decline, the task is in fact much more challenging. If they can do little directly for those already lost to the underclass, they can do much to prevent its growth by helping those constituents who still have or need good jobs, indeed all residents. The business of preserving the quality of urban life is in fact a benefit to all. Economically it brings in revenue from (mostly white) commuters and visitors, some of which comes to benefit those who live in the city, whatever their color. In a host of other ways it helps to remind us that the very word "civilization" comes from the Latin word for "city," and that for most of their history cities have been the centers of all that is best in life. And despite the horror stories represented by smaller places like East St. Louis, to a lesser degree Camden or Newark, the nation's truly great cities are still very much alive.

By a host of indices contemporary Philadelphia, with characteristic moderation, stands squarely in the middle of these. It does not rank at the top in those surveys which sometimes list the best places to live, but the upper middle class can still find attractive residential spots in its very center. The downtown at night is not as lively as Manhattan but is more active than Detroit or Atlanta. It has burned-out black slums as bad as those almost anywhere, segregated black and white neighborhoods of varying prosperity, and large outlying areas where the middle class of both races have long settled near each other in comparative harmony. While the continuing influx of Hispanics and Asians reminds us that the contemporary social landscape must be painted with a palette no longer limited to black and white, the two traditional groups remain the most important. Right now the city's economy is firmly in white hands, its politics just passing into black. This process may be temporarily reversed, as the business community reasserts its authority in time of fiscal crisis, or even interrupted, as by the election of a white mayor. But to the extent that the city's future lies in its own hands, in the long run the quality of its black political leadership will be crucial.

Philadelphia's elective politics are largely but not entirely dominated by the issue of race, far more so than in Los Angeles, less so than in Chicago. Entering the 1990s, the several officers elected citywide include a black mayor, a white district attorney, and an Hispanic councilman; the council's majority is white, the majority leader black. When the changing racial balance was still new, it inspired much extravagant verbiage from both black and white politicians, but while, as in other places, a variety of local factors may lead to white victory in citywide elections, the fact that black power is now an established fact has helped to cool the most confrontational rhetoric.

The growing number of Hispanic—and perhaps in future Asian—voters has also confounded, and in important ways moderated, a number of issues that were once seen only in terms of black and white. These newcomers are still novel enough so that the older groups have not yet gotten used to dealing with them, and early in 1990 the school district, in a slapstick effort to promote recognition of Puerto Rican achievement, published a pamphlet which claimed the tango, enchiladas, pinatas, and tamales as examples of the island's "culture," and William Carlos Williams as one of its leading poets. More important, Hispanic complaints of discrimination by police, educators, and other civil servants have further complicated and in effect diluted the traditional complaint of "racism" in a city with an African-American mayor, police commissioner, and superintendent of schools. In any case, although men and women elected from locally segregated districts may still summon the old bombast and paranoia, those with wider ambitions are now careful not to offend voters of any race. Many of the newer black politicians in particular, perhaps because opportunities are widening for them, seem more able and imaginative than those they are replacing. And they have been far more generous in appointing whites to important jobs than their white predecessors were in appointing blacks, as recognition that the city is in trouble enough without aggravating its divisions.[21]

The biggest troubles are financial, the result of a host of problems which long preceded the achievement of real black power. Like most older cities Philadelphia has a rich history of political corruption and ineptitude, and after a brief political renaissance in the 1950s its local leadership has been unable to meet the challenge of coping with the shrinking population and tax base created by economic change. Through the 1960s and 1970s successive administrations bought short-term political victory through expensive projects, contracts, and benefits to municipal unions. Crime, disorder, bad schools, and racial resentment were long familiar before they were aggravated by the escalating growth of the underclass during the 1970s and 1980s. All contribute to a financial vicious circle involving higher taxes and lowered services, a process which brought the city close to bankruptcy by the summer of 1990, ensuring that Philadelphia will continue to bleed working and middle-class residents and taxpayers.

But not all will leave; many old neighborhood ties are still strong, and overall the old city is too healthy to die of this slow hemorrhaging alone. As a reminder of an earlier heyday, like its counterparts Philadelphia still has major universities, hospitals, and a variety of cultural attractions that will not go away. Powerful financial institutions have a stake in the success of its multiple construction projects, and the formal unemployment rate has for years been lower in city than nation, as corporations look desperately for qualified help. Most important, much of the gap left by "white flight" may be filled with middle-class blacks, a process that political power should help.

Whatever the legal status of affirmative action, any big-city institution dependent on the support of the public must be sensitive to black needs. William Dorsey's great-grandson William Johnson, for example, took up the issue of job discrimination after leaving Lincoln University to do animal research at the Philadelphia Zoo. Although the directors would admit to nothing, early in 1990 the threat of pickets and publicity forced a review of hiring practices at every level, with emphasis on the executive.

But while the zoo and similar organizations will provide some future help, the most direct source of new jobs, however subject to fiscal constraints, will obviously be local government itself. Civil service and other public employees have been very important to the black middle class since the vote was granted in the late 19th century. At the same time, paradoxically, that middle class has been so small that African-Americans as a group have still not reached proportional employment in the better jobs. No one objects to the principle that the city's work force, at all levels, should at least roughly reflect its ethnic composition. But especially in the higher ranks of the police and fire departments, the educational and other local, state, and federal bureaucracies, the number of blacks is still small. As of the summer of 1989 they accounted for only 21 supervisors of the city's more than 300 playgrounds, 12 out of the top 191 jobs in the police department, 34 male principals in 277 schools. There is then much room for improvement, but also serious obstacles.[22]

The first of these obstacles is simply political: the replacement of white civil servants with blacks and other minorities must go slowly and fairly enough so that it does not accelerate the white exodus. Many of the ethnic working- and middle-class whites who remain anchored in the city are in fact here because they work for it. They make up a powerful majority in the most attractive jobs, typified by the police and teachers. Since like most other municipal employees they have a vital stake in voting, turning out in May primaries as well as November elections, they have long been courted by traditional politicians. Already unhappy, seeing black power as a threat, they must at worst be kept merely sullen but not mutinous.

Their greatest bulwark in recent years has been the system of civil-service examinations. And the second great obstacle to continued African-American advancement has been the notorious failure of candidates to score well on either the entrance or promotional exams. While this problem, already noted, goes well beyond the civil service, and will not be dented quickly, civil service reform need not wait that long.

The real problem with written civil-service tests for police, firemen, administrators, and indeed most city employees who work with people more than paper, is that they have notoriously little relation to the jobs themselves. "Bullshitting" is what cops admiringly call the special ability that it takes to get people to do what they ask: answer questions, knock it off, move along, or wait right there. Some of this is instinctive; some, the product of cultural or job experience; some, of physical presence or a natural way with words. Whatever it is, much like the parallel skills required of supervisors in any department, it defies written testing. Worse, the promotional examinations as they stand have long been a major focal point for racial and ethnic jealousies, with cops and schoolteachers ranged against each other in formal Jewish, Irish, Italian, and African-American organizations devoted to "coaching" their members for the tests, and contributing to mutual paranoia about special advantages and even cheating. The only thing about which all groups agree is their dislike for the system itself.

A frontal attack was launched in the summer of 1989 when Philadelphia's police commissioner announced that entry-level examinations would be pass/fail alone, and that hiring decisions would be based more heavily on performance in training school and during the period of probation on the street. If followed in other departments, the new system should substantially increase the number of African-Americans hired and eventually promoted.[23]

City government should also be able to help, if less directly, with the equally needed growth of black business enterprise. Both federal and local governments tried to foster this during the 1970s and part of the 1980s through legally preferential treatment of minority contractors. But blacks involved for over four decades in the bonding business—adequate bonding being one of the traditional hurdles for small businesses and especially minorities to overcome—have testified that there has been no real progress in Philadelphia during the whole of that time. Decades of union discrimination, dating to the late 19th century, have limited the pool from which contractors in the most lucrative construction industry have been drawn. And despite the modest goals set by Congress and city councils, preferential programs were widely resented and accused of holding up important projects. Influential unions and businessmen, who had often cheated to get around their provisions, were cheered when the Supreme Court effectively gutted this special form of affirmative action in 1988.[24]

Nonetheless the history of government contracting suggests that black politicians will find ways of favoring black contractors of every kind, as other ethnic politicians have done before them. The same is true, to a lesser extent, at the federal and state levels. Given the general expansion of government in the second half of the 20th century, the businesses involved may provide anything from architecture to wallpaper.

And there is in the modern city another very different but also promising source of entrepreneurship that was in decline from the very end of the 19th century until the last two decades of our own. The commercially busy streets of the older city, cleared out for three generations by the traffic needs of electrified trolleys and then automobiles, have been coming back. As of 1990 roughly 5000 street vendors of all kinds are again hawking goods in many locations, most conspicuously in the very center of business and commercial districts. They come from many groups, but the city's young blacks are well represented among them, and while the business requires little capital to enter knowledgeable sources estimate that many may gross up to $1000 a day. Established businessmen do not like them, and complain about their impact on pedestrian traffic, taxes, and sanitation. They are in general popular however with strolling visitors, they vote and demonstrate, and in the political push and pull over licenses and the enforcement of sidewalk ordinances they should hold their own. The next step for many should then be to follow an old Anerican tradition by moving on to bigger things.[25]

But the most publicized efforts to help local employment have involved neither civil servants nor businessmen but capital projects. Given the structure of local property taxation, zoning laws, building codes, and the right of eminent domain, every major urban construction project, however financed, is in practice not private but public. Taxpayers may or may not be enthusiastic, but given the financial power of builders and developers and the political power of construction unions, local politicians have always found them irresistible. Ideally they may make the city more livable, an important goal, but few in city government will admit that livability is even an issue. Instead the cost, noise, dust, and inconvenience are all defended, ultimately, in terms of jobs created.

Philadelphia has never lacked for capital spending: since the middle 1960s a sports stadium and indoor arena, a major renovation of the eastern end of the central city, and a downtown commuter tunnel have all kept hardhats at work. Following tradition they have all been far more costly to build and have taken longer than first estimated. The late 19th-century construction of City Hall, squarely at the juncture of the two great axial streets which define Phila-delphia's geography, still holds the record: ground was broken in 1871, construction finished in 1894. Otherwise City Hall has literally been put in the shade, as during the 1980s an unwritten law was shattered when its height was topped by new office skyscrapers, part of the expansion which in 1989 destroyed William Dorsey's old home and gutted his church.

There is no question that the business of approving capital construction is the most glamorous part of running a city. Especially when contrasted with haggling over cost with trash collectors, or trying to get the appropriate bureaucracy to deal more effectively with child abuse, making deals with the movers of the financial world is exciting business. The city's newly powerful black politicians seem to get along with bankers and builders as well as their predecessors, and can negotiate at least as effectively. The real issue is how many more jobs will result.

Construction itself provides relatively few for the money. But the two major projects optimistically scheduled for the 1990s, a convention center and a renovation of the Delaware riverfront, perhaps to be followed by a third, modernization of the port, may in fact add to the number of jobs available to people with few skills. The convention center and riverfront project in particular are designed to cater to visitors, and so expand what economic planners call the "hospitality sector." This at the bottom employs busboys, dishwashers, maids, and parking attendants. The "effective" minimum wage in the area, meaning the hourly rate at which employers can hope to hire reliable men amd women, was by 1990 over $6 an hour, far more than the national minimum. The hope is that at this level, $12,000 a year in 1990 dollars, many thousands of people can be brought into the mainstream economy from below, while others will find employment and profit at other levels.

But even apart from the fact that they never provided many jobs directly, under current conditions new capital projects will not by themselves create an "urban renaissance" through the end of this century. It was federal tax policy which encouraged the boom in high-rise office construction through the 1980s. But Washington over the same period has been far more hurtful than helpful, as its priorities, short-sighted on a grander scale than those of merely local governments, pushed Philadelphia and other cities along the road toward bankrupcty.

The downtown office towers, first, were never filled with tenants; many of the businesses that did rent space were and are highly sensitive to the economic downturn created in part by federal deficits. Federal politicians, too, in the name of tax relief, simply shifted the load instead of truly lightening it. The fiscal policies of all governments are ultimately driven from the top, so that pushing a number of obligations and expectations down to the cities simply helped to push city taxes up. And while there is no escaping the total cost of either social problems or fiscal mismanagement in the United States, the result of all this has been to encourage that vicious circle which squeezes central cities, as exasperated individual businesses and taxpayers can still lighten their own loads by escaping out of the front lines into quieter satellite communities.

The last federal contribution to Philadelphia's fiscal problems is perhaps the example set by playing false with the budget. Beginning in the 1980s the most successful national politicians were able first to convince a people surrounded by affluence that income taxes were their biggest problem, and then for some years to wish away the resulting deficits. In this atmosphere of unreality local politicians could hardly face their own constituents with hard truths. One of the few ways in which Philadelphia leads most other cities is in the weight of its existing tax burden, and the result of the usual political inability to cut expenses was a series of camouflaged shortfalls that were not fully uncovered until the summer of 1990. At that point the two leading investors' guides downgraded the city's municipal obligations to "junk bond" status, and city officials announced that it might shortly be impossible to pay current bills due.

The specter of default, even bankruptcy, has in recent years faced other cities, such as Cleveland and New York, and in bad times may yet spread to more. In Philadelphia, continued problems could mean a double setback, lasting as long as the fiscal crisis, to the promise of black politics. First, effective financial control could pass to a group of unelected and largely white consultants reviving the race issue; and second, any hope of expanding employment through local government would be at best delayed. While the full effect is impossible to predict, it is certainly clear that the city will not build itself many new jobs in the near future, and despite the clamor of various constituencies for a new justice center, a prison, shelters for the homeless, and more, some projects will remain holes in the ground, others castles in the air, and most hopes will be either seriously or calamitously disappointed.

Ultimately, then, the fate of Philadelphia's capital plans reveals more about the limits of local government than its possibilities. Decisions made in city halls are far less important in creating the local economic climate than those made in state capitals, above all in Washington. No city is fully in charge of its own budget, either, with state constitutions limiting the nature and sometimes the amount of local taxes, while state laws or moral obligations demand certain inescapable expenses. The legacies of past governments, too, in the form of civil-service regulations or union contracts, hedge the powers of current politicians. All efforts to find ways around these problems are shadowed by the fact that city-dwellers are typically poorer than most of their fellow Americans, less able to pay taxes, more needful of help. And if this mix of problems makes it hard to count on new capital spending, its impact falls even more dramatically on efforts to cope with existing members of the jobless underclass, and above all on educational efforts to bring them back onto the productive work force, or to keep more young people from tumbling into their ranks.

While city governments did not create the underclass, city governments, with varying aid from state and federal agencies, must pay for its problems. But the severity of the local fiscal situation is inevitably creating a kind of triage mentality in dealing with the most severely handicapped. As surely as economic change and tax pressures are driving productive businesses and residents out, a variety of attractions and conditions continue to bring unproductive people into the metropolis—including helpful suburban policemen, tempted to pick up disturbed or disturbing men and women and deposit them on the other side of the city line. As recently as the middle of the 1980s, Philadelphia provided almost recklessly expensive shelters for the homeless. But as this and other cities have come to serve as poorhouses for the nation, the increasingly minimal services now available to victims of AIDS, drugs, emotional handicaps, and simple unemployment are provided with obvious reluctance, often under court order, the result less of callousness than of hopelessness.

Given the delicate line that politicians have to tread, trying to provide enough basic services to keep productive people in the city without raising their taxes, other problems tend to get shuffled off. The list is endlessly depressing, topped, perhaps, by the victims of drug-induced child abuse; no one denies the need for improvement, but local officials insist, with much justice, that the city should not be responsible for these problems and cannot cure them by itself. Its own priorities are inevitably those of its working taxpayers, reinforced by the interests of well-entrenched municipal unions: in addition to some capital construction, that translates into the need for some visible efforts to keep the streets clean and safe, at least in economically or politically important neighborhoods such as the downtown core locally known as "Center City."

The school district meanwhile faces a fiscal crisis of its own. Its superintendent was during the middle and later 1980s the most highly regarded public servant in Philadelphia, but while one local politician in 1989 suggested that the city council was willing to pass resolutions recommending that she be lifted bodily up to Heaven it was not willing, or able, to fund her budget. And in fact her tenure suggests that while continual deficits are hurtful the underlying problems are even more resistant.

Through the 1980s the superintendent was able to satisfy educational critics on the right by curbing "social promotions," insisting that certain standards be met for moving up in grade. Liberals, teachers, and often resentful parents appreciated her ability to work with the union; the Teacher's Union had been, next to the trash collectors', probably the most unpopular in the city, in part because of its disruptive strikes, but it cannot now be argued that, on a relative basis, its members are underpaid. Meanwhile knowledgeable people from all points on the political spectrum agreed that with a certain toughness the superintendent had "brought the educational bureaucracy under control."

But with all these vaunted accomplishments, the 1980s showed more than anything the limits of the most inspired leadership, even in apparently prosperous times. Philadelphia's new superintendent, like most big-city minority administrators, took office at an already difficult time, when mandates from other agencies had loaded the budget with everything from busing private school students to special programs for the physically and mentally handicapped. More than any other single agency, including the police, the schools have had to face the problems associated with a growing underclass, AIDS, alcohol and drug addiction, homelessness, child abuse, and teenage pregnancy, while they are now bracing for the first big wave of children born with systems full of cocaine. Meanwhile bureaucratic and union rules allow only the smallest room in which to maneuver toward change.

Few people work harder than dedicated schoolteachers, but much like college professors, few at that salary level work less hard than those who have burned out or given up. Even a modest proposal to restore school lunch periods to the high schools accordingly ran into trouble. The lunches were eliminated during the 1960s at many schools in order to cut down on gang-related fights. Now that the problems of the underclass have taken new forms virtually all agree that bringing back the period would both restore flexibility to scheduling and revive sleepily sullen teenagers after noon—but the staff has gotten used to a day that ends at 1:30. The difficulties of firing and hiring were more dramatically illustrated in the spring of 1989 when a former principal of Jacob White's old Vaux Junior High School was twice arrested for threatening the life of the superintendent. Having been removed from his line job, with some trouble, as a result of erratic and sometimes violent behavior, he had been drawing full pay for years while tucked elsewhere into the bureaucracy.[26]

My own work and interests involve me continually with the best and brightest of the city's teachers, those who go to lectures, panel discussions, academic institutes, and workshops, who look for new ways of inspiring and motivating their students. These men and women are often enthusiastic about their own jobs, join earnestly in attempts to change the curriculum, have high hopes for new methods of teaching mathematics, languages, or world cultures. But it is hard to find any who believe that the existing system as a whole can be improved in any dramatic way. While the newspapers are grateful for occasional grade level improvements which move a given class a percentage point or two upward toward the national averages, it is impossible to hide the fact that there has been no real success. During 1989, only 28 percent of Philadelphia's students managed a passing grade in statewide Testing for Essential Learning and Literacy Skills, designed to measure truly minimum competency. The year before, a bare 51 percent of high-school freshmen passed algebra, increasingly the key both to future education and employment. Those who don't make it and still stay in school are then shunted into "General Math," a rehash of essentially sixth-grade arithmetic, taught by rote for as many as three more years. The result is that even the most dutiful youngsters, here as across the country, who listen to the messages which tell them not to drop out, who manage more or less successfully to sit still, take turns, mind the teacher, hold their water, and listen to the bell during twelve long years still find it hard to win a job.[27]

The situation is not entirely hopeless, however; the promise of real jobs is a proven key to success, and here Philadelphia is in many ways a leader. Its "magnet academies," now run out of several high schools in part with the cooperation of the Private Industry Council (PIC), is aimed at eighth graders thought especially likely to drop out. These combine academic and mechanical or business training with the offer of after-school and summer jobs at close to $6 an hour; during the late 1980s a stunning 93 percent of all who entered managed to graduate, 85 percent going on to higher education or employment appropriate to their training.[28]

The PIC further offers a kind of second-chance opportunity for some of the system's dropouts, failures, and even unemployable graduates. Among the bewildering variety of available job training programs, the Council through the 1980s had by far the most successful record. One of approximately 600 set up across the country by the federal Job Training Partnership Act of 1982, Philadelphia's PIC has been one of the best by virtually any standard. The "partnership" involved is one between business and local government, in this case the school district. It offers a full range of programs to those described as "economically disadvantaged," from basic classroom skills to courses in, for example, welding. Its rate of successful placement ranged between 70 percent and 80 percent during the late 1980s, and in fiscal 1988 its graduates furnished fully one-quarter of all new entrants into the city's work force, more than half of them taken off the welfare rolls.[29]

A special study by a team of academic sociologists, after a study of this particular Philadelphia Story, asked rhetorically, "Does Job Training Work?," and reported, resoundingly, that it does. It does indeed, for those students whom the district can afford to enroll, as well as for out-of-school clients who pass through various screenings to sign up. There is still work available to these people, unlike 19th-century products of "industrial education" for blacks. But at current levels, and under current arrangements, the numbers involved are simply not going to make a dent in the ranks of the underclass.[30]

The reasons are both "structural"—resulting from the poverty of the city itself—and "cultural"—the result of resistance from those who need and lack the training. Only some 1,750 of over 100,000 Philadelphia high-school students were enrolled in the magnet academies in 1990; to push that to 5,000 would cost well over a million dollars annually, not an impossible sum, but nearly impossible for the School District of Philadelphia in its current state. The PIC meanwhile handles perhaps 4,000 to 5,000 people a year, most of them the easiest, and cheapest, to deal with: that is, those who already have the equivalent of eighth-grade skills. But during 1988, the last year for which figures were available, properly motivated clients were not easy to find, and voluntary enrollments in job training programs of all kinds dropped off dramatically. And no one pretends that at the current rate either the school district, the PIC, or other programs can shrink the great pool of 300,000 undereducated, sometimes hostile, poor Philadelphians who constitute the underclass, of whom as of 1989 an estimated 100,000 had something between fifth- and eighth-grade skills, and 180,000 even less than that.[31]

Some big-city school districts work better than others, just as some local governments have been shown more fiscal foresight than others, or more imagination in rebuilding their downtown areas, attracting tourists, holding on to core industries. All these things matter, to thousands and even tens of thousands of people. But nothing that any city can do does much to relieve the underclass, and the deadening sameness of the relevant social statistics across the country shows as much as anything that even given vigorous self-help and responsible local government, any wider solution must come from another level entirely.

There has been a sprinkling of good news in the final part of this book to counter the generally sobering, even gloomy, assessment of the modern black city. The middle class, however threatened, has grown much bigger over the past several decades, and racism weaker. There is much that the African-American community is doing voluntarily to help its more isolated members, and much that local black politics may do to help those better connected. There are still great reservoirs of white idealism to draw on, even though history has shown these to be finite, and even though they are short of full capacity in the 1990s. But in a situation full of ironies the ultimate irony may be that the very magnitude of the bad news is the good news, simply because from an entirely new perspective the condition of the underclass is intolerable.

While self-help and philanthropic idealism are long familiar, the new perspective is that of the corporate business community, increasingly concerned about the competitive position of the United States as a whole in the international economic arena. From this view much of the behavior associated with an underclass "culture of poverty" is simply an exaggeration of the behavior of the nation as a whole, as especially during the 1980s Americans have been grabbing at the pleasures of the moment, spending freely on consumer items while piling up massive debts, falling behind educationally, refusing to think realistically about the long-term relationship between means and ends. All of this combined to pull us down; the challenge is to use economic bad news as a stimulus to turn ourselves around.

The obvious need is to think in longer terms about investment, including investment in human beings, a point which may be put in both negative and positive terms. Traditional liberalism, in addition to its appeals to humanity and idealism, has stressed for decades that the effort to fight black urban problems should be seen as such an investment, that prevention is cheaper than cure, schools cheaper than prisons. Through the 1980s that negative case, however powerful, won few converts, and the costs of a growing underclass, in terms of crime control and welfare, treatment for the infant as well as adult victims of crippling disease and addiction, were still disproportionately borne at the local level. But the ever-larger projected future costs can no longer be paid in this way if only because of the near-bankruptcy of local governments, and threaten not only to raise taxes at some level but to act as a severe drag on the national economy as a whole. This prospect has helped to win new converts among corporate economists long resistant to less hardheaded appeals, a development strengthened by the positive case for human investment.

Corporations have long invested in job training, beginning with their own managers; the difference in recent years is that they have extended the investment downward, greatly multiplying the number of dollars spent on newly hired people at entry level. And they are finding that these new people are and will be new indeed, very different from those of the past.

Few sets of projections got more publicity in the late 1980s than the one compiled and endorsed by an eminently conservative group of economists and businessmen, which showed that differences in fertility and immigration patterns pointed inexorably to the fact that only a fraction, estimated at 15 percent, of new entrants into the American work force during the 1990s would be the traditional white males. Many would be women; the fastest growing pool would be members of minority groups, especially blacks and Hispanics. The other side of the fact that ours is economically a common destiny, then, is that the white majority needs these people to be as productive as possible.[32]

What this suggests, posed next to the inexorable need for ever higher computer and other advanced skills, is an enormous educational challenge. Corporations have discovered, or will discover, the huge problems involved in training people with limited educations. To reach further into the pool of those with less than the functional equivalent of an eighth-grade diploma, and usually other handicaps as well, is simply not economical for any individual company;

the deeper the reach, the longer the time required, the greater the risks of dropping out, and of course the greater the cost. The fact that Americans are a highly mobile people, too, means that those trained in one school district or by one corporation may then move on to use their skills in another, and underlines the need to recognize that any successful program must be national in scope. The federal government may then get involved simply because it must; given the need, and unwilling to pay for the needed basic education themselves, corporate managers may swallow their rhetorical objections to big government and appeal to it for help.

So long as the need exists then, the demand for workers, as in World War II, may be an opportunity of many kinds for African-American and other minorities. But the opportunity may be lost unless it is shrewdly managed politically.

The most influential black sociologist of the 1980s is among the many who have pointed out that the dominant majority, certainly since the 1960s, has always been reluctant to grant what it sees as "special favors" to minorities, and it may be added that it is only somewhat less reluctant to pay for programs, such as low-cost housing and welfare increases, that make poverty easier to bear. But education and jobs are as politically appealing as apple pie, and the majority of voters repeatedly tell pollsters that they would be willing even at the price of higher taxes to support policies designed to better both, whatever the color of those who benefit. And during the 1990s the fact that state courts and governments have begun to underline the need for extensive, indeed radical, changes in the structure and financing of American schooling offers a rare opportunity to reverse the political neglect of the past two decades.[33]

The fiscal condition of the federal government, especially in bad times, will frighten politicians, and may paralyze efforts at change. The dramatic unraveling of the Cold War has been marked by violence and desperation in the former Russian empire not anticipated by those who looked forward, in its earliest days, to a massive "peace dividend." International crises, like the Persian Gulf war of 1991, will still occur, and economic downturn will burden Washington with new obligations to add to the costs of the savings and loan bailout. But even in decline we remain the world's richest nation, with much room to cut budgets at every level. Americans still pay far less for social services than the citizens of any western competitor, with the real problem of taxation less one of total weight than of irrational distribution, with poorer places, and people, hit relatively harder than richer ones. And if properly seen as a way of fighting rather adding to economic problems, a well-designed program built around strengthening the long-term links between jobs and schooling could be politically irresistible.

One key to both program and coalition is that the problems are by no means confined either to blacks or other minorities, or indeed to the poor. It cannot be stressed too strongly that the transition to a service economy, which makes educational demands that the species has never experienced before, is creating social dislocation throughout much of the western world. The tens of thousands of non-minority schoolchildren even in a big city like Philadelphia make it, still, the biggest white school district in the state, and much of its underclass, as earlier defined, is also full of longtime white residents. White poverty is of course far more common in Appalachia and other rural areas. And what observers keep calling the national crisis in education affects the richest suburban districts as well as those on Native American reservations: while the President of the United States at the governor's conference held in the fall of 1989 boldly called for American schoolchildren to rank "number one" in science and math by the year 2000, we are currently having a hard time staying abreast of Thailand and Singapore, and our best trail the more developed nations as ominously as our worst.[34]

And just as the problems of our cities should be recognized as part of a larger national problem, the calculus of political demography, too, suggests the need to stress that the problems of African-Americans are those of all Americans. Elections since 1968 have shown repeatedly that the appeal to the black vote by itself has tight limits. Good politics may find alliances and tactics that will keep the Democratic party from taking that vote for granted in the 1990s, as many tried to do, under parallel conditions, in the 1880s. During 1989 the election of Philadelphia's William Gray as Majority Whip in the House of Representatives, Ronald Brown's selection as chairman of the Democratic party, the victories of Governor Douglas Wilder in Virginia and Mayor David Dinkins in New York were all healthy signs. But each of these men won their positions by carefully downplaying, without abandoning, any appeal to a specifically black constituency. Genuine power, as distinct from election in largely black districts or primaries, requires recognition of the brute political facts that the African-American population is officially little more than 12 percent of the whole, an even smaller proportion of the active electorate, and in an age when leverage is measured in campaign dollars is even less influential than its raw numbers would suggest. The estimated number of truly racist white voters roughly equals the black total, and is ready to cancel any movement or cause primarily associated with it.

Specifically black demands will not disappear—Congressman John Lewis, once the champion of higher wages for domestics, has more recently called for a $200,000,000 African-American Museum on the Washington Mall. Many Americans, too, will still respond to appeals for better treatment of our poorest citizens, quite apart from education and jobs. But those two remain the issues most important for the future, and most likely to win success. And the biggest threat to a potentially winning coalition will probably not be distraction from these central goals but disaffection on the part of businessmen looking for shortcuts. Changes in the immigration laws might make it possible to bypass the obvious difficulties of dealing with our own underclass by bringing in

millions of politically appealing Irish, Greeks, or white refugees from European turmoil, with perhaps some Asians or even West Africans to blunt charges
of racism. But while this might have some immediate benefit to employers it
would still leave the rest of us to pay the long-term social bills for dependency
and crime, and it will require imagination and effort to hold the line against
such a strategy.[35]

If, finally, the right coalition can be formed and held, and the right case
made strongly enough, there is much that can be done relatively quickly and
cheaply to begin to bring the urban underclass back into the economy. Two
simple and typical needs for any comprehensive assault on unemployment,
both suggested by people themselves in job training programs, are, for
example, improvements in transportation and information networks and in
day-care. Many outlying or suburban areas have not lost jobs for unskilled
workers as fast as central cities have, and a few have actually gained. In the
greater Philadelphia area a restaurant in, say, Norristown may pay as much as
$2 an hour more than one on Chestnut Street for help, and throw in child care as
well. But people in North Philadelphia are unlikely to hear about this, and
wholly unable to get there. And day-care—itself a major employer of relatively
unskilled women— has always been a problem for working mothers, whether
in need of jobs or education.

The investment in more productive education itself will not pay off nearly
as quickly, and there is of course much skepticism about "throwing federal
money" at it, some of it justified: about $100 billion was spent on employment
and training between 1962 and 1983, with results disappointing to liberals and
conservatives alike. But this money was often appropriated for hidden purposes—in effect bribing potentially rebellious teenagers to keep off the summer
streets, for example—and above all spent naïvely. And given the will there is
now an enormous body of largely unused expertise on how successfully to
educate and eventually hire the jobless.[36]

The common denominator in successful programs is that all, in the words of
one observer, have been "intensive, comprehensive, and flexible." The criterion most usually overlooked, and the one most crucial to the underclass, is
"comprehensive." For unemployed people, and their children, joblessness is
often just the center of a complex of related ills. Job trainees need help in
staying straight just as obviously as recovering addicts need jobs; desertion,
unwanted pregnancy, and a host of other problems may derail anyone or any
program trying to conquer just one of them in isolation. An effort that aims
ultimately at employment must at the same time deal with a range of other
issues, and call on community resources of all kinds, young Greeks and "old
heads," churches and voluntary organizations.[37]

Expectations, finally, must be kept more realistic than during the 1960s War
on Poverty, for example. Any serious attack on long-term unemployment will
be a massive practical test of the two theories as to what creates an "under-

class." Dramatic improvement is within reach, and to the extent that the problem is external or structural, the will and resources to grasp it are at least potentially available. But there will be much discouragement too, and no student of history should expect the elimination of the underclass within a generation. A more realistic definition of success would be simply to win a reversal of current projections, with national productivity on the way up, the great pool of unemployed visibly shrinking and no longer threatening members especially of the black working and middle classes.

And if the whole effort is in fact a test, or experiment, nothing is more appropriate for a nation itself ideally seen as a "Great Experiment" in multi-racial living. We have a second chance now, perhaps a last, to do right what we did not do in the decades after slavery was abolished. With racism much narrowed, and abundance widened, we have more political and social resources than we had then. And it would be a fitting end to the long journey begun with freedom to restore the vitality and optimism of the black city of William Dorsey's day. Only this time it would be as part of a more just, productive, and humane society than that was then, or this is now.

APPENDIX I

The William Henry Dorsey Collection at Cheyney State University

The William Henry Dorsey Collection officially consists of books, manuscripts, biographical clippings, and scrapbooks. Cheyney provides a catalogue entitled "Indexes of the William H. Dorsey Collection, Cheyney State College," with an introduction by Sulayman Clark, which includes a brief biographical sketch as accurate as possible when it was written in 1980. Dr. Clark, together with Dr. James Redpath, was responsible for arranging the collection during 1981–82, following an evaluation by experts in Afro-Americana Charles Blockson and Dorothy Porter-Wesley.

The listed books include 155 titles, some of which have not been conclusively identified as Dorsey's, others which have; most of the latter, and many of the former, deal with slavery, abolition, and the black experience. In contrast only a minority, about 340, of the subjects of the 914 alphabetically arranged biographical files and clippings are African-Americans, as determined either by the cataloguers or myself. Although potentially useful to scholars, these files contain relatively few letters, mostly short, and a handful of autographs or pictures, more of the white subjects—many of them quite obscure Philadelphia officeholders, for example— than of the black. Most of the items in each file are newspaper clippings, often obituaries; the great majority of the subjects have been identified by the cataloguers, the black ones starred for reference.

Of the 388 scrapbooks, the first 261 have been microfilmed; the rest remain tied in red bows in the archive, where they must be treated with great care. With the exceptions of numbers 2, 3, 4, 5, and 7, which are relevant but not strictly African-American in content, the first 130 deal almost exclusively with American black subjects, and so do 242–44, 285, 286, and 287. There are several short scrapbooks, too, which Dorsey titled but are not listed, many of them on microfilm after number 61. These are collectively the backbone of this book. Many of the others are concerned in addition with Africans, American Indians, Pacific Islanders, and other peoples of color. The rest amply show the breadth of Dorsey's interests and curiosity, and deal with subjects such as antiquities, literature, the theater, crime and scandal, famous persons, and above all art in all forms from pyramids to coins.

Dorsey himself indexed most of these books, titled a few, and put none in order;

some of those dealing with blacks were evidently kept on a kind of daily chronological basis, some topically arranged, many a mixture. He was not a tidy man by nature; these books are of varying sizes, those dealing with black subjects averaging perhaps 125 pages, sometimes with 6 or 8 newspaper clippings to a page, sometimes with a whole pamphlet or magazine article. While newspaper clippings comprise about 90 percent of the total, other journals, tickets, menus, programs, and posters are included also. The titles given by the cataloguers are a fair guide to their contents, although there are often items from years other than those indicated. "Miscellaneous," with the year or years, is the most common title, while "Crime," especially in the 1890s, refers simply to the fact that lynchings in the South and various felonies and misdemeanors in the North comprised most of the news devoted to African-Americans in that era.

Not included in the official "Index" is a typewritten guide to approximately 700 catalogues of art shows, auctions, and gallery exhibitions found in the archives and compiled by Charlotte Goodman in 1980. In fact both the cataloguing and the collection itself are clearly incomplete in several respects.

First, since Dorsey himself was "Custodian" of the American Negro Historical Society, many of his items doubtless wound up as part of the Leon Gardiner Collection kept at the Historical Society of Pennsylvania, which contains some posters and tickets quite similar to his, probably collected either by him or by his friend and contemporary Jacob White, Jr. Second, and conversely, the wholly informal and crowded Cheyney State Archives contain a number of items, mixed in with other things, which obviously came from Dorsey—his rent book, for example, and early sketches, plus a scrapbook largely of theatrical items kept by his friend Ira Cliff during the 1860s, a number of others full of clipped prints and portraits, and a stack of unbound copies of the *Peoples' Advocate*. Several other items, such as Joseph Hill's rollbooks from the Institute for Colored Youth, and—to name only the most incongruously mysterious—the manuscript minutes of the Borough of Southwark for several years in the 1790s—were clearly kept by someone with a passion for historical collecting.

Finally, given the careless way in which the whole collection was first given to and then evidently forgotten by Cheyney's long-term President Leslie Pinckney Hill, a number of scrapbooks and clippings were among the items evidently lost. There are virtually no items from 1901, as example, no obituaries of men as important as Robert Purvis and Dorsey's own father Thomas J., just as there is no trace of many of the other kinds of historical memorabilia which his contemporaries describe as occupying his quarters on Dean Street, or at the Church of the Crucifixion where the American Negro Historical Society was headquartered.

APPENDIX II

Sources for William Dorsey
and His Family

Research on Dorsey's family was greatly helped by his granddaughter, Virginia Ramsey Chew, her niece Felicia Blue, and especially the family historian, her nephew Dr. Preston Johnson. Among other materials the family has shared are photographs of Mr. and Mrs. Thomas J. Dorsey, William and Virginia, Sarah, Ira and Thomas J., and several others; documents concerning William's marriage and the birthdates of his children; and letters. Dr. Johnson has done considerable research in archives and cemeteries. But above all he and others have their memories to share, which with a few minor differences check out in all available historical records, and have enabled us to crosscheck each other. The family has some personal memories of William Henry; the major blank spot in both the historical and these living records is his whereabouts and occupation until the early 1860s; he first appears in the city directory of 1861 as a "waiter," afterward as an "artist." His sisters Sarah Seville and Mary Harlan were not known, the latter's memory it seems deliberately suppressed, although there is an awareness of the Seville and especially Harlan connections, as the Harlan daughters grew up in Philadelphia, and there is a photograph of Robert Harlan, Jr., by then nearly 90, presiding over a family reunion in 1939. William's wife Virginia (Cashin) is still recalled vividly; so are their children who remained in Philadelphia, Thomas, John, and above all Sarah Ramsey. Virginia Dorsey Doll is also well remembered, but Ira and Vandyke, only occasional visitors or residents, are more shadowy figures.

Other sources, official, private, and printed, are listed below:

Official Sources:
1. The manuscript census despite the strong caveats suggested in the introduction to Part II remains an essential tool. All census material from 1850 through 1880 may be found, cross-indexed and xeroxed, in the records of the Philadelphia Social History Project, kept at the university of Pennsylvania's Van Pelt Library; and PSHP's data bank has provided a printout of all black Dorseys officially found in the city during those years, with their ages, relationships, occupations, addresses, and birthplaces. The family's effective male founder Thomas J. Dorsey appears in all before his death in 1876, with his wife, to 1870, his children, and sometimes a

servant. William does not appear in 1860; he and his family are there in 1870 and 1880; Mary L. Dorsey—not under her married Harlan name—also appears in 1880, with her (adopted) daughter Nellie. The year 1890 is missing, but William and Virginia appear in 1900 in separate households, she living with her son John and daughter Sarah Ramsey's family.

2. The city directories provide information about occupation and addresses. All male Dorseys except Ira appear at some time, as does Virginia; Mary Dorsey Harlan is listed in 1879 and 1880, her husband Robert Harlan, Jr., in 1879, both without occupations; John C. Seville in 1885. Robert Harlan, Jr., and Dorsey Seville appear in the Washington, D.C., directories, the former only during 1882–84, the latter regularly throughout the late 19th century.

3. The Philadelphia Register of Wills provides a copy of Thomas J. Dorsey's will, probated in 1875; none of his children appear to have filed wills.

4. The records of the Philadelphia Orphan's Court yield eighteen documents relating to Thomas Dorsey's Trust from 1879 to its dissolution in 1926, providing death dates and other information about beneficiaries in addition to financial data. Eight documents listed under Dorsey F. and John C. Seville trace the guardianship of Sarah Dorsey Seville's children.

5. The Philadelphia Municipal Archives contain death certificates for Thomas J., 2/17/75, John, 1/3/07; and William Dorsey, 1/9/23, listing their addresses, place of birth, and occupations; Mary Dorsey Harlan's, dated 1/18/01, is in Washington, D.C. The birth certificates of William's children begin only with Virginia, born 5/18/65; the earlier children may have been born elsewhere or were simply not recorded, as the state's registration act took effect only during 1860, and for some time missed many births at home.

Private Sources:

1. St. Thomas P.E. Church has birth and death and sometimes confirmation records for most family members in Philadelphia.

2. William Dorsey's biographical files (see Appendix I) contain a folder for Dorsey Seville, with newspaper accounts of his Masonic and other activities and a letter to "Uncle Bill." The file for Charles Reason has a letter to Mrs. Thomas J. Dorsey about Sarah Dorsey's 1858 wedding.

3. The Dorsey scrapbooks contain dozens of items about family, from Louise Dorsey's activities on behalf of black soldiers during the Civil War in "Report of the Ladies' Sanitary Association of St. Thomas . . . 1866," scrapbook #27, 2d item, unpaginated, to John's arrest in a gambling raid, 12/26/99, scrapbook #125, p. 73.

4. The Leon Gardiner Collection, Historical Society of Pennsylvania, Box 10G, contains minutes and other records of William Henry Dorsey's participation in the American Negro Historical Society.

5. The Bryn Mawr College Archives have a record of Helen Dorsey's year as a graduate student, in 1926, and the college archivist confirms the family's recollection that she was the first black student enrolled.

Published Sources:

1. Thomas J. Dorsey's story appears in several places, notably W. E. B. Du Bois, *The Philadelphia Negro: A Social Study* (Millwood, N.Y.: Kraus-Thompson, orig. pub. 1899); the Lincoln Inauguration story is in Frederick Douglass, *The Life and Times of Frederick Douglass, Written by Himself* (New York: Macmillan, 1962, orig. pub. 1892), 364–66; Dr. Preston Johnson has provided a copy of the open letter to Grand Duke Alexis published 12/4/71; extensive obituaries appeared in all major Philadelphia papers after his death on 2/17/75.

2. Harrison W. Wayman, "The American Negro Historical Society," *Colored American Magazine* 6, no. 3 (Feb. 1903), has a photograph and account of William Dorsey as custodian.

3. An account of Virginia or Jenny Dorsey's wedding appears in the New York *Age* 12/26/90.

4. The story of Robert J. Harlan, Sr., with some reference to his son and family, appears in Rayford W. Logan and Michael R. Winston, *Dictionary of American Negro Biography* (New York: W. W. Norton, 1982), 287–88.

5. The criminal stories involving William Whitesides and Mary Dorsey Harlan appear in Roger Lane, *Violent Death in the City* (Cambridge: Harvard Univ. Press, 1979), 106–7, and *Roots of Violence in Black Philadelphia* (Cambridge: Harvard Univ. Press, 1986), 31, 131.

APPENDIX III

Philadelphians Most Noted in the Dorsey Collection

The 36 men and women below are taken from alphabetized lists of several thousand names which occur in the Dorsey Collection. These are the ones mentioned most often, a minimum of twelve times each. They do not include mentions in other sources used in this book such as the New York papers, Carl Bolivar's columns in the *Tribune*, the materials in the Leon Gardiner Collection in the Historical Society of Pennsylvania. Mentions in Dorsey scrapbooks numbers 55 and 70 have also been omitted. While the notices may be in any connection, inclusion of the omitted sources would have weighted them in favor of purely social or entertainment functions, raising the relative number given to men like the convivial Doctor Edwin C. Howard, for example, and lowering those of the sober William Still. In counting the references, only one was allowed per story or event, even if a given person was mentioned in different papers or on different days in connection with the school desegregation battle of 1881, for example, or the Douglass Hospital Ball of 1897.

Following each name the total number of mentions is included in parentheses. After that the total is broken into periods: Number of mentions through 1880 follow "A"; from 1881–91, "B"; after 1892, "C." The entries after that refer to the person's dates and birthplace; occupation; education; church affiliation; marital status and number of children if known.

The biographical information is varied both in terms of how much is known—church affiliation is not always clear, for example—and in terms of how reliable it is. The most unreliable information concerns number of children and death dates. The number of children is sometimes taken from biographies or obituaries, sometimes from the census. But the census, in addition to its inaccuracies, at best lists children resident every ten years—with 1890 missing. The effect is to undercount somewhat, an undercount partially balanced by informal adoption arrangements or the mis-attribution of children in a household to its head or most dominant couple. The death date in some cases is taken simply from the last year in which a person was listed in the Philadelphia City Directories; this is usually fairly accurate, but in the case of William Henry Dorsey himself would have been three years off, just as counting children from the census alone would have been one short.

The list includes:

Adger, Robert M. Jr. (14 mentions: A7, B2, C5). 1837–1910, b. Charleston, S.C. Secondhand furniture dealer, postal clerk. ICY. First African Presbyterian. M, 4 children.

Anderson, Rev. Matthew (21 mentions: A0, B4, C17). 1847–1928, b. rural Pennsylvania. Clergyman. Princeton Theological Seminary. Berean Presbyterian. M, no children.

Bassett, Ebenezer (13 mentions: A8, B1, C4). 1833–1900, b. Connecticut. Educator, diplomat. McGrawville College. Religion unknown. M, 2 children.

Ball, Gilbert A. (17 mentions: A1, B15, C1). 1840–90, b. Virginia. Politician, saloonkeeper. No school. First Union Baptist. M, no children.

Bolivar, W. Carl (20 mentions: A7, B4, C9). 1844–1914, b. Philadelphia. Historical columnist, bank clerk. ICY. St. Thomas P.E. Unmarried.

Bowser, David Bustill (15 mentions: A10, B1, C4). 1820–1900, b. Philadelphia. Barber, painter, officer Odd Fellows. Education unknown. St. Thomas P.E. M, 3 children.

Coppin, Fanny Jackson (38 mentions: A8, B12, C18). 1837–1913, b. Washington, D.C. Educator, civic leader. Oberlin. St. Thomas P.E. to Bethel AME. M, no children.

Coppin, Rev. Levi (24 mentions: A2, B8, C14). 1848–1924, b. Maryland. AME Bishop, editor. P.E. Divinity School. AME. Married three times, 1 child.

Creditt, Rev. William (14 mentions: A0, B0, C14). 1864–1921, b. Baltimore. Clergyman. Newton Theological Seminary. First African Baptist. Marital status and children unknown.

Cromwell, Levi (21 mentions: A11, B7, C3). 1835–1904, b. Virginia. Restaurateur. Education and religion unknown. M, no children.

Dorsey, William Henry (21 mentions: A11, B5, C5). 1837–1923, b. Philadelphia. Artist, messenger, landlord. ICY. St. Thomas P.E. M, 6 children.

Durham, John Stephens (13 mentions: A2, B4, C7). 1861–1919, b. Philadelphia. Journalist, diplomat, lawyer. University of Pennsylvania. St. Thomas P.E. M, no children.

Gipson, Stephen (13 mentions: A0, B9, C4). 1853–98, b. Philadelphia. Politician, schoolteacher, government clerk. Lincoln University. St. Thomas P.E. M, no children.

Gould, Rev. Theodore (18 mentions: A1, B7, C10). 1830–1913, b. New Jersey. Clergyman. AME. M, 3 children.

Harper, Frances Ellen Watkins (26 mentions: A4, B7, C15). 1825–1911, b. Baltimore. Writer, WCTU worker. Watkins Academy. Congregationalist. M, 1 child.

Jones, Frank J. R. (28 mentions: A8, B6, C14). 1848–1911, b. Philadelphia. Musician, politician, saloonkeeper. ICY. Religion unknown. M, no children.

Jones, Robert Sr. (22 mentions: A9, B4, C9). 1818–1914, b. Pennsylvania. Barber, civic leader. Education unknown. Central Presbyterian. M, 11 children.

Junior, James (15 mentions: A10, B3, C2). 1838–94, b. Philadelphia. Laborer, political employee. Education and religion unknown. M, 5 children.

Lewis, John D. (15 mentions: A8, B6, C1). 1850–91, b. Canada. Lawyer. Yale Law School. Religion unknown. Married twice, 2 children.

Minton, Theodore J. (26 mentions: A2, B7, C17). 1850–1909, b. Philadelphia. Lawyer, government officeholder. ICY. St. Thomas P.E. M, 2 children.

Mossell, Dr. Nathan (24 mentions: A0, B7, C17). 1856–1946, b. Canada. Physician. University of Pennsylvania Medical School. AME. M, 3 children.

Needham, James F. (33 mentions: A13, B12, C8). 1845–1934, b. Philadelphia. Teacher, government clerk. ICY. St. Thomas P.E. Unmarried.

Perry, Christopher J. (13 mentions: A0, B3, C10). 1854–1921, b. Baltimore. Journalist, publisher, county clerk. ICY. Central Presbyterian. M, 5 children.

Phillips, Rev. Henry L. (30 mentions: A3, B7, C20). 1835–1935, b. British West Indies. Clergyman. Education unknown. P.E. Church of the Crucifixion. M, no children.

Purvis, Robert (32 mentions: A10, B17, C5). 1810–98, b. South Carolina. Gentleman farmer, abolitionist, civic leader. Attended Amherst. Religion unknown. Married twice, 8 children.

Reeve, Rev. John B. (16 mentions: A4, B8, C4). 1832–1915, b. New York. Clergyman. Union Theological Seminary. Central Presbyterian. M, 2 children.

Shadd, Hans Sr. (12 mentions: A4, B6, C2). 1835–1912, b. Philadelphia. Headwaiter. Education unknown. Allen AME. M, 4 children.

Shaeffer, Rev. Cornelius T. (21 mentions: A0, B9, C12). Dates unknown, b. in the South. Clergyman, physician. Medical school. AME. M, 1 child.

Stevens, Andrew Sr. (14 mentions: A4, B5, C5). 1840–98, b. Pennsylvania. Caterer, society leader. Education unknown. First African Baptist. M, 2 children.

Still, William (33 mentions: A14, B9, C10). 1821–1902, b. New Jersey. Coal dealer, abolitionist, philanthropist. No school. Berean Presbyterian. M, 4 children.

Tanner Rev. Benj. T. (31 mentions: A12, B9, C10). 1835–1923, b. Pittsburgh. AME Bishop, editor. Western Theological Seminary. AME. M, 7 children.

Teagle, James H. (14 mentions: A3, B6, C5). 1840–1908, b. Philadelphia. Barber, gambler, politician, restaurateur. Education and religion unknown. M, 2 children.

Turner, Rev. Henry M. (27 mentions: A7, B5, C15). 1834–1915, b. South Carolina. AME Bishop, editor. No school. AME. Married four times, "several" children.

Wears, Isaiah (48 mentions: A21, B15, C12). 1822–1900, b. Baltimore. Barber, notary public, Republican orator. Education unknown. AME. M, 7 children.

White, Jacob C., Jr. (17 mentions: A5, B10, C2). 1837–1900, b. Philadelphia. School principal, cemetery manager. ICY. Central Presbyterian. M, no children.

Williams, Henry P. (33 mentions: A22, B11, C0). Dates and birthplace unknown. Journalist, publisher, political officeholder. Education, religion, marital status, and children unknown.

APPENDIX IV

"Elite" Philadelphians, 1860s and 1890s

The list of elite black Philadelphians described in Chapter 10—confined to males for ease of tracing ancestry through surnames—was compiled from six others. The intent is to create two representative although not quite complete rosters of leading black citizens from two decades about a generation apart. The lists for both the 1860s and the 1890s are each made up of three smaller ones, each involving somewhat different activities and groups of men.

For 1860 there is a list of mostly young to middle-aged admirers who signed a petition to the singer Mary Brown, matched in 1898 by those who played some role in the Frederick Douglass Hospital Grand Charity Ball. The community's most distinguished notables joined with Frederick Douglass in 1863 to sign an open "Call to Arms" in the midst of the Civil War, as a parallel group joined the American Negro Historical Society in 1897. Finally the young men who formed the first three teams of the Pythians Baseball Club may be matched with the gallants who went to the DECAGON ball of 1899.

Some 17 men appear on two or more of the lists from the 1860s, 14 from the 1890s. The total of 130 for the earlier period includes just 107 surnames, on account of the duplication of such common ones as Wilson and Turner; the 137 for the 1890s have 113 different surnames. A few men appear in both generations, including three Joneses, Andrew, F. J. R., and Robert; other long-lasting citizens include Ebenezer Bassett, Alfred Cassey, Thadeus Manning, T. J. Minton, the Reverend John B. Reeve, Isaiah Wears, and Jacob White, Jr.

What keeps either list from being a full roster of the contemporary elite, instead of a representative sample, is that a few important men are left out. Neither Robert Purvis nor William Still, for example, appear in the 1860s; too old to play ball, too serious to petition Madame Brown, and perhaps because of their Garrisonian or Quaker connections unready to sign the "Call to Arms," they appear only in the 1890s, Still as patron of the Douglass ball, both men as members of the ANHS.

The 1860s list includes the following names, with a (1) following the names taken from the Madame Brown petition, a (2) from the Call to Arms, and a (3) from the Pythians Baseball Club.

Robert M. Adger (2), Joshua Adkins (3), William Allen (1), Rev. William Alston (2), James Ash (3), Reverend J. Asher (2), Edward Augustine (1), James

Augustine (1), P. J. Augustine (2), Jacob Ballard (3), Samuel H. Barratt (1), Chesley Bass (1), Ebenezer Bassett (2), Ebenezer Black (2), Rev. James Boulder (2), J. C. Bowers (1), T. J. Bowers (2), David B. Bowser (1, 2), Henry Boyer (3), Joseph Boyer (1), Isaac Brown (1), Joshua Brown (1), Morris Brown, Jr. (3), Charles Bundy (1), John P. Burr (2), Raymond Burr (3), E. M. Burrell (3), George Burrell (3), C. C. Bustill (1), Rev. J. P. Campbell (2), I. N. Cary (1), A. S. Cassey (1, 2), Joseph W. Cassey (1, 2), O. V. Catto (1, 2, 3), Rev. William Catto, (2), Jeffrey Cavens (3), Thomas Charnock (1, 3), John Chew (1), Ira Cliff (1, 2), Charles Colley (1), Daniel Colley (2), Edward Collins (1), John Connor (3), Henry Cropper (2), Eli Davis (2), John H. Davis (3), N. E. Depee (2), Augustus Dorsey (2), Thomas J. Dorsey (1, 2), James Douglass (2), Jonathan Dutton (1), Jacob Farbeaux, Sr. (1), William Forten (2), Horatio Franciscus (3), Daniel George (2), Joshua Gibbs (2), William Gipson (1, 2), Jesse Glasgow (2), Charles Gordon (1), James A. Gordon (2), John Graham (3), A. M. Green (2), Morris Hall (2), Spencer Hanley (3), Augustus Hazzard (3), Edward W. James (1), James Jenkins (3), Augustus Johnson (1), Edward W. Johnson (1), J. B. Johnson (2), Andrew Jones (3), Charles Jones (1), Frank Jones (3), Frank J. R. Jones (3), Robert Jones, Sr. (2), William Jones (1, 3), P. N. Judah (1), Robert Kennedy (1), David Knight (3), Thaddeus Manning (3), James McCrummell (2), Allen McKenna (1), Henry Minton (2), T. J. Minton (3), William H. Minton (1, 3), S. Morgan (2), E. W. Morris (1), James Needham (1, 2), J. W. Page (1, 2), George Price (1), Henry Price (3), J. W. Price (2), J. W. Purnell (3), Jesse Reed (1), Rev. J. B. Reeve (2), Frederick C. Revels (1), William H. Riley (1), Samuel Roberts (1), T. W. Robinson (1), Rev. Alfred Sanford (2), William Shaeff (1), P. T. Smith (1), Steven Smith (2), James Sparrow (3), William H. Stevenson (1), Charles W. Thomas (3), Henry Tobias (1), Rev. J. B. Trusty (2), D. D. Turner (1, 2), Frank Turner (1, 2), Rev. James Underdue (2), S. M. Van Brackle (1), Richard E. Venning (3), Frederick Walker (3), Rev. Eli Weare (2), Isaiah Wears (1), William Whipper (2), Jacob C. White, Jr. (1, 2, 3), Jacob C. White, Sr. (2), Rev. J. A. Williams (2), Dr. James Wilson (1, 2), Charles Wood (1).

The list for the 1890s follows, with a (1) following the names of those at the Douglass Hospital ball, a (2) following those at the DECAGON dance, and a (3) following members of the American Negro Historical Society.

Charles Abele (2), Robert M. Adger, Jr. (3), John Allen (3), William Allmond (2), William Allmond, Jr. (2), George Anderson (1), Rev. Matthew Anderson (3), J. C. Asbury (1), James Ashe (2), James Ashe, Jr. (2), Leon Ashe (2), Rev. J. G. Barksdale (3), Warley Bascom (2), William Bascom (2), Ebenezer Bassett (3), W. A. Baugh (3), Franklin Bell (1), James Bishop (2), W. Carl Bolivar (2, 3), E. A. Bouchet (3), Henry Briggs (3), S. J. M. Brock (1), Charles H. Brooks (1, 3), John Brown (1), Frank Burrell (2), Abel Caldwell (3), J. R. Caldwell (3), Augustus Capps (1), Augustus Capps, Jr. (2), Charles F. Carter (3), Howard Carter (2), John F. Carter (1), A. S. Cassey (3), Jonathan Clifton (2), George Clinton (1), J. H. Coleman (3), Rev. H. H. Cooper (3), Alexander Coots (2), Rev. Levi Coppin (3), Albert Courey (2), Lemuel Cowdery (1, 2), Martin Cowdery (3), Levi Cromwell (3), Barton Curry (1, 2), Frank Curtis (1), George W. Custis (3), Thomas Davis (2), William Davis (2), Frank Dillon (3), William Henry Dorsey (3), John Dorsey (2),

P. A. Dutrieuille (1, 3), M. R. Flint (1), J. G. Galloway (3), Howard Gould (1), S. K. Govern (1), Jonathan Hall (2), Walter Hall (3), Edward Harris (3), Dr. E. C. Howard (3), Theodore Howard, Jr. (2), Dr. Thomas Imes (3), Spencer Irving (2), William A. Jackson (1), Rev. H. K. Johnson (3), William Johnson (1, 3), Andrew Jones (3), Frank J. R. Jones (1), Robert Jones, Sr. (3), J. N. Kelley (1), Henry Klewson (1), William P. Lawrence (3), M. G. Lehman (1), Thaddeus Manning (3), Henry Martin (1, 3), Joshua Matthews (3), Col. John McKee (3), John Miller (2), Stewart Mintess (2), Henry G. Minton (1), T. J. Minton (2), Hiram Montier (3), William Morgan (1), Clifton Moseley (1, 3), Aaron Mossell (1), Dr. Nathan Mossell (1, 3), Alexander Murray (3), Thomas Murray (3), James Field Needham (3), Rev. William O'Connell (1, 3), Levi Oberton (3), E. H. Olds (1), Horace Owen (3), Rev. J. M. Palmer (3), Daniel Parvis (3), Samuel W. Patterson (3), Christopher Perry (3), Rev. Henry L. Phillips (1, 3), Rev. H. H. Pinckney (3), Sydney Pitman (2), William Potter (3), Robert Purvis (3), William Ramsey (2), Rev. John B. Reeve (3), Allen Ricketts (3), Herkimer Rosebone (1), George Ryder (2), Vincent Ryder (2), C. H. Sandridge (1), Joseph Saunders (2), Leonard Sayres (2), Elbert Semby (3), Hans Shadd, Sr. (3), J. H. Smith (1), Joseph Spence (1), Andrew Stevens, Sr. (1, 3), Andrew Stevens, Jr. (1, 3), William Still (1, 3), G. W. Summers (1), Isaac Sutton (2), Charles Taylor (1), J. B. Taylor (1), John Taylor (2), Lawrence Taylor (2), William Thomas (2), Frank Thompson (1), Henry Tobias (1), John Trower (3), Miles Tucker (3), William H. Valentine (3), Harold Warrick (2), Lewis Warrick (2), Richard Warrick, Jr. (2), J. F. Washington (1), Isaiah Wears (3), Jacob White, Jr. (3), J. R. Williams (2), Charles Wilson (1, 3), George H. Wilson (3), Andrew Williams (2), George L. Williams (2), James H. Williams (2, 3).

For the 1860s: The "undersigned gentlemen" who petitioned Mary L. Brown in May of 1860 are listed in Dorsey scrapbook #70, p. 4; the "Call to Arms" in 1863 is located in the Leon Gardiner Collection, Historical Society of Pennsylvania, Box 1G; the first four teams of the Pythians are in Gardiner Collection, HSP, Box 8G.

For the 1890s, those involved in the Frederick Douglass Hospital Grand Charity Ball are listed in Dorsey scrapbook #97, pp. 152–59, *The Evening Telegraph* 12/9/97, *Times* 12/13/97, *Item* 12/17/97, *Tribune* 12/18/97; The American Negro Historical Society's membership list is in Gardiner Collection, HSP, Box 10G; the DECAGON ball is in scrapbook #112, p. 6, *Tribune* 4/15/99.

Notes

Items from the Dorsey Collection (see Appendix I) will be footnoted with the number of the scrapbook first, then the page number, then the date and title of the newspaper or other item. Philadelphia papers will not be given place names. Thus "127.85 *Record* 12/9/79" is the Philadelphia *Record*, Dec. 9, 1879, found in scrapbook number 127, page 85. Note that in many cases either the title or the date of the item may not be available, so that it might be "127.85 12/9/79," or 127.85 *Record -/-/79*." In a very few cases the scrapbooks themselves are either unnumbered or unpaginated. Reprinted materials will be indicated with the paper from which they were clipped, and an asterisk before the one it was taken from, as "127.85 *Chicago *Interocean* in *Record* 12/9/79. Newspaper items from the Dorsey files will be noted as, e.g., "Files, John Smith," with papers given as in forms above.

References to Philadelphia standard census data will not be footnoted. Biographical information, if not taken from contemporary sources, may come from the most convenient rather than the fullest source, notably Rayford W. Logan and Michael R. Winston, eds., *Dictionary of American Negro Biography* (New York: W. W. Norton, 1982), which will be noted as DANB. References to the Philadelphia *Tribune* from 1912 to 1914—prior issues burned in fire—are to the historical columns of W. Carl Bolivar, collected and kindly loaned to me by Harry C. Silcox.

Introduction to Part I

1. W. E. B. Du Bois, *The Philadelphia Negro, A Social Study* (Millwood, N.Y.: Kraus-Thompson, 1973, orig. pub. 1899); among the distinguished recent histories of the city are, for the earlier years, Gary Nash, *Forging Freedom: The Formation of Philadelphia's Black Community 1720–1840* (Cambridge, Harvard Univ. Press, 1980), and for the most recent the moving and partly autobiographical work of Allen B. Ballard, *One More Day's Journey: The Story of a Family and a People* (New York: McGraw-Hill, 1984). Special mention must go to the Philadelphia Social History Project, under the direction of Theodore Hershberg during the 1970s, whose exhaustive studies based on the manuscript census, despite severe flaws in the census, have been helpful to all later researchers. See Theodore Hershberg, ed., *Philadelphia: Work, Space, Family and Group Experience in the Nineteenth Century: Essays Towards an Interdisciplinary History of the City* (New York and Oxford: Oxford Univ. Press, 1981). Harrison W. Wayman, "The American Negro Historical Society," in *Colored American Magazine* 6, no. 3 (Feb. 1903), 287–94. The Dorsey Collection, heavily used by Du Bois, was rediscovered too late to be used by Hershberg et al.

2. Dorsey Collection described in Appendix I.

3. Dorsey family and biography in Appendix II.

4. Quotation from Johns Hopkins University, *Studies in Historical and Political Science* I, no. 1 (1883).

Chapter 1. Of Politics, Religion, and Popular Culture

1. W. E. B. Du Bois, *The Philadelphia Negro, A Social Study* (Millwood, N.Y.: Kraus-Thompson, 1973, orig. pub. 1899), 49–53; John A. Saunders, *100 Years After Emancipation: History of the Philadelphia Negro, 1787–1963* (n.p., n.d.), 146.

2. Bureau of the Census, *Historical Statistics of the United States*, Part I (Washington: U.S. Government Printing Office, 1973), 22–23; Du Bois, *Philadelphia Negro*, 49–53.

3. 43.68 *Bulletin* 2/26/80.

4. 43.1 *New York Times* 4/7/80.

5. 43.1 *New York Times* 4/7/80; 43.3 New York *Herald* 4/7/80; 43.4 *Bulletin* 4/8/80.

6. 43.71 *Day* 4/27/80. For T. Morris Chester and other early black news reporters see Richard Blackett, *Thomas Morris Chester, Black Civil War Correspondent: His Dispatches from the Virginia Front* (Baton Rouge, Louisiana State Univ. Press, 1989).

7. 43.47 *Press* 4/22/80; 43.82 *Bulletin* 4/28/80 *Troy *Times*.

8. 43.86 4/30/80.

9. 43.105 *Bulletin* 5/17/80; 43.127 *Press* 5/31/80; 43.105 *Chicago *Interocean*, n.p., n.d.; 43.120 *Bulletin* 8/8/80; 43.139 *Bulletin* 12/29/80.

10. 43.103 *Press* 3/21/81; 43.104 *Press* 3/29/82.

11. 43.105 *Bulletin* 5/17/80; 43.106 *Press* 4/26/80.

12. 43.105 *Bulletin* 5/17/80; 59.4 *Record* 6/11/77.

13. 8.126 *Inquirer* 4/24/77; 43.3 *New York Times* 4/7/80.

14. 43.40 Pittsburg *Post* 4/20/80.

15. Dorsey scrapbook #122, passim.

16. 93.101 *Tribune* 5/30/96.

17. Fortune in DANB, 236–38.

18. Teagle in Appendix II; Harry Silcox, *Philadelphia Politics from the Bottom Up: The Life of Irishman William McMullen* (Philadelphia: Black Institute Press, 1989), passim.

19. 11.19 Sunday *Leader* 3/9/79; *Tribune* 1/11/13.

20. 49.17 *Times* 11/25/92; 90.39 *North American* 11/24/99.

21. 27 unpaginated Sunday *Mercury* 10/26/73; 65.47 *Times* –/–/86. See Chapter 6.

22. Robert Kelly, *The Shaping of the American Past*, 3rd ed., Vol. I (Englewood Cliffs, N.J.: Prentice-Hall, 1982), 223.

23. Pythian Baseball Club Papers in Leon Gardiner Collection, American Negro Historical Society Papers, HSP.

24. 44.1ff., handwritten.

25. 44.2 *Call* 7/22/88; 44.6 *Item* 11/11/89; 44.10 *Item* 2/2/90.

26. 243.2 *Item* 11/30/93; 243.9 *Times* 1/20/94; 44.17 New York *Illustrated News*, n.d.; 44.26 *Item* 4/22/91.

27. 44.37 *Item* 6/28/90; Dixon in DANB, 180.

28. 44.24 *Item* 8/3/90.

29. 44.37 *Item* 8/3.90; 44.26 *Item* 5/22/91.

30. 243.91 *Press* 10/10/95; 243.71 *Item* 3/7/95; 243.24 *Item* 4/21/94; 44.75 5/24/91.

31. 65.8 *Daily News* 2/12/88; 113.88 11/12/99; 112.24 9/9/03.

32. 242.10 *Press* 12/29/79.

33. Scrapbook #242 passim; Edwin Bancroft Hudson, *The Negro in Sports,* rev. ed. (Washington: Associated Publishers, 1939), 226ff.

34. Scrapbook #242 passim; Andrew Richie, *Major Taylor: The Extraordinary Career of a Champion Bicycle Racer* (New York: Bicycle Books, 1988).

35. Roger Lane, *Roots of Violence in Black Philadelphia, 1860–1900* (Cambridge: Harvard Univ. Press, 1986), 54.

36. Dorsey scrapbook on "The Colored Giants Baseball Club" is not numbered, appears on microfilm reel after #61; from this book Trenton *Times* 5/10/86; Trenton *State Gazette* n.d.; 72.4 *Item* 7/2/90.

37. *Tribune* 8/24/12.

38. On Philadelphia black musicians see Chapter11; 39.74 *Item* 4/1/76.

39. On black musicians see Chapter 11.

40. Scrapbooks #55, 70, passim. 129.70 *Times* 10/24/77; Leon Gardiner Collection, HSP, Box 3G, folder #72.

41. 58.59 *People's Advocate* 11/9/78.

42. Alain Locke, *The Negro and His Music: Negro Art, Past and Present* (New York: Arno Press, 1969, orig. pub. 1930), 17.

43. 13.72 *New York *Herald* in *Press* 2/20/82.

44. Dorothy Gondos Beers, "The Centennial City, 1865–1876," in Russell F. Weigley, ed., *Philadelphia, a 300-Year History* (New York: W. W. Norton, 1982), 444–46.

45. 84.72 1894(?).

46. 32.18 *Chicago *Times* in Trenton *Times* 5/24/86.

47. 50.26 *Times* 7/21/85; 15.45 New York *Sun* 7/21/79.

48. 72.2 7/21/90.

49. 81.150 *Tribune* 4/7/94; 92.50 New York *Sunday World* 7/26/96.

50. 127.69 *North American* 1/17/03; 123.18 *Bulletin* 4/5/03.

51. Scrapbook #45 passim; 45.35 *Times* 8/3/91.

52. 132.53 *Elevator* 2/28/80; 110.14 Bridgeton, N.J., *Pioneer* 11/19/98; Files, Tanner, *Item* 2/3/00.

53. 114.43 –/–/99; 88.12 6/9/94; 46.23 *Christian Recorder* 10/19/76; 15.19 *Inquirer* 12/16/78.

54. John McCarthy, *The Best of Irish Wit and Wisdon* (New York: Dodd, Mead, 1987), 229.

55. 72.7 n.p., n.d.

56. 102.78 n.p., n.d.

57. 91.78 *Lippincott's Magazine* 1/9/86; 129.84 *Press* 1/23/78; New York *Freeman* 9/18/86; 63.19 *Press* 8/10/81.

58. 79.20 n.p., n.d.

59. 101.48 1898; 112.113 n.p., n.d.—the poem is attributed to "Ferguson," also the name of the *Tribune*'s Cape May correspondent.

60. See Robert C. Toll, *Blacking Up: The Minstrel Show in Nineteenth Century America* (New York: Oxford Univ. Press, 1974), passim.

61. Locke, *The Negro and His Music,* 45.

62. 54.49 12/25/82.

63. 15.5ff., several papers 9/15–9/21/79.

64. 15.8 *Press* 9/15/79; 15.9 *Press* 9/16/79; 15.9 *Sunday Transcript* 9/21/79.
65. 58.7 *People's Advocate* 8/24/78.
66. 116.114 *Times* 4/13/94.
67. 74.37 *Press* 9/14/87.
68. 49.19 Chicago *Herald* 10/23/92.
69. 49.138 5/20/93; 30.81 *Press* 7/18/81.
70. 99.1 Boston *Transcript* 7/14/97.
71. *Ibid.*
72. *Ibid.*
73. 119.99 New York *Evening Journal* 7/31/99.
74. 119.55 *Times* 7/30/99.
75. Ernest Hogan's coon songs in Files, Hogan, Indianapolis *Freeman* 2/24/98.
76. *Ibid.;* see Chapter 11; 109.32 3/4/98.

Chapter 2. Of Race, Sex, and Lynching

1. Thomas Jefferson, *Notes on the State of Virginia* (New York: Harper & Row, 1964, orig. pub. 1861), 132–33.

2. John S. Haller, *Outcasts from Evolution: Scientific Attitudes of Racial Inferiority, 1859–1900* (Urbana: Univ. of Illinois Press, 1971), passim; 75.74 *Item* 5/6/90; 97.78 –/–/97; 115.1 –/–/99; 125.76 New York *Evening Journal* 12/11/99.

3. 90.113 *Times* 12/11/99; 93.134 New York *World* 5/2/96; 108.53 *Times* 1/3/98.

4. 50.70 *Press* 12/6/80; 85.141 5/6/94; Louis Aggasiz to E. D. Cope, Feb. 5, 1869, in Quaker Collection, Haverford College Library.

5. 85.136 *Inquirer* 3/4/99, cf. 105.30 New York *Tribune* –/–/98; 53.42 *Press* 2/11/84; 51.57 *Indianapolis *News* in *Press* 8/18/89.

6. 68.9 *Record* 2/28/98.

7. *Inquirer* 6/7/72.

8. 11.93 *Bulletin* –/–/79; 60.12 *Press* 2/22/84; 87.130 12/13/94; 65.25 *Star* 8/25/88; 92.112 8/8/96; 108.49 3/23/98; 98.65 *Times* 8/30/97; 104.30 3/-/98; 107.89 3/4/98.

9. 61.77 *Item* 6/17/90; 113.5 *Item* 10/29/99; 103.51ff., *Item* 9/10/98 and 9/15/98.

10. Robert William Fogel and Stanley Engerman, *Time on the Cross: The Economics of Negro Slavery* (Boston: Little, Brown, 1974). 132–33. The figure arrived at by this procedure was 10 percent; 15.35 Washington *People's Advocate* 7/19/79; 84.131 Letter from "TMR" in *Inquirer* 2/4/94; 59.4 *Record* 6/11/77; 72.44 St. Paul *Daily Globe* 5/25/90.

11. 34.29 4/21/83; 93.14 Washington *Star* 1/22/96; 8.92 *Record* 4/12/79; 121.90 New Brunswick *Fredonian* 2/25/99; 72.36 *Times* 8/17/90; 74.55 *Daily News* 6/2/90.

12. 36.41 New York *Age* 7/19/94; 32/21 *Press* 3/22/86; 72.44 St. Paul *Daily Globe* 5/25/90.

13. 60.45 *Press* 5/18/82.

14. 53.74 *Record* 11/30/77; Bureau of the Census, *Historical Statistics of the United States,* Part I (Washington: U.S. Government Printing Office, 1973, 22.

15. *Ibid.; Inquirer* 8/23/81; 33.24 *New York *Sun* in *Record* 2/19/81.

16. 63.34 *Times* 12/26/87; 51.2 *Press* 7/26/89; Bureau of the Census, *Historical Statistics,* 22.

17. 53.74 *Record* 11/30/77; Michael R. Haines, "Why Were Nineteenth Century U.S. Urban Black Fertility Rates So Low? Evidence from Philadelphia, 1850–1880," unpub. ms., 32–33.

18. The registration system adopted in Philadelphia, as in other cities, usually in the 1860s, was during the 19th century more efficient at recording deaths, through undertakers, than births, which were still done informally at home; see Roger Lane, *Violent Death in the City: Suicide, Accident, and Murder in Nineteenth Century Philadelphia* (Cambridge: Harvard Univ. Press, 1979), 144–47; 58.2 Washington *People's Advocate,* 8/10/78; 127.59 *North American* 1/14/03.

19. 80.8 New York *Sunday World* 3/14/94; 60.101 *Press* 5/2/86.

20. 129.2 n.p., n.d. Population figures cited indicate piece from 1860s.

21. 71.166ff. James Bryce, "Thoughts on the Negro Problem," *North American Review* (Dec. 1891), 654, 651, 652, 653–54, 655–57, 659–60.

22. 101.99 *Literary Digest* in *Tribune* 8/13/98; New York *Age* 10/12/89.

23. Lane, *Roots of Violence,* 45–46 and passim.

24. 69.12 Richmond *Daily Planet* 11/6/89; Arthur F. Raper, *The Tragedy of Lynching* (Chapel Hill: Univ. of North Carolina Press, 1933), 1–2.

25. 49.131 *North American* 2/2/93; 102.101 *Times* 7/16/98.

26. 78.85 Wilmington *Evening Journal* 2/24/92; 95.132 New York *Evening Journal* 10/24/97.

27. Charles Blockson, *The Underground Railroad in Pennsylvania* (Jacksonville, N.C.: Flame International 1981), 37–39; 42.24 n.p., n.d.; Theodore Hershberg and Henry Williams, "Mulattoes and Blacks: Intra-group Color Differences and Social Stratification in Nineteenth Century Philadelphia," in Theodore Hershberg, ed., *Philadelphia: Work, Space, Family and Group Experience in the Nineteenth Century, Essays Towards an Interdisciplinary History of the City* (New York: Oxford Univ. Press, 1981), 399, explains that there were two counts taken in 1870, with the lower figure for African-Americans cited in the text; Lane, *Roots of Violence,* 49.

28. DANB, 510; Files, Gipson, *State Journal* 12/13/90; Files, Offley, *Tribune* 6/13/91; 68.40 1/2/89; see Chapter 6, p. 172 for Minton.

29. 74.43 *Times* 7/15/90; Files, Gibbs, 9/26/74; *Inquirer* 6/8/72; New York *Globe* 11/3/83; 88.51 6/25/94.

30. Frederick A. Norwood, *The Story of American Methodism* (Abington, Mass: Abington Press, 1974), 276.

31. DANB, 609; Files, Heard, *Christian Recorder* 2/21/95.

32. 65.54 *Times* 2/7/86; 65.55 *Press* 3/8/86; 65.61 *Call* 6/7/88; 67.54 *Times* 5/31/90. Lingo in scrapbooks #18–20, from which following paragraphs taken; best single account in 20.12–22 *Inquirer* October 1891.

33. 77.63 *New York Commercial Advertiser* in *Times,* late 1891 or early 1892; 85.94 Camden *Review* 3/8/94; 20.56i poster; 20.55 *Item* 11/15/92, with WHD marginalia.

34. Prior lynching in 85.103–7, esp. *Times* 3/15/94, 3/16/94.

35. Scrapbook #17 on White Lynching, from which following paragraphs taken.

36. 79.121 8/10/92; Paterson *Labor Standard* 3/5/98; 117.77 *Record* 7/4/99.

37. 55.109 *Item* 3/16/94; 85.109 *Item* 3/16/99; New York *World* 9/19/97; 99.69 *Times* 6/13/97.

38. Opinion roundup in 104.48 New York *World* 9/19/97.

39. 17.51 *North American* 6/27/03.

40. 17.33 *Inquirer* 6/24/03; 17.54 *Bulletin* 6/27/03; 17.68 *Record* 6/30/03; 17.51 *North American* 6/27/03.

41. 112.70 *Tribune* 4/29/99.

42. Edward L. Ayers, *Vengeance and Justice: Crime and Punishment in the*

Nineteenth Century South (New York: Oxford Univ. Press, 1984), chap. 7; Ida B. Wells, *The Reason Why* (Chicago, 1894), 7.

43. 77.18 *Item* 9/17/91; 99.18 8/10/97; 115.17 8/3/97; 127.99 *North American* 2/14/03.

44. Scrapbook #43 is devoted to Wilmington, N.C., events.

45. Charles A. Hardy III, "Race and Opportunity: Black Philadelphia During the Era of the Great Migration, 1916–1930," Vol. I (Ph.D. diss. in History, Temple University, 1989), 25; 38.76 *Times* 12/2/99; 38.61 n.p., n.d.

46. 11.38 *Tribune* 2/18/99; 38.51 *Star of Zion* n.p., n.d. with WHD marginalia.

47. See Chapter 7; 66.47 *Press* 5/11/80; 53.55 *Press* 3/2/78; 110.1 New York *World* 11/20/98.

48. See Chapter 7.

49. 86.141 *Inquirer* –/–/1894; 38.53 *Record* 11/23/99; 17.64 *North American* 6/28/03.

50. 81.167 *Tribune* 5/27/93; 114.41 *Tribune* 1/14/99; 38.82 *Tribune* 12/3/99; 17.69 *Record* 6/29/03.

51. 17.69 6/29/03; 17.38 6/24/03; 17.38 6/23/03.

52. 118.50 *Press* 5/23/99; 90.11 *Tribune* 11/14/99; 107.44 *Tribune* 2/29/99.

53. 119.169 New York *Evening Journal* 7/30/99; 31.90 *Item* 11/30/93.

Introduction to Part II

1. Dorothy Gondos Beers, "The Centennial City, 1865–1876," in Russell F. Weigley, ed., *Philadelphia: A 300 Year History* (New York: W. W. Norton, 1982), 417–70, and Nathaniel Burt and Wallace E. Davies, "The Iron Age, 1876–1905," in *ibid.*, 471–523.

2. Figures from Theodore Hershberg et al., "A Tale of Three Cities: Blacks, Immigrants, and Opportunity in Philadelphia, 1850–1880, 1930, 1970," in Hershberg, ed., *Philadelphia: Work, Space, Family and Group Experience in the Nineteenth Century* (New York: Oxford Univ. Press, 1981), 475.

3. Roger Lane, *Roots of Violence in Black Philadelphia, 1860–1900* (Cambridge: Harvard Univ. Press, 1986), 177–79.

4. The Dorsey story is complex: see Chapter 10, and Appendix II.

5. See Appendix III. Missing from 1880 are Gipson, Harper, Turner, and Williams; from 1870 printout from Philadelphia Social History Project, kindly supplied by Henry Williams: Ball, Cromwell, Durham, Still, Tanner, Teagle.

6. Nell Irvin Painter, *Standing at Armageddon: The United States, 1877–1919* (New York: W. W. Norton, 1987), xviii–xxvii; Eudice Glassberg, "Work, Wages, and the Cost of Living: Ethnic Differences and the Poverty Line, Philadelphia, 1880," in *Pennsylvania History* 66, no. 1 (Jan. 1979), 17–58.

Chapter 3. The "Unskilled" Majority

1. 81.167 *Tribune* 5/27/93.

2. Nell Irvin Painter, *Standing at Armageddon: The United States, 1877–1919* (New York: W. W. Norton, 1987), chap. 1.

3. 35.73 St. Louis *Post Dispatch* in *Bulletin* -/-/79; 73.13 1/2 *Evening Telegraph* in *Times* 8/27/90; 112.108 *Record* 5/13/99.

4. Lorenzo J. Greene and Carter Woodson, *The Negro Wage Earner* (New York:

Russell & Russell, 1930), 151; 68.48 *Times* 8/25/81; 38.65 *Inquirer* 9/15/90; 74.19 *Times* 9/12/87; R. R. Wright, Jr., *The Negro in Pennsylvania: A Study in Economic History* (New York: Arno Press, 1967, orig. pub. 1912), 93–94.

5. John W. Cell, *The Highest Stage of White Supremacy: The Origins of Segregation in South Africa and the American South* (Cambridge: Cambridge Univ. Press, 1982), 135–43.

6. See Chapter 4.

7. Theodore Hershberg and Henry P. Williams, "Mulattoes and Blacks: Intragroup Color Differences and Social Stratification in Nineteenth Century Philadelphia," in Hershberg, ed. *Philadelphia: Work, Space, Family and Group Experience in the Nineteenth Century* (New York: Oxford Univ. Press, 1981), 407–8; Lebanon Cemetery Records, Leon Gardiner Collection, HSP, passim; Ms. "Register," Industrial School, Institute for Colored Youth, in Cheyney State University Archives.

8. Philip S. Foner and Ronald L. Lewis, eds., *The Black Worker: A Documentary History from Colonial Times to the Present*, Vol. II, *The Black Worker During the Era of the National Labor Union* (Philadelphia: Temple Univ. Press, 1978), 3–4, 38, 82–108; 52.56 *Press* 3/18/69.

9. Foner and Lewis, *The Black Worker*, Vol. III, *During the Era of the Knights of Labor*, 52, 104–32; unnumbered Dorsey scrapbook, following #63, entitled "The Knights of Labor and the Color Line, 1881."

10. Herbert R. Northrup, *Organized Labor and the Negro* (New York: Harper & Bros., 1944), 7–8.

11. W. E. B. Du Bois, *The Philadelphia Negro: A Social Study* (Millwood, N.Y.: Kraus-Thompson, 1973, orig. pub. 1899), 227; 75.48 4/28/90; *Inquirer* 6/21/98.

12. Foner and Lewis, *Knights of Labor*, 409–41; 87.98 *Christian Recorder* 12/7/94; 80.8 New York *Sunday World* 3/4/94; 85.110 -/-/94.

13. 88.144 *Tribune* 7/21/94; 87.49 *Tribune* -/-/94.

14. Du Bois, *Philadelphia Negro*, 228; 10/5/93; 70.57, printed program, "Third Annual . . . Hod Carriers & Laborers."

15. Du Bois, *Philadelphia Negro*, 227.

16. Dorsey Files, George Sharper, *Tribune* 2/3/94 and 2/16/94; 41.21 *Daily Hotel Report* 11/10/92.

17. Du Bois, *Philadelphia Negro*, 227; see, for balls, etc., scrapbook #70.

18. Printout from 1870 census, Black Occupations, kindly provided by Henry L. Williams of PSHP; Du Bois, *Philadelphia Negro*, 105–7.

19. *Ibid.*, 100.

20. *Ibid.*

21. 10.21 *American & Gazette* 7/13/73; Burt and Davies, "The Iron Age," 506; 59.51 *Day* 11/6/76.

22. *Tribune* 10/5/12; Northrup, *Negro and Labor*, 143; *Tribune* 5/10/13.

23. Du Bois, *Philadelphia Negro*, 135; Michael R. Haines, "Poverty, Economic Stress, and the Family in a Late Nineteenth Century American City: Whites in Philadelphia, 1880," in Hershberg, ed., *Philadelphia*, 247.

24. Du Bois, *Philadelphia Negro*, 105–7, 99; *Tribune*, 6/6/12.

25. *Tribune* 5/10/13; 132.17 *Press* 8/1/81; *Tribune* 5/10/13; *Tribune* 7/20/12; 125.20 -/-/99; 101.88 8/6/98.

26. 119.46 7/18/99; 98.11 8/17/97; Glassberg, "Poverty Line," 26.

27. Glassberg, "Poverty Line," 57; Du Bois, *Philadelphia Negro*, 170–71; Glassberg, "Poverty Line," 56; 75.3 *Times* 11/9/89.

28. 75.48 4/28/90; Lane, *Roots of Violence*, 111–12; 75.48 4/28/90.

29. See Chapter 10.

30. Du Bois, *Philadelphia Negro,* 100.

31. Charles Hardy III, "Race and Opportunity: Black Philadelphia During the Era of the Great Migration, 1916–1930" (Ph.D. diss. in History, Temple University, 1989), chap. 1.

32. See Appendix II.

33. 23.10 *Times* 11/8/85; 49.21 *Daily Hotel Reporter* 11/11/92; *New York Age* 11/29/90.

34. Eaton in Du Bois, *Philadelphia Negro,* 446, 450.

35. *Ibid.,* 446, 490.

36. *Ibid.,* 446; Lane, *Roots of Violence,* 69; *Tribune* 5/10/13.

37. Du Bois, *Philadephia Negro,* 468–69.

38. Printout, 1870 census.

39. Du Bois, *Philadelphia Negro,* 479.

40. *Ibid.,* 102, 103–4.

41. *Ibid.,* 103–4.

42. *Ibid.,* 170.

43. *Ibid.,* 103–4.

44. Dorsey family in Chapter 10; New York *Freeman* 10/16/86; Du Bois, *Philadelphia Negro,* 194.

45. Bruce Laurie and Mark Schmitz, "Manufacture and Productivity: The Making of an Industrial Base, Philadelphia, 1850–1880," in Hershberg, ed., *Philadelphia,* 47; 73.5 *Times* 8/26/90; 73.2 *Record* 8/8/90; 73.2 *Times* 8/19/90.

46. 73.3 *Times* 8/26/90.

47. 73.3 *Item* 8/18/90; *Inquirer* 9/1/90; *Inquirer* 10/18/90; Greene and Woodson, *Negro Wage Earner,* 151; New York *Freeman* 6/19/86.

48. Du Bois, *Philadelphia Negro,* 103–4, 453–54.

49. *Ibid.,* 103, 447.

50. *Ibid.,* 445, 446, 444.

51. 75.58 4/17/90; 99.91 7/31/97; 75.58 4/17/90.

52. 42.39 *New York *Sun* in *Record* 5/11/88; 23.39 *Tribune* 9/29/88.

53. Du Bois, *Philadelphia Negro,* 477.

54. 75.2 *Times* 11/9/89.

55. Du Bois, *Philadelphia Negro,* 139–40.

56. *Ibid.,* 139–40, 440–51; 81.167 *Tribune* 5/2/93; 123.74 *North American* 4/2/63; Du Bois, *Philadelphia Negro,* 138, 449.

57. 72.45 *Times* 7/25/90; 123.74 *North American* 4/21/03.

58. Du Bois, *Philadelphia Negro,* 46–50. Earlier figures are from Philadelphia County, consolidated with the city in 1854.

59. Lane, *Roots of Violence,* 158.

60. 75.28 *Press* 2/3/90.

61. Roger Lane, "John Boyle O'Reilly and the Boston Pilot," unpub. ms., 1957; New York *Freeman* 1/9/86; *People's Advocate* 9/29/77; Dorsey Files, Richard Greener, New York *Age* 11/22/96.

62. Lane, *Roots of Violence,* 44–45; 95.121 *Times* 11/3/97; 90.120 12/11/99; Charles Hardy III, "Race and Opportunity," 230.

63. Dennis Clark, *The Irish in Philadelphia: Ten Generations of Urban Experience* (Philadelphia: Temple Univ. Press, 1973), 74.

64. 89.96 *Sunday World* 12/-/94; 123.63 *Bulletin* 4/12/03.

65. 86.41 *Times* 5/-/94.

66. 106.81 *Times* 1/23/99; 106.82 5/31/98; Lane, *Roots of Violence*, 136; 109.114 4/11/98.

67. 102.42 6/16/98; 88.142 7/8/94; 117.75 6/26/99; 116.77 *Record* 4/15/99; 116.78 *Item* 4/15/99; 116.79 *Record* 4/6/99.

68. 123.63 *Bulletin* 4/21/03; 49.73 12/28/92; 127.42 *North American* 1/6/03; 127.48 *North American* 1/20/03.

69. 87.131 *Times* 12/13/94; 122.114 *Bulletin* 10/15/03; 127.123 2/9/03.

70. 84.1 *Times* 12/23/93.

71. Lane, *Roots of Violence*, 150; 75.58 4/17/90.

72. 75.58 4/17/90; Du Bois, *Philadelphia Negro*, 486; 75.58 4/17/90.

73. Du Bois, *Philadelphia Negro*, 481; 127.87 *North American* 1/29/03.

74. 121.49 *Tribune* 3/18/99; 127.88 Minneapolis *Afro-American Advance*, 1903.

75. Lane, *Roots of Violence*, 147–48, 167.

76. Du Bois, *Philadelphia Negro*, 436; Greene and Woodson, *The Negro Wage Earner*, 80.

77. Ruth Rosen, *The Lost Sisterhood: Prostitution in America, 1900–1918* (Baltimore: Johns Hopkins Univ. Press, 1982), 102, 145–47; Lane, *Roots of Violence*, 127–28.

78. Rosen, *Lost Sisterhood*, chap. 8; Lane, *Roots of Violence*, 125–31.

79. Greene and Woodson, *Negro Wage Earner*, 80; Lane, *Roots of Violence*, 132.

80. 121.91 8/5/98; 119.72 *Times* 7/25/99; 118.91 5/25/99.

81. Claudia Goldin, "Family Strategies and the Family Economy in the Late Nineteenth-Century American City: The Role of Secondary Workers," in Hershberg, ed., *Philadelphia*, 296–304.

82. *Ibid.;* Lane, *Roots of Violence*, 158.

83. On elite families see Chapter 10.

84. Du Bois, *Philadelphia Negro*, 62.

85. Figures calculated from Lane, *Roots of Violence*, 97, 87–89.

86. Lane, *Roots of Violence*, 14 and passim.

87. *Ibid.*, 134–43 and passim.

88. *Ibid.*, 96–105.

89. *Ibid.*, 105–8.

90. *Ibid.*, 157–59.

91. 117.39 *Times* 6/2/99; 117.67 *Times* 6/26/99; 117.67 6/27/99.

92. Lane, *Roots of Violence*, 109–33.

93. 123.30 4/9/03; 117.39 *Item* 6/21/99; Lane, *Roots of Violence*, 159.

94. 121.98 *Item* 3/23/99; 121.100 *Record* 3/29/99; 82.154 9/18/94; 83.48 9/25/94.

95. 112.36 4/22/99; 107.35 *Bulletin* 2/16/98; 108.5 *Times* 10/12/98; 108.5 *Tribune* 10/21/98.

96. 116.86 4/7/99; Allen Steinberg, *The Transformation of Criminal Justice: Philadelphia, 1800–1880* (Chapel Hill: Univ. of North Carolina Press, 1989), passim; 105.72 *Bulletin* 11/15/97.

97. 108.3 *Times* 10/12/98; 88.88 7/2/94; 113.66 11/9/99; 112.24 4/2/99; 112.81 5/4/99.

98. 101.69 *Times* 8/3/98.

99. Du Bois, *Philadelphia Negro*, 208; 106.103 3/11/98; David T. Courtwright, *Dark Paradise: Opiate Addiction in America before 1940* (Cambridge: Harvard Univ. Press, 1982), passim.

100. Du Bois, *Philadelphia Negro*, 66–67, 490.

101. Lane, *Roots of Violence,* 157; 120.87 *Item* 6/9/99; 70.53 12/4/90; New York *Freeman,* 12/13/84.

102. See Appendix II.

Chapter 4. Owners, Artisans, and Entrepreneurs

1. 15.10 Sunday *Times* 7/20/79.

2. W. E. B. Du Bois, *The Negro in Business: Report of a Social Study Made Under the Direction of Atlanta University . . . 1899* (New York: A.M.S. Press, 1971, orig. pub. 1899), 27; Du Bois, *The Philadelphia Negro: A Social Study* (Millwood, N.Y.: Kraus-Thompson, 1973, orig. pub. 1899), 115–26; Theodore Hershberg et al., "A Tale of Three Cities: Blacks, Immigrants, and Opportunity in Philadelphia, 1850–1880, 1930, 1970," in Hershberg, ed., *Philadelphia: Work, Space, Family, and Group Experience in the Nineteenth Century: Essays Towards an Interdisciplinary History of the City* (New York and Oxford: Oxford Univ. Press, 1981), 475.

3. See Appendix III.

4. DANB, 508–10.

5. 15.10 Sunday *Times* 7/20/79; unnumbered Eddy scrapbook after #63, titled "Obituary and Will of Rev. J. P. B. Eddy, Phila. 1882," hereafter cited as 63a; McKee scrapbook is #223.

6. 63a.1 *Bulletin* 9/26/82.

7. *Ibid.*

8. 63a.11 *Evening Telegraph* 9/29/82.

9. *Ibid.;* 63a.13 *Record* 9/30/82; 63a.15 *Bulletin* 10/2/82; 63a.24 *Independent* 7/12/84.

10. 223.12 *Sunday Times* 4/20/02.

11. 223.1 *Evening Telegraph* 4/8/02; 223.12 *Sunday Press* 4/20/02.

12. 223.2 *North American* 4/10/02; 223.5 *Evening Telegraph* 4/12/02.

13. 223.3 *North American* 4/10/02; 223.6 *Press* 4/12/02.

14. 223.6 *Press* 4/12/02; 223.21 *Evening Telegraph* 4/28/02.

15. 223.26 *North American* 5/22/02; 223.30 *Bulletin* 4/8/04; 223.30 *Bulletin* 4/9/04; 223.31 *Record* 9/19/03; 223.31 12/8/04.

16. DANB, 234–35, 566.

17. 63a.11 *Evening Telegraph* 9/29/82; 223.1 *Evening Telegraph* 4/08/02.

18. 63a.11 *Evening Telegraph* 9/29/82.

19. 48.12 New York *Age* 4/17/89; 223.22 *Tribune* 5/3/02.

20. DANB, 573–74, 643.

21. William Still, *The Underground Railroad: A Record of Facts, Authentic Narratives, Letters, Etc.* (Chicago: Johnson Publishing, 1970, orig. pub. 1871), v; see Appendix II.

22. 74.43 *Times* 7/15/90; 91.35 *Record* 2/25/95; Dorsey Files, Robert G. Still obituary, 6/4/91; 40.11, broadside, Pennsylvania Society for the Abolition of Slavery . . . (1889); Roger Lane, *Roots of Violence in Black Philadelphia, 1860–1900* (Cambridge: Harvard Univ. Press, 1986), 48; 111.81 11th *Annual Report,* Berean Building and Loan Association.

23. Receipt in possession of Mrs. Dorothy Warrick-Taylor; Allan W. Turnage to Miss Ella Still, 8/9/02, in William Still Papers, Leon Gardiner Collection, HSP, Box 9G.

24. 23.32 New York *Globe* 3/8/84, WHD marginalia; New York *Globe,* 2/23/84; Benj. Quarles, foreword to Still, *Underground Railroad,* vii; Allan W. Tarnage to Miss

Ella Still, Leon Gardiner Collection, HSP, Box 9G; 83.107 *Public Ledger* 10/5/94; see Chapter 7; Anonymous to "Mr. Nigger," 3/19/74, in Gardiner Collection, HSP, Box 9G.

25. New York *Globe* 2/23/84; William Still, *A Brief Narrative of the Struggle for the Rights of the Colored People of Philadelphia* . . . (Philadelphia, 1867), 23–24.

26. Harry C. Silcox, "Philadelphia Negro Educator: Jacob C. White, Jr., 1837–1902," *Pennsylvania Magazine of History and Biography* 98, no. 1 (Jan. 1973), 87.

27. Jacob C. White, Jr., papers in Gardiner Collection, HSP; see Appendix II.

28. Silcox, "White," 88, 95.

29. *Ibid.*, 76, 85; White to Thomas Hamilton, 2/7/60, JCW, Jr., papers, Box 12G; Silcox, "White," 85–86.

30. JCW, Jr., papers, Box 12G, correspondence with Brown & Rayno, real estate agents, Providence, R.I., 1868–72; Silcox, "White," 85.

31. 75.2 *Times* 11/9/89; 76.73 10/24/94; Gardiner Collection, HSP, Box 11G Lebanon Cemetery Records.

32. *Ibid.;* 113.2 *Tribune* 1/14/99; 123.26 4/6/03.

33. Du Bois, *Philadelphia Negro: A Social Study* (Millwood, N.Y.: Kraus-Thompson, 1973, orig. pub. 1899), 121, 231.

34. This and following account from 113.107 *Press* 11/16/99, and copies of *Press* kindly supplied by Harry C. Silcox, 12/5/82, 12/6/82, 12/7/82, 3/14/83, 3/16/83.

35. 23.5 *Tribune* 3/6/87; 89.33 *Tribune* 9/8/94; 104.55 *Tribune* 5/22/98; 121.43 3/13/99; 113.2 *Tribune* 11/14/99; 123.26 4/10/03.

36. 15.10 Sunday *Times* 7/6/79; Du Bois, *Philadelphia Negro*, 34, 296.

37. *Ibid.*, 32–35; see Appendix III.

38. 16.66 *Record* 3/31/79.

39. *Ibid.;* 9.20, *Address of the Stockholders of Liberty Hall* . . . (Philadelphia: Pub. by the Rev. Elisha Weaver, Agent, AME Book Concern, 621 Pine St.), 9.

40. 16.66 *Record* 3/31/79.

41. 54.52 *Bulletin* 12/11/74; 10.33 *Press* 6/9/77; 73.68 10/4/96; 68.42 *Press* 1/5/89; 62.50 *Times* 5/1/86.

42. Du Bois, *Philadelphia Negro*, 32, 34–35; 15.10 *Sunday Times* 7/26/79; 32.67 *Public Ledger* 4/15/78; 42.72 6/27/92; Richard R. Wright, Jr., *The Negro in Pennsylvania: A Study in Economic History* (New York: Arno Press, 1967, orig. pub. 1912), 88–89.

43. 121.53 *Times* 3/14/99; *Tribune* 5/9/14; Lane, *Roots of Violence*, 71; Charles Fred White, Jr., *Who's Who in Philadelphia* . . . *Biographical Sketches of Philadelphia's Leading Colored People* . . . (Philadelphia: AME Book Concern, 1912), 47–48.

44. Text of Dorsey letter from great-great grandson, Dr. Preston Johnson.

45. Du Bois, *Philadelphia Negro*, 32; New York *Freeman* 4/23/87; Du Bois, *Philadelphia Negro*, 119; 121.53 *Times* 3/14/99.

46. Du Bois, *Philadelphia Negro*, 120; Lane, *Roots of Violence*, 113–15.

47. See Appendix II; James G. Spady, "The Afro-American Historical Society: The Nucleus of Black Bibliophiles," and Harry C. Silcox, unpub. introduction to collection of Bolivar's *Tribune* columns.

48. *Tribune* 6/1/12, 7/20/12, 5/10/13, 9/13/13.

49. *Tribune* 7/20/12; 30.81 *Press* 7/8/81; 102.53 *Times* 6/18/98.

50. Theodore Hershberg and Henry Williams, "Mulattoes and Blacks: Intra-Group Color Differences and Social Stratification in Nineteenth Century Philadelphia," in Hershberg, ed., *Philadelphia*, 410–13.

51. 56.25 8/31/85.
52. *Ibid.*
53. 9.18 *Press* 4/18/73; 61.7 *Press* 8/30/81; Dorsey Files, David Bowser, obituary, *Tribune* 7/7/00, and *Anglo-African* 6/28/62; see Appendix II.
54. 30.54 *Times* 3/11/78; 60.15 *Press* 8/21/80.
55. 60.15 *Press* 8/21/80.
56. 67.36 *Times* 5/6/90; 67.36 4/11/91.
57. 78.100 *Item* 3/3/92; 78.76 3/23/92; 50.83 2/26/94; 115.40 9/9/99; 55.45, Program, 18th Annual Meeting of the Quaker City Association, 5/25/04.
58. Wright, *Negro in Pennsylvania*, 83.
59. 60.15 *Press* 8/21/80.
60. 84.1 *Times* 12/23/93; Alain Locke, *The Negro and His Music: Negro Art, Past and Present* (New York: Arno Press, 1969, orig. pub. 1930), 41; see Appendix II; 61.2 *Ledger* 8/30/81; Lane, *Roots of Violence*, 68.
61. 84.1 *Times* 12/23/93; 42.22 *Globe* 6/2/83; 65.6 *Times* 9/16/88; 73.37 9/16/90; 121.46 *Press* 3/13/99; 74.3 *Item* 7/18/90; 65.6 *Times* 9/16/88; *Tribune* 9/13/13; New York *Globe* 12/1/83; Dr. Henry L. Minton, "Early History of Negroes in Business in Philadelphia: Read Before the American Historical Society" (Philadelphia, 1913), 3.
62. 73.13½, Evening *Telegraph* in *Times* 8/27/90; New York *Age* 3/7/91.
63. 77.48 flyer, "Grand Exposition of the Industry . . . and Artistic Skill of the Colored People," Oct. 14–13, 1891; 77.49 *Weekly Standard* 10/24/91; 77.50 *Public Ledger* 10/15/91; 77.51 *Inquirer* 10/-/91; *Tribune* 1/27/12; cf. Chapter 11.
64. 75.46 *Times* 2/11/90.
65. *Ibid.*
66. DANB, 577–80; Maria M. Matthews, *Henry Ossawa Tanner, American Artist* (Chicago: Univ. of Chicago Press, 1964), chaps. 1–4; DANB, 578.
67. Story in 88.18 *Item* 6/19/94; 88.18 6/19/94; 88.18 6/21/94.
68. Quotes in 88.18 *Item* 6/-/94; 88.18 *Item* 6/19/94.
69. 88.18 *Item* 6/19/94.
70. Dorsey Files, Henry O. Tanner, *Item* 5/26/97. Tanner apparently never mentioned the incident to biographers.
71. H. Harrison Wayman, "The American Negro Historical Society," in *Colored American Magazine* 6, no. 4 (Feb. 1903), 294.
72. 57.1 Washington *People's Advocate* 1/27/77; 57.52 Washington *People's Advocate* 2/3/77; 57.52 Washington *People's Advocate* 1/27/77.
73. 57.9 Washington *People's Advocate* 2/10/77.
74. *Ibid.*
75. *Ibid.*
76. Miscellaneous materials found in Cheyney State University Archives; typed list, "Books (Text and General), Collection of William Henry Dorsey," done by Charlotte Goodman, archivist, 5/6/80; see Appendix I.
77. 75.46 *Times* 2/11/90; Cliff to WHD 11/16/68, Dorsey Files, Ira D. Cliff; Cheyney State Archives, "Catalogue of Art Exhibition, Progressive Workingman's Club, 424 South Eleventh Street"; Gardiner Collection, American Negro Historical Society, HSP, Box 10G. I have seen two small landscapes dated 1880 and 1888, owned by the surviving grandchild, Mrs. Virginia Ramsey Chew.
78. New York *Globe* 11/1/84; 96.74 *Times* 9/5/95; 75.46 *Times* 2/11/90; 57.40 receipt for 56 paintings; 57.34 *North American* 5/14/89; 57.45 *Sentinel* 6/1/89; Silcox, "White," 75; Dorsey Files, Du Bois, Du Bois to W. Carl Bolivar, 3/14/98; Du Bois, *Philadelphia Negro*, iv.

79. 63.3 *Times* 4/16/81; see Appendix II. Cheyney State Archives, "Rent Book: Thoughts," dated 1904, is hard to read but seems to indicate receipts as shown.

80. Gardiner Collection, HSP, Box IG, prospectus for Century Cotton and Woolen Mfg. Co.; Printout, PSHP, 1870 census; New York *Globe* 10/13/83.

81. White, Jr., "Who's Who in Philadelphia," 47–48.

82. *Tribune* 9/13/13; New York *Globe* 12/1/83; *Tribune* 8/10/12; 89.59 1/6/95.

83. Du Bois, *Philadelphia Negro*, 118; 68.9 *Record* 2/28/89; 42.16 *Inquirer* 3/12/78; 42.16 *Evening Express* 3/12/78.

84. Dorsey Files, Gilbert Ball obituary, 12/13/90; Lane, *Roots of Violence*, 115; 75.50 -/-/90.

85. On Whiteside, see Philadelphia Orphan's Court, April Term, 1879, Sur Petition of Mary L. Harlan and Appendix II. Also Roger Lane, *Violent Death in the City: Suicide, Accident, and Murder in Nineteenth Century Philadelphia* (Cambridge: Harvard Univ. Press, 1979), 106–7, and Chapter 11.

86. Dorsey Files, George Sharper, obituary *Tribune* 2/3/94.

87. 57.38 *Press* 5/20/89; New York *Globe* 10/27/83.

88. New York *Freeman* 2/7/85.

89. Lane, *Roots of Violence*, 109–33.

90. *Ibid.*

91. 113.15 *North American* 10/30/99.

92. Lane, *Roots of Violence*, 109–33.

93. *Ibid.*, 107–8.

94. Lane, *Violent Death in the City*, passim; Lane, *Roots of Violence*, 13–16.

95. Du Bois, *Philadelphia Negro*, 262; 75.48 4/28/90; 111.89 *Item* 3/1/99; 111.90 3/2/99.

96. Lane, *Roots of Violence*, 87, 93, 160.

97. *Ibid.*, 160, 92, 93–94, 160–61; *Public Ledger*, April 2–5, 1902; Roger Lane, "On the Social Meaning of Homicide Trends in America," in Ted Robert Gurr, ed., *Violence in America*, Vol. I (Newbury Park: Sage Publications, 1989), 75.

98. Lane, "On the Social Meaning of Homicide Trends," 75.

99. Du Bois, *Philadelphia Negro*, 116–17; Wright, *Negro in Pennsylvania*, 87; *Tribune* 9/13/13; *Tribune* 11/16/12; James Spady, "Afro-American Historical Society," 256; Wendy Ball and Tony Martin, *Rare Afro-Americana: A Reconstruction of the Adger Library* (Boston: G. K. Hall, 1981), 3.

Chapter 5. Education and Educators

1. Harry C. Silcox, "Philadelphia Negro Educator: Jacob C. White, Jr., 1837–1900," *Pennsylvania Magazine of History and Biography* (*PMHB*) 97, no. 1 (Jan. 1973), 86; Dr. Charlene C. Conyers, "A History of Cheyney College to 1951," unpub. ms., 143, 155.

2. W. E. B. Du Bois, *The Philadelphia Negro: A Social Study* (Millwood, N.Y.: Kraus-Thompson, 1973, orig. pub. 1899), 83–89, 86–87, 88.

3. Harry C. Silcox, "Delay and Neglect: Negro Public Education in Antebellum Philadelphia, 1800–1860," *PMHB* 97, no. 2 (Oct. 1973), 449, 454; Du Bois, *Philadelphia Negro*, 86.

4. Harry C. Silcox, "A Comparative Study in School Desegregation: The Boston and Philadelphia Experiences, 1800–1881" (unpub. Ph.D. diss. Temple University, 1971), 202, 200–201; Conyers, "Cheyney," 139; Silcox, "Desegregation," 205–6.

5. Silcox, "Desegregation," 206–7, 207, 208–9.
6. *Ibid.*, 209.
7. Conyers, "Cheyney," 29–30, 43, 29–30.
8. Early history in *ibid.*, 60–97; quotation, p. 103.
9. History in *ibid.*, 109–43.
10. *Ibid.*, 146; "Annual Report of the Board of Managers of the Institute for Colored Youth" (1866), 11.
11. "Annual Report ICY" (1867), 7.
12. *Ibid.*, (1866), 8, 14; Conyers, "Cheyney," 100.
13. "Annual Report ICY" (1868), unpaginated introduction; *ibid.* (1866), 19; *ibid.* (1868), 7–8.
14. Silcox, "Negro Education," 454–56.
15. "Annual Report ICY" (1868), unpaginated introduction; Conyers, "Cheyney," 143–60, 155–62.
16. Leon Gardiner Collection, HSP, Box 6G, ICY Commencement Program for 1867; Conyers, "Cheyney," 143–60.
17. "Annual Report ICY" (1869), 14; Conyers, "Cheyney," 136; "Annual Report ICY" (1868), 13; Conyers, "Cheyney," 161.
18. Linda Marie Perkins, "Fanny Jackson Coppin and the Institute for Colored Youth: A Model of Nineteenth Century Black Female Educational and Community Leadership, 1837–1902" (Ph.D. diss. in Education, University of Illinois at Champaign-Urbana, 1978), 69, 67–68; Conyers, "Cheyney," 123; "Annual Report ICY" (1871), 14.
19. See Appendix III; Conyers, "Cheyney," 162–63; Perkins, "Fanny Jackson Coppin," 85–90.
20. Perkins, "Fanny Jackson Coppin," 76–77.
21. Conyers, "Cheyney," 129; Perkins, "Fanny Jackson Coppin," 69; Harry C. Silcox, "Nineteenth Century Black Militant: Octavius V. Catto. 1839–1871," *Pennsylvania History* 44, no. 1 (Jan. 1977), 53–76; Perkins, "Fanny Jackson Coppin," 70.
22. Silcox, "Catto," 58; Roger Lane, *Roots of Violence in Black Philadelphia, 1860–1900* (Cambridge: Harvard Univ. Press, 1986), 49–52.
23. Perkins, "Fanny Jackson Coppin," 86, 100–101.
24. *Ibid.*, 104–5; Lane, *Roots of Violence*, 45.
25. See Appendix II.
26. Perkins, "Fanny Jackson Coppin," 13–21.
27. *Ibid.*, 21–55.
28. Philip Benjamin, *The Philadelphia Quakers in the Industrial Age, 1865–1920* (Philadelphia: Temple Univ. Press, 1976), 192–93.
29. Gardiner Collection, HSP, Box 13G, St. Thomas Literary and Musical Entertainment Program 11/25/73; Perkins, "Fanny Jackson Coppin," 131, 187.
30. New York *Age* 4/25/91; 27.8 *Public Ledger* 7/1/87; 65.81 -/-/87; 53.36 *Call* 9/5/94; 37.113 *Public Ledger* 10/17/94; 40.1 25th Anniversary Program, Pennsylvania Society for Abolition of Slavery, 1/2/89.
31. Perkins, "Fanny Jackson Coppin," 258–59; Dorsey Files, Cyrus Bustill (ancestor of Douglass), *Sunday Press* 3/23/79.
32. Perkins, "Fanny Jackson Coppin," 103–4, 143–44, 145, 120–22; Conyers, "Cheyney," 168; Perkins, "Fanny Jackson Coppin," 124–25.
33. Perkins, "Fanny Jackson Coppin," 110–12, 116.
34. *Ibid.*, 56, 100–103.
35. *Ibid.*, 122–25, 156, 138–40.

36. *Ibid.*, 127–30, 137.

37. *Ibid.*, 121, 179.

38. August Meier, *Negro Thought in America, 1880–1915: Racial Ideologies in the Age of Booker T. Washington* (Ann Arbor: Univ. of Michigan Press, 1964), 85–99; Perkins, "Fanny Jackson Coppin," 179, 187.

39. Perkins, "Fanny Jackson Coppin," 179–80.

40. *Ibid.*, 179–80; 54.32 *Press* 12/10/79.

41. Perkins, "Fanny Jackson Coppin," 185, 199, 142; 73.52 *Times* 10/7/90.

42. Perkins, "Fanny Jackson Coppin," 203; New York *Freeman* 2/26/87; Perkins, "Fanny Jackson Coppin," 207.

43. Silcox, "White," 88–89.

44. Edmund J. James, ed., *The City Government of Philadelphia: A Study in Municipal Administration* (Philadelphia: Wharton School of Finance and Economy, 1893), 49–73.

45. *Ibid.*, 62; *Annual Report of the Mayor of Philadelphia* (1880), 796, 834; Richard R. Fishbone, "The Shallow Boast of Cheapness: Public School Teaching as a Profession in Philadelphia," *PMHB* (Jan. 1979), 67; William Issel, "The Politics of Public School Reform in Pennsylvania, 1880–1911," *PMHB* (Jan. 1978), 79; *Annual Report of the Mayor* (1880), 876, 783.

46. Fishbone, "Shallow Boast of Cheapness," 70–74, 76–77.

47. *Tribune* 6/22/12; 59.29 *Sunday Dispatch* 5/17/75; Perkins, "Fanny Jackson Coppin," 70–71; Lane, *Roots of Violence*, 69.

48. Silcox, "Catto," 58; 111.39 *Tribune* 2/18/99; *Tribune* 5/11/12; 132.84 *Press* 1/23/78; 33.21 *Press* 3/15/76; Gardiner papers, HSP, Box 6G, Caroline LeCount to Jacob White, Jr., 4/17/79.

49. 35.30 12/14/77; 60.27 *Record* 10/29/80; 28.71 *Inquirer* 9/6/80.

50. *Tribune* 6/22/12.

51. Gardiner papers, HSP, Box 6G, note from James M. McBride, Chair, Committee on Grammar, Secondary, and Primary Schools; 59.21 *Bulletin* 2/11/76; Du Bois, *Philadelphia Negro*, 95; Gardiner papers, Box 13G. Roberts Vaux School Semi-Annual Examination; Fishbone, "Shallow Boast of Cheapness," 75.

52. Silcox, "White," 94–95; Gardiner Papers, Box 3G, Box 4G, Box 1G passim; Box 6G, J. H. Riddick to JCW, Jr., 4/26/80; Box 6G, R. Henry Holly to JCW, Jr., 11/22/87; 67.10 *Times* 10/2/89; Box 6G, Fanny Jackson to JCW, Jr., 8/29/76; Box 6G, Florence Lewis to JCW, Jr., 3/31/81.

53. 49.83 *Public Ledger* 12/24/92; 28.35 *Press* 7/2/77.

54. 35.43 *Press* 6/26/76; 54.1 *Press* 7/-/86; Perkins, "Fanny Jackson Coppin," 138–39.

55. 35.50 *Press* 5/15/69; 35.50 *Sunday Dispatch* 5/10/69; 28.24 Harrisburg *Our National Progress* 5/2/74.

56. Fishbone, "Shallow Boast of Cheapness," 78; 35.98 *Record* 6/17/78, 6/18/78; 35.98A *Record* 6/-/78; 35.98A *Press* 6/26/78.

57. *Christian Recorder* 4/29/80, 11/14/78.

58. 35.98B *Record* 7/3/78; 35.98A *Record* 6/26/78.

59. 35.98A *Press* 6/26/78; 35.98A *Press* 9/26/78; *Christian Recorder* 9/26/78, 11/14/78, 1/29/80, 5/20/80.

60. 28.54 *Press* 9/22/80; 28.55 *Press* 9/24/80; 28.71 *Inquirer* 9/6/80.

61. 28.71 *Inquirer* 9/6/80; 28.76 *Bulletin* 12/1/80; 28.78 *Bulletin* 12/2/80; 28.81 *Day* 12/15/80; 28.81 *Record* 12/3/80; 28.83 *Times* 3/16/81; 28.61 *Press* 4/17/81; 28.60 *Times* 5/8/81.

62. 28.67 *Press* 6/3/81.

63. 28.69 *Press* 7/14/81; 28.70 *Sunday Republic* 7/17/81; 28.71 *Press* 7/30/81.

64. 28.94 *Times* 10/5/81; 28.95 *Evening News* 9/11/81.

65. 48.7 *Tribune* 3/26/87; 93.107 *Inquirer* 5/10/96; 65.8 *Daily News* 2/12/88.

66. New York *Age* 1/11/90; 74.38 *Times* 7/31/88.

67. 74.38 *Times* 7/31/88; 51.20 7/10/88; 74.35 *Times* 7/31/88.

68. James Mulhern, *A History of Secondary Education in Pennsylvania* (Philadelphia: pub. by author, 1933), 533, 535, 535–36; Lane, *Roots of Violence*, 70, 71.

69. Lane, *Roots of Violence*, 70, 71.

70. Perkins, "Fanny Jackson Coppin," 157; 77.28 10/1/91; 93.49 5/25/96; 110.25 *Times* 4/22/98.

71. Perkins, "Fanny Jackson Coppin," 200, 206–8, 218.

72. Cheyney State Archives, ms., "Register, Industrial School, Institute for Colored Youth, Philadelphia, Jan. 2, 1889."

73. New York *Age* 6/7/90; "Register, ICY."

74. 70.46 Program, Academy of Music, Benefit ICY 10/8/90; Perkins, "Fanny Jackson Coppin," 213; 120.16 *Record* 6/1/99; Perkins "Fanny Jackson Coppin," 281.

75. "Register, ICY"; 28.62 *Public Ledger* 6/28/83; Perkins, "Fanny Jackson Coppin," 258.

76. Cf. Silcox, "Catto"; Benjamin, *Philadelphia Quakers;* and Perkins, "Fanny Jackson Coppin," passim, 113–14, 288.

77. Perkins, "Fanny Jackson Coppin," 250–52, 276, 251, 273–74, 286.

78. *Ibid.*, 281, 242, 245; 120.20 *Record* 6/1/99.

79. 120.20 *Record* 6/1/99.

80. Perkins, "Fanny Jackson Coppin," 257.

81. *Ibid.*, 260.

82. *Ibid.*, 282, 286, 318–19.

83. *Ibid.*, 294, 313.

84. 127.30 *Bulletin* 1/3/03; 127.32 1/7/03.

85. New York *Age* 1/13/90; Silcox, "White," 95; 94.116 *Times* 11/19/97; 73.61 *Item* 10/13/90; 75.5 *Record* 1/16/90; 75.7 *Times*; 115.108 *Tribune* 9/23/99.

86. Du Bois, *Philadelphia Negro*, 91; 84.28 *Item* 1/19/93.

87. Allen B. Ballard, *One More Day's Journey: The Story of a Family and a People* (New York: McGraw Hill, 1984), 226; 126.40 5/-/99.

88. Du Bois, *Philadelphia Negro*, 113; New York *Age*, 7/4/91; 117.82 *Tribune* 6/24/99.

89. H. Harrison Wayman, "The Quaker City," in *Colored American Magazine* (Nov. 1903), 770, 771; Ballard, *One More Day's Journey*, 212.

Chapter 6. The Learned Occupations

1. DANB, 669–70; 51.25 *Press* 9/15/76; 42.24; 74.43 *Times* 7/15/90.

2. Robert B. Stevens, *Law School: Legal Education in America from the 1850s to the 1980s* (Chapel Hill: Univ. of North Carolina Press, 1983), 81–82; 120.41 *Tribune* 6/3/99.

3. Geraldine R. Segal, *Blacks in the Law: Philadelphia and the Nation* (Philadelphia: Univ. of Pennsylvania Press, 1983), 28, finds five men listed in the 1850, 1860, and 1870 censuses. No contemporary account mentions them; all are clear that Wright was the first in Pennsylvania, Lewis in Philadelphia, although Lewis is unaccountably

not mentioned in Fleming Tucker's 1964 directory of black lawyers in the city; New York *Age* 4/11/91.

4. *Christian Recorder*, 4/30/76; interview with Dorothy Warrick-Taylor, a niece of Mary Jones and John Lewis, June 1989; *Age* 4/11/91; 9.51 Sunday *Times* 4/17/78; 11.52 *Press* 1/9/78; 11.45 *Press* 6/2/78; 54.4 *Times* 4/8/84; see Appendix II.

5. 16.20 Washington *People's Advocate* 5/7/79; August Meier, *Negro Thought in America, 1885–1915: Racial Ideology in the Age of Booker T. Washington* (Ann Arbor: Univ. of Michigan Press, 1964), 44; 11.62 Washington *People's Advocate* 4/12/79; 65.69 *Times* 10/10/85.

6. 60.49 *Inquirer* 1/27/80.

7. 52.22 *Press* 12/16/81.

8. 28.67 *Press* 12/16/81; 73.61 *Item* 10/13/90.

9. New York *Age* 4/11/91; 13.34 *Item* -/-/75.

10. Account in 42.2 to 42.11, several papers 9/24/75 to 9/28/75; 42.11 *Sunday Dispatch* 11/28/80.

11. 89.103 9/24/87; 127.80 *North American* 1/24/03; 75.23 2/2/90.

12. 13.25 *Times* 3/16/75; 13.96 *Record* 10/17/03; 13.44 *Times* 3/2/76.

13. 13.40 *Inquirer* 4/25/75; 13.55 *Times* 11/25/79; 13.101 *Times* 10/18/83.

14. 13.88 *Press* 10/10/83; 13.99 *Public Ledger* 10/17/83; W. E. B. Du Bois, *The Philadelphia Negro: A Social Study* (Millwood, N.Y.: Kraus-Thompson, 1973, orig. pub. 1899), 418.

15. 68.61 *Press* 11/26/88; New York *Age* 6/8/89.

16. 68.22 *Press* 12/16/81; New York *Age* 4/11/91.

17. 75.45 *Press* 2/1/90; New York *Age* 2/23/95; 116.1 New York *Evening World* 11/20/97; 99.6 *Bulletin* 7/2/97; 122.82 9/23/03.

18. 79.114 8/5/92; New York *Age* 6/8/89.

19. Segal, *Blacks in the Law*, 29; 111.3 *Tribune* 1/28/99; Roger Lane, *Roots of Violence in Black Philadelphia, 1860–1900* (Cambridge: Harvard Univ. Press, 1986), 27; Segal, *Blacks in the Law*, 29.

20. 111.3 *Tribune* 1/28/99.

21. 113.33 *Item* 11/3/99; New York *Age* 9/28/99.

22. Lane, *Roots of Violence*, 153.

23. 127.109 *Telegraph* 2/5/03; 127.112 *Telegraph*.

24. 94.72 11/4/93; 101.61 7/6/98.

25. Linda Marie Perkins, "Fanny Jackson Coppin and the Institute for Colored Youth: A Model of Nineteenth Century Black Female Educational and Community Leadership, 1837–1902" (Ph.D. diss. in Education, Univ. of Illinois at Urbana-Champaign, 1978), 269.

26. 115.41 *Call* 8/25/99.

27. New York *Globe* 12/29/81.

28. See Appendix II; David McBride, *Integrating the City of Medicine: Blacks in Philadelphia Health Care, 1910–1965* (Philadelphia: Temple Univ. Press, 1987), chap. 1.

29. *Tribune* 6/1/12.

30. 1870 census printout supplied by Philadelphia Social History Project; Paul Starr, *The Transformation of American Medicine: The Rise of a Sovereign Profession and the Making of a Vast Industry* (New York: Basic Books, 1982), 134–40, 114–15.

31. Commonwealth of Pennsylvania, PL 40 (1877).

32. *Tribune* 3/18/13; Starr, *Transformation of Medicine*, 52–54, 56–59; Lane, *Roots of Violence*, 154; 10.23 *Baltimore Evening Sun* in *Baltimore American* 7/24/69.

33. Leon Gardiner Collection, HSP, Box 9G, *Mount Holly Herald* 1/8/1962, 4/19/1962; Dorsey Files, Dr. Joseph Still, 1/16/92.

34. 68.36 *Times* 12/22/88; 68.38 *Times* 12/25/88; 68.39 *Times* 6/7/90; 97.80 -/-/97; 68.39 6/6/91.

35. 49.97 *Item* 7/5/92; 82.129 *Press* 9/12/97; 123.5 *North American* 3/30/03.

36. 87.135 *Inquirer* 12/16/94; 105.38 11/23/98; 127.84 *North American* 1/17/03; 75.60; 75.60 *Item* 3/9/90.

37. 55.18 advertisement for Edwin Still; 96.74 *Times* 9/5/98.

38. 60.92 *Item* 8/6/85; 87.34 10/27/94.

39. New York *Freeman* 1/16/86; Pauline E. Hughes, "Famous Women Educators," *Colored American Magazine* (July 1902), 209; New York *Freeman* 3/10/88; Lane, *Roots of Violence*, 69; New York *Age* 7/4/91.

40. Gardiner Collection, HSP, Box 5G, clippings from *Call* 12/5/96 and *Press* 12/6/96; 73.19 *Item* 9/3/90.

41. 73.19 *Item* 9/3/90; 73.20 9/18/90.

42. 73.19 9/18/90.

43. 73.19 *Item* 9/3/90.

44. DANB, 457–58; Herbert B. Morais, *History of the Negro in Medicine* (New York: Publisher's Co., 1977), 80.

45. 15.9 *Inquirer* 12/20/78; 56.10 *Times* 6/6/86; 56.11 *Press* 6/7/88; 67.61 -/-/90.

46. 117.52 *Bulletin* 6/2/99; scrapbook #126, passim, esp. 126.16 *Record* 10/23/06, 126.16 10/24/06.

47. DANB, 458; Gardiner Collection, HSP Box 3G, John McKee to Jacob White, 10/17/95; 97.155 *Times* 12/13/97; 97.157 *Times* 12/4/97; 97.153 Program of Douglass Charity Ball.

48. Gardiner Collection, HSP Box 3G, e.g., Nathan Mossell to Jacob C. White, Jr., 6/18/97 and passim; 109.74 *Times* 4/4/98; 108.68 10/6/98.

49. 118.85 *Times* 5/24/99; Gardiner Collection, HSP, letterheads for Douglass Hospital in Box 3G; Box 3G, H.S.P. Nichols to Jacob C. White, Jr., 10/18/97.

50. 123.85 *Record* 1/6/98; 95.41 10/14/97.

51. 117.57 *Record* 6/29/99; 117.57 *Tribune* 7/8/99.

52. 112.27 -/-/99; New York *Age* 7/4/91; *Tribune* 5/16/14; New York *Age* 7/4/91; 112.94 *Tribune* 4/29/99; Dorsey Files, Robert Abele, *Tribune* 3/26/97.

53. 127.95 *North American* 1/31/03; 35.28 *Record* 12/26/77.

54. DANB, 440–41; H. Harrison Wayman, "The Quaker City," in *Colored American Magazine* 6, no. 12 (Dec. 1903), 888–89; Gardiner Collection, Box 3G, Douglass Hospital letterheads; McBride, *Integrating the City of Medicine*, chap. 1.

55. DANB, 457; note that article has marriage date wrong by ten years, 1883 not 1893; 42.63; 91.117 New York *Age* 3/14/95.

56. 65.47 *Times* -/-/86.

57. New York *Freeman* 11/6/86, 11/13/86.

58. 69.21 *Christian Recorder* 8/15/89. The same incident also inspired James G. Whittier's "Howard at Atlanta."

59. New York *Age* 11/12/89.

60. New York *Freeman* 10/2/86, 7/10/86, 7/24/86, 8/15/86, 7/10/86.

61. *Ibid.*, 7/3/86, 10/30/86.

62. Carl N. Degler, *At Odds: Women and the Family in America, from the Revolution to the Present* (New York: Oxford Univ. Press, 1980), 56, 309.

63. Du Bois, *Philadelphia Negro*, 108–10; Degler, *At Odds*, 390, 160–61.

64. Mrs. N. F. Mossell, *The Work of the Afro-American Women*, 2d ed. (Philadelphia: G. S. Ferguson, 1908), preface; see Appendix II.

65. Margaret Hope Bacon, "One Great Bundle of Humanity: Frances Ellen Watkins Harper (1825–1911)," *PMHB* 108, no. 1 (Jan. 1989), 21–43; New York *Age* 4/25/91.

66. Bacon, "Great Bundle," 42; 74.43 *Times* 7/15/90.

67. Bacon, "Great Bundle," 38; New York *Globe* 6/14/84; 94.51 11/14/97; 40.6 *Sunday Mirror* 1/6/89; 68.40 1/2/89.

68. Mossell, *Afro-American Women*, 17, 16, preface, 14.

69. *Ibid.*, frontispiece, 124, 27, 96–97, 12, 13, 20–21, 166–67.

70. 91.146 Washington *Star* 2/24/95; New York *Freeman* 12/4/87.

71. For journals not cited, see list below.

72. Lane, *Roots of Violence*, 79; *Tribune* 1/11/13.

73. Scrapbook #27, unpaginated, *Sunday Mercury* 10/26/73.

74. New York *Globe* 12/1/83; 48.14 *Sunday Mercury* 5/8/87; Lane, *Roots of Violence*, 79.

75. New York *Globe* 8/24/84; 53.46 *Record* 1/14/81; 61.15 *Day* 1/29/81; New York *Globe* 8/24/84, 10/18/84, 10/25/84.

76. See Appendix II; DANB, 206–7.

77. New York *Age* 9/19/91, 5/17/90, 11/19/92.

78. 88.12 *Tribune* 6/9/94; 89.34 *Tribune* 12/15/94; 87.46 *Tribune* 11/17/94; New York *Age* 5/17/90; John S. Durham, "Labor Unions and the Negro," *The Atlantic Monthly* (Jan. 1898), 222–31.

79. 26.15 *Christian Recorder*, 12/22/87.

80. *Tribune* 1/11/13, 4/4/14; New York *Globe* 1883, 1884, passim.

81. 72.41 *Times* 7/25/90.

82. 72.41 *Times* 7/25/90; Du Bois, *Philadelphia Negro*, 229; New York *Globe* 10/13/83, 11/17/83; *Christian Recorder* 7/20/76.

83. 97.10 Germantown *Astonisher* 11/11/97.

84. 59.56 Sea Isle City *Item* 1/29/76; New York *Globe* 10/25/84, 10/15/84; *Tribune* 5/2/14; New York *Globe* 9/8/83; New York *Freeman* 5/24/86; 46.6. *Sunday Mirror* 46.6 -/-/89; 77.44 *Weekly Standard* -/-/92; 91.142 3/23/95; 105.33 *Defender* 10/22/98; 98.89 *Record* 5/6/98.

85. Dorsey Files, Christopher Perry, *Times* 5/4/95; New York *Globe* 10/27/83.

86. 46.6 *Sunday Mirror* -/-/89; 98.89 *Record* 5/6/98.

87. Lane, *Roots of Violence*, 80.

Chapter 7. *Politics, Politicians, and Civil Servants*

1. 8.132 "Speech of the Hon. Charles O'Neill in the House of Representatives, April 4, 1979"; *Inquirer* 10/12/70.

2. William Gillette, *The Right to Vote: Politics and the Passage of the Fifteenth Amendment* (Baltimore: Johns Hopkins Univ. Press, 1965), 46–48, 116–18; A. K. McClure, *Old Time Notes of Pennsylvania*, Vol. II (Philadelphia: John C. Winston, 1905), 281.

3. 54.13 *Day* 4/13/70; *Inquirer* 10/12/70.

4. Roger Lane, *Roots of Violence in Black Philadelphia, 1860–1900* (Cambridge: Harvard Univ. Press, 1986), 10–11; McClure, *Old Time Notes*, 284.

5. Howard Sprogle, *The Philadelphia Police, Past and Present* (Philadelphia, 1887), 132.

6. *Inquirer* 10/10/71, 10/11/71, 10/12/71; 22.17 *Press* 3/4/77; 22.76 *Public Ledger* 6/19/77.

7. Roger Lane, *Violent Death in the City: Suicide, Accident, and Murder in Nineteenth Century Philadelphia* (Cambridge: Harvard Univ. Press, 1979), passim; Lane, *Roots of Violence*, 140–41.

8. Lane, *Roots of Violence*, 10–12.

9. *Ibid.*, 56–57.

10. 54.52 *Bulletin* 2/11/74; 9.53 "Call of the Sumner Club of Philadelphia, 11/1/73"; Lane, *Roots of Violence*, 73.

11. 60.96 *Record* 12/18/86; 46.46 *Press* 2/15/77; 23.11 *Evening News* -/-/74; Gardiner Collection, HSP, Box 9G, Anon. to "Mr. Nigger," 3/19/74; 54.52 *Bulletin* 2/11/74.

12. Scrapbook #22 passim.

13. *Ibid.*

14. 23.18 *Independent* 8/2/84; 60.6 *Press* 8/18/80; 12.37 *Press* 6/8/77; scrapbook #22 passim; 22.68 *Times* 5/15/77; McClure *Old Time Notes*, 287.

15. 54.46 *Press* 9/15/80.

16. 8.17 *Press* 2/27/79; 40.3 1/3/89.

17. 62.50 *Times* 5/11/86.

18. 37.111 10/23/94; 37.120 New York *Age* 11/11/94; scrapbook #37, passim; 37.119 10/27/94; 37.113 *Public Ledger* 10/17/94.

19. Scrapbook #39 passim; 39.53 *Record* 11/23/98; 39.76 *Times* 12/2/98; 39.82 *Tribune* 12/3/98.

20. Lane, *Roots of Violence*, 30; 102.80 7/3/98; Lane, *Roots of Violence*, chap. 3.

21. 100.42 12/25/95.

22. *Tribune* 12/14/12; 60.85 *Times* 11/11/86; 87.46 *Tribune* 11/17/94.

23. 95.113 10/24/97; 95.113 *Times* 12/14/97; 95.113 12/16/97.

24. 95.113 12/16/97.

25. Lane, *Roots of Violence*, 57–58, 73.

26. 28.132 "Speech of Hon. Chas. O'Neill"; Lane, *Roots of Violence*, 59.

27. 84.11 *Times* 1/27/81; 100.47 12/25/97.

28. 113.63 11/9/99; 107.37 2/16/98; 98.19 8/20/97.

29. 59.51 *Day* 1/16/79; *Tribune* 4/25/14.

30. 90.119 12/10/99; Sprogle, *Philadelphia Police*, 173; U.S. Bureau of the Census, *Historical Statistics of the United States, Colonial Times to 1970, Part I* (Washington: U.S. Government Printing Office, 1975), 168; New York *Age* 11/28/91.

31. *Tribune* 6/6/12; 60.96 *Record* 12/18/80.

32. 9.59 Harrisburg *Our National Progress* -/-/75; 48.91 *Times* 1/4/93.

33. *Tribune* 4/25/14.

34. 9.6 *Press* 4/4/73; Sprogle, *Philadelphia Police*, 210; 52.16 *Record* 12/20/80.

35. Lane, *Roots of Violence*, 62–64.

36. *Ibid.*, 79; 23.24 11/3/79; Harry C. Silcox, "The Black "Better Class" Political Dilemma: Philadelphia Prototype Isaiah C. Wears," *PMHB* 108, no. 1 (Jan. 1989), 45–66, 62; 61.3 *Press* 12/10/80.

37. Lane, *Roots of Violence*, 63–64.

38. 63.5 *Inquirer* 4/16/81; Dorsey was listed as turnkey in City Directory 1881; 63.5 Sunday *Times* 4/17/81; 63.3 *Press* 4/16/81; 63.6 *Press* 8/6/81.

39. 63.26 *Press* 8/22/81; 63.19 *Press* 8/10/81; 63.42 *Sunday Times* 8/21/81; 63.23 *Sunday Transcript* 8/14/81.

40. Scrapbook #63 passim; 63.6 *Press* 8/16/81; 63.11 *Times* 8/6/81.

41. 63.31 *Press* 8/23/81.

42. 63.31 *Press* 8/23/81; 63.38 *Transcript and Ledger* 8/25/81; 63.40 *Sunday Dispatch* 5/28/81.

43. Lane, *Roots of Violence,* 67; Dorsey Files, Jacob Purnell, *Tribune* 3/30/89.

44. Lane, *Roots of Violence,* 67; Edmund James, ed., *The City Government of Philadelphia: A Study in Municipal Administration* (Philadelphia: The Wharton School, 1893), 27–34; New York *Age* 11/28/91; New York *Globe* 3/15/84.

45. Sprogle, *Philadelphia Police,* 173; New York *Globe* 4/12/84.

46. *Inquirer* 8/25/81; *Tribune* 4/25/14; James, *Government of Philadelphia,* 270–72.

47. James, *Government of Philadelphia,* 271–72; New York *Age* 11/28/91; Du Bois, *Philadelphia Negro,* 132; Lane, *Roots of Violence,* 125.

48. 92.41 *Times* 7/26/96.

49. Lane, *Roots of Violence,* 71; 77.1 *Inquirer* 10/16/91; 77.7 *Press* 10/26/91; 77.6 *Item* 10/21/91; 77.10 11/28/91; 77.33 "Council Meeting Phila. Dec. 3, 1891."

50. New York *Age* 11/28/91; 65.22 *Herald* 4/16/88; James, *Government of Philadelphia,* 270–72; New York *Age* 5/10/90.

51. Lane, *Roots of Violence,* 71; 70.60 three tickets to Program at Musical Fund Hall 4/16/91; Lane, *Roots of Violence,* 71.

52. Du Bois, *Philadelphia Negro,* 132.

53. 52.54 *Press* 8/10/68.

54. 23.26 *Press* 8/10/82; 90.7 11/17/99; 89.113 2/2/95.

55. 52.2 *Press* 5/22/82; 115.74 -/-/99; 72.74 *Times* 3/23/90; 89.135 2/2/95; Harry C. Silcox, biographer of both Catto and McMullin, in private conversation; *Inquirer* 12/14/90.

56. New York *Freeman* 6/12/86; 72.74 *Times* 3/23/90; Dorsey Files, Robert Still, *State Journal* -/-/94; 37.71 *Washington Post* 8/12/94.

57. 23.7 *Times* 5/3/84; 58.41 Washington *People's Advocate* 8/21/78; 77.39 *Times* 11/9/91; Silcox, "Isaiah Wears," 64.

58. 23.18 *Independent* 8/2/84; 65.69 *Times* 10/10/88.

59. New York *Age* 11/10/88.

60. 67.61 6/4/90; 37.71 *Washington Post* 8/12/94; 101.50 7/-/98; 101.99 *Tribune* 8/13/98.

61. 110.82 Atlanta *Voice of Missions* -/-/98; 101.47 8/7/98; 110.82 Atlanta *Voice of Missions* -/-/98.

62. 103.101 9/17/98; 118.82 *Tribune* 5/6/99; 114.41 *Tribune* 1/14/99.

63. New York *Freeman* 10/18/84.

64. 63.54 *Times* 1/30/84; New York *Globe* 2/23/84.

65. Unnumbered scrapbook after #61, titled "About Stephen Gipson, Candidate for Legislature 1886", *Record* 9/23/86; *ibid. Sunday Mercury* 9/26/86; *ibid. Sunday Mercury* 9/26/86.

66. Unnumbered scrapbook, "About Stephen Gipson," 10/5/86; unnumbered scrapbook just before "Gipson," titled "John W. Palmer, 1886, Congressman at Large," *Times* 10/18/86; *Inquirer* 11/3/86.

67. New York *Age* 2/22/90; Lane, *Roots of Violence,* 75, 72; 103.121 *Tribune* 9/24/98.

68. Lane, *Roots of Violence,* 75.

69. 9.end roll, unpaginated 4/6/78; 61.2 12/10/80; 63.31 *Press* 8/23/81; *Inquirer* 8/17/90; 107.122 *Tribune* 3/26/98; New York *Globe* 3/15/84; John Stephen Durham, "Labor Unions and the Negro," *Atlantic Monthly* (Jan. 1899), 222–23; New York *Freeman* 2/6/86.

70. 76.101 *Times* 10/31/94.

71. 72.80 *Times* 8/17/90; 72.82 8/19/90.

72. Charles A. Hardy III, "Race and Opportunity: Black Philadelphia during the Era of the Great Migration, 1916–1930" (Ph.D. diss. in History, Temple Univ., 1989), Vol. I, p. 38.

73. 62.43 *Times* 5/4/85; Lane, *Roots of Violence*, 73–74; 72.80 *Times* 8/17/90; Dorsey Files, Gilbert Ball, *Sentinel* 12/13/90.

74. 106.119 *Item* 2/5/98.

75. *Ibid.*

76. *Ibid.*

77. 121.107 *Times* 3/24/99.

78. 22.20 *Public Ledger* 4/24/77; Lane, *Roots of Violence*, 70; 88.21 *Inquirer* 3/29/94; 88.79 *Tribune* 6/23/94; Gardiner Collection, HSP Box 3G, Nathan Mossell to Jacob C. White, Jr., 3/18/97.

79. Du Bois, *Philadelphia Negro*, 113, 133; Du Bois, "The Black Vote of Philadelphia," in Miriam Ershkowitz and Joseph Zigmund, eds., *Black Politics in Philadelphia* (New York: Basic Books, 1973, orig. pub. in Charities, Oct. 1905), 31–39; *Tribune* 4/25/14.

Introduction to Part III

1. W. E. B. Du Bois, *The Philadelphia Negro: A Social Study* (Millwood, N.Y.: Kraus-Thompson, 1973, orig. pub. 1899), 221, for number of black churches; number of Catholic churches founded on or before 1897 found in *A Directory of the Charitable, Educational, and Religious Associations and Churches of Philadelphia . . . Prepared by the Civic Club*, 2d. ed. (Philadelphia, 1903), 665–79, a total of 61 not counting missions. Black population officially estimated at 60,000, Irish Catholic unofficially 360,000. See Roger Lane, *Roots of Violence in Black Philadelphia, 1860–1900* (Cambridge: Harvard Univ. Press, 1986), 179 n.71—rest of Catholic population estimated at an additional 120,000.

Chapter 8. The Churches

1. 26.3 *Christian Recorder* 9/29/87.

2. This is one of the most familiar stories in Afro-American history: see below for some of its sources.

3. 8.47 *Record* 3/29/79.

4. *Ibid.*; Frederick R. Norwood, *The Story of American Methodism* (Abington, Mass.: Abington Press, 1974), 272; 91.144 *Item* 3/23/93.

5. 103.67 12/13/98; 26.1 -/-/92; 94.107 *Times* 11/9/97; W. E. B. Du Bois, *The Philadelphia Negro: A Social Study* (Millwood, N.Y.: Kraus-Thompson, 1973, orig. pub. 1899), 198, 213.

6. Robert Ulle, "A History of St. Thomas Episcopal Church, 1799–1865" (Univ. of Pennsylvania, Ph.D. diss. in History, 1986), 110–11, 80, and passim.

7. *Ibid.*, 45, 79, 116–27.

8. Du Bois, *Philadelphia Negro*, 198.

9. 79.6 *Press* 2/8/92; *History of St. Thomas Protestant Episcopal Church* (n.p., 1905), 3–5; 27.unpaginated, *Press* 11/7/81; Ulle, "St. Thomas," 81–83; 27.unpaginated, *Public Ledger* 7/1/87; Dorsey Files, Rev. George McGuire, *Tribune* 2/23/01.

10. Dorsey Files, Rev. Owen Waller, *Record* -/-/93?; Roger Lane, *Roots of Violence in Black Philadelphia, 1860–1900* (Cambridge: Harvard Univ. Press, 1986), 50; Gardiner Collection, HSP, Box 4G, "Progressive Ticket, St. Thomas Vestry"; 76.37 11/9/91; Du Bois, *Philadelphia Negro*, 199, 218.

11. 8.177 *Inquirer* 5/17/79; 76.37 11/9/91; 25.2 -/-/92; 27.unpaginated *Public Ledger* 10/13/94; 76.37 11/9/91; Du Bois, *Philadelphia Negro*, 209, 213, 216, 218.

12. Dorsey Files, Rev. Owen Waller, *Record* -/-/93?; 27.4 *Report of the Ladies Sunday Association of St. Thomas Church of Philadelphia*; 27.unpaginated *Report of the Sinking Fund . . . 1873*; 27.unpaginated *Public Ledger* 10/13/94; 105.112 *Times* 2/2/98; Du Bois, *Philadelphia Negro*, 218.

13. John A. Saunders, *100 Years after Emancipation: History of the Philadelphia Negro, 1787 to 1963* (n.p., n.d.), 5–6.

14. Albert J. Raboteau, "Richard Allen and the African Church Movement," in Leon Litwack and August Meier, eds., *Black Leaders of the Nineteenth Century* (Urbana and Chicago: Univ. of Illinois Press), 1–20; Norwood, *Methodism*, 276.

15. John Dittmer, "The Education of Henry McNeal Turner," in Litwack and Meier, *Black Leaders*, 253–72; Norwood, *Methodism*, 276.

16. DANB, 484–85.

17. Du Bois, *Philadelphia Negro*, 204.

18. Carolyn Stickney Beck, "Our Own Vine and Fig Tree: The Persistence of an Historic Afro-American Church" (Bryn Mawr College, Ph.D. diss. in History, 1980), 270; M.J.H. in Washington *People's Advocate*, 1/10/80.

19. 101.50 Ocean Grove *Record* 8/3/98; 101.96 8/16/98; 99.133 *Times* 8/6/97; 101.50 7/-/98.

20. Dorsey Files, Rev. Jabez Campbell, *Public Ledger* 9/7/91; Dittmer, "Turner," 261.

21. Dorsey Files, Rev. William H. Yeocum, *Standard-Echo* 7/11/91 and *Christian Recorder* 8/25/87; 62.36 Baltimore *Sun* 1/16/84.

22. Dittmer, "Turner," 263; 80.135 4/9/94; 74.39 *Times* 7/19/90; 65.18 -/-/88; New York *Age* 1/31/91.

23. *Inquirer* 2/18/91; Dittmer, "Turner," 264; New York *Age* 11/29/90; Dorsey Files, Rev. Horace Wayman *Standard-Echo* 12/7/95.

24. 102.44 6/11/98; 101.105 8/13/98; 101.96 8/6/98; 92.29 *Times* 7/27/96; 100.82 12/10/97.

25. Du Bois, *Philadelphia Negro*, 200; 15.106 Sunday *Times* 7/20/79; 25.1 -/-/92; Du Bois, *Philadelphia Negro*, 208–18; 115.26 *Record* 9/2/99.

26. Du Bois, *Philadelphia Negro*, 199; 15.100 Sunday *Times* 7/20/79.

27. Saunders, *History of Philadelphia Negro*, 18–19; 25.3 8/29/91; Du Bois, *Philadelphia Negro*, 216; 25.1 -/-/92; 83.20 *Tribune* 9/29/94; Du Bois, *Philadelphia Negro*, 215.

28. 11.22 Washington *People's Advocate* 2/15/79.

29. New York *Age* 12/15/89, 3/23/89; 75.19 *Times* 2/1/90; New York *Age* 4/19/90, 5/10/92; Du Bois, *Philadelphia Negro*, 219–20.

30. Norwood, *Methodism*, 278–79; 25.1 -/-/92; Du Bois, *Philadelphia Negro*, 213.

31. *Ibid.*, 214, 209; 15.100 Sunday *Times* 7/20/79; 25.1 -/-/92; *A Directory of the Charitable, Educational, and Religious Associations of Philadelphia . . . Prepared by the Civic Club*, 2d. ed. (Philadelphia, 1903), 528–46; 107.12 *Tribune* 2/12/98.

32. Saunders, *History of Philadelphia Negro*, 9–10; 97.63 12/1/97; Du Bois, *Philadelphia Negro*, 214.

33. Saunders, *History of Philadelphia Negro*, 12–13.

34. 62.8 *Press* 8/5/84; 62.9 *Times* 8/6/84.

35. See Appendix II; 120.83 6/12/99.

36. 74.10 *Times* 7/2/90; *Christian Recorder*, passim.

37. 62.9 *Times* 8/6/84; 51.46 *Public Ledger* 7/29/89; 65.1 *Times* 9/10/88; Du Bois, *Philadelphia Negro*, 214; 27.7 8/9/91.

38. 76.33 *Tribune* 10/13/94.

39. Saunders, *History of Philadelphia Negro*, 23; 78.82 2/12/92; Dorsey index to book 78.

40. Arnold Rampersad, *The Art and Imagination of W. E. B. Du Bois* (Cambridge: Harvard Univ. Press, 1976), 19–20, 2, 30, 41; Du Bois, *Philadelphia Negro*, 197–221.

41. Du Bois, *Philadelphia Negro*, 220–21.

42. *Ibid.*, 221, 108.

43. Dorsey Files, Rev. George McGuire, *Tribune* 3/9/01; New York *Age* 10/19/91; 90.49 *Tribune* 11/25/99; 71.117 5/19/95; 106.117 *Tribune* 2/5/98; 107.12 *Tribune* 2/12/98; Dorsey Files, Joseph Cathcart, *Times* 2/24/87.

44. Norwood, *Methodism*, 279–80; 79.92 7/29/92; 114.41 *Tribune* 1/14/99; Dittmer, "Turner," 269–70.

45. Du Bois, *Philadelphia Negro*, 205–7.

46. *Tribune* 4/25/14; Dorsey Files, Rev. Richard Berry, *Tribune* 5/29/97; 67.24 *Press* 3/23/90; Du Bois, *Philadelphia Negro*, 209–13.

47. 25.12 7/4/91; *Tribune* 2/22/12, 5/30/14.

48. *Tribune* 11/16/12; 65.6 *Times* 9/10/88; 73.38 *Inquirer* 9/15/90; 121.46 *Press* 3/13/99.

49. New York *Globe* 9/8/83; New York *Age* 4/13/89; see Appendix II.

50. 107.12 *Tribune* 2/12/98; 94.107 *Tribune* 11/29/97.

51. Clubs listed in *Directory of . . . Churches of Philadelphia;* see Appendix III.

52. *Tribune* 3/16/12.

53. 25.10 7/18/91; 105.112 *Times* 2/2/98; *Tribune* 3/23/12.

54. New York *Globe* 10/6/83, 12/12/85; New York *Freeman* 10/16/86; New York *Age* 2/22/90; *Tribune* 3/23/12; Du Bois, *Philadelphia Negro*, 231–32; *Inquirer* 4/7/93.

55. 83.20 *Tribune* 9/29/94; 74.40 *Times* 7/19/90; Matthew Anderson, *Presbyterianism. Its Relation to the Negro . . .* (Philadelphia: John McGill White, 1897), passim.

56. 74.11 *Times* 6/30/90; 70.21 4th *Annual Report*, Berean Building & Loan Association: 111.85 11th *Annual Report*, Berean Building and Loan Association; 115.23 *Tribune* 9/2/99.

57. 73.29 *Inquirer* 9/10/90; 90.105 12/6/99; 90.106 *Times* 12/9/99; *A Directory of . . . Churches of Philadelphia*, 597–98; 76.60 -/-/94; Harry C. Silcox, "The Search by Blacks for Employment and Opportunity: Industrial Education in Philadelphia," in *Pennsylvania Heritage* 4, no. 1 (Dec. 1977), 40.

58. 123.26 4/7/03; New York *Freeman* 5/16/85; 132.47 *Press* 8/11/69; 83.93 *Public Ledger* 10/3/94.

59. 132.69 Washington *People's Advocate* 10/13/77; 94.92 11/15/97; 118.102 *Times* 5/30/99.

60. 105.33 *Tribune* 12/3/98; 12.30 *Christian Recorder* 12/22/87; 122.40 *Telegraph* 9/12/03.

Chapter 9. Race Pride and Race Relations

1. 60.63 *Inquirer* 1/21/83; 9.70 Washington *People's Advocate* 4/6/78.

2. 76.15 *Arena* (Dec. 1891); New York *Globe* 12/1/83; 49.116 *New Orleans Times-Democrat* in *Evening Telegraph* 1/6/93; 31.93 *Evening Telegraph* 12/22/93.

3. 76.15 *Arena* (Dec. 1891); 23.19 8/9/84; 31.113, Ida. B. Wells, "The Reason Why the Colored American Is Not in the World's Columbian Exposition: The Afro-American's Contribution . . ." (Chicago, 1893), passim.

4. Leon Gardiner Collection, HSP, Box 10G, "Ho! For the West."

5. *Ibid.*

6. Nell Irvin Painter, *Exodusters: Black Migration to Kansas after Reconstruction* (New York: Alfred A. Knopf, 1977), 146–47, 190, 177–78, and passim.

7. *Ibid.*, 176; 8.6 *Bulletin* 1/23/79.

8. Painter, *Exodusters*, 177–78, 184–85, and passim; 11.26 *Press* 4/15/79.

9. 8.90 *Sunday Press* 4/16/79; 8.69 *Bulletin* 4/7/79; 8.111 *Day* 4/19/79; 8.13 *Bulletin* 3/21/79; 8.35 *Public Ledger* 3/21/79; 8.39 *Inquirer* 3/29/79; 8.75 *Times* 4/4/79; *Christian Recorder* 2/7/84; 8.87 *Press* 4/1/79.

10. Painter, *Exodusters*, 228, 231; 8.109 *Press* 4/9/76; 8.155 *Press* 5/3/79; 8.120 "National Executive Committee of the Emigrant Aid Society."

11. New York *Age* 10/12/89; 31.87 11/14/93; 73.45 *Times* 10/12/96; 114.110 *Tribune* 2/11/99; 122.7 9/10/03; 122.23 *Times* 1/3/01; 122.99 New York *Herald* 10/4/01.

12. 9.40 *Press* 3/30/78; 81.95 *Tribune* 3/23/95; 92.106 8/10/96; 95.26 10/12/97; 81.73 3/14/95; 92.106 8/10/96.

13. 95.26 10/12/97; 81.73 3/24/95; Nell Irvin Painter, "Martin R. Delany: Elitism and Black Nationalism," in Leon Litwack and August Meier, eds., *Black Leaders of the Nineteenth Century* (Urbana: Univ. of Illinois Press, 1988), 149–72; Alfred Moss, "Alexander Crummell: Black Nationalist and Apostle of Western Civilization," in *ibid.*, 237–52; John Dittmer, "The Education of Henry McNeal Turner," in *ibid.*, 253–74, 267–68.

14. Dittmer, "Turner," 259–60; New York *Freeman* 4/27/87.

15. See Appendix I, Dorsey scrapbooks 131–52.

16. 134.14 *Bulletin* 5/25/76; 134.18 *Public Ledger* 7/27/76; 133.1 Liberian Catalogue, World's Fair, Chicago 1893; 133.28 3/31/94; 133.27 -/-/94.

17. Carolyn Stickney Beck, "Our Own Vine and Fig Tree: The Persistence of an Historic Afro-American Church" (Bryn Mawr College, Ph.D. diss. in History, 1980), 271; 129.5 Protestant Episcopal Board of Missions Meeting, Oct. 5, 1865, St. Luke's Church, Philadelphia; New York *Freeman* 3/15/84; 45.3 *Bulletin* 4/5/77; DANB, 267–68.

18. *Tribune* 5/9/14; 27.unpaginated *Times* 5/15/90.

19. August Meier, *Negro Thought in America, 1880–1915: Racial Ideologies in the Age of Booker T. Washington* (Michigan, 1963), 63.

20. 95.26 10/12/97; 136.35 3/10/84; 135.20 *Press* 4/28/78.

21. 135.20 *Press* 4/28/78; 135.76 *Record* 4/30/78; 135.39 *Times* 7/9/88; 135.44

Public Ledger 7/26/78; Charles Spencer Smith, D.D., *A History of the A.M.E. Church,* Vol. II (Philadelphia: AME Book Concern, 1922), 127–28; 135.34 *Bulletin* 6/26/78.

22. Dittmer, "Turner," 254; New York *Freeman* 6/30/88; Dittmer, "Turner," 272, 255–56.

23. Mrs. Mossell, *The Work of the Afro-American Women,* 2d ed. (Philadelphia: G. S. Ferguson, 1908), 105; Gardiner Collection, HSP, Box 2G, Robert Purvis to Peter J. Smith, 2/22/67; Gardiner Collection, HSP, Box 9G, Isaiah Wears draft of Purvis Eulogy, 1899; 62.50 *Times* 5/1/86.

24. New York *Age* 1/11/90; 53.64 *Times* 1/19/80; New York *Age* 11/19/92.

25. Smith, *A.M.E. Church,* 174–75; Wilbur Christian Fair, *The Negro as an American Protestant Missionary to Africa* (Univ. of Chicago Ph.D. diss. in History, 1945), 19–26, 37; David H. Bradley, Sr., *A History of the A.M.E. Zion Church,* Part II, *1872–1968* (Nashville: Parthenon Press, 1970), 223–40.

26. Dittmer, "Turner," 262; Smith, *A.M.E. Church,* 110; 56.7 *Times* 6/28/88; 52.68 Camden *Post* 10/12/82.

27. Dittmer, "Turner," 263–64.

28. 31.71 *Tribune* 10/21/93; 31.76 10/4/93; 31.91 12/2/93.

29. Dittmer, "Turner," 264; 93.56 *Times* 5/1/96; 112.111 *Tribune* 5/13/99; 116.64 4/9/99; 125.114 1/8/00; 121.86 *Item* 3/23/99; 122.43 *Telegraph* 9/17/03.

30. 82.142 *Item* 9/16/94; 87.16 11/14/94; 88.38 *Times* 6/27/94; 102.35 10/31/96.

31. 96.60 *Times* 9/5/97.

32. 83.47 9/25/94; 95.95 Bridgeton *Daily Pioneer,* 10/28/97; 95.95 10/18/97, 10/15/97; Gardiner Collection, HSP, Box 1G, African Colonial Enterprise, Philadelphia Executive Board, 2/20/99.

33. Gardiner Collection, HSP, Box 4G, "Farewell Reception for Dr. Thorne, 2/27/97; *ibid.,* Box IG, African Colonial Enterprise; Linda Marie Perkins, "Fanny Jackson Coppin and the Institute for Colored Youth: A Model of Nineteenth Century Black Female Education and Community Leadership, 1837–1902" (Univ. of Illinois, Ph.D. diss. in Education, 1978), 316–17.

34. Dorsey Files, Gilbert Ball, *Times* 12/11/90; 77.12 *Tribune* 10/17/91.

35. 77.27 *Times* 10/14/91; 105.75 *Times* 12/16/98.

36. W. E. B. Du Bois, *The Philadelphia Negro: A Social Study* (Millwood, N.Y.: Kraus-Thompson, 1973, orig. pub. 1899), 220; Washington *People's Advocate* 9/29/77.

37. 118.73 *Irish World* 4/29/99.

38. Roger Lane, *Roots of Violence in Black Philadelphia, 1860–1900* (Cambridge: Harvard Univ. Press, 1986), 140–41.

39. *Ibid.,* 163–64.

40. 62.33 Baltimore *Sun* 6/10/84; 284.unpaginated 12/13/95.

41. See Appendix I; handcopied book in Cheyney State Archives.

42. 52.147 *Item* 9/17/94; 90.70 *Times* 12/5/99; 92.144 8/24/96; Du Bois, *Philadelphia Negro,* 505; 76.35 10/20/99; 108.51 10/1/98.

43. 98.49 9/3/97; 101.72 *Tribune* 8/13/98.

44. 101.72 *Tribune* 8/13/98.

45. Lucy Barber, "The College Settlement," Independent Research Paper, Haverford College, 1985.

46. Allen Davis and John K. Sutherland, "Reform and Uplift among Philadelphia Negroes: The Diary of Helen Parrish, 1888," *PMHB* 94, no. 4 (Oct. 1970), 490–517; 81.165 4/6/95.

47. 34.27 "Speech of S. Laws, D.D.," 4/16/83; *Tribune* 7/13/12.

48. *Tribune* 7/27/12; 79.135 *Standard-Echo* 6/4/92.

49. 79.65 7/24/92; 93.58 *Item* 1/31/96.

50. Lane, *Roots of Violence,* 28–29.

51. Sara Bernard Stein, *Boys and Girls: The Limits of Non-Sexist Childrearing* (New York: Scribner's Sons, 1983), 20–21; Carroll Smith-Rosenberg, "The Female World of Love and Ritual: Relations Between Women in Nineteenth Century America," *Signs* I (Autumn 1975).

52. Lane, *Roots of Violence,* 27; 98.3 *Bulletin* 8/21/97; Louis R. Harlan, *Booker T. Washington: The Wizard of Tuskegee, 1901–1915* (New York: Oxford Univ. Press, 1983), 108–10.

53. Lane, *Roots of Violence,* 29–30.

54. Margaret Hope Bacon, "One Great Bundle of Humanity: Frances Ellen Watkins Harper, 1825–1910," *PMHB* 108, no. 1 (Jan. 1989), 21–22.

55. 98.8 *Item* 8/19/97; 119.28 *Item* 7/11/99; 37.17 4/5/94; 103.101 9/17/98; 112.78 5/2/99.

56. 77.47 *Sunday Republic* 10/23/81; 107.125 *Tribune* 3/8/98; 70.21 Berean Building and Loan Society, 8/25/92; 110.51 11/8/91; 110.51 *Times* 11/14/98.

57. Mrs. Mossell, *Afro-American Women,* 117, 120, 123.

58. Theodore Hershberg and Henry Williams, "Mulattoes and Blacks: Intragroup Color Differences and Social Stratification in Nineteenth Century Philadelphia," in Hershberg, ed., *Work, Space, Family and Group Experience in the Nineteenth Century: Essays Towards and Interdisciplinary History of the City* (New York: Oxford Univ. Press, 1981), 392–94; Charles A. Hardy III, "Race and Opportunity: Black Philadelphia during the Era of the Great Migration, 1916–1930" (Ph.D. diss. in History, Temple Univ., 1989), Vol. I, p. xix, xv, and passim; Allen B. Ballard, *One More Day's Journey: The Story of a Family and a People* (New York: McGraw-Hill, 1984), 198–200; author's interviews with contemporary Philadelphians.

59. Hershberg and Williams, "Mulattoes and Blacks," 425.

60. 51.25 *Press* 6/5/61; 60.90 *Press* 2/14/85.

61. 106.166 *Item* 1/7/98; 106.76 2/-/98.

62. 30.64 *Press* 6/30/77; 53.6 *Record* 5/19/82; 35.114 Washington *People's Advocate* 7/20/78; 11.62 *ibid.* 4/12/79; 68.19 *Record* 1/14/89; 123.16 *Bulletin* 1/29/03.

63. William Still, *The Underground Railroad* (Philadelphia: Porter, 1883), frontispiece; 71.67 -/-/95, photograph of AME Bishops Payne, Tanner, Turner, and Wayman.

64. 81.169 New York *Age* 10/5/93; Dittmer, "Turner," 260; Dorsey Files, H. L. Kealing, *Tribune* 4/1/99; 92.22 *Colored American,* in *Standard-Echo* 1/26/96.

Chapter 10. Organization and Social Class

1. William A. Muraskin, *Middle Class Blacks in a White Society: Prince Hall Freemasonry in America* (Berkeley: Univ. of California Press, 1975), 31–35.

2. *Ibid.,* 35, 36, 34.

3. William J. Whalen, *Handbook of Secret Organizations* (Milwaukee: Bruce Publishing, 1966), 113, 17, 25; Dorsey Files, Dorsey F. Seville, *Colored American* 4/7/00 and Washington *Bee* 10/21/00; 103.88 *Times* 9/9/98.

4. 9.21 *Times* 9/9/77; 14.5 10/10/79.

5. W. E. B. Du Bois, *The Philadelphia Negro: A Social Study* (Millwood, N.Y.:

Kraus-Thompson, 1973, orig. pub. 1899), 224; Washington *People's Advocate* 9/29/77; 127.28 12/28/02; Carolyn Stickney Beck, "Our Own Vine and Fig Tree: The Persistence of an Historic Afro-American Church" (Bryn Mawr College, Ph.D. diss. in History, 1980), 243.

6. New York *Globe* 4/6/83; Dorsey Files, Dorsey Seville, Washington *Bee* 10/21/00; 127.25 12/28/02; 80.126 4/5/94.

7. Whelan, *Secret Organizations*, 56, 119; Dorsey Files, Charles H. Brooks, *Tribune* 7/28/99; 47.16 Bridgeton, N.J., *American Favorite* 10/2/86.

8. 9.32 Washington *People's Advocate* 11/4/77; 47.17 Edward Bassett, Jr., "Origins of Odd Fellows," n.p., n.d.

9. 47.17 Bassett, Jr., "Old Fellows"; 46.16 Bridgeton, N.J., *The American Favorite* 10/2/86.

10. 47.6 *Press* 10/5/86; 47.11 *Sunday Mercury* 10/10/86; 47.6 *Press* 10/6/86; Dorsey Files, Charles H. Brooks, *Tribune* 7/28/99; 47.11 *Sunday Mercury* 10/10/86.

11. 88.132 7/9/94; 88.133 *Tribune* 7/21/94.

12. 108.57 *Times* 10/3/98; 82.95 Reading *Telegram* 9/12/94; Du Bois, *Philadelphia Negro*, 222–24. There is much discrepancy between Du Bois's and newspaper accounts of the numbers in the order, with Du Bois suggesting smaller numbers for Philadelphia and more for the whole U.S.

13. Dorsey Files, David Bustill Bowser, obituary in *Tribune* 7/7/00; Whelan, *Secret Organizations*, 54–56; New York *Age* 11/2/89; 120.106 *Times* 6/19/99.

14. 88.132 *Tribune* 7/2/94; Du Bois, *Philadelphia Negro*, 224; 112.110 New York *Journal* 5/14/99.

15. 103.46 4/24/98; Du Bois, *Philadelphia Negro*, 224.

16. Dorsey Files, Bowser, *Tribune* 7/7/00; *ibid.*, Brooks, *Tribune* 7/28/99.

17. 78.47 12/3/91; 83.84 10/3/93; 72.57 8/3/90.

18. 55.42 Program, Odd Fellows Ball 1/14/89; 72.58 *Item* 8/14/90.

19. John A. Saunders, *100 Years after Emancipation: History of the Philadelphia Negro, 1787–1963* (n.p., n.d.), 54–65, 59.

20. Gardiner Collection, HSP, Box 13G, "Military School for Youths," n.d.

21. PL 218 (1878); 101.91 8/5/98.

22. 9.51 *Times* 11/3/77; 11.52 *Sunday Mercury* 6/9/78; 15.26 *Inquirer* 8/7/79; 15.27 *Public Ledger* 8/14/79.

23. 9.57 *National Republican* 1/24/75; Dorsey Files, James Junior, obituary *Times* 1/15/94; 40.54 *Public Ledger* 7/11/87.

24. 100.23 *Item* 12/22/97; 104.104 6/1/98.

25. 89.34 *Tribune* 12/15/94.

26. 30.39 *Sunday Mercury* 3/16/78; PL 20, sec. 42 (1887).

27. *Tribune* 5/16/14.

28. 93.102 3/4/96; 107.86 *Tribune* 2/26/98; 93.122 5/19/96.

29. 93.122 5/19/96.

30. Gardiner Collection, HSP, Box 13G, Prospectus Philadelphia Building and Loan Association, 9/16/69; *ibid.*, Century Building and Loan, 10/27/86.

31. *Ibid.*, Century B&L, 10/27/86; *ibid.*, Century B&L, 11/27/94; *ibid.*, Century B&L, 10th Annual Report, 10/27/96.

32. *Ibid.*, Pioneer B&L 7th Series; New York *Globe* 11/10/83.

33. Gardiner Collection, HSP, Box 13G, Century B&L 10th Annual Report, 1896; 111.85 11th Annual Report, Berean B&L, 1899.

34. New York *Globe* 3/15/84; 121.53 *Times* 3/14/99.

35. Richard R. Wright, Jr., *The Negro in Pennsylvania: A Study in Economic*

History (New York: Arno Press, 1969, orig. pub. 1912), 178–79; 111.31 *Times* 2/17/99; New York *Globe* 2/17/83.

36. 57.32 *Sunday Mercury* 4/28/89.

37. 55.45 18th Annual Banquet, Quaker City Association.

38. New York *Age* 4/25/88; 79.129 8/6/92; 87.73 *Tribune* 11/24/94; 57.32 *Sunday Mercury* 4/28/89.

39. Unnumbered scrapbook after #61, entitled "About Stephen Gipson, page 1, Flyer August 1888; 57.32 *Sunday Mercury* 4/29/89; 104.51 *Times* 5/29/89.

40. New York *Age* 5/10/90; Du Bois, *Philadelphia Negro*, 225; 109.31 *Tribune* 1/26/98; 121.4 3/3/99; Dorsey Files, obituary William Harvey 11/20/97; New York *Age* 4/19/96; unnumbered scrapbook, following #63, entitled "Obituary and Will of J. B. P. Eddy," no page, *Record* 5/80/82.

41. Du Bois, *Philadelphia Negro*, 224–25.

42. Eudice Glassberg, "Work, Wages, and the Cost of Living: Ethnic Differences and the Poverty Line, Philadelphia, 1880," *Pennsylvania History* 66, no. 1 (Jan. 1979), 57; *A Directory of the Charitable, Educational, and Religious Associations and Churches of Philadelphia . . . Prepared by the Civic Club*, 2d ed. (Philadelphia, 1903), passim.

43. Phillip Benjamin, *The Philadelphia Quakers in the Industrial Age, 1865–1920* (Philadelphia: Temple Univ. Press, 1976), 127; 83.36 *Call* 9/5/94.

44. 83.36 *Call* 9/5/94.

45. *Ibid.;* 10.4 *Bulletin* 9/4/75; 95.108 *Times* 11/1/93; 52.59 *Public Ledger* 10/4/82; 76.18 *Item* 10/14/94; 45.37 *Times* 9/10/92.

46. 67.48 *Public Ledger* 3/1/90; 70.53, Program, Grey's Armory, 12/4/90; 52.89 *Public Ledger* 10/4/82; Benjamin, *Philadelphia Quakers*, 127; 71.55 *Item* 5/7/95.

47. 58.72 5th *Annual Report, Women's Union Christian Association*, 1879; Washington *People's Advocate* 9/29/77; 58.72 5th Annual Report, WUCA. Members are listed in the report, checked in 1879 Philadelphia City Directory; none had occupations of their own, but most had men of same surname at address. Estimate is that less than one-third of residents were not listed in directory as of 1880, most of them "with undistinguished jobs or none"—see Roger Lane, *Violent Death in the City: Suicide, Accident, and Murder in Nineteenth Century Philadelphia* (Cambridge: Harvard Univ. Press, 1979), 129–30.

48. 58.72 *5th Annual Report, WUCA;* 72.17 6/24/90; 94.92 11/15/97.

49. Lane, *Roots of Violence*, 131–32; 91.87 3/8/95; John Robinson, seminar paper on Midnight Mission, Haverford College, 1987; *A Directory of the . . . Churches of Philadelphia* (1903), 158, 156–57.

50. 55.17 First Grand Annual Excursion of the United Southern League of Philadelphia (1894); 95.85 10/-/97; 95.100 10/28/97.

51. 67.81 10/15/89; New York *Age* 4/19/90; 85.71 2/19/94; 89.3 1/2/95; 85.71 2/19/94; Du Bois, *Philadelphia Negro*, 232.

52. New York *Globe* 1883, passim.

53. Scrapbook #70, passim. Population estimate from census is about 45,000. Printout on age structure of black population, 1880, provided by Philadelphia Social History Project, indicates that a little less than two-thirds of population was aged 20 or over. Du Bois, *Philadelphia Negro*, p. 165, puts the average size of a household in the Seventh Ward at five.

54. 27.unpaginated *Tribune* 10/3/94; 77.14 *Tribune* 10/10/91; 69.25 *St. Andrew's Cross*, June 1889.

55. See, e.g., 69.27 Bylaws of the Edwin H. Fitler Club of the Eighth Ward.

56. New York *Age* 5/4/90, 4/23/87, 6/11/87; 87.47 11/17/94.

57. New York *Age* 3/21/95.

58. See Appendix II.

59. 56.33 *Press* 8/16/82; 66.76, n.d. item placed before two others dated 1881; 87.46 *Tribune* 11/17/97, with WHD marginalia.

60. New York *Freeman* 10/16/86.

61. All Dorseys in census in printout from computer files from PSHP; Augustus in 42.26 *Day* 1/16/82; Charles in 96.18 *Bulletin* 9/15/97; second Charles in *Inquirer* 7/8/1989. Most of Dorsey family material below in Appendix II.

62. Virginia Dorsey wedding in New York *Age* 12/26/90.

63. Du Bois, *Philadelphia Negro*, 178; New York *Globe* 11/3/83; 47.11 *Sunday Mercury* 10/10/86; New York *Age* 8/23/90; New York *Freeman* 5/14/87.

64. Linda Perkins, "Fanny Jackson Coppin and the Institute for Colored Youth: A Model of Black Female Educational and Community Leadership, 1837–1902" (Univ. of Illinois Ph.D. diss. in Education, 1978), 97 n.52; Harry C. Silcox, "Nineteenth Century Black Militant: Octavius V. Catto, 1839–1871," *Pennsylvania History* 44 (Jan. 1977), 53–76; Gardiner Collection, HSP, Box 6G, Catto to Cordelia Saunders, 5/25/60; *ibid.*, Catto to Jacob C. White, Jr., 10/2/70; *ibid.*, bill from John Wanamaker's, O. V. Catto, 2/6/71.

65. Charlene C. Conyers, "A History of Cheyney College to 1951," unpub. ms., 168, 156.

66. Du Bois, *Philadelphia Negro*, 195–96.

67. New York *Age* 4/19/96; H. Harrison Wayman, "The Quaker City," *Colored American Magazine* 7, no. 1 (Jan. 1904), 52.

68. See Appendix IV for lists on which the following paragraph is based.

Chapter 11. Recreation, Entertainment, and Postscriptum to
William Henry Dorsey

1. 53.3 *Times* 7/25/89.

2. 55.61 Programs, Academy of Music, 2/20/90; 55.28 3/12/90; 55.30 10/29/03.

3. Dorsey Files, Samuel Adger, obituary, 3/16/92.

4. 132.69 Washington *People's Advocate*, 10/13/77; 132.70 *Times* 10/24/77.

5. Leon Gardiner Collection, Historical Society of Pennsylvania, Box 4G, Program, First African Presbyterian Church, 7/1/68; 55.14 Program 12/1/91 to 12/3/91; Gardiner Collection, HSP, Box 13G, Programs 5/31/94; 1/1/73, 1/13/75, 1/25/77; 11.62 Sunday *Leader* 4/26/79.

6. 55.39 Program 2/14/94.

7. 70.15 Program 8/2/92; 26.12 *Christian Recorder* 11/22/87; 95.35 Program 1/31/94.

8. New York *Globe* 11/28/84.

9. 55.35 Program 1/31/94; New York *Age* 10/17/91.

10. 70.29 Program 3/20/93.

11. Dorsey Files, J. C. Arneaux, Play Poster, *Richard III*, 1/29/87; 78.76 3/23/92; 8.104 Program 4/16/79; 65.47 *Times* -/-/86.

12. Files, Arneaux, *Richard III*, 1/29/87; 78.76 3/23/92.

13. 74.59 *Times* 5/14/94; 70.47 Program 1/21/91.

14. 121.66 3/18/99; Gardiner Collection, HSP, Box 2G handwritten pay scale for performers, 10/21/96.

15. 71.29 4/22/95; 71.29 4/23/95; 101.125 *Item* 8/17/98.

16. 71.29 4/22/95; 71.29 4/23/95; 91.42 2/28/95; 91.60 *Item* 3/7/95; 51.19 1/27/98.

17. New York *Age* 11/15/94.

18. 9.22 n.d., no title, "Composed and Written by John Rhodes, Turnkey of 24th Police District, 25th Ward"; 9.45 "Onward" and "Upward," by JFN, marginalia by WHD; 58.38, "Bingham for Congress"; 58.37 Washington *People's Advocate* 11/-/78.

19. 55.44 "Twenty-fifth Anniversary of Garnett Literary Association"; New York *Globe* 11/17/83, 12/1/83, 5/24/84, 5/10/84.

20. New York *Globe* 4/12/84, 12/27/82; Gardiner Collection, HSP, Box 13G, Bergen Star Concert Program 2/17/87; New York *Freeman* 10/16/86; New York *Age* 5/2/91.

21. 9.34 Washington *People's Advocate* 12/8/77; Gardiner Collection, HSP, Box 1G, "First Amphion Choral Society Meeting," 2/22/76; 9.32 Washington *People's Advocate* 12/8/77.

22. 57.42 *Sentinel* 6/1/89; 57.36 *Tribune* 5/18/89; 77.49 *Standard-Echo* 10/24/91; 120.76 *Tribune* 6/10/99.

23. 77.49 *Standard-Echo* 10/24/91.

24. Ira D. Cliff scrapbook in Cheyney State Archives; 9.57 Washington *People's Advocate* 10/6/77; Wendy Ball and Tony Martin, *Rare Afro-Americana: A Reconstruction of the Adger Library* (Boston: G. K. Hall, 1981), introduction.

25. Dorsey Files, Ira D. Cliff to WHD, 11/16/68; *ibid.*, William C. Nett to WHD, 10/27/65; 29.4 U.S. Commissioner of Education to WHD, 9/21/98; Dorsey Files, E. C. Bassett to WHD, 5/4/98; *ibid.*, Walter. B. Hayner to WHD 9/9/98; 70.1 Frank Johnson Poster, "Presented by A. S. Cassey," 12/6/97; 70.3 Elizabeth T. Greenfield Poster; Dorsey Files, Dorsey Seville to WHD, 8/12/91.

26. W. E. B. Du Bois, *The Philadelphia Negro: A Social Study* (Millwood, N.Y.: Kraus-Thompson, 1973, orig. pub. 1899), introduction by Herbert Aptheker, preface, iv.

27. Gardiner Collection, Box 10G, American Negro Historical Society notes, 10/18/97, 10/25/97, and flyer 11/19/97.

28. H. Harrison Wayman, "The American Negro Historical Society," *Colored American Magazine* 6, no. 3 (Feb. 1903), 294; Gardiner Collection, Box 10G, American Historical Society Notes, 10/25/97; box 10G, passim.

29. 70.24 Fitler Club Excursion 6/15/91; 55.29 Knights Templars Excursion 9/19/89; 70.10 Knights Templars Excursion 9/15/91.

30. Roger Lane, *Roots of Violence in Black Philadelphia, 1860–1900* (Cambridge: Harvard Univ. Press, 1986), 117–18; 55.25 Major Wright Poster 7/10/97.

31. 98.93 flyer "Colored People's Day," n.d.

32. 82.51 *Times* 9/9/94; 103.56 9/1/95; 115.39 *Evening Telegraph* 9/7/99; 115.39 *Star* 9/8/99.

33. 103.56 9/1/95; 92.132 8/20/96; 103.108 *Record* 9/4/98.

34. 49.62 12/25/92; 125.6 *North American* 12/22/02.

35. 242.1 *Times* 11/18/88; 242.2 *Item* 8/22/90; 242.5 *Times* 8/26/90; 242.7 *Times* 8/27/90; 242.8 *Times* 8/31/90; 242.34 *Item* 2/13/96; 242.33 *Item* 6/7/95.

36. Lane, *Roots of Violence*, 117–18.

37. DANB, Dixon, 180.

38. 243.92 New York *World* 2/2/96.

39. 244.43 *Times* 2/5/99; 77.25 2/8/92; John A. Saunders, *100 Years after Emancipation: History of the Philadelphia Negro, 1787–1963* (n.p., n.d.), 186; Lane, *Roots of Violence*, 119; 116.55 *Times* 3/26/94.

40. 243.32 6/10/94; 243.32 6/11/94.

41. *Tribune* 5/3/13; 101.119 *Inquirer* 8/7/98; *Tribune* 8/24/12.

42. Gardiner Collection, HSP, Box 8G, Daniel Adger to Jacob C. White, Jr., 10/2/67, Charles McCullough to Aaron Brown, 7/8/70; Harry C. Silcox, "Nineteenth Century Black Militant: Octavius V. Catto, 1839–1871," *Pennsylvania History* 44 (Jan. 1977), 53–77; Lane, *Roots of Violence*, 54.

43. 70.31 "Strong Rest v. Strong Unique," 9/20/93.

44. 110.29 *Times* 11/24/98.

45. New York *Age* 5/24/90; 122.35 9/19/03; 113.88 11/12/99.

46. 85.29 *Press* 2/21/94; 70.52 Grand Prize Tournament, Crescent Club 3/8/93.

47. 79.129 8/6/92; 112.104 5/10/99; 108.65 *Times* 10/7/98; see Appendix III.

48. Lawrence W. Levine, *Highbrow/Lowbrow: The Emergence of Cultural Hierarchies in America* (Cambridge: Harvard Univ. Press, 1988), 108, chap. 2, and passim.

49. *Tribune* 2/3/12; 70.3 Concert Program, Madame Brown, 1860.

50. 55.15 Young Men's Social Club, 4/13/79; 35.38 *Sunday Mercury* 2/14/69; 55.38 Laura Shepard 11/5/90; 127.5 *North American* 12/26/02; 55.40 "Grand Calico . . ." 2/26/84.

51. 70.38 Union Beneficial Association 3/25/70; New York *Freeman* 5/5/88; 70.16 Hotel Brotherhood Ball 11/10/92; 70.37 Third Annual Hodcarriers' Ball 10/5/93; 55.1 Pennsylvania Beneficial Association Ball 5/8/90.

52. 97.154 Evening *Telegraph* 12/9/97; 97.159 *Tribune* 12/18/97; Du Bois, *Philadelphia Negro*, 320; 9.70 Washington *People's Advocate* 1/26/78.

53. Lane, *Roots of Violence*, 77; New York *Age* 2/22/90.

54. 55.11 5/3/90.

55. 70.37 Young Men's Social Club 1/29/91; 78.89 n.d., in context 1891 or '92.

56. 52.42 *Press* 12/12/76; 65.72 New York *Times* 7/27/84; 49.74 12/24/92.

57. Lane, *Roots of Violence*, 115, 146.

58. Arnold Shaw, *Black Popular Music in America: From the Spirituals, Minstrels, and Ragtime to Soul, Disco, and Hip-Hop* (New York: Schirmer Brothers, 1986), 43; Dorsey Files, Ernest Hogan, Indianapolis *Freeman* 12/24/98.

59. 97.151 Program Douglass Hospital Ball 12/8/97; 55.41 Program Odd Fellows Ball 1/14/89; 97.151 Program Douglass Hospital Ball 12/8/97.

60. 109.11 *Tribune* 4/16/98.

61. 119.76 7/22/99; 119.104 7/9/99.

62. 96.19 New York *Journal* -/-/97; 116.114 *Item* 4/16/99.

63. 110.38 New York *Journal* 11/13/98; 115.105 n.d.

64. 110.38 New York *Journal* 11/13/98.

65. James G. Spady, "The Afro-American Historical Society: The Nucleus of Black Bibliophiles," *Negro History Bulletin* (June/July 1974), 254–57. The Leon Gardiner Collection of the Historical Society of Pennsylvania contains what is left of the society's papers, other than those left by Dorsey himself. Most of the private papers are those of Jacob C. White, Jr., Isaiah Wears, and William Still, all of whom died between the founding of the society in 1897 and 1903. Dorsey did not leave his things to the society, nor did Robert M. Adger, Jr.

66. "Thoughts" in small "Rent Book, 1904," in Cheyney State Archives.

67. Scrapbook #255, although not the last of those arbitrarily numbered in the 1980s—see Appendix I—contains clippings dated later than those in any other.

68. 255, unpaginated. Crime in *Record* 8/21/07, conviction *Bulletin* 9/2/07; executions in 12/17/07. The author has a certified copy of State of New Jersey Bureau of Vital

Statistics, Certificate of Record of Death, Stephen Dorsey, black, 26 years old, laborer: birthplace, kin, and length of residence in state are all "unknown."

Introduction to Part IV

1. Some of the people interviewed for this final part are listed in the preface. In general they and others I have more briefly consulted over the phone, or as fellow participants in talk shows, television panels, teacher-education programs, political rallies, receptions for minority businessmen, or simply as old friends or acquaintances will not be quoted directly or formally footnoted. Notes in general during this last part will be strictly limited to sources which give specific statistics or hard facts.

Chapter 12. Survivals and Evolution: The Black City Today

1. Eric King, "Social Indicators Report of African-Americans in Philadelphia 1984 to 1988," in King, ed., *The State of Black Philadelphia*, Vol. VIII (Philadelphia: Urban League, 1989), 75–112.

2. ANHS in James Spady, "The Afro-American Historical Society: Nucleus of Black Bibliophiles, (1897–1923)," *Negro History Bulletin* (June/July 1974).

3. Story from conversation with Sulayman Clark, one of those who worked on the Dorsey Project, June 1989.

4. Charlene C. Conyers, "A History of Cheyney College to 1951," unpub. ms., chaps. 7–11; *Inquirer* 9/20/88, 3/16/89.

5. *Inquirer* 10/20/88.

6. *Inquirer* 6/8/89.

7. Carolyn Stickney Beck, "Our Own Vine and Fig Tree: The Persistence of an Historic Afro-American Church" (Bryn Mawr College, Ph.D. diss. in History, 1980), passim.

8. Edward Sims, "The African-American Church: Its Rich History, Its Present Dilemma, Its Mandate for the Twentieth Century," in Urban League of Philadelphia, *The State of Black Philadelphia*, Vol. VII (Philadelphia, 1987), 37–46.

9. *Inquirer* 7/8/89.

10. *Inquirer* 7/15/89.

11. I have been an honorary member of the Main Line Interdenominational Choir for about ten years, having helped to found it. The only condition is that I not sing—a rule which I break routinely from the back of various halls and churches when they are up front.

12. Erving poll in *Philadelphia Magazine* (July 1989), 9.

13. Poll for *Life Magazine* 11, no. 5 (Spring 1988), 70.

14. *Inquirer* 1/12/89; *New York Times* 1/12/89; *Wall Street Journal* 1/12/89.

15. *Inquirer* 5/31/89, 6/14/89.

16. W. E. B. Du Bois, *The Philadelphia Negro: A Social Study* (Millwood, N.Y.: Kraus-Thompson, 1973, orig. pub. 1899), 390.

17. Eric King, "Social Indicators Report on African-Americans in Philadelphia, 1984 to 1988," in Urban League of Philadelphia, *The State of Black Philadelphia*, Vol. VIII, pp. 75–110, 84, 80, 78, 101.

18. *In The Black: A Magazine-Style Directory of Black-Owned Businesses and Other Organizations* 1, no. 1 (1987–88), 39; Eric S. King, "A Social Indicators Report

on African-Americans in Philadelphia: A Beginning," in Urban League of Philadelphia, *The State of Black Philadelphia*, Vol. VII, p. 9.

Chapter 13. Transition: From There to Here

1. U.S. Bureau of the Census, *The Social and Economic Status of the Black Population of the United States: An Historical View, 1790–1970* (Washington: U.S. Government Printing Office, n.d.), table 8, p. 15.

2. Roger Lane, *Roots of Violence in Black Philadelphia, 1860–1900* (Cambridge: Harvard Univ. Press, 1986), 162–66.

3. John A. Saunders, *100 Years After Emancipation: The History of the Philadelphia Negro, 1787–1963* (n.p., n.d.), 87.

4. Harrison Wayland, "The Quaker City," in *Colored American Magazine* 6, no. 11 (Nov. 1903), 772; DANB, Bland, 46–47; Allen B. Ballard, *One More Day's Journey: The Story of a Family and a People* (New York: McGraw-Hill, 1984), 227–28.

5. Harry C. Silcox, "The Search by Blacks for Employment and Opportunity: Industrial Education in Philadelphia," *Pennsylvania Heritage* 4, no. 1 (Dec. 1976), 42–43.

6. Charles A. Hardy III, "Race and Opportunity: Black Philadelphia During the Era of the Great Migration" (Ph.D. diss. in History, Temple Univ., 1989), chap. 1, esp. pp. 12–15.

7. *Ibid.*, chaps. 1, 9, 10.

8. Arthur Dudden, "The City Embraces 'Normalcy,'" in Russell Weigley, ed., *Philadelphia, a 300-Year History* (New York: W. W. Norton, 1982), 592–93; U.S. Census, 1920, Vol. IV, Table 2, pp. 1194ff.

9. David McBride, *Integrating the City of Medicine: Blacks in Philadelphia Health Care, 1910–1965* (Philadelphia: Temple Univ. Press, 1989), Table 1, p. 11; Hardy, "Race and Opportunity," Table 14, p. 283.

10. Geraldine R. Segal, *Blacks in the Law: Philadelphia and the Nation* (Philadelphia: Univ. of Pennsylvania Press, 1983), 29.

11. *Status of the Black Population*, Table 8, p. 15.

12. Hardy, "Race and Opportunity," Table 3, p. 102; Lane, *Roots of Violence*, 143, 166.

13. Roger Lane, "On the Social Meaning of Homicide Trends in America," in Ted Robert Gurr, ed., *Violence in America: Vol. 1, The History of Crime* (Newbury Park: Sage Publications, 1989), 55–79, 75.

14. Hardy "Race and Opportunity," Table 2, p. 17, Table 9, p. 270, Table 10, p. 271.

15. McBride, *City of Medicine*, 88, Table 14, p. 89; U.S. Census (1920), Vol. IV, Table 2, 1194ff.

16. Hardy, "Race and Opportunity," 282–96; U.S. Census (1930), Vol. IV, Table 2, pp. 1412ff.

17. Allen B. Ballard, *One More Day's Journey: The Story of a Family and a People* (New York: McGraw-Hill, 1984), 231–32.

18. U.S. Census (1940), Vol. III, Part 5, Table 13, pp. 408ff.

19. *Status of the Black Population*, Table 8, p. 15; Philip M. Hauser, "Demographic Factors in the Migration of the Negro," in Talcott Parsons and Kenneth B. Clark, eds., *The Negro in America* (Boston: Houghton Mifflin, 1965), 71–101.

20. Margaret B. Tinkom, "Depression and War, 1929–1946," in Russell F. Weigley, *Philadelphia: A 300-Year History* (New York: W. W. Norton, 1982), 642–44.

21. *Status of the Black Population,* Table 54, p. 75; Lane, *Roots of Violence,* 168.

22. Ted Robert Gurr, "Historical Trends in Violent Crime," in Gurr, ed., *Violence in America,* 39.

23. U.S. Census (1960), Vol 1, Part 10, Table 122, p. 749ff.

24. Segal, *Blacks in the Law,* 4–5, 64–70.

25. U.S. Census (1960), Vol. 1, Part 10, Table 122, p. 749ff.; Herbert M. Morais, *The History of the Negro in Medicine* (Miami: International Book Corporation, 1967), 192.

26. *Status of the Black Population,* Table 53, p. 74, Table 74, p. 103.

27. *Ibid.,* Table 47, p. 69; Gurr, "Historical Trends in Violent Crime," 39.

28. *Status of the Black Population,* Table 8, p. 15.

29. Reynolds Farley, *Blacks and Whites: Narrowing the Gap?* (Cambridge: Harvard Univ. Press, 1984), 19, 48.

30. McBride, *City of Medicine,* chap. 8.

31. Segal, *Blacks in the Law,* 54, 55, 270–75.

32. Gerald David Jaynes and Robin M. Williams, Jr., eds., *A Common Destiny: Blacks and American Society* (Washington: National Academy Press, 1989), 588.

33. On liberal silence, see Julius W. Wilson, *The Truly Disadvantaged: The Inner City, the Underclass, and Public Policy* (Chicago: Univ. of Chicago Press, 1987), chap. 1.

34. *Status of the Black Population,* Table 47, p. 69.

35. Wilson, *The Truly Disadvantaged,* 95–100.

Chapter 14. A Common Destiny: Prospects for the Black City

1. An entire issue of the *Annals of the American Academy of Political and Social Science* (Jan. 1989), edited by William Julius Wilson, was devoted to the urban underclass; its several perceptive articles agreed on no definition, and none attempted an estimate of its size.

2. *Inquirer* 5/2/89; notes from presentation by David Lacey, former head of Philadelphia's Private Industry Council.

3. John D. Kasarda, "Urban Industrial Transition and the Underclass," in Wilson, ed., *Annals of AAPSS,* 26–47, 34.

4. Mark Alan Hughes, "Poverty in Cities," a research report of the National League of the Cities (Feb. 1989), makes a compelling case for the effects of geographical isolation.

5. On social isolation see Elijah Anderson, "Moral Leadership and Transitions in the Urban Black Community," in Harold Bershady, ed., *Essays in Honor of E. Digby Baltzell* (Philadelphia: Univ. of Pennsylvania Press, 1988), and Julius W. Wilson, *The Truly Disadvantaged: The Inner City, the Underclass, and Public Policy* (Chicago: Univ. of Chicago Press, 1987), 60–62 and passim.

6. Ted Robert Gurr, "Historical Trends in Violent Crime: Europe and the United States," in Gurr, ed., *Violence in America,* Vol. I, *The History of Crime* (Newbury Park: Sage Publications, 1989), 21–54.

7. *Ibid.*

8. David Courtwright, *Dark Paradise: Opiate Addiction in American before 1940* (Cambridge: Harvard Univ. Press, 1982), passim.

9. *Inquirer* 2/23/90.

10. Family Court in David C. Drake, "The Lost Generation," in Philadelphia *Inquirer Magazine* 7/23/89, p. 7.

11. Herbert C. Gutman's *The Black Family in Slavery and Freedom, 1750–1925* (New York: Vintage Books, 1977) is the best-known book in the field; although for later years its reliance on answers to the census weakens its credibility, many other scholars confirm its picture of the family under slavery.

12. Mark Testa et al., "Employment and Marriage among Inner-City Fathers," in Wilson, ed., *Annals of AAPSS*, 84.

13. Eric S. King, "Social Indicators Report on African-Americans in Philadelphia 1984–1988," in King, ed., *The State of Black Philadelphia*, Vol. VIII (Philadelphia: Urban League of Philadelphia, 1989), 75–110, 101, 78.

14. Report cited in *Inquirer* 1/16/90.

15. *Ibid.* 8/5/89.

16. *Ibid.* 6/19/89.

17. *Ibid.* 9/18/89.

18. Study summarized in talk by Marcia Hall at Haverford College, 2/6/90, "The Talented Tenth Reconsidered: Race Consciousness in Black Students on White Campuses"; program by Alpha Pi Alpha, University of Pennsylvania, and associated sororities.

19. *Inquirer* 2/4/89.

20. *Ibid.* 3/6/90.

21. *Ibid.* 2/9/90.

22. *Ibid.* 8/3/89.

23. *Ibid.*

24. Interviews at reception by Minority Business Enterprise Council, June 1989.

25. Interview with Curtis Jones, head Minority Business Enterprise Council, June 1989.

26. *Inquirer* 1/30/89, 6/23/89.

27. *Ibid.* 12/30/89, 2/11/90.

28. Academies in *New York Times* 2/17/90.

29. Private Industry Council of Philadelphia, *Annual Report*, 1988.

30. Eli Ginsberg, Terry Williams, and Anna Dutka, *Does Job Training Work? The Clients Speak Out* (Boulder: Westview Press, 1989).

31. *New York Times* 2/17/90; *Inquirer* 6/23/89.

32. William B. Johnson and Arnold E. Packer, *Workforce 2000: Work and Workers for the Twenty-first Century* (Indianapolis: Hudson Institute, 1987), 95.

33. Wilson, *Truly Disadvantaged*, chap. 5 and passim.

34. U.S. in 1987 ranked 14th out of 17 nations surveyed by a team from Columbia Teacher's College, reported in *The Science Report Card* (Princeton: Educational Testing Service, 1988). The situation worsens with each age or grade level.

35. *Black Issues in Higher Education* 6, no. 17 (11/9/89).

36. Ginsberg et al., *Does Job Training Work?*, 1.

37. Lisbeth B. Schorr, *Within Our Reach: Breaking the Cycle of Disadvantage* (New York: Anchor Press, 1988), 259.

Index

Brown, Isaiah, 22, 23, 244, 245
Brown, John, 105
Brown, Louis L., 27, 351
Brown, Mary L., 326
Brown, Michael, 250
Brown, Morris, 235
Brown, Ronald, 407
Brown, William M., 51
Brown family, 234, 307
Browne, Hugh, 162
Brown vs. Board of Education, 363
Bruce, Blanche K., 10
Bruce, David, 178
Bruce, H. K., 207
Bruce, John Edward ("Bruce Grit"),
    29–30
Bruce, Josephine, 174
Bryant, "Bear," 363
Bryce, James, 41, 265
Bryn Mawr College, 356, 359
Building and Loan Associations, 289–90
Burns, Benjamin, 48–49
Burns, Bobby, 37
Burns, John, 69
Burr, R. Emery, 282
Burr, Raymond J., 101, 102
Burrell, George T., 287
Burrell, Ida, 159
Burrell family, 307
Burton, Guy, 110, 126, 190, 209
Burton, John, 103
Bush, Cornelius, 173
Business. *See* Entrepreneurs
Business-government coalition, 403,
    406–9
Bustill, Amanda, 153, 154, 155, 164
Bustill, Joseph, 254
Bustill family, 120. *See also* Bowser,
    David Bustill; Mossell, Gertrude
    Bustill
Butler, Benjamin, 220
Butler, James, 207
Butler, Joe, 322
Butler, Matthew, 258

Cable, George Washington, 143
Cain, R. H., 256, 261
Cakewalk, 329, 331. *See also*
    Dance
Caldwell, Alexander, 193
Caldwell, Richard, 212
"Calico" dance, 327, 329
Callendar, Charles, 27
Cameron, Donald, 217
Campbell, Frazelia, 188

Campbell, J. P., 47
Campbell, Jabez, 237, 264
Camp meetings, 22, 231, 237–38, 239–
    40
Camp William Penn, 105, 286
Capital punishment, 131, 132, 360. *See
    also* Lynching
Carroll, Charles, 212, 214
Carter, Jimmy (president), 369
Carter, Joseph, 249
Case, Fanny, 294
Cassey, Alfred S., 101, 210, 317, 318
Cassey, Inez, 188
Cassey family, 234
Caterers' Association, 113
Catering business, 111–15
Cathcart, Joseph, 246, 317
Catto, Octavius V., 135, 136, 137, 139,
    144, 149, 167, 218, 227, 234, 305–
    6, 323
    at ICY, 140–41
    killing of, 141, 198, 200, 202–3, 217
Catto School, 150, 340
Cemetery business, 106–10, 126
Census, reliability of figures in, 5, 39,
    59–61, 119, 371
Centenarians, 23–24, 35
Centennial Exhibition of 1876, 146,
    156
Central High School for Boys, 148,
    155–56, 157
Central Presbyterian Church, 143, 241
Century Building and Loan Associa-
    tion, 289–90, 290
Century Cotton and Woolen Manufac-
    turing Company, Ltd., 125
Chamberlain, Wilt, 348
Chaplin, John G., 123
Charismatic churches. *See* Unaffiliated
    churches
Charitable organizations, 293–97
    churches and, 249–51
    private, 293–97
    public, 293
Charity, 73
Chase, Elias, 119
Chase, Isaac, 200
Chatelaine, Heli, 265
Cherry Street Baptist Church (Mother
    Church), 242–43
Chester, David, 213
Chester, T. Morris, 13
Chew, Benjamin, 154
Chew, Levi, 110
Chew, Robert, 110

Reconstruction (*Cont.*)
  failure of, 7–8, 160, 259, 332–33
  Harper's efforts in, 187
  Southern violence and, 42
Record, 11, 12, 51, 65, 153, 154, 209, 277
Recreation. *See also* Entertainment
  churches and, 310
  hunting and fishing, 320
  social class and, 325–32
  summer excursions, 319–20
  team sports and, 320–25, 321–25
Reeve, John B., 240, 267, 276
Religion. *See also* Churches; *specific churches*
  black music and, 20–22
  news coverage on, 21–23, 38
  vitality of, 240
Republican party. *See also* Government jobs
  black disaffection with, 216–19
  black vote and, 220–23
  political dependence and, 197–98, 203–4, 222–23, 224–26
  surrender of the South by, 7–8
Republic of Liberia, 260, 261–65
Residential segregation, 89, 129–30, 212, 378–79, 391–92
Restaurants, discrimination in, 171–72
Revels, Hiram K., 12
Rhodes, John W., 315
Richmond Planet, 12, 42
Richmond *Rankin Institute,* 185
Ringgold, Thomas P., 318
Rives, Hallie Erminie, 43
Roberts, Madame J. J., 179
Roberts Vaux School. *See* Vaux School
Robeson, Paul, 359
Robinson, Charles, 174
Robinson, Jackie, 363
Role models
  flight of black middle class and, 391–92
  need for, in 1990s, 378, 383, 387
  prominent blacks as, in 1990s, 388–89
Rollin, J. D., 316
Roman Catholic Church, 150, 241–42
  African-American Congregation, 345
Roosevelt, Eleanor, 359–60
Roosevelt, Franklin (president), 359, 362
Roosevelt, Theodore (president), 17, 284, 321
Roots (televised series), 389
Rossell, David, 175, 254

Rotherty, William E., 260
Rural to urban migration. *See* In-migration
Rush, Banjamin, 236
Ryan, John P. (archbishop of Philadelphia), 82, 102, 104, 241, 267

Sadler, Clara, 164, 165
St. George's Methodist Episcopal Church, 232, 233
St. Louis Browns (baseball club), 65
St. Michael's and All Angels mission, 235–36, 250
St. Peter Clavers mission, 241, 242, 267
St. Thomas P. E. Church, 55, 102, 143, 149–50, 179, 261, 341
  history of, 232, 233
  membership in, 298
  Williams's article on, 189–90
Satire, 26
Sayings, 25–26
Sayres, Benjamin, 183, 304
Schindler, Azeno, 122
Schofield, J. M., 9, 10
School segregation,148, 150
  black challenges to, 152, 154–56, 169
Schultz, Charles, 387
Science, late 19th-century attitudes and, 21, 33, 34–35, 37, 56
Scott, J. F. K., 173
Scott, J. Howard, 168
Scott, William, 66, 126, 132, 168
Secondhand shops, 115, 129
"Second Reconstruction." *See* Post-World War II era
Secret orders, 279–85
Segregation. *See* Civil rights; Racism; School segregation
Self-help
  activities classified as, 393
  in late 19th century, 146, 192
  need for, in 1990s, 376, 387
  potential for, in 1990s, 391–400
Selika, Madame, 19, 20, 312
Sentinel, 124, 156, 194, 222, 243
Service economy, shift to
  educational demands of, and underclass, 377, 406–7
  1990s wage earners and, 352
  poor blacks and, 371–73, 380
Settlement house, 270–71
Seville, Dorsey F. (WD's nephew), 60, 280, 281, 301, 303, 317
Seville, John C. (WD's nephew), 60, 301, 303